# CRIMINAL JUSTICE
## 93/94

### Editor

**John J. Sullivan**
**Mercy College, Dobbs Ferry, New York**

John J. Sullivan, professor and chairman of the Department
of Law, Criminal Justice, and Safety Administration at
Mercy College, received his B.S. in 1949 from Manhattan
College and his J.D. in 1956 from St. John's Law School.
He was formerly captain and director of the Legal Division
of the New York City Police Department.

### Editor

**Joseph L. Victor**
**Mercy College, Dobbs Ferry, New York**

Joseph L. Victor is professor and assistant chairman of the
Department of Law, Criminal Justice, and Safety
Administration at Mercy College, and coordinator of
Criminal Justice Graduate Study at the Westchester Campus
of Long Island University. Professor Victor has extensive
field experience in criminal justice agencies, counseling, and
administering human service programs. He earned his B.A.
and M.A. at Seton Hall University, and his Doctorate of
Education at Fairleigh Dickinson University.

Cover illustration by Mike Eagle

Annual Editions
*A Library of Information from the Public Press*

**The Dushkin Publishing Group, Inc.**
**Sluice Dock, Guilford, Connecticut 06437**

# The Annual Editions Series

Annual Editions is a series of over 55 volumes designed to provide the reader with convenient, low-cost access to a wide range of current, carefully selected articles from some of the most important magazines, newspapers, and journals published today. Annual Editions are updated on an annual basis through a continuous monitoring of over 300 periodical sources. All Annual Editions have a number of features designed to make them particularly useful, including topic guides, annotated tables of contents, unit overviews, and indexes. For the teacher using Annual Editions in the classroom, an Instructor's Resource Guide with test questions is available for each volume.

## VOLUMES AVAILABLE

Africa
Aging
American Government
American History, Pre-Civil War
American History, Post-Civil War
Anthropology
Biology
Business Ethics
Canadian Politics
China
Commonwealth of Independent States
Comparative Politics
Computers in Education
Computers in Business
Computers in Society
Criminal Justice
Drugs, Society, and Behavior
Dying, Death, and Bereavement
Early Childhood Education
Economics
Educating Exceptional Children
Education
Educational Psychology
Environment
Geography
Global Issues
Health
Human Development
Human Resources
Human Sexuality
India and South Asia

International Business
Japan and the Pacific Rim
Latin America
Life Management
Macroeconomics
Management
Marketing
Marriage and Family
Microeconomics
Middle East and the Islamic World
Money and Banking
Nutrition
Personal Growth and Behavior
Physical Anthropology
Psychology
Public Administration
Race and Ethnic Relations
Social Problems
Sociology
State and Local Government
Third World
Urban Society
Violence and Terrorism
Western Civilization, Pre-Reformation
Western Civilization, Post-Reformation
Western Europe
World History, Pre-Modern
World History, Modern
World Politics

Library of Congress Cataloging in Publication Data
Main entry under title: Annual editions: Criminal justice. 1993/94.
    1. Criminal Justice, Administration of—United States—Periodicals.
I. Sullivan, John J., comp. II. Victor, Joseph L., comp. III. Title: Criminal justice.
HV 8138.A67          364.973.05          LC 77-640116
ISBN: 1-56134-193-2

Seventeenth Edition

Manufactured by The Banta Company, Harrisonburg, Virginia 22801

Printed on Recycled Paper

# To the Reader

In publishing ANNUAL EDITIONS we recognize the enormous role played by the magazines, newspapers, and journals of the *public press* in providing current, first-rate educational information in a broad spectrum of interest areas. Within the articles, the best scientists, practitioners, researchers, and commentators draw issues into new perspective as accepted theories and viewpoints are called into account by new events, recent discoveries change old facts, and fresh debate breaks out over important controversies.

Many of the articles resulting from this enormous editorial effort are appropriate for students, researchers, and professionals seeking accurate, current material to help bridge the gap between principles and theories and the real world. These articles, however, become more useful for study when those of lasting value are carefully *collected, organized, indexed,* and *reproduced* in a *low-cost format*, which provides easy and permanent access when the material is needed. That is the role played by *Annual Editions*. Under the direction of each volume's *Editor*, who is an expert in the subject area, and with the guidance of an *Advisory Board*, we seek each year to provide in each *ANNUAL EDITION* a current, well-balanced, carefully selected collection of the best of the public press for your study and enjoyment. We think you'll find this volume useful, and we hope you'll take a moment to let us know what you think.

During the 1970s, criminal justice emerged as an appealing, vital, and unique academic discipline. It emphasizes the professional development of students who plan careers in the field, and attracts those who want to know more about a complex social problem and how this country deals with it. Criminal justice incorporates a vast range of knowledge from a number of specialties, including law, history, and the behavioral and social sciences. Each specialty contributes to our fuller understanding of criminal behavior and of society's attitudes toward deviance.

In view of the fact that the criminal justice system is in a constant state of flux, and because the study of criminal justice covers such a broad spectrum, today's students must be aware of a variety of subjects and topics. Standard textbooks and traditional anthologies cannot keep pace with the changes as quickly as they occur. In fact, many such sources are already out of date the day they are published. *Annual Editions: Criminal Justice 93/94* strives to maintain currency in matters of concern by providing up-to-date commentaries, articles, reports, and statistics from the most recent literature in the criminal justice field.

This volume contains units concerning crime and justice in America, victimology, the police, the judicial system, juvenile justice, and punishment and corrections. The articles in these units were selected because they are informative as well as provocative. The selections are timely and useful in their treatment of ethics, punishment, juveniles, courts, and other related topics.

Included in this volume are a number of features designed to make it useful for students, researchers, and professionals in the criminal justice field. These include a topic guide for locating articles on specific subjects; the table of contents abstracts, which summarize each article and feature key concepts in bold italics; and a comprehensive bibliography, glossary, and index. In addition, each unit is preceded by an overview that provides a background for informed reading of the articles, emphasizes critical issues, and presents challenge questions.

We would like to know what you think of the selections contained in this edition. Please fill out the article rating form on the last page and let us know your opinions. We change or retain many of the articles based on the comments we receive from you, the user. Help us to improve this anthology—annually.

John J. Sullivan

Joseph L. Victor

*Editors*

# Contents

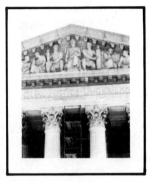

## Unit 1

# Crime and Justice in America

Eight selections focus on the overall structure of the criminal justice system in the United States. The current scope of crime in America is reviewed; topics such as criminal behavior, drugs, and organized crime are discussed.

The concepts in bold italics are developed in the article. For further expansion please refer to the Topic Guide, the Index, and the Glossary.

# Unit 2

## Victimology

Eight articles discuss the impact of crime on the victim. Topics include the rights of crime victims, the consequences of family violence, rape, and incest.

# Unit 3

## Police

Eight selections examine the role of the police officer. Some of the topics discussed include police response to crime, utilization of policewomen, and ethical policing.

The concepts in bold italics are developed in the article. For further expansion please refer to the Topic Guide, the Index, and the Glossary.

# Unit

# The Judicial System

Seven selections discuss the process by which the accused are moved through the judicial system. Prosecutors, courts, the jury process, and judicial ethics are reviewed.

# Unit 5

# Juvenile Justice

Seven selections review the juvenile justice system.
The topics include effective ways to respond to violent
juvenile crime, juvenile detention, female delinquency,
and children in gangs.

# Unit 6

# Punishment and Corrections

Seven selections focus on the current state of America's penal system and the effects of sentencing, probation, overcrowding, and capital punishment on criminals.

The concepts in bold italics are developed in the article. For further expansion please refer to the Topic Guide, the Index, and the Glossary.

The concepts in bold italics are developed in the article. For further expansion please refer to the Topic Guide, the Index, and the Glossary.

# Charts and Graphs

The concepts in bold italics are developed in the article. For further expansion please refer to the Topic Guide, the Index, and the Glossary.

# Topic Guide

This topic guide suggests how the selections in this book relate to topics of traditional concern to students and professionals involved with the study of criminal justice. It is useful for locating articles that relate to each other for reading and research. The guide is arranged alphabetically according to topic. Articles may, of course, treat topics that do not appear in the topic guide. In turn, entries in the topic guide do not necessarily constitute a comprehensive listing of all the contents of each selection.

| TOPIC AREA | TREATED IN: | TOPIC AREA | TREATED IN: |
|---|---|---|---|
| **Attorneys** | 26. Public Defenders<br>27. Abuse of Power in the Prosecutor's Office | **Crime Victims** | See Victimology |
| **Battered Families** | 13. When Men Hit Women<br>15. Abused Women Who Kill<br>16. Incest: A Chilling Report | **Criminal Behavior** | 3. Are Criminals Made or Born?<br>8. Understanding Mass Murder |
| **Boot Camps** | 43. New Chain Gangs | **Criminal Justice** | 1. Overview of the Criminal Justice System<br>2. What Is Crime?<br>26. Public Defenders<br>27. Abuse of Power in the Prosecutor's Office<br>28. Search for Justice |
| **Children** | See Juveniles | | |
| **Community Policing** | 19. Blacks and Cops: Up Against a Wall<br>21. Are Women Better Cops?<br>23. Cops Get Up-Close and Personal | **Cultural Awareness** | 18. Law Enforcement in a Culturally Diverse Society |
| **Constitutional Rights** | 31. Court's 2 Visions of Free Speech | **Death Penalty** | 44. Costliest Punishment<br>45. 'This Man Has Expired' |
| | | **Defense Counsel** | 26. Public Defenders |
| **Corrections** | 39. Sentencing and Corrections<br>40. Women in Jail: Unequal Justice<br>41. Doubling the Prison Population<br>42. Crime of Black Imprisonment<br>43. New Chain Gangs | **Delinquency** | See Juveniles |
| | | **Discrimination** | 4. Race: Our Dilemma Still<br>7. Siege of L.A.<br>18. Law Enforcement in a Culturally Diverse Society<br>19. Blacks and Cops: Up Against a Wall<br>22. Preventing Hate Crime<br>28. Search for Justice |
| **Courts** | 25. Judicial Process<br>26. Public Defenders<br>27. Abuse of Power in the Prosecutor's Office<br>28. Search for Justice<br>29. Jurors Hear Evidence and Turn It Into Stories<br>30. Grand Illusion<br>31. Court's 2 Visions of Free Speech<br>32. Handling of Juvenile Cases<br>35. Juvenile Court | **Drugs** | 5. 20 Years of War on Drugs, and No Victory Yet |
| | | **Ethics** | 24. Higher Education and Ethical Policing<br>27. Abuse of Power in the Prosecutor's Office |
| **Crime** | 1. Overview of the Criminal Justice System<br>2. What Is Crime?<br>3. Are Criminals Made or Born?<br>5. 20 Years of War on Drugs, and No Victory Yet<br>9. Fear of Crime<br>22. Preventing Hate Crime | **Family Violence** | 10. Hunted<br>13. When Men Hit Women<br>15. Abused Women Who Kill<br>16. Incest |

# Crime and Justice in America

The past few years have been explosive ones in so far as crime and justice have been concerned. We have witnessed riots in several cities because of unpopular jury verdicts, a rise in "hate crimes," an increase in racial tensions, and drugs remain a scourge on society.

The articles found in this section are intended to serve as a foundation for the materials presented in subsequent sections. "An Overview of the Criminal Justice System" charts the flow of events in the administration of the criminal justice system. "What Is Crime?" presents definitions of some of the most serious crimes.

"Are Criminals Made or Born?" explores some of the causative factors of criminal behavior. Racial tensions are explored in "Race: Our Dilemma Still" and "The Siege of L.A." Both articles concern the 1992 riots in Los Angeles after a jury acquitted several police officers in the Rodney King alleged police brutality case. "20 Years of War on Drugs, and No Victory Yet" paints a bleak picture, and "Organized Crime: Past, Present, and Future" indicates that organized crime is not going to go away.

"Understanding Mass Murder: A Starting Point" deals with police tactics being developed to handle mass murder cases.

### Looking Ahead: Challenge Questions

What impact did the Rodney King alleged police brutality case have on the criminal justice system?

Do you think the criminal justice system is racially biased?

# Unit 1

# An Overview of the Criminal Justice System

**The response to crime is a complex process that involves citizens as well as many agencies, levels, and branches of government**

## The private sector initiates the response to crime

This first response may come from any part of the private sector: individuals, families, neighborhood associations, business, industry, agriculture, educational institutions, the news media, or any other private service to the public.

It involves crime prevention as well as participation in the criminal justice process once a crime has been committed. Private crime prevention is more than providing private security or burglar alarms or participating in neighborhood watch. It also includes a commitment to stop criminal behavior by not engaging in it or condoning it when it is committed by others.

Citizens take part directly in the criminal justice process by reporting crime to the police, by being a reliable participant (for example, witness, juror) in a criminal proceeding, and by accepting the disposition of the system as just or reasonable. As voters and taxpayers, citizens also participate in criminal justice through the policymaking process that affects how the criminal justice process operates, the resources available to it, and its goals and objectives. At every stage of the process, from the original formulation of objectives to the decision about where to locate jails and prisons and to the reintegration of inmates into society, the private sector has a role to play. Without such involvement, the criminal justice process cannot serve the citizens it is intended to protect.

## The government responds to crime through the criminal justice system

We apprehend, try, and punish offenders by means of a loose confederation of agencies at all levels of government. Our American system of justice has evolved from the English

### What is the sequence of events in the criminal justice system?

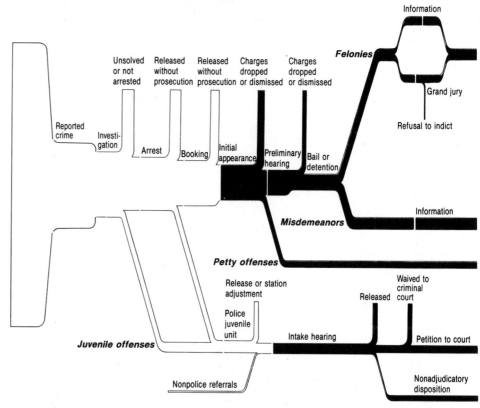

Note: This chart gives a simplified view of caseflow through the criminal justice system. Procedures vary among jurisdictions. The weights of the lines are not intended to show the actual size of caseloads.

common law into a complex series of procedures and decisions. There is no single criminal justice system in this country. We have many systems that are similar, but individually unique.

Criminal cases may be handled differently in different jurisdictions, but court

decisions based on the due process guarantees of the U.S. Constitution require that specific steps be taken in the administration of criminal justice.

The description of the criminal and juvenile justice systems that follows portrays the most common sequence of events

From *Report to the Nation on Crime and Justice*, Bureau of Justice Statistics, U.S. Department of Justice, March 1988, pp. 56-60.

in the response to serious criminal behavior.

### Entry into the system

The justice system does not respond to most crime because so much crime is not discovered or reported to the police. Law enforcement agencies learn about crime from the reports of citizens, from discovery by a police officer in the field, or from investigative and intelligence work.

Once a law enforcement agency has established that a crime has been committed, a suspect must be identified and apprehended for the case to proceed through the system. Sometimes, a suspect is apprehended at the scene; however, identification of a suspect sometimes requires an extensive investigation. Often, no one is identified or apprehended.

### Prosecution and pretrial services

After an arrest, law enforcement agencies present information about the case and about the accused to the prosecutor, who will decide if formal charges will be filed with the court. If no charges are filed, the accused must be released. The prosecutor can also drop charges after making efforts to prosecute *(nolle prosequi)*.

A suspect charged with a crime must be taken before a judge or magistrate without unnecessary delay. At the initial appearance, the judge or magistrate informs the accused of the charges and decides whether there is probable cause to detain the accused person. Often, the defense counsel is also assigned at the initial appearance. If the offense is not very serious, the determination of guilt and assessment of a penalty may also occur at this stage.

In some jurisdictions, a pretrial-release decision is made at the initial appearance, but this decision may occur at other hearings or may be changed at another time during the process. Pretrial release and bail were traditionally intended to ensure appearance at trial. However, many jurisdictions permit pretrial detention of defendants accused of serious offenses and deemed to be dangerous to prevent them from committing crimes in the pretrial period. The court may decide to release the accused on his/her own recognizance, into the custody of a third party, on the promise of satisfying certain conditions, or after the posting of a financial bond.

In many jurisdictions, the initial appearance may be followed by a preliminary hearing. The main function of this hearing is to discover if there is probable cause to believe that the accused committed a known crime within the jurisdiction of the court. If the judge does not find probable cause, the case is dismissed; however, if the judge or magistrate finds probable cause for such a belief, or the accused waives his or her right to a preliminary hearing, the case may be bound over to a grand jury.

A *grand jury* hears evidence against the accused presented by the prosecutor and decides if there is sufficient evidence to cause the accused to be brought to trial. If the grand jury finds sufficient evidence, it submits to the court an indictment (a written statement of the essential facts of the offense charged against the accused). Where the grand jury system is used, the grand jury may also investigate criminal activity generally and issue indictments called grand jury originals that initiate criminal cases.

Misdemeanor cases and some felony cases proceed by the issuance of an *information* (a formal, written accusation submitted to the court by a prosecutor). *In some jurisdictions*, indictments *may be* required in felony cases. However, the accused may choose to waive a grand jury indictment and, instead, accept service of an information for the crime.

### Adjudication

Once an indictment or information has been filed with the trial court, the accused is scheduled for arraignment. At the arraignment, the accused is informed of the charges, advised of the

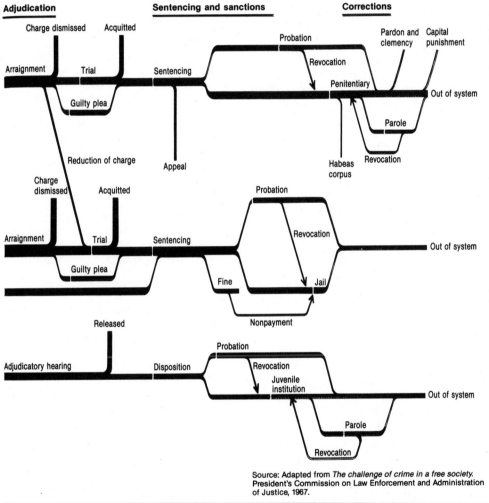

**Adjudication** · **Sentencing and sanctions** · **Corrections**

Source: Adapted from *The challenge of crime in a free society*. President's Commission on Law Enforcement and Administration of Justice, 1967.

rights of criminal defendants, and asked to enter a plea to the charges. Sometimes, a plea of guilty is the result of negotiations between the prosecutor and the defendant, with the defendant entering a guilty plea in expectation of reduced charges or a lenient sentence.

If the accused pleads guilty or pleads *nolo contendere* (accepts penalty without admitting guilt), the judge may accept or reject the plea. If the plea is accepted, no trial is held and the offender is sentenced at this proceeding or at a later date. The plea may be rejected if, for example, the judge believes that the accused may have been coerced. If this occurs, the case may proceed to trial.

If the accused pleads not guilty or not guilty by reason of insanity, a date is set for the trial. A person accused of a serious crime is guaranteed a trial by jury. However, the accused may ask for a bench trial where the judge, rather than a jury, serves as the finder of fact. In both instances the prosecution and defense present evidence by questioning witnesses while the judge decides on issues of law. The trial results in acquittal or conviction on the original charges or on lesser included offenses.

After the trial a defendant may request appellate review of the conviction or sentence. In many criminal cases, appeals of a conviction are a matter of right; all States with the death penalty provide for automatic appeal of cases involving a death sentence. However, under some circumstances and in some jurisdictions, appeals may be subject to the discretion of the appellate court and may be granted only on acceptance of a defendant's petition for a *writ of certiorari*. Prisoners may also appeal their sentences through civil rights petitions and writs of habeas corpus where they claim unlawful detention.

## Sentencing and sanctions

After a guilty verdict or guilty plea, sentence is imposed. In most cases the judge decides on the sentence, but in some States, the sentence is decided by the jury, particularly for capital offenses such as murder.

In arriving at an appropriate sentence, a sentencing hearing may be held at which evidence of aggravating or mitigating circumstances will be considered. In assessing the circumstances surrounding a convicted person's criminal behavior, courts often rely on presentence investigations by probation

agencies or other designated authorities. Courts may also consider victim impact statements.

The sentencing choices that may be available to judges and juries include one or more of the following:
• the death penalty
• incarceration in a prison, jail, or other confinement facility
• probation—allowing the convicted person to remain at liberty but subject to certain conditions and restrictions
• fines—primarily applied as penalties in minor offenses
• restitution—which requires the offender to provide financial compensation to the victim.

In many States, State law mandates that persons convicted of certain types of offenses serve a prison term.

Most States permit the judge to set the sentence length within certain limits, but some States have determinate sentencing laws that stipulate a specific sentence length, which must be served and cannot be altered by a parole board.

## Corrections

Offenders sentenced to incarceration usually serve time in a local jail or a State prison. Offenders sentenced to less than 1 year generally go to jail; those sentenced to more than 1 year go to prison. Persons admitted to a State prison system may be held in prisons with varying levels of custody or in a community correctional facility.

A prisoner may become eligible for parole after serving a specific part of his or her sentence. Parole is the conditional release of a prisoner before the prisoner's full sentence has been served. The decision to grant parole is made by an authority such as a parole board, which has power to grant or revoke parole or to discharge a parolee altogether. The way parole decisions are made varies widely among jurisdictions.

Offenders may also be required to serve out their full sentences prior to release (expiration of term). Those sentenced under determinate sentencing laws can be released only after they have served their full sentence (mandatory release) less any "goodtime" received while in prison. Inmates get such credits against their sentences automatically or by earning it through participation in programs.

If an offender has an outstanding charge or sentence in another State, a

detainer is used to ensure that when released from prison he or she will be transferred to the other State.

If released by a parole board decision or by mandatory release, the releasee will be under the supervision of a parole officer in the community for the balance of his or her unexpired sentence. This supervision is governed by specific conditions of release, and the releasee may be returned to prison for violations of such conditions.

## The juvenile justice system

The processing of juvenile offenders is not entirely dissimilar to adult criminal processing, but there are crucial differences in the procedures. Many juveniles are referred to juvenile courts by law enforcement officers, but many others are referred by school officials, social services agencies, neighbors, and even parents, for behavior or conditions that are determined to require intervention by the formal system for social control.

When juveniles are referred to the juvenile courts, their *intake* departments, or prosecuting attorneys, determine whether sufficient grounds exist to warrant filing a petition that requests an *adjudicatory hearing* or a request to transfer jurisdiction to criminal court. In some States and at the Federal level prosecutors under certain circumstances may file criminal charges against juveniles directly in criminal courts.

The court with jurisdiction over juvenile matters may reject the petition or the juveniles may be diverted to other agencies or programs in lieu of further court processing. Examples of diversion programs include individual or group counseling or referral to educational and recreational programs.

If a petition for an adjudicatory hearing is accepted, the juvenile may be brought before a court quite unlike the court with jurisdiction over adult offenders. In disposing of cases juvenile courts usually have far more discretion than adult courts. In addition to such options as probation, commitment to correctional institutions, restitution, or fines, State laws grant juvenile courts the power to order removal of children from their homes to foster homes or treatment facilities. Juvenile courts also may order participation in special programs aimed at shoplifting prevention, drug counseling, or driver education. They also may order referral to criminal court for trial as adults.

Despite the considerable discretion associated with juvenile court proceedings, juveniles are afforded many of the due-process safeguards associated with adult criminal trials. Sixteen States permit the use of juries in juvenile courts; however, in light of the U.S. Supreme Court's holding that juries are not essential to juvenile hearings, most States do not make provisions for juries in juvenile courts.

## The response to crime is founded in the intergovernmental structure of the United States

Under our form of government, each State and the Federal Government has its own criminal justice system. All systems must respect the rights of individuals set forth in court interpretation of the U.S. Constitution and defined in case law.

State constitutions and laws define the criminal justice system within each State and delegate the authority and responsibility for criminal justice to various jurisdictions, officials, and institutions. State laws also define criminal behavior and groups of children or acts under jurisdiction of the juvenile courts.

Municipalities and counties further define their criminal justice systems through local ordinances that proscribe additional illegal behavior and establish the local agencies responsible for criminal justice processing that were not established by the State.

Congress also has established a criminal justice system at the Federal level to respond to Federal crimes such as bank robbery, kidnaping, and transporting stolen goods across State lines.

## The response to crime is mainly a State and local function

Very few crimes are under exclusive Federal jurisdiction. The responsibility to respond to most crime rests with the State and local governments. Police protection is primarily a function of cities and towns. Corrections is primarily a function of State governments. More than three-fifths of all justice personnel are employed at the local level.

| | Percent of criminal justice employment by level of government | | |
|---|---|---|---|
| | Local | State | Federal |
| Police | 77% | 15% | 8% |
| Judicial (courts only) | 60 | 32 | 8 |
| Prosecution and legal services | 58 | 26 | 17 |
| Public defense | 47 | 50 | 3 |
| Corrections | 35 | 61 | 4 |
| Total | 62% | 31% | 8% |

Source: *Justice expenditure and employment, 1985,* BJS Bulletin, March 1987.

## Discretion is exercised throughout the criminal justice system

Discretion is "an authority conferred by law to act in certain conditions or situations in accordance with an official's or an official agency's own considered judgment and conscience."[1] Discretion is exercised throughout the government. It is a part of decisionmaking in all government systems from mental health to education, as well as criminal justice.

Concerning crime and justice, legislative bodies have recognized that they cannot anticipate the range of circumstances surrounding each crime, anticipate local mores, and enact laws that clearly encompass all conduct that is criminal and all that is not.[2] Therefore, persons charged with the day-to-day response to crime are expected to exercise their own judgment within *limits* set by law. Basically, they must decide—
• whether to take action

• where the situation fits in the scheme of law, rules, and precedent
• which official response is appropriate.

To ensure that discretion is exercised responsibly, government authority is often delegated to professionals. Professionalism requires a minimum level of training and orientation, which guides officials in making decisions. The professionalism of policing discussed later in this chapter is due largely to the desire to ensure the proper exercise of police discretion.

The limits of discretion vary from State to State and locality to locality. For example, some State judges have wide discretion in the type of sentence they may impose. In recent years other States have sought to limit the judges' discretion in sentencing by passing mandatory sentencing laws that require prison sentences for certain offenses.

## Who exercises discretion?

| These criminal justice officials. . . | . . .must often decide whether or not or how to— |
|---|---|
| **Police** | Enforce specific laws<br>Investigate specific crimes<br>Search people, vicinities, buildings<br>Arrest or detain people |
| **Prosecutors** | File charges or petitions for adjudication<br>Seek indictments<br>Drop cases<br>Reduce charges |
| **Judges or magistrates** | Set bail or conditions for release<br>Accept pleas<br>Determine delinquency<br>Dismiss charges<br>Impose sentence<br>Revoke probation |
| **Correctional officials** | Assign to type of correctional facility<br>Award privileges<br>Punish for disciplinary infractions |
| **Paroling authority** | Determine date and conditions of parole<br>Revoke parole |

# 1. CRIME AND JUSTICE IN AMERICA

## More than one agency has jurisdiction over some criminal events

The response to most criminal actions is usually begun by local police who react to violation of State law. If a suspect is apprehended, he or she is prosecuted locally and may be confined in a local jail or State prison. In such cases, only one agency has jurisdiction at each stage in the process.

However, some criminal events because of their characteristics and location may come under the jurisdiction of more than one agency. For example, such overlapping occurs within States when local police, county sheriffs, and State police are all empowered to enforce State laws on State highways.

Congress has provided for Federal jurisdiction over crimes that—
• materially affect interstate commerce
• occur on Federal land
• involve large and probably interstate criminal organizations or conspiracies
• are offenses of national importance, such as the assassination of the President.[3]

Bank robbery and many drug offenses are examples of crimes for which the States and the Federal Government both have jurisdiction. In cases of dual jurisdiction, an investigation and a prosecution may be undertaken by all authorized agencies, but only one level of government usually pursues a case. For example, a study of FBI bank robbery investigations during 1978 and 1979 found that of those cases cleared—

• 36% were solved by the FBI alone
• 25% were solved by a joint effort of the FBI and State and local police
• 40% were solved by the State and local police acting alone.

In response to dual jurisdiction and to promote more effective coordination, Law Enforcement Coordinating Committees have been established throughout the country and include all relevant Federal and local agencies.

## Within States the response to crime also varies from one locality to another

The response differs because of statutory and structural differences and differences in how discretion is exercised. Local criminal justice policies and programs change in response to local attitudes and needs. For example, the prosecutor in one locality may concentrate on particular types of offenses that plague the local community while the prosecutor in another locality may concentrate on career criminals.

## The response to crime also varies on a case-by-case basis

No two cases are exactly alike. At each stage of the criminal justice process officials must make decisions that take into account the varying factors of each case. Two similar cases may have very different results because of various factors, including differences in witness cooperation and physical evidence, the availability of resources to investigate

and prosecute the case, the quality of the lawyers involved, and the age and prior criminal history of the suspects.

## Differences in local laws, agencies, resources, standards, and procedures result in varying responses in each jurisdiction

The outcomes of arrests for serious cases vary among the States as shown by Offender-based Transaction Statistics from nine States:

| | % of arrests for serious crimes that result in... | | |
|---|---|---|---|
| | Prosecution | Conviction | Incarceration |
| Virginia | 100% | 61% | 55% |
| Nebraska | 99 | 68 | 39 |
| New York | 97 | 67 | 31 |
| Utah | 97 | 79 | 9 |
| Virgin Islands | 95 | 55 | 35 |
| Minnesota | 89 | 69 | 48 |
| Pennsylvania | 85 | 56 | 24 |
| California | 78 | 61 | 45 |
| Ohio | 77 | 50 | 21 |

Source: Disaggregated data used in *Tracking offenders: White-collar crime*, BJS Special Report, November 1986.

Some of this variation can be explained by differences among States. For example, the degree of discretion in deciding whether to prosecute differs from State to State; some States do not allow any police or prosecutor discretion; others allow police discretion but not prosecutor discretion and vice versa.

# What is crime?

## Crimes are defined by law

In this report we define crime as all behaviors and acts for which a society provides formally sanctioned punishment. In the United States what is criminal is specified in the written law, primarily State statutes. What is included in the definition of crime varies among Federal, State, and local jurisdictions.

Criminologists devote a great deal of attention to defining crime in both general and specific terms. This definitional process is the first step toward the goal of obtaining accurate crime statistics.

To provide additional perspectives on crime it is sometimes viewed in ways other than in the standard legal definitions. Such alternatives define crime in terms of the type of victim (child abuse), the type of offender (white-collar crime), the object of the crime (property crime), or the method of criminal activity (organized crime). Such definitions usually cover one or more of the standard legal definitions. For example, organized crime may include fraud, extortion, assault, or homicide.

## What is considered criminal by society changes over time

Some types of events such as murder, robbery, and burglary have been defined as crimes for centuries. Such crimes are part of the common law definition of crime. Other types of conduct traditionally have not been viewed as crimes. As social values and mores change, society has codified some conduct as criminal while decriminalizing other conduct. The recent movement toward increased "criminalization" of drunk driving is an example of such change.

New technology also results in new types of conduct not anticipated by the law. Changes in the law may be needed to define and sanction these types of conduct. For example, the introduction of computers has added to the criminal codes in many States so that acts such as the destruction of programs or data could be defined as crimes.

## What are the characteristics of some serious crimes?

| Crime | Definition | Facts |
|---|---|---|
| **Homicide** | Causing the death of another person without legal justification or excuse, including UCR crimes of murder and nonnegligent manslaughter and negligent manslaughter. | • Murder and nonnegligent manslaughter occur less often than other violent UCR Index crimes.<br>• 58% of the known murderers were relatives or acquaintances of the victim.<br>• 20% of all murders in 1985 occurred or were suspected to have occurred as the result of some felonious activity. |
| **Rape** | Unlawful sexual intercourse with a female, by force or without legal or factual consent. | • Most rapes involve a lone offender and a lone victim.<br>• About 32% of the rapes recorded by NCS in 1985 were committed in or near the victim's home.<br>• 73% of the rapes occurred at night, between 6 p.m. and 6 a.m.<br>• 58% of the victims of rape in 1985 were under 25 years old. |
| **Robbery** | The unlawful taking or attempted taking of property that is in the immediate possession of another, by force or threat of force. | • Robbery is the violent crime that most often involves more than one offender (in almost half of all cases in 1985).<br>• About half of all robberies reported by NCS in 1985 involved the use of a weapon. |
| **Assault** | Unlawful intentional inflicting, or attempted inflicting, of injury upon the person of another. Aggravated assault is the unlawful intentional inflicting of serious bodily injury or unlawful threat or attempt to inflict bodily injury or death by means of a deadly or dangerous weapon with or without actual infliction of injury. Simple assault is the unlawful intentional inflicting of less than serious bodily injury without a deadly or dangerous weapon or an attempt or threat to inflict bodily injury without a deadly or dangerous weapon. | • Simple assault occurs more frequently than aggravated assault.<br>• Most assaults involve one victim and one offender. |

(continued on next page)

## What are some other common crimes in the United States?

**Drug abuse violations**—Offenses relating to growing, manufacturing, making, possessing, using, selling, or distributing narcotic and dangerous nonnarcotic drugs. A distinction is made between possession and sale/manufacturing.

**Sex offenses**—In current statistical usage, the name of a broad category of varying content, usually consisting of all offenses having a sexual element except for forcible rape and commercial sex offenses, which are defined separately.

**Fraud offenses**—The crime type comprising offenses sharing the elements of practice of deceit or intentional misrepresentation of fact, with the intent of unlawfully depriving a person of his or her property or legal rights.

**Drunkenness**—Public intoxication, except "driving under the influence."

**Disturbing the peace**—Unlawful interruption of the peace, quiet, or order of a community, including offenses called "disorderly conduct," "vagrancy," "loitering," "unlawful assembly," and "riot."

**Driving under the influence**—Driving or operating any vehicle or common carrier while drunk or under the influence of liquor or drugs.

From *Report to the Nation on Crime and Justice,* Bureau of Justice Statistics, U.S. Department of Justice, March 1988, pp. 2-3, 8-9.

# 1. CRIME AND JUSTICE IN AMERICA

**Liquor law offenses**—State or local liquor law violations, except drunkenness and driving under the influence. Federal violations are excluded.

**Gambling**—Unlawful staking or wagering of money or other thing of value on a game of chance or on an uncertain event.

**Kidnaping**—Transportation or confinement of a person without authority of law and without his or her consent, or without the consent of his or her guardian, if a minor.

**Vandalism**—Destroying or damaging, or attempting to destroy or damage, the property of another without his or her consent, or public property, except by burning, which is arson.

**Public order offenses**—Violations of the peace or order of the community or threats to the public health through unacceptable public conduct, interference with governmental authority, or violation of civil rights or liberties.

Weapons offenses, bribery, escape, and tax law violations, for example, are included in this category.

## How do violent crimes differ from property crimes?

The outcome of a criminal event determines if it is a property crime or a violent crime. Violent crime refers to events such as homicide, rape, and assault that may result in injury to a person. Robbery is also considered a violent crime because it involves the use or threat of force against a person.

Property crimes are unlawful acts with the intent of gaining property but which do not involve the use or threat of force against an individual. Larceny and motor vehicle theft are examples of property crimes.

In the National Crime Survey a distinction is also made between crimes against persons (violent crimes and personal larceny) and crimes against households (property crimes, including household larceny).

## How do felonies differ from misdemeanors?

Criminal offenses are also classified according to how they are handled by the criminal justice system. Most jurisdictions recognize two classes of offenses: felonies and misdemeanors.

Felonies are not distinguished from misdemeanors in the same way in all jurisdictions, but most States define felonies as offenses punishable by a year or more in a State prison. The most serious crimes are never "misdemeanors" and the most minor offenses are never "felonies."

## What is organized crime?

Although organized crime has been considered a problem throughout the century, no universally accepted definition of the term has been established. The President's Commission on Organized Crime, for example, defines the criminal group involved in organized crime as "a continuing, structured collectivity of persons who utilize criminality, violence, and a willingness to corrupt in order to gain and maintain power and profit."

Some characteristics of organized crime are generally cited:
- **Organizational continuity:** Organized crime groups ensure that they can survive the death or imprisonment of their leaders and can vary the nature of their activities to take advantage of changing criminal opportunities.
- **Hierarchical structure:** All organized crime groups are headed by a single leader and structured into a series of subordinate ranks, although they may vary in the rigidity of their hierarchy. Nationwide organizations may be composed of multiple separate chapters or "families," each unit generally headed by its own leader who is supported by the group's hierarchy of command. Intergroup disputes, joint ventures, and new membership are generally reviewed by a board composed of the leaders of the most powerful individual chapters. For example, La Cosa Nostra currently is estimated to include 24 individual "families" all under the general authority of a "National Commission" comprised of an estimated nine bosses.
- **Restricted membership:** Members must be formally accepted by the group after a demonstration of loyalty and a willingness to commit criminal acts. Membership may be limited by race or common background and generally

## What are the characteristics of some serious crimes?

| Crime | Definition | Facts |
|---|---|---|
| **Burglary** | Unlawful entry of any fixed structure, vehicle, or vessel used for regular residence, industry, or business, with or without force, with the intent to commit a felony or larceny. | • Residential property was targeted in 2 out of every 3 reported burglaries; nonresidential property accounted for the remaining third.<br>• In 1985, 42% of all residential burglaries occurred without forced entry.<br>• About 37% of the no-force burglaries were known to have occurred during the day between 6 a.m. and 6 p.m. |
| **Larceny-theft** | Unlawful taking or attempted taking of property other than a motor vehicle from the possession of another, by stealth, without force and without deceit, with intent to permanently deprive the owner of the property. | • Less than 5% of all personal larcenies involve contact between the victim and offender.<br>• Pocket picking and purse snatching most frequently occur inside nonresidential buildings or on street locations.<br>• Unlike most other crimes, pocket picking and purse snatching affect the elderly about as much as other age groups. |
| **Motor vehicle theft** | Unlawful taking or attempted taking of a self-propelled road vehicle owned by another, with the intent of depriving him or her of it, permanently or temporarily. | • Motor vehicle theft is relatively well reported to the police. In 1985 89% of all completed thefts were reported.<br>• The stolen property is more likely to be recovered in this crime than in other property crimes. |
| **Arson** | The intentional damaging or destruction or attempted damaging or destruction by means of fire or explosion of property without the consent of the owner, or of one's own property or that of another by fire or explosives with or without the intent to defraud. | • Single-family residences were the most frequent targets of arson.<br>• 16% of all structures where arson occurred were not in use. |

Sources: BJS *Dictionary of criminal justice data terminology*, 2nd edition, 1981. BJS *Criminal victimization in the U.S.*, 1985. FBI *Crime in the United States 1985.*

# Organized crime includes many traditional crimes as well as offenses such as racketeering

involves a lifetime commitment to the group, which can be enforced through violent group actions.

• **Criminality/violence/power:** Power and control are key organized crime goals and may be obtained through criminal activity of one type or in multiple activities. Criminal activity may be designed directly to generate "income" or to support the group's power through bribery, violence, and intimidation. Violence is used to maintain group loyalty and to intimidate outsiders and is a threat underlying all group activity. Specific violent criminal acts include, for example, murder, kidnaping, arson, robbery, and bombings.

• **Legitimate business involvement:** Legitimate businesses are used to "launder" illegal funds or stolen merchandise. For example, illegal profits from drug sales can be claimed as legitimate profits of a noncriminal business whose accounting records have been appropriately adjusted. Legitimate business involvement also elevates the social status of organized crime figures.

• **Use of specialists:** Outside specialists, such as pilots, chemists, and arsonists, provide services under contract to organized crime groups on an intermittent or regular basis.

## Organized crime groups often are protected by corrupt officials in the government and private sector

Such officials include inspectors who overlook violations, accountants who conceal assets, financial officers who fail to report major cash transactions, law enforcement officers who provide enforcement activity information to drug traffickers, and attorneys who have government witnesses intimidated to change their testimony. The public also supports organized crime by sometimes knowingly or unknowingly purchasing illegal goods and "hot" merchandise.

## Organized crime groups are involved in many different activities

In addition to its well known involvement in illegal drugs, organized crime is also involved in prostitution, gambling, and loan sharking operations and has been shown to have infiltrated legitimate industries such as construction, waste removal, wholesale and retail distribution of goods, hotel and restaurant operations, liquor sales, motor vehicle repairs, real estate, and banking.

## How much does organized crime cost?

A recent survey for the President's Commission on Organized Crime estimates that 1986 net income from organized crime activity ranged between $26.8 billion (a low estimate) and $67.7 billion (the high estimate).

The indirect costs of organized crime affect all consumers through increased consumer prices. Kickbacks, protection payments, increased labor and material costs, and lack of competition in industries controlled by organized crime all increase consumer costs. Unpaid taxes on illegal activities result in higher tax burdens for legal wage earners.

## Racketeer Influenced and Corrupt Organization (RICO) statutes are key tools in the fight against organized crime

The Federal RICO statute was enacted in 1970 and was amended most recently in 1986. Unlike other existing statutes that address individual criminal acts such as murder or robbery, the RICO statute was specifically designed to target the overall and continuing operations of organized crime organizations. Specifically, the act prohibits the use of racketeering activities or profits to acquire, conduct, or maintain the business of an existing organization or "enterprise." Racketeering activities are defined to include any act or threat involving murder, kidnaping, gambling, arson, robbery, bribery, extortion, dealing in narcotic or dangerous drugs, fraud, and other crimes. The act also provides for forfeiture of illegally obtained gains and interests in enterprises.

Twenty-three States had enacted RICO statutes by 1986. Most of them are very similar to the Federal statute.

The government also has other tools to fight organized crime, including witness protection programs, electronic surveillance procedures, and immunity statutes.

## There is much debate about how to define "white-collar" crime

Reiss and Biderman define it as violations of law "that involve the use of a violator's position of significant power,

influence or trust . . . for the purpose of illegal gain, or to commit an illegal act for personal or organizational gain." Another researcher, Sutherland, defines white-collar crime as "a crime committed by a person of respectability and high social status in the course of his occupation." Edelhertz defines it as "an illegal act or series of illegal acts committed by nonphysical means and by concealment or guile to obtain money or property, to avoid the payment or loss of money or property, or to obtain business or personal advantage."

Although specific definitions vary, the term is generally construed to include business-related crimes, abuse of political office, some (but not all) aspects of organized crime, and the newly emerging areas of high-technology crime. White-collar crimes often involve deception of a gullible victim and generally occur where an individual's job, power, or personal influence provide the access and opportunity to abuse lawful procedures for unlawful gain.

Specific white-collar crimes include embezzlement, bribery, fraud (including procurement fraud, stock fraud, fraud in government programs, and investment and other "schemes"), theft of services, theft of trade secrets, tax evasion, and obstruction of justice.

## Unlike violent crimes, white-collar crimes do not necessarily cause injury to identifiable persons

White-collar crime instead can cause loss to society in general as in cases of tax evasion, for example. For this reason, white-collar crimes, unlike violent crimes, may not always be detected and are more difficult to investigate.

## Little data are available on the extent of white-collar crime

Measuring white-collar crime presents special problems:

• **No uniform definitions** exist that define either the overall scope of white-collar crime or individual criminal acts.

• **Wide variations** in commercial recordkeeping procedures make it difficult to collect and classify data on the loss.

• **Uncertainty over the legal status** of financial and technical transactions complicates the classification of data.

# White-collar crime refers to a group of nonviolent crimes that generally involve deception or abuse of power

• **Computer technology** can conceal losses resulting from computer crimes.
• **Crimes may not be reported** to protect consumer confidence.

**Almost three-fourths of the white-collar crimes prosecuted at the State level resulted in convictions**

A study of 8 States and the Virgin Islands found that 12% of the white-collar crime cases that originated with an arrest and for which dispositions were reported in 1983 were not prosecuted. The study defined white-collar crimes as forgery/counterfeiting, fraud, and embezzlement.

Prosecution rates for white-collar crimes were similar to those for violent crimes (murder, rape, robbery, kidnaping, and assault), property crimes (stolen vehicles, burglary, and arson), and public order crimes (drug and weapons offenses and commercial vice). Because the study focused on white-collar crime cases that were reported through the criminal justice system, the sample does not take into account the large number of white-collar crimes that were not discovered, not reported to authorities, or did not result in an arrest.

The study also found the conviction rate for cases prosecuted to be about 74%, slightly higher than for violent crimes (66%) and public order crimes (67%) and about the same as for property crimes (76%).

About 60% of the persons convicted for white-collar crime vs. about 67% of those convicted for violent crimes were sentenced to prison. Eighteen percent of white-collar offenders sentenced to prison were sentenced to more than 1 year (about the same as persons convicted of public order offense) vs. 39% of violent offenders.

# ARE CRIMINALS MADE OR BORN?

## Evidence indicates that both biological and sociological factors play roles.

**Richard J. Herrnstein and
James Q. Wilson**

*Richard J. Herrnstein is a professor of psychology
and James Q. Wilson a professor of government at
Harvard.*

A revolution in our understanding of crime is quietly overthrowing some established doctrines. Until recently, criminologists looked for the causes of crime almost entirely in the offenders' social circumstances. There seemed to be no shortage of circumstances to blame: weakened, chaotic or broken families, ineffective schools, antisocial gangs, racism, poverty, unemployment. Criminologists took seriously, more so than many other students of social behavior, the famous dictum of the French sociologist Emile Durkheim: Social facts must have social explanations. The sociological theory of crime had the unquestioned support of prominent editorialists, commentators, politicians and most thoughtful people.

Today, many learned journals and scholarly works draw a different picture. Sociological factors have not been abandoned, but increasingly it is becoming clear to many scholars that crime is the outcome of an interaction between social factors and certain biological factors, particularly for the offenders who, by repeated crimes, have made public places dangerous. The idea is still controversial, but increasingly, to the old question "Are criminals born or made?" the answer seems to be: both. The causes of crime lie in a combination of predisposing biological traits channeled by social circumstance into criminal behavior. The traits alone do not inevitably lead to crime; the circumstances do not make criminals of everyone; but together they create a population responsible for a large fraction of America's problem of crime in the streets.

Evidence that criminal behavior has deeper roots than social circumstances has always been right at hand, but social science has, until recent years, overlooked its implications. As far as the records show, crime everywhere and throughout history is disproportionately a young man's pursuit. Whether men are 20 or more times as likely to be arrested as women, as is the case in Malawi or Brunei, or only four to six times as likely, as in the United States or France, the sex difference in crime statistics is universal. Similarly, 18-year-olds may sometimes be four times as likely to be criminal as 40-year-olds, while at other times only twice as likely. In the United States, more than half of all arrests for serious property crimes are of 20-year-olds or younger. Nowhere have older persons been as criminal as younger ones.

It is easy to imagine purely social explanations for the effects of age and sex on crime. Boys in many societies are trained by their parents and the society itself to play more roughly and aggressively than girls. Boys are expected to fight back, not to cry,

# Intelligence and temperament have heritable bases and influence behavior.

and to play to win. Likewise, boys in many cultures are denied adult responsibilities, kept in a state of prolonged dependence and confined too long in schools that many of them find unrewarding. For a long time, these factors were thought to be the whole story.

Ultimately, however, the very universality of the age and sex differences in crime have alerted some social scientists to the implausibility of a theory that does not look beyond the accidents of particular societies. If cultures as different as Japan's and Sweden's, England's and Mexico's, have sex and age differences in crime, then perhaps we should have suspected from the start that there was something more fundamental going on than parents happening to decide to raise their boys and girls differently. What is it about boys, girls and their parents, in societies of all sorts, that leads them to emphasize, rather than overcome, sex differences? Moreover, even if we believed that every society has arbitrarily decided to inculcate aggressiveness in males, there would still be the greater criminality among *young* males to explain. After all, in some cultures, young boys are not denied adult responsibilities but are kept out of school, put to work tilling the land and made to accept obligations to the society.

But it is no longer necessary to approach questions about the sources of criminal behavior merely with argument and supposition. There is evidence. Much crime, it is agreed, has an aggressive component, and Eleanor Emmons Maccoby, a professor of psychology at Stanford University, and Carol Nagy Jacklin, a psychologist now at the University of Southern California, after reviewing the evidence on sex differences in aggression, concluded that it has a foundation that is at least in part biological. Only that conclusion can be drawn, they said, from data that show that the average man is more aggressive than the average woman in all known societies, that the

sex difference is present in infancy well before evidence of sex-role socialization by adults, that similar sex differences turn up in many of our biological relatives—monkeys and apes. Human aggression has been directly tied to sex hormones, particularly male sex hormones, in experiments on athletes engaging in competitive sports and on prisoners known for violent or domineering behavior. No single line of evidence is decisive and each can be challenged, but all together they convinced Drs. Maccoby and Jacklin, as well as most specialists on the biology of sex differences, that the sexual conventions that assign males the aggressive roles have biological roots.

That is also the conclusion of most researchers about the developmental forces that make adolescence and young adulthood a time of risk for criminal and other nonconventional behavior. This is when powerful new drives awaken, leading to frustrations that foster behavior unchecked by the internalized prohibitions of adulthood. The result is usually just youthful rowdiness, but, in a minority of cases, it passes over the line into crime.

The most compelling evidence of biological factors for criminality comes from two studies— one of twins, the other of adopted boys. Since the 1920's it has been understood that twins may develop from a single fertilized egg, resulting in identical genetic endowments— identical twins—or from a pair of separately fertilized eggs that have about half their genes in common—fraternal twins. A standard procedure for estimating how important genes are to a trait is to compare the similarity between identical twins with that between fraternal twins. When identical twins are clearly more similar in a trait than fraternal twins, the trait probably has high heritability.

There have been about a dozen studies of criminality using twins. More than 1,500 pairs of twins have been studied in the

United States, the Scandinavian countries, Japan, West Germany, Britain and elsewhere, and the result is qualitatively the same everywhere. Identical twins are more likely to have similar criminal records than fraternal twins. For example, the late Karl O. Christiansen, a Danish criminologist, using the Danish Twin Register, searched police, court and prison records for entries regarding twins born in a certain region of Denmark between 1881 and 1910. When an identical twin had a criminal record, Christiansen found, his or her co-twin was more than twice as likely to have one also than when a fraternal twin had a criminal record.

In the United States, a similar result has recently been reported by David Rowe, a psychologist at the University of Oklahoma, using questionnaires instead of official records to measure criminality. Twins in high school in almost all the school districts of Ohio received questionnaires by mail, with a promise of confidentiality as well as a small payment if the questionnaires were filled out and returned. The twins were asked about their activities, including their delinquent behavior, about their friends and about their co-twins. The identical twins were more similar in delinquency than the fraternal twins. In addition, the twins who shared more activities with each other were no more likely to be similar in delinquency than those who shared fewer activities.

**No single method of inquiry should be regarded as conclusive. But essentially the same results are found in studies of adopted children. The idea behind such studies is to find a sample of children adopted early in life, cases in which the criminal histories of both adopting and biological parents are known. Then, as the children grow up, researchers can discover how predictive of their criminality are the family histories of their adopting and biological parents. Recent studies show that the biological family his-**

**tory contributes substantially to the adoptees' likelihood of breaking the law.**

**For example, Sarnoff Mednick, a psychologist at the University of Southern California, and his associates in the United States and Denmark have followed a sample of several thousand boys adopted in Denmark between 1927 and 1947. Boys with criminal biological parents and noncriminal adopting parents were more likely to have criminal records than those with noncriminal biological parents and criminal adopting parents. The more criminal convictions a boy's natural parents had, the greater the risk of criminality for boys being raised by adopting parents who had no records. The risk was unrelated to whether the boy or his adopting parents knew about the natural parents' criminal records, whether the natural parents committed their crimes before or after the boy was given up for adoption, or whether the boy was adopted immediately after birth or a year or two later. The results of this study have been confirmed in Swedish and American samples of adopted children.**

**Because of studies like these, many sociologists and criminologists now accept the existence of genetic factors contributing to criminality. When there is disagreement, it is about how large the genetic contribution to crime is and about how the criminality of biological parents is transmitted to their children.**

**Both the twin and adoption studies show that genetic contributions are not alone responsible for crime — there is, for example, some increase in criminality among boys if their adopted fathers are criminal even when their biological parents are not, and not every co-twin of a criminal identical twin becomes criminal himself. Although it appears, on average, to be substantial, the**

precise size of the genetic contribution to crime is probably unknowable, particularly since the measures of criminality itself are now so crude.

We have a bit more to go on with respect to the link that transmits a predisposition toward crime from parents to children. No one believes there are "crime genes," but there are two major attributes that have, to some degree, a heritable base and that appear to influence criminal behavior. These are intelligence and temperament. Hundreds of studies have found that the more genes people share, the more likely they are to resemble each other intellectually and temperamentally.

Starting with studies in the 1930's, the average offender in broad samples has consistently scored 91 to 93 on I.Q. tests for which the general population's average is 100. The typical offender does worse on the verbal items of intelligence tests than on the nonverbal items but is usually below average on both.

Criminologists have long known about the correlation between criminal behavior and I.Q., but many of them have discounted it for various reasons. Some have suggested that the correlation can be explained away by the association between low socioeconomic status and crime, on the one hand, and that between low I.Q. and low socioeconomic status, on the other. These criminologists say it is low socioeconomic status, rather than low I.Q., that fosters crime. Others have questioned whether I.Q. tests really measure intelligence for the populations that are at greater risk for breaking the law. The low scores of offenders, the argument goes, betray a culturally deprived background or alienation from our society's values rather than low intelligence. Finally, it is often noted that the offenders in some studies have been caught for their crimes. Perhaps the ones who got away have higher I.Q.s.

But these objections have proved to be less telling than they once seemed to be. There are, for example, many poor law-abiding people living in deprived environments, and one of their more salient characteristics is that they have higher I.Q. scores than those in the same environment who break the law.

Then, too, it is a common misconception that I.Q. tests are invalid for people from disadvantaged backgrounds. If what is implied by this criticism is that scores predict academic potential or job performance differently for different groups, then the criticism is wrong. A comprehensive recent survey sponsored by the National Academy of Sciences concluded that "tests predict about as well for one group as for another." And that some highly intelligent criminals may well be good at eluding capture is fully consistent with the belief that offenders, in general, have lower scores than nonoffenders.

If I.Q. and criminality are linked, what may explain the link? There are several possibilities. One is that low scores on I.Q. tests signify greater difficulty in grasping the likely consequences of action or in learning the meaning and significance of moral codes. Another is that low scores, especially on the verbal component of the tests, mean trouble in school, which leads to frustration, thence to resentment, anger and delinquency. Still another is that persons who are not as skillful as others in expressing themselves verbally may find it more rewarding to express themselves in ways in which they will do better, such as physical threat or force.

For some repeat offenders, the predisposition to criminality may be more a matter of temperament than intelligence. Impulsiveness, insensitivity to social mores, a lack of deep and enduring emotional attachments to others and an appetite for danger are among the temperamental characteristics of high-rate offenders. Temperament is, to a degree, heritable, though not as much so as intelligence. All parents know that their children, shortly after birth, begin to exhibit certain characteristic ways of behaving — they are placid or fussy, shy or bold. Some of the traits endure, among them aggressiveness and hyperactivity, although they change in form as the child develops. As the child grows up, these traits, among others, may gradually unfold into a disposition toward unconventional, defiant or antisocial behavior.

Lee Robins, a sociologist at Washington University School of Medicine in St. Louis, reconstructed 30 years of the lives of more than 500 children who were patients in the 1920's at a child guidance clinic in St. Louis. She was interested in the early precursors of chronic sociopathy, a condition of antisocial personality that often includes criminal behavior as one of its symptoms. Adult sociopaths in her sample who did not suffer from psychosis, mental retardation or addiction, were, without exception, antisocial before they were 18. More than half of the male sociopaths had serious symptoms before they were 11. The main childhood precursors were truancy, poor school performance, theft, running away, recklessness, slovenliness, impulsiveness and guiltlessness. The more symptoms in childhood, the greater the risk of sociopathy in adulthood.

Other studies confirm and extend Dr. Robins's conclusions. For example, two psychologists, John J. Conger of the University of Colorado and Wilbur Miller of Drake University in Des Moines, searching back over the histories of a sample of delinquent boys in Denver, found that "by the end of the third grade, future delinquents were already seen by their teachers as more poorly adapted than their classmates. They appeared to have less regard for the rights and feelings of their peers; less awareness of the need to accept responsibility for their obligations, both as individuals and as members of a group, and poorer attitudes toward authority."

Traits that foreshadow serious, recurrent criminal behavior have been traced all the way back to behavior patterns such as hyperactivity and unusual fussiness, and neurological signs such as atypical brain waves or reflexes. In at least a minority of cases, these are detectable in the first few years of life. Some of the characteristics are sex-linked. There is evidence that newborn females are more likely than newborn males to smile, to cling to their mothers, to be receptive to touching and talking, to be sensitive to certain stimuli, such as being touched by a cloth, and to have less upper-body strength. Mothers certainly treat girls and boys differently, but the differences are not simply a matter of the mother's choice — female babies are more responsive than male babies to precisely the kind of treatment that is regarded as "feminine." When adults are asked to play with infants, they play with them in ways they think are appropriate to the infants' sexes. But there is also some evidence that when the sex of the infant is concealed, the behavior of the adults is influenced by the conduct of the child.

Premature infants or those born with low birth weights have a special problem. These children are vulnerable to any adverse circumstances in their environment — including child abuse — that may foster crime. Although nurturing parents can compensate for adversity, cold or inconsistent parents may exacerbate it. Prematurity and low birth weight may result from poor prenatal care, a bad diet or excessive use of alcohol or drugs. Whether the bad care is due to poverty, ignorance or anything else, here we see criminality arising from biological, though not necessarily genetic, factors. It is now known that these babies are more likely than normal

17

babies to be the victims of child abuse.

We do not mean to blame child abuse on the victim by saying that premature and low-birth-weight infants are more difficult to care for and thus place a great strain on the parents. But unless parents are emotionally prepared for the task of caring for such children, they may vent their frustration at the infant's unresponsiveness by hitting or neglecting it. Whatever it is in parent and child that leads to prematurity or low birth weight is compounded by the subsequent interaction between them. Similarly, children with low I.Q.s may have difficulty in understanding rules, but if their parents also have poor verbal skills, they may have difficulty in communicating rules, and so each party to the conflict exacerbates the defects of the other.

THE STATEMENT that biology plays a role in explaining human behavior, especially criminal behavior, sometimes elicits a powerful political or ideological reaction. Fearful that what is being proposed is a crude biological determinism, some critics deny the evidence while others wish the evidence to be confined to scientific journals. Scientists who have merely proposed studying the possible effects of chromosomal abnormalities on behavior have been ruthlessly attacked by other scientists, as have those who have made public the voluminous data showing the heritability of intelligence and temperament.

Some people worry that any claim that biological factors influence criminality is tantamount to saying that the higher crime rate of black compared to white Amer-

icans has a genetic basis. But no responsible work in the field leads to any such conclusion. The data show that of all the reasons people vary in their crime rates, race is far less important than age, sex, intelligence and the other individual factors that vary within races. Any study of the causes of crime must therefore first consider the individual factors. Differences among races may have many explanations, most of them having nothing to do with biology.

The intense reaction to the study of biological factors in crime, we believe, is utterly misguided. In fact, these discoveries, far from implying that "criminals are born" and should be locked up forever, suggest new and imaginative ways of reducing criminality by benign treatment. The opportunity we have is precisely analogous to that which we had when the biological bases of other disorders were established. Mental as well as physical illness — alcoholism, learning disabilities of various sorts, and perhaps even susceptibilities to drug addiction — now seem to have genetic components. In each case, new understanding energized the search for treatment and gave it new direction. Now we know that many forms of depression can be successfully treated with drugs; in time we may learn the same of Alzheimer's disease. Alcoholics are helped when they understand that some persons, because of their predisposition toward addiction to alcohol, should probably never consume it at all. A chemical treatment of the predisposition is a realistic possibility. Certain types of slow learners can already be helped by special programs. In time, others will be also.

Crime, admittedly, may be a more difficult program. So many different acts are criminal that it is only with considerable poetic license that we can speak of "criminality" at all. The bank teller who embezzles $500 to pay off a gambling debt is not engaging in the same behavior as a person who takes $500 from a liquor store at the point of a gun or one who causes $500 worth of damage by drunkenly driving his car into a parked vehicle. Moreover, crime, unlike alcoholism or dyslexia, exposes a person to the formal condemnation of society and the possibility of imprisonment. We naturally and rightly worry about treating all "criminals" alike, or stigmatizing persons whom we think might become criminal by placing them in special programs designed to prevent criminality.

But these problems are not insurmountable barriers to better ways of thinking about crime prevention. Though criminals are of all sorts, we know that a very small fraction of all young males commit so large a fraction of serious street crime that we can properly blame these chronic offenders for most such crime. We also know that chronic offenders typically begin their misconduct at an early age. Early family and preschool programs may be far better repositories for the crime-prevention dollar than rehabilitation programs aimed — usually futilely — at the 19- or 20-year-old veteran offender. Prevention programs risk stigmatizing children, but this may be less of a risk than is neglect. If stigma were a problem to be avoided at all costs, we would have to dismantle most special-needs education programs.

Having said all this, we must acknowledge that there

is at present little hard evidence that we know how to inhibit the development of delinquent tendencies in children. There are some leads, such as family training programs of the sort pioneered at the Oregon Social Learning Center, where parents are taught how to use small rewards and penalties to alter the behavior of misbehaving children. There is also evidence from David Weikart and Lawrence Schweinhart of the High/Scope Educational Research Foundation at Ypsilanti, Mich., that preschool education programs akin to Project Head Start may reduce later deliquency. There is nothing yet to build a national policy on, but there are ideas worth exploring by carefully repeating and refining these pioneering experimental efforts.

Above all, there is a case for redirecting research into the causes of crime in ways that take into account the interaction of biological and social factors. Some scholars, such as the criminologist Marvin E. Wolfgang and his colleagues at the University of Pennsylvania, are already exploring these issues by analyzing social and biological information from large groups as they age from infancy to adulthood and linking the data to criminal behavior. But much more needs to be done.

It took years of patiently following the life histories of many men and women to establish the linkages between smoking or diet and disease; it will also take years to unravel the complex and subtle ways in which intelligence, temperament, hormonal levels and other traits combine with family circumstances and later experiences in school and elsewhere to produce human character.

# RACE :
# OUR DILEMMA STILL

**Again, a city was in flames. And again, race was back on the national agenda. In a NEWSWEEK forum, blacks and whites, liberals and conservatives, reflect on a horrible week.**

In the prescient film "Grand Canyon," about life in Los Angeles, Danny Glover, the black lead, turns to a young gang member who is brandishing a gun and says, "This is not the way the world is supposed to be." There is no better epigram for last week's events.

The L.A. riots are now part of our modern racial history, added to a list that stretches from Birmingham through Boston to Howard Beach. Here are some Americans wrestling with our lingering national dilemma:

### Spencer Holland
*Director, Center for Educating African-American Males*

**M**y first reaction was, what am I going to tell my children?

I'm still grappling with that. We told them that this kind of thing was finished in America. We're on them to do their academics, to stay in school, and then something like this happens.

I say to our children all the

time that if it hadn't been for white citizens of good standing, slavery would not have ended. If it hadn't been for white citizens of good standing, the civil-rights movement wouldn't have taken hold the way it did. So white people should let their children know that white people who do things like the police in the King case are wrong, just like black people in the ghetto who sell drugs are wrong.

But there is no need to burn down your own community. We learned those lessons in the '60s. You don't burn down your community. You mobilize and you wake up and you help each other.

### Bill Bradley
*Senator, New Jersey*

**I** had prayed I would never see this again. I hoped I'd never have to worry about another war at home.

The key thing now is to avoid a chain reaction, to stabilize the situation. Then we have to use these events as a pretext for rather dramatic action. We have to fight for and build democracy in every generation. We have to do it at every level: the presidency, every state, every community, every family.

Federal money is necessary—but not sufficient. We do need a sizable infusion of federal money. If we decided to spend $15 billion to $20 billion a year on rebuilding our infrastructure, much of that money would wind up being spent in the cities. We need to do that. We also need to spend more on the Job Corps, neighborhood development, unemployment benefits, welfare reform. We need to fund what are called 15-month houses, where new mothers can care for their newborns in the first, crucial months, in a residential setting that gives the children a chance. We need honesty and straight talk. Go home tonight and reread the Kerner Commission report. And ask yourself what it is we've managed to do in all the years since it was written. The answer is: not nearly enough.

### Norman Amaker
*Loyola (Chicago) U. law prof.*

**A**frican-Americans will draw from this the lesson we've always known. Our lives aren't worth shit. It's as though my entire career has been a waste of time. Same situation I encountered in the South when

defending Martin Luther King.

White people must determine where we go from here. The outrage that ought to be pouring forth is that of the white majority. Black America did not create this problem. We cannot solve it. Now it's time for some white people to step up and say enough is enough. If they don't, it means they don't care enough. It's that simple.

### Armstrong Williams
*Graham Williams Group, a D.C.-based public-relations firm*

**A** few weeks ago I would have told black high-school students there was a justice system that would protect them. After the King verdict I cannot tell them that they're not being discriminated against because they're black. I can't tell them that anymore because I don't believe it anymore. It's horribly painful. It makes me want to weep.

How can I as an African-American conservative tell kids to "stop harping on racism" and, "If you work you'll succeed"? Everything I've ever said and been working for has been shattered in that verdict. For a juror to say that the baton wasn't even hitting. You know what that's like? It's like the crazy people saying the Holocaust never happened.

I would like to say that there was no need for an NAACP. But I can see the need for it now. I'm going to silently wait and give the white community the benefit of the doubt. But I can understand why a lot of these black kids feel the way they do, that the legal system is not designed for them and nothing will ever change that, not when you can see that videotape like I did.

### Keaven Dollery
*President, Afro-American Patrolmen's League*

I was an African-American before I ever thought of becoming a police officer—in fact I never thought I would ever be a police officer. Maybe white officers need to take a sensitivity course to know how to handle black people because we demand respect as well.

I'm afraid for my kids right now out in the street, knowing that there is a possibility of an officer stopping them and beating them and being acquitted. Right now I don't feel like putting the uniform back on.

### Jonathan Rubinstein
*Author, 'City Police'*

Why is it that we have a profound division in this country along racial lines, yet black people in America only feel moved to public protest around issues of police brutality? White people and large numbers of black people feel threatened by the crime that plagues them all the time, black people in particular. Black people are so far out of politics, so far out of the context of American life that the only time they feel legitimized to make a protest is when they feel their lives threatened by the "white master."

We try to explain away the problems of the black community because of poverty, lack of education, unemployment. But we have to recognize that living in these neighborhoods is a pathology—they are a dumping ground of crime and all that is unsavory, as ghettos have been for centuries. We have to recognize that the black community has a special problem, which

has a history. It doesn't just mean we need more cops with more sticks, it means we need more policing. Until we can establish some kind of public order there will be no hope, no employment and no education.

### Brenda J. Muhammad
*President, Mothers of Murdered Sons (MOMS)*

We can't trust the police and we can't trust each other. Last year we lost more than 25,000 people on the streets of America. Of that 25,000, more than 70 percent were blacks who were killed by other blacks. When are we going to raise up in arms about that? We need this same vigor every day when a black person has been killed on our streets. But not until we rise up as we have in this particular case will we make a difference. The cheapness of black life perpetuates the attitudes expressed by the King jury. I feel that what a lot of those jurors were saying is, "Black folk don't care about black folk, why should we care about black folk?"

### Roy Innis
*Chairman, the Congress of Racial Equality*

I don't believe that this one incident—the beating of Rodney King in Los Angeles and the miscarriage of justice in Simi Valley—will turn back that real social revolution that we should be so proud of, a revolution greater than the French Revolution in the 18th century or the Russian Revolution at the beginning of this century. I'm convinced that the romance America had with overt racism is over.

The justice system has protected and shielded us from the worst effects of prejudice and hate in the '50s and '60s. The judiciary has been the bulwark of black freedom in this country. Black America, and the rest of America, needs to hear from honest black leaders who will not attempt to alibi for the pillagers. There should be a legitimate protest at the way the trial was conducted, a protest to insist that the federal government move quickly and with great determination. But the only thing those riots are

about is criminals acting like criminals.

### Henry Louis Gates Jr.
*Chair of Afro-American Studies at Harvard*

I haven't felt this depressed about race relations in the United States since the assassination of Martin Luther King, and like that assassination, I think this is going to be a watershed event in history.

I have always been paranoid around the police. I often find myself moving into upper-middle-class white neighborhoods, and the first thing I do when I move into a neighborhood is to check in with the police and introduce myself. "Hi. I am Doctor Gates. I go away often and I was wondering if there are any security precautions I should take during vacations." But of course that's not it. It's that sooner or later someone is going to see this Negro in a car and ask what he is doing there. I do it so they see this face. I've lived in all-white neighborhoods in Durham, N.C., and in Ithaca, N.Y., and now in predominantly white Lexington, Mass. I think it's disgusting to feel that you have to do that. It's just a bizarre form of behavior that's required by the racist nature of this society, and the police.

I don't think that any of us who have quote unquote made it understand what it means to have no hope. It's time for leadership to stop repeating tired, worn-out civil-rights slogans. It's time to work with scholars to find out the intersections of race and class in society. We need something new and I don't know what it is. But what has all this success of ours individually been about except to work together?

### Andrew Hacker
*Queens College political scientist*

The jury saw the tapes over and over. You have to wonder about these people, to ask what is going on in the Ventura counties out there, these white suburbs. And the mentality is, "The police are there to protect us; they have to be able to do anything they can to keep them away." Rodney King repre-

sents the "them." Simi Valley is 40 miles away from L.A., but these people are afraid of the Willie Hortons out there.

White America is doing fairly well and yet it feels that it has in its midst these former slaves who never adapted—never mind whether we let them or not—and now they're threatening us. They're supposed to know their place.

### Tom McClintock
*State assemblyman from Ventura County*

It is difficult to separate the social from the economic issues. Particularly in California, as the economy implodes, those at the lower rungs of the social-economic scale are feeling the pain the greatest and it is difficult to separate those emotions from social developments. Throughout the 1980s the economic expansion benefited all classes and race relations seemed to be clearly improving as economic opportunity improved. But that does not appear to be the case in the last year or two, and incidents like the King verdict compound the economic pressures that are building.

To the extent that economic opportunity is expanded, race relations are improved. But in the last few years we have unleashed the four horsemen of the recession: taxation, regulation, litigation and waste. To the extent that we can rekindle the economic expansion of the Reagan years we will see improvements in race relations.

### Matty Rich
*Filmmaker*

The riots are an excuse for white society to sit back and laugh. "I told you, these Negroes don't know how to act; they're dangerous." America breeds the hatred in these white police officers, these jurors. This is the way America sets a tone, the beatings of blacks and minority people. We're tired of the reminders that we're just niggers.

I feel real angry and upset. I've seen friends die. But I've never been through anything where my black friends and my white friends both have felt such *shame*. Something like this takes us back years. It strips everything away. If they don't show us the respect we are due, kids on the street are going to start plucking off cops —they've got more gunpower than the cops. The only way people will listen is violence.

If we had our black political leaders, this rioting wouldn't be happening. There is no black political leader. I'm talking about our, not everybody's, leader. I'm not talking about a rainbow coalition. I have nothing against Jackson, but I think the rainbow is an illusion. I think we need somebody who can relate to us on a street level, who can understand our frustration. Someone who can go to the high-up leaders and say, if you don't pay attention, your streets are going to be burned, not our streets but your streets.

### Charles Murray
*American Enterprise Institute*

I don't think the jurors' reaction had as much to do with race as fear of violent crime. But most of the fear of violent crime is fear of black crime. That is not irrational and it's something for leaders, black and white, to talk about openly. Frightened whites are responding to reality. If blacks say, "It's whites who have been frightened by the Willie Horton ad," we're never going to get anywhere. They've got to say, "Whites are scared of something that they're justified in being scared of."

When blacks say they've suffered years of neglect, a lot of whites are looking at pictures on TV of black looters taking things from stores as a disconsolate Asian sits by and watches his life's work go down the drain. They're saying, "How is it that this Asian guy, who we've not done one damn thing for in terms of social programs, how come he doesn't deserve our sympathy instead of the looters?" Unless blacks come to grips with that reaction, we're never going to get anywhere.

### Candace An
*Big One Market, Los Angeles*

When we saw the destruction we just cried and cried, the whole family cried. My parents worked for 15 years; in one night it's all gone. We called for police protection and they said, "Sorry." That's not fair. That's injustice. We didn't have guns, but when we saw what happened we wished we had had a gun to protect ourselves. My parents want to rebuild but they're afraid.

Everybody was rioting. It wasn't just black people. Mexicans did it too. They're hurting themselves. Who's going to cash their checks now? They need us as much as we need them. We just lost the American Dream. That's the dream that everyone has that you'll be able to support a family, have a business and make a better life for your children.

### Lu Palmer
*Chicago Black*
*United Communities*

The only remedy is from within. The problem is, because we do not control any institutions in our community or outside of it, we have virtually no chance of bringing about that remedy. Power comes from institutions. We control no institution. Not our schools, mass media, politics. Consequently, white men, in essence, control those institutions—and they thus control our minds. Our only way to escape that reality is through the building and maintenance of institutions.

### Martin Luther King III
*Fulton County commissioner*

I would like to see a massive economic protest. This case took place in Hollywood. It would be ideal if African-Americans chose for three months not to go to the movies, and not to patronize just for a month the record industry. When we affect white America in the pocketbook, it has always responded.

We have to address justice, and the way we do it is to utilize our power to vote. I would also like an effort of massive voter registration to come out of this.

### Jawanza Kunjufu
*Educational consultant*

I want our young people to read a book a month about their history and their culture and I want them to start with Malcolm X and Marcus Garvey . We have young people wearing Malcolm X caps who haven't read a book about him.

I tell young people to be very careful about the friends they choose. I tell young males specifically that where you are between 10 o'clock at night and 3 o'clock in the morning will determine where you will spend the rest of your life.

I ask them to remember the numbers 28, 30, 2 and 4: don't get married until you're 28, don't have children until you're 30, only have 2 children and have them 4 years apart. Last, but not least, we want them to put God first in their lives because then they would have a natural high.

### Adam Jones
*Writer, Peninsula magazine*
*Harvard University senior*

I'm horrified by the state of anarchy in Los Angeles. At least 44 people dead: that to me is much worse, at least in a statistical sense, than the occasional problems that result from excessive police force. A lot of people may be using this as an excuse to commit random acts of violence and looting. When people see that the power structure is breaking down, they lose their inhibitions. It seems to be a natural inclination. When one group starts to commit violence, then others say, "Wow, maybe I can get away with that, too."

Here at Harvard people look at you and they assume by the color of your skin that you have certain values. I think that's just wrong. I think things like affirmative action can promote racism; by saying you need someone from a particular background, you're assuming all of them are the same. It promotes resentment on the part of majorities, who assume that they may lose to a less qualified person.

### Angela
*Clark Atlanta*
*University student*

It's Angela. Just Angela. If we cannot have justice there's not going to be any peace. We can't just sit there and say, "Oh, gee, that was so unfair." It doesn't work. It does not work. White people do not care. They can smile in your face but they don't care. We're tired of it. I want something better, and I'm sick of it. I am sick of it. I've had it.

### William Julius Wilson
*University of*
*Chicago sociologist*

The problems in the inner cities have actually gotten worse since the Kerner report. There's a growing concern over poverty, increased joblessness and greater economic disparity. At the same time, however, since Reagan entered office, urban problems have received less attention on the national agenda.

I think there is an association between declining resources in the neighborhoods and increasing social problems. A lot of people important for maintaining stability in inner-city neighborhoods have left. This leaves behind what I call the truly disadvantaged population. As the higher-income black and white families depart, you have less stability, and in time you have the potential for a violent uprising if you get the right spark. It didn't shock me that Los Angeles blew up. Unfortunately the problem with that incident is that it aggravates an already tense racial atmosphere across the country.

If the violence in Los Angeles had been minimal, I think there would have been general sympathy for the rioters. People could appreciate that folks are upset over this shocking verdict. But as the rioting goes on and the looters come out of stores, people shift their anger toward the rioters.

We need political leadership to direct frustration in a positive direction. If only we could get people of all races to realize they have mutual problems and mutual interests in addressing them. We need to tell lower-income whites that we're aware of their anxieties and concerns and convince them that we should not be fighting each other for diminishing resources.

# 20 Years of War on Drugs, and No Victory Yet

## Joseph B. Treaster

Standing on a bleak corner in the South Bronx littered with old heroin syringes and empty crack vials, it is hard to imagine that the United States has poured nearly $70 billion into fighting drugs in the last 20 years.

"I look at the message coming out of Washington that we're winning the war on drugs and I don't know what city they're talking about," New York's Police Commissioner, Lee P. Brown, said in a recent interview. "It's certainly not New York City."

It also does not appear to be Washington, Chicago, Los Angeles or any other big city.

In 1971, when Richard M. Nixon became the first President to declare war on drugs, the country had perhaps 1.5 million heroin addicts—up from perhaps 50,000 in 1960—and legions of rebellious young people puffing marijuana.

Then in the 1980's a cocaine epidemic cut a swath through the heart of American society, starting as an expensive nose powder and changing into a cheap-per-dose but ferociously addictive crack-pipe load. Each President since Mr. Nixon has thrown more money into the battle. But the problem has persisted.

Now national surveys show middle-class cocaine use on the decline; it has dropped 22 percent since 1988. But Federal officials say 6.4 million Americans used it last year. Marijuana use has seen a similar decline from its 1979 peak but is now at roughly the same level among young adults—with about half having tried it—as it was 20 years ago, when war was declared.

In the meanest neighborhoods, where jobs are scarce and hope flutters on crippled wings, cocaine snorting and smoking is rising again. And the police say a flood of potent heroin is creating new addicts.

Drug-related crime is far worse than it was 20 years ago. Articles about machine-gun battles on street corners and children hit by dealers' bullets have become routine. Jittery addicts are still killing their grandmothers—or other peoples'—for drug money. Radios are still flying out of parked cars.

It may be too harsh to say the war has been lost. But on many fronts there seems to have been little progress.

Since 1971, the Drug Enforcement Administration has been created, Federal "drug czars" have come and gone and the military has been ordered into the fray. Different states have passed laws ranging from traffic tickets for smoking a marijuana cigarette to life sentences for selling heroin. The Governments of Turkey, Mexico, Thailand, Colombia, Peru and Bolivia have been threatened with diplomatic isolation or offered bribes for their farmers, herbicides for their drug crops and helicopters for their police. Panama has been invaded—a drug bust that took 26 American lives and more than 500 Panamanian ones.

Many drug experts contend that the United States, driven by Congresses and Presidents trying to look tough on crime, follows a fundamentally flawed policy: spending most of the money on law enforcement.

*Drug-related crime is far worse than it was 20 years ago. Articles about children hit by dealers' bullets have become routine.*

No one knows what will work against drugs—or whether the war, like an earlier one called Prohibition, ought to be abandoned as a failure, and drug abuse treated as a medical problem like alcoholism.

But experts say far more money should go for other tactics: anti-drug education for children, treatment for addicts and a search for more chemicals that, like methadone, block addictive drugs.

These are not new ideas. The bulk of the $3 billion that Mr. Nixon spent was for treatment and education. But it was soon outpaced by spending for enforcement.

For most of the Reagan years, even as crack sent overdose deaths and crime rates soaring, only about 20 percent of the budget went to treatment and education.

This year, the Bush Administration will spend nearly $12 billion on drugs,

# Billions for Enforcement, but the Flood Still Gushes In

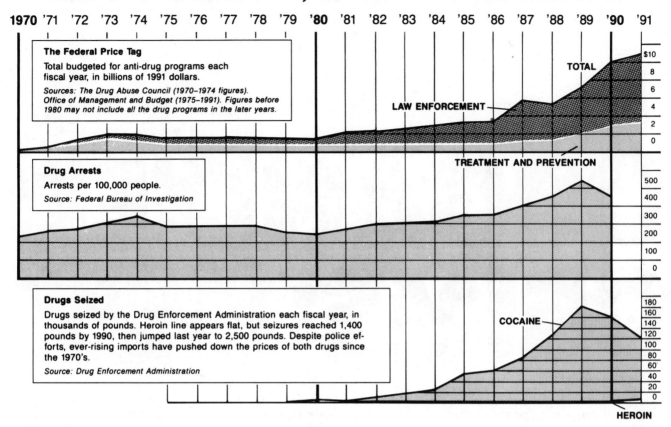

**1970** '71 '72 '73 '74 '75 '76 '77 '78 '79 **'80** '81 '82 '83 '84 '85 '86 '87 '88 '89 **'90** '91

**The Federal Price Tag**

Total budgeted for anti-drug programs each fiscal year, in billions of 1991 dollars.

*Sources: The Drug Abuse Council (1970–1974 figures). Office of Management and Budget (1975–1991). Figures before 1980 may not include all the drug programs in the later years.*

TOTAL

LAW ENFORCEMENT

TREATMENT AND PREVENTION

**Drug Arrests**

Arrests per 100,000 people.

*Source: Federal Bureau of Investigation*

**Drugs Seized**

Drugs seized by the Drug Enforcement Administration each fiscal year, in thousands of pounds. Heroin line appears flat, but seizures reached 1,400 pounds by 1990, then jumped last year to 2,500 pounds. Despite police efforts, ever-rising imports have pushed down the prices of both drugs since the 1970's.

*Source: Drug Enforcement Administration*

COCAINE

HEROIN

---

more than double what was spent in Mr. Reagan's last year in office. More than two-thirds of it is going to tactics that have consistently failed to cap the gushers of drugs: police training for South America, swarms of planes and boats, a picket of radar balloons and drug agents at the borders, more jails and battalions of police officers.

"It reminds me of that cartoon," said Dr. Herbert Kleber, professor of medicine at Columbia University and a former deputy director of the Office of National Drug Control Policy who quit when he couldn't get more money shifted to treatment. "This king is slamming his fist on the table, saying 'If all my horses and all my men can't put Humpty Dumpty together again, then what I need is *more* horses and *more* men.' "

Bob Martinez, who heads the Office of National Drug Control Policy, which makes him the current "drug czar," insists that the Bush strategy is to apply "pressure against all fronts." He says the drop in middle-class use implies "substantial, undeniable progress."

**Cocaine Still Easy to Find**

Critics of the law-enforcement emphasis believe that many Americans, seeing cocaine destroy friends, dropped it on their own, and that marijuana and cocaine use declined naturally as baby-boomers aged.

One indicator of how little effect the police have had in closing markets is that more than half the high school seniors questioned by University of Michigan researchers just last year said that finding cocaine was "fairly easy" or "very easy." Nearly 40 percent said the same for crack and about a third for heroin.

In the late 1980's, there was a flurry of support for legalizing drugs. Doing so, advocates said, would rout the gangs, cut crimes by addicts, and save billions in police, court and prison costs. Opponents argued that it would increase addiction, overdoses and hospital costs. But these days, said Dr. David F. Musto, a drug expert at Yale University, "Americans are moving increasingly toward seeing drugs as having no redeeming qualities whatsoever."

Still, many believe the drug budget should be spent differently.

Mark A. R. Kleiman, a drug specialist at Harvard, suggests focusing on addicted thieves and robbers, offering treatment and letting them stay out of jail by passing frequent urine tests. If three-quarters of them stopped using drugs, he estimates, crime would drop substantially and half the cocaine market would dry up.

The National Institute for Drug Abuse hands out grants for the search for a "methadone for cocaine," but has only $40 million of this year's budget.

In any case, many experts believe the solution lies not in foreign lands, at the borders or in prisons, but in the towns and cities of America. "If the 'war' is to be won, it will be won in the hearts and minds of people who might be inclined to consume drugs," said F. LaMond Tullis, a political scientist at Brigham Young University. Changing attitudes, he said, takes time, yields no get-tough-on crime headlines "and is not amenable to someone's four-year cycle on his political campaign."

# ORGANIZED CRIME: PAST, PRESENT, AND FUTURE

*"The new gangs have not expanded beyond their racial and ethnic borders in any significant way, which may explain much of their fierceness and violence as they compete for limited criminal opportunities."*

## Robert J. Kelly

*Dr. Kelly is professor of social sciences and criminal justice at Brooklyn College and the Graduate School of The City University of New York and president of the International Association for the Study of Organized Crime.*

ORGANIZED CRIME in the U.S. has been the object of morbid fascination in the popular culture and of abiding concern among law enforcement agencies nationwide. Still, we are jaded by the spiraling number of films and books, punctuated by real-life gangland assassinations, that reinforce an image of the underworld as a natural manifestation of ethnic urban life. La Cosa Nostra seems like a romantic, updated version of the western movie, played out on the streets of the big cities where the good guys and the wiseguys who share many of the same instincts and values do battle before an enthralled public.

Though organized crime was fertilized in the same urban environments as oppressive poverty, blind racism, and widespread alienation, it differs from these social ills. Because it has become so deeply embedded in our politics and economic life, most Americans do not see it as a serious problem. Where ambivalence and some degree of tolerance start and end is not clear. Consequently, a variety of activities that officially are defined as organized crime—drug trafficking, extortion, prostitution, sports betting, loansharking, and the sale of stolen goods—are not seen by everyone as equally criminal and socially enervating.

Some crimes are viewed as little more than harmless personal vices or victimless crimes. Thus, many who play illegal numbers self-righteously may condemn drug-dealing, considering their preference as entertainment and maybe providing some hope for a better life that hurts no one except the tax collectors. The specific crimes change over time, with crack replacing bootleg liquor and video pornography competing with street prostitution.

Nevertheless, the organizations and mechanisms that deliver illicit goods and services, whatever their precise structure or name—Mafia or Cosa Nostra—persist and transcend changing tastes and definitions of what is illegal.

Organized crime thrives in America's cities and has roots implanted deeply in the early tumultuous history of the U.S. The outlaw gangs of the Old West constitute part of our criminal heritage. Sanitized for pop consumption, these have passed into our romantic legendary social history. However, the modern concern with organized criminality is associated less with bandits raiding trains and stagecoaches and more with the cities filling up with immigrants.

For European arrivals at the turn of the century and contemporary waves of immigrants from the Pacific and Caribbean rims, the quick illicit profits from crime represented rapid advancement up the first rungs of a ladder of social mobility, promising an escape from the ignominious squalor of slum life. The history of this ethnic succession has described a demonstrable relationship among minority status, politics, and crime. It first infected the Irish, who formed notorious street gangs in the large cities where they settled. By the end of World War I, the Irish virtually dominated both crime and big city machine politics. Eventually, the political influence they nursed into being enabled them to shift into legitimate occupations in construction, trucking, public utilities, and the burgeoning civil services, where Irish ethnicity became synonymous with police work.

The aftermath of the war also brought Prohibition, a defining moment in the American crime scene. The Volstead Act, the crowning achievement of the Temperance Movement, forbade the sale and distribution of alcoholic beverages for personal consumption. The legislation morally was intended to rescue the masses from enslavement to liquor, but created unprecedented criminal opportunities for Jewish and Italian gangsters who cooperated and competed with the Irish underworld. The subsequent outbreak of murder and mayhem connected with the enormously lucrative bootleg business aroused fear of crime throughout the U.S. Anticipating Repeal, the shrewder gangsters invested their money in other businesses. By the late 1930s, the criminal syndicates that emerged during Prohibition attached themselves to other important sources of both legitimate and illicit income by leveraging themselves into growth industries such as gambling and labor unions.

In the early 1940s, shocked by indiscriminate violence in the streets, prosecutors and citizen groups grew militant and responded to public outcries that crime be brought under control and contained. The exposure in New York City of a secret organization of professional killers-for-hire, labeled Murder, Inc., stunned the nation.

It was not until 1951 that an official style was set for the investigation of organized crime which continues to this day. The Kefauver Committee conducted public hearings across the nation seeking maximum press exposure and openly identified what it called an American Mafia. That criminal organization was said to control a vast network of vice activities stretching from coast to coast that had corrupted all levels of government. These sensational claims received wide publicity, but were not taken too seriously by law enforcement agencies until the accidental discovery of a major gangster summit in Appalachia, N.Y., in 1957. On top of this came the 1963 testimony of Joseph Valachi before a Congressional committee in which he announced the existence of La Cosa Nostra. Valachi

was a "soldier" in the Genovese "crime family" who had soured on the mob and decided that the best way to get revenge was to expose it.

Even after Valachi's disclosures of an Italian-American crime network composed of 24 "families" whose tentacles reached across the country and whose activities were coordinated by a governing body of Mafia chiefs called the "Commission," the attack on organized crime was remarkably feeble. In 1967, the President's Task Force meticulously charted family lineages and analyzed the organizational structure of La Cosa Nostra. Its most important recommendations were RICO statutes and electronic surveillance legislation that took many years to implement.

The lack of a vigorous response to organized crime may be explained by a confluence of events and factors that remain more or less chronic problems for law enforcement. First, many local law enforcement officials had been compromised, tempted by bribes into allowing "harmless" vices to operate, and therefore had become too enmeshed in the web of corruption spun by crime syndicates. Second, even those with the will and determination to resist easy money to look the other way often lacked the manpower and sophisticated skills to investigate complex illegal business enterprises. Third, the vaunted code of silence that is part of the subculture of organized criminal behavior prevailed in spite of efforts to lure informants. *Omerta*, the idea that one sees and says nothing, was enforced with a vengeance until fairly recently, when the government put together

a Witness Protection Program that can afford some assurance of safety for those who cooperate with prosecutions against mobsters.

Finally, the FBI, which logically was the agency best equipped to confront organized crime nationally, had to be dragged into the battle. During J. Edgar Hoover's long reign as director, it did virtually nothing for reasons that are not entirely clear. He chose to ignore organized crime and often contended—before Robert Kennedy forced him to acknowledge its existence—that it was a figment of the imagination. Perhaps, in his cunning calculations, he realized that organized crime was a more formidable foe, and corruption threat, to his agents than car thieves, communists, and bank robbers. So, in order to maintain an unblemished record as the nation's premier crime fighter, the one who always gets his man, Hoover declined to join the war on the underworld.

Since the late 1960s, when the government began to show some interest, public hearings, prosecutions, and the testimony of members of crime groups have focused attention on Italian-dominated criminal activities. For the public, organized crime and Italian Mafia or La Cosa Nostra became essentially synonymous. This slanderous impression was and is more fiction than fact; other ethnic groups also were deeply involved in vice and rackets.

## Into the future: the new Mafias

As the apotheosis of organized crime, La Cosa Nostra reflects not so much an obses-

Special Senate Committee to Investigate Organized Crime, chaired by Estes Kefauver (fourth from right), first brought Mafia activities before the U.S. public in 1951.

sion with the folklore of feudal bandits descending on Brooklyn and Little Italy as it betrays an ignorance of the facts. The fabrications have become glossed so creatively and ingeniously, they have created an intrinsic fascination that even the participants in the real thing, who ought to know better, are tempted to believe. Not unlike the debates about the existence of God, all there is to know about the Mafia seems to be known by now except whether it actually exists. Many scholars still find the evidence conflicting and unreliable—particularly the idea of a nationally coordinated conspiratorial brotherhood. Scholars demythologize the legend as quickly as popular writers and filmmakers re-mythologize the grandeur of the Godfather. The question, nonetheless, is not whether the Mafia has a sordid or glittering past, but whether it has a future.

Black and Hispanic street gangs seem to flourish quite well without the apparatus of a myth. Obviously there is Big Crime. Must this mean there are Big Players? The current consensus—a fragile one to be sure—among law enforcement specialists is that Big Crime is organized more broadly than it used to be and that La Cosa Nostra families continue to play some part in it—decisive in some illegal enterprises, marginal in others. To count La Cosa Nostra out, to think that the Pizza Connection trials spell the end of the Mafia, is to write a premature obituary.

The End of the Mafia school of thought maintains that sustained law enforcement pressures over the past decade, coupled with lethal competitive pressures from aspiring minority gangs, will drive the Mafia out or force it to go relatively straight, and that organized crime, like prizefighting, will be seized by the ambitious poor. This point of view overlooks the sheer size of modern criminal markets and enterprises. Common street punks can not start small as they once did and hope to compete with international drug cartels, multi-state rackets, and a law enforcement community organized to stymie low-level hoods. Capitalization, contacts, and experience are entry requirements, and these resources and assets are what traditional La Cosa Nostra groups can provide.

What seems likely through the last decade of the 20th century is that the Mafia will assume an entrepreneurial role—remote from the raucous street crime and vice activities, but bankrolling and protecting a new generation of gangsters. La Cosa Nostra may have the dubious honor of seeing its name generically applied descriptively to other ethnic criminal groups, with talk in the media about Chinese godfathers and Colombian capos. These young, aspiring Corleones in the UN of crime have been nurtured in the managerial revolution so that they may find themselves manning computers, rather than machine guns. Out of nostalgia or need, the Mafia will retain some small niche in the underworld since it has promulgated the best image and public relations gimmicks and because it simply got there first and set the tone and style for the bad guys and the good guys thereafter.

As La Cosa Nostra goes through a meltdown, what other organized crime groups will emerge and seek the top of the hill? The acquisition of power may be more complicated than the question indicates. Some surely will fall in with the Mafia and collude to achieve influence and authority, but others may strike out brazenly against the Mafia establishment and carve out their own territories, daring others to challenge them.

While the Mafia tends to its familiar illicit activities, the highly profitable and dangerous business of drug trafficking has attracted younger criminals whose greed and ambition scarcely are coarsened by experience. True to the traditions bequeathed by Prohibition, many of the new criminals are recent immigrants to the U.S. Many of the new arrivals—Chinese, Vietnamese, Jamaicans, Mexicans, Colombians, Dominicans, and even Sicilians—turn to crime not because the society is closed off to them, but because it is so wide open. In many cases, they come from societies noted for draconian police methods. Consequently, the freedom and anonymity possible in the U.S. and the diffusion of law enforcement are inviting to those who wish to skirt legitimacy, make money as quickly as possible doing whatever it takes, and hide themselves in the protective cocoons of impenetrable ethnic enclaves.

Black organized criminals are an anomaly in this inventory of lawbreakers. Involved since the 1920s in the policy (numbers) rackets and drug dealing, their ranks have expanded as Italian inner-city neighborhoods turned blacker in the social upheavals of the 1960s. Black gangsters moved up and commanded their own turfs. In Buffalo, Newark, Detroit, and Los Angeles, black criminal organizations took control of vice. With the possible exception of the Crips and Bloods—black gangs that have grown stronger and stabilized, displacing the dominant Italians—they have not developed a national structure like the Mafia.

Criminals from Cuba and Latin America have been washing ashore for some time as economic and political conditions worsen. The political revolutions and drug epidemics two decades ago were accompanied by the establishment of small, tightly knit colonies of Cubans, Colombians, and Mexicans in Miami, New York, Chicago, and Los Angeles, where the smuggling and distribution of narcotics in massive quantities fueled the explosive American consumer demand.

The Asian criminal figures in the U.S. at first came primarily through legal immigration agencies and social help organizations assisting people to settle in Chinatowns. Given the size of their migration (second only to the Mexicans), declining employment opportunities for unskilled labor, and the difficulties lawmen have with Chinese dialects, the criminal spinoffs of the tongs and local street gangs they influence absorbed many FOBs (Fresh Off the Boat). The gangs war incessantly over territory in the constricted neighborhoods of Chinatowns for control of gambling, extortion, prostitution, and drugs.

Jamaican "posse" gangs also arrived in the U.S., fleeing political turmoil at home. Members are drawn from the slums of East Kingston in Jamaica and drift into Miami, New York, and other cities where there are black-controlled drug centers. As with the Chinese and Latinos, these groups are very violent.

Riven from within by informants, threatened from without by government electronic surveillance, and beseiged by challengers, the Mafia has retreated. Yet, none of the emerging criminal groups enjoy the entrenched linkages with labor unions and businesses that have been the distinctive signature of the Mafia. The new gangs have not expanded beyond their racial and ethnic borders in any significant way, which may explain much of their fierceness and violence as they compete for limited criminal opportunities. Few of the new gangsters have flexed their muscles with labor unions and fewer still flirt with corrupted politicians and police. The Mafia may not have been deposed, but it has been shaken. There is much disorganization in organized crime, and this condition is likely to remain so in the future.

# THE SIEGE OF L.A.

## Denied the justice they demanded for Rodney King, protesters and looters unleashed the deadliest riot in 25 years—and issued a wake-up call to the rest of America

AMERICA ON TRIAL

"We've got shooting all over the city."

"They're destroying their own neighborhoods— it's as bad as an earthquake."

"Let's bang that motherf—."

Like bulletins from a war zone, the words and images came flying out of a city going up in smoke and flames. In Los Angeles last week it was full-metal-jacket time—lock and load. Downtown, a mob of blacks, whites and Hispanics torched the guardhouse outside police headquarters, lit a fire in city hall, then trashed the criminal courts building. Across town, hammers banged down storefront security gates. Flames shot 100 feet into the night. Giddy looters lurched off with carts of groceries and cases of beer, armloads of clothes, bundles of everything from running shoes to guns. The upscale trundled away TV and stereo sets, microwave ovens and personal computers, even office furniture. Standing in the firestorm, tears streaming down his face, Charles Kim, an immigrant from Korea, looked at a burned-out shop and cried, "This is not America.... We are all brothers. Why are they doing this?"

After years of neglecting the pent-up misery of the inner cities, the country shuddered at the bloody wake-up call. Out of a city endlessly burning, out of the heart of Simi Valley and the soul of South-Central Los Angeles, a verdict seen as a miscarriage of justice induced a convulsion of violence that left 44 dead, 2,000 bleeding and $1 billion in charred ruins. The 56 videotaped blows administered by Los Angeles police to Rodney King last year had landed hard on everyone's mind. But they fell like feathers on a suburban jury that acquitted the cops of using excessive force. "That

verdict was a message from America," said Fermin Moore, owner of an African artifacts shop near Inglewood. The reply from the inner city was a reciprocal "F— you." First South-Central blew. Then fires licked up to Hollywood, south to Long Beach, west to Culver City and north to the San Fernando Valley. The nation's second largest city began to disappear under billows of smoke.

Inevitably, the catastrophe summoned up memories of Watts; but the differences were more striking than the similarities. "All you had then was bottles and bricks," said one blood, opening his trunk to show

> From what you know of the Rodney King beating case, do you think the verdict finding the policemen not guilty was justified or not?
>
> | | WHITES | BLACKS |
> |---|---|---|
> | Justified | 12% | 4% |
> | Not justified | 73% | 92% |
>
> The federal government may be able to take action against the policemen involved in the case under U.S. civil-rights laws. Would you favor such action?
>
> | | WHITES | BLACKS |
> |---|---|---|
> | Yes, would favor | 77% | 91% |
> | No, would not favor | 17% | 6% |
>
> From the Newsweek Poll of April 30-May 1, 1992

his stash of automatic weapons. "That ain't it now—this ain't gonna be like the '60s." Despite his bravado, the incendiaries this time were a more mixed bag. Instead of enraged young black men shouting, "Kill Whitey," Hispanics and even some whites—men, women and children— mingled with African-Americans. The mob's primary lust appeared to be for property, not blood. In a fiesta mood, threadbare looters grabbed for expensive consumer goods that had suddenly become "free." Better-off black as well as white and Asian-American businesspeople all got burned. "This wasn't a race riot," said urban sociologist Joel Kotkin of the city's Center for the New West. "It was a class riot."

The elements of race and class mingled and combusted with tremendous heat, setting off secondary eruptions in San Francisco, Seattle and Atlanta. In New York City, stores closed and panicky whites left work early when a small protest flared up in Times Square. The conflagration surprised the authorities and singed them badly. Mayor Tom Bradley expressed his equal dismay with the verdict and determination to restore order; but he seemed tired and out of touch with the new forces surging through the streets. For a few hours President Bush wavered between offering sympathy for those who found the verdict astounding and politically safer homilies on the rule of law. Then, belatedly regrouping, he dispatched a team of Justice Department prosecutors to press federal civil-rights charges against the acquitted officers and he sent 5,000 troops to stiffen the LAPD. Once again soldiers with guns patrolled the streets of an American city. "We have seen images ... we will never forget," he told the nation. "None of this is what we wish to think of as America."

Could you trust your own eyes—that was the unsettling question. The 81 seconds of the King-beating video gave way to 72 hours of riot coverage. The combination threatened to fragment the country along its worst fault lines. Never had two worlds seemed farther apart than Simi Valley and South-Central, a microcosm of suburban and inner-city America. The King video did to the jury what freeze frames and instant replay can do to discredit a referee. But this was no game. At risk was one standard of justice for all, the fairness of the courts, the majesty of the law. The irony was that as tempers spilled over and Los Angeles toppled into anarchy, it was left to the victim to implore everyone else to come to their senses. Voice trembling, King suddenly reappeared on television. "Can we stop making it horrible?" he said. "It's just not right. We can get along—we just gotta."

**'Big Time':** The siege of Los Angeles began after defense lawyers turned what had looked like a clear case of police brutality into a shrewd exercise in reverse English. Pretrial publicity was relentless. The defense got a change of venue from Los Angeles to Simi Valley, a comfortable, white middle-class suburb favored by officers retiring from the LAPD. Even so, the evidence looked overwhelming. In addition to the video, prosecutors had transcripts of conversations in which Officers Laurence Powell, Timothy Wind and Sgt. Stacey Koon talked about "a Big Time use of force." ("I haven't beaten anyone this bad in a long time.") Then the fourth defendant, Officer Theodore Briseno, testified *against* the others. "Everyone from the president to the dogcatcher had their necks in a noose," recalled John Barnett, Briseno's lawyer. "I thought we'd be presiding over a hanging—my biggest worry was just getting the jury's attention at all."

The jurors—six men and six women equally divided between Republicans and Democrats—fairly represented the sense and sensibility of their own communities: places like Simi Valley, Thousand Oaks, Camarillo and Ventura. There were 10 whites, one Hispanic, one Asian; they ranged in age from 38 to 65. It was the genius of the defense to neutralize the video by playing up the high-speed chase that preceded King's beating and the contempt he had shown for the police. One juror told talk-show host Larry King that the video was "ludicrous." She argued that Rodney King had "dictated all of the actions." And when asked if the use of the word "gorillas" during the trial had bothered her, she said, "Not at all." Her conscience was clear, she added: the riot would have broken out in any case because "these individuals were . . . just waiting for a cause." Another juror said on "Nightline," "The only input I had was what the judicial system, the judge, the defense attorneys, the prosecutors gave me to work with—the law's the law."

**'Not guilty':** The verdict suggested that the jurors believed the officers were simply doing their job, which consisted at least in part of allaying the anxieties of Simi Valley about people like Rodney King and places like South-Central. In the courtroom, the foreman stood up and called "Not guilty" to the charges of assault and falsifying police reports. The jurors couldn't agree on the brutality rap against Officer Laurence Powell, and the judge declared a mistrial on that count. The words "not guilty" shot from the jury box like Taser stun darts. Witnesses shook their heads as the defendants patted their lawyers on the back, hugged their families. Outside, on the courthouse steps, Councilwoman Patricia Moore called the result "a modern-day lynching." John Singleton, the young director of "Boyz N the Hood," wrapped his arm around her. "This is a time bomb," he said. "It's going to blow up."

The clock was already ticking. King's supporters and friends of the policemen were shoving one another when the courthouse door flew open and Koon stepped out. "Guilty. Guilty. Guilty," roared voices in the crowd. A tight smile masking his nerves, Koon hotfooted it to his car; people kicked at his doors and shook their fists at him as he sped away. Reporters flashed bulletins, and within an hour protests were tying up the phones at newspapers, radio and television stations. Saying the acquitted policemen were "not fit to wear a uniform," Mayor Bradley called the verdict "senseless" and said it could "never blind what the world saw." "It's not just. It's not right," said Steve Lerman, King's lawyer. "It may be that 12 white jurors aren't going to convict four white cops for beating a black man—it may be as simple as that."

It was not as simple as that; the more agonizing question was how far a verdict honestly rendered could miscarry and whether those who had chosen sides over the matter would go back to the courts—or settle it in the streets. The answer came soon enough. At the intersection of Normandie and Florence avenues in South-Central, black kids began throwing stones and bottles at passing cars. The mob swelled. They hauled two white motorists from their cars and stomped them. Then Reginald Oliver Denny, 36, a gravel-truck driver with long blond hair, drove into the melee. Five men grabbed him, kicked him, smashed him on the head with a fire extinguisher and stole his wallet. For nearly an hour panicked drivers drove around him. A news chopper filmed the assault, possibly even encouraged it. T. J. Murphy, 30, an aerospace engineer, saw the beating on TV

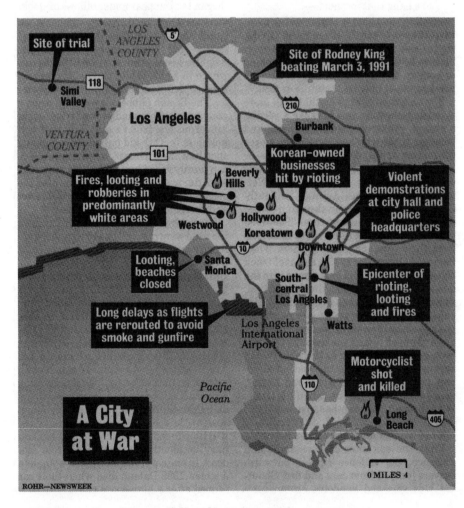

A City at War

ROHR—NEWSWEEK

and drove to the scene. He found Denny, eyes swollen shut, in the cab of his truck. With the help of three other African-Americans, Murphy shielded the critically injured trucker and got him to a hospital.

From the epicenter of Normandie and Florence, the violence rippled outward. Drivers jumped from cars and fled. Shouting kids smashed windows, tromped on hoods and roofs, torched the abandoned vehicles. Then they turned to a liquor store, small shops, a gas station. Before long, flames and black smoke engulfed the neighborhood. And the LAPD was nowhere in sight. White journalists became targets. Jeff Kramer, a freelance reporter for The Boston Globe, played dead when a gang smashed his windows and tried to tear him from his driver's seat. His seat belt held him in. One kid pulled out a gun and shot him three times. An African-American family found him and called paramedics. After waiting vainly for 30 minutes, the good Samaritans hid him under a blanket and smuggled him to the hospital.

**Fire fight:** As the violence swelled, most of the dead were men: all but 15 were African-Americans; there were 9 Hispanics, 5 whites and one Asian. Arturo Miranda, 20, was driving home from soccer practice with his family when a bullet tore through his car, hit him in the head and killed him. Scott Coleman, 26, and Matthew Haines, 32, were knocked from a motorcycle. Coleman was shot three times, but lived; Haines died instantly with a bullet in his brain. Los Angeles patrolmen got into a fire fight with snipers at the Nickerson Gardens housing project; a V-100 armored car rescued them, and Dennis Jackson, 38, was later found dead at the scene. But the police have not had time to separate out what may be ordinary accidents and homicides from riot dead. In one case, two men and a woman in a stolen 1982 Datsun died when their car flipped after a high-speed chase with cops in Beverly Hills. The emergency situation will make it hard to determine precisely the sum and complexion of the body count.

The riot did not play out in neatly drawn ranks of black against white. As dusk approached, more than 1,500 peaceful demonstrators assembled at South-Central's First African Methodist Episcopal Church. The group sang gospel songs, prayed that there would be no bloodshed. Mayor Bradley acknowledged that many felt outraged over the verdict, but he stressed that the anger was shared by whites as well as African-Americans. Blacks themselves appeared to split along generation lines. While parents called for peace, one young woman stood up and said, "We can no longer afford to listen to pretty speeches." Outside, gang leaders brandishing pipes, sticks and baseball bats whipped up hotheads, urging them not to trash their own neighborhoods but to attack richer turf to the west. "You have a car—then get your white

ass out of here," one friendly elder advised a NEWSWEEK reporter. As the church service came to an end, the sound of gunfire rattled through the darkness. A band of kids chased the reporter as he gunned his car across a front lawn and wheeled away.

In the days of raw nerves before the verdict, Police Chief Daryl Gates—whose style of L.A. law had started the trouble in the first place—boasted of having a special, $1 million contingency plan to cope with any trouble; but it turned out that the secret weapon was nothing more than a long-standing design for handling earthquakes and riots. At 2:30, about an hour before the jury rendered the verdict, bean counters worried about overtime let 1,000 officers go off duty. At South-Central's 77th Division, there were fewer than three dozen cops. At 6:30 Gates was nowhere to be found. He had gone to Brentwood to raise money to defeat an initiative aimed at police reform. "I asked him where he was going," says Police Commission president Stanley Sheinbaum. "He didn't tell me."

The city's nerve center, such as it was, was four floors below the lobby of city hall east in downtown Los Angeles. The first few hours after the verdict were near chaos. The speed of the riots startled the police and the fire department. "With the Watts riots in 1965 it built and built and on the third day the city went mad," says Police Commander Robert Gil. "This was completely different—the city went wild in just an hour and a half." The danger should have been clear. There were fierce protests at the Parker Center; a fire-rescue unit was missing in South-Central; the Foothill Station in the San Fernando Valley had come under fire.

Even so, no one ordered a "mobilization" until about 7:30. Gates did not get back until about 9 p.m. Only then did the LAPD lurch into action. A command post in South-Central did pull the city's 18 divisions together, and 600 heavily armed officers poured in. But the first results were mixed at best. It took a lot of time to get off-duty cops back, and the blue line was spread so thin it frightened no one. Many men with experience in South-Central were sent to the perimeter of the riot; many without it wound up in the thick of things. By 10 p.m., 25 square blocks of central Los Angeles were ablaze. Fans emerging from a Lakers game wandered into a combat zone. Shortly before midnight, Gov. Pete Wilson announced that he was sending 750 highway patrolmen and 2,000 National Guardsmen. "The situation," Chief Gates said lamely, "is not under control."

The sun came up on a city that had lost its center of gravity and was spinning out of orbit. Buses and trains stopped running. Schools closed. In a panicky rush to get out of town, drivers clogged the freeways; some bumped up onto cross-country bike paths to

beat the hopeless roads. Stores and offices shut their doors. The smoke from 1,000 fires grew so dense that air-traffic controllers could keep open only one runway at Los Angeles International Airport. Instead of a saccharine "Have a nice day," flight attendants looked anxiously at the arriving passengers and said, "Be careful."

Looters of all races owned the streets, storefronts and malls. Blond kids loaded their Volkswagen with stereo gear; a Yuppie jumped out of his BMW and scrounged through a gutted Radio Shack near Hancock Park. Filipinos in a banged-up old clunker stocked up on baseball mitts and sneakers. Hispanic mothers with children browsed the gaping chain drug marts and clothing stores. A few Asians were spotted as well. Where the looting at Watts had been desperate, angry, mean, the mood this time was closer to a manic fiesta, a TV game show with every looter a winner. Toting a Hefty bag full of electronic calculators, a 13-year-old black kid looked up dizzily and said, "My mom's not gonna believe the stuff I got today."

With the looters such a wild rainbow of races, it seemed more plausible to look elsewhere for what had possessed them. Richard Cunningham, 19, a clerk with a neat goatee, ran 10 blocks from his home to defend the Wherehouse from looters who were swiping CDs and videos. "Get out. Get out," he yelled, and they left. Standing by the cash register, he said, "They don't care for justice, they don't care for anything. Right now they're just on a spree." Three men lurched down the street toting a couch from a furniture store up the block. Cunningham shook his head. "They want to live the lifestyle they see people on TV living," he said. "They see people with big old houses, nice cars, all the stereo equipment they want, and now that it's free, they're gonna get it."

Throughout the city black merchants spray-painted their doors and awnings or put signs in their windows to distinguish them from white and Asian shops. Sometimes it worked; mostly it didn't. When Hispanic looters missed the JUSTICE FOR KING sign in the window of the Land of the Little Ones—a children's furniture store— and started to bang down the door, two blacks in Malcolm X baseball caps ran up and yelled, "Hey, motherf——. Don't hit that." Other black stores went up with all the rest. Looking on in disgust, Hector Ybarra said, "Where we gonna shop tomorrow? Where those people gonna live? Who's gonna be able to hold their heads up? This just ain't right." Nearby an African-American filmed the looters on his camcorder. He said he wanted the tape to show kids so they could see how the community was tearing itself apart, the same mistake it had made in the '60s.

Perhaps the most immediate racial ten-

# How the Defense Dissected the Tape

### Telling the jury how to interpret what they saw

How could they? Across an incredulous nation, that was the question everyone asked when they learned of the verdict in the Rodney King case. Most of the jurors weren't talking—indeed, some were hiding—but those who gave interviews were swayed by several aspects of the trial: King never took the stand in his own behalf, the four cops seemed believable and the prosecution failed to explain what they should have done differently. The strategy was to shift the focus away from the police officers.

In that sense, King was an easy target. He had led the police on a high-speed chase, reaching 115 miles per hour on the freeway, and then laughed at the officers who surrounded him with guns drawn. All this happened, the defense told the jury, before the video rolled and the beating began. And King could have ended the violence simply by "assuming the position"—face down, legs spread, arms outstretched—the defense argued. The two other black men in King's Hyundai—who submitted to handcuffs—were unharmed by the police.

There was still the videotape to deal with, though. How could the camera lie? For the defense, the key was to confront the damning tape head-on. "There were positive things to point out," Michael Stone, the lawyer for Officer Laurence Powell, told NEWSWEEK. The defense played the tape forward and backward, freeze-frame and fast-motion. "A picture is worth a thousand words," says Darryl Mounger, the lawyer for Sgt. Stacey Koon, "but a lot of times it takes a thousand words to explain a picture. What you think you see isn't always what you see." Here are three examples of what the defense—and jurors—saw.

## AM 12:52:41

**Roughly 30 seconds into** the beating, King struggles to his knees even as the four police officers order him to lie face first on the ground so he can be handcuffed. Defense lawyers dwelt on these early scenes in the videotape, where King repeatedly tries to get up. In a frame 25 seconds earlier, King made it to his feet and lunged at Officer Powell. The defense's message to the jury: King refused to obey orders and posed a threat to the officers. "They were not going to let him get into a position where he could stand again," says Stone, Powell's lawyer. That's why they used their batons on a man the lawyers said was 6 feet 3 and 250 pounds. Expert witnesses explained that under LAPD regulations, officers are permitted to use force to subdue a suspect or overcome resistance. The judge's instructions to the jury further emphasized that such force is "reasonable" if the typical cop would use it under similar circumstances.

Other defense witnesses testified that King had already been hit with two Taser darts, each carrying 50,000 volts of electricity—enough juice to immobilize almost any suspect. Tim Singer, a highway-patrol cop who was not charged, testified that the scene reminded him of a movie "where the monster gets shot and still is coming at you." This shows King's willingness to resist arrest, Stone says. "The strategy was to put the jury in the shoes of the police officer so they see things through his eyes." It apparently worked. One juror told CNN, "They did what they had to do in order to get him under control in extreme conditions."

## AM 12:53:20

**King lies on the ground** face first, having already sustained numerous blows from the four policemen. Officer Theodore Briseno has his leg on King's neck. Yet the defense believed this frame critical to their success in winning over the 12 jury members. Why? Because, much as it might appear otherwise, Briseno isn't really attacking King. He's keeping him down for his own good. Briseno testified that he feared that his exhausted colleagues would escalate the violence—maybe even shoot the suspect—if King didn't stay on the ground at this late point in the highly charged confrontation. Under this view of the videotape, Briseno's lawyer John Barnett told the jury, Briseno may have saved King's life rather than causing him gratuitous injury.

The frame also shows, as the defense team argued it, that Officer Powell has moved his baton out of his strong right hand and, in preparation for an arrest, is reaching for handcuffs in his rear pocket. This is the only point in the 81-second taped beating that the officers testified that they believed King was ready to stop resisting and comply with orders. But, as shown in subsequent frames of the video, King began to move yet again. Powell quickly shifted his baton back to his right hand and delivered more blows in an attempt to subdue him. "In my opinion," a juror told Reuters, King "was in full control." Only later did King finally ask the officers, "Please stop." Though King still wasn't in the proper position, Sergeant Koon instructed the officers to "cuff him."

## AM 12:53:29

**The latter part of the** videotape potentially was the most damaging to the four police officers. King is virtually motionless on the ground and is offering no visible resistance. But the officers, according to their lawyers, continued to beat King because he refused to comply with their demands. The cops also said that the tape hardly shows everything they were dealing with—King's expression, for example. "This guy had a look of determination," says Mounger, Sergeant Koon's lawyer. "He did not have a look of pain or fear on his face." And they pointed out that King appeared to be on PCP, a drug that sometimes gives users unusual strength. (Tests showed no PCP, but King was legally drunk.)

Stone concedes that these frames "put us in a terrible hole. When I first saw the tape, my knees were shaking." But Stone and the other defense attorneys figured that it could show that the officers complied with rules for escalating degrees of force.

Police are trained to use the baton first to cause pain. That usually stops a suspect. "A little pain is a great incentive," says Mounger, who served 10 years with the Los Angeles Police Department. "When you get hit with a metal baton by someone who knows how to swing it, you're supposed to do what they say so they don't hit you again." If the pain doesn't deter, the officers are trained to use the baton to break bones—wrists, elbows, clavicles—bones that break easily. One juror's conclusion: "The officers simply did what they are trained for, using the tools that they are given."

BOB COHN and DAVID A. KAPLAN

sion in the city divided blacks and Koreans, not blacks and whites. A year ago a Korean grocer shot and killed Latasha Harlins, a black 15-year-old, after a fight in a market; the black and Korean communities have been at each other's throats ever since then. Well over 100 Asian-owned stores went up in flames last week. "We've been here 400 years. Our blood is here, in the land. You don't shoot our children," said one middle-aged African-American studying the fires on Pico Street. "F–k them." Among many hardworking Koreans, the feeling was mutual.

**'No trouble':** With the police in disarray, some Koreans formed their own vigilante groups for self-defense. They strapped metal grocery carts together in a line across the parking lot at the Korean Supermarket on Olympic. Then they drew their Volvos, Mercedeses and other high-end cars into a Maginot line. Behind the cars crouched a dozen men with shotguns and pistols. Some had cellular phones strapped to their belts; others set up fields of fire from a supermarket roof. "No trouble," said one of the defenders with a wave. "Come back tomorrow."

The people whose job it was to protect Los Angeles took a little longer to pull together. After their initial fuddlement, Mayor Bradley, Governor Wilson and Chief Gates regained their equilibrium. They imposed a dawn-to-dusk curfew; they mustered more National Guardsmen. President Bush put the U.S. Army at Ford Ord at their disposal, along with 1,000 federal officers trained in riot control, and declared the city a disaster area. "We will take back our streets," the mayor vowed—and they did.

It was a victory with no parades. There was nothing to celebrate. The smoking rubble gave off a sour smell that drifted over entire neighborhoods. Mayor Bradley named Peter Ueberroth, the former baseball commissioner, to head a committee to rebuild neighborhoods damaged in the rioting. One city official estimated that even before the riots most of South-Central's businesses were just getting by, that perhaps 30 percent were not insured. Even those that had insurance will probably not

recover full damages. "I'm black, I'm proud. I love my people," says Thomas Hill, owner of a shop on Western Avenue. "But I'm a businessman and I've got a family to support. I'll never come back here again." Watts never recovered from the 1965 riots. Now, predicts sociologist Kotkin, "South-Central L.A. will become an economic Mojave Desert."

If the economic wreckage was awful, the damage to institutions and human trust was far worse. And no one was going to get a breather. King has brought an $83 million civil suit against the city. The city must now decide whether to retry Powell. The Justice Department investigation seemed

---

Compared with whites charged with crimes, are black people charged with crimes treated more harshly or more leniently, or are blacks and whites treated about the same in this country's justice system?

|  | WHITES | BLACKS |
|---|---|---|
| **More harshly** | 46% | 75% |
| **More leniently** | 5% | 3% |
| **The same** | 38% | 16% |

For this special NEWSWEEK Poll, The Gallup Organization interviewed a national sample of 242 black adults and 350 white adults by telephone April 30–May 1. The margin of error: plus or minus 5 percentage points (6 for whites, 7 for blacks). Some "Don't know" and other responses not shown. The NEWSWEEK Poll © 1992 by NEWSWEEK, Inc.

---

likely to produce federal indictments against the four cops, and who knew how many reruns of the video. It was hard to see how relations between the community and the police could get much worse. "You take the aggression out of a stud and see what happens," muttered one cop. "We were a bull. We feel we've been castrated." "I've been worried for my life since this whole thing began," added Rich-

ard Sanchez, a nine-year veteran of the force. "A lot of guys are talking about retirement."

**'The system':** Community trust, race relations, the delicate arrangements of class were all in tatters. Not since the 1960s had so many people talked so furiously about "the system" and the way it ran down the powerless. Talk, of course, meant little. After the verdict, a Washington Post/ABC News Poll showed that three quarters of the whites questioned agreed with the all-but-unanimous feeling of African-Americans that the system of justice was loaded against them. But the riots have probably wrecked whatever chance there might have been for a reconciliation. "It will be much harder to push through any meaningful reform of the LAPD," predicted Ramona Ripston of the American Civil Liberties Union. The more likely outcome was a backlash that will lend itself to the hot rhetoric and manipulations of politicians.

Over the past century there have been four cycles of major riots involving race, and now class, and each time things seem to cut to the same pattern: a long accumulation of grievances at the bottom, a studied indifference at the top, finally a catalyst—then an explosion. How awful, everyone says. Then the rush to scapegoats instead of solutions begins. It has been more than 20 years since the Kerner Commission said the United States was drawing itself up into two societies, separate and unequal. It took the combined eruptions of Watts, Detroit, Newark and Washington, D.C., just to get that on the record. There has been progress since then, but nowhere near enough. Now the Big One has hit Los Angeles—not an earthquake as everyone feared, but a tectonic jolt in the nation's soul. It will take nerve and new ideas to ride through the aftershocks.

TOM MATHEWS *with* MICHAEL MEYER, DONNA FOOTE, ANDREW MURR, LYNDA WRIGHT, JOSHUA HAMMER, MARCUS MABRY, HOWARD MANLY, KAREN SPRINGEN *and* REBECCA CRANDALL *in Los Angeles*

# Understanding Mass Murder: A Starting Point

## Ronald M. Holmes and Stephen T. Holmes

*Ronald M. Holmes is professor, School of Justice Administration, University of Louisville. Stephen T. Holmes is research assistant, University of Cincinnati.*

There is a great deal of misunderstanding about mass murder. Often, the terms mass murder, serial murder, and spree murder are used interchangeably. But there are fundamental differences in these three forms of "multicide," the killing of three or more victims. Motivation, anticipated gains, selection of victims, methods of murder, and other important elements are unique to each type. Here, one type of multicide—mass murder—is examined.

## WHAT IS MASS MURDER?

Obviously, the complexities of mass murder cannot be explained in a simple definition. However, briefly stated, mass murder is the killing of a number of persons at one time and in one place. What constitutes "a number of persons," however, has been the topic of debate. Although some authorities have stipulated four as the minimum number of victims necessary for an incident to be called a mass murder (Hazelwood & Douglas, 1980), others have set the number at three (Holmes and De-Burger, 1985, 1988; Hickey, 1991). Dietz also offers the number three " . . . if we define mass murder as the willful injuring of five or more persons of whom three or more are killed by a single offender in a single incident" (1986, p. 480).

The concern with numbers becomes complicated when injured victims are factored into the definition. Of course, if only two persons are killed and 30 are saved by the heroic actions of medical personnel, is this not also a mass murder? One can see the danger of limiting the definition to the number of victims killed.

Time is another critical element in the basic definition of mass murder. Typically, mass murder is a single episodic act of violence, occurring "at one time and in one place." One such case occurred at a McDonald's restaurant in San Ysidro, California. The victims, 40 in all shot dead, just happened to be in the same place in the restaurant. Many similar situations have occurred. However, one must recognize that incidents may occur at slightly different times, say minutes or even a few hours apart, and also at different locales, perhaps only a few blocks away, and still constitute mass murder. For example, a mass murderer may go into a business establishment and kill several customers and then go across town and kill another person. This must be considered a single act of mass murder despite the slightly varying times and locations.

Thus, a definition of mass murder should take into consideration 1) the number of victims, 2) the location of the murders, 3) the time of the killings, and 4) the possibility of distance between murder sites. These components become vitally important when differentiating between mass murder, serial murder, and spree murder. The determination of the type of homicide holds the key to understanding the character of the person who would commit such an act and enables law enforcement to put into motion the procedures and protocol called for in such a situation.

No matter how you define it, mass murder is neither an American nor a modern phenomenon. Cases spreading across history depict acts of mass murder. In recent times, however, mass murder seems to be on the increase—or is it? It may seem that such crimes have escalated because of the manner in which they are currently detected and reported. Table 1—which shows the names, locations, and the number of victims of mass killers in the past 50 years in the United States—gives some idea of the magnitude of mass murder.

## DIFFERENCES BETWEEN MASS AND SERIAL MURDER

There are significant differences between mass and serial killers. One difference is that mass murderers often die at the scene of the multiple slayings. They either commit

# TABLE 1.   MODERN MASS MURDERS

| Year | State | Murderer | Death Toll |
|------|-------|----------|------------|
| 1949 | New Jersey | Howard Unruh | Shot 13 neighbors |
| 1950 | Texas | William Cook | Shot 5 family members |
| 1955 | Colorado | John Graham | Bomb on a plane, 44 died |
| 1959 | Kansas | Richard Hickock | Stabbed/shot 4 members of Culter family |
| 1959 | Kansas | Perry Smith | Stabbed/shot 4 members of Culter family |
| 1966 | Illinois | Richard Speck | Stabbed/strangled 8 student nurses |
| 1966 | Texas | Charles Whitman | Shot 16, mostly students |
| 1966 | Arizona | Robert Smith | Shot 5 women in a beauty salon |
| 1969 | California | Charles Watson | Stabbed 9 persons for Charles Manson |
| 1969 | California | Patricia Krenwinkel | Stabbed 9 persons for Charles Manson |
| 1969 | California | Linda Kasabian | Stabbed 7 persons for Charles Manson |
| 1969 | California | Susan Adkins | Stabbed 9 persons for Charles Manson |
| 1970 | N. Carolina | Jeff MacDonald | Stabbed 3 members of his family |
| 1971 | New Jersey | John List | Shot 5 family members |
| 1973 | Georgia | Carl Isaacs | Shot 5 members of a family |
| 1973 | Georgia | Billy Isaacs | Shot 5 members of a family |
| 1974 | Louisiana | Mark Essex | Shot 9, mostly police officers |
| 1974 | Long Island | Ronald DeFeo | Shot 6 family members |
| 1975 | Florida | Bill Ziegler | Shot 4 adults in a store |
| 1975 | Ohio | James Ruppert | Shot 11 family members |
| 1976 | California | Edward Allaway | Shot 7 coworkers |
| 1977 | New York | Frederick Cowan | Shot 6 coworkers |
| 1978 | Guyana | Jim Jones | Poisoned/shot 912 cult members |
| 1982 | Pennsylvania | George Banks | Shot 13 family and acquaintences |
| 1983 | Louisiana | Michael Perry | Shot 5 family members |
| 1983 | Washington | Willie Mak | Shot 13 people in the head |
| 1983 | Washington | Benjamin Ng | Shot 13 people in the head |
| 1984 | California | James Huberty | Shot 21 at McDonald's |
| 1985 | Pennsylvania | Sylvia Seigrist | Shot several at a mall, 2 died |
| 1986 | Oklahoma | Patrick Sherrill | Shot 14 coworkers |
| 1986 | Arkansas | Ronald Simmons | Shot 16 family members |
| 1987 | Florida | William Cruse | Shot 6 persons at a mall |
| 1988 | California | Richard Farley | Shot 7 in a computer company |
| 1988 | Illinois | Lauri Dann | Shot, poisoned many, 1 death |
| 1988 | California | James Purdy | Shot 5 children in a playground |
| 1988 | N. Carolina | Michael Hayes | Shot 4 neighbors |
| 1989 | Kentucky | Joseph Wesbecker | Shot 8 coworkers |
| 1990 | Michigan | Lawrence DeLisle | Drowned his 4 children |
| 1990 | Florida | James Pough | Shot 13 in an auto loan company |
| 1990 | New York | Julio Gonzalez | 87 people died in a night club fire |
| 1991 | Michigan | Ilene Russell | 4 adults and 1 child in a fire |
| 1991 | Ohio | Kim Chandler | Shot her 3 children |
| 1991 | Kentucky | Michael Brunner | Shot girlfriend, her 2 children |
| 1991 | New Jersey | Joseph Harris | Shot 4 people at post office |
| 1991 | New York | Andrew Brooks | Shot father and 3 men |
| 1991 | Hawaii | Orlando Ganal | Shot 4 people including inlaws |
| 1991 | Texas | George Hennard | Shot 22 people in a restaurant |
| 1991 | Iowa | Gang Lu | Shot 5 college students and officials |
| 1991 | New Hampshire | James Colbert | Strangled wife, suffocated 3 daughters |
| 1991 | Kentucky | Robert Daigneau | Shot wife and three strangers |
| 1991 | Michigan | Thomas McIlwane | Shot 3 workers in a post office |

suicide or place themselves in situations where they "force" the police to take lethal action. Only occasionally do they turn themselves into the police after the deed is done. Serial killers, on the other hand, take great pains to avoid detection and take elaborate measures to elude apprehension.

Community reaction to the two types of murders is also different. Typically when a mass murder occurs, the immediate community, as well as the rest of the nation, is stunned by the event and abhorred by it. The community's pain is direct and severe but short-lived in that the mass murder is almost always either apprehended immediately or winds up dead. Shortly the social climate returns to what it was before the incident. Such is not the case with serial murder. The terror instilled by a serial murderer permeates the community's consciousness. There is no perceived end to the situation—it only ends when the killer is apprehended. Such situation existed in Seattle, which was terrorized for more than a decade by the Green River Killer, who murdered 49 women—some prostitutes, some not—and remained unapprehended. The news media recently reported that the Green River Killer may have returned to Seattle. Forty more victims— a quantity similar to the number originally attributed to this killer—have been found. The community's fears remain unassuaged. The mass murderer is often painted as a demented, mentally ill person. People interviewed on TV after the fact of a mass murder will make such statements as the killer had been seeing a mental health professional, had been on medication, or had been threatening fellow employees. In other words, the killer was displaying certain signs that should have made him or her detectable had society used appropriate expertise and resources to do so. The serial murderer, on the other hand, gives no such clues. Ted Bundy, Gerald Stano, Randy Craft, one and all, were not easily discernable serial killers. They walked into the lives of many, often invited, and fatally dispatched them with little concern. Serial killers generate a social paranoia that mass murderers do not; people feel a personal vulnerability when a serial killer is at large.

Surrette (1992) discusses two types of social behavior: front stage and back stage. Front stage behavior is that which is public and displayed to others. The mass murderer has often been judged in an ex post facto manner as angry, raging with outward-directed hatred, or displaying other behaviors which those who bother to notice would see as certainly atypical. Those interviewed after the recent mass slaying in Killeen, Texas, all saw the killer as an angry and hostile person. One survivor of the Wesbecker killings in Louisville, Kentucky, upon hearing what were simply loud and unusual sounds, remarked, "I bet that's crazy Joe Wesbecker coming back to kill us all." Another employee in the plant said Wesbecker told him of a plan to arm a model airplane and fly it into the plant, exploding it once it was inside (Yates, 1992). This is front stage behavior typical of mass murderers.

The front stage behavior of serial killers is typically a "normal" picture of societal adjustment: The person functions as a law student, the owner of a construction company, a social worker, or an engineer. But the secret behavior—the back stage behavior—is something only the victim sees. It is the early detection of the front stage behavior of the mass killer that may alert to the catastrophic back stage behavior which may follow.

## CLASSIFICATION OF MASS MURDER

As with many forms of human conduct and behaviors, sociologists and other social and behavioral scientists have taken it upon themselves to organize mass murder into social constructs. Such constructs are often based upon behavioral dynamics, motivation, victim characteristics and selection methodologies, loci of motivations, and anticipated rewards. This methodology was used by Holmes and DeBurger in their development of a typology of various types of serial killers (1988, pp. 46–60). This typology has been widely cited as an instrument for analysis and discussion and will be employed here.

### Behavioral Background: Basic Sources

The exact etiology of the mass murderer is unclear. As it is true that mass murderers are different from serial killers, it is true that the root causes of such personalities are also different. It is the unique combination of the biology, the sociology, and the personal psychology of an individual which accounts for the personality and thus the behavior of an individual.

No one factor causes a person to become a mass murderer. The total personality of multicidal offenders cannot easily be explained by simple biological inheritance (Hickey, 1991). Moreover, brain disorders, a blow to the head (Norris, 1988), or simple chemistry cannot totally explain behavior (Podolsky, 1964). The same is true of sociogenic factors. The root causes of delinquency, which many held dear in the 1960's—poverty, female-headed families, etc.—do not explain mass murder any more than they explained delinquency. If these factors were direct causative factors, then all who experienced poverty as a child or who were raised in a home with an absent father or father-figure would become delinquent. Holmes and DeBurger relate:

"Bad" neighborhoods, economic stress, family instability, and violence in the culture do not directly produce serial murderers. Out of a cohort that experiences the worst possible combinations of social stresses, relatively few will engage in outright criminal behavior and fewer still will become homicidal. . . . (1988, p. 48)

Another important distinction regarding mass and serial killers is that, based on the analysis of more than 400 cases of serial murder, there is overwhelming evidence that serial murderers do not wish to be apprehended.

## TABLE 2.   TRAITS OF MASS MURDER TYPES

|  | Discipline | Family Annihilator | Pseudo-commando | Disgruntled Employee | Set & Run |
|---|---|---|---|---|---|
| **Motivation** | | | | | |
| Intrinsic |  | X | X | X |  |
| Extrinsic | X |  |  |  | X |
| **Anticipated Gain** | | | | | |
| Expressive | X | X | X | X |  |
| Instrumental |  |  |  |  | X |
| **Victim Selectivity** | | | | | |
| Random | X |  | X |  | X |
| Nonrandom |  | X |  | X |  |
| **Victim Relationship** | | | | | |
| Affiliative |  | X |  | X |  |
| Strangers | X |  | X |  | X |
| **Spatial Mobility** | | | | | |
| Stable |  | X | X | X |  |
| Transient | X |  |  |  | X |
| **Victim Traits** | | | | | |
| Specific |  |  |  |  |  |
| Nonspecific | X | X | X | X | X |

They wish to continue their killings for whatever motivation impels them to do so. Very few surrender themselves to the police. Edmund Kemper is an exception to the rule. He said that "the killings had to stop" (HBO, Murder No Apparent Motive). Kemper killed his mother in California one day, her friend the next day, and then drove to Colorado. He turned himself in to the police after driving back to California. Such behavior is unlike that of all other known serial killers. As for the mass murderer, apprehension is not an issue. The mass murderer has no intent to kill again unless he is a revenge or mercenary type of mass killer. As mentioned earlier, most of the time the mass murderer will be willing to die at the scene of the crime, either committing suicide or forcing those in authority to kill him.

### Victim Characteristics

Victim traits do not appear to be a crucial element in mass murder. The victim is in the wrong place at the wrong time. The customers at the McDonald's restaurant had no role in the Huberty mass murder scene other than simply being there. The victims of the Tylenol killer shared no common trait other than buying a particular brand of medicine at varied and unrelated stores.

### Motivation

Another element used to categorize mass murderers is motivation. What is the motivation for a person to commit such an act of human atrocity as the murder of a large number of people? This is not an easy question to adequately address. A partial answer lies in the location of motivation, either intrinsic or extrinsic. For example, is there something deep within the person, something over which the person has no control? This is a common theme often heard in interviews with multicidal offenders, e.g., serial killers. They identify an "entity" within their personality, an entity which impels them to kill. This entity is a small part of the serial killers' personality, but this one percent can take over the other 99 percent (Michaud & Aynesworth, 1983). Such phenomenon does not appear to be true with mass murderers.

More likely the motivation rests outside the individual, something which commands to kill. For example, Charles Manson commanded Tex Watson, Susan Atkins, Leslie Van Houten, and Patricia Krenwinkel one night to kill Sharon Tate, Steven Parent, Abigail Folger, Voytek Frykowski, and Jay Sebring, and Leno and Rosemary LaBianca the second night. This instruction to kill rested outside the personalities of the killers themselves; Manson served as the motivational locus.

With James Huberty the motivation to kill rested within Huberty himself. For a myriad of reasons ranging perhaps from occupational and social class frustrations to other stresses, he killed—not because someone commanded him to, but because he believed that society was operating against him, and he was reacting to the injustices he perceived in society.

## Anticipated Gain

The anticipated gains are also something to consider in any typology. What is the person to realize from his personal behavior? Is it revenge at a former supervisor in the workplace for giving a poor job performance rating (Wesbecker)? Is it to acquire a monetary reward by setting a fire in a business building? Clearly, the anticipated gains here are entirely different. The results, however, are the same: the deaths of a number of innocent persons. The gains are either expressive (psychological) gains or instrumental (material) gains. Examination of perceived gains is important in the consideration of the type of mass killer, not only from a law enforcement point of view, but from a social/behavioral perspective as well.

## Spatial Mobility

Much has been discussed about geographical mobility as a trait of serial killers. Spatial mobility was a significant factor in Holmes and DeBurger's development of the four types of serial killers: Visionary, Mission, Hedonistic, and Power/Control (Holmes & DeBurger, 1985). However, spatial mobility as related to victim selection does not play a critical role in mass murder. Unless the person is involved in mass murder for pay, e.g., an arsonist who is compensated by others to set fires for the personal profit of a business, most mass murderers are geographically stable.

One exception to spatial mobility is the Disciple Killer. Falling under the spell of a charismatic leader, these mass killers are often runaways or castoffs from a family. They are not necessarily indigenous to the area where they fall under the spell of their leader. However, the domicile is often semi-permanent, and the victims unfortunately live in the same locale as the killers and their leader.

## TYPOLOGY OF MASS MURDER

The development of a typology of mass murderers is an arduous task. The first decision, discussed earlier, concerns what is the base number of victims for a mass murder case. Already decided in the baseline number of three.

The next task is the development of a taxonomy predicated upon the following elements: basic sources, victim characteristics, motivation, anticipated gain, and spatial mobility. There are also other elements to consider, e.g., type of weapon used, lifestyle of the killer himself, relational closeness or affinity of the victims, and personal mental/physical health of the killer. Four raters

placed 47 known mass murderers—responsible for a total of 437 victims—into one of the five theoretical categories discussed below. The agreement rate among the raters was 93 percent. Table 2 illustrates the traits of the five categories of mass murderers.

## The Disciple

The Disciple follows the dictates of a charismatic leader. There are more than a few examples of a disciple mass killer. Consider Leslie Van Houten. A former high school cheerleader and beauty queen, this young woman of 16 fell under the spell of Charles Manson. Of course, she was not alone. Lynette Fromme, Tex Watson, Bobbie Beausoleil, and others fell under the spell of their leader.

What caused these "nice, normal" young people of the peace generation to become ruthless and merciless killers? There is no easy answer. But what is known is that in the case of the disciple mass murderer, selection of victims is at the discretion of the leader. Manson allegedly told his followers to kill those who happened to be at a formerly rented home at 10050 Cielo Drive. The house was the former residence of Doris Day's son, Terry Melcher, and actress, Candice Bergen (Bugliosi, 1974, p. 4).

The motivation for mass murder for the Disciple Killer rests outside the killer. The leader of the group demands the action. The killer wants acceptance by the leader—this is the psychological gain, the expressive gain. This psychological acceptance is paramount in the need hierarchy of the mass killer; he feels he deserves psychological approbation only if he carries out the wishes of the leader. Money, revenge, or sex are not the motivating factors nor the anticipated gain. The disciple scenario was also played out by the followers of Jim Jones at the massacre at Jonestown in Guyana.

Spatial mobility is a consideration here. Typically the acts of violence associated with the slaughter of innocents are near the location of the leader. So, a Disciple Killer would not be a traveler in the same sense as would a geographically transient serial killer. However, the mass murderer will follow the leader and is unlikely to be from the area where the homicide occurred. The types of weapons used in this form of multicide are usually restricted to hand weapons, knives, guns, etc. The Jonestown case, where death was by poison, was an exception.

With the Disciple Killer, unlike others, there does not appear to be a general dislike of the world around the killer. Neither is the person placed in a situation in which the only way to remove himself from the situation is to kill. The Disciple Killer is murdering because of the effect the leader has upon him. There are no particular victims (the victim trait is inspecific) to be dispatched. The victims, typically strangers, are selected by the leader, and the orders are carried out by the dispatched disciple. One may compare the case of a soldier in war who leads prisoners to their certain demise not because of the soldier's fear for his own life, but because of his dedication to following the orders of the leader. By the same token, a certain amount of personal responsibility is relieved in this scenario. Many defendants at Nuremburg raised this point as part of their defense.

The Disciple Killer may have an additional dimension, a trait more likely found in the serial killer. If a Disciple Killer's leader demands further action—and since the killer's "reason to be" centers around the approbation of the leader—the killer will not be willing to die through suicide or police interdiction. The Disciple Killer will live to kill again.

### The Family Annihilator
Dietz (1986) has offered another type of mass murderer. The Family Annihilator is one who kills an entire family at one time. This killer may even murder the family pet. The murderer is the senior male in the family, depressed, often with a history of alcohol abuse, and exhibits great periods of depression. The motivation typically lies within the psyche of the individual. Oftentimes feeling alone, anomic, and helpless, this killer launches a campaign of violence against those who share his home. Because of the despair in his own life, the killer wishes to change the situation by reacting in the most bizarre fashion.

Concerning spatial mobility, the Family Annihilator is indigenous to the area in which the crime occurs. A lifelong member of the community, he chooses to end the life of his own family for reasons which may be unclear not only to the investigators but to the killer as well. In 1988, David Brown in Minnesota axed four family members to death for no clear reason. George Banks in 1982 shot 13 family members and relatives for unknown reasons. These killers were well known in their communities. Ronald Simmons, recently executed in Arkansas for his crimes, killed 16 members of his family. James Colbert killed four in his home in New Hampshire. Spatial mobility plays little role in this type of mass murder.

### Pseudocommandos
Dietz offers yet another type of mass murderer. The Pseudocommando is preoccupied with weaponry. Often the killer stockpiles exotic weapons in his home. Assault weapons, machine guns, even hand grenades are not unknown to this mass murderer. This killer's homicide usually occurs after a long period of deliberation and careful planning. There is no clear understanding of the etiology of the Pseudocommando. Certainly there are social components to the behavior—the killer's world plays an integral part in his behavior. But the Pseudocommando lashes out at society in a most grotesque way. Something in his world is not correct, and he will "teach the world a lesson" by his behavior.

Victim characteristics play no role in the victim selection process. Unlike the case of the serial killer with a shoe fetish (Jerry Brudos) or preoccupation with hair style (as Rule [1980] arguably claims about Ted Bundy), the victims here may simply be in the wrong place at the wrong time. When Huberty walked into McDonald's in 1984, the only relationship he shared with the victims was that they were all in the same place at the same time.

Motivation rests within the psyche of the Pseudocommando. There is something inside him which impels, or commands, that the massacre occur. There is nothing outside the personality exacting the killing of innocent persons, as with the Disciple Killer. Anticipated gain of the Pseudocommando is twofold. First, the activity of the mass kill calls attention to the issue which the killer believes to be important. In Huberty's case, the nation's economic state—which resulted in his moving to California from Ohio—was certainly one of the reasons he committed the act. The second anticipated gain is that the name of the killer will live in infamy. Most of us recognize the name of James Huberty; how many know any of the names of his 40 victims? Most of us recall the name of Charles Whitman; what is the name of even one of his more than a score of victims? Such is the point.

Concerning spatial mobility, there is little evidence to suggest that it is a significant factor for Pseudocommandos. Huberty, for example, moved to California and committed his murders there; Whitman lived in Texas, the site of his crime.

### Disgruntled Employees
Disgruntled Employees are often former employees of a company who have been dismissed or placed on some form of medical leave or disability. Many times, as a result of psychiatric counseling, the person perceives that he is suffering a great personal injustice beyond his control. He retaliates by going to the place where he was once a valued employee and searching for those who have wronged him. Both Joseph Wesbecker and Patrick Sherrill played out such scenario. In 1986, Sherrill returned to the post office where he had been an employee. Looking for supervisors, he started firing in the rooms and corridors of the post office, wounding and killing indiscriminately. Even though Sherrill's primary motive was to kill supervisors, he actually wounded and killed many coworkers. Joseph Harris also killed his fellow workers in the post office, partly in response to his perception that he was unfairly treated there.

The psychological sources of a Disgruntled Employee's mentality are certainly worthy of consideration. This type of killer often has severe psychological problems which interfere with normal day-to-day functioning. The person either may be on some form of medication or undergoing counseling or psychotherapy for a condition which is often diagnosed as paranoia. The anticipated gain is also psychological. There is no money to be realized, no social justice issues, nothing outside the world of work and the imagined injustices which were committed against him there.

The victim selection process for the Disgruntled Employee is nonrandom. He seeks a particular group of persons to kill, those who shared the workplace. However, once inside the workplace, the killer will then randomly fire, shooting anyone who happens to be there. The motivation to kill here—a drive to "right a wrong"—rests within the murderer's personality. He is there to call attention to a wrong directed and carried out against him.

Spatial mobility with this type of mass murderer is quite limited. Often this person has been employed with the same company and has lived in the same community for years. Wesbecker, for example, worked for Standard Gravure Company for more than 15 years. Sherrill was a postal worker for over a decade. Wesbecker was a native of Louisville, Kentucky, where he committed his murders; Sherrill had lived in the same community for more than 20 years. The danger to citizens in the community, however, is quite limited. This may mollify the citizens in the community at large but does little to placate the families of the victims.

### Set-and-Run Killers

Another type of mass murderer is the Set-and-Run Killer (Dietz, 1986). Spurred sometimes by a motive for revenge, sometimes for anonymous infamy, and sometimes simply for creature comfort reasons, this type of killer is qualitatively different from the others discussed.

Most mass killers either commit suicide at the scene or force law enforcement officials to kill them. Such is not true with the Set-and-Run Killer. This murderer will employ techniques to allow escape before the act itself occurs. For example, a Set-and-Run Killer may plant a bomb in a building, setting a time device so that the murderer is far removed from the scene when the explosion occurs. In other cases, this killer tampers with a food product or a medicine, places the container back upon the shelf, and leaves. The killer, then, does not directly observe the consequences of his act. He may be across town or even in another country when the results of his actions become evident.

Obviously depending on the movtivation of the act itself, victim selection varies. For example, if a person is employed to set a building afire for insurance purposes and a hundred people are inside the building at the time of the blaze, the characteristics of the victims are of no significance. The anticipated gain here is monetary. The owner of the building is paying the killer, perhaps an arsonist, to do the deed. There is no psychological motivation; there is no injustice to prove to society. The motivation lies not within the personality of the killer but is instrumental gain, money.

In some instances, the victim of the Set-and-Run Killer may be once removed. Take, for example, someone who tampers with a food product from Company X. Five people purchase and ingest the food. All five die. But in the mind of the killer in this scenario, Company X is truly at fault and is actually the intended victim. Therefore, the motivation here is psychological, exacting revenge on the company for a perceived wrong. The gain is also psychological. No money is realized. Moreover, Company X may lose money because customers will no longer purchase the product for fear that it may be contaminated.

Because he flees the scene before the killings actually occur, the Set-and-Run Killer is very difficult to apprehend. Realizing the motivation, anticipated gain, and victim characteristics (in this instance, once removed) is crucial to understanding and apprehending the Set-and-Run Killer.

### CONCLUSION

Since the authors started this article, at least nine more cases of mass murder have occurred in the United States. And there is no indication that incidences of such crimes will subside. There will always be persons who will be motivated by personal, economic, or social pressures to commit multicide. This is not an easy truth for society to accept, if only because the murder of innocent victims reminds us of our own personal vulnerability.

The first step in dealing with a concern as somber as mass murder is a clear understanding of the nature of the act itself. A theoretical typology, such as the one outlined in this article, can aid in this understanding. The typology offered here, which is unique in the literature, not only helps to explain the anticipated gains and behavioral motivations of mass murderers, but also considers victim selectivity, victim relationship, and perpetrator mobility. Such information will give a somewhat clearer picture of what types of persons would commit such heinous acts.

This is not to give the impression that it is easy to spot potential mass murderers. What separates mass murderers from persons with similar traits who do not resort to violence is a question that is difficult to answer. Indeed, there may be no sufficient response. But what is known is that friends and relatives often report—unfortunately all too late—"danger signs" which should have been recognized. For example, the individual who has verbalized a plan to kill is not taken seriously, and he later kills eight persons in his workplace. Such situation is not unique. The person who exhibits gross signs of depression, an anomalous interest in exotic weapons, a stated sense of anomie, or other such behavioral traits may be only a step away from carrying out an act of multicide.

Mental health professionals and probation/parole officers, among others, may be in a position to recognize potentially dangerous individuals who are physically—and more importantly psychologically—poised for fatal violence on a large scale. In becoming aware of the behavioral and psychological traits of mass murderers, mental health and criminal justice practitioners at least open the door to the possibility of circumvention. Law enforcement officers, too, need to be apprised of their unique position in relation to mass murderers. As mentioned earlier, mass murderers often place themselves in situations that force law enforcement officers to kill them. Other times, the murderers commit suicide. In either case, the officers are placed in a situation where their own lives are in jeopardy.

What can society do about mass murder? Unfortunately, little can be done once an attack commences. As far as stopping the crime before it happens, some say that effective gun control legislation is the answer. Certainly, if gun control could be rigorously enforced, it might deter some mass murderers, but it is not the answer for society's protection from the mass killer. Except in the case of mass murderers who kill for pay, underlying the actions of most of these killers are problems which stem from pressure, real or imagined. These pressures may arise at a societal level or from the individual's own position in a work situation or family unit. Mass murderers lack the motivations commonly associated with serial murderers—a point that must be recognized and appreciated.

Recognizing that mass murder is fundamentally dissimilar from other forms of homicide and must be dealt with differently is important. Certainly, a better understanding of mass murder will not be the pivitol element in eradicating this form of violence. What it is, however, is a recognition of the problem—a first step, a starting point.

## BIBLIOGRAPHY

Bugliosi, V. (1974). *Helter skelter.* New York: Bantam Books.

Dietz, M. (1983). *Killing for profit.* Chicago: Nelson-Hall.

Dietz, P. (1986). Mass, serial and sensational homicides. *Bulletin of the New York Academy of Medicine.* 62(5), 477–491.

Fox, J., & Levin, J. (1989). Satanism and mass murder. *Celebrity Plus,* 49–51.

Graysmith, R. (1976). *Zodiac.* New York: Berkley Books.

Hazelwood, R., & Douglas, J. (1980). The lust murder. *FBI Law Enforcement Bulletin,* 49(4), 1–8.

Hickey, E. (1991). *Serial murderers and their victims.* Belmont, CA: Brooks/Cole Publishing Co.

Holmes, R., & DeBurger, J. (1985). Profiles in terror: The serial murderer. *Federal Probation,* 49(3), 29–34.

Holmes, R., & DeBurger, J. (1988). *Serial murder.* Beverly Hills: Sage Publications.

Howard, C. (1979). *Zebra,* New York: Berkley Books.

Levin, J., & Fox, J. (1985). *Mass murder.* New York: Plenum Press.

Lunda, D. (1976). *Murder and madness.* San Francisco: San Francisco Book Company.

Michaud, S., & Aynesworth, H. (1983). *The only living witness.* New York: Signet books.

*Murder: No apparent motive.* (1980). HBO Undercover Series.

Norris, J. (1988). *Serial killers: The growing menace.* New York: Dolphin Books.

Podolsky, E. (1964). The chemistry of murder. *Pakistan Medical Journal,* 15, 9–14.

Rule, A. (1980). *The stranger beside me.* New York: Signet.

Surette, R. (1992). *Media: Images and realities.* Belmont, Ca: Brooks/Cole Publishing Co.

Yates, C. (1992, November 13). Personal interview.

# Victimology

Victimology focuses on crime victims. The popularity of this area of study can be attributed to the early work of Hans von Hentig and the later work of Stephen Schafer. These writers were the first to assert that crime victims play an integral role in the criminal event, that their actions may actually precipitate crime, and that unless the victim's role is considered, the study of crime is not complete.

In recent years, a growing number of criminologists have devoted increasing attention to the victim's role in the criminal justice process. Generally, areas of particular interest include calculating costs of crime to victims, victim surveys that measure the nature and extent of criminal behavior, establishing probabilities of victimization risks, studying victim precipitation of crime and culpability, and designing services expressly for victims of crime. As more criminologists focus their attention on the victim's role in the criminal process, victimology will take on even greater importance.

Articles in this unit provide sharp focus on key issues. From the lead essay, "The Fear of Crime," we learn that fear of being victimized is pervasive among people, including some who have never been victims of crime. This article addresses the effects of crime on its victims. The horror of family violence and limitations of the criminal justice system in dealing with it are clearly evident in "Hunted: The Last Year of April LaSalata." The spreading national menace called "stalking," with its obvious connection to violence, is the focus of the next article, "In the Mind of a Stalker."

Most women who are raped are raped by people they know. This phenomenon, called "acquaintance rape," is examined in "When Is It Rape?"

The intractability of the problem of battering is made evident in "When Men Hit Women." Though widely considered the model for the rest of the country, a Duluth, Minnesota, program for battered women has its limitations.

"The Unbearable Loss" by Chip Brown reflects upon the increase in child murders in the United States. Many of the victims' families are seeking channels for their grief as well as new legal rights.

Brenda Clubine was convicted of killing her husband after he had beaten her for years. "Abused Women Who Kill Now Seek Way Out of Cells" tells of Clubine's fight for clemency for inmates at the California Institute for Women.

The unit closes with "Incest: A Chilling Report." This article provides a revealing look at victims and offenders of child abuse.

## Looking Ahead: Challenge Questions

Is the fear of crime realistic?

What life-style changes might you consider to avoid becoming victimized?

Are you familiar with victim service programs in your area?

How does crime affect the victim's psyche?

What exactly is acquaintance rape?

# Unit 2

# The Fear of Crime

## The fear of crime affects many people, including some who have never been victims of crime

### How do crime rates compare with the rates of other life events?

| Events | Rate per 1,000 adults per year* |
|---|---|
| Accidental injury, all circumstances | 242 |
| Accidental injury at home | 79 |
| Personal theft | 72 |
| Accidental injury at work | 58 |
| Violent victimization | 31 |
| Assault (aggravated and simple) | 24 |
| Injury in motor vehicle accident | 17 |
| Death, all causes | 11 |
| Victimization with injury | 10 |
| Serious (aggravated) assault | 9 |
| Robbery | 6 |
| Heart disease death | 4 |
| Cancer death | 2 |
| Rape (women only) | 2 |
| Accidental death, all circumstances | .5 |
| Pneumonia/influenza death | .3 |
| Motor vehicle accident death | .2 |
| Suicide | .2 |
| Injury from fire | .1 |
| Homicide/legal intervention death | .1 |
| Death from fire | .03 |

These rates approximate your chances of becoming a victim of these events. More precise estimates can be derived by taking account of such factors as your age, sex, race, place of residence, and lifestyle. Findings are based on 1982–84 data, but there is little variation in rates from year to year.

*These rates exclude children from the calculations (those under age 12–17, depending on the series). Fire injury/death data are based on the total population, because no age-specific data are available in this series.

Sources: *Current estimates from the National Health Interview Survey: United States, 1982*, National Center for Health Statistics. "Advance report of final mortality statistics, 1983," *Monthly Vital Statistics Report*, National Center for Health Statistics. *Estimates of the population of the United States, by age, sex, and race: 1980 to 1984*, U.S. Bureau of the Census. *The 1984 Fire Almanac*, National Fire Protection Association. *Criminal victimization 1984*, BJS Bulletin, October 1985.

### The chance of being a violent crime victim, with or without injury, is greater than that of being hurt in a traffic accident

The rates of some violent crimes are higher than those of some other serious life events. For example, the risk of being the victim of a violent crime is higher than the risk of death from cancer or injury or death from a fire. Still, a person is much more likely to die from natural causes than as a result of a criminal victimization.

### About a third of the people in the United States feel very safe in their neighborhoods

The fear of crime cannot be measured precisely because the kinds of fears people express vary depending on the specific questions asked. Nevertheless, asking them about the likelihood of crime in their homes and neighborhoods yields a good assessment of how safe they feel in their own immediate environment.

In the Victimization Risk Survey, a 1984 supplement to the National Crime Survey, most people said that they felt at least fairly safe in their homes and neighborhoods. Yet, the people who said that they felt "fairly safe" may have been signaling some concern about crime. Based on a "very safe" response, a little more than 4 in 10 people felt entirely safe in their homes and about 1 in 3 felt totally safe in their neighborhoods—
• homeowners felt safer than renters
• people living in nonmetropolitan areas felt safer than those living in cities
• families with incomes of $50,000 or more were most likely to report their neighborhoods were very safe from crime.

The Victimization Risk Survey found that—
• 9 in 10 persons felt very or fairly safe in their places of work
• few persons—about 1 in 10—felt in danger of being a victim of a crime by a fellow employee, but persons working in places that employ more than 50 people were more likely to express fear of possible victimization.

### The groups at the highest risk of becoming victims are not the ones who express the greatest fear of crime

Females and the elderly generally express a greater fear of crime than do people in groups who face a much greater risk. The Reactions to Crime project found that such impressions are related to the content of information about crime. Such information tends to emphasize stories about elderly and female victims. These stories may influence women and the elderly in judging the seriousness of their own condition. Perhaps groups such as females and the elderly reduce their risk of victimization by constricting their activities to reduce their exposure to danger. This behavior would account, at least in part, for their high levels of fear and their low levels of victimization.

### Relatives, friends, and neighbors who hear about a crime become as fearful as the victim

When one household in a neighborhood is affected by a crime, the entire neighborhood may feel more vulnerable. This suggests that people who have not been victimized personally may be strongly affected when they hear about how others have been victimized. The Reactions to Crime project found that

From *Report to the Nation on Crime and Justice*, Bureau of Justice Statistics, U.S. Department of Justice, March 1988, pp. 24-25.

# How does crime affect its victims?

indirect reaction to crime is often very strong.

### $13 billion was lost from personal and household crimes in 1985

The direct cash and property losses from personal robberies, personal and household larcenies, household burglaries, and privately owned motor vehicle theft in 1985 was slightly more than $13 billion. This NCS finding probably underestimates the amount covered by insurance because the claims of many respondents had not been settled at the time of the NCS interview.

UCR data show that in 1985 losses from reported robberies, burglaries, and larceny/theft surpassed $5.9 billion. Among the many economic consequences of crime are lost productivity from victims' absence from work, medical care, and the cost of security measures taken to deter crime.

Other costs of crime include the economic costs of the underground economy, lowered property values, and pain and suffering of victims, their families, friends, and neighbors.

### The economic impact of crime differs for different groups

The cost of crime is borne by all segments of society, but to different degrees. A study on the economic cost of crime using NCS data for 1981 shows that the dollar loss from crimes involving money, property loss, or destruction of property rises with income.

• Median losses were higher for households with incomes of $15,000 or more than for households with incomes of

less than $7,500 from burglary ($200 vs. $100) and from motor vehicle theft ($2,000 vs. $700).

• Median losses from personal crimes were higher for blacks ($58) than for whites ($43).
• Median losses from household crimes were higher for blacks ($90) than for whites ($60).
• More than 93% of the total loss from crime was in crimes without victim-offender contact (such as burglary, theft without contact, and motor vehicle theft).

### Many victims or members of their families lose time from work

Along with injuries suffered, victims or other members of their household may have lost time from work because of a violent crime. Lost worktime was reported in 15% of rapes and 7% of assaults (11% of aggravated assaults, 6% of simple assaults).

### Violent crimes killed 19,000 and injured 1.7 million in 1985

NCS data for 1985 show that of all rape,

robbery, and assault victims—
• 30% were injured
• 15% required some kind of medical attention
• 8% required hospital care.

The likelihood of injury was—
• greater for females than males even when rape was excluded from the analysis
• about the same for whites and blacks
• greater for persons from lower than from higher income households.

### Who is injured seriously enough to require medical attention?

An analysis of NCS data for 1973–82 found that—
• Female victims are more likely than male victims to be injured, but they have about the same likelihood of requiring medical attention (13% of female vs. 12% of male victims).
• Blacks are more likely than whites to require medical attention when injured in violent crimes; 16% of black violent crime victims and 16% of the victims of all other racial groups required medical attention, while 11% of white victims required such care.

---

### How seriously a victim is injured varies by type of crime

| | Percent of all violent victimizations requiring: | | | Median stay for those hospitalized overnight |
|---|---|---|---|---|
| | Medical attention | Treatment in hospital emergency room | Overnight hospital stay | |
| Rape | 24% | 14% | 3% | 4 days |
| Robbery | 15 | 7 | 2 | 5 |
| Assault | 11 | 5 | 1 | 5 |
| Aggravated | 18 | 9 | 3 | 5 |
| Simple | 7 | 3 | — | 2 |

—less than .5%

Source: BJS National Crime Survey, 1973–82.

# HUNTED

## THE LAST YEAR OF APRIL LaSALATA

She thought the criminal-justice system would protect her from her ex-husband. But the system was no match for his lethal rage.

## Richard C. Firstman

*Richard C. Firstman is a contributing writer of*
The Newsday Magazine.

Her body a pattern of scars, April LaSalata stared up at the young woman standing uneasily at her bedside.

"How old are you?" April asked warily.

Frances Radman, a 27-year-old assistant district attorney with a gentle manner, had heard that one before. "How old are *you*?" she asked gamely.

April laughed; she was feeling better this March day in 1988. But still she worried: It seemed to her that the prosecutor was as vulnerable as she was. For her part, Radman hadn't expected April to be so tiny, just 85 pounds and barely five feet tall. When April displayed the scars that split her upper body in two, Radman was amazed that such a delicate woman had managed to survive so brutal an attack.

"He won't get out of jail, will he?" April asked.

Knowing the events of the past months, now seeing this torn body before her, Radman knew this was not a trivial question.

"No," she said, "he won't."

Four months before, in the fall of 1987, a Suffolk County judge had signed the papers terminating the marriage of April and Anthony LaSalata, high school sweethearts from Brentwood. To the mind of her ex-husband, April had been the winner in this divorce; he had been the loser. She got the kids, the house and freedom from a calamitous marriage. He got a trailer and a court order barring him from menacing his ex-wife. It had been the kind of divorce that had produced almost monthly police reports: domestic dispute, 110 McKinley.

On the ninth call to the Third Precinct, in February, the police had found Anthony LaSalata trying to get into the house with a crowbar. They had arrested him for harassment. Then he had been released.

After work on Friday, Feb. 26, April, as was her custom, drove to her mother's house to pick up her sons, Justin, 10, and Anthony Jr., 4. She decided to leave Anthony overnight and drove the few blocks home with Justin. They scanned the front lawn, then walked into the house. The phone in the kitchen, the red one with "911" written on it, was ringing. Justin answered; it was his grandmother, checking to see that they had gotten home all right. Justin said they were fine.

And then, the closet door flew open.

April screamed. Justin cried out, "Dad, what are you doing here?" His father told him to be quiet and then cut the telephone cord. The receiver fell onto a sweater on the floor.

LaSalata, according to the police, pushed his son into a bedroom and closed the door. He grabbed April, dragged her downstairs and started stabbing her. He twisted the knife inside her abdomen. She screamed to Justin to get out of the house, and Justin bolted and began banging on the doors of neighbors.

When LaSalata heard Justin leave, he looked up reflexively, stabbed April a third time, and stopped. He left her bleeding in the basement and fled the house. April dragged herself to the basement phone. After all her instructions to Justin about how to call for emergency help, it was Gerard, her brother who lived 25 miles away, whom she called first.

*"Whatsa matter? Whatsa matter?"* Gerard screamed into the phone. In his house, a room full of guests stood horrified. April was describing her wounds to her brother. "Close your arms around them! Hold them tight!" Gerard yelled into the phone. When rescue came, April was bleeding so relentlessly that she kept sliding off the stretcher.

She was in surgery through the night. The doctors did not believe she would live — her wounds suggested to them an autopsy had already been performed. But somehow, she reached the recovery room. She spent the next week on life-support machines.

LaSalata was charged with attempted murder and held in the Riverhead jail.

No, Fran Radman told April in the hospital room, he would not get out. His lawyer was arguing that LaSalata was not competent to stand trial, and so there would be no bail until there was a decision on that issue. Or so Radman thought.

TWO weeks later, in what Radman would later describe as a critical bureaucratic "mix-up," Judge Morton Weissman set cash bail at $25,000 while she was appearing in another court on another case. Kevin Fox, LaSalata's attorney, told Radman not to worry: LaSalata would never raise that kind of money.

But five months later, in midsummer, LaSalata's parents decided to mortgage their house to get him out of jail. And from that day forward, as her life was defined by a collection of motions and briefs, April LaSalata came to know on the deepest level that she would not survive.

On New Year's Eve, 1988, when a radio announcer reported on the second woman in Suffolk County in three days to be killed by her estranged husband, despite orders of protection, April turned to her oldest friend and said, "Sharon, I'm next."

* * *

April LaSalata, 34 at her death, was not an anonymous victim crying in the dark. In her world, she was surrounded by many people who cared a great deal about her, a prosecutor who fought for her, a cop who tried to protect her.

And still, she died.

The questions raised by her death a year ago have less to do with why some men are driven to such desperate acts of domestic terrorism than with why the legal system sometimes fails to protect the women they kill. April LaSalata's case played to the fears of all women who saw her death as a confirmation of a terrible truth: that even at its best, the system is not designed to keep a hunted woman alive.

Her case is closed now, her onetime husband having seen to that with five shots from

## 'WHAT APRIL SAW WAS THAT HE WAS SO MACHO.'

a rifle last January, three to her, two to himself. But her death touched so many lives — people who knew her intimately, others who were more familiar with her case file — and they struggle still for acceptable explanations, to place blame on someone or something other than Anthony LaSalata alone.

April's family is suing the Suffolk County Police Department for failing to protect her, but others argue that the police did all they could. An examination of the last year of her life shows that many factors contributed to her death, including miscalculations by some members of the criminal justice system, perhaps an insensitivity by others, and some ambiguities born of the bureaucracy itself.

In the end, despite the depth of April's fears and the brutality of the stabbing attack, Anthony LaSalata was just another defendant awaiting trial on a charge of attempted murder. The case dragged on as many cases do. LaSalata was released on bail as many defendants are.

And April LaSalata was left to wonder on what night in the near future her ex-husband would come again to kill her.

* * *

April Principio, a bricklayer's daughter, was in the eleventh grade at Brentwood High when she met Tony LaSalata, a senior. April liked to read and Tony liked to fix cars, but they shared ethnic background and neighborhood ties, and April was not attracted to gentle boys. Among the things she found appealing about Tony was the strength of his wrists: She liked the way he shifted his car. When he was 18, LaSalata acquired a tattoo: *Live and Let Die.*

"Tony was the first person who paid attention to her," recalled Sharon Millard, April's close friend. "What April saw was that he was so macho, in total control, which she felt she needed, someone to guide her."

But Tony's control bordered on compulsion. If April was out with a girlfriend, Tony was likely to turn up agitated, demanding her return to his car. April was ambivalent about Tony's tyrannical tendencies. Of course, she found them annoying — his jealousy became so much a part of her daily life that she was moved to write about it, prophetically if with some bemusement, in her yearbook inscription to Millard, her friend since kindergarten:

*I'll never forget the time [we] had to hide on wet grass behind Debbie Mann's car because LaSalata was passing, and many more of those "times" to come.*

But in her innocence, April took Tony's attentions as a sign of love. "You get all sorts of attention from someone and it makes you feel good," Millard said. "You go on the assumption that it's true love. Tony was her first one, and that was it."

Her parents were so opposed to the rela-

## 'SHE SLEPT WITH THE DRESSER IN FRONT OF THE BEDROOM DOOR.'

tionship that they begged her to go away to college. But April was headstrong, a lifelong trait, and at the time reasonably rebellious. Despite her parents' urgings, she cast her lot with Tony. She went to work in a bank, Tony got a job on the pie line at Entenmann's Bakery, and in June, 1975, they were married.

In those early years, April and Tony continued the rancor that often marked their courtship. In an interview with a court-appointed psychiatrist after his arrest in 1988, LaSalata said: "The only complaint she ever had about me and our marriage early on was that I smoked too much pot. Other than that there were no other complaints except me yelling at her."

She had one other complaint, however: Tony's employee file was getting thick with reprimands and warnings for missing work and for not getting along with co-workers. April felt at times that she was doing more than her share of supporting the family.

The turning point in the marriage — the point from which it would deteriorate beyond hope of repair — came in 1982, when April and Tony went to the wedding of a friend from high school. April wasn't feeling well and left early with a friend of theirs, and when Tony came home and found the friend in the house, he believed that April had been unfaithful to him. April insisted that she had not.

Whatever happened that night, the incident became so much a point of contention in the marriage that nearly everyone who knew the LaSalatas — their friends, their relatives and ultimately the corps of lawyers, prosecutors and psychiatrists who would populate their lives — would hear a version of it.

WAS always angry with her," LaSalata told the psychiatrist in 1988. "I wouldn't let that night go. She swore she didn't, then she said if she did or didn't, she would swear that she didn't. That one incident for over five years has been constantly on my thoughts. I keep asking friends and they are all sticking together and telling me I was crazy. It was like a conspiracy. When they all looked at my wife, I know they all wanted her. They all wanted to take turns with my wife. They didn't give a —— if I was their friend, they just wanted her."

April would later tell Radman, "You'd think I was Christie Brinkley, the way he was acting."

In 1983, LaSalata was fired from Entenmann's. He found work at Fairchild Republic, and later at Grumman. Down in the basement, which he had finished himself, he also cooked up get-rich-quick schemes. The marriage grew more acrimonious, and then abusive. April would vilify Tony for not working, Tony would bring up the wedding incident. And Jus-

tin would follow his mother around with a bow and arrow to protect her. April taught him how to dial 911.

Finally, in 1986, April decided to see a lawyer about divorcing Tony. The following April, she called the police for the first time. She said that Tony was threatening her. She went to court and was granted an Order of Protection.

"He would be mean one day, begging her the next," said Millard. "Some days he stuck to her like glue. He would follow her around the house. She hated that. She couldn't wait to go to work."

The couple slept in separate rooms, but a few times April woke up with Tony standing over her. For a while, she slept with the dresser in front of the bedroom door. At one point, she told friends, Tony put a gun to her head and threatened to kill her. During the divorce proceedings April called the police eight times.

April decided to move with her sons to her mother's house, but her lawyer advised her to move back in so she would be on firmer ground when she asked the judge to award her the house.

But when she moved back in, she told friends and Radman, her husband raped her. Her lawyer, William Griffin, says April never told him this.

The divorce was granted in the fall of 1987, with April getting custody of the children and sole occupancy of the house. Family Court Judge John Dunn gave LaSalata 60 days to find another place to live, leaving a bitterly divorced couple living under the same roof.

In December, LaSalata moved into a $90-a-month house trailer in Bay Shore. But the terms of the divorce decree only seemed to intensify his violent tendencies. When April gave her brother Gerard a shotgun for Christmas, he told her, "You're the one that needs this."

It is difficult to learn much about LaSalata's view of what was happening in his life because nearly all of his friends and relatives declined to be interviewed for this article. But one friend said that LaSalata had become fixated on April's refusal to sell the house and split the money.

"The guy was strapped," said the friend, who asked not to be identified. "He was working nights at Grumman, he was living in this dinky trailer, he couldn't even watch TV except for Channel 12 because he couldn't afford an antenna. He wanted some money so he could start his life over."

Wary of LaSalata, Gerard Principio, who taught martial arts, arranged for one of his students, Billy Woods, to live in the basement apartment Tony had finished. Billy was 25, slightly built and wore longish hair and an earring. He worked as a maintenance man for Slomin's fuel oil. April was glad to have someone else in the house. Billy was glad to know April. Soon they became involved, and Woods' mission took on greater importance.

April had iron gates installed over the front door.

One late night in February, 1988, LaSalata went to the house and found Woods' fuel truck parked outside. When he saw Woods in the house, he tried to break through the gates with a crowbar. April called the police and Tony was arrested for harassment. Out on bail, he called her and said he would shoot her.

In a few days, April was scheduled to go to court for a stronger Order of Protection. But Tony had other ideas.

"Tony told me that if the judge didn't modify his decision, it was time for this," an acquaintance of LaSalata's said in a statement to police. "As he said this, he picked up a big Rambo-type knife off the table. Tony said that he was going to 'kill the bitch.' . . . Tony then said that he was at the house a few nights before to kill April, that he had cut the telephone lines and then he changed his mind. . . . I got in touch with April and told her what Tony had said. April told me that she would be careful."

**S**HE came in dead," recalls Dr. Alexander Melman, the surgeon at Southside Hospital in Bay Shore who sewed April back together on the night of Feb. 26. "She had no blood pressure, she had wounds to the lungs and the diaphragm and part of her liver was sticking out. The son of a bitch turned the blade, an old trick to create more injuries. It reminded me of a wartime injury."

April spent six days on life-support systems as her hosptial room filled with flowers, balloons, cards and visitors. Members of the Long Island Women's Coalition came to offer their help, but April didn't feel a part of them, didn't feel they were living in her world. To April this was not a political issue. This was *her* issue.

"I thought I was going to die," she told Newsday reporter Dan Fagin, who was preparing a story on how local police respond to domestic violence. "It's been getting worse and worse, but I never thought it would come to this. I'm terrified. You can't imagine what it's like to be living with this every day."

Another visitor was Vincent O'Leary. He had known April since high school, and now he was a police detective, working in their home precinct, the Third. He was assigned to her case. Though such a convenience has the ring of a cheap trick by a screenwriter, in this true story O'Leary was the friend on the force. But it did not seem to relieve April's fear. "I just think of what his jail sentence is going to be and him getting out and getting me," she told Fagin.

LaSalata was initially charged by police with first-degree assault and held on $25,000 bail by District Court Judge Francis Caldeira.

From jail, he wrote a letter to his older son:

*Dear Justin,*

*I am writing you this letter to tell you how sorry I am about what happened to your mother. If you hate me now and never want to see me again I can understand why. I just wanted to tell you that I was very very sick that night and that I did not know what I was doing. I hope and pray to God that you and your mother can forgive me. I wish that there was some way that the pain that your mother has in her body now can somehow be transformed into my body . . . I miss you and Anthony so much. Take care and be a good boy. Please send me a letter. I wish there was something that I could send you but right now I have nothing to send you other than my love. I love you Justin!*

On the same day that LaSalata wrote the letter, he was served in jail with this County Court decree: "It is ordered that the above named defendant observe the following conditions of behavior: Stay away from the home, school, business, or place of employment of: April LaSalata."

The next day, LaSalata appeared before County Court Justice Morton Weissman, to whose court the case was transferred after a grand jury indicted him on a charge of attempted murder. Kevin Fox, LaSalata's attorney, indicated he would argue that his client was not competent to stand trial, and Weissman, as is customary when a competency issue is raised, held him without bail.

Fran Radman was brand new to the district attorney's family crimes bureau when she was handed a pile of cases from a departing prosecutor. She had been handling drunk-driving and misdemeanor, child sex-abuse cases in the District Court bureau, and People vs. Anthony LaSalata would be her biggest case to date. A couple of years out of Brooklyn Law School, she had joined the district attorney's office because she felt that was where she could do the most good. Her sympathies lay with victims of crime.

Radman's inexperience was disquieting to April and her family. But what she lacked in seasoning she would try to make up for with dedication. Like April, she was the daughter of a working-class family, had grown up in western Suffolk County and had never wandered far. Now, Radman was living with her parents in East Northport. And when she met April for the first time in the hospital, she felt more than the usual compassion.

"She said that even in the hospital she was afraid he would come get her," Radman recalls. "But she was composed. She always was. Usually she would be kidding, smiling, pleasant, but when it was about being afraid, she got very straight-faced. I thought when I walked out, Wow, that is some strong woman."

\* \* \*

Thursday, April 7, 1988, was a very busy day in the Suffolk County criminal courts.

Radman was scheduled to present evidence to a grand jury on a sex abuse case that day, so she asked another member of the bureau, Gaetan Lozito, to stand in for her at a conference with Judge Weissman on the LaSalata case. Radman's primary concern — for April's peace of mind, as well as her own — was that LaSalata remain in jail. And Fox, she says, had assured her in a phone conversation that he wouldn't be making a bail application. So Radman didn't regard the conference as key.

But there was a crack, after all, and April was about to fall through it.

Weeks before, Dr. Allen Reichman, a psychiatrist who judges the competency of defendants in Suffolk's criminal cases, had found that LaSalata did, in fact, understand the charges against him and was capable of aiding his defense. Now, in the conference in the judge's chambers, a kind of dress rehearsal for open court, Fox told Weissman and Lozito that he would seek to have his own psychiatrist contradict that finding, and also advance his defense of mental impairment on the night of the attack. At Radman's instruction, Lozito told Weissman that April was afraid that her ex-husband would be released, and showed photographs of the weapon he had used.

Then Lozito had to leave for another case. She handed the file over to Matthew Parella, an assistant district attorney who had never seen the case but who was covering Weissman's courtroom for the major crimes bureau. "Nothing's going to happen," he says Lozito told him.

In the courtroom, Fox repeated his intentions for the record. Then Weissman surprised everyone.

"Do you have a bail application?" he asked Fox, according to a transcript of the session.

"No," Fox said, "we reserve it."

"You never made a bail application before this?" Weissman persisted. He seemed to be indicating he wanted to set bail.

Fox was unprepared, but he took his shot. He asked that bail be set at $25,000, the same amount as when the charge was assault.

Weissman looked at Parella. "We'll ask that no bail be continued until the results of the defense psychiatric exam," Parella said.

"No, I won't do that," Weissman said. "Give me a monetary recommendation."

Parella asked for $100,000, but he did not present arguments for the higher bail.

"Hundred thousand bond, twenty-five thousand cash," Weissman said.

To this day, Radman sees that moment as the "mix-up" that made the job of protecting April much more difficult. She says that had she been been there, she would have argued strenuously that the bail wasn't high enough. But now she was stuck with it.

Later, she called Fox. "You said you weren't going to make a bail application," she recalls telling him. Fox explained the circumstances, then said, "Don't worry, Fran, he'll never make that kind of bail."

(Asked to comment for this article, Weissman said he could not recall the case and, anyway, did not discuss cases he had handled.)

MEANWHILE, Fox was finding that his client was still obsessed with his divorce. "Obviously [in retrospect] there was something boiling inside, but it didn't show," he said. "He seemed very subdued, polite, sort of defeated. He wasn't a raving lunatic."

In the spring, April went back to work in the credit department at J.C. Penney, but she was still in pain from her wounds and preoccupied by the court case against Tony. She believed in the *victim's* right to a speedy trial.

The case was transferred to Judge Rudolph Mazzei, and on Aug. 5, a conference was scheduled. April told Radman she wanted to be there.

Also in attendance that day were John and Otille LaSalata, Tony's father and mother. They were like a lot of parents of accused criminals — they were sick over it. And in their sadness, they had an inverted view of the situation. To them, Tony was the victim, April the victimizer.

Afterward, as April walked toward her car with Gerard and Radman, John LaSalata drove up beside them. Throughout, April feared him as much as she feared Tony.

"You slut!" LaSalata screamed at April, according to Radman. "You're the reason my son's in jail!"

John LaSalata was charged with harassment, and although it was later dismissed at April's behest, the incident set the tone for his son's defense.

"His parents saw their son as being sick, and they felt she was one of the causes," said Charles Russo, Fox' law partner. "They didn't say [the stabbing] was justified, but they didn't understand why the criminal justice system was involved. They wanted to get help."

Three days after the incident in the parking lot, and 163 days after their son went to jail, the LaSalatas decided to mortgage their home to get him out.

In April's world, alarms went off. Vinnie O'Leary was the first to call: *He's out.* April couldn't believe it, and when Radman called, the prosecutor found a very nervous woman on the other end of the line.

"Do you have any place to go?" Radman asked.

"*Any place to go?*" April repeated angrily. "He did this to me, and now I have to change my whole life? I live here. My kids go to school here."

A siege mentality set in as word of LaSalata's release spread. Radman had a portable panic button delivered to April's house; she could wear it around her neck and summon the police instantly. And a tape recorder was installed on her kitchen phone. When Det.

Frank Fallon came to install the tape machine, April showed him a picture of her wounds after surgery. "Every noise, every sound, a car or somebody starting a lawn mower, made her nervous," Fallon recalls. "She didn't sleep at night. I told her, 'That's a hell of a way to live. Why don't you move?' "

At home, Justin took to following his mother around with a baseball bat. "He follows me everywhere," April told Radman. "It drives me crazy."

At work, April was allowed to park in the fire zone directly outside the store. A security guard escorted her to her car each night after work.

And at the district attorney's office, the case took on the qualities of a cause. The family crimes unit was staffed mainly by young women whose caseloads were dominated by crimes against women and children, usually involving sexual and physical abuse. It was not unusual for the prosecutors to become emotionally involved with their "clients," and this was especially true of the case of April LaSalata. Radman, whose office was decorated with artwork by victims of child abuse, felt that this time she carried the burden of keeping the victim alive. And she would not play it safe.

Among prosecutors, Mazzei had a reputation, justified or not, as a "defendant's judge." In late August, with Mazzei on vacation, Radman went to Judge Charles Cacciabaudo to try to have LaSalata returned to jail, at a higher bail. To do this, she needed some new evidence. She told Cacciabaudo that April had been receiving "unusual phone calls," since her ex-husband's release, related the incident involving his father, and said that LaSalata had been found competent to stand trial.

Kevin Fox told the judge that LaSalata, suffering from depression, would be voluntarily admitted to South Oaks Hospital in Amityville on that day.

Cacciabaudo rejected Radman's bail request. Then he looked at LaSalata and warned him not to go near his ex-wife.

"Yes, sir," LaSalata said.

As LaSalata underwent psychiatric treatment in South Oaks, Radman pushed for a trial date. To impress upon Mazzei the seriousness of the case, she showed him the photographs of April after the attack. This was an off-the-record move not generally regarded as proper. But LaSalata was due to get out of South Oaks in 60 days, and Radman wanted to jar Mazzei into action. The judge said the case ought to come up soon. But he gave no commitments.

On Sunday, Oct. 16, as Tony's stay in South Oaks was drawing to a close, April was outside the house with Justin and Anthony when a gray car slowed as it passed. In the passenger seat, April was sure, was Tony, wearing a red shirt she had bought him years before.

April called the police, who said they couldn't make an arrest because Tony hadn't come close enough. But Radman said it was enough for her, and had two detectives go to South Oaks to pick him up on charges of criminal contempt.

Radman took the case to District Court

Judge William Bennett. But there was one problem: Fox produced a letter from Dr. Nicholas Samios, LaSalata's physician at South Oaks, saying that the record showed LaSalata had not left the hospital on the day in question.

Radman went to see Bennett in his chambers. "Judge, he's going to kill her," Radman says she told Bennett. "He should be nowhere near this house. We're trying to protect her."

But Bennett said his hands were tied — LaSalata had an alibi. He released him on his own recognizance.

Radman was furious. "His defense [in the stabbing] was mental defect," she says now. "He wasn't saying he didn't do it. So why not keep him in jail? Why not be safe? The problem is we don't have preventative detention in New York and we should."

In New York, as in most other states, the purpose of bail is to insure that a defendant will appear for trial. There, a cornerstone of the criminal justice system, the presumption of the accused's innocence, comes in conflict with the victim's presumption of danger.

After Bennett's decision, Radman called and visited April frequently, if only to let her know she wasn't alone. "I was so afraid," she said. "I don't know if she knew that. Now what do we do? I was afraid that this aggravated everything. April was angry, afraid and wiped out."

In her anxiety, knowing Tony was about to be released from South Oaks, did April imagine seeing him that Sunday? Or did Samios assume that because there was no record of his absence LaSalata must have been in the hospital?

Radman decided to take the South Oaks case to a grand jury and let April tell her story. The grand jury indicted LaSalata, but on Nov. 15, Mazzei, clearly angered at Radman, called it "the proverbial ham sandwich indictment" — referring to a legal truism that prosecutors can lead a grand jury to indict anybody for anything. Mazzei refused to impose bail.

A few weeks before, while Radman was planning her strategy on the South Oaks incident, she had asked Mazzei to move the attempted-murder case up on the calendar. When Mazzei refused, Radman suggested April come to court to make a personal pitch. That day, Radman asked Mazzei again to raise or revoke bail. Mazzei again rejected the request. Then April approached the bench. She spoke softly and nervously.

"I just would like to know how long it's going to take to get a court date. I mean, from Aug. 7 since he's been out on bail, I have been living in fear. I have an 11-year-old son walking around with a baseball bat."

"I understand your concern," Mazzei told her. "The problem is at the present time there are more than 35 defendants who are in custody on murder charges and attempted murder charges who have to be given preference and they have been in custody over a year. Constitutionally that's the way I have to do it."

One factor in the waiting time was the temporary transfer of four criminal court judges to the civil part in April, 1988, to relieve a backlog there. They would not return until December. But another factor that might have been working against April was the trial record of the judge assigned to her case.

AMONG some lawyers, Mazzei is a jurist who has a reputation for delaying or avoiding trials. In 1988, the year the LaSalata case was before him, Mazzei presided over just two trials, according to the court clerk's office. The year before, he had three. In terms of numbers of trials, this placed him 14th among the 15 County Court judges working in Suffolk during those two years.

Mazzei declined to be interviewed for this article, saying through a secretary that he was too busy.

At every turn, Radman felt she was coming up against a rigid legal system whose arbiters were insensitive to the peril that was consuming a woman's life and unresponsive to the urgings of a young, female prosecutor.

"It's still the old boys' network," she said. "I'm little, I'm young. You can sense they treat you differently."

Indeed, her adversaries, Fox and Russo, agree that a different prosecutor might have gotten an earlier trial date. But they lay some of the blame on the district attorney's office for assigning the case to a young prosecutor working in a bureau with a relatively low profile in the office.

"Fran became very involved," Fox said. "She did a good job, but somebody with more authority could have pushed things along." Some of April's family felt likewise. But a former member of the family crimes unit, who asked not to be identified, said a more experienced prosecutor might not have fought as hard: "Fran did more than any other prosecutor would have. She saw the injustice and she went in to Mazzei and kept fighting. A lot of people would have been afraid to."

Chief Assistant District Attorney Mark Cohen added that Radman was well supervised and took counsel from others. "The attention and dedication that assistant paid to the case are beyond question," he said. "To suggest that she was 'inexperienced' and somehow that becomes a logical connection to what happened is misplaced."

As Radman struggled with the system, Fox had troubles of his own. In recent months, LaSalata's parents had been insisting that their son's defense be based on his ex-wife's character. In effect, they wanted Fox to blame April for pushing Tony too far. In October after a series of heated arguments with John LaSalata, Fox took the unusual step of asking to be released from the case. Mazzei granted the request. Fox's withdrawal would delay matters further, as a new attorney would have to be appointed by the court.

Mazzei took the opportunity to remind Anthony LaSalata about the Order of Protection. "I don't want you to go anywhere near your wife," Mazzei said, apparently unaware that they were no longer married.

"No sir," LaSalata said.

But despite his courtroom passivity, it is clear now that LaSalata remained a man possessed. "Some people's self-involvement is so unreasonable that they have enormous trouble dealing with rejection," Dr. Reichman, the court-appointed psychiatrist who examined LaSalata, said in an interview.

April knew this better than anyone. All these months, Fran Radman fought for her and Vinnie O'Leary checked on her. Pictures of LaSalata were kept in the Third Precinct's sector cars. But April told friends she was sure she would not survive Tony's rage. She wrote her will and selected an urn to hold her ashes.

"She *knew* he was going to kill her," Billy Woods said. "She told everybody. Her mother, her brother. She told me every day."

Despite her resignation, April's determination was seen in the way she lived her last months. She went to work in the credit department, shepherded her children to soccer practice, cared for her plants, mowed her mother's lawn.

"A lot of people would have given in," said Kevin Mack, a family friend. "But that was not April's way. She was resolute. She loved her boys and worked hard. And she didn't want to hide. People would say, 'Go away for a while,' or 'Carry a weapon.' "

"We all approached her," Radman said. "I knew she had relatives in New Jersey. But all I got was screaming: 'Here I am, raising two kids, why should we have to leave?' Was it worth it more to her to maintain her life here? Hard question. I think she felt that no matter where she went he would find her. I suggested Ridge, where her brother lives. And she said, 'It's all wide open spaces, he can get me from anywhere.' "

APRIL went to court in Riverhead on Dec. 20. She sat on the opposite side of the room from LaSalata. The defense asked for a three-week adjournment, setting a trial date of Jan. 11. April slipped into the next courtroom to watch the proceedings there. It was the murder trial of Matthew Solomon, accused of strangling his wife the previous Christmas.

The next day, Tony LaSalata went to Edelman's Sporting Goods store in Farmingdale and bought a .22-cal. Marlin rifle, the same model he'd carried with him the night he stabbed April. He filled out the requisite form, which asked, "Are you under indictment . . .?" LaSalata wrote, "No."

On Dec. 26, Lydia Grohoski was shot to death by her estranged husband, Joseph, in the basement of their home in Cutchogue. An Order of Protection was in effect at the time. On Dec. 29, Elizabeth Croff was shot by her estranged husband, William, in front of a cookie factory in Islip. An Order of Protection was in effect at the time. Both men then killed themselves.

On New Year's Eve, Sharon Millard brought her children to April's house for dinner. From the radio in the kitchen they heard a newscaster discussing the cases of Grohoski and Croff. April looked squarely at her oldest friend.

"Sharon," she said. "I'm next."

On the evening of Tuesday, Jan. 3, LaSalata left his parents' house in his mother's car. He said he was going to visit a woman friend. He was wearing his red-and-black hunter's jacket.

At the holidays, he had been feeling low, detectives would learn later. He was living with his parents, was about to come to trial, but was still obsessed with his divorce.

LaSalata drove to 110 McKinley St. He began walking back and forth out front. Justin and

Anthony were inside with their grandmother, who was preparing dinner. The television was on, the volume high. The boys were waiting for Woods to come home with two mice for their pet boa constrictor. Woods had a last-minute call from Slomin's, so he couldn't meet April at work and escort her home, as he liked to do.

April arrived on McKinley Street about 6:30. As she reached the concrete steps in front of her door, LaSalata came out from behind some shrubs. He aimed his sawed-off rifle at her chest and fired. Then he stood over her body and shot her twice in the head. Inside, Justin and Anthony watched television and their grandmother cooked dinner. Their mother lay in the bushes until Woods came home and found her.

"Frannie," Mary Werner, the chief of the family crimes bureau, told Radman over the phone an hour after the fatal shots were fired, "they got April." Radman cried; she didn't sleep for three days. "I kept thinking of her children, of the little boy coming to my office saying he'll do anything to help his mother."

In the end, Radman realized she was part of a system that couldn't help enough. "I had tried to be optimistic," she said. "Gerard wanted to get a gun. I said no, don't do that. I should have told him, yeah. Going to law school, you think the system works, but here's someone I knew and liked and she's dead."

People in the office asked Radman if she'd request a transfer out of family crime, but she felt that would be letting April down somehow. Now, she takes some comfort from the belief that judges in her part of the world seem to be setting higher bails in domestic abuse cases. And in the year since the murders of April and the two other women, reports and arrests for family violence increased dramatically in Suffolk County. But still, when battered women descend the stairs to her basement office and sit before her, it is April whom Radman sees in her mind. And she worries for them.

"We all feel part of it," said Charles Russo, Fox' partner. "When you wake up in the morning and hear, 'April LaSalata is killed,' you feel part of the system. . . . You can't help but have this big empty hole in you."

It was, Mazzei said a day after the murder, "a judge's nightmare."

On Jan. 6, the police discovered LaSalata's frozen corpse slumped in the front seat of his mother's car at a rest stop beyond Exit 52 of the Long Island Expressway. There were two gunshot wounds.

Two days later, more than 100 people crowded into St. Luke's Church in Brentwood for April's funeral mass. "She will never be forgotten," a friend told a reporter. "She will be in our hearts forever." April was cremated, her ashes placed in the urn she had picked out.

In the spring, LaSalata's family petitioned for guardianship of Justin and Anthony, who were living with their grandmother Lillian Principio. April's friends gathered 2,000 names on petitions opposing the idea, and in the fall the petition was withdrawn.

Last month, over the airwaves of radio station WBLI came the voice of Steve Harper, the afternoon disc jockey.

"We've got a special request right now for two little guys, Anthony and Justin, who've had a very tough year. And I understand . . . they're on their way to New York City to see the tree at Rockefeller Center. And we want to wish them all the best. We've got a song for them."

He played "This One's for the Children."

# In the mind of a stalker

*The man who killed actress Rebecca Schaeffer is a symbol of a spreading national menace*

On the morning of the last free day of his life in 1989, 19-year-old Robert Bardo ordered onion rings and cheesecake at a Los Angeles diner. He nodded over his food, then went into the restroom. Inside, he pulled a .357 Magnum pistol out of a red and white plastic grocery bag and put one more hollow-point cartridge into its six-round cylinder, fully loading the gun.

Carrying the sack, he walked a few blocks in brilliant sunshine to the doorstep of TV actress Rebecca Schaeffer. Bardo had been there an hour before, when he had a one-minute conversation with the young star and handed her a note. "Take care, take care," she had said as she quickly closed the glass security door and backed down the hallway. On his second visit, as Schaeffer opened the door, Bardo killed her with one shot in the chest and ran away. In December 1991, after a Los Angeles Superior Court trial, Bardo was sentenced to life in prison without parole. And his case became a frightening symbol of a growing phenomenon in the past decade—stalking.

Besides its obvious connection to violence, stalking raises crucial public-policy questions. Stalkers seem to slip between the cracks of law-enforcement and mental-health agencies—neither of those institutions has the responsibility or capacity for identifying stalkers or protecting victims. In most states, police cannot act unless there is an overt threat, even if they recognize danger signals, while civil libertarians object to law-enforcement officials' maintaining files on the mentally ill.

Stalking is now commonplace in many high-profile locales. There have been dozens of other recent cases spotlighting entertainment celebrities, sports figures, broadcasters and politicians. A surprisingly large number of Hollywood stars have been subject to "strange, unwanted attention," according to Park Dietz, a California psychiatrist recognized as an expert on stalking. Congressional officials say the number of threats to members rose to 566 last year from 394 in 1987.

But stalking cases also have involved thousands of ordinary Americans otherwise anonymous except to their pursuers. One study estimates that 1 in 20 adults will be stalked in her or his lifetime, and other researchers suggest that up to 200,000 people exhibit a stalker's traits. Usually, the harassment constitutes little more than annoyance, such as repeated phone calls or unsolicited letters. The worst episodes, however, result in the death or injury of the person being stalked. And the threat has become so widespread that California became the first state to enact an antistalking law in 1990 after a grotesque quadruple murder. Several other states are considering similar measures.

**Who they are.** Stalkers range from coldblooded killers to lovesick teens, huddled beneath an umbrella of psychological syndromes: paranoia, erotomania, manic depression and schizophrenia. To some degree, all are mentally or emotionally disturbed; many share a family history of similar illness.

No one knows for sure what causes a person to become a stalker, though theories abound. Gavin de Becker, an authority on protecting celebrities and politicians, has compiled a database of some 9,000 potential and actual stalkers, up from 1,500 names in 1985. His research reveals several common characteristics, which he calls pre-incident indicators. Culled from behavioral records and some 200,000 letters, the indicators include things like references to obsessive love, weapons, death, suicide, religious themes and a common destiny with the stalked figure. There is no single stalker profile. But many stalkers share certain behavioral traits: an intense interest in the media, an inability to develop meaningful relationships, a history of unsuccessful efforts to establish an identity and a desire for recognition and attention.

Robert Bardo was an archetypal stalker, who, in the words of one of his high-school teachers, "was a time bomb waiting to explode." He was the youngest of seven children; his father was a noncommissioned officer in the Air Force who met his mother, a Korean resident of Japan, at Yokota Air Force Base. The family moved frequently before winding up in Tucson in 1983, when he was 13.

The first signs of trouble began months later, after Bardo visited a sister who was a topless dancer and bar waitress in Florida. At the end of the year, he stole $140 from his mother's purse and took a bus to Maine, searching for Samantha Smith, the teenager who became famous by writing to then Soviet President Mikhail Gorbachev. She had also replied to a letter Bardo wrote her. Unable to locate her, he was picked up by juvenile authorities and held briefly before being returned to his family. While in Maine, he stabbed himself in the wrist with a pen.

**Outcast.** In junior high school, he was a straight-A student but a social outcast. He never talked to other students, preferring to stand alone, nodding, on the school sidewalks. He began writing letters, often three times a day, to one of his teachers, signing them "Scarface," "Dirty Harry Callahan" and "James Bond." In the letters, which he wrote while listening to the radio, he said he would have to kill her and others, and he also wrote of suicide.

Although school officials told his parents he needed psychiatric help, the parents denied it and, except for one week at Palo Verde Hospital, refused to enroll him in counseling. In one form sent home for the parents to fill out, Bardo himself wrote: "Help. This house is hell. I'm going to run away again. I can't handle it anymore. Please help. Fast."

At Pueblo High School, Bardo remained both an A student and a loner. After he sent his English teacher a 10-page letter vowing to kill himself, he was temporarily removed to a foster home. Again, his parents denied that he was disturbed, and the boy was returned home. His last hospitalization came for a month in the summer of 1985, when he was diagnosed as "severely emotionally handicapped" and coming from a "pathological and dysfunctional family." He was described as a "model patient, eager for all therapy," who discouraged other adolescent patients from using street drugs. Despite the apparent progress, his parents took him out of the hospital, and a few weeks later, he dropped out of high school. That was 1985.

"My mistake was dropping out of high school," Bardo said six years later to a visitor at the Los Angeles County Jail. "I was isolated. I didn't have any friends, never had a girlfriend. I felt alienated, but I liked watching movies or TV. That's when I lost my place."

Bardo doesn't like to talk about his home life, other than to say, "I got my ass kicked a lot." But Dietz, the psychiatrist who testified at Bardo's trial, and John Stalberg, another psychiatrist who interviewed Bardo three times, believe Bardo's family contributed substantially to his problems. They suggest that his father is an alcoholic, his mother displays paranoid symptoms and that at least one older brother physically abused him, making him drink urine and forcing him to shoplift. Bardo's father said, "We've been staying away from the press," and declined further comment about these allegations.

After dropping out of school, Bardo became, in his own words, a "geek who worked at Jack in the Box." Every morning before 5, he walked 2 miles to the fast-food restaurant, where he was employed as a janitor. Other than sleeping 15 hours a day, his only activities were trying to learn to play the guitar, listening to music and watching television. He was never in trouble with the law and says he never took illegal drugs or drank alcohol. He never made more than $3,000 a year, never had a date and never lost his virginity. In psychoanalytic terms, Bardo suffered from dysphoria,

intolerably unpleasant emotions. "He began to live a fantasy life," says Stalberg, "to give him some sort of relief from the mental pain and torture."

**"I worshiped her."** The fantasy life included near-total absorption in the music of Bruce Springsteen, U2, Guns 'n' Roses, the Beatles and other groups. In August 1986, it began to include Rebecca Schaeffer. "She just came into my life at the right time, when I was 16," he recalls. "She was bright, beautiful, spunky—I was impressed with her innocence. She was like a goddess for me, an icon. I was an atheist out there. I worshiped her."

After watching the actress on "My Sister Sam," Bardo began writing her. She sent him one handwritten postcard, saying his first letter was "the nicest, most real" she had received, drawing a peace symbol and heart on the card and signing it "Love, Rebecca."

Not long after receiving the card, Bardo wrote in his diary, "When I think about her I feel that I want to become famous and impress her." Below, on the same page, he wrote: "How do you I [sic] know if the table and paper before me is just a field of electronic pulses. How can I be sure if this is reality?"

He traveled in June 1987 to the Burbank studios where the series was filmed, carrying a large teddy bear and a letter for Schaeffer. Security guards rebuffed him. He returned a month later, this time carrying a knife ("because I thought she was turning arrogant"). But he again failed to meet Schaeffer and went back to Arizona.

For much of 1988, Bardo forgot about the actress, shifting his fixation to singers Debbie Gibson and Tiffany. In mid-1989, though, Schaeffer acted in "Scenes From the Class Struggle in Beverly Hills," a film described in promotions as "just another weekend of shameless sexual adventure, ill-fated romance and accidental death." The actress appeared in one scene in bed with an actor, incensing Bardo, who believed she had become just "another Hollywood whore."

The denouement came quickly. After reading in *People* magazine how Arthur Jackson, a stalker who stabbed actress Theresa Saldana numerous times, had obtained her address, Bardo paid $250 to a private detective, who learned Schaeffer's address from California's motor vehicle department. He got his older brother to buy him a gun (Arizona requires firearms purchasers to be 21), put it in a plastic bag with a letter to Schaeffer. The bag also contained a U2 tape (whose song "Exit" contains the lyrics, "Deeper into the black/Deeper into the white/Pistol weighing heavy") and a copy of "The Catcher in the Rye," the book carried by John Hinckley Jr. when he shot President Reagan. In his shirt

pocket, Bardo carried hollow-point cartridges, which explode on impact.

**The murder.** He took an overnight bus to Los Angeles Union Station and a local bus to the Fairfax district where Schaeffer lived. After walking aimlessly for 90 minutes, he went to her apartment and pushed her buzzer; she came down and he handed her the letter. Then, he went to the diner, called his sister in Tennessee (who told him to leave immediately and come there) and returned to Schaeffer's door.

After the shooting, Bardo hopped a bus to Tucson and was spotted wandering among the cars on a freeway ramp by a police officer. After he told the officer that he had killed Rebecca Schaeffer, he was arrested, extradited to Los Angeles and held for trial. The death sentence was ruled out when his defense attorney, Stephen Galindo, waived Bardo's right to a jury trial. He was convicted in October 1991 of first-degree murder. Bardo didn't deny the prosecution's version of events, except to claim that he didn't ambush Schaeffer. Judge Dino Fulgoni found otherwise and imposed the toughest available sentence.

Marcia Clark, the attorney who prosecuted Bardo's case, believes the ease with which Bardo could contact Schaeffer was her main attraction for him. Bardo patterned himself after assassins, she says, not romancers. She downplays suggestions Bardo is mentally ill, arguing that he is a "con man" who is adept at persuading people to believe "his poor little me" stories. She also asserts that Bardo killed Schaeffer solely for the publicity: "He wanted to be famous."

Bardo, now 22, says he understands the fantasy into which he retreated. "I don't think I'm insane," he says. "I'm just emotional. If it wasn't for my obsession, I'd be law-abiding. But Hollywood is a very seductive place. There are a lot of lonely people out there seduced by the glamour."

Even today, however, Bardo can't completely let go of the young woman he killed. In Los Angeles County Jail, he insists to a visitor that his name and phone number were in Schaeffer's appointment book the day she died. The jail interview room phones suddenly go dead because of a mechanical glitch, and, one wrist manacled to a steel bar, Bardo writes with a stubby pencil on legal paper, "She was going to call me," and holds it up to the protective glass.

"How do you know?" the visitor writes back.

Bardo scribbles furiously: "Why else would she put it in there?"

MIKE THARP IN LOS ANGELES

# When Is It RAPE?

## He was a classmate, a co-worker or a date. He says she wanted it. She calls it a crime. A battle of the sexes rages over drawing the line.

**NANCY GIBBS**

Be careful of strangers and hurry home, says a mother to her daughter, knowing that the world is a frightful place but not wishing to swaddle a child in fear. Girls grow up scarred by caution and enter adulthood eager to shake free of their parents' worst nightmares. They still know to be wary of strangers. What they don't know is whether they have more to fear from their friends.

Most women who get raped are raped by people they already know—like the boy in biology class, or the guy in the office down the hall, or their friend's brother. The familiarity is enough to make them let down their guard, sometimes even enough to make them wonder afterward whether they were "really raped." What people think of as "real rape"—the assault by a monstrous stranger lurking in the shadows—accounts for only 1 out of 5 attacks.

So the phrase "acquaintance rape" was coined to describe the rest, all the cases of forced sex between people who already knew each other, however casually. But that was too clinical for headline writers, and so the popular term is the narrower "date rape," which suggests an ugly ending to a raucous night on the town.

These are not idle distinctions. Behind the search for labels is the central mythology about rape: that rapists are always strangers, and victims are women who ask for it. The mythology is hard to dispel because the crime is so rarely exposed. The experts guess—that's all they can do under the circumstances—that while 1 in 4 women will be raped in her lifetime, less than 10% will report the assault, and less than 5% of the rapists will go to jail.

When a story of the crime lodges in the headlines, the myths have a way of cluttering the search for the truth. The tale of Good Friday in Palm Beach landed in the news because it involved a Kennedy, but it may end up as a watershed case, because all the mysteries and passions surrounding date rape are here to be dissected. William Kennedy Smith met a woman at a bar, invited her back home late at night and apparently had sex with her on the lawn. She says it was rape, and the police believed her story enough to charge him with the crime. Perhaps it was the bruises on her leg; or the instincts of the investigators who found her, panicked and shaking, curled up in the fetal position on a couch; or the lie-detector tests she passed.

On the other side, Smith has adamantly protested that he is a man falsely accused. His friends and family testify to his gentle nature and moral fiber and insist that he could not possibly have committed such a crime. Maybe the truth will come out in court—but regardless of its finale, the case has shoved the debate over date rape into the minds of average men and women. Plant the topic in a conversation, and chances are it will ripen into a bitter argument or a jittery sequence of pale jokes.

Women charge that date rape is the hidden crime; men complain it is hard to prevent a crime they can't define. Women say it isn't taken seriously; men say it is a concept invented by women who like to tease but not take the consequences. Women say the date-rape debate is the first time the nation has talked frankly about sex; men say it is women's unconscious reaction to the excesses of the sexual revolution. Meanwhile, men and women argue among themselves about the "gray area" that surrounds the whole murky arena of sexual relations, and there is no consensus in sight.

In court, on campus, in conversation, the issue turns on the elasticity of the word *rape,* one of the few words in the language with the power to summon a shared image of a horrible crime.

At one extreme are those who argue that for the word to retain its impact, it must be strictly defined as forced sexual intercourse: a gang of thugs jumping a jogger in Central Park, a psychopath preying on old women in a housing complex, a man with an ice pick in a side street. To stretch the definition of the word risks stripping away its power. In this view, if it happened on a date, it wasn't rape. A romantic encounter is a context in which sex *could* occur, and so what omniscient judge will decide whether there was genuine mutual consent?

Others are willing to concede that date rape sometimes occurs, that sometimes a man goes too far on a date without a woman's consent. But this infraction, they say, is not as ghastly a crime as street rape, and it should not be taken as seriously. The New York *Post,* alarmed by the Willy Smith case, wrote in a recent editorial, "If the sexual encounter, *forced or not,* has been preceded by a series of consensual activities—drinking, a trip to the man's home, a walk on a deserted beach at 3 in the morning—the charge that's leveled against the alleged offender should, it seems to us, be different than the one filed against, say, the youths who raped and beat the jogger."

This attitude sparks rage among women who carry scars received at the hands of men they knew. It makes no difference if the victim shared a drink or a moonlit walk or even a passionate kiss, they protest, if the encounter ended with her being thrown to the ground and forcibly violated. Date rape is not about a misunderstanding, they say. It is not a communications problem. It is not about a woman's having regrets in the morning for a decision she made the night before. It is not about a "decision" at all. Rape is rape, and any form of forced sex—even between neighbors, co-workers, classmates and casual friends—is a crime.

A more extreme form of that view comes from activists who see rape as a metaphor, its definition swelling to cover any kind of oppression of women. Rape, seen in this light, can occur not only on a date but also in a marriage, not only by violent assault but also by psychological pressure. A Swarthmore College training pamphlet once explained that acquaintance rape "spans a spectrum of incidents and behaviors, ranging from crimes legally defined as rape to verbal harassment and inappropriate innuendo."

No wonder, then, that the battles become so heated. When innuendo qualifies as rape, the definitions have become so slippery that the entire subject sinks into a political swamp. The only way to capture the hard reality is to tell the story.

A 32-year-old woman was on business in Tampa last year for the Florida supreme court. Stranded at the courthouse, she accepted a lift from a lawyer involved in her project. As they chatted on the ride home, she recalls, "he was saying all the right things, so I started to trust him." She agreed to have dinner, and afterward, at her hotel door, he convinced her to let him come in to talk. "I went through the whole thing about being old-fashioned," she says. "I was a virgin until I was 21. So I told him talk was all we were going to do."

But as they sat on the couch, she found herself falling asleep. "By now, I'm comfortable with him, and I put my head on his shoulder. He's not tried anything all evening, after all." Which is when the rape came. "I woke up to find him on top of me, forcing himself on me. I didn't scream or run. All I could think about was my business contacts and what if they saw me run out of my room screaming rape.

"I thought it was my fault. I felt so filthy, I washed myself over and over in hot water. Did he rape me?, I kept asking myself. I didn't consent. But who's gonna believe me? I had a man in my hotel room after midnight." More than a year later, she still can't tell the story without a visible struggle to maintain her composure. Police referred the case to the state attorney's office in Tampa, but without more evidence it decided not to prosecute. Although her attacker has admitted that he heard her say no, maintains the woman, "he says he didn't know that I meant no. He didn't feel he'd raped me, and he even wanted to see me again."

Her story is typical in many ways. The victim herself may not be sure right away that she has been raped, that she had said no and been physically forced into having sex anyway. And the rapist commonly hears but does not heed the protest. "A date rapist will follow through no matter what the woman wants because his agenda is to get laid," says Claire Walsh, a Florida-based consultant on sexual assaults. "First comes the dinner, then a dance, then a drink, then the coercion begins." Gentle persuasion gives way to physical intimidation, with alcohol as the ubiquitous lubricant. "When that fails, force is used," she says. "Real men don't take no for an answer."

The Palm Beach case serves to remind women that if they go ahead and press charges, they can expect to go on trial along with their attacker, if not in a courtroom then in the court of public opinion. The New York *Times* caused an uproar on its own staff not only for publishing the victim's name but also for laying out in detail her background, her high school grades, her driving record, along with an unattributed quote from a school official about her "little wild streak." A freshman at Carleton College in Minnesota, who says she was repeatedly raped for four hours by a fellow student, claims that she was asked at an administrative hearing if she performed oral sex on dates. In 1989 a man charged with raping at knife point a woman he knew was acquitted in Florida because his victim had been wearing lace shorts and no underwear.

From a purely legal point of view, if she wants to put her attacker in jail, the survivor had better be beaten as well as raped, since bruises become a badge of credibility. She had better have reported the crime right away, before taking the hours-long shower that she craves, before burning her clothes, before curling up with the blinds down. And she would do well to be a woman of shining character. Otherwise the strict constructionist definitions of rape will prevail in court. "Juries don't have a great deal of sympathy for the victim if she's a willing participant up to the nonconsensual sexual intercourse," says Norman Kinne, a prosecutor in Dallas. "They feel that many times the victim has placed herself in the situation." Absent eyewitnesses or broken bones, a case comes down to her word against his, and the mythology of rape rarely lends her the benefit of the doubt.

She should also hope for an all-male jury, preferably composed of fathers with daughters. Prosecutors have found that women tend to be harsh judges of one another—perhaps because to find a defendant guilty is to entertain two grim realities: that anyone might be a rapist, and that every woman could find herself a victim. It may be easier to believe, the experts muse, that at some level the victim asked for it. "But just because a woman makes a bad judgment, does that give the guy a moral right to rape her?" asks Dean Kilpatrick, director of the Crime Victim Research and Treatment Center at the Medical University of South Carolina. "The bottom line is, Why does a woman's having a drink give a man the right to rape her?"

Last week the Supreme Court waded into the debate with a 7-to-2 ruling that protects victims from being harassed on the witness stand with questions about their sexual history. The Justices, in their first decision on "rape shield laws," said an accused rapist could not present evidence about a previous sexual relationship with the victim unless he notified the court ahead of time. In her decision, Justice Sandra Day O'Connor wrote that "rape victims deserve heightened protection against surprise, harassment and unnecessary invasions of privacy."

That was welcome news to prosecutors who understand the reluctance of victims to come forward. But there are other impediments to justice as well. An internal investigation of the Oakland police department found that officers ignored a quarter of all reports of sexual assaults or attempts, though 90% actually warranted investigation. Departments are getting better at educating officers in handling rape cases, but the courts remain behind.

## 2. VICTIMOLOGY

A New York City task force on women in the courts charged that judges and lawyers were routinely less inclined to believe a woman's testimony than a man's.

The present debate over degrees of rape is nothing new: all through history, rapes have been divided between those that mattered and those that did not. For the first few thousand years, the only rape that was punished was the defiling of a virgin, and that was viewed as a property crime. A girl's virtue was a marketable asset, and so a rapist was often ordered to pay the victim's father the equivalent of her price on the marriage market. In early Babylonian and Hebrew societies, a married woman who was raped suffered the same fate as an adulteress—death by stoning or drowning. Under William the Conqueror, the penalty for raping a virgin was castration and loss of both eyes—unless the violated woman agreed to marry her attacker, as she was often pressured to do. "Stealing an heiress" became a perfectly conventional means of taking—literally—a wife.

It may be easier to prove a rape case now, but not much. Until the 1960s it was virtually impossible without an eyewitness; judges were often required to instruct jurors that "rape is a charge easily made and hard to defend against; so examine the testimony of this witness with caution." But sometimes a rape was taken very seriously, particularly if it involved a black man attacking a white woman—a crime for which black men were often executed or lynched.

Susan Estrich, author of *Real Rape*, considers herself a lucky victim. This is not just because she survived an attack 17 years ago by a stranger with an ice pick, one day before her graduation from Wellesley. It's because police, and her friends, believed her. "The first thing the Boston police asked was whether it was a black guy," recalls Estrich, now a University of Southern California law professor. When she said yes and gave the details of the attack, their reaction was, "So, you were really raped." It was an instructive lesson, she says, in understanding how racism and sexism are factored into perceptions of the crime.

A new twist in society's perception came in 1975, when Susan Brownmiller published her book *Against Our Will: Men, Women and Rape*. In it she attacked the concept that rape was a sex crime, arguing instead that it was a crime of violence and power over women. Throughout history, she wrote, rape has played a critical function. "It is nothing more or less than a conscious process of intimidation, by which *all men* keep *all women* in a state of fear."

Out of this contention was born a set of arguments that have become politically correct wisdom on campus and in academic circles. This view holds that rape is a symbol of women's vulnerability to male institutions and attitudes. "It's sociopolitical," insists Gina Rayfield, a New Jersey psychologist. "In our culture men

hold the power, politically, economically. They're socialized not to see women as equals."

This line of reasoning has led some women, especially radicalized victims, to justify flinging around the term rape as a political weapon, referring to everything from violent sexual assaults to inappropriate innuendos. Ginny, a college senior who was really raped when she was 16, suggests that false accusations of rape can serve a useful purpose. "Penetration is not the only form of violation," she explains. In her view, rape is a subjective term, one that women must use to draw attention to other, nonviolent, even nonsexual forms of oppression. "If a woman did falsely accuse a man of rape, she may have had reasons to," Ginny says. "Maybe she wasn't raped, but he clearly violated her in some way."

Catherine Comins, assistant dean of student life at Vassar, also sees some value in this loose use of "rape." She says angry victims of various forms of sexual intimidation cry rape to regain their sense of power. "To use the word carefully would be to be careful for the sake of the violator, and the survivors don't care a hoot about him." Comins argues that men who are unjustly accused can sometimes gain from the experience. "They have a lot of pain, but it is not a pain that I would necessarily have spared them. I think it ideally initiates a process of self-exploration. 'How do I see women?' 'If I didn't violate her, could I have?' 'Do I have the potential to do to her what they say I did?' Those are good questions."

Taken to extremes, there is an ugly element of vengeance at work here. Rape is an abuse of power. But so are false accusations of rape, and to suggest that men whose reputations are destroyed might benefit because it will make them more sensitive is an attitude that is sure to backfire on women who are seeking justice for all victims. On campuses where the issue is most inflamed, male students are outraged that their names can be scrawled on a bathroom-wall list of rapists and they have no chance to tell their side of the story.

"Rape is what you read about in the New York *Post* about 17 little boys raping a jogger in Central Park," says a male freshman at a liberal-arts college, who learned that he had been branded a rapist after a one-night stand with a friend. He acknowledges that they were both very drunk when she started kissing him at a party and ended up back in his room. Even through his haze, he had some qualms about sleeping with her: "I'm fighting against my hormonal instincts, and my moral instincts are saying, 'This is my friend and if I were sober, I wouldn't be doing this.'" But he went ahead anyway. "When you're drunk, and there are all sorts of ambiguity, and the woman says 'Please, please' and then she says no sometime later, even in the middle of the act, there still may very well be some

kind of violation, but it's not the same thing. It's not rape. If you don't hear her say no, if she doesn't say it, if she's playing around with you—oh, I could get squashed for saying it—there is an element of say no, mean yes."

The morning after their encounter, he recalls, both students woke up hung over and eager to put the memory behind them. Only months later did he learn that she had told a friend that he had torn her clothing and raped her. At this point in the story, the accused man starts using the language of rape. "I felt violated," he says. "I felt like she was taking advantage of me when she was very drunk. I never heard her say 'No!,' 'Stop!,' anything." He is angry and hurt at the charges, worried that they will get around, shatter his reputation and force him to leave the small campus.

So here, of course, is the heart of the debate. If rape is sex without consent, how exactly should consent be defined and communicated, when and by whom? Those who view rape through a political lens tend to place all responsibility on men to make sure that their partners are consenting at every point of a sexual encounter. At the extreme, sexual relations come to resemble major surgery, requiring a signed consent form. Clinical psychologist Mary P. Koss of the University of Arizona in Tucson, who is a leading scholar on the issue, puts it rather bluntly: "It's the man's penis that is doing the raping, and ultimately he's responsible for where he puts it."

Historically, of course, this has never been the case, and there are some who argue that it shouldn't be—that women too must take responsibility for their behavior, and that the whole realm of intimate encounters defies regulation from on high. Anthropologist Lionel Tiger has little patience for trendy sexual politics that make no reference to biology. Since the dawn of time, he argues, men and women have always gone to bed with different goals. In the effort to keep one's genes in the gene pool, "it is to the male advantage to fertilize as many females as possible, as quickly as possible and as efficiently as possible." For the female, however, who looks at the large investment she will have to make in the offspring, the opposite is true. Her concern is to "select" who "will provide the best set up for their offspring." So, in general, "the pressure is on the male to be aggressive and on the female to be coy."

No one defends the use of physical force, but when the coercion involved is purely psychological, it becomes hard to assign blame after the fact. Journalist Stephanie Gutmann is an ardent foe of what she calls the date-rape dogmatists. "How can you make sex completely politically correct and completely safe?" she asks. "What a horribly bland, unerotic thing that would be! Sex is, by nature, a risky endeavor, emotionally. And desire is a violent emotion. These people in the date-rape movement have erected so many rules and regulations that I don't know how people can have erotic or desire-driven sex."

Nonsense, retorts Cornell professor Andrea Parrot, co-author of *Acquaintance Rape: The Hidden Crime*. Seduction should not be about lies, manipulation, game playing or coercion of any kind, she says. "Too bad that people think that the only way you can have passion and excitement and sex is if there are miscommunications, and one person is forced to do something he or she doesn't want to do." The very pleasures of sexual encounters should lie in the fact of mutual comfort and consent: "You can hang from the ceiling, you can use fruit, you can go crazy and have really wonderful sensual erotic sex, if both parties are consenting."

It would be easy to accuse feminists of being too quick to classify sex as rape, but feminists are to be found on all sides of the debate, and many protest the idea that all the onus is on the man. It demeans women to suggest that they are so vulnerable to coercion or emotional manipulation that they must always be escorted by the strong arm of the law. "You can't solve society's ills by making everything a crime," says Albuquerque attorney Nancy Hollander. "That comes out of the sense of overprotection of women, and in the long run that is going to be harmful to us."

What is lost in the ideological debate over date rape is the fact that men and women, especially when they are young, and drunk, and aroused, are not very good at communicating. "In many cases," says Estrich, "the man thought it was sex, and the woman thought it was rape, and they are both telling the truth." The man may envision a celluloid seduction, in which he is being commanding, she is being coy. A woman may experience the same event as a degrading violation of her will. That some men do not believe a woman's protests is scarcely surprising in a society so drenched with messages that women have rape fantasies and a desire to be overpowered.

By the time they reach college, men and women are loaded with cultural baggage, drawn from movies, television, music videos and "bodice ripper" romance novels. Over the years they have watched Rhett sweep Scarlett up the stairs in *Gone With the Wind;* or Errol Flynn, who was charged twice with statutory rape, overpower a protesting heroine who then melts in his arms; or Stanley rape his sister-in-law Blanche du Bois while his wife is in the hospital giving birth to a child in *A Streetcar Named Desire*. Higher up the cultural food chain, young people can read of date rape in Homer or Jane Austen, watch it in *Don Giovanni* or *Rigoletto*.

The messages come early and often, and nothing in the feminist revolution has been able to counter them. A recent survey of sixth- to ninth-graders in Rhode Island found that a fourth of the boys and a sixth of the girls said it was acceptable for a man to force a woman to kiss him or have sex if he has spent money on her. A third of the children said it would not be wrong for a man to rape a woman who had had previous sexual experiences.

Certainly cases like Palm Beach, movies like *The Accused* and novels like Avery Corman's *Prized Possessions* may force young people to re-examine assumptions they have inherited. The use of new terms, like acquaintance rape and date rape, while controversial, has given men and women the vocabulary they need to express their experiences with both force and precision. This dialogue would be useful if it helps strip away some of the dogmas, old and new, surrounding the issue. Those who hope to raise society's sensitivity to the problem of date rape would do well to concede that it is not precisely the same sort of crime as street rape, that there may be very murky issues of intent and degree involved.

On the other hand, those who downplay the problem should come to realize that date rape is a crime of uniquely intimate cruelty. While the body is violated, the spirit is maimed. How long will it take, once the wounds have healed, before it is possible to share a walk on a beach, a drive home from work or an evening's conversation without always listening for a quiet alarm to start ringing deep in the back of the memory of a terrible crime?　　**—*Reported by Sylvester Monroe/Los Angeles, Priscilla Painton and Anastasia Toufexis/New York***

# WHEN MEN HIT WOMEN

*A program for battered women in Duluth, Minn.—though widely considered the model for the rest of the country—has enjoyed only limited success. Nothing speaks more eloquently to the intractability of the problem.*

## Jan Hoffman

*Jan Hoffman, a staff writer for* The Village Voice, *recently completed a journalism fellowship at Yale Law School.*

This Saturday night shift has been excruciatingly dull for the police in Duluth, Minn., a brawny working-class city of 90,000 on the shoreline of Lake Superior. The complaints trickle into the precinct, the callers almost embarrassed: black bear up a tree; kids throwing stuffed animals into traffic. But it's 1 A.M. now, and the bars are closing. People are heading home.

1:02 A.M.: Couple arguing loudly. Probably just "verbal assault," the dispatcher tells the car patrols.

1:06 A.M.: Two squad cars pull up to the address. A tall blond man opens the door as a naked woman hurriedly slips on a raincoat. The man looks calm. The woman looks anything but.

"We were just having a squabble," he begins.

"He was kicking the [expletive] out of me," she yells.

"Let's go in separate rooms and talk," says one of the officers, following the Duluth Police Department procedure for domestic disputes.

In the living room, George G. tells his side of the story. "We've been trying to work on things. And so we were talking. And wrestling."

How does he explain the blood oozing from the inside of her mouth? "She drinks, you know. She probably cut herself." From inside the bedroom, Jenny M., whose face is puffing up, screams: "Just get him out of here! And then you guys leave, too!"

The police officers probe for details, telling her that something must be done now, or there will probably be a next time, and it will hurt much worse. Jenny M. glares, fearful but furious. "He slapped me and kicked my butt. He picked me up by the hair and threw me against the wall."

"She lies, you know," George G. confides to an officer, who remains stone-faced. Jenny M. starts crying again.

"I don't want him hurt. This is my fault. I'm the drinker. He's not a bad guy."

Following protocol, the officers determine that the couple live together. And that she is afraid of him. Next, they snap Polaroids of her bruised face, and of his swollen, cut knuckles. Then the police head toward George G. with handcuffs. He looks at her beseechingly. "Jenny, do you want me to go?"

An officer cuts him short. "George, it's not her choice."

George G. thrusts his chin out and his fists deep into the couch. "But this is just a domestic fight!"

One cop replies: "We don't have a choice, either. We have to arrest you." They take him away, handcuffed, leaving Jenny M. with leaflets about the city's Domestic Abuse Intervention Project (D.A.I.P).

By 1:34 A.M. George G. has been booked at the St. Louis County jail, where he will sit out the weekend until arraignment on Monday morning. Within an hour, a volunteer from the city's shelter will try to contact Jenny M., and in the morning, a man from D.A.I.P. will visit George and explain the consequences in Duluth for getting into "a domestic fight."

It was 10 years ago this summer that Duluth became the first local jurisdiction in America to adopt a mandatory arrest policy for misdemeanor assaults—the criminal charge filed in most domestic-violence cases. But the arrest policy alone is not what makes Duluth's perhaps the most imitated intervention program in the country. Its purpose is to make every agent of the justice system—police, prosecutors, probation officers, judges—deliver the same message: domestic violence is a crime that a community will not tolerate. The program's centerpiece is D.A.I.P., which acts as a constant, heckling monitor of all the organizations. The project, which also runs batterers' groups and supervises custody visits between batterers and their children, chugs along on $162,000 a year. Financing comes from the state's Department of Corrections, foundation grants and fees for D.A.I.P.'s manuals and training seminars.

The Duluth model—pieces of which have been replicated in communities throughout Minnesota, in cities like Los Angeles, Baltimore, San Francisco, Nashville and Seattle, and in countries like Canada, Scotland, New Zealand and Australia—has been admiringly described by Mary Haviland, a New York City domestic-abuse expert, as "an organizing miracle."

Typically, a first-time offender is incarcerated overnight. If he pleads guilty, he'll be sentenced to 30 days in jail and put on probation, pending completion of a 26-week batterer's program. If he misses three successive classes, he is often sent to jail. Men who are served with civil orders of protection are routinely sent into the same treatment program. Staff members and volunteers from the shelter maintain contact with victims throughout the process.

Many experts regard Duluth as embodying the best of what the almost 20-year-old battered-women's movement has sought to achieve. The movement, inspired by the grass-roots feminist campaign that opened rape-crisis centers in the late 60's, sprang up in the mid-70's as a loose coalition of emergency shelters. Duluth's own shelter, the Women's Coalition, was founded in 1978. Reflecting the national movement's multiple approaches a few years later, Duluth activists then prodded local law-enforcement agencies to take the issue seriously and eventually urged that batterers be offered treatment as well as punishment.

Nowadays in Duluth, women who seek help from the legal system do receive some protection, and their batterers are usually held accountable. After a decade of many trials and many errors, Ellen Pence, one of the project's founders and its national proselytizer, estimates that 1 out of every 19 men in Duluth has been through the program. During that same period, not one Duluth woman died from a domestic homicide. Given the rate of Duluth's domestic homicides in the 70's, says Pence, "there are at least five women alive today that would have otherwise been killed."

The results from Duluth are not, however, wholly triumphant. One study shows that five years after going through the Duluth program and judicial system, fully 40 percent of the treated men end up reoffending (or becoming suspects in assaults), either with the same woman or new partners. Pence thinks the real number may be closer to 60 percent. And the number of new cases each year that come before either criminal or family court judges has remained constant—about 450 a year.

"The changes in the country have been enormous," says Elizabeth M. Schneider, a Brooklyn Law School professor and expert on battered women. "But we seriously underestimated how wedded our culture is to domestic violence." Upward of four million American women are beaten annually by current and former male partners, and between 2,000 to 4,000 women are murdered, according to the National Woman Abuse Prevention Center. C. Everett Koop, the former Surgeon General, has identified domestic violence as the No. 1 health problem for American women, causing more injuries than automobile accidents, muggings and rapes combined. The connection with child abuse in a family has been well documented: between 50 and 70 percent of the men who physically harm their partners also hit their children.

At this point, while intervention may be possible, prevention seems all but unimaginable. Despite the community's exceptional efforts, as Pence flatly admits: "We have no evidence to show that it has had any general deterrent effect. The individual guy you catch may do it less. But in Duluth, men don't say, 'Gee, I shouldn't beat her up because I'll get arrested.' After 10 years, we've had a lot of young men in our program whose dads were in it.

"I have no idea where the next step will come from," she adds. "We're too exhausted just trying to stay on top of things as they are."

Ellen Pence's commitment to ending family violence is hard-earned. An aunt was shot to death by her husband, a sister is a former battered wife and, one night about 20 years ago, a neighbor fleeing an abusive partner left her boy with Pence, who subsequently helped raise him. In 1981, D.A.I.P. received a $50,000 state grant for Pence's bold new experiment. Duluth was chosen for a simple but powerful reason: the city's judges and police chief were the only ones in Minnesota willing to take her proposal seriously. A Minnesota native, Pence, now 43, is an exasperating, indefatigable earthshaker, who, by dint of her salty wit and impassioned outbursts, simply will not be denied.

Duluth, she concedes, is not exactly the mayhem capital of the Midwest. In 1990, homicides hit a record high of three. The local scourge is predominantly alcoholism, not drug addiction. The people are mostly Scandinavian and Eastern European, with a modest minority of Ojibwa Indians, blacks and Southeast Asians. With fir-dotted hills that swoop sharply down to the largest fresh-water lake in the world, Duluth appears to be a pretty decent place to live—particularly for those with a fondness for ice fishing and months of subfreezing weather. Its incidence of domestic violence is probably no worse than anywhere else in the country, and, a decade ago, was treated just as casually. In 1980, there were just 22 arrests for domestic assault, and only four convictions.

First, Ellen Pence took on the cops.

Traditional practice: If an officer doesn't witness a misdemeanor assault, the officer won't arrest.

New practice: If an officer has probable cause, including a victim's visible injury, to believe a misdemeanor domestic assault occurred within four hours of the arrival of the police, the officer must arrest. In 1990, the Duluth police arrested 176 men and 23 women for misdemeanor domestic assaults—of whom almost all were convicted. (Experts agree that violence by women against men is usually in self-defense or retaliation, and is often less severe.)

Over the years, mandatory arrest has become increasingly popular, having been adopted, though inconsistently enforced, in dozens of municipalities and 15 states—although recent studies have called into question whether police arrests are the best way to protect domestic-abuse victims.

Still, mandatory arrest earns favorable reviews from police and prosecutors, and a D.A.I.P. survey found that 71 percent of the victims approved of the Duluth police's handling of their situations. But some battered-women's advocates remain skeptical, particularly because the policy can be disproportionately tough on poor minority families. Most experts point out that while battering occurs across all races and classes, poor people are more likely to be reported to authorities and punished than men from middle-class households. "For people who are more disadvantaged economically, like Native Americans, blacks and Hispanics, there are higher levels of all kinds of victimization, including family violence," says Angela Browne, the author of "When Battered Women Kill."

Another significant problem with mandatory arrest is that it can backfire: on occasion, when faced with two bloodied people accusing each other of attacking first, police have arrested the woman as well as the man. When this happens, children may be sent into foster care. In Connecticut, which has one of the country's toughest domestic-violence policies, the dual-arrest rate is 14 percent.

Many police are still reluctant to arrest because prosecutors tend to put the cases on the back burner. Prosecutors, in turn, blame their lack of action on the victims, who, they say, often refuse to press charges, fearing a batterer's revenge or believing his promise of reformation. Duluth, however, has what officials call a "flexible no-drop" policy: regardless of the victim's wishes, the prosecutor will almost always pursue the case.

"I assume that victims won't cooperate," says Mary E. Asmus, the chief prosecutor of Duluth's city attorney's office. Asmus has a working procedure for obtaining evidence independent of the victim's cooperation. At trial, she'll offer police photographs, tapes of calls to 911 and medical records. She also subpoenas all victims. If the victim recants on the stand, Asmus, making unusual use of a state rule of evidence, will offer the woman's original statement to police—not to impeach her witness, but to assert the facts of the incident. In her nine years as a Duluth prosecutor, Asmus has lost only three domestic-violence cases in court.

Nationwide, some of the most aggressive domestic-violence prosecutors are in Philadelphia, San Francisco and San Diego, which files at least 200 new cases each month. To pressure women to testify, some prosecutors have gone so far as charging them with filing false police reports and perjury, issuing contempt-of-court citations, and, in rare instances, even jailing them. The no-drop policy has ignited fiery debate. One prosecutor argued in a recent national District Attorneys Association Bulletin that it "smacks of the worst kind of paternalism." In Westchester County, N.Y., Judge Jeanine Ferris Pirro retorts, "Some jurisdictions allow a victim to drop charges, and that's sending a subtle message that they don't take the crime seriously."

Not surprisingly, a no-drop policy often puts prosecutors at odds with the same activists who are demanding that the justice system go after batterers. Susan Schechter, author of "Women and Male Violence," contends that such a policy can erode a battered woman's sense of self-esteem and control, "particularly when she has a good sense of her own danger and what's best for her and the kids." Pence says that in Duluth, D.A.I.P. has managed to cut the dual-arrest rate way down. "We trust our system," she says, "so we're willing to force a woman into it." But Pence doesn't condone mandatory arrest or no-drop prosecutions unilaterally.

While tougher policies have diverted more cases into criminal court, women just want their abusers out of the house but not sent to jail seek relief through a different route: the civil order of protection, which limits the batterer's contact with the woman and her children. Applying for such an order can be a labyrinthine undertaking—even on a good day. Every jurisdiction has its own criteria for who qualifies, as well as for the duration of the protection order. Women with mixed feelings about getting the order in the first place can quickly become frustrated.

And judges become frustrated with them. Gender-bias studies of various state court systems have sharply criticized judges for penalizing battered women. In Duluth, the D.A.I.P. targeted the judiciary. "We explained why they were seeing what they were seeing," Pence recalls. "They were interpreting a woman's fear as ambivalence and masochism. We showed them what happened in cases when they just gave a guy a lecture or a fine." Now she occasionally trots out one or two Duluth judges on her judicial-training sessions around the country. One grumbles fondly that "Ellen Pence is turning us into feminist tools."

Judge Robert V. Campbell of Duluth's District Court presides over most of its order-of-protection hearings. If a woman fails to appear in court because her abuser may be present, "I'll continue the order for a month or so, on the theory that she's being intimidated," Campbell says. A Duluth woman named Brenda Erickson, whose request for an order against her husband alleged that he'd raped her, had her first brush with the justice system before Judge Campbell. Her husband's attorney argued that his client could not have raped her. "Your honor," Erickson remembers the lawyer protesting, "she's his wife!"

The judge, she says, all but leaped down from the bench, sputtering, "If she'd been raped by a stranger, would you expect her to live with him, too?" "And I thought, Oh God, he understands how I feel," Erickson says.

Six glum faces, 12 crossed arms—nobody thinks they did anything wrong, so why do they have to be here? Ty Schroyer, a D.A.I.P. group leader, assumes an expression of determined cheeriness as he greets this week's recruits, all ordered by the court to the batterer's program. Some ground rules:

"We don't call women 'the old lady,' 'the wife,' 'that slut,' 'that whore,' 'the bitch,' 'that fat, ugly bitch.' . . ." The list quickly becomes unprintable.

"So what should we call her—'it'?" says a man who calls himself Dave, as the others snicker.

"How about her name?" snaps Schroyer, who himself was arrested nearly a decade ago for pounding his wife's head against a sidewalk.

Trying to change a batterer's behavior toward women makes pushing boulders uphill look easy. Nonetheless, at least 250 different programs around the country, filled with volunteer and court-referred clients, are having a go at it. Among them, no consensus has emerged about philosophy or length of treatment: Phoenix courts send their batterers to 12 weeks or more of counseling sessions; San Diego batterers must attend for a year.

Edward W. Gondolf, a Pittsburgh sociologist who has evaluated and developed batterers' programs for 12 years, says, "We're making a dent with garden-variety batterers"—first-time or sporadic offenders—"but there's another cadre, the most lethal, who are still out of our reach." Batterers who go through the legal system should be more carefully screened, he says, and some confined. Men whom he would categorize as antisocial or even sociopathic batterers—about 30 percent—not only resist intervention, but may be further antagonized by it.

He cautions women not to be taken in when their partners enter counseling. "Counseling is the American way to heal a problem," he says. "She'll think, 'If he's trying, I should support him,' while he's thinking, 'I'll go to the program until I get what I want—my wife back.' But his being in counseling may increase the danger for her because she has got her guard down."

In Duluth, when a batterer enters D.A.I.P., officials at the Women's Coalition shelter will stay in close touch with the victim; a woman who is reluctant to report another beating to police can confide in a shelter counselor, who will tell a group leader, who may confront the man in the following week's session.

Nearly half of all batterers have problems with substance abuse, especially alcohol, and D.A.I.P. group leaders often have difficulty persuading men not to blame their violence on their addictions. John J., 35, a Duluth man who once beat a marine senseless with a lug wrench, raped the women he dated and kicked the first of four wives when she was pregnant, thought he'd become violence-free after going through the D.A.I.P. batterers' program and Alcoholics Anonymous. One night several years later, though sober, he shoved his third fiancée so hard that she went flying over a coffee table. "Men have more courage when we're drunk," he says, teary-eyed with shame, during an interview. "But the bottle didn't put the violence there in the first place."

Why do men hit women? "Men batter because it works," says Richard J. Gelles, director of the Family Violence Research Program at the University of Rhode Island. "They can not only hurt a woman but break down her sense of self-worth and belief that she can do anything about it."

Some programs use a therapeutic approach, exploring family history. Others employ a model inspired by the psychologist Lenore Walker's "cycle of violence" theory of battering: the man goes through a slow buildup of tension, explodes at his partner and begs her forgiveness during a honeymoon period.

But Pence criticizes both approaches for failing to confront a batterer's hatred of women, as well as his desire to dominate them. Duluth's 26-week program is divided in two sections. The first, usually run by a mental-health center, emphasizes more traditional counseling that tries to teach men to walk away from their anger. The second, run by D.A.I.P., provokes men to face up to their abuse and to identify the social and cultural forces underlying it. (In 1990, Duluth sent 350 men through its program. By comparison, Victim Services in New York City sent 300.)

Bill, 30, admits that he once believed "you were allowed to hit a woman if you were married—the license was for possession." A sense of entitlement pervades the men's groups: when Schroyer asked one man why he cut telephone cords in his house, the man shouted, "Why should she talk on something I paid for?"

Duluth batterers don't necessarily have to slap, punch, choke, kick with steel-toed boots or crush empty beer cans against a cheekbone to keep their partners terrified. During arguments, abusers will floor the gas pedal, clean hunting rifles or sharpen knives at the kitchen table, smash dishes and television sets, call her office very two minutes and hang up. One man smeared a peanut butter and jelly sandwich in his wife's hair. One woman's ex-husband wrote her phone number in the men's rooms of Duluth's seediest bars, with an invitation to call for a good time.

Then there are the outright threats. If she leaves him, he'll tell child-welfare services that she's a neglectful mother. Or he'll kill her. Or himself.

## 2. VICTIMOLOGY

Schroyer and the other group leaders stress that when the violence does erupt, contrary to a batterer's favorite excuse, he has not lost control. "You chose the time, the place, the reason, how much force you'd use," Schroyer tells them. "She didn't."

But convincing men that they are better off without that control is perhaps the most challenging impediment to treatment. One night a batterer huffily asked, "Why should men want to change when we got it all already?"

Brenda Erickson, one of the Duluth women who appeared before Judge Campbell, had been thinking about leaving her husband, Mike, for a long time. Mike had always told her that she was fat, ugly and stupid, and besides, no man would want a woman with three children, so she'd better stay with him. Brenda never thought she was a battered woman, because Mike had never punched her.

The social psychologist Julie Blackman points out that a byproduct of the attention given to the Lisa Steinberg tragedy several years ago is that the public now mistakenly associates battered women with the smashed, deformed face of Hedda Nussbaum. Susan Schechter finds that many abused women who are not as bloodied as the character portrayed by Farrah Fawcett in "The Burning Bed" do not believe they deserve aid. "Many battered women see themselves as strong, as keeping together a family, in spite of what's going on," Schechter says.

Mike often assured Brenda that if he went to jail, it wouldn't be for wife-beating—it would be for her murder. When he was angry, he would shatter knickknacks or punch a hole in the wall right next to her head. Brenda is 5 foot 1 and Mike is 6 foot 3. "Imagine an 18-wheeler colliding with a Volkswagen," she says. "So I learned how to say 'yes' to him, to defuse situations."

Over the eight years of their marriage, the family subsisted on welfare and Mike's occasional earnings as a freelance mechanic. In the final years, Brenda cooked in a restaurant, worked as an aide for Head Start and cared for their three sons. According to Brenda, Mike chose not to seek a full-time job in order to keep an eye on her. She couldn't even go to the grocery store alone.

Frequently, he raped her. "He'd rent pornographic films and force me to imitate them," Brenda says. The sex was often rough and humiliating. "He thought that if we had sex a lot I wouldn't leave him." Mike acknowledges that there was "mental abuse" in their marriage, but not what he'd call rape. "I'm oversexed, but there's nothing wrong with that."

A friend at work, sensing Brenda's distress, gave her the number of the Women's Coalition shelter. Brenda would call anonymously, trying to figure out if she could possibly escape. Finally, she just picked a date: Feb. 9, 1988.

That morning, she told Mike she was taking the kids to school. Once there, a shelter official picked them up. When Brenda walked into the handsome Victorian house filled with women and children, she felt an overwhelming sense of relief.

Women stay in abusive relationships too long for many reasons. Susan Schechter says it can take years before physical abuse starts, even longer for a woman to learn "not to blame herself or his lousy childhood for his violence." Brenda refused for years to believe her marriage wasn't working. Another Duluth woman, who endured a decade of stitches and plaster casts, sobbed, "We did have some wonderful times, and he was my entire world."

Some women stay because they may have reasonable expectations that they will die leaving. As many as three-quarters of the domestic assaults reported to authorities take place after the woman has left.

Some women stay because they can't afford to leave—or because, long since alienated from friends and family, they have no place to go. There are about 1,200 shelters scattered across the country, many reporting that they must turn away three out of every four women who ask for help. Duluth's shelter can house up to 30 women and children; the shelter in Las Vegas, Nev. (population: 850,000), has only 27 beds.

But when Brenda finally made the decision to leave, she had more options than most battered women in the country—the full resources of the shelter and D.A.I.P. were available to her. Shelter staff members screened her phone calls, and Pence spoke with Mike on Brenda's behalf; she joined a women's support group, and a counselor led her through the first of what would be many appearances before Judge Campbell in family court. But things did not go smoothly.

Mike did manage to complete the batterers' group program and made several passes through substance-abuse treatment. Yet, even though Brenda had filed for three separate orders of protection, the net effect was negligible: she claims to have suffered harassing phone calls, slashed tires and broken car windows. D.A.I.P. officials pressed police to investigate, but because the officers never caught Mike on the premises, he was never arrested.

After the divorce was granted, they continued to battle over visiting the children. Brenda had ultimately left Mike because of her children—the eldest, then in kindergarten, was already angry and traumatized. Research indicates that children exposed to family violence are 10 times as likely to be abused or abusive in adult relationships.

Two years ago, D.A.I.P. opened a visitation center at the Y.W.C.A. for noncustodial parents whom the court has granted supervised time with their children. The entrances and exits are such that neither parent has to see the other, and, under the watchful gaze of a D.A.I.P. staff member, parent and children have the run of two large living rooms, a small kitchen and a roomful of toys. This is where Brenda's boys have been seeing their father and his new wife.

Brenda Erickson is now an honor student at the University of Minnesota in Duluth, majoring in family life education. "Mike has some good qualities," she allows, "but this sure as hell beats walking around on eggshells. The boys and I are so much more relaxed and able to love each other. And I found a strength I never knew I had."

On a Friday night last fall, Mike Erickson was finally arrested for domestic assault and violently resisting arrest. The victim was not Brenda, however, but his new wife, Deborah, and her teen-age son. In the ensuing brawl, it took four officers and a can of Mace to get him into the squad car, as he howled: "I wasn't domesticating with her. I was drinking!" He pled guilty to all charges and served 36 days on a work farm. Mike is now enrolled in the D.A.I.P. program. "That night I pushed my stepson and backhanded my wife because she pulled the phone out and I got irritated," he says. "It's hard for me to shut up when I get going."

But Deborah Erickson refused to file charges against Mike or even to speak to a volunteer from the Women's Coalition. She has been in abusive relationships be-fore, but she's certain this marriage is different. "I told the cops, 'Hey, it happened, but it's not happening again.'"

Those who are in a position to help battered women tend to deny the gravity of the problem. "Doctors still believe the falling-down-stairs stories, and clergy still tell women to pray and go to a marriage counselor," says Anne Menard of the Connecticut Coalition Against Domestic Violence.

But Congress has begun to act. In 1990, it passed a resolution, adapted by 30 states, urging that domestic violence by a parent be a presumption against child custody. The most dramatic policy reform, however, may be Senator Joseph R. Biden Jr.'s pending Violence Against Women Act, which proposes, among other things, to stiffen penalties for domestic abusers.

But while the use of the criminal-justice system to quash domestic violence has gained currency around the country, Ellen Pence's advice to women in battering relationships is simply this: leave. Leave because even the best of programs, even Duluth's, cannot insure that a violent man will change his ways.

# THE UNBEARABLE LOSS

With the rise in child murders,
victims' families are seeking new legal rights
and channels for their grief

## CHIP BROWN

Life is arrested in the quilt. The muddy pictures of the dead stare out like faces in a yearbook. Some squares have bric-a-brac or heartfelt verse below the dates of birth and death. *Forever in our hearts.* Under Raynell Muskwinsky's picture, her mother, Gilda, satin-stitched a yellow rose of Texas; the faint red stain is lipstick from where she bit the thread.

Glen Enright, who would have taken over his father's business, smiles from his parents' family room. Kimberly Strickler is settled happily on the knee of a department-store Santa. Daniel Ward beams at the camera in a picture taken a month before his father shot him in the head. The photo of Elena Semander comes from the session she hoped would show her potential as a model; she was strangled by a serial killer. The youngest face belongs to Sam McClain Jr., murdered with his mother, Linda, six weeks after his first birthday. She was found on the floor of the living room, Sam in the kitchen freezer, frozen solid, with many small cuts on the soles of his feet.

The keeper of the quilt is Shirley Parish, mother of Kimberly. Shirley is a warm and hospitable woman, a former nurse, but in parts of Fort Bend County, where her only daughter was shot in the trunk of a car in January 1979, she is known as "the crazy lady." For ten years she has made no secret of her determination to see the state of Texas execute Roger Leroy DeGarmo, the con-

victed killer of her daughter, a man who testified at his own trial that the guilty verdict was correct, and that, furthermore, the jury should put him to death because if he ever got out he was going to track them all down and kill them too—and if they were sleeping he would wake them up first.

Many pictures on the quilt are all the more poignant because they were never envisioned as images of commemoration. Some of the parents Shirley asked for photos were reluctant to part even temporarily with what had become their most precious possessions. A Houston T-shirt shop called Street Smart agreed to transfer the pictures onto fabric for free, and Shirley got a book of quilting patterns. She picked out a blue border with a calico backing. A year ago last February she started sewing. By the fall she had filled twenty-seven of the thirty spaces. She laid the squares out boy, girl, boy, girl, like a dinner party, but the pattern didn't hold, because there were too many murdered men.

On the second Tuesday of every month Shirley removes the quilt from her bed and bundles it downtown to St. Paul's United Methodist Church, where she hangs it on a stand in a room on the second floor of the youth building. As people drift in they gather around it. Some fall to reminiscing cheerfully. Others just stand there in a kind of stone communion, as if they were staring into an abyss. The people arriving are mostly white middle-

aged women, but there are a number of men and some younger faces, and you would not know from their disparate looks and backgrounds what they have in common, why they are all here—not until the meeting starts and everyone takes a seat in the circle of folding chairs, and a grave ceremony commences.

"We will begin tonight by introducing ourselves and telling our stories. I'm Gilda Muskwinsky, president of the Houston Chapter of Parents of Murdered Children. My daughter, Raynell, was murdered August 15, 1984."

Gilda turns to her left.

"I'm Paul E. Martin and my son, Todd, was murdered November 26."

"I'm Linda Kelley and on August 29, 1988, my two children were murdered by an ex-con who came into a pawnshop and shot them in the head. My two children are gone and my life is destroyed."

"I'm Gloy Redden. James Goss was my son. I didn't say anything at the last meeting."

And so they go around the room telling their stories, quilt songs, rote summaries of privation and grief. Now it is the turn of an attractive young Korean woman.

"My name is Caroline Min and my younger brother, Walter, was killed by two men."

It is only her second meeting, and she begins to lose her composure. As a new member, she has been cited in the September newsletter piled on the table: "Into our circle of friends we cordially welcome..." Shirley Parish has already had

**The Supreme Court is considering whether to allow "victim-impact statements," telling the jury of a family's suffering.**

Walter's picture inked onto cloth, and she has presented the square to Caroline. Now, with forty pairs of eyes on her, Caroline starts to weep. She clutches the quilt square like a handkerchief she can't use.

"He was supposed to graduate from high school..." she says. Her last words come out in a vehement sob. "They didn't just kill my brother, they killed a part of my life!"

For all the lives that terminate in the quilt, the quilt is a point of departure, the place from which survivors can start back from the dead. It is a long road. That nothing is harder to bear than the death of a child is axiomatic, but the truth is the death of a child by homicide is a hundred times worse. "You can't prepare for it," Shirley Parish told me one day. "One minute you're waving good-bye, expecting to see your child at home that night, the next you're looking at a tag on a toe." These years after Kim's death, she still cannot stop herself from running after a stranger in the mall because a flashing resemblance makes her think it's Kim.

Scarcely ten years ago, family members who had been victimized by a violent crime often felt injured twice—once by the crime and a second time by the criminal-justice system. Judges excluded them from courtrooms lest they prejudice juries. Prosecutors dropped charges or fashioned plea bargains without notifying them. Their emotional losses were not taken into account. They were shunned, perhaps out of some superstitious fear of murder, or judged morally defective when they voiced the natural desire for revenge. Grieve, but privately, was the message. Express your anger, but not too loudly. Seek justice, but don't get in the way of the law.

With nowhere to turn, they turned to one another.

The Parents of Murdered Children was founded in 1978 by a Cincinnati couple whose daughter had been murdered. Today the organization claims 30,000 members in seventy chapters. P.O.M.C. is one of a raft of groups in the victims'-rights movement, which has improved the treatment of the survivors of violent crimes. In death-penalty cases, the Supreme Court is reconsidering whether to allow "victim-impact statements" that describe for juries the suffering of a victim's family. Many states have adopted restitution laws and passed victims' bills of rights. Many prosecutors now make a point of keeping families apprised of legal developments. "I was one of the very first parents allowed to be present at the trial in Texas," Shirley Parish recalled.

But these victories have been won in the face of greater losses. Murder rates continue to rise, and in the late eighties criminal homicide was the second-most-common cause of death for Americans between the ages of fifteen and twenty-four. Congress, which will declare August 12 to 18 National Parents of Murdered Children Week, has been locked in debate over a more substantive response to violence in America. The Brady Bill, passed by the House, would impose a waiting period on handgun purchases. And President Bush has submitted a crime bill that would expand the use of the death penalty, limit legal appeals for death-row inmates, and permit "good faith" exceptions to existing restrictions on the use of evidence by police and prosecutors.

Congressman Charles Schumer, the New York Democrat who chairs the House subcommittee on crime, believes that P.O.M.C. is a valuable outlet and hopes the commemorative legislation will "generate a broader base of support and assistance."

In Houston, where there's a murder every fifteen hours, P.O.M.C. has one of its most active branches. A core of about forty people regularly attend meetings. Newcomers are referred by police and victims'-assistance officers. Active members canvass the morgue and drop brochures off at funeral homes. ("A lot of men think we just sit around and cry," said one member.) The format is not for everybody, and the attrition rate is high.

"Nobody can tell you what to do," said Jack Enright, sitting in the office that had once belonged to his thirty-two-year-old son, Glen, murdered in the summer of 1989. "We needed help and we knew it. We were going in all crazy directions. My wife and I went to one meeting of Parents of Murdered Children and we didn't get a lot out of it, but I stuck it out, and she started coming, too. It's the best thing we've done. They don't perform miracles, but they can help you mentally or with things you don't know about."

The purpose of the meetings is "to give sorrow words," but often parents unburden themselves of darker emotions that can't be expressed anywhere else in public. They voice their rage, the violence in themselves that tempts them to take the law into their own hands. They are bound as much by the effort to articulate a loss that beggars description as by their special suffering. Their stories, repeated month after month, acquire a kind of liturgical power. As in the text of a Mass, the language is both literal and symbolic. Even at the extremes of despair, the ritual of telling the tale reflects some faith in the power of the word. In saying what happened, somehow there's hope.

And so that night newcomers and long-standing members alike were introduced to Terri Jeffers: "I'm Terri Jeffers and my son, Daniel, was murdered by my ex-husband while I listened on the telephone."

A few days later, I visited her at her home in an apartment development twenty miles north of Houston. Now thirty-seven, she works as a scrub technician for an ophthalmologist, and lives alone with ten-year-old Melissa, her daughter from her first marriage. James Ward was her second husband, and at the time, they had been divorced a month. He had three-year-old Daniel. She had attached a tape recorder to the phone, trying to get proof that he was dangerous. She played the tape of the phone call for me.

Ward's voice is flat and purposeful, and filled with calmly insane logic. She is sobbing and screaming as she pleads for the life of their son.

"Honey, I do love you," he said.

"Don't kill my baby. How could you threaten to kill my baby?" she said.

"You want to tell him good-bye?"

"You're going to kill him?"

"Yes I am. Here he is."

**"I'm Terri Jeffers and my son was murdered by my ex-husband while I listened on the telephone."**

''Don't you dare!''

''You made the decision. You called my bluff.''

''Don't you dare!''

''Huh?''

''Don't you dare touch my baby!''

''Hey, you're the one who called the cops. You thought you were cool, bitch. You did what you thought was right, huh? Think about it.''

Then two light, flat pops that on the tape sound almost inconsequential. Terri shut off the recorder and removed the tape. It was raining outside. I didn't know what to say.

She had met James Ward in May 1983 through friends of friends. He was a carpenter, and as she wrote in notes made after Daniel's death, ''He seemed to be everything I wanted—hard worker, family man, churchgoer, [and he] liked Melissa.'' She said that his temper surfaced eight months later. He drank caseloads of beer. Extremely jealous, he accused her of being a whore, and threatened to cut her hands off. Eventually she moved out; they reconciled when he agreed to see a counselor. In February 1988 he smashed her against the headboard of their bed, and she fled to a women's shelter and filed for divorce. He received the news with what seemed to her to be ''an eerie calm,'' and persuaded the court to let him have visitation rights. While she believed he might try to kill her, and Melissa too, she was sure he would not harm Daniel. When Daniel kept saying ''Daddy's got a gun and he's going to kill me,'' she reassured him, ''No, Daniel, Daddy loves you.''

At the hospital on August 6, 1988, Terri held her son's hands. He was brain-dead, but his heart flailed on at two hundred beats a minute. She cradled him until the organ-donor team arrived.

Now, two years later, in her bedroom, she pulled down the books of Daniel, four blue volumes of photographs showing Daniel being born, Daniel standing up, Daniel wearing a fire hat with a siren in the crown. Terri paged through his short life: ''This is when he was three—he was so proud that he was tall enough to jump up and turn off the light switch. And here he's bobbing for apples. And this is Daniel at his last birthday, at Show Biz pizza. I bought him a banjo and his cowboy hat, and some six-shooters because I had them as a kid. That's Jim loading them with caps.''

The last pages are filled with pictures of the funeral: three days after Daniel died, she was spending money she didn't have to buy him a white shirt, a double-breasted navy blazer with gold buttons, and a bow tie. She bought him shoes too, even though no one would be able to see his feet in the casket.

Melissa came through the living room. Terri stopped me from opening a manila envelope until Melissa left. ''She's never seen it.'' Inside was Daniel's autopsy photograph: one of those pictures that register before you mean to look. A .22-caliber slug smashed open a raw red crater of tissue and blood in Daniel's forehead. Jim Ward recovered from his self-inflicted wound. Six months after his son's death, he was convicted of murder. He is serving a life sentence, and in 2003 he may be eligible for parole.

''I just don't think I can forgive him,'' Terri said. ''If it was a drowning, or something accidental, but to deliberately pull a gun and pull the trigger—to say 'I've got him now and I'm going to hurt you'...I believe in God, but I'm angry at God because he'd let somebody like Jim go to heaven. If he repents, he can go to heaven. There's something terribly wrong with that. My heart has been ripped out. All the plans I had, all the love—you raise your child, you teach them, you nurse them, you stay up at night when they're sick. Daniel never got to play baseball. He never got to go to AstroWorld. One of my last vivid memories is of him standing in the bathtub, saying, 'I love you, Mama.' It's all I've got...''

She began to cry. Every time she opened the newspaper she found more evidence of man's depravity. And now the atrocities were impossible to ignore: ''Christopher Kalmbach—his mother's boyfriend poured pepper down his throat. Tommy Lott—he was tortured to death in 1981. I just wrote the parole board. A man just got fifty years for raping an eight-month-old baby—she had semen in her chest cavity, her chest cavity had been penetrated. Another child was thrown out a window and died, and the man who did it got ten years. A father shot his two kids in the head; that was on the one-year anniversary of Daniel's death. I listen to all the little details. Just last week a mother stabbed her daughter twenty-seven times because she broke a music box. There's a lot of us in Parents of Murdered Children who are considered crazy because we're talking about what happened, because we're not afraid to say how we feel. I just get this rage—how can these people do this and get away with it? I'm stunned. I can't believe it. There are some people in this world that are evil.''

She was stunned, and that rage which had given her strength also threatened to consume her. It had eroded her faith. She used to read lessons at Mass, but after Daniel's death biblical homilies made her restless, and the doctrine of forgiveness, the axis of the New Testament, outraged her sense of justice. She had bought a .38 with a four-inch barrel —a present to herself one Christmas. There was a bullet-riddled target taped to the back of her closet.

Parents of Murdered Children helped channel her feelings. She'd toured death row with members from the group. Campaigning to make child murder a capital offense, she'd taken her autopsy photo to Austin to show to state legislators. She'd played the tape of her son's execution on TV talk shows. Now she'd shown the picture to me, and played the tape for me, and as I stood up to leave she thanked me profusely.

Was it simply that she needed someone to hear her out? To help her come to terms with the evil she had encountered, the grief, the pointlessness of her days, which made her not care if she got fat or ever met anyone again?

It was more than that. One could venture that she was stuck in her story, telling it over and over, but not getting anywhere. She was still devoured by rage at what people did—what your own family could do. Such feelings were only human, but they had trapped her. Anyone who listened had to know there was a plea for help in her confidences, her willingness to review the most harrowing episodes. There was an appeal not that one endorse her bitter feelings but that perhaps one could show her the way beyond them. There had been meaning and purpose in the days before Daniel was killed. There had been peace of mind too. Whatever rage might accomplish (and she had sworn to return violence for violence if the occasion should arise), it could not beget peace of mind. However much vengeance might satisfy her, it did not contain the germ of new life. She could not build happiness around brutal newsclips and a .38, and yet she could not get her mind around forgiveness, the untenable idea that the murderer, who once had been her husband, had a place in heaven with her son. The rain had quit, and the air on the

## Families often felt injured twice—once by the crime and a second time by the criminal-justice system.

front porch was fresh. We shook hands, and Terri thanked me again. Then she summoned Melissa inside, pulled the door, and threw the lock.

If Terri Jeffers was stuck, her friend Sam McClain had moved on, or at least seemed to. He had made a new life for himself. He had remarried. He had a new son. His days had been redeemed, and yet he still viewed his life through the prism of the past, and on the second Tuesday of the month, sometimes accompanied by his new wife, he went to the Parents of Murdered Children meeting, where he said, "My name is Sam McClain and my wife and son were murdered and no one was ever caught."

A few days later I drove out to see him at his house in northeast Houston. He let me in while Jumbo, his black "bark-and-hide" lapdog, bounded about like a keyed-up cat. His new wife, Kerry, was holding their boy, Ricky, born four months earlier. On the living-room shelf were pictures of Sam's first wife, Linda Annette Flora, and his first son, Sam junior.

At twenty-seven Sam was younger than most members in the group, lanky and soft-spoken, with large liquid eyes. Two years ago he had been living with Linda and Sam junior in a house in Woodland Acres, a short drive away. He worked as a machinist; Linda had a job at a Wal-Mart store. They had been together for a year and a half, but had dated since high school. The baby had been born prematurely, and pulled through only after five dicey weeks in neonatal intensive care.

Shortly after two on the afternoon of August 7, 1988, Sam returned from a trip to Trinity County. The door was shut but not latched. The stereo was playing, the air-conditioning was on. Linda was sprawled on the floor on top of some of baby Sam's toys. By the eerie pallor of her legs and the glazed, milky color of her eyes, Sam knew the situation was dire. Baby Sam was nowhere to be found. Sam called the police.

At eight that night, after the cops had combed the house, a patrolman on guard noticed a couple of loaves of bread on top of the refrigerator. On a hunch, he opened the freezer. Sam junior's naked body was curled up in the fetal position, frozen solid. It had to be pried out. The morgue was unable to type the blood, and the coroner noted evidence of torture: thirty-three cuts on the boy's feet and buttocks, abrasions on his penis, fractures on both sides of his head.

"I went in to see him for ten or fifteen seconds," Sam recalled in a soft, halting voice. "I had to see him—I couldn't let them take this object off under a blanket and me accept it. It was a gruesome sight, but if I hadn't seen it, I might have trouble believing it."

For a week he was a suspect. He was interviewed by detectives all night, and several days later took six hours of polygraph tests. No money or jewelry was missing, and there was no sign of forced entry. The horror of being a suspect himself scarcely registered as he struggled to come to grips with the annihilation of his family. "If the police were suspicious of me, I didn't care. Their deaths were such a giant idea. It was so big you couldn't conceive of it all at once in your mind. I'd go home and pick a little piece of it to think about."

Eventually the police ruled out Sam. They videotaped the funeral, but turned up few clues. Today the case remains unsolved.

A month after the murder, Sam went to a neighborhood hangout called the Junction with Linda's brother. He met Kerry, who had read about the case, but didn't recognize him. She sympathized. She let him go on. Not long afterward, he asked her to go with him to a meeting of Parents of Murdered Children. He felt out of place among the older members of the group, who were in their forties and fifties, but he could relate to Terri Jeffers. Their children were killed on the same day.

Two months after Sam met Kerry, he gave her an emerald ring. "You helped me," he said. "You were there to talk to. You weren't involved."

"I had some reservations about getting married," she recalled now, shifting little Ricky to her shoulder. "I knew he wasn't over it, I know now he'll never be over it. There are some people at Parents of Murdered Children whose children died twelve years ago and they're not over it. I just thought, This is

what he wanted. I knew I loved him, I knew it was going to be tough, and he told me he needed me."

"Most people at the meetings are able to tell their stories," Sam said. "What I say is: 'My wife and son were murdered and I have had a hard time.' It's easier to avoid it than to say my little boy was cut up and Linda was stabbed eleven times. When I try to wonder what Linda felt, all I can feel is panic.... Sometimes I get real mad. I drove by the house once; a lady with a little kid was sitting outside. Part of me wanted to stop and say, 'Do you know what happened here? How can you live here?' But I've had a second chance. It's harder on an older person. If I'd have been twenty years older, I would have lost out. I had Sam for thirteen months. That's not a long time. I'm wondering how these people whose children are my age, how they manage. It's not like somebody being sick. It's just all of a sudden, boom, like lightning striking. Everything in my whole life changed the moment I walked through that door. I lost my wife, I lost the person I talk to, I lost my son, I lost the place I lived. It took everything. I almost feel it took part of my life sometimes."

A year after the murder Sam and his brother Jim had leaflets printed up offering a $1,500 reward. On the night of the first anniversary of the murders, Sam stayed up all night assembling a model of a gold Jeep. Kerry slept beside him on the living-room floor. He is afraid of losing his new family, and insists Kerry spend the night at her mother's if he has to go out of town. For months he used to time her trips to the Laundromat. He moved Ricky's crib away from the window. He always phones before he comes home, not wanting to enter an empty house. He'll check the closets. For months it was impossible for him to open the refrigerator and get ice.

His keepsakes are few: two pairs of baby shoes, one outfit, and the blue scrub suit he wore in the delivery room —the smock stamped with his son's inky footprint. And photographs, including the pictures of Linda and Sam that Shirley Parish sewed into the quilt. And there is the videotape: baby Sam's first birthday, June 26, 1988, at Pistol Pete's Pizza in Pasadena. We watched it that night, laughed about all the *p*'s as Sam slipped the cassette into the VCR. Suddenly baby Sam's face appeared on the screen, prodigally

## More than anyone I met in Parents of Murdered Children, Harriett Semander has divined meaning in her daughter's death.

smiling. He was dressed in a red-striped shirt and shorts and a party hat. Kerry glanced at her husband's face and at the video. The camera zoomed in on Linda.

"She's perfect now," Kerry said. "I can never be that perfect person."

Jumbo climbed off the couch. On the screen, the party unrolled with no dramatic developments. "This is probably pretty boring for you," Sam said to me.

"Not at all."

"Look at this part. He's on a merry-go-round and somebody calls his name, and he almost falls off trying to look back over his shoulder. He'd just started walking. He was killed four days after he took his first steps."

On the sound track a voice called, "Sam! Sam! Sam!"

"He's smiling a lot."

"He'd smile at anything. You see him there, and then what happened...You wonder how anybody could...It's two totally different deals...I wonder..."

Little Ricky began to fuss in the other room. "I better throw a bottle in the microwave," said Kerry, getting up.

"It's really helped since he came along," said Sam.

When Kerry was pregnant, she had a baby shower; Terri Jeffers came. She gave them Daniel's stroller.

"Two and a half years ago," said Sam, "if somebody showed me a picture of where I'd be now I'd say, 'No, that's not me, that's somebody else . . .'"

His voice trailed off; he seemed embarrassed by his frailty. In some ways he would never catch up to the events that had engulfed him; he would always be dislocated by his life's violent turn, and the tenacity of grief, and the mystery of never having answers, much less the satisfaction of justice. Perhaps he would always struggle with the miracle of deliverance too, as the possibility of happiness now hovered before him in the form of his new wife and son.

The camera zoomed in on baby Sam and then panned to Linda, who was holding up a large yellow T-shirt, a gift

to the birthday boy from Pistol Pete's. She looked into the camera and said, "One of these days it'll fit."

Last fall many parents in the Houston Chapter were outraged when two federal judges ordered inmates released from the county jail to ease a severe overcrowding problem. When the release date approached, Shirley Parish stayed on the phone all week mustering a crowd to protest; Jack Enright called local TV and radio stations, and even the White House. He had the idea to form a human chain around the jail. Also, he was hunting around for a coffin, the idea being to dramatize the impact of violent crime by having the parents fill it with copies of their children's death certificates.

By the time Harriett Semander got to the jail on Friday night an angry crowd had assembled, and sheriff's deputies had established a cordon between the protesters and the prisoners coming out. Some parents had taped pictures of their murdered children to plastic Halloween tombstones, although the inmates being released were not murderers, or even felons, but people like the guy who'd been in jail a week awaiting trial for driving with a suspended license.

Someone handed Harriett Semander a Marks-A-Lot and some poster board. She didn't know what to put on her placard, and so in big letters she scrawled a message that had less to do with the issues of overcrowded jails than with her own imprisonment and the story of her daughter Elena, who was strangled to death eight years ago by a serial killer named Coral Watts. Her message was simply: NO, NO, NO!

And yet more than anyone I met in Parents of Murdered Children, more than Sam McClain and surely more than Terri Jeffers, Harriett Semander has divined meaning in her daughter's death. If her conclusions betray the compulsion to twist and bend inscrutable events so that they fit some pattern in our heads, her efforts have at least produced a kind of reckoning. The journal she kept traces her struggle.

*Holy Week April 1982: The similarity of Christ's death and Elena's was revealed to me—the humiliation, the nakedness, pain, beatings, and in the end, both were wrapped in a sheet and taken away. This was on Holy Thursday. Holy Friday was confusing—whose funeral, Elena's or Christ's?*

Elena was the oldest of the four kids Harriett raised with her husband, Zack. Zack taught math, and Harriett worked in the office at an exclusive Houston private school. Elena was educated there, a whiz in math, with a talent for sculpture and drawing. She also excelled at sports, enough to earn a field-hockey scholarship to the University of Denver. She had gorgeous chestnut hair, and was flirting with the idea of being a model.

On the night of February 6, a night cold enough for her to have worn her rabbit jacket, she stopped by a friend's apartment. He wasn't home. It was after midnight. As she was getting back in her car, she was jumped by Coral Watts, a twenty-eight-year-old mechanic who had been under surveillance by Houston police as a suspect in a number of other killings. Six months later, when he confessed that hers was the fifth of nine murders he had committed in the Houston area, Watts told the story of Elena's death.

"Did she fight?" detectives asked him.

"Yeah."

"Was she still wearing that coat?"

"Yeah."

"Remember what she said during the struggle?"

"No."

"Then what happened? What was this that you choked her with?"

"My hands."

"O.K., then what happened?"

"Then I took her coat and her pants and shirt off.... I tied the shirt around her neck and one end around her leg."

"What did you do this for?"

"I don't know."

"...All right, then what did you do?"

"Picked her up and put her in the Dumpster."

"Remember what the Dumpster looked like? What color was it?"

"Gray, I believe."

"Was it a tall Dumpster?"

"A short one."

"Was she heavy to lift?"

"Yeah."

Stripped and hog-tied, Elena was discovered that morning by a garbageman. Harriett was able to identify the body when she recognized her daughter's crooked toe. The only reason Watts was caught three months after Elena's murder was that a woman he had tied up escaped while he was busy trying to drown another woman in a bathtub. In exchange for telling police where nine of his victims were, the state of Texas allowed him to plead guilty to one

**She mapped out the
sequence of killings,
drawing up an
elaborate chart,
annotating news
accounts, digging for
information.**

count of burglary. He was sentenced to
60 years; because the judge found that
the water in the bathtub was the equivalent of a deadly weapon and therefore
an aggravating factor, Watts would not
be eligible for parole for twenty years.

*Mother's Day 1982: Love never dies,
it just grows. I felt Elena's love on Mother's Day and she felt mine. Our love
continues to grow throughout eternity.
What a glorious resurrection it will be
when we are all again united. I wonder
if Elena's murderer celebrated Mother's Day and what kind of woman his
mother is?*

Harriett had survived the first years
pretending Elena was away at college.
She would sign Elena's name to Christmas presents for her other kids. Once,
she sat by a pool for four hours watching
a twelve-year-old girl who looked like
Elena at that age. Even picking up an
apple could trigger grief: it reminded
her of Elena, who was afraid of red
apples because of what had happened
to Snow White.

The second year, she started to har-
ness her feelings. She opened files on
Watts. She tried to contact the mothers
of some of his other victims. She
mapped out the sequence of killings,
drawing up an elaborate chart, annotating news accounts, digging for information from the police. She worked for
four years to audit a tape of his confession. She attended his sentencing. And
in August 1989 she and Zack won a $1.1
million wrongful-death judgment against
him. (They were represented by Shirley
Parish's husband, whom they had met
through Parents of Murdered Children.)

"I was at the beginning of the victims'-rights movement, and the police
and the district attorney didn't know what
to do with me. I was asking for things no
other parents had asked for. They thought I
was crazy, my husband thinks I'm crazy,
but it was part of the grief I had to deal
with."

When Watts was sentenced, Harriett

thought she could move on. In July 1987
she wrote in her journal: "I find myself
moving out of the 'justice' stage to the
more healing area of 'acceptance' by sharing Elena's story. . . . The type of built-in
anger that I can't seem to shake is giving
way to an inner voice that tells me life is
too short."

Then in August 1989 she called the
Board of Pardons and Paroles and
learned the astonishing news that Watts
was eligible for parole. The judicial
finding that a deadly weapon—the water
in the bathtub—had been used in the
commission of the burglary had been
overturned on appeal, and though it
was unlikely that Watts would be released on parole, he nevertheless qualified for review.

"My husband and I are getting old,"
she said. "We'd like to do something
together in the five or ten years of good
health we have left. Then one fatal
phone call and I'm back in it." She
alerted the national headquarters of
Parents of Murdered Children to put
out the word, and more than one thousand letters arrived decrying the possibility of parole. The experience impressed upon her the necessity of un-
ceasing vigilance.

*June 4, 1986: I was reading through
my journal meditation from 1979 to
1981. So many prayers were written for
Elena to find a meaningful Christian relationship with a boyfriend! I never understood why the Lord didn't answer
that prayer for me before she died, when
tonight it suddenly dawned on me that
He did answer those prayers. Every
boy Elena dated has probably given
their relationship Christian meaning
since her death. There is no time element with God.*

The Semanders are Greek Orthodox;
like Terri Jeffers, a Roman Catholic,
they are as troubled by the doctrine of
forgiveness as by God's purpose in taking their child's life. They have struggled to reconcile religious precepts on
life's sanctity with their personal experience of evil, which has made them advocates of the death penalty.

As they are Greek-Americans, I asked
if they had read Nicholas Gage's book
*Eleni*, which tells the story of how the
author returned to Greece and tracked
down the man who had murdered his
mother. In the climactic scene Gage
stands over his mother's murderer with a
gun but does not pull the trigger. They
had read the book, and had in fact dis-

cussed that very scene with the author
when he came to Houston to speak.

"I went up to him afterwards," Harriett said. "I said, 'My daughter's been a
murder victim, and there's something
bothering me. Do you regret not shooting him?' He said there were moments
when he wakes up and wishes he had.
In God's eyes he did the right thing,
but I don't know how he did it. How
did he control himself? If Coral Watts
was in this room I would start beating
on him. It's not hate—it's an uncontrollable urge to fight back, to protect,
to revenge.

"The first time we went to church
after Elena's death, we had to kneel
down and thank Him for everything
good and bad. I had to thank Him for
Elena's death. I couldn't do it, not
at first. It took a couple of years. I
had a list of people to pray for, the
living and the dead, and I had to put
Coral Watts in the living list and Elena
in the dead."

Her husband was staring at a classical
clay bust on the den table—Elena had
made it. "Wiping Watts out of my
mind, I don't know if I could do that,"
said Zack.

"When I think of Elena, I think of
Watts," said Harriett. "I know his
birthday. I think about his daughter.
I would like to go back to school some-
day and study painting; I'm interested
in portraits, and one of the first I would
do is Coral Watts. His face is embedded in my mind. He's part of my
family."

Could there be a more wrenching introduction to our condition as pawns
of fate than having to cope with
homicide? Two cases I heard about seem
now to exemplify the beginning and the
end of what is a long procession of
wounded people struggling to go on. A
few years ago, a woman in the Houston
Chapter came to the meetings mourning
her murdered daughter. She seemed to
be mending on schedule, and then suddenly she took her own life on her
daughter's grave.

And then there was the late Kitty
Yonley, who stands out as the only person anyone can think of in the Houston
Chapter who was opposed to capital
punishment. She forgave the man who
had stabbed her daughter, Nina, to death
in August 1979. She sent him a copy of
the Bible.

Some parents are stuck; some adjust.

# Vengeance would never be blind. It was personal. It was, in a strange way, like family.

Some cannot pick up the burden of catastrophe; others are able to find grace, a balance between the yearning to remember and the need to forget. A lot of success has to do with ritualizing a connection with the murdered child. For ten years after Kim's death, Shirley Parish, who had never smoked before, would start her day smoking one of her daughter's brand of cigarettes.

Success also often seems to depend on what sort of understanding parents can reach about the people who killed their children. To understand is not necessarily to make peace or to forgive. Time, which according to the platitude heals all wounds, has in many cases turned parents into ferocious advocates of capital punishment. Nearly two-thirds of P.O.M.C. members support the death penalty. In Texas, a fair number would relish the chance to start the lethal solution dripping into the vein of the condemned. They know the appeal-laden process of imposing the death penalty can be more expensive than committing a murderer to life in prison. They know the New Testament injunctions against killing, the plea for forgiveness. They know Camus's famous argument that no murderer's deed can compare with the evil of capital punishment, "the most premeditated of murders."

To Camus, many parents would reply that, however great the agony of the condemned, no doubt exists about what debt is being paid. A condemned man knows why he is to die; their children did not. In advocating capital punishment, what many parents seem to be seeking is not so much the extermination of a killer as an equivalency of feeling:

they want their suffering communicated and shared. They want the people who murdered their children to know the torture of their loss. The desire for revenge is the ugliest emotion in the human psyche, but it often collapses into something almost poignant—the longing to find a shred of conscience in people whose moral capacity is grotesquely diminished. Why did you do this? they ask, and they pore over criminal records and family histories, hunting for answers, for any trace of that sympathetic faculty by which one person can know and even suffer another's pain.

Murder ultimately was a measure of *their* moral capacity. Many found themselves wanting. Their innocence had been stripped away; their values and beliefs had been badly gouged, if not wrecked. For most parents, murder ruptured the idea of unalloyed goodness. But for others, honest or brave enough to look within, it ruptured the idea of unalloyed evil too. Evil was nothing apart from them anymore—no longer "the Other." It had stolen into their homes and seeped into their hearts. They had to live with the vengeful impulse to return death for death, and, conversely, had to find the resolve to hold themselves back. In their extremes of emotion, nothing was black-and-white; the world was a palette of grays. One could as glibly pay sanctimonious lip service to the idea of forgiveness as join the ignorant masses clamoring for the executioner. Forgiveness would never come cheap for parents, but then, vengeance would never be blind. It was personal. It was, in a strange way, family.

So they marched on courthouses and mailed off Bibles and stitched together quilts. They did something because they needed to *do* something, if only to fend off the full experience of loss. More than from grief, they needed to save themselves from their own powerlessness. If murder was a book of lessons in fragility, ephemeral happiness, the irrevers-

ible arrow of fate, the hardest lesson of all was that life is not organized around human needs; for every one thing they could control there were a million they could not.

After Captain Bill Edison from the Houston Homicide Division gave a little talk, and somebody joked that maybe they should get Charles Bronson to speak at the next meeting, and after the group rejected the idea of putting the names of the killers on the quilt below their victims ("Why would you want that scum on the quilt?" "We can make another quilt and let it burn"), and after Terri Jeffers made a pitch for the fifteen-dollar heart-shaped lockets, the proceeds to go to the national organization, and after some discussion as to what might be done to counteract the anti-death-penalty slant of a new movie on Home Box Office (resolved to write a letter to HBO), and after more discussion as to whether the chapter ought to include a rose when distributing brochures to funeral homes, the September meeting broke up.

"Y'all remember to bring your death certificates next meeting," said Gilda Muskwinsky as the circle of friends dispersed. The cake plates and the truth-in-sentencing petitions were packed up. The quilt came down. Shirley Parish carried it out to her car. The air after the rain was clean and sweet. Caroline Min would return the cloth square fixed with Walter's face, and tomorrow or the next day, or sometime soon, Shirley would sew it into the Houston Chapter's tapestry of phantoms. They'd likely seen the last of Caroline. She was moving back to Seattle to be with her parents—heartbroken immigrants from Korea. Walter was their American future. Walter was going to be a lawyer...Face after face, story after story. It had occurred to Shirley as the quilt came together that it could never be finished. It could only be kept up-to-date.

# Abused Women Who Kill Now Seek Way Out of Cells

*A prison group aims to break a cycle of victimization.*

## Jane Gross

*Special to* The New York Times

FRONTERA, Calif., Sept. 9—When Brenda Clubine arrived in prison 7 years ago to serve 15 years to life for killing a husband more than twice her size, she was beginning to ask herself questions about the violence she had suffered and in turn had meted out, about the Gordian knot that ties the abuser and the abused.

"I had two choices," said Ms. Clubine, a tiny, 41-year-old former nurse who said she had endured years of savage beatings by her husband. "I could commit suicide, or I could try to understand what was going on in my life."

At the California Institution for Women here, a gentle-looking place except for the perimeter of coiled razor wire, she asked other women why they were imprisoned, and heard stories that matched her own.

But when she asked if there was a group for battered women who had killed their mates, she was told there was not. So Ms. Clubine set about organizing one. A three-year battle with the prison bureaucracy ended in 1988 with the first weekly meeting of Convicted Women Against Abuse. It began with 10 members and has grown to 45.

### 22 Petitions for Clemency

Today, in her 8-foot-by-6-foot cell, in the prison mail room where she works, as a clerk, and in the classroom where she leads the support group, Ms. Clubine carries pressed to her chest a copy of a commutation petition she hopes will win her release. The thick document is the most tangible evidence of what the women have accomplished.

The original document and 21 others like it sit on the desk of Gov. Pete Wilson. Each pleads the case of a woman convicted of first- or second-degree murder in California before last year's passage of a state law that made admissible testimony about battered women's syndrome, in which prolonged abuse can convince a victim that violence is the only way out.

About 20 more petitions are expected to be filed next month, all the outgrowth of the group Ms. Clubine started here after she was convicted of the 1983 killing of her husband, a retired Los Angeles police detective, who she says broke her ribs and jaw, stabbed her and tore the skin off her face during a stormy marriage that ended when she shattered his skull with an empty wine bottle.

Mr. Wilson is expected to rule on the petitions in the next few weeks, Dan Schnur, the governor's director of communications, said. Mr. Schnur said each petition would be "treated on an individual basis."

Here as in other states, the primary opponents of clemency for such women have been prosecutors, who are divided about whether battered women's syndrome is a valid defense

or an exaggerated claim by someone grasping for a way out of a murder conviction.

The California petitions were inspired by mass clemencies in late 1990 and early 1991 of 26 women in Ohio and 8 in Maryland. And they come at a time when rising public interest in domestic violence has propelled similar clemency drives in at least 20 states, New York among them.

### Movement Built in Prisons

But the movement is different in California. Elsewhere in the nation it has been instigated by elected officials, like former Gov. Richard F. Celeste of Ohio, or by advocates for battered women, like the House of Ruth in Baltimore. Both of those movements drew criticism afterwards, with opponents complaining that prosecutors had not been consulted or that cases had not been scrutinized closely enough.

Here the women themselves initiated the clemency drive, writing Governor Wilson last year, imploring him to consider commutation of their sentences and inviting him to one of their meetings so he could better understand what had brought them to this place.

The invitation to visit drew a polite "no thank you" from Mr. Wilson. But the letter attracted the attention of lawyers and advocates from throughout the state who banded together and offered free representation.

At about the same time, Jackie Spier, a state assemblywoman, held legislative hearings at Frontera at which Ms. Clubine, who has a parole hearing on Sept. 16, and seven other women in her group told their stories.

### 'Go Home and Try Harder'

Among those testifying was Frances Caccavale, a 78-year-old Italian immigrant who described snatching a knife from the kitchen drain board and stabbing her elderly husband as he threatened her with a gun. Mrs. Caccavale said she had earlier wept to her priest about a half-century of beatings. 'Go home and try harder,' she said the priest told her.

The coalition of lawyers, from community organizations like the San Francisco Neighborhood Legal Assistance Foundation and from premier firms like Gibson, Dunn & Crutcher of Los Angeles, which represents Ms. Clubine, understood that a simple two-page letter would not win clemency. So each lawyer took a case, visited the prison for an interview and began drafting the arguments and gathering the exhibits that together constitute a clemency petition.

The team of lawyers, now grown to more than 100, determined that 22 women in Ms. Clubine's group were candidates for clemency: they met the accepted definition for battered women's syndrome, had killed abusers and had exhausted appeals.

If there is anything striking about the women it is how ordinary they seem. Ranging in age from 25 to 78, some with sheets of long hair like graduate students, others with age spots on their hands, they wear blue-jeans and T-shirts or state-issued muumuus, makeup, nail polish and perfume. Alternating between devilish humor and sodden tears, they sound like women gathered anywhere to talk about their men.

In this prison classroom, unlike the police stations where they filed complaints against their husbands and the courtrooms where they were tried, nobody asks: Why did you put up with it?

At this week's meeting, many talked of loving and hating their abusers at the same time. They said they once believed that they were to blame for the violence they suffered and that they could stop it if they only figured out how to behave. They recalled the terror of facing a beating if they came home 10 minutes late or served a lukewarm dinner.

Many of them said they had been turned away from overcrowded women's shelters and had been treated dismissively by police officers. They said they had tried to flee their husbands, only to be stalked and beaten worse.

Most said they had been threatened with death if they left and had been told, "If I can't have you nobody else can." Glenda Virgil observed dryly that those words should be the "password into this club and the motto on our T-shirts."

All of the women said that if they had not killed their mates they were certain they would be dead. "I ask myself what I could have done different," said Rose Parker. "And I still can't see no other way of getting out alive."

Most of the women said they had grown up in families where violence was common, and that the events they had witnessed as children later had been duplicated with uncanny precision in their relationships with men.

Ms. Virgil remembers her father throwing her mother out of a moving car on Highway 101 near the California coast, and she said that years later, at that very spot, her husband did the same to her. Now, Ms. Virgil says, her 22-year-old daughter is being beaten by her mate. "She's making the same excuses I made," Ms. Virgil said.

Rosemary Dyer once lay in bed with her mother after church, moments after the older woman had been beaten. "Mama, can we run away now?" she asked. Her mother said no, they would have to stay because, "I love him, and anyway, he wouldn't let us."

Years later, when she was black-and-blue herself, Ms. Dyer's mother pleaded with her, "Honey, come home. I'll come get you." Her answer echoed the past: "I can't, mama. I love him, and he won't let me go."

Ms. Dyer, like others in the group, said that prison sometimes feels like a sanctuary. "We may be locked up," she said, "but we can look in the mirror without seeing black eyes and knocked-out teeth. We don't have to be afraid to flush the toilet or cough at the wrong time. We can like ourselves and know who we are for the first time."

And it is that knowledge that the women hope to carry outside the fences. "To leave here with the information we have in our heads," Ms. Virgil said. "If we can get outside and talk to other women, I know we can make a difference."

# INCEST

## A Chilling Report

**Do you want to know what incest is? What it really is? No euphemisms, evasions, excuses, or intellections? Are your sure? Then read this. Every word of it is true. The horror is unimaginable. But in the end, at least you will know.**

### Heidi Vanderbilt

*Heidi Vanderbilt is an award-winning writer who lives in New England.*

*Where there is no last name identifying details have been changed.*

### The Children

I am five. The July sun shines on my shoulders. I am wearing a dress I have never seen before, one I don't remember putting on. The door opens and a little girl runs to me her face delighted. I have never seen her before. I am completely terrified and try to hide behind my astonished and irritated mother.

---

### CASE STUDIES

Rikki and Nick's parents were members of a satanic cult. The children were sexually abused and tortured. When the parents left the cult, they got their children into therapy. Rikki is three. Nick is four. Both have full-blown multiple personality disorders.

Lauren was five when she told her mother that a family friend who often took care of her had "fooled" with her. Her mother was relieved when the doctors found no physical evidence of sexual abuse. She wondered if her daughter's story was true. Then Lauren told her mother that the friend had taken photos of her. The photos were found; they revealed that Lauren had been raped and sodomized over a period of more than a year.

Sharon's mother masturbated her to sleep from the time she was born. As Sharon grew older, her mother would sometimes stare at her for long periods. "I love you too much," she would repeat, over and over. Now 44, Sharon says, "I still don't know where my mother ends and I begin."

"I take responsibility for what happened," she says. "I bought into it. I know my mother shouldn't have done it, but I'm responsible, too."

"How could you be responsible for something that began when you were only a baby?" a friend asks.

"I just am," she insists.

Sharon has been in Freudian analysis for 15 years.

---

"But she's your best friend!" my mother says, and tells me that I played at the girl's house just yesterday. I don't remember. When my mother tells me her name, I've never heard it before.

Other children arrive. I remember some of them, but from long ago. They're older now. They've grown. Some have lost their teeth.

I pretend that everything is all right.

At night I lie awake as I have for years, listening. I hear footsteps coming down the hall. I hold my breath. I watch the edge of the door to my bedroom. I watch for the hand that will push it open. If it is my mother's hand or my father's, I am all right. For now. If it is the hand of the woman who lives with us and sticks things into me, I move out of my body. I disappear into a painting on the wall, into my alarm clock with its rocking Gene Autry figure, into imaginary landscapes. Usually I come back when the woman leaves. But not always.

I am eight. I have spoken French from the time I was three. I attended a French kindergarten, and now the Lycée Français. I have just spent the summer in France. My French is fluent when we leave Nice. Four days later, after my return to the woman who hurts me, I can no longer understand or speak a single word of French. Sitting at my gouged wooden desk, my classmates sniggering around me, I feel terrified and ashamed, certain that whatever is wrong is my fault.

She told me she would cut out my tongue. She told me I would forget. I remember how tall she was, how she wore her hair pulled back with wisps breaking loose at the temples. I knew then that I would never forget.

I am 40. There are things I have always remembered, things I have forgotten, things that exist in shadows only, that slip away when I try to think about them. I can't remember all that she did that sent me "away." Nor do I know what I was doing while I was "away." I only know that these episodes began with periods of abuse so frightening, painful, and humiliating that I left my body and parts of my mind.

I rarely talk about what happened to me. I have never discussed the details with my parents, my husband, or anyone else. Whenever I think of telling, she returns in my dreams.

I dream that I am a child and she chases me with a sharp knife, catches me, and gouges out my eyes. I dream that I have to protect little children at night, even though I am alone and a child myself. I tuck in the other children and get into my bed. Her arm reaches for me and pulls me down. I dream that I run for help, enter a phone booth, hear a dial tone. When I reach up I see the phone has been torn from the wall. I dream of animals skinned alive while I scream.

Sometimes when I sleep I stop breathing and can't make myself start until I wake gasping, my fingers blue.

Incest can happen to anyone: to rich and to poor; to whites, blacks, Asians, Native Americans, Jews, Christians, and Buddhists. It happens to girls and to boys, to the gifted and to the disabled. It happens to children whose parents neglect them, and those—like me—whose parents love and care for them.

What exactly is incest? The definition that I use in this article is: any sexual abuse of a child by a relative or other person in a position of trust and authority over the child. It is the violation of the child where he or she lives—literally and metaphorically. A child molested by a stranger can run home for help and comfort. A victim of incest cannot.

Versions of this definition are widely used outside the courtroom by therapists and researchers. In court, incest definitions vary from state to state. In many states, the law requires that for incest to have taken place, vaginal penetration must be proved. So if a father rapes his child anally or orally he may be guilty of child sexual abuse but may not, legally, be guilty of incest.

I believe that if incest is to be understood and fought effectively, it is imperative that the definition commonly held among therapists and researchers—the definition I have given here—be generally accepted by the courts and public. I am not alone in this belief. As therapist E. Sue Bloom, for one, writes in *Secret Survivors: Uncovering Incest and Its Aftereffects in Women:* "If we are to understand incest, we must look not at the blood bond, but at the emotional bond between the victim and the perpetrator.... The important criterion is whether there is a real relationship in the experience of the child."

"The crucial psychosocial dynamic is the *familial* relationship between the incest participants," adds Suzanne M. Sgroi, M.D., director of the Saint Joseph College's Institute for Child Sexual Abuse Intervention in West Hartford, Connecticut, writing in the *Handbook of Clinical Intervention in Child Sexual Abuse.* "The presence or absence of a blood relationship between incest participants is of far less significance than the kinship roles they occupy."

Incest happens between father and daughter, father and son, mother and daughter, mother and son. It also happens between stepparents and stepchildren, between grandparents and grandchildren, between aunts and uncles and their nieces and nephews. It can also happen by proxy, when live-in help abuses or a parent's lover is the abuser; though there is no blood or legal relationship, the child is betrayed and violated within the context of family.

No one knows how many incest victims there are. No definitive random studies on incest involving a cross section of respondents have been undertaken. No accurate collection systems for gathering information exist. The statistics change depending on a number of variables: the population surveyed, the bias of the researcher, the sensitivity of the questions, and the definition of incest used. This is an area "where each question becomes a dispute and every answer an insult," writes Roland Summit, M.D., a professor of psychiatry at Harbor-UCLA Medical Center in Torrance, California, in his introduction to *Sexual Abuse of Young Children.* "The expert in child sexual abuse today may be an ignoramus tomorrow."

As recently as the early '70s, experts in the psychiatric community stated that there were only 1 to 5 cases of incest per one million people. When I began work on this article, I thought that maybe one person in a hundred was an incest victim. How wrong I was. Sometimes called "rape by extortion," incest is about betrayal of trust, and it accounts for most child sexual abuse by far. To be specific:

In 1977, Diana E. H. Russell, Ph.D., professor emeritus at Mills College in Oakland, California, and author of *The Secret Trauma: Incest in the Lives of Girls and Women* and *Sexual Exploitation: Rape, Child Sexual Abuse and Workplace Harassment,* questioned 930 San Francisco women and found that 38 percent had been sexually abused by the time they had reached the age of 18. She further found that of those women who were victims, 89 percent were abused by relatives or family acquaintances. Using Russell's figures as my guide—they are widely cited by other authorities in the field and have been duplicated in other studies—the estimate of the incidence of incest that I came up with is one in three; which is to say that incest happens to about one person in three before the age of 18.

Incestuous acts range from voyeurism and exhibitionism to masturbation, to rape and sodomy, to bestiality, to ritualized torture in cults. Incest may or may not include penetration, may or may not be violent. It may happen only once or continue for decades. It usually exists in secret, but not always.

Kim Shaffir was four and a half years old when her divorced mother remarried. Her stepfather, John Hairsine, showed Kim pornographic photographs and read aloud to her from pornographic novels. He took Polaroids of himself and Kim's mother having sex and showed Kim the pictures. He arranged for her to watch him and her mother having intercourse; he told her when they would be doing it and left the door open. Hairsine kept Kim quiet with the threat that if she told anyone, her mother would send her away.

From exhibitionism and voyeurism, Hairsine moved on to fondling. He made Kim perform oral sex on him. Then he forced her to have anal sex. As he had photographed himself with her mother, he now photographed himself with Kim.

When Kim was 13 her mother discovered the blurred backings of the Polaroid pictures of her husband and Kim. She broke the camera as a symbolic statement. "We're going to put it all behind us," she announced. But she was wrong.

Hairsine made peepholes throughout their Maryland house so he could spy on Kim. He drilled through the bathroom door. Kim repeatedly stuffed the hole with soap and toilet paper, which he would remove and she would replace. For three years she tried to avoid showering when her mother was out of the house.

Every morning, under the guise of waking

her for school, Hairsine entered her room and masturbated in her presence. Kim, now 30 and living in Washington, D.C., says, "That's how I'd wake up, to him coming into a dish towel as he stood by my bed."

One reason for the imprecise nature of the incest statistics is that when children try to tell, they aren't believed. Another is that many victims don't recognize certain behaviors as abusive. My parents would never have let anyone abuse me—if they had known. They didn't know because I didn't know to tell them.

Small children understand very little about sex. Even kids who use "dirty" words often don't understand what those words mean. And as little as they know about normal sex, they know less about deviant sex. They simply trust that whatever happens to them at the hands of those who take care of them is supposed to happen. Children know that adults have absolute power over them, and even in the face of the most awful abuse, they will obey.

The victim who does tell is almost always asked: Why didn't you tell sooner? The answers are:

I didn't know anything was wrong.
I didn't know it was illegal.
I didn't know who to tell.
I did tell and no one believed me.
I was ashamed.
I was scared.

The abuser keeps the incest secret through threats:

If you tell, I will kill you.
If you tell, you'll be sent away.
If you tell, I'll kill your little sister.
If you tell, I'll molest your little brother.
If you tell, I'll kill your dog.
If you tell, it will kill your mother.
If you tell, no one will believe you.
If you tell, then you will go to the insane asylum.
If you tell, I'll go to jail and you'll starve.
If you tell, they'll give you to someone who will really hurt you.
If you tell, you'll go to hell.
If you tell, I won't love you anymore.

Many abusers make good on their threats, but most don't need to. "Small creatures deal with overwhelming threat by freezing, pretending to be asleep, and playing possum," says Dr. Roland Summit, the Harbor-UCLA Medical Center psychiatrist who, in a paper titled "The Child Sexual Abuse Accommodation Syndrome," sets forth a widely accepted explanation of how children behave when molested.

The classic paradigm for an incestuous union is between an older male (father or stepfather or grandfather or uncle) and a younger female. The male is pictured as seduced by a conniving and sexually precocious child who wants sex, power, and presents. Or he is seen as a snaggletoothed tree dweller with an IQ below freezing who rapes his daughter because she is female, his, and nearer to hand than a cow. Yet Massachusetts therapist Mike Lew, author of *Victims No Longer: Men Recovering from Incest and Other Sexual Child Abuse,* told me that as many as 50 percent of victims may be boys. As therapist Karin C. Meiselman, Ph.D., writes in *Resolving the Trauma of Incest,* "The fact that many males are abused as children and adolescents is only beginning to receive adequate professional attention."

**D**ifficult as it is for girls to talk about their abuse, it is even harder for boys. Boys are taught that they must be strong and self-reliant. For a boy to report that he was abused, he must admit weakness and victimization. If he was molested by a male, he will fear that this has made him homosexual.

Then, too, many boys simply don't know they have been abused. Deborah Tannen, Ph.D., professor of linguistics at Georgetown University and author most recently of *You Just Don't Understand: Women and Men in Conversation,* suggests that girls and boys are raised in different cultures. The world expects one set of behaviors and attitudes from girls and another, quite different set from boys.

We teach girls to avoid sex, to wait, and to protect themselves. We teach them that men are not allowed to do certain things to them. But we teach boys that any sex—any heterosexual sex—is good, the earlier the better. We tell them they "scored," they "got lucky." But consider the impact when a boy "gets lucky" with his mother.

"My first really clear memory," says Michael Smith, 30, "is of my mother performing oral sex on me. I was seven. My parents would make me watch them have sex before or after my mother had oral sex with me."

Ralph Smith, the family patriarch, is now 65 years old. His wife, Betty, is 58. They are gray-haired, churchgoing, God-fearing people whose eight children range in age from 20 to 40. The Smiths say they tried to give their kids a good childhood.

"What happened to me was bad," says Michael, "but it was nothing compared to what happened to Lisa." Lisa is Michael's sister. Her earliest memory is of being five and her father fondling her and performing oral sex on her. She told her mother. "I was in the bathtub when I told her," Lisa says. "She slapped me around. She said, 'You're dirty. Don't ever say that again.'"

Lisa's parents had sex in front of her, and when she turned 12 her father had intercourse with her—a pattern he continued until she turned 23 and left home. "I didn't like it," she says. "But he said it was right. He said it even said in the Bible that it was okay to have sex with your children and sex with your parents. He quoted Job. I begged my mother not to leave me alone with him anymore. She said, 'I know you love him.' I asked her to help me, but she wouldn't."

Lisa's sister Michelle slept in a room next to Lisa's. She would hear her father go into Lisa's bedroom at night. "I would hear Lisa crying and screaming and telling him no," Michelle recalls.

Ralph and Betty Smith made Michael and Lisa perform oral sex on each other while they watched and gave instructions. "They said they were teaching us about sex," Michael says. "They were teaching us how to be good mates when we grew up, how to keep a mate satisfied. I would know how to please a woman. I could stay married."

Ralph and Betty kept the children silent by beating them and threatening to kill them and their brothers and sisters. Ralph Smith regularly held a gun to Lisa's head while he had intercourse with her.

Lisa believed that she and Michael were the only ones being molested. She believed that her being abused was protecting her younger siblings. "Until Michelle came and told me she was also being molested," Lisa says, "I thought I had protected them. My whole goal was to protect them. When I found out they had all been abused . . . " Her voice trails off. "We were afraid of our parents and the outside world. The very few people we tried to tell didn't believe us or only believed a little, not enough to do anything."

"I even told a priest once," Michael says. "He gave me a bunch of leaflets and told me to go home and work it out with my family."

Abused children assume that they are responsible for the abuse, believing they brought it on themselves. One man said to his 13-year-old victim, "I'm sorry this had to happen to you, but you're just too beautiful." Some victims feel guilty because they accepted presents or felt pleasure. Victims who experience orgasms while being molested suffer excruciating guilt and conflict.

## 2. VICTIMOLOGY

While there have been articles by pedophiles arguing that incest is good and natural and that its prohibition violates the rights of children, psychiatrist Judith Lewis Herman, M.D., writes in her pioneering book, *Father-Daughter Incest,* that the actual sexual encounter, whether brutal or tender, painful or pleasurable, "is always, inevitably, destructive to the child." And Maryland psychotherapist Christine A. Courtois, Ph.D., author of *Healing the Incest Wound: Adult Survivors in Therapy,* is firm in her belief that incest "poses a serious mental-health risk for a substantial number of victims."

Mariann's father began taking her into his shower when she was five. He washed her and taught her to wash him. He took her into his bed for snuggling, which turned into fondling. He taught her to masturbate him and made her perform oral sex on him. When she was ten he forced her to have vaginal and anal intercourse.

Mariann's father told her he was teaching her about sex. He said he was teaching her to control her sexual feelings so she wouldn't get swept away. He told her that if she was ever with a boy and got sexually aroused, she was to come to him and he would "help" her.

When Mariann's mother caught her husband fondling their daughter, she called Mariann a whore and accused her of trying to seduce her father. Yet when Mariann's father got a job in another state that required him to move early one spring, her mother stayed behind until summer but insisted that Mariann go with him.

As Mariann grew older her father experienced periods of impotence. When he could no longer manage penetration, he masturbated between his daughter's breasts, ejaculated onto her chest, and rubbed his semen over her.

"There was no escaping it, no safety," Mariann remembers. "I started to feel crazy. I wanted to be crazy. I remember thinking, I want to take LSD and go crazy so they'll lock me up and I can stay there for the rest of my life." At 17, Mariann cut her wrists. The wounds were superficial, but she bled into her sheets all night and came down to breakfast with Band-Aids lined up along her arms. No one asked what had happened.

In spite of her objections and efforts to avoid her father, he continued to have sex with her, until he died when she was in her 20s. She has been hospitalized several times for severe depression and suicidal impulses. "I was invisible," she says. "That's all I was—a vagina. Nothing else existed."

If incest can lead to suicide, it can also lead to homicide. Witness Tony Baekeland. Tony's mother, Barbara, seduced him when he was in his early teens. She openly boasted of their affair, and Tony talked of it as well. When he became violent in his late teens and early 20s, neither of his parents got him psychiatric help. At 26, Tony stabbed his mother to death in their apartment. He was incarcerated at a facility for the criminally insane. His grandmother rallied friends and family to have him released. It took six years. Once freed, Tony stabbed his grandmother eight times at her apartment in New York. She survived. He was imprisoned on Rikers Island, where he suffocated himself with a plastic bag.

In young children who are victims of incest, the vast array of physical and psychological symptoms suffered include injuries to the mouth, urethra, vagina, and anus; bedwetting and soiling; fear of everyone of the perpetrator's gender; nightmares and/or sleep loss; compulsive masturbation, precocious sexual knowledge, and sexual acting out; running away, suicide attempts, and sexually transmitted diseases. Judge Jeffry H. Gallet of the New York State Family Court, sitting in Manhattan, perhaps best known as the judge who heard the Lisa Steinberg case, told me he had once seen a baby with pelvic inflammatory disease so severe that as an adult she will never be able to conceive. And as is well known to health workers and court officials, not all AIDS babies contract the virus before they are born.

It is not at all unusual for victims to grow up with sexual problems. Some can't touch or be touched. Others become wildly promiscuous. Or act out in other sexual ways. That was the case with my friend Nina, who told me that she had been her "father's mistress."

Nina then went on to defend her father. "I hate it," she said, "when people say, 'Any man who'd do that is sick.' He wasn't sick. Except for the incest my dad was totally reliable and helpful and loving. He was the only loving parent I had. He was my role model when I was growing up. He taught me about morals and gave me all the important lessons of my life. If I have to give up my love for my father, what will I have left? I hate what he did, but I love him."

In what she now understands was an unconscious need to reenact in adulthood her secret, duplicitous life with her father, Nina became a bigamist. She married two men, maintained two households, and simultaneously raised three children—two of them in one house and a stepchild in the other.

Some victims become prostitutes. Others believe that incest forced them into lifelong sexual behaviors that they would not have chosen for themselves, including homosexuality. Victims experience not only guilt, shame, fear, and a broad range of psychosocial disorders. They are unable to trust. They have severe problems maintaining intimate relationships, including those with their children.

Journalist Betsy Peterson, in *Dancing with Daddy: A Childhood Lost and a Life Regained,* describes how incest with her father affected her relationship with her sons. "To know how much I love them is to know what I didn't give them, what they missed and what I missed," she writes. "I use my hands to stuff the sobs back in, to eat the terrible grief . . . because I spent their childhood as I spent my own, trying to protect myself."

Michigan therapist Kathy Evert, author of the autobiographical *When You're Ready: A Woman Healing from Childhood Physical and Sexual Abuse by Her Mother,* recently completed a study of 93 women and 9 men abused by their mothers. She found that almost a fourth of the men and more than 60 percent of the women had eating disorders. "I can't tell you the number of women I've seen who weigh over five hundred pounds," Evert says. One woman told her she ate to get bigger and more powerful than her mother. Another woman in the group weighed more than 600 pounds. "Food was my weapon against her," she said of her mother.

More than 80 percent of the women and all the men in Evert's study had sexual problems as adults that they attributed to the abuse by their mothers. And almost two thirds of the women said they rarely or never went to the doctor or dentist because to be examined was too terrifying for them. Thus they are unable to avail themselves of the diagnostic benefits of modern medicine, such as pelvic exams, PAP smears, breast examinations, and mammography.

Some victims are unable to feel physical pain. Some self-mutilate—they burn or cut themselves. Mariann told me that the impulse to cut herself is almost constant and almost uncontrollable. "You get to feeling like your body is full of something rotten," she says. "If you can make an opening, somehow the pressure will be relieved and everything will come out."

Dr. Roland Summit says that a victim of incest "will tend to blame his or her own body for causing the abuse." Some victims may go so far as to seek repeated cosmetic surgeries in an attempt to repair physically the damage that was done to them psychologically, according to a 1990 paper written by Elizabeth Morgan, M.D., a plastic surgeon, and Mary L. Froning, who holds a doctorate in psychology. (Dr. Morgan herself had made headlines in the late '80s, when she sent her daughter into hiding to keep her away from the father that Dr. Morgan alleged had sexually abused the child.) Perpetual plastic surgery, in fact, was to become one of the consequences of incest for Cynthia, who was raped by her father and her brother Eugene but had blocked all memory of the assaults.

Even when her brother sexually abused Cynthia's daughter Kit, Cynthia failed to recall her own assaults. Kit was three and a half when Eugene came to visit and, one afternoon, took her upstairs to the bathroom. When Cynthia discovered them, both were naked. Kit was sitting on the sink and Eugene, standing between her legs, was slowly rocking back and forth. Cynthia threw her brother out of the house. Then she said to the confused child, "This never happened. Understand? Forget it ever happened." By the time Kit was 20, she had only vague memories of childhood trips to the doctor for pelvic examinations and ointments.

Cynthia spent years in psychoanalysis, which didn't seem to help her severe depressions—nor restore her memory of having been sexually assaulted as a child. She kept telling Kit—who didn't understand why she was being told—that incest is so rare that it almost never happens. Kit was in her 30s when she remembered that afternoon in the bathroom with her uncle, and she understood then that he had probably given her a sexually transmitted disease.

Cynthia began to have plastic surgery in her middle 40s. She approached each operation as if it were The Solution, and she was briefly delighted with the results. Within months of each lift, tuck, or suction, however, she began to prepare for the next one. Cynthia didn't remember her own abuse until she was in her late 60s and a grandmother. Now in her middle 70s, she is planning on having a breast reduction as soon as she can find the right surgeon.

Also prevalent among incest victims is post-traumatic stress disorder (PTSD), which I discussed at length with Mary W. Armsworth, Ed.D., the author of dozens of articles on incest and its aftermath, as well as a professor of educational psychology at the University of Houston who teaches one of the few courses in this country on trauma. In the early '80s, Armsworth

noticed that incest patients, who "live in a bath of anxiety," had the same PTSD symptoms demonstrated by some Vietnam War veterans and most victims of torture. These symptoms include but are not limited to amnesia, nightmares, and flashbacks. People who have PTSD may "leave their bodies" during the abuse, and they may continue to dissociate for decades after the abuse ends.

(In 1990, *The New York Times* reported that Dennis Charney, M.D., a Yale psychiatrist and director of clinical neuroscience at the National Center for Post-Traumatic Stress Disorder, had found that even one experience of overwhelming terror permanently alters the chemistry of the brain. The longer the duration and the more severe the trauma, the more likely it is that a victim will develop PTSD.)

Most of the dreams told to me by victims of incest involve being chased and stabbed, suffocated, made immobile and voiceless. I myself have a recurring dream of a man who gouges out my eyes and of a woman who rips out my tongue. One woman who has been in long-term therapy owing to years of abuse by her aunt, uncle, and mother told me she dreamed she was at a beautiful, crowded picnic in the woods when she vomited feces. The dream so revolted and shamed her that she had never before told it to anyone, not even her therapist.

Children forced to perform fellatio may grow up to be adults with flashbacks triggered by the smell of Clorox, the feel of melted butter, the sight of toothpaste in their mouth. It is difficult for people who don't have flashbacks to know what one is like. Flashbacks are not memories—memories have distance, are muted and selective. A flashback is a memory without distance. It can bring all the terror of an original event, triggered by something utterly innocuous.

A few months ago I was daydreaming in a friend's kitchen. Her husband, on his way to get the mail, came up quietly behind me, speaking softly to himself. The sensation of being approached (sneaked up on) from the rear by a much larger person who was muttering triggered a flashback—terror so acute that I had to get him away from me with the same urgency I would feel if my shirt were on fire.

Flashbacks can be almost continuous and overwhelming. People who experience them without knowing what causes them can feel crazy. An incest survivor's friend, seeing her run to hide for no apparent reason, might agree that she is. When flashbacks come less frequently, they can be handled almost as fast

as they happen. The man who accidentally terrified me never knew it, and I was able to check back in with where I really was and what had really happened almost as quickly as I had checked out.

At the extreme edge of post-traumatic stress disorder lies multiple personality disorder (MPD). It was once thought to be rare and is still disbelieved entirely by some (one of the more noted skeptics is Paul McHugh, M.D., head of psychiatry at Johns Hopkins in Baltimore). But while MPD has been called the UFO of psychiatric disorders, a growing number of cases are being treated.

Researchers believe that children develop multiple personalities as a way of coping with abuse so violent and sadistic that the mind fractures. Each assault is then handled by one or more personalities—"selves," or "alters." Some personalities hold pain, others grief, others rage. Even happiness may be segregated into a discrete "self." The personalities often have no knowledge of one another, so a person with MPD "loses time" when one personality gives way to another, and can "come to" hours or years later without any way of knowing what had happened in the interim.

Brad, a victim of incest who suffers MPD, has learned to recognize a particular feeling that warns him he is about to switch into one of his alters. It happens under stress, he says. "My eyes all of a sudden blur and everything goes to gauze."

I met another sufferer of multiple personalities—a young woman—the day after she fled a cult. My husband and I were guests of the people she ran to, and I sat up with her until early morning because she was afraid to be alone. She had been sexually tortured by her father, brothers, and other cult members for all of her 28 years. As we talked, she switched personalities.

One of her alters was suicidal. Another wanted to call her family and tell them where she was. One was very young, five or six. One knew the dates of satanic holidays and the rituals she had performed on them. At one point during the night she closed her eyes, then opened them again and looked at me with such an evil stare that the hair on my neck stood up. Later, she asked me to put my arms around her and hold her, and I did.

"I was my mother's gift to my father," says Sylvia, yet another woman who suffers multiple personalities. "My dad's a pedophile. He had sex with me until I was seven. My mom's a sociopath. She tried to suffocate me many, many times. She slept with my brother until he was fourteen. She made him her husband, even though my father lived with us. The last time I saw her was twenty years ago. I came by the house where she was living with my brother. He opened the door with a gun in his hand. She had told him to shoot me."

Sylvia and her family lived in a cult that practiced blood sacrifices. When she was three, she was ritualistically raped and sodomized by the cult leaders. Her life was so torturous that she split into alternate selves who carried on when she couldn't.

"The one thing a child learns from sexual abuse," Dr. Summit told me, "is how to be abused." Sexually abused children teach themselves to endure assault. Instead of learning to protect themselves, they learn that they *can't* protect themselves. As adults they can be blind to dangers others would find obvious. They may freeze or go limp when threatened. Someone who has never been abused can say no, can walk or run away, can scream and fight. The incest victim often doesn't know what to do except to wait for the danger to be over.

Child incest victims often become adult rape victims. Almost one quarter of the incest victims Mary W. Armsworth studied went on to be sexually abused by their therapists. Many incest victims as adults choose abusive partners.

Judy, who was abused from infancy by her grandmother, grew up with what she describes as free-floating feelings of shame. "I always felt there was something wrong about me," she says, "something loathsome."

She married a violent man. She believed that when he beat her it was her fault and what she deserved. She believed the beatings were a sign of his love. She stayed with him for more than a decade, leaving him only when she became afraid that her suicidal feelings would overwhelm her and that she would die, leaving her child alone and in danger from his father.

Only later did Judy remember the abuse at the hands of her grandmother. "Every night, I lay awake listening for the sound of her feet on the hall carpet," she now recalls. "I taught myself to leave my body when she came into the room, and to forget. I forgot so well that whole years vanished from my life."

When victims do finally remember their abuse, they are often hushed by friends and told to "put it in the past," to "forgive and forget." But that is precisely what they unwittingly had done so very long ago. In *Incest and Sexuality: A Guide to Understanding and Healing,* psychotherapists Wendy Maltz and Beverly Holman point out that "many women (estimates run as high as 50 percent) do not remember their incestuous experiences until something triggers the memory in adulthood."

"Sometimes my body remembered," says therapist Roz Dutton of Philadelphia, "and sometimes my mind remembered." Roz was an infant when her father began coming into her room at night. He placed one hand on her back and inserted a finger in her anus. He continued doing this until she was two and her baby sister was born. As a teenager and young woman Roz had no conscious memory of these events, though her life had been punctuated with "nudging feelings and disturbing thoughts."

Roz became a therapist with a thriving practice. In working with her clients, she noticed that she had "triggers"—things she heard or saw that sent her into a dissociative state. These things tended to have to do with certain settings but included once the unexpected sight at a professional meeting of a man's hairy hands. Though she questioned herself for years in therapy and in clinical supervision, it wasn't until she was in her early 40s that a chance remark to a colleague about brainwashing—and the colleague's reply that maybe Roz was afraid of brainwashing herself—evoked memories of her father.

Says Roz: "As I talked about myself and my symptoms—eating disorders, depression, inability to protect myself from emotional danger, dissociating emotionally—I began to make clear connections between myself and other abuse victims." Roz's memories were of early infancy. She remembered feelings of dread and terror associated with her father coming into her room. Images came to her of his hands reaching over the slats of her crib, and she experienced body memories from infancy of being held facedown and penetrated.

Just how reliable are memories? Can they be manufactured? How reliable, especially, is the memory of a child? Do leading questions by parents, therapists, or investigators—or the use of anatomically detailed dolls in the questioning of children who may have been abused—create false accusations that lead to false convictions? These were the sort of questions addressed by Gail S. Goodman, a psychologist at the State University of New York, Buffalo, and her colleagues in studies designed to test not only the accuracy of children's recall under stress and over time but also how children respond to leading or strongly suggestive questions devised to bring about false accusations. "If children are indeed as suggestible as some have claimed, then we should be able in our studies to create false reports of abuse," Goodman writes in the chronicle of her studies, published in 1990. Child-abuse charges, after all, have often been dismissed by judges on this ground.

The scenes acted out in one of Goodman's studies were based on actual child-abuse cases. Pairs of four- and seven-year-olds were taken into a dilapidated trailer where they encountered a man who talked to them while using hand puppets. Then he put on a mask. While one of the children observed, he played a game of Simon Says with the other child, during which he and the child touched knees. He photographed the children and played a game where one child tickled him while the other child watched. All of this was videotaped through a one-way mirror so that researchers could have a precise record.

Ten to 12 days later the children were asked the kinds of questions that might lead to a charge of sexual abuse: "He took your clothes off, right?" The seven-year-olds remembered more than the four-year-olds, but whatever both groups remembered they remembered accurately and could not be led into sexualized answers. They became embarrassed by the leading questions, looked surprised, covered their eyes, or—according to Goodman—"asked in disbelief if we would repeat the question."

Goodman and her colleagues used anatomically detailed dolls when questioning the children to see if the dolls would encourage false reports. The study's conclusion on this point: "Whether or not the children were interviewed with anatomically detailed dolls, regular dolls, dolls in view, or no dolls did not influence their responses to the specific or misleading abuse questions."

Because some people believe that a child under stress can't remember accurately and may escalate what really happened in order to match the stress felt, Goodman also studied children who had to go for shots at a medical clinic. "We know of no other scientific studies in which the stress levels were as high as they were for our most stressed children," she writes. The children had to sit in the clinic waiting room and listen to other children scream as they got a needle, knowing they would get one, too.

"These children's reports were completely accurate," Goodman writes. "Not a single error in· free recall was made." The most stressed children remembered best and in the greatest detail. One year later Goodman and her colleagues reinterviewed as many participants as they could find. Even after the children had listened repeatedly to leading questions, most persisted in reporting the incident exactly as it had taken place. "Child abuse involves actions directed against a child's body," Goodman writes. "The violation of trivial expectations would probably not be very memorable. The violation of one's body is."

## The Offenders

Jerry "Bingo" Stevens was born in 1910 in New Orleans. He was the third of five children and the first and only boy, hence his nickname. Bingo's father, Joe, was tall, handsome, redheaded, and smart. A supremely successful real estate developer, Joe believed that men should be strong and that women should smell good, keep the house clean, and serve dinner on time. He smoked a cigar and drank quietly and steadily from the moment he came home from the office until he went to bed.

Bingo's mother, Trudy, sometimes took the boy to bed with her to relieve her loneliness. She snuggled him in the dark, trying to block the sounds Joe made on his way into the girls' rooms, and any sounds that came later.

Joe died of cirrhosis of the liver when Bingo was 13. "You're the man of the house now," his mother told him.

By the time Bingo was 30, he had molested not only his sisters but most of their children. Trained from infancy to keep sexual abuse a secret, they never talked about it, even among themselves.

Bingo fell in love and married. The marriage was, apparently, a happy one. He had three daughters of his own, a son, and, eventually, an infant granddaughter. When his wife died he mourned. Then, after an interval, he married again and had a happy second marriage. He owned and operated a successful real estate business. In addition, he was a champion polo player and a member of the Explorers Club.

Bingo died of a heart attack in 1988 while sailing on Lake Pontchartrain with the nine-year-old daughter of his best friend.

He was, as anyone who knew Bingo was quick to say, brilliant, funny, charming, gifted, and successful with women. There was nothing about him that would have identified him as an incestuous father, brother, uncle, cousin, and grandfather. I am one of the children he abused.

After Bingo's death I visited his psychiatrist. "Bingo was one of my favorite patients ever," he told me.

"He molested me," I said.

"He molested everyone," his psychiatrist said. "Why not you?"

Everyone reading this article probably knows—whether aware of it or not—more than one incestuous man or woman. "Offenders don't have horns and a tail," says incest survivor Kim Shaffir. "They look like nice guys. They are not strangers. Everyone tells you to say no to strangers. No one tells you to say no to your family."

In *Broken Boys, Mending Men: Recovery from Childhood Sexual Abuse*, incest survivor Stephen D. Grubman-Black points out that "perpetrators who commit sex crimes are rarely the wild-eyed deviants who stalk little boys. They are as familiar and close by as the same room in your home, or next door, or at a family gathering."

Offenders come from the ranks of doctors, construction workers, hairdressers, building contractors, teachers, landscapers, philosophers, nuclear physicists, and women and men in the armed forces. David Finkelhor, Ph.D., director of the Family Research Laboratory at the University of New Hampshire, and his associate, Linda Meyer Williams, Ph.D., had just concluded *Characteristics of Incest Offenders*, their landmark study of incestuous fathers, when they saw nearly half of their subjects sail off to the Persian Gulf to serve their country.

Some offenders prefer girls, others boys. Some abuse both. Some are interested only in adolescents, or preteens, or toddlers, or newborns. Some, though not most, molest only when they are drinking or depressed or sexually deprived. Some don't abuse until they are adults, but more than half start during their teens.

Like Bingo, some victims go on to become abusers. Seventy percent of the incestuous fathers in the Finkelhor study admitted that they were abused during their own childhood. Judith V. Becker, Ph.D., a professor of psychiatry and psychology at the University of Arizona College of Medicine who has supervised or been involved in the assessment and/or treatment of more than 1,000 abusers, reports that some 40 percent said they had been sexually abused as children. Ruth Mathews, a psychologist who practices with Midway Family Services—a branch of Family Services of Greater St. Paul—has seen a similar number of adolescent offenders, male and female, and has arrived at a similar conclusion.

Mathews went on to tell me about a girl whose father abused her with vibrators after her mother's death. He also brought in other men to abuse her and, with his new wife, had sex in front of her. When she was 12, a city agency, acting on a neighbor's complaint, removed her from her father's house and placed her in a foster home. There she inserted knitting needles into her foster sister's vagina. Asked why, she replied, "For fun." In therapy, asked to draw a picture of herself, she chose a black magic marker and wrote, over and over again, the words *hate, disgust,* and *hell*.

In another instance of children acting out their own abuse on other children (animals are also frequent targets), one little boy was referred for therapy because he tried to mount most of the children in his kindergarten. His parents told the therapist that they made him ride on his father's back while they had intercourse. They said that this excited them.

Although we want to believe that we can spot evil when we confront it, the truth is that nothing about a perpetrator would alert us. Offenders are good at hiding what they do. They are master manipulators, accomplished liars. Those few who aren't get caught; the others molest dozens or even hundreds of children over many decades.

On January 15, 1991, 67-year-old Raymond Lewis, Jr., a retired aerospace designer, son of the founder of the Lewis Pharmacies in Los Angeles, wrote to his middle-aged daughter Donna that he "was the father who begat you; the knight on a white horse who protected you. The guy who had no lover other than your mom till well past his teens. A no smoking, no drinking, no drugs man of restraint."

This man of restraint had raped his five daughters (Donna's first memory of abuse is of her father molesting her while he was taking her to her first day of school in the first grade) and each of the female granddaughters he had access to—five out of seven. In the letter, Lewis wrote: "What is going on in Marlon's twisted mind when he tells of me, deathly ill and post-operative from my prostectomy, licking Nicole's vagina making slurping noises? . . . Why would I *lick* a female? Wrong modus operandi. Wrong age. And a relative! A grandchild! Totally insane! Granddaughters have fathers and no father would permit such a thing to happen. Nor would any mother. Had it happened, hell would have been raised."

But for more than 40 years, hell had not been raised. When Lewis's daughters tried to avoid him, when they cried and told him it hurt, when they threatened to tell on him, he showed them photographs of decapitated murder victims. They endured his rapes in silence, convinced from earliest childhood that they were protecting one another and themselves.

Says DeeDee, now 38: "My father said, 'People who betray their father are like people who betray their country. They should be executed.' He carried a gun in his car, in some black socks. He also kept a gun between the mattress and box spring.

"At first he'd molest me in the bathtub. He'd say, 'I'm the baby. Clean me up. Here's the soap.' Every time before he molested me and my sisters, he'd put his foot on the bed and beat on his chest like King Kong. He penetrated me when I was eight. When I was thirteen he bought me a ring. He told me we could cross out of California and get married, because I was illegitimate. He said exactly the same thing to my daughter when *she* was thirteen. I fooled around with the first boy I could. I got pregnant. I thought, Thank goodness, Dad won't touch me now. For a while, he didn't.

"When my little sister was fifteen she was living alone with Dad. I waited one day until he'd gone out, and went in the house. I found her in a corner, naked, crying. She said, 'I'll be okay. Don't tell. Don't tell.' I thought that if I told, Dad would find out and kill me."

One daughter broke away from Lewis when she was in her 30s and went into therapy. Then, recognizing signs of sexual abuse in her five-year-old niece, Nicole, DeeDee's youngest child, she reported her father to the authorities. In his letter to Donna, Lewis wrote about Nicole: "I fooled with the petite perjurer's pudendum! She said it! Crazy story! Totally insane!" He denied that he had done anything. At first his other daughters defended him. Then they began to talk—16 relatives, including his daughters, told the same story.

Most of his crimes were wiped out by the statute of limitations. He was charged with only four counts of child sexual abuse against his five-year-old granddaughter, and one count of incest—a lesser charge in California, as in most states—against her mother, DeeDee, whom he had coerced into sex when she was a grown woman by promising to leave her daughter alone.

During the trial Lewis's daughters—all professional women, one a college professor—were unable to meet his gaze in the courtroom. It fell to his five-year-old granddaughter

to face him. Although Lewis had threatened that he would kill her if she ever talked about what he had done, the judge ordered her to tell the truth. Seated on the witness stand, shaking and crying, she testified for two days. Lewis denied everything.

Three times the judge asked him if there wasn't anything he was sorry for. "How could they say such terrible things about me?" Lewis asked by way of an answer. "I drove a rusted wreck of a car so that I could give them good cars."

"Isn't there something you think you did to make your family say these things about you?" the judge asked.

"Well, maybe," Lewis replied. "A long time ago."

The five-year-old handed the judge a note she had written. "My granddaddy is a bad man," it read. "I want him to go to jail for two hundred years."

Lewis was convicted of one count of incest against his daughter and three counts of lewd acts, including oral copulation, involving his granddaughter. Expressing the opinion that Raymond Lewis, Jr., represented a threat to all females and that the only place where he would have no access to them was in prison, Superior Court Judge Leslie W. Light sentenced him to the maximum: 12 years and 8 months. But with time off for good behavior, he will probably serve only half his sentence, which means that he will be released from Mule Creek Prison in 6 years.

Says DeeDee: "Until I was twenty-three, I thought I was retarded. He told me I was brain damaged. He told me I was neurotic, manic-depressive, a damaged genius. He thought he was a genius. He said we could have a child together and it would be a genius. Six months before going to jail, he offered me one hundred thousand dollars to bear his child.

"I always hoped he would love me. I just wanted to be his daughter. But now I have my own home, my own checking account. I give sit-down dinners. I feel special. I have knowledge. I am a great mom and I'll be a great grandmom. I love myself, finally. And now I can die without that secret."

Lewis never said he was sorry. In the letter to Donna—one of a stream that he continues to send to his daughters—he wrote: "Loneliness was the reason that I had enslaved myself in my youth to raise kids, and now in the illnesses of old age 14 of my loved ones had abruptly dumped me! *Licked!* How bizarre! A puzzle."

Lack of empathy for the victim is typical of offenders. Every therapist I spoke to commented on this characteristic. All said that for offenders to be rehabilitated they must take responsibility for what they did and develop empathy for their victims. With one possible exception, not one of the offenders I interviewed had done this.

I am talking to Joe. His daughter accused him of sexually abusing her. He pleaded nolo contendere. "But I didn't do it," he says. His sentence: four years probation, with therapy. He has been in treatment for two years. "When I first came to therapy," he says, "I had an attitude that I was being punished for what I didn't do. I had no rights, when you got right into it."

I ask how he feels about the therapy he is required to undergo now. "It's a little inconvenient," he says, "but it helps me in dealing with other people to understand them. I think it would be helpful if a lot of people could go through a program to give them understanding and another outlook, instead of being negative or feeling put down."

I ask him again about his daughter. "I never touched her," he says.

Later I talk with Joe's therapist. "Is he in denial?" I ask.

"Denial," the therapist replies, "is when someone says 'She asked for it' or 'She didn't say no.' Joe's not in denial. He's lying."

I am talking to Chris. His sentence: 8 to 23 months in jail plus 5 years probation, with therapy. He has served 8 months and has been in therapy for 2 years.

"My stepdaughter and I had an affair when she was thirteen," he says. "It lasted a year. I got sick and had to go on dialysis. My wife was working. My stepdaughter was taking care of me. She was like the wife. She never refused me or anything. I really believe she fell in love with me. More than like a father. She met a boy and fell in love. He was into selling cocaine. I didn't want him in the house. I slapped her. She ran to her grandmother and told. She didn't want to take it to court, didn't want me to go to jail. But her grandmother and Women Against Rape stepped in. The grandmother never did like me anyway. They blew it out of proportion and it got all stinky. I did what I could to keep it out of the paper. I could have beat it. I have to come here [to therapy] or I'd have to serve all my time. But if I didn't have to come, I wouldn't."

"Is there a message you would like me to pass on to the people who read this?" I ask him. "Can you tell me something that would help them?"

"Yes!" he replies. "I want you to tell them that if their child gets a boyfriend, don't stand in the way. Don't say no. If I hadn't said no to her, this would never have happened."

I am talking to Bob. He, too, is in court-ordered therapy. Two and a half years ago he was convicted of indecent assault on his girlfriend's 15-year-old daughter. "She was curious about drinking," he says. "Her mother and I decided we would all get together and drink. Better at home, you know?"

The first time, all three drank together. But later the drinking took place when Bob's girlfriend was away. "The first time it went okay," he says. "Then two weeks later, we did it again. I talked her into giving me a back rub. Then I gave her one. I felt her breasts. She didn't say no. I was very attracted. She got up and went upstairs. She got on the phone, but she didn't say 'Stop.' Then she pretended to fall asleep facedown. I fondled her buttocks, pulled her pants down, felt her vagina.

"She was crying. I started to get scared. For myself. I really got scared. I'm trying to figure out how to react. I ask her, 'You want me to leave?' She says to me, 'No. Mom loves you.' She went outside and didn't come back. She called her girlfriend whose mom works at the courthouse. The cops showed up. I was thinking, Oh shit, this is real."

Bob was given a two-year probation, with therapy. (The sentence was light because this was his first offense and the molestation hadn't progressed beyond fondling.) "She would have dropped it," Bob says, "but the courts already had it."

I ask Bob about his therapy. "I have a lot more knowledge now than I had," he replies—"about how many lives I can screw up. Every time she goes through something in the future I'm going to have to ask myself, 'Was I responsible for that?'"

**M**ales who molest children have traditionally been lumped into two broad categories, violent and nonviolent. Included in the latter are offenders who are fixated and regressed. Psychologist A. Nicholas Groth, Ph.D., founder of the Sex Offender Program at the Connecticut Correctional Institution at Somers, describes fixated offenders as adult men who "continue to have an exclusive or nearly exclusive sexual attraction toward children." Regressed offenders are attracted to their peers, but under

stress—illness, loss of job or spouse—turn to children as substitutes.

To refine these categories, Robert A. Nass, Ph.D., a Pennsylvania therapist who treats sex offenders, suggests a third group: quasi-adult sex offenders—men who yearn for a loving relationship with another adult but, because of their own immaturity, are unable to have one and turn to children instead.

In researching *Characteristics of Incest Offenders,* the most detailed study of male perpetrators to date, David Finkelhor and Linda Meyer Williams of the University of New Hampshire questioned 118 incestuous fathers in exacting detail. Based on the men's explanations about why and how the incest started and how the men felt about what they had done, the researchers identified five distinct types of incestuous father: the sexually preoccupied—men who are obsessed about sex and tend to sexualize almost every relationship; adolescent regressives—men who have adolescentlike yearnings for young girls generally and direct them toward their daughter; instrumental self-gratifiers—men who molest their daughter while fantasizing about someone else; the emotionally dependent—men who turn to their daughter for emotional support they feel deprived of from others; and angry retaliators—men who assault their daughter out of rage at her or someone else.

And what of the women who sexually abuse children in their care? What patterns, if any, are they cut from? Psychologist Ruth Mathews of St. Paul, in a study of more than 100 female sex offenders—65 adult women and 40 adolescent girls—found that they fall into four major categories.

The first is teacher-lover—usually made up of older women who have sex with a young adolescent. This category often goes unnoticed by society as well as by the offender because the behavior is socially sanctioned. For confirmation, one has only to look to films such as *The Last Picture Show, Summer of '42,* and *Le Souffle au Coeur.*

The second category is experimenter-exploiter, which encompasses girls from rigid families where sex education is proscribed. They take baby-sitting as an opportunity to explore small children. Many of these girls don't even know what they are doing, have never heard of or experienced masturbation, and are terrified of sex. One girl who had seen a movie with an orgasm scene said, "I wondered if *I* could get that 'ah' feeling. I was waiting for the 'ah' to happen, then I got into all this trouble."

The third category is the predisposed,

meaning women who are predisposed to offend by their own history of severe physical and/or sexual abuse. The victims are often their own children or siblings. As one woman in this category said, "I was always treated as an animal when I was growing up. I didn't realize my kids were human beings."

Mathews's final category is male-coerced women—women who abuse children because men force them to. These women were themselves abused as children, though less severely than the predisposed. As teens they were isolated loners but anxious to belong. Many are married to sex offenders who may abuse the kids for a long time without the wife's knowledge. Ultimately, she is brought into it. Witness a typical scenario.

He: "Let's play a game with the kids."
She *(surprised and delighted):* "Great!"
He: "Let's play spin the bottle."
She: "No!"
*(He slaps her face, then beats her head on the floor. The child tries to stop him.)*
Kid *(yelling):* "Mom, do it. *He's* been doing it for years."

Deeply dependent and vulnerable to threats, these women are easily manipulated. As one of them said, "If he would leave me, I would be a nobody." Once such a woman molests a child, however, she may go on to offend on her own. As the mother of a five-year-old put it, "Having sex with my son was more enjoyable than with my husband."

While more than a third of the survivors I interviewed told me that they had been molested by women, true female pedophiles, Mathews says, are relatively rare—about 5 percent of her sample. Those she interviewed had themselves been abused from approximately the age of two onward by many family members. They received virtually no other nurturing—most of the nurturing they received was from the offender—and came to link abuse with caring.

Like male offenders, some females molest many, many children, their own and those in their care. But Mathews feels that women may take more responsibility for their acts than men do. Only one girl she worked with blamed her victim. Seventy percent of the females took all the blame if they acted alone. One half took 100 percent of the responsibility if they molested with a man. Where the men minimized what had happened—"We were only horsing around"—the women were "stuck in shame."

In Atlanta at a poetry reading, the woman sitting next to me asks what I write about. When I tell her, she leans close. "I molested my son," she whispers. I ask if she wants to talk about it. "No," she says. "But I will say that it will take me the rest of my life to even begin to deal with it."

Therapist Kathy Evert of Michigan, extrapolating from her 450-question survey of 93 women and 9 men who were abused by their mothers, sees a more general problem. "I believe that no one, including me," she says, "knows the extent of sexual abuse by females, especially mothers. About eighty percent of the women and men reported that the abuse by their mothers was the most hidden aspect of their lives. Only three percent of the women and none of the men told anyone about the abuse during their childhood." Instead they endured their own suicidal and homicidal feelings.

A. Nicholas Groth, the Connecticut psychologist, suggests "the incidence of sexual offenses against children perpetrated by adult women is much greater than would be suspected from the rare instances reported in crime statistics." He further suggests that women offenders may not be recognized as such because it is relatively easy to get away with abusive behavior under the guise of child care.

Female offenders wash, fondle, lick, and kiss the child's breasts and genitals, penetrate vagina and anus with tongue, fingers, and other objects: dildos, buttonhooks, screwdrivers—one even forced goldfish into her daughter. As one survivor told me, "My mom would play with my breasts and my nipples and insert things into my vagina to see if I was normal. 'I'm your mother,' she'd say. 'I need to know you're growing properly.' She'd give me enemas and make me dance for her naked. It lasted until I was twenty. I know it's hard to believe, but it's true. I was petrified of her. Absolutely."

It has long been believed that any woman who sexually abuses a child is insane and sexually frustrated but that her abuse is less violent than a man's. None of this is true. Only a third of the women and men in Kathy Evert's study, for example, said they thought that their mother was mentally ill. (According to Ruth Mathews, a tiny percentage of abusing mothers are severely psychotic.) Not only were most of the mothers in the study sane, but almost all had an adult sexual partner living with them. Furthermore, the mothers in Evert's study abused their daughters violently, beat and terrorized them, and raped them with objects. But they treated their sons like substitute lovers. Evert postulates that the abusing mothers projected self-hate from their own history of sexual abuse onto their daugh-

# A PIONEERING NEW

David Finkelhor, Ph.D., and Linda Meyer Williams, Ph.D., who are sociologists at the Family Research Laboratory of the University of New Hampshire, have recently completed the most thorough study to date of men who have sexually abused their daughters. The sample consisted of 118 incestuous fathers—55 men in the U.S. Navy and 63 civilians from treatment centers around the country—and a carefully matched control group of nonincestuous fathers.

In this landmark study on the characteristics of incest offenders, Finkelhor and Williams set out to determine whether men are socialized to see all intimacy and dominance as sexual, whether fathers separated from their daughter for long periods soon after birth are more likely to molest her than fathers who have not been absent, and whether incestuous men had themselves been abused as children more than had nonoffenders. The researchers also sought to learn each man's feelings about his daughter, his outlook on sex, and his attitudes toward incest.

Many theories have been posited about why fathers molest their daughters. Everything from alcoholism to a frigid wife has been blamed. With this study, Finkelhor and Williams have shed new light on the subject and produced much new insight. They have established, for example, that there are distinct differences in the onset of abuse: Daughters ranged in age from 4 weeks to 15 years old when the incest began. "Fathers were more likely to start abuse when their daughter was four to six years old or ten to twelve years old," the study reveals, "than to initiate abuse when she was seven, eight, or nine years old." Men reported various behaviors leading up to the abuse. Some of the fathers said they had masturbated while thinking of their daughter, had exposed themselves to her, or had made her touch their genitals before they began touching hers. A substantial percentage of the men—63 percent—had been sexually attracted to their daughter for a period of years before the abuse began. Most significantly, the findings reveal that there are many paths to incestuous behavior and that there is not just one type of man who commits such abuse.

Each man was interviewed for at least six hours and was asked hundreds of questions. The results—many presented here for the first time—dispel some common myths and prompt the following typology.

# Type 1.

**SEXUALLY PREOCCUPIED**

Twenty-six percent of the fathers studied fell into this category. These men had "a clear and conscious (often obsessive) sexual interest in their daughters." When they told what attracted them to their daughter, they talked in detail about her physical qualities—the feel of her skin, for example, or the smell of her body.

Type 1 subcategory: *Early sexualizers*

Among the sexually preoccupied fathers, many regarded their daughter as a sex object almost from birth. "One father reported that he had been stimulated by the sight of his daughter nursing and that he could never remember a time when he did not have sexual feelings for her. . . . He began sexually abusing her when she was four weeks old."

Many of the offenders were themselves sexually abused as children.

# STUDY OF INCESTUOUS FATHERS

"These men are so sexualized that they may simply project their sexual needs onto everybody and everything. . . . The children may be those who are most easily manipulated to satisfy the preoccupations."

## Type 2.
**ADOLESCENT REGRESSIVES**

About a third of the fathers—33 percent—became sexually interested in their daughter when she entered puberty. They said they were "transfixed" by her body's changes.

For some the attraction began when the daughter started to act more grown up, before her body changed. Some of the fathers in this group became aroused by a daughter after having been away from her for a long time. Her new maturity and developing body caught them by surprise. Sometimes the fathers let the attraction build for years, masturbating to fantasies of the daughter, before they acted.

These men acted and sounded like young adolescents themselves when they talked about their daughter. One said, "I started to wonder what it would be like to touch her breasts and touch between her legs and wondered how she would react if I did."

"The father-adult in me shut down," said another offender, "and I was like a kid again."

## Type 3.
**INSTRUMENTAL SELF-GRATIFIERS**

These fathers accounted for 20 percent of the sample. They described their daughter in terms that were nonerotic. When they abused her, they thought about someone else—their wife, even their daughter as an adult.

In contrast to the sexually preoccupied and adolescent-regressive fathers who focused on their daughter, the instrumental self-gratifiers blocked what they were doing from their mind: "They used their daughter's body as a receptacle." The fact that they were abusing a daughter or that a daughter was so young was actually "a distracting element" that these fathers had to work to ignore. While one man was giving his seven-year-old a bath, she rubbed against his penis. "I realized that I could take advantage of the situation," he said. "She wasn't a person to me." Another man said, "I abused her from behind so I wouldn't see her face."

Instrumental self-gratifiers abused sporadically, worried about the harm they were causing, and felt great guilt. To alleviate the guilt, some convinced themselves that their daughter was aroused.

## Type 4.
**EMOTIONALLY DEPENDENT**

Just over 10 percent of the sample fit this category. These fathers were emotionally needy, lonely, depressed. They thought of themselves as failures and looked to their daughter for "close, exclusive, emotionally dependent relationships," including sexual gratification, which they linked to intimacy and not to their daughter's real or imagined sexual qualities.

One man, separated from his wife, saw his five-year-old daughter only on weekends. "It was companionship," he said. "I had been alone for six months. We slept together and would fondle each other. The closeness was very good and loving. Then oral sex began."

The average age of the daughter when the incest began was six to seven years. But it happened with older daughters as well. The fathers of older daughters described the girls as their "best friends," and the relationships had a more romantic quality: The men described their daughter as they might have described an adult lover.

## Type 5.
**ANGRY RETALIATORS**

About 10 percent of the men were in this category. These fathers were the most likely to have criminal histories of assault and rape. They abused a daughter out of anger at her or, more often, at her mother for neglecting or deserting them. Some denied any sexual feelings for the daughter. One father of a three-year-old said, "My daughter has no sex appeal for me at all. What I did was just an opportunity to get back at my daughter for being the center of my wife's life. There was no room for me."

Sometimes the daughter was abused because she resembled her mother, sometimes because of the father's desire to desecrate her or to possess her out of an angry sense of entitlement. Some angry retaliators tied up, gagged, beat, and raped their daughter and were aroused by the violence.

**OTHER FINDINGS** Alcohol and drugs: While 33 percent of the men reported being under the influence of alcohol when the abuse occurred, and 10 percent reported that they were using drugs, only 9 percent held alcohol or drugs responsible. "Preliminary analysis indicates that the incestuous fathers are not more likely than the comparison fathers to have drug or alcohol abuse problems, although they may use alcohol or drugs to lower their inhibitions to abuse."

Marital discord: Forty-three percent of the men felt that their relationship with their wife was part of the reason for the incest. "However, the wife was rarely the only factor mentioned. . . . Different men probably come to incestuous acts as a result of different needs, motives, and impairments."

Sexual abuse of the offender as a child: Significantly, 70 percent of the men said they themselves had been sexually abused in childhood. Half were physically abused by their father and almost half—44 percent—had been physically abused by their mother. "Although not all who are abused go on to become perpetrators, it is critical that we learn more about how child sexual victimization affects male sexual development and male sexual socialization."

**RECOMMENDATIONS** Finkelhor and Williams suggest, considering the "intergenerational transmission of sexual abuse," men be given improved opportunities for positive fathering—including paternity leave and more liberal visitations in cases of divorce or separation. Also that they be encouraged to be intimate in nonsexual ways, beginning in boyhood. The study argues that, based on the evidence, it's very likely that people can become more aware of the precursory signs of incest. "It is conceivable," Finkelhor and Williams conclude, "that the sequence of events that leads to abuse can be interrupted."

## CASE STUDIES

When Anne-Marie's 17-year-old daughter, Maureen, left home, she told an aunt that her father had molested her and her brothers and sisters. While the case was being investigated, Maureen's father killed her mother. Out on bail pending trial, he moved back in with his younger children. When a child-welfare worker came to question him, he said, "Get out of my face or I'll do to you what I did to my wife."

Jenny, who had been sexually abused as a child, refused to believe it when a neighbor filed a complaint charging that her ten-year-old had been molested by Jenny's husband, Norman. Then her own child, five-year-old Emma, told Jenny that her father had abused her and her baby brothers while Jenny was at work. Norman went to prison.

Jenny poured gasoline over herself and her children and struck a match. The mother and both sons were enveloped in flames, but Emma was able to escape. Jenny, two-year-old Adam, and three-year-old Gerry burned to death.

Alison was eight when she was raped by her stepfather, Buddy, a drug user. HIV positive, Buddy had infected his wife, who later gave birth to an HIV-positive son and, the following year, a second daughter, who is HIV negative. In 1987, Alison's mother, who was carrying twins at the time, died of AIDS in her seventh month of pregnancy. Convicted of Alison's rape, Buddy is currently serving time. From prison he is seeking visitation rights to his son and daughter, who are now in foster care.

ters. "This causes rage and anger that don't go away," she says.

Not all incest is intergenerational, committed by adult against child. "There is more sibling incest than parent-child," David Finkelhor told me. And in *Sibling Abuse: Hidden Physical, Emotional, and Sexual Trauma*, Vernon R. Wiehe, Ph.D., professor of social work at the University of Kentucky, writes: "There is evidence . . . that brother-sister sexual relationships may be five times as common as father-daughter incest."

There are problems with numbers and definitions in this area, as in others. How, for example, does one define consensual versus forced sexual contact between siblings? Finkelhor says that an age gap of five years implies coercion. Others feel that a five-year gap is too wide. What about children who are close in age but different in size? What about children who have much more or much less power in the family? What about children who are more gifted or less gifted physically or intellectually?

Coercion aside, "sibling abuse has been ignored in part," writes Vernon Wiehe, "because the abusive behavior of one sibling toward another is often excused as normal behavior. Sibling rivalry must be distinguished from sibling abuse."

Certainly, sibling sexual abuse is no different from other sexual abuse in that it is self-perpetuating. According to the Fin-

kelhor study: "The role of physical and emotional abuse in childhood should not be overlooked. . . . Arousal to very young children may be the result of early sexual victimization."

The Finkelhor study has profound implications for the possible prevention of father-daughter incest. Over 50 percent of the men in the study reported that their sexual interest in the daughter developed slowly. Is it possible that prevention programs could have helped them clarify and deal with their feelings about her before sexual contact occurred? According to the researchers, "It is conceivable that men can interrupt the sequence of events which led to the abuse."

Currently, the statistics on recidivism are predictably dismal. The rehabilitation of offenders has always been approached as a matter of jail, probation, or court-ordered therapy. Only some few medical institutions in the country—notable among them, Baltimore's Johns Hopkins—offer impressive inpatient treatment involving drugs and therapy, but treatment is expensive, and not all medical-insurance plans will cover it.

While some nonmedical rehab programs claim up to a 95 percent "cure" rate, they are misleading in their optimism. Jim Breiling of the National Institutes of Mental Health says

that the results of many studies are suspect owing to the unreliability of statements by offenders, many of whom lie. According to one study, a 38 percent dropout of participants can be anticipated in any program. Of those who receive the full course of treatment, 13 percent reoffend during the first year. After that, who knows?

The rare offender who voluntarily seeks help can get trapped in a bind. Therapists are legally required to inform the local police if they hear about a specific child-abuse crime. Massachusetts therapist Mike Lew cautions his clients at the outset that if they tell him they have offended, he must report them. Even so, the authorities tend to look more favorably on those who turn themselves in than on those who get caught or accused.

Ruth Mathews believes that women may be easier to rehabilitate than men because, as noted, they may feel more empathy for their victims than male offenders do. But she points out that her opinion is based on the women she sees, who have come voluntarily for treatment. A sample of women in prison for sex crimes would probably yield very different results. Child offenders who receive treatment, on the other hand, do much better than adults. They need less long-term help and are less likely to reoffend.

Mental-health providers are key to spotting and treating offenders and their victims. But, says psychologist Mary W. Armsworth, the Houston trauma specialist, "we don't train mental-health providers properly." Incest victims who need psychiatric care are often misdiagnosed. Victims of child sexual abuse who suffer symptoms of posttraumatic stress disorder have been hospitalized for everything from manic depression to schizophrenia and have been subjected to shock treatments, insulin shock, and other inappropriate therapies.

Misdiagnosis occurs because the therapist, psychiatrist, or doctor doesn't know what to look for, doesn't consider childhood sexual abuse a possibility, or doesn't believe the patient's account of what has occurred. For almost a century, Freud and his followers have led us astray.

Vienna, Austria. April 21, 1896. Sigmund Freud stands before his colleagues at the Society for Psychiatry and Neurology, reading his paper "The Aetiology of Hysteria." He informs his listeners that mental illness is the result of childhood sexual abuse. The words he uses to describe the abuse are *rape, assault, trauma, attack*.

He has based his findings—which he has used to formulate what he terms the seduction theory—on the testimony of his patients. These are both women and men who have told him of their childhood abuse, often by their fathers. He has listened to them, understood them, and believed them. He has reason to. As he has written to his friend and colleague Wilhelm Fliess, "My own father was one of these perverts and is responsible for the hysteria of my brother . . . and those of several younger sisters."

But Freud is soon under attack by his colleagues, many of whom denounce his argument. He retracts the seduction theory. The accounts of incest, he now says, were fabricated by hysterical women who were not assaulted. Like Oedipus, he says, they yearned for intercourse with one parent and wanted to murder the other, and these yearnings produced such a profundity of guilt and conflict that they caused a lifetime of mental illness.

Unlike the seduction theory, for which Freud was ostracized, the Oedipal theory finds favor with the great majority of his colleagues. It becomes the cornerstone, the bible, of all psychoanalysis to come.

Jeffrey Moussaieff Masson, Ph.D., former project director of the Sigmund Freud Archives in Washington, D.C., and a self-described "former psychoanalyst," has written three books detailing first his affection for, then his disaffection from, Freud and his teachings. According to Masson, Freud's reversal of his position represented a monumental loss of moral courage that served to save his professional skin to the detriment of his patients.

In *Banished Knowledge: Facing Childhood Injuries,* Alice Miller, Ph.D., like Masson a former Freudian psychoanalyst, argues that Freud suppressed the truth to spare himself and his friends the personal consequences of self-examination. "Freud has firmly locked the doors to our awareness of child abuse and has hidden the keys so carefully that ensuing generations have been unable to find them."

Miller goes on to make a startling revelation about Freud's great friend Wilhelm Fliess. She writes that many decades after Freud suppressed his data, Wilhelm's son Robert found out that "at the age of two,

[Robert] had been sexually abused by his father and that this incident coincided with Freud's renunciation of the truth."

Some scholars have expressed the wish that the seduction theory and the Oedipal theory could work together. But they can't. The seduction theory states that child sexual abuse is the cause of most—or even all—mental illness. The Oedipal theory, on the other hand, states that child sexual abuse almost never happens, that a person's memories are false, and that mental illness and neuroses come from a child's conflicted desires for sex and murder.

Ever since Freud, the Oedipal theory has been used to refute claims of child sexual abuse. In *Healing the Incest Wound,* Dr. Christine Courtois, the Maryland psychotherapist, writes that "many survivors report that they were medically examined and treated for their various symptoms, but for the most part the symptoms were never attributed to abuse even when the evidence was obvious. Instead, symptoms were most frequently described as psychosomatic or without basis or another diagnosis was given." Some therapists still tell their patients that their memories—no matter how degrading, detailed, or sadistic—are really their wishes. Freud placed the responsibility for the deed and the memory not with the offending adult but with the child victim—and his adherents continue the sham. As Alice Miller writes: "I often hear it said that we owe the discovery of child abuse to psychoanalysis. . . . In fact it is precisely psychoanalysis that has held back and continues to hold back knowledge of child abuse. . . . Given our present knowledge of child abuse, the Freudian theories have become untenable."

But most people don't know this. To accept that Freud lied means that nearly a century of child rearing, analytic training, law enforcement, and judicial and medical attitudes must be reconsidered. As the matter rests now, the men and women who should be able to identify abuse and help prevent and punish it have never even learned the basics. Our doctors, analysts, and judges have been taught to mistake victim for offender. They allow offenders to remain untreated, free to infect the next generation.

Alice Miller writes that Freud "wrote volume after volume whose style was universally admired and whose contents led humanity into utter confusion." His legacy has been in part to blind us to the prevalence of incest, to make the offenders in our midst invisible.

At the Sexual Abuse Center of the Family Support Line in Delaware County, Pennsylvania, therapists who work with perpetrators and survivors showed me paintings done by children aged 7 to 12 who had participated in an incest survivors' support group.

Monica, 10, had drawn the outline of an adult, six feet tall, on butcher paper. With the help of her therapist she titled it *Diagram of a Perpetrator.* She drew in hair, a brain, eyes, ears, nose, mouth, shoulders, big hands, a heart, and a penis. Next to each feature, down each finger, and around the penis, she wrote the things her father had said to her:

TRUST ME.

I'LL PROTECT YOU.

I'M NOT GOING TO HURT YOU.

IT'LL FEEL GOOD.

DON'T FIGHT ME.

DON'T MOVE.

THEY'RE SOFT.

I THINK WITH MY PENIS.

I DON'T CARE WHAT YOU SAY.

I NEED SOME.

BETTER ME THAN SOMEONE ELSE.

IT'LL MAKE YOU A WOMAN.

I'M BIG.

**Editor's note:** This is a four-part report, of which two parts are included here. Parts two and three addressing the courts and recovery factors may be found in the February 1992 issue of *Lear's.*

# Police

The police officer of today faces a wide range of problems that were not the concern of the police a generation ago. Racial tensions are high, the criminal is more violent and heavily armed, and drug use is on the increase, bringing with it more violent crime. As the police turn to new technologies, new methods of patrolling, and so forth, the human impact of the tensions of the work load are being felt.

The spotlight has been on the police, as never before, since the Los Angeles Rodney King alleged police brutality incident of March 3, 1991. That case highlighted the issues of racial tension, police tactics, and community relations.

The articles in this section address several aspects of the role of the police in society. "Police Response to Crime" traces the primary and secondary roles of the police in the enforcement of the law. It is interesting to note just how small a proportion of crime is actually dealt with by the police.

The articles "Law Enforcement in a Culturally Diverse Society" and "Blacks and Cops: Up Against a Wall" deal with several aspects of police relationships with minority groups.

The stressful nature of the police job is outlined in "The Most Stressful Job in America: Police Work in the 1990s," and a provocative article asks, "Are Women Better Cops?" The phenomenon of hate crime is highlighted in "Preventing Hate Crime: New Tools, New Expectations for Law Enforcement," and "Cops Get Up-Close and Personal" evaluates community policing.

The section closes out with a report on studies that concern "Higher Education and Ethical Policing."

**Looking Ahead: Challenge Questions**

Are the police of today being adequately trained to deal with the diverse cultures in modern society?

Do you believe that women make better cops?

Is community policing working?

Is there a correlation between education and ethical police behavior?

# Unit

# 3

# Police Response to Crime

## The system responds directly to a fraction of crime

### Most crime is not reported to police

. . . [O]nly about a third of all crimes are reported to police. The crimes most likely to be reported are those most serious in terms of injury and economic loss.

The criminal justice system responds to crimes brought to its attention by reports from citizens or through direct observation by law enforcement officers. Crimes are reported most often by the victim or a member of the victimized household. Police discover 3% of reported personal crimes and 2% of reported household crimes.

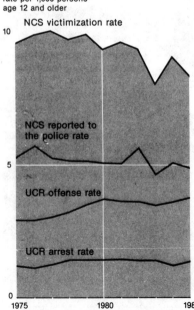

Aggravated assault
rate per 1,000 persons
age 12 and older

NCS victimization rate

NCS reported to
the police rate

UCR offense rate

UCR arrest rate

1975    1980    1985

Most reported crimes are not solved by arrest. For that reason the proportion of crimes handled directly by the criminal justice system through the processing of suspects is relatively small. Indirectly, the criminal justice system may be dealing with more crime than appears from arrest data because the offenders who are processed may have committed much more crime than that for which **they are arrested.**

Fallout for the crime of aggravated assault is shown in this chart:

### The first contact with the criminal justice system for most citizens is the police dispatcher

In many cities citizens can report crimes through a universal number, such as 911. In other cities the citizen must call the police directly. The dispatcher will ask for facts about the crime, such as what happened, where, when, whether or not it involved injury or loss. This information helps the police to select the most appropriate response.

### Law enforcement is one of several police roles

The roles of police officers are—
• **Law enforcement**—applying legal sanctions (usually arrest) to behavior that violates a legal standard.
• **Order maintenance**—taking steps to control events and circumstances that disturb or threaten to disturb the peace. For example, a police officer may be called on to mediate a family dispute, to disperse an unruly crowd, or to quiet an overly boisterous party.

• **Information gathering**—asking routine questions at a crime scene, inspecting victimized premises, and filling out forms needed to register criminal complaints.
• **Service-related duties**—a broad range of activities, such as assisting injured persons, animal control, or fire calls.

Wilson's analysis of citizen complaints radioed to police on patrol showed that—
• 10% required enforcement of the law
• more than 30% of the calls were appeals to maintain order
• 22% were for information gathering
• 38% were service-related duties.

### Most crime is not susceptible to a rapid police response

A study by the Police Executive Research Forum suggests that police response time is important in securing arrests only when they are called while the crime is in progress or within a few seconds after the crime was committed. Otherwise, the offender has plenty of time to escape.

In a study of response time in Kansas City, only about 6% of the callers reported crimes in progress. Where discovery crimes are involved (those noticed after the crime has been completed), few arrests may result even if citizen reporting immediately follows discovery; by this time the offender may be safely away. If a suspect is arrested, the length of delay between the offense and arrest may crucially affect the government's ability to prosecute the suspect successfully because of the availability of evidence and witnesses.

From *Report to the Nation on Crime and Justice,* Bureau of Justice Statistics, U.S. Department of Justice, March 1988, pp. 62-63, 66.

# A variety of public agencies provide protection from crime

## Today, police officers do not always respond to calls for service

Based on research and the desire for improved efficiency, many police departments now use a number of response alternatives to calls for service. The type of alternative depends on a number of factors such as whether the incident is in progress, has just occurred, or occurred some time ago and whether anyone is or could be injured. Police officers may be sent, but the call for service may also be responded to by—

• **Telephone report units** who take the crime report over the telephone. In some departments, more than a third of the calls are initially handled in this way.

• **Delayed response** if officers are not needed at once and can respond when they are available. Most departments state a maximum delay time, such as 30 to 45 minutes, after which the closest unit is assigned to respond.

• **Civilian personnel** trained to take reports; they may be evidence technicians, community service specialists, animal control officers, or parking enforcement officers.

• **Referral to other noncriminal justice agencies** such as the fire department, housing department, or social service agencies.

• **A request for a walk-in report** where the citizen comes to the police department and fills out a report.

## Law enforcement evolved throughout U.S. history

In colonial times law was enforced by constables and a night watch made up of citizens who took turns watching for fires and unruly persons. By the beginning of the 19th century, most citizens who could afford it paid for someone else to take their watch.

The first publicly supported, centralized, consolidated police organization in the United States was established in New York in 1844. It was modeled after the London Metropolitan Police created in 1829 by Sir Robert Peel. Other major American cities adopted the same system soon after. Today, more than 90% of all municipalities with a population of 2,500 or more have their own police forces.

## Rural policing in the United States developed from the functions of sheriffs

The office of sheriff, a direct import from 17th century England, was used primarily in the rural colonies of the South. As elected county officials, sheriffs had detention and political functions along with law enforcement responsibilities.

Originally responsible for large, sparsely populated areas, many sheriffs were faced with big city law enforcement problems because of urban growth after World War II. In some counties the sheriff's office has retained its detention functions, but law enforcement functions are handled by county police departments. In other counties the sheriff's office resembles many big city police departments. There are more than 3,000 sheriff's departments in the United States today.

## Traditionally, the police function has been dominated by local governments

• In 1986 there were 11,743 municipal, 79 county, and 1,819 township general-purpose police agencies in the United States. Together, they employ 533,247 full-time equivalent employees.

• Other State and local law enforcement groups include State agencies such as the 51 State police and highway patrols and some 965 special police agencies including park rangers, harbor police, transit police, and campus security forces. Along with their independent responsibilities, these agencies often support local law enforcement on technical matters such as forensics and identification.

• The Federal Government employs 8% of all law enforcement personnel. Among the more than 50 Federal law enforcement agencies are the Federal Bureau of Investigation (FBI), the Drug Enforcement Administration (DEA), the Bureau of Alcohol, Tobacco, and Firearms (BATF), the Secret Service, and the Postal Inspection Service.

## Urbanization and social change have had great impact on policing

• The dramatic shift in population to urban areas since World War II has had great impact on the demand for police service. The percentage of police officers employed in urban areas rose from 68% in 1977 to 82% in 1982.

• During the recent period of increasing concern about employment discrimination against women and minorities, mostly white, male police departments have added women and minorities to their ranks. The proportion of sworn officers who were women went from 2% in 1971 to almost 7% in 1985. The proportion of police officers and detectives who were black went from 9% in 1983 to 12% in 1985.

## Professionalism and advanced technology have also transformed policing in the past half century

• In 1982, 79% of police officers in a sample survey conducted by the FBI reported that they had done some college work. 23% of the respondents had received baccalaureate degrees.[1] Basic and in-service training is now regarded as indispensable. More than 670 training academies now exist in the United States.[2]

• In 1964 only one major police department was using automated data processing.[3] More recent surveys suggest that virtually all jurisdictions of 50,000 or more population were using computers by 1981.[4]

• In 1922 less than 1,000 patrol cars were in use in the entire country.[5] At that time, only one city had radio-equipped cars. Today, the patrol car has almost replaced the "beat cop" and police communications enable the patrol officer to have access to citizen calls for service as well as data banks on a variety of critical information, including outstanding warrants and stolen property.

## Private security continues to grow

After public police agencies were formed in the mid-1800s, organized pri-

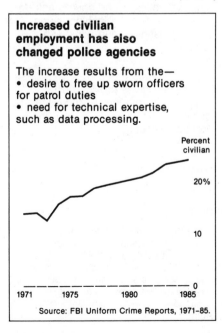

**Increased civilian employment has also changed police agencies**

The increase results from the—
• desire to free up sworn officers for patrol duties
• need for technical expertise, such as data processing.

Percent civilian

Source: FBI Uniform Crime Reports, 1971–85.

## 3. POLICE

# Private security plays an important role in crime control

vate law enforcement developed in response to—
• the lack of public police protection in the expanding West
• problems with interstate jurisdiction
• development of the railroad
• increased industrialization.

The first private security officer, Allan Pinkerton, had a tremendous impact on private security through his work with the railroads and through his establishment of the first private security firm. Owing to the lack of a Federal law enforcement agency, Pinkerton's security agency was hired by the Federal Government in 1861. More recently there has been increased need for private security, particularly to protect defense secrets and defense supplies provided by the private sector. More recent growth in private security is in response to growth of crime and security needs in businesses.

### The private security industry protects private concerns against losses from accidents, natural disasters, or crime

This for-profit industry provides—
• personnel, such as guards, investigators, couriers, bodyguards
• equipment, including safes, locks, lighting, fencing, alarm systems, closed circuit television, smoke detectors, fire extinguishers, and automatic sprinkler systems
• services, including alarm monitoring; employee background checks and drug testing; evacuation planning; computer security planning; and polygraph testing.

Private security is provided either by direct hiring (proprietary security) or by hiring specific services or equipment (contract security).

### 1.1 million people are estimated to be employed in private security

| | |
|---|---|
| **Proprietary security** | **448,979** |
| Guards | 346,326 |
| Store detectives | 20,106 |
| Investigators | 10,000 |
| Other workers | 12,215 |
| Manager and staff | 60,332 |
| **Contract security** | **640,640** |
| Guards and investigators | 541,600 |
| Central alarm station | 24,000 |
| Local alarm | 25,740 |
| Armored car/courier | 26,300 |
| Security equipment | 15,000 |
| Specialized services | 5,000 |
| Security consultants | 3,000 |
| Total | 1,100,000 |

Source: Cunningham and Taylor, *Private security and police in America: The Hallcrest report* (Portland, Oreg.: Chaneller Press, 1985).

### The authority of private security personnel varies among States and localities

Many States give private security personnel authority to make felony arrests when there is "reasonable cause" to believe a crime has been committed. Unlike sworn police officers, private personnel are not obligated to tell arrestees of their rights. Private security usually cannot detain suspects or conduct searches without the suspect's consent. In some States laws give private security authority to act as "special police" within a specific jurisdiction such as a plant, a store, or university campus.

### Many private security firms are licensed or regulated

In some jurisdictions both State and local requirements must be met to obtain a license to provide private security.

At the State level—
• 35 States license guard and patrol firms.
• 22 States and the District of Columbia require the registration of guards.

• 37 States license private investigators.
• Alarm companies must obtain a license in 25 States and are regulated in 10 States.
• 8 States license armored car companies and 6 States license couriers.
• In fewer than 12 States, the same agency or board regulates alarm companies and armored car firms, as well as guard, patrol, and investigative firms.
• 3 States have independent regulatory boards; 6 States have such boards in State agencies.
• Private security is regulated by the department of public safety or State police in 15 States, the department of commerce or occupational licensing agency in 7 States, and the department of state in 5 States.

### Public police are often employed by private security firms

Some police officers "moonlight" as private security officers in their off-duty hours. According to the Hallcrest survey, 81% of the surveyed police departments permit moonlighting, but most estimated that 20% or less of their officers are working as private security personnel. Acting like a contract security firm, some police departments provide personnel to private concerns and use the revenue for the department.

### Private security has continued to outnumber public police since the 1950s

Public police protection grew most rapidly in the late 1960s and early 1970s in response to increasing urbanization and crime rates. Public police protection has stabilized in the 1980s, but private security has continued to grow. Further growth of the private security industry is expected, particularly in relation to products using high technology, such as electronic access control and data encryption units for computer security systems.

---

### Notes

1. FBI, *A study of factors influencing the continuing education of police officers,* LeDoux and Tully, July 1982.

2. O'Leary and Titus, *Monograph,* vols. I and II, National Association of State Directors of Law Enforcement Training (Columbia: South Carolina Criminal Justice Authority, 1986).

3. Kent Colton, "Police and computers: Use, acceptance, and impact of automation," in *The municipal yearbook, 1972* (Washington: International City Management Association, 1972).

4. *Survey of police operational and administrative practices 1978* (Washington: Police Executive Research Forum, 1978).

5. Herbert G. Locke, "The evolution of contemporary police service," in *Local government police management,* 2nd edition, Bernard L. Garmine, ed. (Washington: International City Management Association, 1982).

# Law Enforcement in a Culturally Diverse Society

## Gary Weaver, Ph.D.

*Dr. Weaver is a professor of international and intercultural communications in The School of International Service at The American University, Washington, D.C.*

This article focuses on the cultural aspects of communication and behavior. It describes the basic nature of culture and then addresses the naive assumptions held by many Americans regarding cultural diversity. The article concludes with recommendations to overcome barriers to cross-cultural communication.

### The Basic Nature of Culture

The complexity of culture can best be explained by comparing it to an iceberg. The tip of the iceberg

T o better serve citizens from increasingly diverse backgrounds, law enforcement officers need to understand the cultural aspects of communication and behavior. Frustrations will only mount if the criminal justice community ignores diversity or assumes that it can continue to function according to traditional expectations and norms. In short, officers need to know the dynamics of cross-cultural communications.

represents the external or conscious part of culture—language, customs, food, etc. The portion that lies beneath the water's surface, which makes up by far the larger part of the iceberg, corresponds to the internal or subconscious aspects of culture. This includes the beliefs, thought patterns, and world views shared by all people in the same social group.[1]

Furthermore, internal culture determines behavior. To realize what motivates other peoples' behavior and how they explain their behavior, it is important to appreciate their internal culture.

When internal cultures come together, it is as if a collision occurs at the base of the two icebergs. The effects of this impact depend on the understanding that exists between the two cultures.

### Naive Assumptions Regarding Cultural Diversity

While we all know that people from other cultures eat different types of food and speak different languages, we often fail to realize that they also have different values, beliefs, and thought patterns. More importantly, we seldom recognize that our own cultures also program us with a particular set of values, beliefs, and thought patterns.

People hold a number of assumptions about those from cultures other than their own. These

assumptions must be examined before any consideration can be given to overcoming barriers to cross-cultural communication.

*Assumption #1: As society and the workforce become more diverse, differences become less important.*

Simply mixing culturally different people together does not resolve misunderstandings and conflict. Quite the contrary. Differences usually become more apparent and hostilities can actually increase during encounters between culturally diverse individuals.[2]

As long as individuals surround themselves with those who share basic values, beliefs, and behaviors, culture can be taken for granted. However, when these individuals interact with people who are culturally different, they see contrasts and make comparisons. In turn, they become more aware of their own culture.

Ironically, the best way to discover one's culture is to leave it and enter another. This is especially true of internal culture. For example, the black identity movement among college students in the late 1960s did not begin on black campuses. Rather, it started when predominantly white colleges recruited large numbers of black students. When these African-American students

Reprinted from *FBI Law Enforcement Bulletin*, September 1992, pp. 1-7.

91

found themselves literally surrounded by white people, they didn't become white. They simply became more aware of what it means to be black. The value and importance of their racial identities didn't diminish; they increased.

*Assumption*  *#2: "We're all the same" in the American melting pot.*

The notion that "we are all the same" spins off the so-called "melting pot" myth. Granted, some truth lies in the idea that America is a nation of immigrants. Traditionally, people came from around the world, threw their culture into the American "melting pot," and advanced economically because of their own individual efforts. Unfortunately, this notion represents an exaggerated and romanticized truth. All cultures did not melt into the pot equally.

What many immigrants found could be described as a cultural cookie cutter—a white, male, Protestant, Anglo-Saxon mold. Those who could fit in the mold more easily advanced in the socioeconomic system. The Irish, Italians, and Poles could get rid of their accents, change their names, and blend into the dominant white community. But, African Americans, American Indians, and Latinos couldn't change the color of their skin or the texture of their hair to fit the mold. They were identifiably different.[3]

During the various cultural and racial identity movements of the 1960s and 1970s, people asserted their right to be different within a pluralistic society. These people continually asked, "Why couldn't individuals retain their differences and still have an equal opportunity? Why is it necessary to give up these differences to become part of the mainstream or dominant culture?" They wanted to be recognized not for fitting into the white, middle class, male mold, which people of color and women could never do, but for their differences.

Along these same lines, all cultural, racial, and gender differences do not disappear when someone dons a uniform. Even though law enforcement asserts that everyone is the same when wearing blue, it becomes practically impossible to deny the diversity that shows itself in the ranks. What law enforcement needs to do is to accept and to manage this diversity. In the long run, this only strengthens law enforcement organizations.

**...as society and the law enforcement workforce become more diverse, the ability to manage cultural diversity becomes essential.**

*Assumption #3: It's just a matter of communication and common sense.*

At least 90 percent of the messages that people send are not communicated verbally, but by posture, facial expressions, gestures, tone of voice, etc.[4] These nonverbal messages express and shape attitudes and feelings toward others. No one teaches their meanings in school. Rather, people subconsciously learn the meaning of nonverbal messages by growing up in a particular culture. At the same time, they assume that everyone shares these meanings. In reality, just the opposite is true.

Consider the following scenario:

A Nigerian cab driver runs a red light. An officer pulls him over in the next block, stopping the patrol car at least three car lengths behind the cab. Before the police officer can exit the patrol car, the cabbie gets out of his vehicle and approaches the officer.

Talking rapidly in a high-pitched voice and making wild gestures, the cab driver appears to be out of control, or so the officer believes.

As the officer steps from his car, he yells for the cab driver to stop, but the cabbie continues to walk toward the officer. When he is about 2 feet away, the officer orders the cabbie to step back and keep his hands to his sides. But the cab driver continues to babble and advance toward the officer. He does not make eye contact and appears to be talking to the ground.

Finally, the officer commands the cab driver to place his hands on the patrol vehicle and spread his feet. What began as a routine stop for a traffic violation culminates in charges of disorderly conduct and resisting arrest.

This scene typifies many of the encounters that take place daily in the United States between law enforcement and people of other cultures. A simple traffic violation escalates out of control and becomes more than a matter of communication and common sense. It represents two icebergs—different cultures—colliding with devastating results.

To understand the final outcome, we need to examine the breakdown in nonverbal communication. First, most Americans know to remain seated in their vehicles when stopped by the police. But the Nigerian exited his cab because he wanted to show respect and humility by not troubling the officer to leave his patrol car. The suspect used his own cultural rule of thumb (common sense), which conveyed a completely different message to the officer, who viewed it as a challenge to his authority.

The Nigerian then ignores the command to "step back." Most likely, this doesn't make any sense to him because, in his eyes, he is not even close to the officer. The social distance for conversation in Nigeria is much closer than in the United States. For Nigerians, it may be less than 15 inches, whereas 2 feet represents a comfortable conversation zone for Americans.

Another nonverbal communication behavior is eye contact. Anglo-Americans expect eye contact during conversation; the lack of it usually signifies deception, rudeness, defiance, or a means to end a conversation. In Nigeria, however, people often show respect and humility by averting their eyes. While the officer sees the cabbie defiantly "babbling to the ground," the Nigerian believes he is sending a message of respect and humility.

Most likely, the cab driver is not even aware of his wild gestures, high-pitched tone of voice, or rapid speech. But the officer believes him to be "out of control," "unstable," and probably, "dangerous." Had the cab driver been an Anglo-American, then the officer's reading of the cabbie's nonverbal behavior would have been correct.

One of the primary results of a breakdown in communications is a sense of being out of control; yet, in law enforcement, control and action are tantamount. Unfortunately, the need for control combined with the need to act often makes a situation worse. "Don't just stand there. Do something!" is a very Anglo-American admonition.

With the Nigerian cab driver, the officer took control using his cultural common sense when it might have been more useful to look at what was actually taking place. Of course, in ambiguous and stressful situations, people seldom take time to truly examine the motivating behaviors in terms of culture. Rather, they view what is happening in terms of their own experiences, which comes off being ethnocentric—and usually wrong.

Law enforcement professionals need to develop *cultural empathy*. They need to put themselves in other people's cultural shoes to un-

derstand what motivates their behavior. By understanding internal cultures, they can usually explain why situations develop the way they do. And if they know their own internal cultures, they also know the reasons behind their reactions and realize why they may feel out of control.

> ## " *Law enforcement professionals need to develop cultural empathy.* "

*Assumption # 4: Conflict is conflict, regardless of the culture.*

During face-to-face negotiations with police at a local youth center, the leader of a gang of Mexican-American adolescents suddenly begins to make long, impassioned speeches, punctuated with gestures and threats. Other members of the group then join in by shouting words of encouragement and agreement.

A police negotiator tries to settle the group and get the negotiations back on track. This only leads to more shouting from the Chicano gang members. They then accuse the police of bad faith, deception, and an unwillingness to "really negotiate."

Believing that the negotiations are breaking down, the police negotiator begins to leave, but not before telling the leader, "We can't negotiate until you get your act together where we can deal with one spokesperson in a rational discussion about the issues and relevant facts."

At this point, a Spanish-speaking officer interrupts. He

tells the police negotiator, "Negotiations aren't breaking down. They've just begun."

Among members of certain ethnic groups, inflammatory words or accelerated speech are often used for effect, not intent. Such words and gestures serve as a means to get attention and communicate feelings.

For example, during an argument, it would not be uncommon for a Mexican-American to shout to his friend, "I'm going to kill you if you do that again." In the Anglo culture, this clearly demonstrates a threat to do harm. But, in the context of the Hispanic culture, this simply conveys anger. Therefore, the Spanish word "matar" (to kill) is often used to show feelings, not intent.

In the gang scenario, the angry words merely indicated sincere emotional involvement by the gang members, not threats. But to the police negotiator, it appeared as if the gang was angry, irrational, and out of control. In reality, the emotional outburst showed that the gang members wanted to begin the negotiation process. To them, until an exchange of sincere emotional words occurred, no negotiations could take place.

Each culture presents arguments differently. For example, Anglo-Americans tend to assume that there is a short distance between an emotional, verbal expression of disagreement and a full-blown conflict. African-Americans think otherwise.[5] For black Americans, stating a position with feeling shows sincerity. However, white Americans might interpret this as an indication of uncontrollable anger or instability, and even worse, an impending confrontation. For most blacks, threatening movements, not angry words, indicate the start of a fight. In fact, some would argue that fights don't begin when people are talking or arguing, but rather, when they stop talking.

Mainstream Americans expect an argument to be stated in a factual-inductive manner.[6] For them, facts presented initially in a fairly unemotional way lead to a conclusion. The greater number of relevant facts at the onset, the more persuasive the argument.

African-Americans, on the other hand, tend to be more affective-intuitive. They begin with the emotional position, followed by a variety of facts somewhat poetically connected to support their conclusions. Black Americans often view the mainstream presentation as insincere and impersonal, while white Americans see the black presentation as irrational and too personal. Many times, arguments are lost because of differences in style, not substance. Deciding who's right and who's wrong depends on the cultural style of communication and thinking used.

Differences in argumentative styles add tension to any disagreement. As the Chicano gang leader presented his affective-intuitive argument, other gang members joined in with comments of encouragement, agreement, and support. To the police negotiator, the gang members appeared to be united in a clique and on the verge of a confrontation.

Sometimes, Anglo-Americans react by withdrawing into a super-factual-inductive mode in an effort to calm things down. Unfortunately, the emphasis on facts, logical presentation, and lack of emotion often comes off as cold, condescending, and patronizing, which further shows a disinterest in the views of others.

Law enforcement officers should remember that racial and cultural perceptions affect attitudes and motivate behavior. In close-knit ethnic communities, avoiding loss of face or shame is often very important. Combatants find it difficult to back away or disengage from a conflict. As a result, third parties must intervene to avoid loss of face. These intermediaries must know all disputants. Their goal is to bring about compromise because everyone has to continue living together in the community.

This is exactly the role President Carter played in negotiations between Israel and Egypt. Begin and Sadat could not have signed the Camp David Accords without President Carter being the third-party intermediary. Compromise was necessary because Israelis and Egyptians must live together in the Middle East.

In complex urban societies, there is no assumption of indirect responsibility. If a matter must be resolved by intervention, then the judge and jury must appear neutral or uninvolved. Resolution is determined by a decision of right or wrong based on the facts or merit of the case. Compromise is seldom a desired goal.

### Cross-cultural Training

Because of naive assumptions, the criminal justice community seldom views cross-cultural awareness and training as vital. Yet, as society and the law enforcement workforce become more diverse, the ability to manage cultural diversity becomes essential. Those agencies that do not proactively develop cultural knowledge and skills fail to serve the needs of their communities. More importantly, however, they lose the opportunity to increase the effectiveness of their officers.

Unfortunately, cross-cultural training in law enforcement often occurs after an incident involving cross-cultural conflict takes place. If provided, this training can be characterized as a quick fix, a once-in-a-lifetime happening, when in reality it should be an ongoing process of developing awareness, knowledge, and skills.

At the very least, officers should know what terms are the least offensive when referring to ethnic or racial groups in their communities. For example, most Asians prefer not to be called Orientals. It is more appropriate to refer to their nationality of origin, such as Korean-American.

Likewise, very few Spanish speakers would refer to themselves as Hispanics. Instead, the term "Chicano" is usually used by Mexican-Americans, while the term "Latino" is preferred by those from Central America. Some would rather be identified by their nationality of origin, such as Guatemalan or Salvadoran.

Many American Indians resent the term "Native American" because it was invented by the U.S. Government. They would prefer being called American Indian or known by their tribal ancestry, such as Crow, Menominee, or Winnegago.

The terms "black American" and "African American" can usually by used interchangeably. However, African American is more commonly used among younger people.

The criminal justice community needs to weave cross-cultural awareness into all aspects of law enforcement training. Law enforcement executives must realize that it is not enough to bring in a "gender" expert after someone files sexual harassment charges or a "race" expert after a racial incident occurs. Three-hour workshops on a specific topic do not solve problems. Cross-cultural issues are interrelated; they cannot be disconnected.

### Overcoming Barriers to Cross-cultural Communication

What can the criminal justice community do to ensure a more culturally aware workforce? To begin, law enforcement professionals must *know their own culture*. Everyone needs to appreciate the impact of their individual cultures on their values and behaviors. Sometimes, the best way to gain this knowledge is by intensively interacting with those who are culturally different. However, law enforcement professionals must always bear in mind that culture, by definition, is a generalization. Cultural rules or patterns never apply to everyone in every situation.

The next step is to *learn about the different cultures found within the agency and in the community.*

However, no one should rely on cultural-specific "guidebooks" or simplistic do's and don'ts lists. While such approaches to cultural awareness are tempting, they do not provide sufficient insight and are often counterproductive.

First, no guidebook can be absolutely accurate, and many cover important issues in abstract or generic terms. For example, several different nations comprise Southeast Asia. Therefore, when promoting cultural awareness, law enforcement agencies should concentrate on the nationality that is predominant within their respective communities, i.e., Vietnamese, Laotian, Cambodian, etc. At the same time, these agencies should keep in mind that cultures are complex and changing. Managing cultural diversity also means being able to adjust to the transformations that may be occurring within the ethnic community.

Second, relying on a guidebook approach can be disastrous if it does not provide the answers needed to questions arising during a crisis situation. It is much more useful to have a broad framework from which to operate when analyzing and interpreting any situation. Such a framework should focus on internal, not just external, culture. Knowing values, beliefs, behaviors, and thought patterns can only assist law enforcement when dealing with members of ethnic communities.

Law enforcement professionals should also *understand the dynamics of cross-cultural communication, adjustment, and conflict.* When communication breaks down,

frustration sets in. When this happens, law enforcement reacts. This presents a very serious, and potentially dangerous, situation for officers because of the emphasis placed

*The criminal justice community cannot afford to ignore the diversity of cultures in American society or within the profession itself.*

on always being in control. Understanding the process of cross-cultural interaction gives a sense of control and allows for the development of coping strategies.

Finally, law enforcement should *develop cross-cultural communicative, analytical, and interpretative skills.* Awareness and knowledge are not enough. Knowing about the history and religion of a particular ethnic group does not necessarily allow a person to communicate effectively with someone from that group. The ability to communicate effectively can only be learned through experience, not by reading books or listening to lectures. At the same time, being able to analyze and interpret a conflict between people of different cultures can also only be mastered through experience.

## Conclusion

Culture regulates people's be-

havior and thought patterns. During an encounter between individuals of different cultures, the dynamics of cross-cultural interaction comes into play. An inability to communicate on the part of those involved raises barriers that oftentimes magnify the differences and escalate the conflict.

The criminal justice community cannot afford to ignore the diversity of cultures in American society or within the profession itself. Maintaining traditional expectations and norms only serves to broaden the chasm between law enforcement agencies and the citizens whom they serve.

Police professionals need to understand the cultural aspects of communication. They also need to realize that the issue centers not on eliminating diversity, but rather on how to manage it, and more importantly, on how to learn from it.

**Endnotes**
[1] Edward Hall, *Beyond Culture* (Garden City, New York: Doubleday), 1976.
[2] Nancy Adler, *International Dimensions of Organizational Behavior,* 2d ed. (Cambridge, Massachusetts: Kent Publishing, Co.), 1991; Richard Brislin, *Cross-Cultural Encounters,* (Elmsford, New York: Pergamon Press, 1981).
[3] Gary Weaver, "American Identity Movements: A Cross-Cultural Confrontation," *Intellect,* March 1975, 377-380.
[4] Albert Mehrabian, "Communication Without Words," in *Readings in Cross-Cultural Communication,* 2d ed., Gary Weaver (ed.) (Lexington, Massachusetts: Ginn Press, 1987), 84-87.
[5] Thomas Kochman, *Black and White Styles in Conflict* (Chicago, Illinois: University of Chicago Press), 1981.
[6] Edmund Glenn, D. Witmeyer, and K. Stevenson, "Cultural Styles of Persuasion," *International Journal of Intercultural Communication,* 1, 1977, 52-66.

# Blacks and Cops: Up Against a Wall

*Exploring ways to break the cycle of dependence and distrust*

Like many African-Americans, Dr. Calvin Cunningham has had his share of encounters with the police. Not all of them were bad. For instance, the police were prompt and courteous after a burglary at his Westchester, N.Y., home. But while he hardly fits the stereotype of marauding youth, the distinguished-looking, 62-year-old physician has been pulled over by cops on the road and hassled for such minor infractions as a broken light. "I think I am treated better because of my M.D. plates than I would be without them, but they don't afford the level of protection they would afford a white doctor," he says. Young black men have an even harder time escaping the presumption that they are guilty until proven innocent. "I have students who are stopped at random by police on the roads, legs apart, hands on the roof," says Andrew Hacker, a Queens College professor and author of "Two Nations: Black and White, Separate, Hostile, Unequal." "Black people are angry because police can't seem to tell the difference between a minister and a mugger."

The relationship between blacks and cops is paradoxical to the core. Nobody needs the police more than African-Americans, yet no community harbors greater resentment toward them. The two groups have plenty of opportunity to cultivate this mutual distrust, particularly in the inner city. "We have thousands of kids in these neighborhoods who have had endless contact with cops, who've been arrested, who see people get arrested," says Jonathan Rubinstein, a former Philadelphia policeman and crime expert. Blacks disproportionately commit violent crimes; they are also, disproportionately, the victims. In recent years an increasing number of police departments have implemented community policing programs, in which cops and residents work together to fight crime. But there has been a growing consensus among many blacks that the police can only do so much to impose order; the missing ingredient is self-help. Says Darnell Hawkins, a sociologist at the University of Illinois at Chicago: "The alternatives are empowerment from within or destruction from within."

Long-simmering antagonisms provided the tinder for last week's unrest. "In every black person, there is an almost instinctual suspicion of the white police," says the Rev. Wyatt Tee Walker, pastor of the Canaan Baptist Church in Harlem. By the time inner-city kids reach fourth grade, says Chicago priest Michael Pfleger, they view cops with "distrust and fear and, worse, anger." In every sense, they remain worlds apart. Most cops reside far from the high-risk areas they police—a distance that fosters alienation and smugness. New York Police Commissioner Lee Brown has asked the state legislature for the authority to make city cops live within its borders.

In recent years police departments have taken pains to hire and promote minorities. Major cities with black police chiefs include New York, Detroit, Philadelphia and Washington. While some law-enforcement experts believe black cops' visible presence has helped foster better feelings, skepticism remains over whether they are really different from their white brethren in blue. "Blacks can be more brutal toward blacks than whites are," says Calvin Rolark, chairman of the Police Chief's Advisory Council for the District of Columbia. "Their whole personality changes when they become members of the police force." "In effect," says Walker, "they join the enemy."

When cops and blacks clash, many African-Americans feel divided loyalties. "For me it's always been tough to be a defender of the police," says the Rev. Imagene Bigham Stewart, who runs a shelter for the homeless in Washington, D.C. "But you cannot live in the inner city without

## The Word on the Street Is Heard in the Beat

Anyone surprised by the outrage last week hasn't been listening to rap music. Rap and films like "Boyz N the Hood" have reported the tensions leading up to last week's rioting better than the news media. "Rap," says Chuck D of the group Public Enemy, "is Black America's TV station . . . Black life doesn't get the total spectrum of information through anything else."

Poverty, drugs, violence, bad schools, family breakdowns, racial tension: all have made it into the music of young blacks and—increasingly—whites. "Rap music has warned the Bushes and Reagans and politicians," says Luther Campbell of the 2 Live Crew. "If people would just take these rap tapes and analyze them, they'd find out what makes us tick."

In 1989, two years before Rodney King brought LAPD into the national consciousness, the Compton, Calif., rappers N.W.A. wrote a song about relations between blacks and police. It was called "—— tha Police." Widely criticized for possibly inciting violence, the song is an articulate description of fear and anger. With lines like "Some police think/They have the authority to kill the minority" and "Taking out a police will make my day," the group anticipated both the King incident and the community response.

"We're journalists," says B-Real, of the Los Angeles crew Cypress Hill. "I'll take an experience that involves one of us or a friend, and I'll explain what happened and why." Last year, he says, an LAPD officer pushed him onto a parked car. He wrote a song about it, "Pigs": "This pig thought he got away but they caught his ass on videotape." A week later the King video hit the news. "We've been reporting this," says Tupac Shakur, an Oakland rapper and star of the upcoming film "Poetic Justice," directed by John Singleton. "We've warned, 'If you don't clean up, there's going to be a mass destruction'."

**'Not alone':** But rap doesn't just report. "When you hear Ice Cube or Public Enemy, you know you're not alone," says Shakur. "It's like being in Vietnam and seeing another soldier on the battlefield." He believes that "the music has stirred people up to the point that they don't care if they get killed . . . Now [with rap becoming more popular among whites] we see it isn't a black movement, it's a youth movement. It comes from poverty, not from race."

In the name of reportage, some rappers have claimed a license not just for profanity but for misogyny, homophobia and racism. They've met heavy-handed—and sometimes substantial—resistance. Two weeks ago prosecutors in Omaha, Neb., brought charges against six retailers for selling 2 Live Crew tapes to minors. Rappers call this blaming the messenger. Says Campbell, "We're screaming out what the problem is, and they're screaming back, 'Don't say what you're saying'." Maybe now more people will see that rap's most offending messages often come with its most prescient ones.

JOHN LELAND

---

police." William E. Francis, a black policeman in Houston, embodies the dilemma. Francis, 31, grew up on stories of police brutality, but a steady diet of thefts, murders and assaults in his neighborhood changed his views. "I wanted to make a difference, right some wrongs," says the 10-year veteran. With more blacks moving into the middle class and beyond, blacks have a greater stake than before in the system; they, like middle-class whites, want the police to protect their person and property.

**Best hope:** Community policing seems law enforcement's best hope for changing the "us-versus-them" mentality. An updated version of the cop on the beat, it involves assigning foot patrols to a particular neighborhood and giving them the chance to become a trusted presence. Hundreds of cities have implemented programs over the last few years with impressive results. New York Commissioner Brown attributes last year's 4.4 percent drop in reported crimes in his city to expanded foot patrols. But the most important measure of success may be how people *feel* in their neighborhoods. "Policemen are viewed as partners," says Newark Mayor Sharpe James, "not members of an occupying force." Los Angeles, by contrast, offers "the antithesis of community policing," says Wesley Skogan, a Northwestern University professor and national expert on policing. "The department was cool, aloof, disconnected from the community."

Beyond the burned-out buildings, the Rodney King verdict has done incalculable damage in the ghetto. Since the '80s, black conservatives have argued that African-Americans should stop blaming their troubles on discrimination and begin bettering their own lot; some now say the verdict in fact proves there is systemic racism and worry that black youth will repudiate the message of self-help. Mark H. Moore, a professor at Harvard's Kennedy School of Government, suggests that the acquittals strain the contract that exists between police and society to protect its poor as well as its rich. Given the historic animosity between blacks and cops, it won't be easy to rebuild lost faith; the civil violence last week demonstrated the urgency of that task.

ELOISE SALHOLZ WITH STEVEN WALDMAN IN WASHINGTON, ANNE UNDERWOOD IN NEW YORK, JOHN MCCORMICK IN CHICAGO AND BUREAU REPORTS

# The most stressful job in America: Police work in the 1990s

*The news media have so sensationalized recent brutality reports that many segments of the public are now suspicious of all policemen. Yet police today face a gauntlet of stresses and obstacles so formidable that it is a wonder they can do their job at all.*

**David Kupelian**
**With reports by Robert Just, Elizabeth Newton, Jeanne A. Harris, and Jacqueline Hewko.**

*David Kupelian is Managing Editor of* New Dimensions.

In 1991, America's police are subject to greater scrutiny, second-guessing, and Monday-morning quarterbacking than at any other time in history. Their misdeeds and mistakes, real or alleged, are given saturation publicity. The videotaped beating of Rodney King was aired so many times that most Americans have its image etched permanently in their minds.

Yet, there are other videos that the public rarely sees. One month before the Rodney King beating, a Texas policeman, having routinely stopped a truck, was shot as he approached the driver. That video was shown on national TV for about one day. A week later a North Carolina state trooper was intentionally run over by a truck—also video taped. It received very little air time. Is there a double standard here?

By sensationalizing and endlessly harping on several isolated incidents, the media, in conjunction with grandstanding politicians, have fostered a new and increasingly widespread perception of America's police as the enemy, rather than the protector, of decent society. Los Angeles is a city "under siege by occupying forces," claims Roland Coleman of the Southern California Civil Rights Coalition. Jesse Jackson practically accused the entire Los Angeles Police Department of being racist.

Rep. John Conyers (D, Mich.) warns that the nation faces "a crisis of confidence in law enforcement." Responding to this intense political pressure, the U.S. Justice Department has mounted a major effort to review its file of 15,000 cases of alleged brutality, some of which are six years old.

Did all this hysteria really result from three L.A. cops beating Rodney King?

Police brutality has always existed, and it *is* a problem today. But is it true, as current media reporting implies that American law enforcement is increasingly populated by racists and bullies? "Any police brutality is a serious matter and deserves attention and correction," says former Attorney General Edwin Meese. "But you also have to maintain a perspective that these events are relatively rare." Meese faults the media for distorting the issue. "More and more of the police-beat reporters just do not understand what the police go through, as the older reporters did. Instead, they are young hot-shots fresh out of journalism school who want to make a name for themselves by castigating the police."

In fact, police brutality may actually be *less* prevalent today than it was twenty years ago. Civil liberties groups and police departments report *fewer* brutality complaints filed in recent years, not more. And while the FBI's Civil Rights Division reports 2,450 complaints involving law enforcement in 1989, during the same period, 62,172 law enforcement officers were victims of assaults.

This month (*August, 1991*) *New Dimensions* takes a close look at the men and women who make up America's police force—their almost impossible job, their frustrations, and their pain at being judged so harshly by the public. It is a shocking story, so far unreported by the popular media, of life on the front lines of America's increasingly violent crime war.

## THE VERY THIN BLUE LINE

"Every time you go out on duty you're going out there with a full deck of cards, and you have absolutely no idea how they are going to be dealt to you," muses Gary Steiner, an eight-year member of the Santa Monica Police Department in Los Angeles County. "Very often officers are put into situations where one minute everything is fine and next second, literally, you are going to be killed unless you act."

During street training as a San Francisco police officer, Peggy Wu discovered what was required of her. "I was called to one of the housing projects in the Mission District. My partner and I, who were the first police officers to arrive, found a child who had just been scalded to death in the tub by her mother. There were heroin and drug paraphernalia all over that squalid apartment. We arrested the mother as a suspect for the murder of her child, who was scalded and basically drowned in the tub. It was absolutely horrifying," she said.

"I spent most of the night there, talking with the woman for hours and hours. It was basically a negligence situation. She was high and the child ended up dead." According to Wu, nothing from her former life as a civilian could possibly have prepared her for being a policewoman.

Every cop has his or her own personal horror stories, nightmarish dramas into which the police willingly thrust themselves to play their valiant roles. Indeed, the only thing standing between average citizens and the hellish world of murder, drugs, and violent crime is a thinning blue line of beleaguered police men and women. Their task is formidable. Crime is up, way up. Police in New

---

## Cop-bashing media-style

■ On a recent episode of "L.A. Law," a black motorist is signalled by Los Angeles Police to pull over after failing to make a complete stop at a stop sign. But just the sight of police flashers in his rear view mirror terrifies the motorist—it is one week after the Rodney King incident—so he takes off at high speed. A dangerous 60 mph chase through a residential area ends at the man's house, where he threatens the police, "If you try to get me, I'll shoot."

Arrested and charged with running a red light, speeding, reckless endangerment, and failing to obey a police officer, the man pleads innocent on all charges. At his trial, he argues that he was afraid for his life and feared putting himself at the mercy of a police department with a reputation—recently documented—of brutality, especially against minorities.

The jury's verdict: not guilty.

Just in case any viewers missed the show's point that Los Angeles Police are brutes, "L.A. Law's" scriptwriters arranged to have the black man's attorney, Jonathan Rawlings, also be brutalized by L.A.'s finest while being stopped for a minor traffic violation.

Clearly, the belief that police brutality is rampant in American is becoming integrated into the thought-stuff of current popular mythology, one of the hot new prejudices that Hollywood writers can exploit in the creation of prime time entertainment. And no wonder, Hollywood borrows its subject matter from the news media, who are currently engaged in one of their favorite armchair sports: cop-bashing.

Ever since the brutal beating of Rodney King by three Los Angeles policemen on March 5, a seemingly end-less stream of stories in the print and television media have been painting America's law enforcement community as brutal, racist, and trigger-happy.

■ After the network news shows kicked off the cop-bashing season, ABC's "The West" picked up the ball and trounced the San Diego Police Department. "In Los Angeles," reported anchor Joe Oliver, "what begins as a routine traffic stop (*Editor's note: Rodney King actually led police on a high-speech chase.*) ends with a violent beating, while in San Francisco, highway patrol officers use riot batons against passive protesters. In each of those confrontations, the citizen lived to testify. But further south in San Diego, people have not been so lucky."

In an almost embarrassing display of one-sided reporting, Oliver proclaimed: "On a per-capita basis, San Diego police are killing people at a greater rate than anywhere in the West . . . San Diego police killed 12 people in 1990. . . ." Oliver made very little mention of the circumstances surrounding the killings.

■ On ABC's "Prime Time Live," Sam Donaldson's report on the U.S. Border Patrol, which focused on two police shootings, suggested that the Patrol wantonly shoots innocent Mexicans trying to cross the border. Rep. Edward Roybal (D, Calif.), a member of the House Hispanic Caucus, is seen on camera stating: "[The Border Patrol] think that they have a God-given right to abuse people, to violate individuals and human rights." Yet, while there were 53 cases of alleged abuse in 1989, the Patrol arrested 945,000 illegal aliens that year—one charge of abuse for every 17,000 arrests.

York City answered 4 million 911 calls last year alone, up from 2.7 million in 1980. But the numbers tell only half the story.

## IN COLD BLOOD

Criminals, many experts agree, are simply worse today than in previous eras. Vaguely reminiscent of the Biblical warning of an age "when love of one for another will grow cold," a new, more violent, more death embracing trance of hatred seems to have captivated armies of social outcasts, especially in the inner cities.

Whereas 20 years ago a fender bender might have resulted in an argument or fist fight, today it is not uncommon to hear reports of one driver shooting the other in cold blood, then coolly getting back into his car and driving off.

David Kalich, a Houston policeman, contemplates this modern phenomenon: "Two brothers were fighting over a pork chop that their mother had left one of them," he says, recalling a recent incident he investigated. "The other one got mad enough that he stuffed it down his brother's throat and choked him to death. When I got there, he said, 'Yeah. I killed him. He took my pork chop.' Then he kicked the body lying there in the living room and said, 'I'd kill him again if he was alive.' "

Fueled by the lust of drug trafficking profits, tens of thousands of gang members have turned many of America's inner cities into Beiruts of gang warfare. "In the 1940s and 1950s, a single police officer could face down a crowd of two or three dozen young people," says Meese. "Just by his presence, he would restore order. If he asked them to move on, they would move. Today that isn't necessarily the case." Indeed, for many youths who have known nothing from the day they were born except violence and abuse, killing a cop is a badge of honor.

There is a new meanness on the streets. The Jamaican drug gangs, for instance, which control much of the U.S. crack trade, "are absolutely the most vicious organized crime group today," says Joe Vince of the Miami office of the bureau of Alcohol, Tobacco, and Firearms. With a combined membership of over 10,000, the Jamaican gangs, or "posses," turn to violence and torture at the slightest provocation. They often dispose of rival gang members, or just someone who gets in their way, by cutting that person into pieces in a bathtub, and then disposing of the pieces in dumpsters all over town. They call it "jointing."

## HOLDING BACK THE TIDE

To fight back these incarnated demons of the underworld, police must play the role of combat soldier, referee, psychologist, urban negotiator, social worker, doctor, and older brother. To do all this, they must be supermen. "I will keep my private life unsullied as an example to all,"

*Criminals, many experts agree, are simply worse today than in previous eras. . . . 20 years ago a fender bender might have resulted in an argument or fist fight, today it is not uncommon to hear reports of one driver shooting the other in cold blood, then coolly getting back into his car and driving off.*

reads the National Law Enforcement Code of Ethics, "maintain courageous calm in the face of danger, scorn, or ridicule, develop self-restraint and be constantly mindful of the welfare of others, honest in thought and deed in both my personal and official life." While there are some rotten apples, most cops try diligently to live up to their profession's call for Herculean strength and nobility. Indeed, as any cop will tell you, sometimes the most difficult recruitment of the job is simply being strong and calm in the midst of chaos and tragedy.

"I responded to a traffic accident where a two-year-old boy had broken away from his bigger sister and run across the street," recalls Philip Hurtt, an El Cajon Police Officer in San Diego County. "The boy made it as far as the middle of the street before a car hit and killed him. My responsibility was to stay with his mother, brothers, and sisters. Just having to be strong in dealing with trauma of his brothers and sisters, who were only eight or nine at most, talking to the mother, trying to keep her and the kids calm while her son was being picked up off the street and taken to the hospital—that was really hard."

## OVER THE EDGE

Such are the formidable stresses police must deal with—the need to remain calm, strong, and in control in the face of tragedy, frequent danger, and constant exposure to the worst side of life. But police today are burdened by a whole slew of additional—mostly politically motivated—stresses that too often push them over the edge.

Race relations has emerged as an explosive law enforcement issue. While the Rodney King case virtually *invited* the charge of racism, the shooting of an Hispanic man by a black female officer in Washington, D.C.—after the suspect had pulled a knife on the policewoman—also resulted in racial riots. Why?

In an age when an increasing number of Al Sharptons and Jesse Jacksons purposely stir up racial resentments to galvanize a power base to support their own agendas, the nation's police are fighting a no-win war. It does not matter how tactfully, professionally, and impartially they might perform their jobs. They can, on a political whim, be branded racists.

America's increasing factionalization—one Los Angeles precinct hosts 43 different languages and dialects—has made the policeman's job extremely difficult. He inevitably feels like an outsider, and is viewed as one—far from the ideal of the neighborhood cop who knows and befriends the people on his beat. In such neighborhoods, which generate a disproportionate number of calls for serious problems compared to less divided communities, the value placed on human life is often low. Going into such a neighborhood knowing that their lives are on the line, it is easy for cops to develop a siege mentality—an "Us vs. Them" attitude.

Lewis Alvarez is all too familiar with the dangers of being a cop in a racially explosive powder keg. In 1982, Alvarez, then a Miami police officer, shot and killed a black man in self-defense. "I went to arrest him and he pulled his gun, so I shot and killed him. That's all that happened."

But that wasn't all. In an area already boiling with racial tensions, there was tremendous public pressure to "get" Alvarez, and the state attorney succumbed, indicting the young officer for homicide. Seven months and $200,000 in attorney's fees later, a jury found him not guilty. Alvarez's case is a prime example of politics at war with law enforcement. "The justice system and law enforcement cannot withstand the weight of politics," says Alvarez, who is now in private business. "It's like putting a 300-pound brick on a 40-pound scale. It just cannot hold it."

### THE INJUSTICE SYSTEM

Indeed, one of the worst stresses for police today is the criminal justice system, the very system that is supposed to back them up. "A lot of people get into police work because they believe they can do something about criminals and crime," remarks Detective Jack Luther, an 18-year veteran of the Los Angeles Police Department. "They get a rude awakening when they realize that felonies get knocked down so easily it's pathetic."

Police today are constantly frustrated and frequently betrayed by a judicial system that has become skewed in favor of criminals at the expense of victims and police. The universal frustration cops feel when they risk their lives to make an arrest, only to hear that the criminal is back on the street before the paperwork is completed, has led to widespread cynicism, burnout, and sometimes corruption and brutality.

Disillusion with the system "has a serious impact on police," says Meese, "which we have seen in the increased cynicism, and which has led, I think, in some cases to misconduct by police over the last 25 years." Learning from experience how quickly many offenders exit the system's revolving door may tempt some police officers to mete out a distorted version of "curbside justice" a la Rodney King. Frustrated at seeing criminals go free and getting rich off their crimes can lead to the temptation, to which a few cops succumb, to get rich off

*"Over the years, the justice system has had more and more technicalities imposed upon it that have nothing to do with the guilt or innocence of the accused, and which frequently turn a trial into an inquisition into the conduct of the police officer rather than the misconduct of the defendant."*
—Former Attorney General Edwin Meese

of *their* work, i.e., by taking a payoff for not busting a rich drug lord.

More commonly, however, frustration with the justice system results in burnout. Officers who feel that arresting dangerous suspects just doesn't produce results often stop trying. "I guess you'd call it the 'on-the-job retirement syndrome,' " says Steiner. "A burned out police officer basically gives up and just answers radio calls, and spends hours filling out reports." Wu refers to this syndrome as the "four reports a day formula."

What has happened to America's justice system? In the '60s and the early '70s, Americans virtually enshrined personal freedom. Mass demonstrations involving violence to people and the destruction of property became an everyday occurrence, but were considered expressions of free speech to be contained, rather than crimes to be punished. The free speech movement became a kind of on-going drug party. As the national preoccupation with self-gratification grew it took on increasingly bizarre forms. (Of course, varieties of self-expression considered "normal" today—obscene rap music, sacrilegious art, homosexual marriages—would have been viewed as outrageous even during the '60s and '70s.)

During that period of "personal freedom" mania, the Warren Court, controlled by a liberal majority, rendered a series of opinions which inserted into the laws of criminal procedure restrictions on police behavior that had never even been considered throughout America's history. For instance, the birth of the "exclusionary rule" meant that evidence could not be used in prosecuting a suspect unless it was seized in exactly the right way—and "the right way" seemed to change from case to case. "The rights of the accused," says Meese, "must be protected, but in a way that doesn't defy common sense, and which provides for getting all the truth in front of the jury."

The Supreme Court does not exist in a vacuum. Although the Warren Court's decisions dealt with technical areas of criminal procedure, they reflected, at the highest level of America's judiciary, the prevailing attitude of the times: the elevation of personal liberty over every other consideration.

The result? "Over the years," says Meese, "the justice system has had more and more technicalities imposed upon it that have nothing to do with the guilt or innocence of the accused, and which frequently turn a trial into an inquisition into the conduct of the police officer rather than the misconduct of the defendant. This disturbs police officers, who have an innate sense of fairness and justice, which is often violated."

Don Baldwin, Executive director of the National Law Enforcement Council, agrees: "Today, there is the likelihood that somebody can commit a heinous crime and get off almost scot-free because there is a violation under the exclusionary rule. You go out and risk your life to bring a criminal in, and a shrewd lawyer points out that you overstepped the bounds of proper procedure in some small way."

What would police like to see in the way of system reform? According to Baldwin, whose organization serves as an umbrella for 14 law enforcement organizations with a combined membership of 450,000 officers: "The thing that would help law enforcement the most is to get some laws on the books that have teeth in them, that would mandate that if a person commits a crime, that they have to pay for it. If the sentence says ten years, they get ten years."

Besides mandatory sentencing and modification of the exclusionary rule, says Baldwin, many police would also like to see speedier court action, more jails and prisons, the death penalty, and *habeas corpus* reform—limiting the number of times a convicted felon can appeal his case, since his opportunities currently are virtually unlimited.

## REPEATING THE VIETNAM MISTAKE

Struggling against a web of criminal brutality, personal tragedy, racial politics, and a lenient judicial system, America's police force today finds itself in a war zone. But not just any war zone. As in the Vietnam War—a conflict in which America's young soldiers fought as bravely as in any war before or since, but who were not allowed to win—today's police, particularly in the nation's troubled inner cities, increasingly feel as though they, too, are fighting a war that they are not being allowed to win.

Whereas U.S. troops in Vietnam were hamstrung by confused an indecisive administration policies, today's domestic troops find their efforts being sabotaged by a judicial system overly concerned with the rights of the accused at the expense of the victim. In Vietnam, isolated reports of atrocities, such as at My Lai, led to the grossly unjust spectacle of American anti-war demonstrators condemning all U.S. soldiers. Today, isolated reports of police brutality are resulting in much the same thing: mass condemnation of America's police force.

Without the support of the public, a nation's soldiers simply cannot win the war they have been sent off to fight. As General Schwarzkopf said at the stunning conclusion of the gulf ground war: If U.S. troops had to fight using Iraq's inferior weapons, and Iraq had fought us using our superior weapons, the U.S. still would have won—because our troops had great morale, and theirs didn't. Without the strong support of the public and the backing of the justice system, America's police are in danger of losing the war they have been asked to fight.

## THE HIGH COST OF POLICE STRESS

The stress of being a soldier in a no-win war results in many casualties among our troops:

• **23 percent of police officers are alcoholics.** In one study of 2,300 police officers, it was found that 23 percent had serious alcohol problems. One contributing problem is that drinking is very much a part of the police subculture.

• **28 percent are at high risk for heart attacks.** 15 percent of police have cholesterol levels twice the level required to render them coronary heart disease risks.

• **36 percent have serious health problems.** More than thirty-five physiological and many other psychological problems have been attributed to job-related stress.

• **Divorce is a serious problem.** In the United States, police divorce rates have been found to be as high as 75 percent. The critical period for police marriages appears to be the first three years when the anxiety of "reality shock" is at peak for new officers.

• **Cops are prone to suicide.** Compared to workers in other occupations, police officers are particularly prone to killing themselves. Some believe that the police suicide rate is artificially low due to the tendency of departments to report any suicide that can possibly be viewed in another way as accidental. Most often, they list the cause as "heart attack."

## WHEN COPS CROSS THE THIN BLUE LINE

Given the nature of the job, it is understandable that police suffer greater physical and family problems than does the average person. While the police officer who turns his stress inward may end up with the kind of problems that add to these statistics, the individual who turns his frustration and rage outward can find himself taking unnecessary risks, isolating himself from friends (particularly friends who are not police), becoming increasingly callous, and even turning to extortion and other criminal behavior, as well as using unnecessary violence in dealing with citizens.

On the other hand, some individuals are attracted to police work in the first place simply because they are bullies looking for the opportunity to push other people around. These are the rotten apples of law enforcement. Stress management programs and system reform will not help them. They just need to be weeded out. But this is not easily done because of the code of silence among police. "There are so many good officers, but they all protect the worst officer. That's just the code," says Wu. "It's a shame."

Most policemen agree that brutality would not go on if the administration didn't approve it, or at least tolerate it. Decent cops who become brutal are overreacting to the stresses of their job—and that overreaction should be caught by supervisors before it becomes a problem. Unfortunately, many departments still do not have adequate stress training programs to help supervising officers find and diffuse overstressed officers. In addition, cops wrestle with their own macho image, says Ed Donovan, a retired 32-year veteran of the Boston Police Department and founder of the first organization to deal with cops under stress.

"What police have in common all over the world is that tough-guy image, the John Wayne syndrome," says Donovan. "That is what they die from."

To Donovan, the problem is simple: A cop who is stressed and has become a problem is ignored by his supervisors because they don't want to acknowledge there is a problem—it's bad PR to advertise that your cops are not well. Second, the cop takes refuge in his own macho image, which he believes he must maintain in order to do his job. These two factors, says Donovan, lead police, who are seldom adequately prepared to deal with stress anyway, to ignore it.

The department sometimes ignores it as well. Supervising officers have been notorious for transferring troubled officers out of one assignment into another precinct, just to get rid of the problem. But problems that are not addressed get worse—sometimes much worse.

## THE SERPICO SYNDROME

The most disturbing part of her police job, says Wu, was the occasional brutality on the part of certain cops. "Once, in the Mission Station, one particular officer who had a terrible temper brought in a handcuffed prisoner. I didn't see what started it, but he angered that officer who started beating this cuffed man. He pulled him out of the bookies room and brought him into the common room in front of all the officers, and continued to beat up on him.

"I couldn't take it," Wu remembers. "I just stood up and went over to the training officer and said, 'He can't do that in front of me because I have to do something about it. You make him stop because I'll report to you.' He went to the officer and pointed me out and said, 'Don't do it in front of her, because she's going to do something about it.' So they pushed him into the men's locker room and continued to beat him. The captain never looked up, and that was the end of it for that night—but not the end of it for me.

"The next time I worked, I was out on the street on a call, and called for a 1025, 'officer needs assistance.' My sergeant and someone else came. But as we were leaving, the sergeant said, 'You know, you called for a 1025. Sometimes you never get the backup when you need it.' I

knew immediately that was a warning, so I confronted my partner and said, 'Hey, I'm here for you, you're here for me or I assume you are, but if I needed help, and if this sergeant's telling me that I'm not going to get it, you'd better tell me right now, because I'm not going to work under those conditions.' "

Such incidents have always been an ugly part of the police world. The film "Serpico" portrayed the true story of New York City police officer Frank Serpico, who exposed the corruption that was rampant in that department during the 1960s. In retaliation for "ratting," Serpico was denied the crucial backup he needed during a drug raid—and was shot. He lived to testify and subsequently his department was cleaned up.

Unfortunately, the "code of silence" among police—the powerful taboo against "ratting" on a fellow officer who is crooked or brutal—makes it almost impossible to weed out the bad members. Feeling they have no other friends—the criminals, the justice system, the press, the politicians, and frequently the public all arrayed against them—police feel they have no other natural allies except each other. Like soldiers at war, who, during the heat of the battle find themselves fighting not for God, mother, country, or freedom, but for each other, so do cops protect one another fiercely, including the rotten ones. They are all cops, and cops don't rat on other cops.

"Cops stick together right or wrong because they get screwed all the time," says Alvarez. "If the standards were changed and things were done by the book, by the law, cops would not stick together when they are wrong. A good cop is not going to put up with an individual who violates the law or tarnishes everything he stands for when there is no need."

## SOLUTIONS

In the war between good and evil, there are casualties on the front lines. Cops are only human, made of the same mortal flesh and blood as the rest of us. The stresses can be overwhelming, and when they are, something has to break.

"Most policemen in this country—and I've been involved in numerous shootings, so I can tell you from personal experience—are crying on the inside," says Bill Arnado, who was a S.W.A.T. instructor for the Los Angeles Police Department until an injury forced him off the force in 1976. "They're torn up on the inside. They have that macho image on the outside, but if you could really look into a policeman, most of them are real emotional. They're very pro-American, but they're crying on the inside and they don't know how to let it out."

Policemen have got to learn to open up and show their emotions, says Arnado. It can be difficult. "If you shot somebody, it's hard to go home and tell your wife 'I just shot a person' or 'My partner was killed in front of me.' You can't take that home. So it builds up and pretty soon you explode. I almost exploded. I've been through it.

"Let's say the police officer responds to a robbery in progress. Maybe he gets into a fight, or a shooting, or an argument. Afterwards, he gets in his car and heads down the road. He pulls over a speeder, but he still hasn't come down from the stress level of the robbery—his heart is still pounding. The speeder just so much as says something wrong, and right away *boom*. Then the cop goes right out on another hot call. You have to walk in his shoes to understand what I'm trying to tell you. The stress is there. It's how he controls that stress, that's what counts."

Arnado, now a Sheriff of Josephine County, Oregon, echoes the voice of many in law enforcement that say there may indeed be a way out, a way to allow America's police to win the no-win war—not only against crime, but against the stress that is killing them.

"The first thing I do when I get a new employee," he says, "is to sit him down and tell him, 'Law enforcement is *not* the most important thing in your life.' The first, most important thing you have is faith in God, your family, and your community. . . . While you're on duty, give 110 percent, but once your tour of duty is up, when you hang up your gun and badge and get away from the job, go home and be with your family and loved ones."

The biggest danger a police officer has, says Arnado, is becoming just a police officer. "A lot of cops—especially young ones, the three-to-five year cops—think everybody's a dirtbag. But after they get a little more time on the job, they realize it's not true."

### THE RETURN OF THE PEACE OFFICER

"Police badly need to move into a new era," says Arnado. "They need to go into what is called Community Oriented Policing." Currently being employed in over 300 cities and towns nationwide—including Boston and San Francisco—Community Oriented Policing (COP) is essentially the resurrection of the traditional "beat cop" style of policing. "Since the '60s," says Arnado, who trains departments throughout the Northwest in COP principles, "policemen have mainly responded to radio calls." Whereas cops once knew their neighborhoods intimately, talked to its residents, engaged in social work, rounded up stray animals, and generally befriended the community, for the last three decades police work has been reduced to an endless stream of 911 calls—"You call, we haul," in police lingo. The cop sees only the worst side of the community and constantly reacts to trouble, instead of stopping it before it happens.

The COP approach: Many calls coming from one area may signal a root problem. If police and the community can solve that root problem, then there will be less need for law enforcement. Example: a broken window in a building encourages disrespect, and then more windows are broken by kids. Or a bar in a neighborhood may be a problem. When police focus on eliminating specific problems they tend to plug the leak in the boat, so to speak, rather than constantly bail out the boat without plugging the leak.

"This is an important thing," says former Attorney General Meese, "where police officers get out of their cars, become acquainted with the local population they serve, deal with people as human beings in a one-to-one relationship, obtain information from the public about community conditions, about criminal activity that's going on, about specific suspects—and then use this cooperation to do a better job of protecting the community."

Already, COP has paid handsome dividends in many communities throughout the nation. "Police who have

## Balancing the scales

The police and public alike have become cynical over a justice system that sentences Lawrence Singleton—a man who raped a 15-year-old girl, cut off her arms, and left her for dead—to 14 years, only to release him after eight. On the other extreme, evangelist Jim Baker received a 45-year sentence for fraud in a country where convicted murderers are sentenced to an average of 20 years.

As a stem in rectifying this imbalance, the Federal Sentencing Commission set up guidelines that went into effect on November 1, 1987. Before then, sentencing had been totally up to the discretion of individual judges. And whatever sentence *was* handed down wasn't real. The average convicted criminal served only one-third of the time imposed, at which time the parole commission would decide whether or not he was to be released.

Congress scrapped the system due to its obvious inequities. Now the sentences generated under the guidelines are so-called "real time sentences." Parole has been abolished in the Federal Courts; it is no longer available for anyone sentenced under these guidelines.

"I think the system is more fair now, especially to the defendants," says Paul Martin of the Federal Sentencing Commission. "It used to be that if one man robs a bank in South Carolina and another robs a bank in New York City, the first man could get 20 years and the second could get three." That kind of discrepancy "breeds disrespect for the law," says Martin. "Oftentimes it mattered more who the particular judge was than what particular crime a person had committed." Martin believes the new system will also benefit the victims of crime.

tried community policing have found that they can be a catalyst for developing neighborhoods," says Meese. This is important, he says, because "one of the reasons people have given up is there doesn't seem to be anybody in a position of authority who is going to take an interest in them."

In a rural community like Arnado's, Community Oriented Policing comes naturally. Officers live in the community they serve, they know its people and its problems, and COP just extends and enhances an on-going process. It is in the big cities of the nation that community policing offers the greatest challenges.

Looking at the nation's major cities, Ed Donovan is pessimistic. "With the layoffs of police, with the recession, with the lack of housing and the homeless and the drugs and AIDS and the lost youth of America, I only see more and more fear. I see television condoning violence. It's nothing for a kid to go to a movie and see someone kick somebody in the stomach or hit him over the head with a baseball bat and then laugh about it afterwards.

"If it gets any worse, we're going to have to put the National Guard in the streets of major cities. In 1991 we're already ahead of 1990's murder record, which is an all-time high."

Yet, through the gloom, Donovan sees a solution: "The public has to take a hand in this. It's not going to turn around by itself." Indeed, community involvement seems to be the wave of the future. According to the FBI, the 1990s will be the decade of greatly increased citizen participation in helping the police to enforce the laws and make America's communities livable again. But in some communities, such as Macon, Georgia, the future is now.

## THE CIVIL RESPONSIBILITY MOVEMENT

"No one could have disliked law enforcement [more] than I did," admits Rev. Charles Jones, a Macon, Georgia, Baptist minister. "I constantly blamed the police for the problems in the community." In Jones's neighborhood of Bellevue, residents were close to despair. The combined effect of gangs and drugs had devastated the area and created a siege mentality.

Macon Police Chief Jim Brooks was just as frustrated. "We used every kind of police technique you can imagine and still we didn't accomplish anything over there."

Rev. Jones confronted Chief Brooks at every opportunity, demanding that he do more to clean up the drug- and crime-infested community. "He wore me out," remembers Brooks, referring to Jones's angry calls for everything from more cops and patrol cars to a whole new police precinct in Bellevue. Jones recalls: "I took busloads of people down there to 'give them hell'—but that wasn't the answer."

Jones laughs about it now. So does Brooks. They discovered a secret weapon: "The answer," says Jones, "was the community standing up, *with* the police, and saying 'we've had enough!' "

Who gave them the answer? A man named Herman Wrice from a tough Philadelphia neighborhood called Mantua. Wrice and his group, *Mantua Against Drugs*, spend their time organizing citizens who are sick of seeing their children die—either suddenly on the streets or slowly in a drugged haze of lost hope and broken dreams. "When a city or a small town can find no resources to meet this epidemic, then they go back to basics," says Glenn McCurdy, an early member of MAD. The "basics" in this case is *citizen action*.

## CONFRONTING THE PROBLEM

Wrice's method is simple confrontation on a mass scale. His method is the essence of elegant simplicity: He and concerned citizens in the community walk through crime-infested neighborhoods and order the drug dealers out. Amazingly, it works. "The drug dealer is someone who has never had to deal with real confrontation in his life," says Wrice. But the drug dealers weren't the only ones afraid. After years of living under a siege mentality, the citizens themselves weren't too eager for confrontation. "First time out people are afraid," Wrice admits. "They are under the impression that these dealers are invincible." Wrice corrects that impression as fast as he can. "I always take the worst corner first," he chuckles. His reasoning is simple—after that it can only get easier, and the citizens know it.

Although his intent is to intimidate the criminal through direct action, Wrice has no interest in vigilantism. Involving law enforcement is the key to the whole idea. When he started *Mantua Against Drugs*, Wrice did it with full police involvement as members, and within the first three weeks, the group had closed down 14 crack houses. With patrol cars parked nearby, citizens chanting "Up with hope—Down with dope" would approach the crack houses and surround them using bullhorns to scold the dealers inside.

"The drug dealers get moving for one simple reason," says Wrice. "Someone is putting the light on them." Chief Brooks is more specific: "The single greatest weapon that we have used against them to date is the video camera. I guess you could take an Uzi out there but I don't think you'd move them any faster," he jokes. Of course, the crowd itself makes a big impression, and although the dealers wave guns and make threats, they eventually take off into the night.

Wrice and his movement don't threaten easily. He has obvious contempt for the dealers who he complains are portrayed falsely on TV as tough guys. "They remind me of Saddam Hussein—if you go after them, they'll surrender. You can't go believing that 'Republican Guard' line—remember that?—how deep they were dug in, and how many body bags we were going to need. You can't believe that fear stuff. The enemy came at us through psychology, not through warfare. We gave Iraq the psychological

# Building shattered lives

When people have their backs to the wall, who do they call? A cop. When a cop has his back to the wall, who does he call? When Boston patrolman Ed Donovan was in trouble, the answer was a resounding "nobody." A cop at age 26, a full-fledged alcoholic by 29, Donovan found himself outside Boston's Fenway Park one steamy summer day in 1969 pushing the barrel of his .38-caliber service revolver into his mouth, panicked, depressed, ready to end his life.

As a police photographer Donovan had spent 10 years looking through a camera lens at an endless stream of victims of brutal murders, rapes, car accidents, and violent assaults. He coped with the constant images of carnage by attending "choir practice" (police jargon for drinking with their buddies) and popping anti-depressants, never once daring to face the grim reality that his life was falling apart.

To this day Donovan doesn't know what stopped him from pulling the trigger. But the near-suicide marked the turning point in his shattered life. From that moment forward, Donovan—almost without realizing it—began devoting his life to helping stressed-out cops.

With the encouragement of some tough cop friends, Donovan checked himself into a detox center in the summer of 1970, joined Alcoholics Anonymous after sobering up, and started putting his life back together. Fellow cops who had witnessed the dramatic change in Donovan began coming to him for help with their own problems. By 1972 he had teamed up with fellow Boston policeman Joe Ravino to form what would become, in 1974, the Boston Police Stress Program. The success of that program prompted Donovan to establish the International Law Enforcement Stress Association (ILESA), located in Matapan, Massachusetts, in 1978.

Donovan's near 20-year odyssey into the world of police stress management has been the focus of a 1986 book, *The Shattered Badge*, by Canadian Bill Klankewitt, and a soon-to-be-aired TV movie starring David Soul (of "Starsky and Hutch" fame).

Whether he's running weekly meetings of the Boston stress program, lecturing on police stress around the world, or talking to a single, distressed cop, Donovan's message is the same: When you're in trouble, get out from behind your badge.

The job of police officer comes complete with a macho image, he explains, a "tough guys don't cry" syndrome that teaches cops to hold in their feelings—on and off the job—at any cost. "The enemy within, the silent killer, is cops suppressing their feelings and thinking they can handle it. Instead, it handles them," he says.

Treating stressed-out law enforcement officers has its hitches, as Donovan discovered early on. Because police departments had no way of treating overstressed officers, most dealt with the problem simply by ignoring it. For their part, troubled officers were reluctant to admit problems for fear they would lose their jobs. This combination of factors made cops unwilling to open up to anyone outside of the police's tightly knit rank and file. But they listen to the likes of Donovan—a tough, non-nonsense cop like themselves who had been in their shoes—and survived.

While there has been a gradual change in police work during Donovan's 32-year career—there is more violence and less respect for police officers today, he comments—the stress has always been there. That's why Donovan likes to counsel young police academy recruits; it gives him a chance to stop problems before they start. "Prevention is the key," he explains. "We can't just keep patching up cops and putting them back on the streets."

Donovan's persistence in this field is beginning to pay off. Stress management courses are becoming an integral part of police training. "Police academies are letting recruits know beforehand that they are human," he says, "that when they hurt they have a place to go."

One place troubled officers go is Seafield 911, a Davie, Florida treatment center exclusively for chemically dependent and stressed-out cops. Begun in 1989, a brainchild of Donovan and George Benedict, owner of Seafield Treatment Centers, Seafield 911 has helped hundreds of cops overcome their alcohol and drug dependencies. Seafield is different from many treatment centers in that it is staffed mostly by former law enforcement professionals—men and women who can readily relate to the unique stresses that tip cops over the edge.

Despite the stress of police work, Donovan says there is no shortage of young men and women wanting to become cops. Their reasons are still altruistic, he says; they want to make a difference in society. Donovan sees his role as injecting a bit of cool reality into their sometimes rosy expectations, giving recruits a good, hard look at what it really takes. And if the going gets tough, thanks to Donovan's tireless efforts, there's a safety net—a place to fall back and regroup.

Retired for 2 years now, Donovan has not slowed down. His latest endeavor is to revive *Police Stress* magazine, ILESA's house publication. Lack of funds prompted him to suspend publication several years ago, even though the demand for it has remained high. If he can line up the funding, Donovan intends to market the new *Police Stress* magazine to a huge readership of law enforcement personnel around the world.

The need to get the message to cops is still great, says Donovan. "There are still many cops who have the Neanderthal attitude that 'we don't have problems,' that 'we don't air our troubles to anybody,' " he says. "As long as they have that attitude, cops are going to get sicker and sicker."

Donovan won't rest until that attitude is wiped out. "I'm a survivor. "I'm the guy who had the gun in my mouth cocked many times," he says. "When I think about it, I just thank God I didn't die."

attitude that they were going to win. 'It's going to be another Vietnam!' we said. The heck with that!'"

## UP WITH HOPE

A former coach, Boy Scout leader, and father of 7, Herman Wrice has begun what could fairly be called a *civil responsibility movement*. Although his effort to get citizens to take back the streets began locally, it is growing into an impressive national campaign dedicated to training and inspiring citizens and local law enforcement officials to join together to throw the drug dealers out.

It's easy to see why President Bush has referred to Wrice as "the John Wayne of Philadelphia," but John Wayne walked alone and Wrice is very much a team player. "I've never seen a coming together between a law enforcement agency and a community like this," says Chief Brooks. These days the Chief is a true believer. "I can tell you about cold nights when there were 14 young black children inside a police van to stay warm with a white police officer demonstrating an in-car computer. I can tell you about a 76-year-old woman who came to me and said, 'Chief, I haven't been out of my house after dark in 7 years, and it's a wonderful feeling to be able to do it now.'" Bellevue's crime rate is substantially down since the program started last November.

Brooks's stories aren't just about civilians. He tells of a 17-year police veteran who was so burnt out from the hopeless crime situation that he was ready to quit the department. The Wrice method turned him around. "The second or third night we were out," says Brooks, almost incredulous, "he was off duty, but he and his family were there, marching in the streets. It's that powerful."

Today, police from many towns and cities are asking Herman Wrice to give them training in his methods. As a result, from Akron to Savannah to St. Louis to Chicago, citizens and police are reaching out to each other as friends. "You don't need a national guard. You don't need 50 police officers," says Reverend Jones, "All you need is just a few folks in the streets telling those drug dealers they've got to go." Says Brooks, looking back on the experience of community and cops standing by each other. "It's more grand than anything that I'm capable of telling you about."

## EPILOGUE

Why do well-armed criminals leave communities where cops and housewives march around chanting slogans and shouting at them through bullhorns? What is the magic that melts the invincible drug dealer?

They are literally shamed out. Such demonstrations of solidarity between the community and the police breathe conscience back into the nation's communities. Run-down neighborhoods where nobody cares are irresistibly inviting to the criminal element, which regards broken windows and the like as engraved invitations to move in. Dope dealers simply feel comfortable in a community that doesn't care. But when people do care, and care courageously, the dealer feels unbearable discomfort and shame, and runs off into the night.

Why does fixing that broken window prevent crime and delinquency in a neighborhood? It is a clear signal of that community's caring and vigilance. Like the human body, where an open wound can result in infection, neighborhoods must also clean up their wounds to keep out the infection of crime. The cooperation of police and community produces a profound change of chemistry in a community's body politic. It reaffirms the value of the police, who are no longer looked upon as hired guns, but as true representatives of the people.

For what they do, for what we pay them, police are the best employee value there is. And because cops are under such stress, Americans would do well to exercise a little compassion toward them. Cops have a difficult job to do, and that job becomes nearly impossible without the support of both the court system and the public. Lacking such support, there will be no incentive for good people to go into law enforcement, and they will gradually dropout. The only incentive left will be for people to work with unworkable options—the perfect excuse for abusing power, taking bribes, and being brutal.

After all, if it's a no-win game, why play by the rules? If there's no way out and no options, why even try?

We expect our police not only to protect us from the criminal underworld, but increasingly to solve every problem of our own making, from child abuse and domestic fights to drunk driving accidents and drug addiction. We created the problems; they have to deal with the results—and they are the ones that end up with suicide, alcoholism, and divorce rates doubles those of the rest of the population.

It does not have to be so. The individual citizen holds the key: First support your police then get involved in helping them, not blaming them.

Like troops in a foreign land, unless they are supported and loved by those on the home front whom they are defending, police all the more easily become demoralized, and fall to corruption and cynicism. They are soldiers, and just as some of our soldiers in Vietnam found it easier to take dope and break the rules when they heard reports that many Americans did not support their efforts, so are America's police also made more vulnerable to temptation through our abuse of them. Public support provides the stability and faith that these men and women need in order to fight the good fight for the rest of us.

# Are Women Better Cops?

## In some important ways, yes, especially as the job evolves. Cool, calm and communicative, they help put a lid on violence before it erupts.

**JEANNE MC DOWELL** LOS ANGELES

Among the residents, merchants and criminals of Venice, Calif., officer Kelly Shea is as well known as the neighborhood gang leaders. The blond mane neatly tied back, slender figure and pink lipstick violate the stereotype of guardian of law and order; but Shea, 32, has managed to win the respect of street thugs who usually answer more readily to the slam of a cop's billy club. She speaks softly, raising her voice only as needed. While her record of arrests during her 10 years on patrol is comparable to those of the men in her division, she has been involved in only two street fights, a small number by any cop's standard. Faced with hulking, 6-ft. 2-in. suspects, she admits that her physical strength cannot match theirs. "Coming across aggressively doesn't work with gang members," says Shea. "If that first encounter is direct, knowledgeable and made with authority, they respond. It takes a few more words, but it works."

Hers is a far cry from the in-your-face style that has been the hallmark of mostly male police forces for years. But while women constitute only 9% of the nation's 523,262 police officers, they are bringing a distinctly different, and valuable, set of skills to the streets and the station house that may change the way the police are perceived in the community. Only on television is police work largely about high-speed heroics and gunfights in alleys. Experts estimate that 90% of an officer's day involves talking to citizens, doing paperwork and handling public relations. Many cops retire after sterling careers never having drawn their gun.

As the job description expands beyond crime fighting into community service, the growing presence of women may help burnish the tarnished image of police officers, improve community relations and foster a more flexible, and less violent, approach to keeping the peace. "Policing today requires considerable intelligence, communication, compassion and diplomacy," says Houston police chief Elizabeth Wat-

son, the only female in the nation to head a major metropolitan force. "Women tend to rely more on intellectual than physical prowess. From that standpoint, policing is a natural match for them."

Such traits take on new value in police departments that have come under fire for the brutal treatment of suspects in their custody. The videotaped beating of motorist Rodney King by four Los Angeles cops last year threw a spotlight on the use of excessive force by police. The number of reports continues to remain high across the country after the furor that followed that attack. Female officers have been conspicuously absent from these charges: the independent Christopher commission, which investigated the L.A.P.D. in the aftermath of the King beating, found that the 120 officers with the most use-of-force reports were all men. Civilian complaints against women are also consistently lower. In San Francisco, for example, female officers account for only 5% of complaints although they make up 10% of the 1,839-person force. "And when you see a reference to a female," says Eileen Luna, former chief investigator for the San Francisco citizen review board, "it's often the positive effect she has had in taking control in a different way from male officers."

Though much of the evidence is anecdotal, experts in policing say the verbal skills many women officers possess often have a calming effect that defuses potentially explosive situations. "As a rule, they **tend to be much more likely to go in and talk rather than try to get control in a way that makes everyone defensive," says Joanne Belknap, an associate professor of criminal justice at the University of Cincinnati. Women cops, she has found, perceive themselves as peacekeepers and negotiators. "We're like pacifiers in these situations," says Lieut. Helen DeWitte, a 21-year veteran of the Chicago force who was the first woman in the department to be shot in the line of duty. Having women partners for 14 years taught San Francisco sergeant Tim Foley to use a softer touch with suspects,** instead of always opening with a shove. "It's nonthreatening and disarming," he says, "and in the long run, it is easier than struggling."

Such a measured style is especially effective in handling rape and domestic-violence calls, in which the victims are usually women. In 1985 a study of police officers' treatment of spousal-abuse cases by two University of Detroit professors concluded that female officers show more empathy and commitment to resolving these conflicts. While generalizations invite unfair stereotyping, male officers often tend not to take these calls as seriously, despite improved training and arrest policies in almost half of all states. "Men tend to come on with a stronger approach to quiet a recalcitrant male suspect," notes Baltimore County police chief Cornelius Behan, whose 1,580-member force includes 143 women. "It gets his macho up, and he wants to take on the cop."

Despite the research, the notion of "female" and "male" policing styles remains a controversial one. Individual temperament is more important than gender in the way cops perform, argues Edwin Delattre, author of *Character and Cops: Ethics in Policing*. Other experts contend that aggressiveness among officers is more a measure of a department's philosophy and the tone set by its top managers. "When cops are trained to think of themselves as fighters in a war against crime, they come to view the public as the enemy," observes James Fyfe, a criminal-justice professor at The American University.

Some female officers have qualms as well about highlighting gender-based differences in police work, especially women who have struggled for years to achieve equity in mostly male departments. The women fear that emphasizing their "people skills" will reinforce the charge that they don't have the heft or toughness to handle a crisis on the street. But while women generally lack upper-body strength, studies consistently show that in situations in which force is needed, they perform as effectively as their male counterparts by using alternatives, such as karate, twist locks or a baton instead of their fists.

Yet the harassment that persists in many precinct houses tempts female cops to try to blend in and be one of the boys. All too often that means enduring the lewd jokes transmitted over police-car radios and the sexist remarks in the halls. In most places it means wearing an uncomfortable uniform designed for a man, including bulletproof vests that have not been adapted to women's figures. The atmosphere is made worse because about 3% of supervisors over the rank of sergeant are women, in part owing to lack of seniority. Milwaukee police officer Kay Hanna remembers being reprimanded for going to the bathroom while on duty. Chicago Lieut. DeWitte found condoms and nude centerfolds in her mailbox when she started working patrol.

Women cops who have fought discrimination in court have fared well. Los Angeles officer Fanchon Blake settled a memorable lawsuit in 1980 that opened up the ranks above sergeant to women. Last May, New York City detective Kathleen Burke won a settlement of $85,000 and a public promotion to detective first-grade. In her suit she had alleged that her supervisor's demeaning comments about her performance and his unwillingness to give her more responsible assignments impeded her professional progress. He denied the charges. But many women still fear that complaining about such treatment carries its own risks. Beverly Harvard, deputy chief of administrative services in Atlanta, says a female officer would have to wonder "whether she would get a quick response to a call for backup later on."

Resistance toward women cops stems in part from the fact that they are still rela-

tive newcomers to the beat. In the years after 1910, when a Los Angeles social worker named Alice Stebbins Wells became the country's first full-fledged female police officer, women served mostly as radio dispatchers, matrons, and social

## "Policing requires intelligence, communication, compassion and diplomacy."

Elizabeth Watson,
Houston police chief

workers for juveniles and female prison inmates. Not until 1968 did Indianapolis become the first force in the country to assign a woman to full-time field patrol. Since then, the numbers of women in policing have risen steadily, thanks largely to changes in federal antidiscrimination laws. Madison, Wis., boasts a 25% female force, the highest percentage of any department in the country.

Because female cops are still relatively few in number, a woman answering a police call often evokes a mixed response. Reno officer Judy Holloday recalls arriving at the scene of a crime and being asked, "Where's the real cop?" Detective Burke, who stands 5 ft. 2 in. and has weighed 100 lbs. for most of her 23 years on the force, says she made 2,000 felony arrests and was never handicapped by a lack of physical strength. Burke recalls subduing a 6-ft. 4-in., 240-lb. robbery suspect who was wildly ranting about Jesus

Christ. She pulled out her rosary beads and told him God had sent her to make the arrest. "You use whatever you got," she says. When it looks as though a cop may be overpowered, the appropriate response for any officer—male or female—is to call for backup. "It's foolish for a cop of either sex to start dukin' it out," says Susan Martin, author of *On the Move: The Status of Women in Policing.*

A growing emphasis on other skills, especially communication, comes from a movement in many police departments away from traditional law enforcement into a community-oriented role. In major cities such as New York, Houston and Kansas City, the mark of a good officer is no longer simply responding to distress calls but working in partnership with citizens and local merchants to head off crime and improve the quality of life in neighborhoods. In Madison, which has been transformed from a traditional, call-driven department into a community-oriented operation in the past 20 years, police chief David Couper says female officers have helped usher in a "kinder, gentler organization." Says Couper: "Police cooperation and a willingness to report domestic abuse and sexual assaults are all up. If a person is arrested, there is more of a feeling that he will be treated right instead of getting beat up in the elevator."

In Los Angeles the city council is expected to pass a resolution next month that will lead to a 43% female force by the year 2000, up from 13.4% now. "We have so much to gain by achieving gender balance, we'd be nuts not to do it," says councilman Zev Yaroslavsky. Ideally, the solution in all cities and towns is a healthy mix of male and female officers that reflects the constituency they serve and the changing demands of the job. —*With reporting by Georgia Pabst/Milwaukee*

## *Law Enforcement and the Preservation of Civil Rights*

# Preventing Hate Crime: New Tools, New Expectations for Law Enforcement

*Michael Lieberman, Associate Director and Counsel, Anti-Defamation League, Washington, D.C.*

The violence on the streets of Los Angeles following the announcement of the jury's verdict in the Rodney King police brutality case has riveted the nation's attention on race relations and raised concerns about our criminal justice system. The widely viewed, graphic videotape of the beating of Rodney King has adversely affected the reputations of good officers across the country and put police behavior in the spotlight. Citizens are now looking to law enforcement executives for assurances that what happened to King, as well as what happened on the streets of Los Angeles after the verdict, will not happen in their communities.

This increased public awareness and concern has both raised expectations for those government officials charged with confronting these difficult problems and served to underline the critical importance of initiatives to promote enhanced police-community cooperation. The national spotlight, however, also presents exciting new opportunities for law enforcement agencies to enhance relationships with community groups.

Police agencies with a proven track record on outreach to minority groups and community organizations—like the Boston Community Disorders Unit, the Neighborhood Relations Unit in Chicago and the Baltimore County Police Department—have offered compelling testimonies that effective responses to hate or bias crimes can deter crime and will advance police-community relations.

Forty-six states and the District of Columbia have now enacted statutes addressing criminal activity motivated by prejudice. Yet, even the toughest laws are irrelevant absent a commitment by law enforcement authorities to address each hate crime in the most effective manner possible. Too frequently, these acts are dismissed as "pranks" or ordinary cases of vandalism, assault or arson. The failure to recognize and effectively address this unique type of crime, however, could cause an isolated incident to fester and explode into widespread community tension.

## Counting Hate Crimes

In the past, both local and national responses to hate crimes have been severely hampered by the almost total lack of hard, comprehensive and comparative data concerning the number, location and types of hate crimes. To date, only 17 states and several municipal police departments have established systematic hate crime data collection procedures.

However, several private organizations also track hate crimes. The Anti-Defamation League (ADL) has conducted an annual audit of one type of hate crime—anti-Semitic incidents—reported to ADL regional offices around the country since 1979. The findings of the league's 1991 "Audit of Anti-Semitic Incidents" were particularly disturbing: 1,879 separate incidents of vandalism, violence or harassments. Not only was this the fifth straight year of increase, but these are the largest figures in the audit's history, representing an 11 percent increase over 1990.

Moreover, the league's analysis revealed an unhealthy tendency toward increasing confrontations with Jews as individuals—for the first time, there were more attacks on Jewish individuals than against their institutions and property.

Evidence suggests that documented attacks against individuals on the basis of their sexual orientation have increased as well. A recent National Gay and Lesbian Task Force report revealed an increase in attacks on gays and lesbians in each of five major metropolitan areas in 1991—a 31 percent increase overall from 1990.

State law enforcement authorities, too, generally have reported increases in the number of hate crimes reported to them. Of the states that have tabulated 1991 data, New Jersey, Massachusetts, Pennsylvania, Connecticut and Florida, as well as the Chicago Police Department, recorded varying degrees of increase, while Maryland, which enacted the first data collection law in 1980, recorded a slight decrease. Also noteworthy is the fact that there has been a steady increase in the number of agencies participating in the hate crime reporting system within these states.

This is a welcome trend. In supporting hate crime data collection initiatives across the country, ADL and other community groups have recognized an important byproduct of efforts to accurately report hate crime: training for police officers in how to identify and respond appropriately to this damaging criminal activity. For organizations representing minority groups that are frequently the targets of hate violence, the aggregate numbers are far less important that the response of law enforcement authorities to each incident.

## The Hate Crime Statistics Act

The federal Hate Crime Statistics Act (HCSA) is a powerful new mechanism with which to confront violent bigotry against individuals on the basis of their race, religion, sexual orientation or ethnicity—and provides government and law enforcement officials with a tangible, practical tool to enhance police-community relations. The act requires the Justice Department to acquire data on crimes that "manifest prejudice based on race, religion, sexual orientation or ethnicity" and to publish an annual summary of the findings.

During congressional consideration of the measure, the HCSA received crucial support from a number of prominent law enforcement organizations, including the IACP, the Fraternal Order of Police (FOP), the National Sheriffs' Association (NSA), the Police Foundation, the National Organization of Black Law Enforcement Executives (NOBLE) and the Police Executive Research Forum.

Attention has now turned to implementation of the act by the FBI, as well as by state and local law enforcement officials. From the beginning, the FBI's Uniform Crime Reporting (UCR) unit treated its hate crime data collection mandate as more than just another administrative task. The bureau has shaped its outreach and education efforts on the new act with substantial input from both law enforcement agencies and human relations organizations with prior experience in both collecting hate crime data and responding to hate violence. To its credit,

the FBI utilized existing resources in developing its excellent training manual and data collection guidelines. These two well-crafted and inclusive documents have now been distributed to over 16,000 law enforcement agencies nationwide. In testimony before the House Judiciary Subcommittee on Crime and Criminal Justice in mid-May, the bureau indicated that it considers hate crime data collection a permanent addition to the UCR program, even though its congressional mandate expires in 1994.

Recognizing that the credibility and usefulness of this data will depend on the quality of the reports, the FBI has arranged training seminars on how to identify, report and respond to hate crimes for state and local law enforcement authorities. These programs have featured presentations on the nature of prejudice,

the utility of the data and the impact of hate violence. ADL and other groups with expertise in analyzing and responding to hate crimes have participated in these sessions. The FBI has now provided training for officials from over 300 of the nation's largest cities. Resolutions urging comprehensive implementation of the act have been passed by the IACP, the NSA, the FOP, the U.S. Conference of Mayors and the International Association of Directors of Law Enforcement Standards and Training.

As efforts to implement the HCSA continue and expand, we will learn more about the perpetrators of these especially hurtful crimes—and how to prevent them. Moreover, comprehensive implementation of the HCSA should have a significant impact on treatment of hate

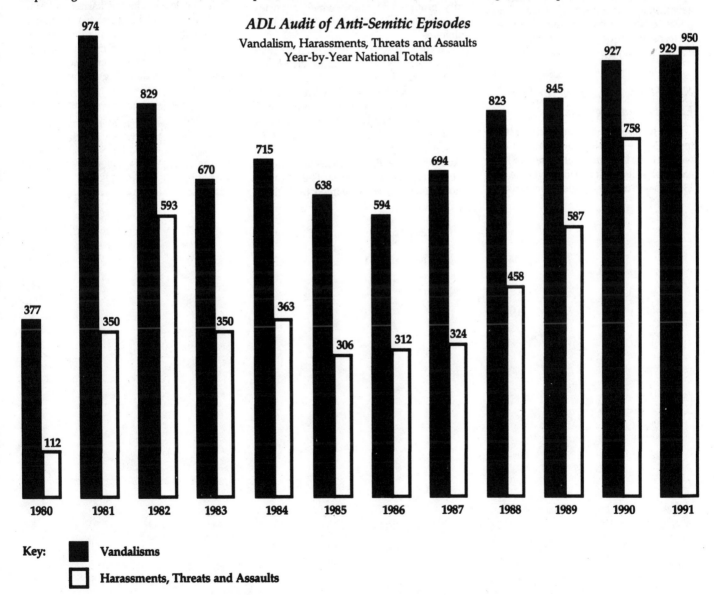

### ADL Audit of Anti-Semitic Episodes
Vandalism, Harassments, Threats and Assaults
Year-by-Year National Totals

Key:
■ Vandalisms
□ Harassments, Threats and Assaults

*Note: 1979 report recorded only "Anti-Semitic Incidents," without separate category of threats, harassments, etc. The 1979 total was 129.*

violence throughout the criminal justice system. This "trickle up" impact begins with the responding officer's initial hate crime designation and continues with an investigator's verification of the incident. Prosecutors, especially in states with enhanced penalty provisions for hate crimes, can be expected to press hard for convictions in these frequently well-publicized cases—with judges then under scrutiny to mete out deterrent sentences after convictions.

The establishment of specifically focused departmental policies and procedures for addressing hate violence is a proactive step that sends a strong message to victims and would-be perpetrators that the police take hate crimes seriously. In addition, tracking hate crimes can help police officials craft preventive strategies. By compiling statistics and charting the geographic distribution of these crimes, police officials may be able to discern patterns and anticipate an increase in racial tensions in a given jurisdiction.

### Next Steps: Resources for Law Enforcement Agencies

The Justice Department's first HCSA report is due out this summer. The data will likely be used in exactly the way ADL has utilized its audit findings over the past 13 years—to make statistical comparisons, chart trends and tailor appropriate responses. Like other data collected by the FBI and published in *Crime in the United States*, national hate crime figures will be made public on a jurisdiction-by-jurisdiction basis.

Before that time, police agencies would be well-served to establish an integrated hate crime response network, including liaisons to local prosecutors, city or county human rights commissions and private victim advocacy organizations. Local human relations groups, like ADL, can be helpful in a number of ways—including helping to analyze the data for both their own constituents and the media. This context can be especially useful in the case of aggressive, diligent agencies who are called upon to expain why their hate crime numbers are higher than neighboring, less attentive departments. Community groups will know which agencies have made serious efforts to confront hate violence.

Excellent resources now exist to help departments establish hate crime response procedures—or to help modify existing practices to comply with the FBI's UCR program. The previously mentioned FBI training manuals, model practices developed by NOBLE and the comprehensive model policy developed by IACP's National Policy Center last August are invaluable references. The center's model policy is accompanied by a thorough and thoughtful *Concepts and Issues Paper*.

ADL, too, has developed a number of hate crime training resources that are available to communities and law enforcement officials, including a 17-minute hate crime training video on the impact of hate crime and appropriate responses (produced in cooperation with the New Jersey Department of Law and Public Safety), a handbook of existing hate crime policies and procedures at both large and small police departments and a general human relations training program to examine the impact of discrimination, while promoting both better cultural awareness and increased appreciation for diversity.

The success of the HCSA will be determined at the local level—and it will be measured by the response of police officials to each criminal act motivated by prejudice. While bigotry, hatred and anti-Semitism cannot be legislated, tabulated or regulated out of existence, effective response to this type of criminal activity by public and police officials can play an essential role in deterring and preventing the violence.

*ADL's hate crimes training video and policies and procedures handbook are available from the ADL National Office, 823 United Nations Plaza, New York, NY 10017; 212/490-2525.*

# Cops Get Up-Close and Personal

Micah Morrison

**Summary:** Sgt. Joe Friday's impersonal style just won't cut it in today's crime-plagued cities. Some communities have found that police interaction is more effective in halting crime or stopping it before it happens. In cities such as New York, residents and police are working together to regain order and safety on the streets.

He has become an American icon, a direct descendant of the stranger who rides in to clean up the town in scores of classic Westerns and kissing cousin to the larger-than-life cops in the *Lethal Weapon* movies. He is the cool, professional, modern urban cop, Sgt. Joe Friday at the door, asking for "just the facts, ma'am." In the popular mind and the popular culture, he is that vaguely menacing figure behind the mirror sunglasses, aloof and austere, yet ready to break a few heads to keep order.

However, the public belief that order is not being kept is growing increasingly firm. Despite statistical signs that crime has leveled off and even dropped in some areas, the public perception in American cities is exactly the opposite: Crime is skyrocketing, the streets are becoming ever more dangerous, and the contemporary cop is at best hamstrung and overwhelmed, at worst criminally brutal. Now when the stranger rides through town, he leaves Rodney King and the Los Angeles riots in his wake.

But in some parts of America a movement is under way to dramatically reshape the roles of both police officers and the communities they serve. It is being led by a handful of police chiefs, criminal justice experts and community activists such as Felice Kirby.

"It shouldn't take an L.A. riot to show that policing in America is broken," says Kirby, a community organizer in the Williamsburg section of Brooklyn and director of the Neighborhood Anti-Crime Center of the Citizens Committee for New York City. "Taxpayers, the funders of police services, are terribly dissatisfied. Here in New York, we're working on a radical shift in traditional police-community relationships."

"Part of what we're talking about," explains George Kelling, professor of criminal justice at Northeastern University and consultant to many police departments and unions, "is burying the Sergeant Friday mentality. Think of what Joe Friday really meant: Here's this cool, remote figure who comes to the door and greets a terribly upset woman with 'just the facts, ma'am, just the facts.' His definition of responsibility is to get the information and make the arrest. He shows no concern about dealing with the conditions that gave rise to the crime, minimizing the psychological damage to the woman or restoring her to functioning."

The new model of policing would replace the Sgt. Fridays — the "remote-stranger professionals," in the jargon of criminology — with the friendly faces of neighborhood cops. "Officers who are active in the community have a stake in the community and are there to assist the community in defending itself," says Kelling.

In the words of New York City Police Commissioner Lee Brown, the most prominent police administrator backing the new model, "the beat cop is coming back."

The catchall buzzword for the new model is "community policing," and according to its proponents it is a lot more than simply putting cops back on the block. "Community policing," says Kelling, "is essentially a strategy of policing that emphasizes collaboration with citizens in the identification of neighborhood problems and the resolution of those problems."

Kirby says, "What community policing does is put an officer out among the people he's supposed to be serving and have him ask: 'What do *you* care about, how can *you* help me solve the problem?' This is part of what we mean by a radical break with traditional relationships. No longer does the officer say, 'Tell me what I can do for you.' Instead he says, 'Tell me what you want us to do together.' "

And no longer does the community sit back passively, asking, "What have you done for me lately?" Says Kirby: "In the community, it creates among the citizens a mentality of being a thoughtful participant in, rather than a passive receptacle of, police services."

Well, maybe.

Critics of community policing say that friendly beat officers addressing the concerns of the citizenry are fine, but the idea that this is some magic-bullet solution for serious crime — murders, rapes, assaults, big-time drug dealing and a rising tide of violence fueled by crack cocaine — is laughable to them.

One of the most prominent critics is the former chief of the Los Angeles Police Department, Daryl Gates. In his recently published autobiography, *Chief*, he writes that "too many people mistake community policing as a cure-all for crime. It is not."

The LAPD is widely viewed as the epitome of the remote-stranger, war-on-crime, SWAT team model of professional policing. In fact, it was Gates who pioneered the Special Weapons and Tactics team model.

Gates's view commands great sympathy in the closed world of policing. He writes that with drugs and high-powered weapons plaguing the streets of the inner cities, "being tough — no, being hard as granite" is what keeps a cop alive.

He characterizes community policing as "a bunch of cops grinning at people and patting kids on the head." Gates thinks he has seen the community policing future and it doesn't work.

This is also the view from Houston. In February, the new mayor, Bob Lanier, fired Police Chief Elizabeth Watson partly because of controversy over the community policing policy — "a policy in which," the *Houston Post* tartly observed, "police spend a lot of time interacting with a neighborhood rather than catching crooks."

So what, exactly, is community policing? Cynics would call it a feel-good term, rhetoric, window-dressing for police chiefs seeking to appease critics. Indeed, no two advocates agree on all the details of community policing, and the term has been promiscuously invoked in public policy discussions. This is one reason that it has been viewed by many police departments as suspiciously squishy, more of an academic fad than a serious strategy.

"Most everywhere you go and ask people how they like community policing, they say they like it, even though they're not quite clear what it means," says Thomas Reppetto, a former Chicago policeman and president of the Citizens Crime Commission of New York City. "To some people, it simply means more cops. They like that. To others it means not only more cops, but more neighborhood-oriented cops. We're still in the process of learning a great deal about community policing, however, and I don't think there will emerge one exact model that you can stamp on every American city."

Most experts agree that one important element of community policing is more neighborhood cops. Yet the key to understanding the community policing concept seems to lie not with the police, but with looking at crime in a different way.

The advocates of community policing, by and large, downplay statistical measures of crime and put a premium on community perceptions: Disorderly conditions in a neighborhood may or may not show up in crime reports and numbers of arrests, but they undermine the community's sense of confidence and hasten its decay. In other words, disorder disrupts civil norms.

Since the 1960s, writes Kelling in the spring edition of *NY: The City Journal*, "research has confirmed that crime, as well as fear of crime, is closely associated with disorder. Disorder includes petty crime and inappropriate behavior such as public drunkenness, panhandling, and loitering; its physical manifestations include graffiti, abandoned cars, broken windows, and abandoned buildings."

For most people, he writes, the crime problem "comes down to the fear they endure as a consequence of disorder — the well-founded belief that in disorderly places society has ceded control to those who are on the margin or outside the law, and therefore anything might happen in those places. . . . Fighting disorder, by solving the problems that cause it, is clearly one of the best ways to fight serious crimes, reduce fear, and give citizens what they actually want from the police force."

"When you go out to neighborhoods and start talking to people," Kelling adds in an interview, "it is inevitable that although they are concerned about serious crime, the primary thing they are concerned about is what [political scientist] James Q. Wilson and I called [in a widely circulated article in the *Atlantic*] the 'broken windows syndrome.' That is, citizens are concerned about disorder — the abandoned buildings with broken windows, the youths drinking and doing drugs in the parks, the inability to use the parks because of boisterous gangs, low-level drug dealing on the corners, the deinstitutionalized mentally ill homeless, streets darkened by broken streetlamps, prostitutes rampant in the area, cars speeding by. The things that bother citizens most are the things they experience. And what most citizens experience are disorderly conditions, which often are precursors of crime."

Such disorder does not show up on the statistical crime indexes that the media and politicians focus on and that therefore drive police policy. In bureaucratic terms, disorder is unimportant; police officers do not advance through the ranks by attacking the conditions or working to solve the problems caused by disorder.

"Suppose," says Kelling, "an officer comes across a cabbie and a client arguing over a fare. Now, most good cops will step in and resolve the conflict. If the officer stands back and lets them get into a brawl, however, the officer can go in and arrest them. The interesting thing is, the intervention to resolve the conflict wouldn't show up on any crime index, but the arrest would. Statistically, the arrest would be a 'good thing,' but in reality it would be a sign of the officer's negligence in resolving the conflict."

Kelling rejects the idea that community policing is a "softer" form of policing or essentially a public relations effort. "In fact," he says, "community policing is very aggressive and has the potential for being much more intrusive in community life than the current model, because you're not waiting for things to happen. Instead, you're trying to identify problems that are going to lead to continual criminal activity or new criminal activity."

As an example of aggressive community policing, Kelling points to rowdy neighborhood bars known for late-night sidewalk brawls and frequented by low-level drug dealers. "Why wait to be called to that bar night after night?" he asks. "An effective community policing program — a program with strong support from the community — would give a police officer the political and moral and social authority to go knock on the door and say, 'Excuse me, we know you're having problems here. Maybe it's in your own interest as well as your neighbors' to keep the brawlers sober and the drug dealers away. Maybe there's something we can work out together.'"

Another example would be household disputes. "Say a husband and wife have been fighting and an officer has gotten five or six calls to a household. Well, you know you're going to be back there," says Kelling, "but instead of waiting for the call and going back when they're drunk and angry and fighting, why not go by early and knock on the door and say, 'Hey, you're hurting each other and it's going to get worse if you don't get some help. Can we refer you to a social service agency or a priest or a rabbi?'"

Community policing techniques, Kelling further argues, are appropriate for more serious crimes as well. "Once one starts analyzing who does what to whom, one finds that to the extent people do experience serious crime — especially assault and rape and murder — often the crime is committed by someone they know, and often know quite intimately," Kelling says. "The thing that people fear most about crime — and police institutions are built around responding to that fear — is the predatory stranger. Yet when one breaks down serious crimes, 'the predatory stranger' often turns out to be a date, an uncle, a husband, an acquaintance. So we have police departments that are oriented around predatory stranger crimes on the street, when as a matter of fact a good share of these crimes involve some form of community problems or family breakdown."

He has called for rethinking both the nature of the crime problem and the role of the police in crime control. Rethinking the crime problem means a shift—significant but not absolute—away from the predatory stranger strategies and crime indexes and to-

ward notions of what constitutes disorder and how it can be contained and reversed before it leads to serious crime.

Rethinking the role of the police includes abandoning traditional notions of what it means to fight crime. Says Kelling: "Notice how it seems to be aggressive policing to lie back and wait until something happens, then go in with the lights flashing and sirens screaming. As a matter of fact, that is relatively passive in comparison to the model of saying, 'Hey, we've been called here five times and we think you need some help.' [The latter] is much more aggressive, but not in the lights-and-siren style. It is a very, very intrusive style, too. But I think it is a level of intrusiveness that is being invited by neighborhoods."

To go by the fragmentary evidence trickling in from New York, community policing's high degree of intrusiveness is indeed being welcomed. The program has a tireless booster in Police Commissioner Brown, who once was chief of police in Houston. Brown is in the second year of a five-year plan to transform the institutions of the NYPD — a bureaucratic leviathan with a uniformed force of more than 29,000 — into a paradigm of community policing.

Brown's vision is set out in a cumbersome NYPD document, *Policing New York City in the 1990s: The Strategy for Community Policing.* In it, he gives his definition of community policing, calling it an "evolving strategy that alters the fundamental way in which police fight crime and respond to other problems in the community. It means having officers in neighborhoods work cooperatively with the people to address problems of crime, drugs, disorder, fear and other elements that have a disruptive influence on the quality of life in the city."

Even before Brown's 1990 arrival from Houston, which is in the process of gutting his ambitious strategy there, a small-scale community policing program was reaping benefits in New York. The C-POP, or Community Patrol Officer Program, started in 1985, is the acorn from which Brown hopes to grow an oak.

"C-POP," explains activist Kirby, "was an experiment in community policing at a unit level within the precinct houses. A small unit would be charged with the responsibility of walking a beat, identifying problems and participating in problem solving with the community. Lee Brown's vi-

sion recognizes that you can't conduct effective community policing unless the entire NYPD assumes responsibility for and ownership of this new style of policing."

In 1985, however, few people had heard of community policing — certainly not Marie Christopher. The mother of two had been burned out of her Harlem tenement and was homeless for seven months, leaving her children in the care of their grandmother. Finally she was accepted at the Pueblo Nuevo housing complex on Manhattan's Lower East Side.

Unfortunately, Pueblo Nuevo turned out to be a Felliniesque nightmare peopled with addicts in the hallways, prostitutes turning tricks in the stairwells and a bustling drug dealing operation — the magnet for the hookers and addicts — overseen by a wheelchair-bound hustler with a sawed-off shotgun under his lap quilt and goons at his side. After a year, Christopher decided she wasn't going to take it anymore. A housing official put her in touch with Felice Kirby, who put her in touch with Sgt. Mike Walsh, then head of the C-POP unit at the local 7th Precinct.

Christopher was not optimistic, to say the least, about getting cooperation from the police. But Walsh was no Joe Friday. With his support and aid from Kirby's center, Christopher began to organize the tenants of Pueblo Nuevo. They learned how to gather evidence to make a case that would not be thrown out of court. They provided police with detailed information on drug dealing activities. At the same time, Walsh's unit made daily sweeps of the building, disrupting the drug trade and driving customers and prostitutes away.

After a year of work, the careful community-police cooperation paid off. The drug dealers were busted and sent away to do hard time. Without drugs, the hookers and crack addicts departed. Life at Pueblo Nuevo started looking a whole lot better. "It's important to remember that half of community policing is community," says Kirby. "It's about changing community norms regarding what is acceptable and what isn't."

Kirby's activism in her own Williamsburg neighborhood has carried her on an unlikely odyssey. She is one of only a half dozen full-time community policing trainers in the country. Although Kirby had a background in community organization, having worked on tenant-landlord disputes and participated in a lengthy battle to save a local firehouse, her real introduction to community policing came from the prostitutes of Kent Avenue.

In 1984, with construction under way on a housing project in the Hasidic section of Williamsburg, the powerful Orthodox Jewish community had driven away prostitutes who had worked the previously neglected area. The hookers headed for Kent Avenue, a stretch of abandoned waterfront property on the north side of Williamsburg. Soon it was known as an easy-access and hassle-free area.

"Up to a hundred prostitutes a day were working the waterfront," Kirby recalls, "taking off their clothes, soliciting children, turning tricks in front of residential housing. Pimps, drugs and murders followed."

The socially conservative, working-class residents of the neighborhood were appalled. The community's neglect and apathy had sent a signal to pimps and prostitutes that it was all right to operate there, and standard police sweeps were netting few arrests and fewer convictions.

Kirby, already known to the community as an organizer, was approached for help. "The community was ready to help itself," she says. "For two weeks, we marched up and down the strip with cameras, pretending we were taking pictures of the johns and their license plates. If we found out who the johns were, we'd call their homes and ask females answering the phones if they knew what the guy was doing at a known sex trade location. We strung banners with warnings about hookers with AIDS. We would circle cars where girls were turning tricks and [we would] chant and harass."

They also met with the police. "At first," says Kirby, "the meetings were not pleasant. We'd yell and scream for action, and they'd tell us the legal barriers to effective prosecution — the girls carried no positive identification, it was difficult to prove repeat offenses and make jail time stick, it was difficult to gather evidence. The court system would bounce them with time served or a fine."

In what would turn out to be one of the key lessons of community policing, the concerned residents learned how to gather evidence, file complaints and make a court case stick. They worked with the police to develop an effective strategy.

"It wasn't good that the girls would get out with time served or a fine," Kirby says. "They'd be back on the street in no time. We told the police and the district attorney, 'This is not an appropriate strategy. The strategy should be strong enforcement, harassment and negative publicity for a concentrated period of time to convey the message that this type of activity will not be tolerated in this area.'"

In this case, with an effective community-police partnership, the results were dramatic. The community could do what the police could not do without raising cries of outrage from civil libertarians, and the police, in turn, could make "quality arrests" — ones that would not get thrown out of court.

But Kirby warns that such success does not come easy. "At the moment, there still isn't enough 'community' in community policing, not in New York or anywhere else in America."

Kirby finds an odd ally in this sentiment in L.A.'s Daryl Gates. For the community policing concept to work, Gates writes in his autobiography, "the neighborhood must be actively involved, and many people don't want to bother. They want to come home at night, know they can rest safely, walk the streets after dark and maybe say a friendly hello to the officer—but that's all the interaction with the police they want. Their attitude is: It's their job to stop crime—let them do it."

If community policing has a core tenet, it's that the attitudes of police and citizens must change. Changing attitudes is a big part of Kirby's job. Following the hooker skirmish on the waterfront, she was recruited by the Citizens Committee for New York City to train C-POP officers. She now conducts training sessions for cops and communities all over America.

"Due to the stress of the job, a lot of officers over time tend to look at the community as 'them versus us,'" Kirby says. "The community, in this view, is made up of victims, potential victims, informants, assailants and [jerks]. The community similarly develops a black-and-white perception of the police: as uncaring, or lazy, or corrupt or an occupying army."

With both police and community groups, Kirby works to break down stereotypes. The Citizens Committee also provides individuals and groups with nuts-and-bolts information about starting neighborhood organizations and helping police turn arrests into convictions in court.

In training police officers, says Kirby, "I spend time working with small groups, doing exercises and providing information that enhances their ability to see the community as a resource in preventing crime, solving tough crime problems and improving living conditions. We try to build interview, communication, community assessment and problem solving skills.

"Exercises are usually very interactive, involving some role-playing and some field-based work," Kirby adds. "All this, of course, is diametrically opposed to the standard military style of instruction, which approaches an officer as an empty glass to be filled up with precisely the knowledge the instructor wishes to convey."

But does an emphasis on community work and building problem solving skills adequately prepare officers for what they have to face on the streets? Or, as Gates believes, do cops have to be tough as nails to do the job?

"Frankly," says criminal justice expert Kelling, "one thing that is rarely communicated is the very high level of fear on the part of the police. And yes, they do encounter real depravity. But that's the problem: Police often only encounter the really bad, [the] subgroups of the community. So when you do reintroduce the police into neighborhood life, you're going to have to do that in close collaboration with citizens.

"People are going to have to patrol with police, introduce the police to good citizens of the neighborhood and get officers to know where and who the good citizens are, because a lot of officers are very, very scared," he continues. "Yet whenever officers have started working in the communities, they start getting a lot of satisfaction out of it. The problem with the remote-stranger model of policing is that cops don't get to know the good people of the community."

With its oblique suggestion that it might be soft on criminals by abandoning the war-on-crime mentality, community policing does have an aura of touchy-feely liberalism. Yet on close examination, the community policing model seems genuinely tough, and radical in ways that could appeal to conservatives and liberals alike.

At the bottom, community policing emphasizes grass roots networks and citizen empowerment. At the top, it suggests a radical decentralization of power in police bureaucracies, shifting authority away from hierarchical chains of command and out toward precinct houses and line officers working with communities to develop local strategies.

Decentralization, of course, is radical in both a Jeffersonian and Reaganist sense and has implications beyond the community policing effort. In a broad survey of the welfare, education and criminal justice reforms of the 1960s, sociologist Charles Murray, writing in the July issue of *Commentary*, observes that while most of the big centralized federal programs were undeniable failures, the "handful of successes that survive scrutiny are local, small-scale, initiated and run by dedicated people, and operated idiosyncratically and pragmatically — all the things that large-scale federal programs cannot be." Community policing fits Murray's definition of a successful program.

Felice Kirby, for one, does not care whether it is labeled liberal or conservative. "The point is there's a crisis, and community policing is a viable part of the strategy for making life better," she says. "There are never enough government resources to do everything for people, and even if there were, it's debilitating for people to be 'done for' all the time. It produces unhealthy people."

It's a hot summer day in Williamsburg, and Kirby is watching her 3-year-old daughter, Corrina, play on the sidewalk. A few blocks away, a siren sounds.

"We've got to take care of each other," Kirby says. "If that's a radical notion, so be it."

# Higher Education and Ethical Policing

**MITCHELL TYRE and
SUSAN BRAUNSTEIN, Ed.D.**

*Chief Tyre commands the Juno Beach, Florida, Police Department.*

*Dr. Braunstein is an associate professor of communications at Lynn University, Boca Raton, Florida.*

I n March 1991, the now famous Rodney King videotape was first broadcast to television viewers across the Nation and around the world. Suddenly, police ethics were being discussed in editorials, news programs, and on radio and television talk shows. However, concern about ethical police behavior predated this blinding media spotlight by many years. In fact, since the introduction of organized law enforcement agencies, communities and departments have agonized over the sometimes unethical decisions made by individual officers that resulted in criminal acts, decreasing departmental morale, and increased public dissatisfaction.

This article presents a brief overview of the prevailing beliefs among researchers concerning the effects of higher education on ethical policing and explains how these beliefs developed. In addition, the article discusses the results of two recent studies of Florida police officers that measure the relationship between higher education and the ethical behavior expected of law enforcement officers.

## ETHICS IN POLICING

The nature of policing dictates that officers must consistently make immediate and demanding decisions. These decisions call into play ethical and moral, as well as procedural and legal, questions and are most often made without recourse to specific directions from superiors or specific policy directives.

Another factor that forces officers to make difficult decisions is the changing role of law enforcement in today's society. As William Scott noted in his article on college education requirements for police officers, the role of officers is

Reprinted from *FBI Law Enforcement Bulletin*, June 1992, pp. 6-10.

changing "... from pure enforcement of the law to one of dealing with people and their problems. Police...are taking a more holistic approach to the community."[1] This social work/community problem-solving approach creates even more demands on officers, as such a technique often requires them to choose between criminal justice or community service solutions. These decisions may be made with reference to policy, ethical standards, or on the basis of expediency, among other factors.

A further, but often overlooked, reason for ethics education is the myth of full enforcement. In *Police Training for Tough Calls: Discretionary Situations*, Frank Vandall argues that most formal police training relies on the principles of full enforcement. Practitioners, of course, are aware that full enforcement is impossible, impractical, and undesirable. Consequently, officers often make enforcement decisions with little formal guidance from their training or their departments.

According to Vandall, one result of this is inadequate recruit training in applied ethics. He states, "Since the task of the officer is thought to be simply to arrest when there is a violation, little attempt is made in training to distinguish similar calls or to give examples of how a particular law or department rule (if any) might be applied in different situations."[2]

In practice, enforcement policy is generally determined by the lowest ranks, i.e., patrol officers who interact with the public. In many cases, the decision for arrest is based solely on their discretion.[3] Nevertheless, much police training and education fails to deal with the concept of discretion in law enforcement.[4]

### The Benefits of Higher Education

Higher education has been cited as an advantage and even a cure-all since at least 1917,[5] and numerous studies have called for college edu-

cation for police personnel.[6] Nevertheless, many police administrators meet such proposals with less than whole-hearted enthusiasm.

This could rest in the fact that many police supervisors do not believe that college education produces better officers.[7] Indeed, a field survey of police administrators and supervisors in Florida revealed that many administrators believe that much of the research undertaken at universities is purely theoretical and unsupported by real life experience.[8]

This belief, however, seems contrary to the findings of other surveys gauging the relationship between higher education and policing. In M.S. Meagher's 1983 study of 183 officers at one agency, the frequency of occurrence of specific positive acts was statistically different when controlled for higher education. Meagher did not claim that higher education was the sole cause, but the study showed a clear relationship between higher education and the performance of desirable police tasks, such as the ability to communicate, the capacity to evaluate personal characteristics of others, and the ability to analyze and synthesize data logically.[9] All these are important factors in making ethical decisions.

David Murrell's 1982 doctoral dissertation took as its working hypothesis the assertion that an educated officer would be a better officer.[10] To test this hypothesis, he compiled a list of measurable factors that constituted good police work and compared the performance of educated and noneducated officers in two departments. The results conformed closely with his expectations. He concluded, "... college education makes for superior police work performance...."[11]

In a 1988 study of the Los Angeles Police Department, Hooper concluded that there were "no appreciable differences across educational levels in the performance of police duties [but] generally, educational level accounts for some dif-

ference in proficiency of police tasks."[12] Among the specific revelations of this study was the finding that officers who have completed 2 years of college are less likely to be accused of misconduct.[13]

A New York City-Rand Institute Study of the NYPD concluded that "... college educated officers in New York performed at a level well above average."[14] The study also found that more educated officers were "... less likely to incur civilian complaints."[15]

Although such research is helpful in pointing out relationships between education and performance, it rarely focuses directly on ethics. Often, however, the subject is examined through such measures as disciplinary records and civilian complaints. Although studies are not unanimous on the subject, research seems to indicate that there is a positive correlation between higher education, fewer disciplinary actions, and fewer citizen complaints.

### A Moral Code

To educate police officers adequately in the ethical sense, they must be encouraged to create a "moral code."[16] It is this internalized code to which officers turn when decisions must be made without recourse to specific direction from superiors or policy, and such occasions are frequent in police work.

Traditionally throughout American history, a liberal education has been viewed as the means by which citizens are grounded in the principles of an ethical, educated life. It is the liberal education portion of the college curriculum that is expected to lay the basis for cultural literacy and to provide the foundation for cultural values.[17]

One characteristic of general education, as opposed to career training, is the emphasis general education puts on the ethical and aesthetic development of the individual. As may be expected, there is evidence that such an education does positively affect student val-

*...research seems to indicate that there is a positive correlation between higher education, fewer disciplinary actions, and fewer citizen complaints.*

ues.[18] In short, a liberal education helps to define and foster an individual's moral code.

## CURRENT STANDARDS

In spite of government incentives and increasing departmental practices to encourage higher education, most police officers in this country have not completed a higher education degree. In Florida, for example, only about 35 percent of the State's police officers have earned a college degree.[19]

Most officers still must complete an academy curriculum that bears little similarity to higher education. For instance, in Florida, police officer candidates must complete a 520-hour, rigidly defined curriculum at a designated police academy. This curriculum includes no "humanities" or general education courses, and only a 1-hour class on ethics.

## FLORIDA STUDIES

In an effort to expand the data relating ethical policing to higher education, the authors initiated two research studies of Florida police officers. The first study concentrated on forced choice scenarios; the other centered on decertification proceedings by the Florida Department of Law Enforcement (FDLE).

### Study One: Forced Choice Scenarios

This study required respondents to choose between various responses to three different scenarios that posed ethical dilemmas. Fifty active duty police officers from two departments and 60 control subjects (persons who were not sworn officers) were given forced choices,

ranging from ethically sound, to unethical, to outright illegal.

The results indicated that educational levels had a direct positive effect upon *all* individuals surveyed—those with more advanced education were more likely to make ethically sound choices. However, for police officers, the correlation between a college degree and ethical decisions was 12 times greater than for the control group. [20]

The importance of this study is not that the attitudes described will accurately predict behavior, but that at least under scrutiny, educated police officers choose ethically better answers. They may or may not act

according to those answers in real-life situations, but they have demonstrated that they know the morally acceptable behaviors and will choose them in a controlled study situation. That is less true of the officers who have not completed a college degree program.

### Study Two: Examination of Decertifications

The second study examined 1987-1988 data concerning the statistical relationship between probable cause for decertification hearings by the FDLE and educational levels of officers. The FDLE, through the Criminal Justice Standards and Training Commission (CJSTC), holds probable cause hearings to determine if an officer's certification should be suspended for a specific period of time or revoked.

The 1987 statistics revealed that officers who had not attained a 2-year college degree were roughly four times more likely to be brought

**Example of Forced Choice Scenario**

You are on assignment to the Drug Squad and are in the process of serving a search warrant on a suspected drug dealer's house. The suspect is handcuffed, sitting on the bed in the back bedroom, where you find a suitcase with what appears to be a small amount of marijuana on top of several stacks of $20 bills, which you approximate to total $50,000. The suspect says, "That stuff was left here by a friend—forget the dope and I'll forget the money." No other detective is present or has seen the money. Your son, a leukemia victim, is in need of a bone marrow transplant that insurance will not cover.

**Would you:**

1) Arrest the suspect for possession of marijuana and bribery

2) Take the money and forget the marijuana, since its only marijuana and not cocaine or harder drugs

3) Take only that part of the money needed for the operation

4) Take part of the money and arrest the suspect anyway

5) Call your partner and ask his opinion

before the commission for illegal or unethical behavior. In 1988, FDLE figures indicated that 1 in 217 officers with less than an associate's degree was brought before the commission to face disciplinary action. However, only 1 in 686 with an associate's degree was brought before the commission.

In 1989, the figures were quite similar. Sixty-five percent of all officers in the State had less than a 2-year degree; 35 percent had at least a 2-year degree. Yet, only 15 percent of the officers brought before the CJSTC for disciplinary hearings had a 2-year degree.

This research is preliminary. No effort has been made to control for age, length of service, type of degree, or other variables that other studies indicate might be significant. However, the research indicates that possession of a college degree acts as a predictor of behavior in that those officers who have a degree are statistically less likely to be involved in the decertification process.

## RECOMMENDATION

The research available on the subject, though admittedly preliminary, appears to confirm the concept that better educated officers generally can be expected to perform in an ethically sound way. Therefore, it may be advisable to consider integrating the learning objectives of the police academy (currently required in at least 20 States)[21] into a 2-year college curriculum. The proposed curriculum would include task-specific skill courses for officers, such as traffic stops and defensive tactics, but would also require liberal arts courses.

For this proposal to become a reality, however, will require support not only from community leaders but also from law enforcement managers. To break from traditional training methods will result in resistance from some quarters, but police administrators should insist on the very best training, education, and preparation for their officers. Modern societal expectations demand that law enforcement officers have a broad-based education.

## CONCLUSION

The need for ethical officers is clear. The complexity of American society, the nature of police work, and the problems inherent in discretionary enforcement all require officers who are solidly grounded in applied ethics.

In all of the areas analyzed here—review of literature, scenario studies of sworn and nonsworn personnel, and examination of FDLE statistics on probable cause hearings—officers who had at least a 2-year college degree performed better than those who did not. There is no question that a behavior as complex as practicing ethical standards is influenced by many factors—education is but one among them. It does seem clear, however, that a positive correlation exists between college education, better police performance, and ethical police behavior.

Given the tremendous challenges facing law enforcement today and in the years to come, community and police administrators must consider any steps that could improve the capability of officers to ensure community safety. Research indicates that to promote ethical conduct, one step may be to integrate the traditional police academy curriculum with general college degree courses.

### Endnotes

1 William Russell Scott, "College Education Requirements for Police Entry Level and Promotion: A Study," *Journal of Police and Criminal Psychology*, 1986, 16-17.

2 Frank J. Vandall, *Police Training for Tough Calls: Discretionary Situations* (Atlanta: Center for Research in Social Change, Emory University, 1976), 4.

3 Kenneth Culp Davis, *Police Discretion* (St. Paul, Minnesota: West Publishing Co., 1975), 39.

4 Supra note 2.

5 Herman Goldstein, *Policing in a Free Society* (Cambridge: Ballinger, 1977), 283.

6 Mitchell Tyre and Susan Braunstein "Colleges May Provide Alternatives to Traditional Academies," *The Florida Police Chief*, Oct. 1989, 31 - 37; also Charles B. Saunders, Jr., *Upgrading the American Police: Education and Training for Better Law Enforcement* (Washington, D.C., 1970: The Brookings Institution), 112, 113; also Lawrence Sherman and the National Advisory Commission on Higher Education for Police Officers, *The Quality of Police Education: A Critical Review with Recommendations for Improving Programs in Higher Education* (San Francisco: Jossey-Bass, 1987).

7 See, e.g., Dennis D. Powell, "An Assessment of Attitudes Toward Police Education Needs," *Journal of Police & Criminal Psychology*, March 1986, 4.

8 Mitchell Tyre and Susan Braunstein, telephone and personal interviews conducted in Florida, 1989.

9 William Russell Scott, "College Education Requirements for Police Entry Level and Promotion: A Study," *Journal of Police and Criminal Psychology,* March 1986, 4.

10 David Murrell, *The Influence of Education in Police Work*, dissertation, Florida State University (1982).

11 Ibid.

12 Michael Kent Hooper, *The Relationship of College Education to Police Officer Job Performance*, dissertation, University of Michigan (1988).

13 Ibid.

14 Bernard Cohen and Jan M. Chaiken, *Police Background Characteristics and Performance* (Lexington, Massachusetts: Lexington Books D.C. Heath & Co., 1973).

15 Ibid.

16 Callahan concludes that teaching students the necessary analytical and critical skills and encouraging them to create their own moral systems encourages the development of such systems. Daniel Callahan, "Goals in the Teaching of Ethics," in *Ethics Teaching in Higher Education.,* ed. Daniel Callahan and Sissela Bok (New York: Plenum Press, 1980), 61-80.

17 Howard R. Bowen, *Investment in Learning: The Individual and Social Value of Higher Education* (San Francisco: Jossey-Bass, 1977).

18 Eric Donald Hirsh, Jr., *Cultural Literacy: What Every American Needs to Know* (New York: Vintage Books, 1988).

19 Florida Department of Law Enforcement/ DOE Criminal Justice Training Grant Task Force Seminar (May 1989).

20 Study developed and administered by Susan Braunstein and Mitchell Tyre. Questionnaires administered to sworn officers of the Stuart, Florida, and Port St. Lucie, Florida, Police Departments and college students matched for age at Barry University and the College of Boca Raton, Florida, 1990. Authors assisted in statistical analysis by Robert Foresman, Florida Institute of Technology.

21 Supra note 19.

# The Judicial System

Our system of criminal justice is an adversarial system and the protagonists are the state and the criminal defendant. The courtroom is where the drama is played out, and we look to the courts to preserve our liberties and ensure a fair trial.

"The Judicial Process: Prosecutors and Courts" outlines the roles of prosecutors, defense counsel, and the courts in the criminal justice process. "Public Defenders" discusses the role of the public defender and the adequacy of representation.

"Abuse of Power in the Prosecutor's Office" is a critical analysis of the office of prosecutor. The article is presented, not as an indictment of all prosecutors, but to stimulate discussion as to the potential for abuse.

"The Search for Justice: Is Impartiality Really Possible?" touches on a current problem, namely the difficulty of impaneling an impartial jury, and "Jurors Hear Evidence and Turn It Into Stories" discusses some ways that juries evaluate evidence. The grand jury system comes under scrutiny in "Grand Illusion."

In June of 1992, the U.S. Supreme Court wrestled with the question of whether or not the Constitution permits the government to declare that some speech is so hateful that it may be punished as a crime. "The Court's 2 Visions of Free Speech" discusses how a divided Court handled this matter.

## Looking Ahead: Challenge Questions

What can be done to ensure fairness in the prosecutor's office?

Is the grand jury system archaic?

How should the courts handle "hate crimes"?

# Unit 4

# The Judicial Process: Prosecutors and Courts

## The courts participate in and supervise the judicial process

**The courts have several functions in addition to deciding whether laws have been violated**

The courts—
• settle disputes between legal entities (persons, corporations, etc.)
• invoke sanctions against law violations
• decide whether acts of the legislative and executive branches are constitutional.

In deciding about violations of the law the courts must apply the law to the facts of each case. The courts affect policy in deciding individual cases by handing down decisions about how the laws should be interpreted and carried out. Decisions of the appellate courts are the ones most likely to have policy impact.

**Using an arm of the State to settle disputes is a relatively new concept**

Until the Middle Ages disputes between individuals, clans, and families, including those involving criminal acts, were handled privately. Over time, acts such as murder, rape, robbery, larceny, and fraud came to be regarded as crimes against the entire community, and the State intervened on its behalf. Today in the United States the courts handle both civil actions (disputes between individuals or organizations) and criminal actions.

**An independent judiciary is a basic concept of the U.S. system of government**

To establish its independence and impartiality, the judiciary was created as a separate branch of government co-equal to the executive and the legislative branches. Insulation of the courts from political pressure is attempted through—
• the separation of powers doctrine
• established tenure for judges
• legislative safeguards
• the canons of legal ethics.

Courts are without the power of enforcement. The executive branch must enforce their decisions. Furthermore, the courts must request that the legislature provide them with the resources needed to conduct their business.

**Each State has a system of trial and appeals courts**

Generally, State court systems are organized according to three basic levels of jurisdiction:

• **Courts of limited and special juris-** diction are authorized to hear only less serious cases (misdemeanors and/or civil suits that involve small amounts of money) or to hear special types of cases such as divorce or probate suits. Such courts include traffic courts, municipal courts, family courts, small claims courts, magistrate courts, and probate courts.

• **Courts of general jurisdiction**, also called major trial courts, are unlimited in the civil or criminal cases they are authorized to hear. Almost all cases originate in the courts of limited or special jurisdiction or in courts of general jurisdiction. Most serious criminal cases are handled by courts of general jurisdiction.

• **Appellate courts** are divided into two groups, intermediate appeals courts, which hear some or all appeals that are subject to review by the court of last resort, and courts of last resort, which have jurisdiction over final appeals from courts of original jurisdiction, intermediate appeals courts, or administrative agencies. As of 1985, 36 States had intermediate appellate courts, but all States had courts of last resort.

**The U.S. Constitution created the U.S. Supreme Court and authorized the Congress to**

From *Report to the Nation on Crime and Justice,* Bureau of Justice Statistics, U.S. Department of Justice, March 1988, pp. 81-82, 71-72, 74-75.

## establish lower courts as needed

The Federal court system now consists of various special courts, U.S. district courts (general jurisdiction courts), U.S. courts of appeals (intermediate appellate courts that receive appeals from the district courts and Federal administrative agencies), and the U.S. Supreme Court (the court of last resort). Organized on a regional basis are U.S. courts of appeals for each of 11 circuits and the District of Columbia. In Federal trial courts (the 94 U.S. district courts) more than 300,000 cases were filed in 1985; there was one criminal case for every seven civil cases. In 1985 more than half the criminal cases in district courts were for embezzlement, fraud, forgery and counterfeiting, traffic, or drug offenses.

## Court organization varies greatly among the States

State courts of general jurisdiction are organized by districts, counties, dual districts, or a combination of counties and districts. In some States the courts established by the State are funded and controlled locally. In others the court of last resort may have some budgetary or administrative oversight over the entire State court system. Even within States there is considerable lack of uniformity in the roles, organization, and procedures of the courts. This has led to significant momentum among States to form "unified" court systems to provide in varying degrees, for uniform administration of the courts, and, in many cases, for the consolidation of diverse courts of limited and special jurisdiction.

## Most felony cases are brought in State and local courts

The traditional criminal offenses under the English common law have been adopted, in one form or another, in the criminal laws of each of the States. Most cases involving "common law" crimes are brought to trial in State or local courts. Persons charged with misdemeanors are usually tried in courts of limited jurisdiction. Those charged with felonies (more serious crimes) are tried in courts of general jurisdiction.

In all States criminal defendants may appeal most decisions of criminal courts of limited jurisdiction; the avenue of appeal usually ends with the State supreme court. However, the U.S. Supreme Court may elect to hear the case if the appeal is based on an alleged violation of the Constitutional rights of the defendant.

## Courts at various levels of government interact in many ways

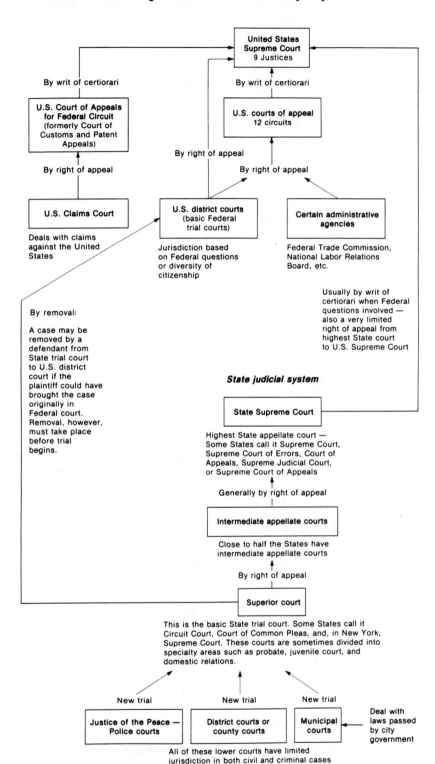

Updated and reprinted by permission from *The American Legal Environment* by William T. Schantz. Copyright © 1976 by West Publishing Company. All rights reserved.

## State courts process a large volume of cases, many of them minor

In 1983, 46 States and the District of Columbia reported more than 80 million cases filed in State and local courts. About 70% were traffic-related cases, 16% were civil cases (torts, contracts,

## Differences in how prosecutors handle felony cases can be seen in 4 jurisdictions

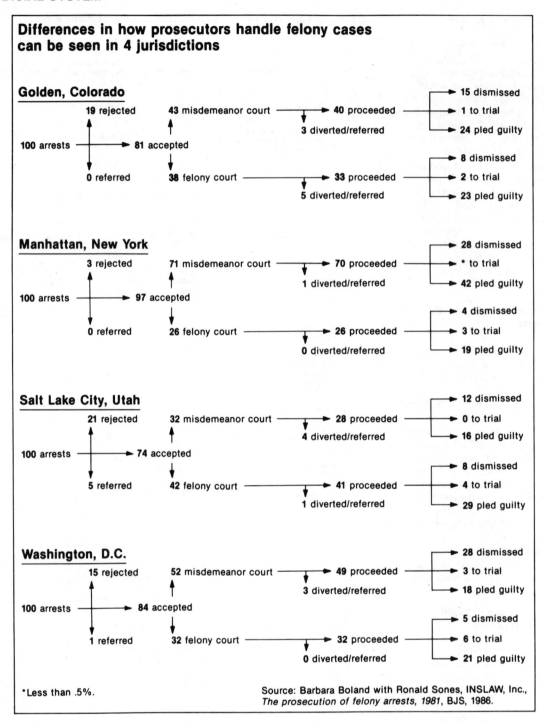

### Golden, Colorado

| 100 arrests → 81 accepted |
| 19 rejected |
| 0 referred |
| 43 misdemeanor court → 40 proceeded |
| 3 diverted/referred |
| 15 dismissed / 1 to trial / 24 pled guilty |
| 38 felony court → 33 proceeded |
| 5 diverted/referred |
| 8 dismissed / 2 to trial / 23 pled guilty |

### Manhattan, New York

| 100 arrests → 97 accepted |
| 3 rejected |
| 0 referred |
| 71 misdemeanor court → 70 proceeded |
| 1 diverted/referred |
| 28 dismissed / * to trial / 42 pled guilty |
| 26 felony court → 26 proceeded |
| 0 diverted/referred |
| 4 dismissed / 3 to trial / 19 pled guilty |

### Salt Lake City, Utah

| 100 arrests → 74 accepted |
| 21 rejected |
| 5 referred |
| 32 misdemeanor court → 28 proceeded |
| 4 diverted/referred |
| 12 dismissed / 0 to trial / 16 pled guilty |
| 42 felony court → 41 proceeded |
| 1 diverted/referred |
| 8 dismissed / 4 to trial / 29 pled guilty |

### Washington, D.C.

| 100 arrests → 84 accepted |
| 15 rejected |
| 1 referred |
| 52 misdemeanor court → 49 proceeded |
| 3 diverted/referred |
| 28 dismissed / 3 to trial / 18 pled guilty |
| 32 felony court → 32 proceeded |
| 0 diverted/referred |
| 5 dismissed / 6 to trial / 21 pled guilty |

*Less than .5%.

Source: Barbara Boland with Ronald Sones, INSLAW, Inc., *The prosecution of felony arrests, 1981*, BJS, 1986.

small claims, etc.), 13% were criminal cases, and 1% were juvenile cases. Civil and criminal cases both appear to be increasing. Of 39 States that reported civil filings for 1978 and 1983, 32 had increases. Of the 36 States that reported criminal filings for both years, 33 showed an increase in the volume of criminal filings.

In the 24 States that could report, felony filings comprised from 5% to 32% of total criminal filings with a median of 9%.

### Victims and witnesses are taking a more significant part in the prosecution of felons

Recent attention to crime victims has spurred the development of legislation and services that are more responsive to victims.
• Some States have raised witness fees from $5-10 per day in trial to $20-30 per day, established procedures for victim and witness notification of court proceedings, and guaranteed the right to speedy disposition of cases

• 9 States and the Federal Government have comprehensive bills of rights for victims

• 39 States and the Federal Government have laws or guidelines requiring that victims and witnesses be notified of the scheduling and cancellation of criminal proceedings

• 33 States and the Federal Government allow victims to participate in criminal proceedings via oral or written testimony.

# The prosecutor provides the link between the law enforcement and adjudicatory processes

## The separate system of justice for juveniles often operates within the existing court organization

Jurisdiction over juvenile delinquency, dependent or neglected children, and related matters is vested in various types of courts. In many States the juvenile court is a division of the court of general jurisdiction. A few States have statewide systems of juvenile or family courts. Juvenile jurisdiction is vested in the courts of general jurisdiction in some counties and in separate juvenile courts or courts of limited jurisdiction in others.

## The American prosecutor is unique in the world

First, the American prosecutor is a public prosecutor representing the people in matters of criminal law. Historically, European societies viewed crimes as wrongs against an individual whose claims could be pressed through private prosecution. Second, the American prosecutor is usually a local official, reflecting the development of autonomous local governments in the colonies. Finally, as an elected official, the local American prosecutor is responsible to the voters.

## Prosecution is the function of representing the people in criminal cases

After the police arrest a suspect, the prosecutor coordinates the government's response to crime—from the initial screening, when the prosecutor decides whether or not to press charges, through trial. In some instances, it continues through sentencing with the presentation of sentencing recommendations.

Prosecutors have been accorded much discretion in carrying out their responsibilities. They make many of the decisions that determine whether a case will proceed through the criminal justice process.

## Prosecution is predominantly a State and local function

Prosecuting officials include State, district, county, prosecuting, and commonwealth attorneys; corporation counsels; circuit solicitors; attorneys general; and U.S. attorneys. Prosecution is carried out by more than 8,000 State, county, municipal, and township prosecution agen-

cies.[1] In all but five States, local prosecutors are elected officials. Many small jurisdictions engage a part-time prosecutor who also maintains a private law practice. In some areas police share the charging responsibility of local prosecutors. Prosecutors in urban jurisdictions often have offices staffed by many full-time assistants. Each State has an office of the attorney general, which has jurisdiction over all matters involving State law but generally, unless specifically requested, is not involved in local prosecution. Federal prosecution is the responsibility of 93 U.S. attorneys who are appointed by the President subject to confirmation by the Senate.

## The decision to charge is generally a function of the prosecutor

Results of a 1981 survey of police and prosecution agencies in localities of over 100,000 indicate that police file initial charges in half the jurisdictions surveyed. This arrangement, sometimes referred to as the police court, is not commonly found in the larger urban areas that account for most of the UCR Index crime. Usually, once an arrest is made and the case is referred to the prosecutor, most prosecutors screen cases to see if they merit prosecution. The prosecutor can refuse to prosecute, for example, because of insufficient evidence. The decision to charge is not usually reviewable by any other branch of government.

## Some prosecutors accept almost all cases for prosecution; others screen out many cases

Some prosecutors have screening units designed to reject cases at the earliest possible point. Others tend to accept most arrests, more of which are dismissed by judges later in the adjudication process. Most prosecutor offices fall somewhere between these two extremes.

Arrest disposition patterns in 16 jurisdictions range from 0 to 47% of arrests rejected for prosecution. Jurisdictions with high rejection rates generally were found to have lower rates of dismissal at later stages of the criminal process. Conversely, jurisdictions that accepted most or all arrests usually had high dismissal rates.

## Prosecutorial screening practices are of several distinct types

Several studies conclude that screening

decisions consider—
• evidentiary factors
• the views of the prosecutor on key criminal justice issues
• the political and social environment in which the prosecutor functions
• the resource constraints and organization of prosecutorial operations.

Jacoby's study confirmed the presence of at least three policies that affect the screening decision:
• Legal sufficiency—an arrest is accepted for prosecution if, on routine review of the arrest, the minimum legal elements of a case are present.
• System efficiency—arrests are disposed as quickly as possible by the fastest means possible, which are rejections, dismissals, and pleas.
• Trial sufficiency—the prosecutor accepts only those arrests for which, in his or her view, there is sufficient evidence to convict in court.

## The official accusation in felony cases is a grand jury indictment or a prosecutor's bill of information

According to Jacoby, the accusatory process usually follows one of four paths:
• arrest to preliminary hearing for bind-over to grand jury for indictment
• arrest to grand jury for indictment
• arrest to preliminary hearing to a bill of information
• a combination of the above at the prosecutor's discretion.

Whatever the method of accusation, the State must demonstrate only that there is probable cause to support the charge.

## The preliminary hearing is used in some jurisdictions to determine probable cause

The purpose of the hearing is to see if there is probable cause to believe a crime has been committed and that the defendant committed it. Evidence may be presented by both the prosecution and the defense. On a finding of probable cause the defendant is held to answer in the next stage of a felony proceeding.

## The grand jury emerged from the American Revolution as the people's protection against oppressive prosecution by the State

Today, the grand jury is a group of ordinary citizens, usually no more than 23, which has both accusatory and investigative functions. The jury's proceedings are secret and not adversarial so that most rules of evidence for trials do not apply. Usually, evidence is presented by the prosecutor who brings a case to the grand jury's attention. However, in some States the grand jury is used primarily to investigate issues of public corruption and organized crime.

## Some States do not require a grand jury indictment to initiate prosecutions

| Grand jury indictment required | Grand jury indictment optional |
|---|---|
| **All crimes** | Arizona |
| New Jersey | Arkansas |
| South Carolina | California |
| Tennessee | Colorado |
| Virginia | Idaho |
| | Illinois |
| **All felonies** | Indiana |
| Alabama | Iowa |
| Alaska | Kansas |
| Delaware | Maryland |
| District of Columbia | Michigan |
| Georgia | Missouri |
| Hawaii | Montana |
| Kentucky | Nebraska |
| Maine | Nevada |
| Mississippi | New Mexico |
| New Hampshire | North Dakota |
| New York | Oklahoma |
| North Carolina | Oregon |
| Ohio | South Dakota |
| Texas | Utah |
| West Virginia | Vermont |
| | Washington |
| **Capital crimes only** | Wisconsin |
| Connecticut | Wyoming |
| Florida | |
| Louisiana | **Grand jury lacks authority to indict** |
| Massachusetts | |
| Minnesota | |
| Rhode Island | Pennsylvania |

Note: With the exception of capital cases a defendant can always waive the right to an indictment. Thus, the requirement for an indictment to initiate prosecution exists only in the absence of a waiver.
Source: Deborah Day Emerson, *Grand jury reform: A review of key issues*, National Institute of Justice, U.S. Department of Justice, January 1983.

## The secrecy of the grand jury is a matter of controversy

Critics of the grand jury process suggest it denies due process and equal protection under the law and exists only to serve the prosecutor. Recent criticisms have fostered a number of reforms requiring due process protections for persons under investigation and for witnesses; requiring improvements in the quality and quantity of evidence presented; and opening the proceeding to outside review. While there is much variation in the nature and implementation of reforms, 15 States have enacted laws affording the right to counsel, and 10 States require evidentiary standards approaching the requirements imposed at trial.

## The defense attorney's function is to protect the defendant's legal rights and to be the defendant's advocate in the adversary process

Defendants have the right to defend themselves, but most prefer to be represented by a specialist in the law. Relatively few members of the legal profession specialize in criminal law, but lawyers who normally handle other types of legal matters may take criminal cases.

## The right to the assistance of counsel is more than the right to hire a lawyer

Supreme Court decisions in *Gideon* v. *Wainwright* (1963) and *Argersinger* v. *Hamlin* (1972) established that the right to an attorney may not be frustrated by lack of means. For both felonies and misdemeanors for which jail or prison can be the penalty, the State must provide an attorney to any accused person who is indigent.

The institutional response to this Constitutional mandate is still evolving as States experiment with various ways to provide legal counsel for indigent defendants.

# *Public Defenders*

AGNES A. SERPE

*Agnes A. Serpe is a student at Creighton University in Omaha, Nebraska. She is pursuing Creighton's Three Plus Three program, a combination Business Administration/Law program.*

They [public defenders] are a fraternity of righteous, these low-paid lawyers, dogmatists of the criminal justice system, who often find themselves lining up on the sides of rapists, murderers, child-molesters, and drug dealers.[1]

A public defender is an attorney appointed to aid indigent persons, usually in cases involving possible imprisonment. Because the Supreme Court guarantees that all persons accused of felonies, regardless of their ability to pay for counsel, have the right to a publicly provided defense lawyer during police questioning, pretrial hearings, the trial, and appeal, the public defender is a busy attorney.[2]

With the rate of crime in the United States continuing to rise, the demand for defense counsel increases. Public defenders are expected to begin research and representation early on in their cases, and they are expected to follow through to the appeals stages and probation revocation hearings.[3] The problem is that there are more cases in need of public defense counsel than there are attorneys with the time, money, and expertise to handle such cases. The result is that cases involving indigent clients are often delayed or expedited, hampering the public defender in effectively representing his client.[4]

Although the problems facing public defense counsel in the United States today are severe ones, the present judicial system has a strong foundation. The U.S. bases its whole judicial system on the fundamental principle ". . . laid down by the greatest English judges . . ."[5] The system holds that it is better to let many guilty persons escape than it is to let one innocent person be imprisoned.[6]

Since the primary goal of the judicial system is to protect the innocent, the system holds that every individual has the right to counsel. In 1791, Congress passed the Sixth Amendment to the Constitution, guaranteeing in all criminal prosecutions, the accused person has the right to a ". . . speedy and public trial, by an impartial jury of the state and district wherein the crime shall have been committed. . . and to have the assistance of counsel for his defense.'"[7] According to the Sixth Amendment, 'counsel' does not include lay persons, but rather refers only to persons authorized to practice law.[8]

Despite the amendment, flaws still remained in the system. Only until after 1961 did the Supreme Court rule that the guarantees found in the Sixth Amendment apply to the state trial courts as well as the federal trial courts.[9] Also, court-appointed attorneys were expected to serve the public without compensation, burdening the practicing bar of attorneys and forcing the judges to appoint young, inexperienced counsel.[10] Moreover, a public defender program was not established until the early 1920's.[11]

## History

At first, public defenders were part of the legal aid societies that were supported by charities. The society handled both civil and criminal cases and had the authority to accept or reject cases. The earliest legal aid society was Der Deutsche Rechtsschutz

Verein (the German Legal Defense Society) which was organized in 1876 to help German immigrants. Later, in 1888, New York City created the New York Legal Aid Society, and Chicago established the Chicago Bureau of Justice.[12]

Early legal aid societies, such as the ones in New York and Chicago, did not take many criminal cases because they lacked the time, money, and personnel to conduct criminal investigations and absorb the trial work.[13] By 1962, the burden of criminal caseloads shifted from the legal aid societies to the 110 newly established public defender offices across America. The number of public defender offices was very few in proportion to the population of the country, but enough to provide minimal service in some major cities. Accordingly, the offices were noted for being understaffed.[14]

Furthermore, up until 1963, any legal assistance providing defense services for indigent criminals had been a matter left up to the judge to decide, depending heavily upon the charitable time and money contributions from the bar association. The demand for sufficient funding resulted in the Ford Foundation's decision to create the National Defender Project in 1964. Donating $6,000,000 to the National Legal Aid and Defender Association over a five-year period, the foundation provided the funds that were needed to improve and establish organized defense systems in over sixty cities across the nation.[15]

The Ford Foundation's sudden display of generosity occurred immediately after the landmark court case Gideon v Wainwright in 1963. In this case, Clarence Earl Gideon, the defendant, who was tried and convicted in a Florida state court, committed the felony of breaking and entering (a pool-room) with the intent to commit a misdemeanor theft. When he requested an attorney for his trial, the judge refused him. The judge claimed that he could not assign an attorney to Gideon because Gideon was not charged with a capital offense (that is, one punishable by death). Since the judge did have the power to appoint counsel, the judge had made an obvious mistake.[16] As a result, the Supreme Court ruled that Gideon's quality of defense was inadequate

and "about as well as could be expected from a layman."[17]

Therefore, the outcome of Gideon v Wainwright was an emphasis on what the Sixth Amendment is all about. "The right to legal representation must be granted to all indigent defendants in all felonies."[18]

"This noble idea [right to counsel] cannot be realized if the poor man charged with crime has to face his accusers without a lawyer to defend him," stated Mr. Justice Black, who was in harmony with the majority opinion in Gideon v Wainwright.[19]

*Although there was a time when public defenders were paid a great deal less than the state's prosecuting attorney, today the difference between the public defender's salary and the state's prosecuting attorney's salary has decreased.*

Thus, the Gideon v Wainwright decision came at the right time, prompting the Ford Foundation to donate money. Also, the case proved that ". . . lawyers in criminal courts are necessities, not luxuries."[20] The foundation had heard the pleas for the funding and had solved some problems for the time being.

Later, in 1964, The Criminal Justice Act was passed, making the federal government provide funds for judges to pay attorneys to represent indigent defendants. At first, however, these funds were available only to attorneys who defended federal crimes, not state crimes. The earliest response was from the state of New Jersey which enacted a state-wide public defender program.[21]

### Public Defenders Today

Generally, there are two main means of appointing defense counsel in the U.S. One is the ad hoc, or random, appointment of counsel, and the other is the coordinated assigned counsel program.[22] With ad hoc appointments, the more predominant of the two methods, attorneys are appointed case by case rather than in accordance with an organized plan. The attorneys who are appointed to a case are often the ones who just happen to be in the courtroom at the time of the client's arraignment. As a result the allocation of the burdens placed on defense attorneys is often unfair, and often denies the accused person competent and prepared defense counsel.[23]

On the other hand, the coordinated assigned counsel programs have systematic methods and procedures for the assignment of defense counsel. Some of the programs have loosely structured control over appointments; whereas, others maintain a strict level of control.[24] The coordinated assigned counsel system may be administered by the organized bar, as in San Mateo County, California;[25] a defender office, as in the state of New Jersey;[26] the county, as in King County, Washington;[27] an independent agency, as in the state of Wisconsin;[28] a judge or other court official who provides a rotating list of attorneys;[29] or a client who selects his own attorney, as in Ontario, Canada.[30]

It seems clear that lawyers join the public defender's office to gain trial experience and to make a positive contribution to society through public service.[31] However, the number of attorneys interested in this type of work is declining because of low salaries, and also due to the attraction of big law firms and corporate law,[32] and the extensive and specialized expertise needed for public defender work.[33] As a result, all too often the poor accused of crimes in our country do not receive the fair trial and the full attention to which they are entitled.

## Problems and Solutions

Nowadays, the public defender's problem with money is not so much related to salary as it is the lack of sufficient funding for research provided by the federal government. Although there was a time when public defenders were paid a great deal less than the state's prosecuting attorney, today the difference between the public defender's salary and the state's prosecuting attorney's salary has decreased.[34] For example, in 1931, the public defender's salary was $300 per year; whereas, the state's attorney's salary was $1,000 per year. However, in 1984, public defenders were paid approximately $29,863 per year; and the state's attorneys were paid approximately $30,680

per year—a difference of only $817.[35] That is to say that public defenders no longer are justified to complain about the major salary difference between themselves and the state's attorneys.

On the other hand, public defenders are justified in complaining about the difference between their salaries and the salaries of young lawyers who enter legal aid groups. An entry level attorney at a legal aid group will be guaranteed a salary of at least $32,500 per year, along with some extra help with paying back student loans. Although the entry level attorney's pay at legal aid groups is under one-half of what entry level attorneys at major law firms earn, it is still higher than the public defender's salary.[36]

Furthermore, many salaried public defenders, like the ones in New York City and St. Louis, Missouri,[37] have valid reasons to complain about heavy caseloads because the federal government does not provide the necessary funds required for the adequate defense of indigents.[38] Even though public defenders are tireless and dedicated workers, they lack the resources and government funding needed for their overwhelming caseload.[39] For example, in 1983 in St. Louis, Missouri, twenty-two public defenders handled 12.000 cases on a budget of $695,000. At the same time, forty-five attorneys in the state prosecutor's office had a budget of $2.4 million.[40] Therefore, all too often, the public defender does not or cannot find the time and the money to spend researching and preparing a client's case to the best of his ability. Accordingly, indigent clients often do not receive adequate representation.

A second problem that hinders a public defender from effectively defending his client is the lack of manpower. Even though about one-half of all criminal cases in New York City and St. Louis, Missouri, involved defendants who were too poor to pay for their counsel, state and federal levels failed to support the proposed increase in the staff of the public defender office in both these cities.[41]

Furthermore, the problems stem from the attorneys themselves who do not want to become public defenders. The American Bar Association reports that 17.7% of our nation's 659,000 private attorneys practice pro bono work. In Los Angeles, Public Counsel—a group that provides the poor with legal assistance—has lost its participation from outside law firms. The total drop in participation from outside law firms is 30% since 1986.[42] The point is that not enought attorneys are willing to spend their time and money representing the poor free of charge, even though a held belief of the profession is that all lawyers should devote part of their time to pro bono work in either a public defender's office or legal aid society.[43]

Accordingly, Circuit Court Judge, Byron Kinder of Jefferson City, Missouri, subpoenaed 100 lawyers who work for Missouri agencies based in Jefferson City—the state's capital—to press them into service as public defenders for indigent criminal defendants. The U.S. Constitution guarantees a lawyer to all poor defendants. However, Cole County—the county in which Jefferson City is located—has only one public defender. Also, the county has run out of money to pay private attorneys to help out.[44]

One solution to the lack of attorneys is to make pro bono work mandatory for all private attorneys. The proposed system would allow courts, legislatures, and bar associations to force attorneys into donating their time to public defense. However, in some cases, attorneys may avoid their service obligation by paying a fee. Recently, a mandatory pro bono program has been imposed in Westchester County, New York, and El Paso, Texas.[45]

The problem with mandatory pro bono work is that its requirements are not fair to small law practices. Solo practitioners and small law firms, unlike large law firms with many young associates who can be assigned to meet pro bono requirements, will find it nearly impossible to meet pro bono quotas.[46]

Moreover, mandatory pro bono work is a problem for the indigent defendant as well as the solo practitioner. For example, some legal aid attorneys testify that 'drafting' attorneys is not the answer because it may lead to the attorney's lack of conviction and/or his lack of legal skills needed to defend the poor.[47]

The third and final problem contributing to ineffective defense counsel in the U.S. is

that few attorneys possess the expertise needed to defend the poor and carry out the functions of a public defender. All public defenders need special skills and knowledge, an unorthodox philosophy, and patience. All too often, the defense counsel in the U.S. is lacking in one or more of the aspects of expertise, resulting in ineffective public counsel for the poor.[48]

To begin with, law school students gain practical trial experience working for public defender organizations and legal aid departments. As a result, clients may be getting help from students rather than professional counsel who have acquired skill through past experience.[49] Also, the past few years, younger lawyers tend to serve people who are too poor to afford their own lawyers—especially poor persons accused of narcotics law violations. The accused person's defense in drug-related crimes requires technical statutes and procedures that many lawyers are not familiar with. Therefore, young attorneys are the ones who tend to handle the bulk of these cases, resulting in questionable representation.[50]

Furthermore, effective defense counsel need skills and knowledge to deal with the problems of the indigent. As one attorney explains, "Your clients have no funds. . . no witnesses. . . only have one name. . . hang out on the streets. . . don't have phones. . . don't have a life like the rest of us."[51]

Adding to the problem, most of the accused are not articulate and tend to be less intelligent and more sociopathic than the general population.[52] Thus, the public defender needs special skills for dealing with the poor.

Second, the problem with the lack of expertise is the lack of attorneys who are capable of having an unconventional philosophy. Since the basis of legal ethics is loyalty to the client, public defenders have ethics which are practically opposite of what is commonly understood to be ethical. If, in fact, the client did commit a crime, the defense attorney is supposed to prevent the "coming out" of the crime and the jury's recognition of the crime.[53] In other words, it would be legally unethical for a defense attorney to refrain from doing everything in his power to protect his client. For example, even when a lawyer knows that his client is a thief, the public defender must attempt to prevent the search for the victim's stolen property.[54] Because justice under the law is not always the same as true justice, public defenders often find it difficult to uphold and believe in their legal ethics. James S. Kunen, a former public defender who found it difficult to believe in legal ethics, stated the following:

> . . . my job was to get what my client wanted. . . [Judge Ugast] flew into one of his daily earnest, rages, upbraiding me for being 'an idealist' with abstract notions of legal duty and no contact with reality, adding that I typified everything that was wrong with the Public Defender Service. I was pleased . . . because. . . I shared the judge's preference for doing what you think is right, as opposed to what you are supposed to do . . . .[55]

If public defenders find it difficult to believe in legal ethics, then what are their motives to defend the indigent criminal? Aside from striving to "legitimize themselves as professionals," the public defenders' motives stem from the belief that a person is innocent until proven guilty beyond reasonable doubt. Also, they believe that it is right to defend the guilty client because—although he is guilty—he needs protection from police, prosecutorial, and judicial abuse.[56]

Finally, the third essential to defense expertise is patience. The rest of the judicial system—that is, the police, the prosecuting attorney, and the judges—along with the clients and the general public, all test the patience of the public defender.

For instance, not only must a public defender accept that he will probably not win his cases,[57] but also, he must deal with the habitual postponements of his cases. Public defenders' cases get postponed more often than cases involving private defense attorneys.[58] Some judges act as if they are being considerate of private attorneys by calling their cases before public defenders' cases because "time is money for the private attorney."[59]

In reality, some of these judges lack respect for the public defender. All too often judges are "prosecution-minded and. . . generally tougher on the defense attorney."[60] They tend to treat public defenders as "second-class lawyers."[61] One public

defender explains just how some judges treat public defenders:

> [Judges] view the public defenders very similar to how they view court clerks. We are gophers, we run for things. Whenever there's something the judge needs done, if there is not a clerk available, the judge gives it to the public defender and has him do it. They would never think of having the state's attorney do it. But public defenders have to do the silly stuff.[62]

*Not only do public defenders need patience with the judicial system, but they need to have patience with their clients.*

Not only do public defenders need patience with the judicial system, but they need to have patience with their clients. Clients often doubt the public defender's ability as a trial lawyer. As a result, public defenders are continually swallowing their pride for their clients—most of whom lack faith in the legal profession. One public defender protested, "I am a real lawyer, I went to a real law school, I passed a real bar exam!"[63]

Because of unappreciative clients, public defenders believe, and have the right to believe, that the people in their community do not appreciate them as competent attorneys.[64] Even though a small portion of the population does respect public defenders, the profession has clearly been degraded time and time again:

> Public defenders in America have been both maligned and idealized. Some [people] view them as champions of individual rights, the defenders of the poor and down trodden. Others see them as 'cop-out' artists who are too quick to bargain away the precious rights of their underprivileged clients.[65]

Furthermore, the public defender has the problem of developing the expertise of patience with a judicial system that delays cases to the point where witnesses disappear, and expedites trials so that the defense is at a disadvantage.[66]

## Conclusion

The search for an improved public defender program continues. The ideal program would have adequate staffing and more than enough funding to assign cases to attorneys according to their experience and workload. The primary goals of the program would be efficiency, effectiveness, and productivity.[67]

The productivity measurement would include a high quality of service, which will be the most difficult to render.[68] However, despite the rocky history and recent beginning of the public defender program, the level of expertise that exists among attorneys now is much better than it was a few years ago. Therefore, the office of the public defender—although it has major problems—is improving, and will continue to improve as long as it attempts to solve its problems.

> Thirty years ago the public defender office seemed to be little more than a beneficent (though ultimately benign) gesture, on the part of a few county governments, toward poor people in trouble with the law. . . But. . . public defenders today play such an important role in the administration of criminal justice that without them, the work of our urban criminal courts especially would come to a standstill.[69]

[1] Lisa McIntyre, *The Public Defender* (Chicago, Illinois: The University of Chicago Press, 1987), p. 86.

[2] "Public Defenders," *Funk and Wagnalls New World Encyclopedia,* 1983.

[3] William McDonald, *The Defense Counsel* (Beverly Hills, California: Sage Publications, 1983), p. 79.

[4] "Public Defenders Assail Felony Judges' New Rules to Speed Court Cases," *Milwaukee Journal,* October 28, 1988, p. A1, Col. 1–6.

[5] James Kunen, *How Can You Defend Those People?* (New York: Random House, 1983), p. vii.

[6] *Ibid.,* p. vii.

[7] United States Constitution, Amendment 6.

[8] *Ibid.,* p. 314.

[9] McIntyre, p. 21.

[10] McDonald, p. 76.

[11] Robert Janosik, *Encyclopedia of the American Judicial System* (New York: Charles Scribner's Sons, 1972), p. 645.

[12] *Ibid.,* p. 645.

[13] *Ibid.,* p. 645.

[14] *Ibid.,* p. 646.

[15] McDonald, p. 81.

[16] McIntyre, p. 21.

[17] *Ibid,,* p. 21.

[18] *Ibid,,* p. 21.

[19] McDonald, p. 76.

[20] McIntyre, p. 21.

[21] Janosik, p. 645.

[22] McDonald, p. 85.

[23] *Ibid.,* p. 86.

[24] *Ibid.,* p. 87.

[25] *Ibid.,* p. 87.

[26] *Ibid.,* p. 88.

[27] *Ibid.,* p. 88.

[28] Richard J. Phelps, *Office of the State Public Defender Biennial Report* (Madison, Wisconsin: 1987), p. 5.

[29] McDonald, p. 89.

[30] *Ibid.,* p. 89.

[31] McIntyre, p. 86.

[32] R. Lacayo, "The Sad Fate of Legal Aid," *Time,* June 20, 1988, p. 59.

[33] B. Kinder, "Lawyer Round-up in Jeff City," *Time,* May 4, 1981, p. 44.

[34] McIntyre, p. 90.

[35] *Ibid.,* p. 90.

[36] Lacayo, p. 59.

[37] Janosik, p. 645.

[38] Denise Shekerjian, *Competent Counsel: Working With Lawyers* (New York: Dodd, Mead, and Co., 1985), p. 55.

[39] *Ibid.,* p. 55.

[40] Janosik, p. 645.

[41] *Ibid.,* p. 645.

[42] Lacayo, p. 59.

[43] *Ibid.,* p. 59.

[44] Kinder, p. 44.

[45] Lacayo, p. 59.

[46] *Ibid.,* p. 59.

[47] *Ibid.,* p. 59.

[48] Kinder, p. 44.

[49] Henry Poor, *You and the Law* (New York: Reader's Digest, 1984), p. 733.

[50] *Ibid.,* p. 736.

[51] McIntyre, p. 144.

[52] *Ibid.,* p. 144.

[53] James Kunen, "How Can You Defend Those People?" *Harper's,* April, 1982, p. 83.

[54] *Ibid.,* p. 86.

[55] *Ibid.,* p. 82.

[56] McIntyre, p. 169.

[57] *Ibid.,* p. 162.

[58] Kunen, p. 83.

[59] McIntyre, . 87.

[60] *Ibid.,* p. 87.

[61] *Ibid.,* p. 87.

[62] *Ibid.,* p. 88.

[63] *Ibid.,* p. 89.

[64] *Ibid.,* p. 87.

[65] McDonald, p. 67.

[66] Kunen, p. 83.

[67] McDonald, p. 299.

[68] *Ibid.,* p. 299.

[69] McIntyre, p. 1.

# ABUSE OF POWER IN THE PROSECUTOR'S OFFICE

*Bennett L. Gershman*

*Bennett L. Gershman is professor of law at Pace University. He is the author of* Prosecutorial Misconduct *and several articles on law dealing with such topics as entrapment and police and prosecutorial ethics. For ten years, he was a prosecutor in New York.*

The prosecutor is the most dominant figure in the American criminal justice system. As the Supreme Court recently observed, "Between the private life of the citizen and the public glare of criminal accusation stands the prosecutor. [The prosecutor has] the power to employ the full machinery of the State in scrutinizing any given individual." Thus, the prosecutor decides whether or not to bring criminal charges; whom to charge; what charges to bring; whether a defendant will stand trial, plead guilty, or enter a correctional program in lieu of criminal charges; and whether to confer immunity from prosecution. In jurisdictions that authorize capital punishment, the prosecutor literally decides who shall live and who shall die. Moreover, in carrying out these broad functions, the prosecutor enjoys considerable independence from the courts, administrative superiors, and the public. A prosecutor cannot be forced to bring criminal charges, or be prevented from bringing them. Needless to say, the awesome power that prosecutors exercise is susceptible to abuse. Such abuses most frequently occur in connection with the prosecutor's power to bring charges; to control the information used to convict those on trial; and to influence juries.

The prosecutor's charging power includes the virtually unfettered discretion to invoke or deny punishment, and therefore the power to control and destroy people's lives. Such prosecutorial discretion has been called "tyrannical," "lawless," and "most dangerous." Prosecutors may not unfairly select which persons to prosecute. But this rule is difficult to enforce, and the courts almost always defer to the prosecutor's discretion. In one recent case, for example, a prosecutor targeted for prosecution a vocal opponent of the Selective Service system who refused to register, rather than any of nearly a million nonvocal persons who did not register. The proof showed that the defendant clearly was selected for prosecution not because he failed to register but because he exercised his First Amendment rights. This was a legally impermissible basis for prosecution. Nevertheless, the courts refused to disturb the prosecutor's decision, because there was no clear proof of prosecutorial bad faith. Many other disturbing examples exist of improper selection based on race, sex, religion, and the exercise of constitutional rights. These cases invariably are decided in the prosecutor's favor. The reasoning is circular. The courts presume that prosecutors act in good faith, and that the prosecutor's expertise, law enforcement plans, and priorities are ill suited to judicial review.

Unfair selectivity is one of the principal areas of discretionary abuse. Another is prosecutorial retaliation in the form of increased charges after defendants raise statutory or constitutional claims. Prosecutors are not allowed to be vindictive in response to a defendant's exercise of rights. Nevertheless, proving vindictiveness, as with selectiveness, is virtually impossible. Courts simply do not probe the prosecutor's state of mind. For example, prosecutors often respond to a defendant's unwillingness to plead guilty to a crime by bringing higher charges. In one recent case, a defendant charged with a petty offense refused to plead guilty despite prosecutorial threats to bring much higher charges. The prosecutor carried out his threat and brought new charges carrying a sentence of life imprisonment. The court found the prosecutor's conduct allowable. Although the prosecutor behaved in a clearly retaliatory fashion, the court nevertheless believed that the prosecutor needed this leverage to make the system work. If the prosecutor could not threaten defendants by "upping the ante," so the court reasoned, there would be fewer guilty pleas and the system would collapse.

Finally, some prosecutions are instituted for illegitimate personal objectives as opposed to ostensibly valid law enforcement objectives. Such prosecutions can be labeled demagogic and usually reveal actual prosecutorial malice or evil intent. Telltale signs of demagoguery often include the appearance of personal vendettas, political crusades, and witch hunts. Examples of this base practice abound. They have involved prosecutions based on racial or political hostility; prosecutions motivated by personal and political gain; and prosecutions to discourage or coerce the exercise of constitutional rights. One notorious example was New Orleans District Attorney James Garrison's prosecution of Clay Shaw for the Kennedy assassination. Other examples have included the prosecutions of labor leader James Hoffa, New York attorney Roy Cohn, and civil rights leader Dr. Martin Luther King.

## HIDING EVIDENCE

A prosecutor's misuse of power also occurs in connection with legal proof. In the course of an investigation, in pretrial preparation, or even during a trial, prosecutors often become aware of information that might exonerate a defendant. It is not unusual for the prosecutor to have such proof, in view of the acknowledged superiority of law enforcement's investigative resources and its early access to crucial evidence. The adversary system relies on a fair balance of opposing forces. But one of the greatest threats to rational and fair fact-finding in criminal cases comes from the prosecutor's hiding evidence that might prove a defendant's innocence. Examples of prosecutorial suppression of exculpatory evidence are numerous. Such conduct is pernicious for several reasons: It skews the ability of the adversary system to function properly by denying to the defense crucial proof; it undermines the public's respect for and confidence in the public prosecutor's office; and it has resulted in many defendants being unjustly convicted, with the consequent loss of their liberty or even their lives.

Consider the following recent examples. Murder convictions of Randall Dale Adams in Texas, James Richardson and Joseph Brown in Florida, and Eric Jackson in New York all were vacated because the prosecutors hid crucial evidence that would have proved these defendants' innocence. The Adams case—popularized by the film *The Thin Blue Line*—depicts Texas "justice" at its worst. Adams was convicted in 1977 of murdering a policeman and sentenced to die largely on the testimony of a juvenile with a long criminal record who made a secret deal with the prosecutor to implicate Adams, and the testimony of two eyewitnesses to the killing. The juvenile actually murdered the policeman, as he later acknowledged. At Adams' trial, however, the prosecutor suppressed information about the deal and successfully kept from the jury the juvenile's lengthy record.

The prosecutor also withheld evidence that the two purported eyewitnesses had failed to identify Adams in a line-up, and permitted these witnesses to testify that they had made a positive identification of Adams. A Texas court recently freed Adams, finding that the prosecutor suborned perjury and knowingly suppressed evidence.

Richardson—whose case was memorialized in the book *Arcadia* was condemned to die for poisoning to death his

tor misrepresented to the jury that ballistics evidence proved the defendant's guilt, when in fact the prosecutor knew that the ballistics report showed that the bullet that killed the deceased could not have been fired from the defendant's weapon.

Eric Jackson was convicted of murder in 1980 for starting a fire at Waldbaum's supermarket in Brooklyn in which a roof collapsed and six firefighters died. Years later, the attorney who repre-

---

*Abuses most frequently occur in connection with the prosecutor's power to bring charges, to control the information used to convict those on trial, and to influence juries.*

---

seven children in 1967. The prosecutor claimed that Richardson, a penniless farm worker, killed his children to collect insurance. A state judge last year overturned the murder conviction, finding that the prosecutor had suppressed evidence that would have shown Richardson's innocence. The undisclosed evidence included a sworn statement from the children's babysitter that she had killed the youngsters; a sworn statement from a cellmate of Richardson's that the cellmate had been beaten by a sheriff's deputy into fabricating his story implicating Richardson; statements from other inmates contradicting their claims that Richardson confessed to them; and proof that Richardson had never purchased any insurance.

Brown's murder conviction recently was reversed by the Eleventh Circuit. Brown was only hours away from being electrocuted when his execution was stayed. That court found that the prosecutor "knowingly allowed material false testimony to be introduced at trial, failed to step forward and make the falsity known, and knowingly exploited the false testimony in its closing argument to the jury." The subornation of perjury related to the testimony of a key prosecution witness who falsely denied that a deal had been made with the prosecutor, and the prosecutor's misrepresentation of that fact to the court. In addition, the prosecu-

sented the families of the deceased firemen in a tort action discovered that one of the prosecutor's expert witnesses at the trial had informed the prosecutor that the fire was not arson related, but was caused by an electrical malfunction. At a hearing in the fall of 1988, the prosecutor consistently maintained that nothing had been suppressed and offered to disclose pertinent documents. The judge rejected the offer and personally inspected the prosecutor's file. The judge found in that file two internal memoranda from two different assistant district attorneys to an executive in the prosecutor's office. Each memorandum stated that the expert witness had concluded that the fire had resulted from an electrical malfunction and had not been deliberately set—and that the expert's conclusion presented a major problem for the prosecution. None of this information was ever revealed to the defense. On the basis of the above, the court vacated the conviction and ordered the defendant's immediate release.

To be sure, disclosure is the one area above all else that relies on the prosecutor's good faith and integrity. If the prosecutor hides evidence, it is likely that nobody will ever know. The information will lay buried forever in the prosecutor's files. Moreover, most prosecutors, if they are candid, will concede that their inclination in this area is not to reveal information that might damage his or her case. Ironically, in this important area in which the prosecutor's fairness, integrity, and good faith are so dramatically put to the test, the courts have defaulted. According to the courts, the prosecutor's good or bad faith in secreting evidence is irrelevant. It is the character of the evidence that counts, not the character of the prosecutor. Thus, even if a violation is deliberate, and with an intent to harm the defendant, the courts will not order relief unless the evidence is so crucial that it would have changed the verdict. Thus, there is no real incentive for prosecutors to disclose such evidence.

Hopefully, in light of the recent disclosures of prosecutorial misconduct, courts, bar associations, and even legislatures will wake up to the quagmire in criminal justice. These bodies should act vigorously and aggressively to deter and punish the kinds of violations that recur all too frequently. Thus, reversals should be required automatically for deliberate suppression of evidence, and the standards for reversal for nondeliberate suppression relaxed; disciplinary action against prosecutors should be the rule rather than the exception; and legislation should be enacted making it a crime for prosecutors to willfully suppress evidence resulting in a defendant's conviction.

## MISBEHAVING IN THE COURTROOM TO SWAY THE JURY

Finally, the prosecutor's trial obligations often are violated. The duties of the prosecuting attorney during a trial were well stated in a classic opinion fifty years ago. The interest of the prosecutor, the court wrote, "is not that it shall win a case, but that justice shall be done. As such, he is in a peculiar and very definite sense the servant of the law, the twofold aim of which is that guilt shall not escape or innocence suffer. He may prosecute with earnestness and vigor—indeed, he should do so. But, while he may strike hard blows, he is not at liberty to strike a foul one."

Despite this admonition, prosecutors continually strike "foul blows." In one leading case of outrageous conduct, a prosecutor concealed from the jury in a murder case the fact that a pair of undershorts with red stains on it, a crucial piece of evidence, was stained not by blood but by paint. In another recent case, a prosecutor, in his summation, characterized the defendant as an "animal," told the jury that "the only guarantee against his future crimes would be to execute him," and that he should have "his face blown away by a shotgun." In another case, the prosecutor argued that the defendant's attorney knew the defendant was guilty; otherwise he would have put the defendant on the witness stand.

The above examples are illustrative of common practices today, and the main reason such misconduct occurs is quite simple: It works. Indeed, several studies have shown the importance of oral advocacy in the courtroom, as well as the effect produced by such conduct. For example, a student of trial advocacy often is told of the importance of the opening statement. Prosecutors would undoubtedly agree that the opening statement is indeed crucial. In a University of Kansas study, the importance of the opening statement was confirmed. From this study, the authors concluded that in the course of any given trial, the jurors were affected most by the first strong presentation that they saw. This finding leads to the conclusion that if a prosecutor were to present a particularly strong opening argument, the jury would favor the prosecution throughout the trial. Alternatively, if the prosecutor were to provide a weak opening statement, followed by a strong opening statement by the defense, then, according to the authors, the jury would favor the defense during the trial. It thus becomes evident that the prosecutor will be best served by making the strongest opening argument possible, thereby assisting the jury in gaining a better insight into what they are about to hear and see. The opportunity for the prosecutor to influence the jury at this point in the trial is considerable, and many prosecutors use this opportunity to their advantage, even if the circumstances do not call for lengthy or dramatic opening remarks.

An additional aspect of the prosecutor's power over the jury is suggested in a University of North Carolina study, which found that the more arguments counsel raises to support the different substantive arguments offered, the more the jury will believe in that party's case. Moreover, this study found that there is not necessarily a correlation between the amount of objective information in the argument and the persuasiveness of the presentation.

For the trial attorney, then, this study clearly points to the advantage of raising as many issues as possible at trial. For the prosecutor, the two studies taken together would dictate an "action-packed" opening statement, containing as many arguments as can be mustered, even those that might be irrelevant or unnecessary to convince the jury of the defendant's guilt. The second study would also dictate the same strategy for the closing argument. Consequently, a prosecutor who through use of these techniques attempts to assure that the jury knows his case may, despite violating ethical standards to seek justice, be "rewarded" with a guilty verdict. Thus, one begins to perceive the incentive that leads the prosecutor to misbehave in the courtroom.

Similar incentives can be seen with respect to the complex problem of controlling evidence to which the jury may have access. It is common knowledge that in the course of any trial, statements fre-

dence on the decisions of jurors. The authors of the test designed a variety of scenarios whereby some jurors heard about an incriminating piece of evidence while other jurors did not. The study found that the effect of the inadmissible evidence was directly correlated to the strength of the prosecutor's case. The authors of the study reported that when the prosecutor presented a weak case, the inadmissible evidence did in fact prejudice the jurors. Furthermore, the judge's admonition to the jurors to disregard certain evidence did not have the same effect as when the evidence had not been mentioned at all. It had a prejudicial impact anyway.

However, the study also indicated that when there was a strong prosecution case, the inadmissible evidence had little, if any, effect. Nonetheless, the most significant conclusion from the study is that inadmissible evidence had its most prejudicial impact when there was little other evidence upon which the jury could base a decision. In this situation, "the controversial evidence becomes quite salient in the jurors' minds."

Finally, with respect to inadmissible evidence and stricken testimony, even if

---

*In one leading case of outrageous conduct, a prosecutor concealed from the jury in a murder case the fact that a pair of undershorts with red stains on it, a crucial piece of evidence, was stained not by blood but by paint.*

---

quently are made by the attorneys or witnesses despite the fact that these statements may not be admissible as evidence. Following such a statement, the trial judge may, at the request of opposing counsel, instruct the jury to disregard what they have heard. Most trial lawyers, if they are candid, will agree that it is virtually impossible for jurors realistically to disregard these inadmissible statements. Studies here again demonstrate that our intuition is correct and that this evidence often is considered by jurors in reaching a verdict.

For example, an interesting study conducted at the University of Washington tested the effects of inadmissible evi-

one were to reject all of the studies discussed, it is still clear that although "stricken testimony may tend to be rejected in open discussion, it does have an impact, perhaps even an unconscious one, on the individual juror's judgment." As with previously discussed points, this factor—the unconscious effect of stricken testimony or evidence—will generally not be lost on the prosecutor who is in tune with the psychology of the jury.

The applicability of these studies to the issue of prosecutorial misconduct, then, is quite clear. Faced with a difficult case in which there may be a problem of proof, a prosecutor might be tempted to try to sway the jury by adverting to a matter that might be highly prejudicial. In this connection, another study has suggested that the jury will more likely consider inadmissible evidence that favors conviction.

Despite this factor of "defense favoritism," it is again evident that a prosecutor may find it rewarding to misconduct himself or herself in the courtroom. Of course, a prosecutor who adopts the unethical norm and improperly allows jurors to hear inadmissible proof runs the risk of jeopardizing any resulting conviction. In a situation where the prosecutor feels that he has a weak case, however, a subsequent reversal is not a particularly effective sanction when a conviction might have been difficult to achieve in the first place. Consequently, an unethical courtroom "trick" can be a very attractive idea to the prosecutor who feels he must win. Additionally, there is always the possibility of another conviction even after an appellate reversal. Indeed, while a large number of cases are dismissed following remand by an appellate court, nearly one-half of reversals still result in some type of conviction. Therefore, a pros-

moral standards, the problem of courtroom misconduct will inevitably be tolerated by the public.

Moreover, when considering the problems facing the prosecutor, one also must consider the tremendous stress under which the prosecutor labors on a daily basis. Besides the stressful conditions faced by the ordinary courtroom litigator, prosecuting attorneys, particularly those in large metropolitan areas, are faced with huge and very demanding caseloads. As a result of case volume and time demands, prosecutors may not be able to take advantage of opportunities to relax and recover from the constant onslaught their emotions face every day in the courtroom.

Under these highly stressful conditions, it is understandable that a prosecutor occasionally may find it difficult to face these everyday pressures and to resist temptations to behave unethically. It is not unreasonable to suggest that the conditions under which the prosecutor works can have a profound effect on his attempt to maintain high moral and ethical standards. Having established this hy-

---

*An unethical courtroom ''trick'' can be a very attractive idea to the prosecutor who feels he must win.*

---

ecutor can still succeed in obtaining a conviction even after his misconduct led to a reversal.

An additional problem in the area of prosecutor-jury interaction is the prosecutor's prestige; since the prosecutor represents the "government," jurors are more likely to believe him. Put simply, prosecutors are the "good guys" of the legal system, and because they have such glamor, they often may be tempted to use this advantage in an unethical manner. This presents a problem in that the average citizen may often forgive prosecutors for ethical indiscretions, because conviction of criminals certainly justifies in the public eye any means necessary. Consequently, unless the prosecutor is a person of high integrity and able to uphold the highest

pothesis, we see yet another reason why courtroom misconduct may occur.

## WHY PROSECUTORIAL MISCONDUCT PERSISTS

Although courtroom misconduct may in many instances be highly effective, why do such practices continue in our judicial system? A number of reasons may account for this phenomenon, perhaps the most significant of which is the harmless error doctrine. Under this doctrine, an appellate court can affirm a conviction despite the presence of serious misconduct during the trial. As one judge stated, the "practical objective of tests of harmless error is to conserve judicial resources by enabling appellate courts to cleanse the judicial process of prejudicial error without becoming mired in harmless error."

Although this definition portrays harmless error as having a most desirable consequence, this desirability is undermined when the prosecutor is able to misconduct himself without fear of sanction. Additionally, since every case is different, what constitutes harmless error in one case may be reversible error in another case. Consequently, harmless error determinations do not offer any significant precedents by which prosecutors can judge the status of their behavior. Moreover, harmless error determinations are essentially absurd. In order to apply the harmless error rule, appellate judges attempt to evaluate how various evidentiary items or instances of prosecutorial misconduct may have affected the jury's verdict. Although it may be relatively simple in some cases to determine whether improper conduct during a trial was harmless, there are many instances when such an analysis cannot be properly made but nevertheless is made. There are numerous instances in which appellate courts are deeply divided over whether or not a given error was harmless. The implications of these contradictory decisions are significant, for they demonstrate the utter failure of appellate courts to provide incentives for the prosecutor to control his behavior. If misconduct can be excused even when reasonable judges differ as to the extent of harm caused by such misbehavior, then very little guidance is given to a prosecutor to assist him in determining the propriety of his actions. Clearly, without such guidance, the potential for misconduct significantly increases.

A final point when analyzing why prosecutorial misconduct persists is the unavailability or inadequacy of penalties visited upon the prosecutor personally in the event of misconduct. Punishment in our legal system comes in varying degrees. An appellate court can punish a prosecutor by simply cautioning him not to act in the same manner again, reversing his case, or, in some cases, identifying by name the prosecutor who misconducted himself. Even these punishments, however, may not be sufficient to dissuade prosecutors from acting improperly. One noteworthy case describes a prosecutor who appeared before the appellate court on a misconduct issue for the third time, each instance in a different case.

Perhaps the ultimate reason for the ineffectiveness of the judicial system in curbing prosecutorial misconduct is that prosecutors are not personally liable for their misconduct. During the course of a trial, the prosecutor is absolutely shielded from any civil liability that might arise due to his or her misconduct, even if that misconduct was performed with malice. To be sure, there is clearly a necessary level of immunity accorded all government officials. Without such immunity, much of what is normally done by officials in authority might not be performed, out of fear that their practices would later be deemed harmful or improper. Granting prosecutors a certain level of immunity is reasonable. Allowing prosecutors to be completely shielded from civil liability in the event of misconduct, however, provides no deterrent to courtroom misconduct.

For the prosecutor, the temptation to cross over the allowable ethical limit must often be tremendous, because of the distinct advantages that such misconduct creates with respect to assisting the prosecutor to win his case by effectively influencing the jury. Most prosecutors must inevitably be subject to this temptation. It takes a constant effort on the part of every prosecutor to maintain the high moral standards necessary to avoid such temptations. Despite the frequent occurrences of courtroom misconduct, appellate courts have not provided significant incentives to deter it. Inroads will not be made in the effort to end prosecutorial misconduct until the courts decide to take a stricter, more consistent approach to this problem.

# The Search for

# JUSTICE:

## Is Impartiality Really Possible?

*"Defining and impaneling 'impartial' juries have proven to be daunting tasks, particularly in trials involving issues, events, or people of public interest."*

### Newton N. Minow and Fred H. Cate

*Mr. Minow is director, The Annenberg Washington Program in Communications Policy Studies, Northwestern University, Evanston, Ill.; a partner in the Chicago law firm Sidley & Austin; and former chairman of the Federal Communications Commission. Mr. Cate is associate professor of law, Indiana University School of Law, Bloomington; and of counsel to the Washington, D.C., law firm Fields & Director.*

IN 1871, Mark Twain described the system by which jurors are selected as putting "a ban upon intelligence and honesty, and a premium upon ignorance, stupidity, and perjury." His concern was that judges were responding to the expansion of the media —in that time, telegraph and newspapers— and news reports about people and events which later were the subject of a trial by banning informed citizens from juries. Twain wrote about the selection process in one case: "I remember one of those sorrowful farces, in Virginia, which we call a jury trial. A noted desperado killed Mr. B., a good citizen, in the most wanton and cold-blooded way. Of course the papers

were full of it, and all men capable of reading read about it. And of course all men not deaf and dumb and idiotic talked about it. . . .

"A minister, intelligent, esteemed, and greatly respected; a merchant of high character and known probity; a mining superintendent of intelligence and unblemished reputation; a quartz-mill owner of excellent standing, were all questioned . . . and all set aside. Each said public talk and the newspaper reports had not so biased his mind but that sworn testimony would overthrow his previously formed opinion and enable him to render a verdict without prejudice and in accordance with the facts. But of course such men could not be trusted with the case. Ignoramuses alone could mete out unsullied justice."

More than a century later, *The Daily Telegraph* wrote about jury selection in U.S. courts for another trial—that of Lt. Col. Oliver North. "Ignorance is the path to enlightenment. . . . The slightest taint of interest in the world beyond home and work is enough to win dismissal."

The issues raised by Mark Twain in 1871 and by *The Daily Telegraph* in 1989 demand more attention than ever today. Satellites, mobile equipment, broadcast and cable television, and other new technologies, combined with an insatiable public curiosity, have led to an explosion in news coverage and dramatic re-enactments of criminal activities. Average hours of television usage by household is a staggering 7.2 per day; average radio usage is almost three hours a day; and more than 64% of American households read newspapers. "L.A. Law" is seen by more people than even were eligible for jury service in Twain's day.

Because of mass media proliferation in American life, it is impossible for any responsible citizen to be unaware of major crimes in his or her local community. Even on the national level, Oliver North, former Washington, D.C., Mayor Marion Barry, *Exxon Valdez* Captain Joseph Hazelwood, billionaire hotel-keeper Leona Helmsley, or Panamanian leader Manuel Noriega are household names.

The Sixth Amendment to the Constitution requires that criminal defendants be tried by "an impartial jury of the State and district wherein the crime shall have been committed." Defining and impaneling "impartial" juries have proven to be daunting tasks, particularly in trials involving issues, events, or people of public interest. The press—vigorously exercising its First Amendment rights—may saturate the public with news and opinions about every facet of the case.

During the 1980s, the public was inundated with courthouse steps claims by defense lawyers that "my client can't get a fair trial because of pretrial publicity." The national newspapers and wire services alone carried more than 3,100 such statements.

These claims are a far cry from the jury system's common law roots. Originally, it was a gathering of people specifically chosen *because of* their knowledge of the parties and facts involved in the case. This was exemplified by Henry II's Grand Assize of Clarendon of 1166, which called for "the 12 most lawful men of the hundred" and "the four most lawful men of every vill" to give testimony about accused felons in the region. "If it developed that the jurors testified under oath that they were unacquainted with the facts, other jurors were summoned until there were 12 who had knowledge and who agreed."

Beginning in the early days of the republic, however, U.S. courts began to struggle with the issue of whether exposure to media coverage biases potential jurors. Perhaps the earliest case to deal squarely with the issue was the 1807 treason trial of Aaron Burr, over which Chief Justice John Marshall presided. Publicity about the feud between Burr and Pres. Thomas Jefferson had heightened interest in the sensational trial. Burr's attorneys argued that finding citizens for the jury who were unfamiliar with the parties and the incident—a virtually impossible task—was essential to protect the rights of their client.

Marshall disagreed. According to the Chief Justice, requiring jurors without any opinions "would exclude intelligent and observing men, whose minds were really in a situation to decide upon the whole case according to the testimony." Such a strident rule "therefore will not be required." He further stated: "Light impressions which may fairly be supposed to yield to the testimony that may be offered, which may leave the mind open to a fair consideration of that testimony, constitute no sufficient objection to a juror. . . . "

More than a century later, the U.S. Supreme Court ruled in *Irvin v. Dowd* that knowledge of the facts and issues alone will not necessarily disqualify a person from jury service. "It is not required, however, that the jurors be totally ignorant of the facts and issues involved." The Court's rationale was practical: "In these days of

swift, widespread and diverse methods of communication, an important case can be expected to arouse the interest of the public in the vicinity, and scarcely any of those best qualified to sit as jurors will not have formed some impression or opinion as to the merits of the case." It concluded: "It is sufficient if the juror can lay aside his impression or opinion and render a verdict based on the evidence presented in court."

## Inadequate remedies

Judges rely on a variety of techniques in attempting to identify partiality and minimize its impact in the courtroom. These techniques include change of venue (moving the trial), continuance (delaying it), *voir dire* (questioning potential jurors), jury instructions, and jury deliberation. Judges and prosecutors generally believe that these existing remedies work. Many social scientists, however, argue that they are ineffective at identifying and remedying bias.

Consider change of venue. Courts are extraordinarily reluctant to grant such motions for fear of admitting that the defendant can't get a fair trial in their jurisdiction. Even in the case of Jack Ruby—where every citizen of Dallas might be expected to have seen the film clip of him shooting Lee Harvey Oswald—the judge refused to grant a motion for change of venue. It also may be wholly ineffective as a remedy for pretrial publicity in nationally reported cases. Where in the U.S. can a jury unfamiliar with the acts of Manuel Noriega and the American invasion of Panama be impaneled?

Instructions from the judge to ignore information learned outside of the courtroom, though relied upon in almost every case, widely have been demonstrated to be ineffective. Judge Learned Hand called such instructions a "placebo," requiring of the jury "a mental gymnastic which is beyond, not only their powers, but anybody else's." At The Annenberg Washington Program's forum, "Selecting Impartial Juries: Must Ignorance Be a Virtue in Our Search for Justice?," psychologist Norbert Kerr stated: "Instructions—there's not a single study anywhere—good study, bad study—that shows that this does a bit of good. In fact, it may do harm."

The remedy for pretrial publicity most favored by judges, and the primary means through which most courts seek to determine the qualifications of citizens to sit on a jury, is *voir dire*. Through a series of questions, the judge and/or, in some jurisdictions, attorneys question potential jurors in an effort to determine whether they can be impartial.

Existing research suggests that *voir dire* is ineffective as a means of identifying prejudice. Many critics charge that it fails to elicit accurate or honest responses from

potential jurors or members of the venire (the panel from which they are chosen). Repeated studies have concluded that "Jurors do not speak out during *voir dire,* nor do they acknowledge their prejudices and preconceptions. Further, they occasionally lie when questioned in public." For instance, who is going to admit publicly to being a bigot? In addition, many attorneys and judges believe jurors use confessions of prejudice as a convenient method to avoid jury duty.

Many jurors underestimate their exposure, but, with follow-up questions, may demonstrate considerable knowledge about the case. For instance, in *State v. Copeland,* in which a black defendant was tried in Medart, Fla., for the brutal 1978 murder of a 19-year-old white woman, one juror denied having any knowledge of the case, but admitted upon further questioning to having "discussed it and read it in the newspapers."

Judges and lawyers all too frequently indicate the answers they want. Judge Stanley Sporkin of the U.S. District Court for the District of Columbia stated at the Annenberg forum that he asks potential jurors, "Could you forget about what you've read or heard about this case and just take the facts as you hear [them] in this courtroom and decide the case on those facts? And nine times out of 10 they certainly can."

Effective *voir dire* questions are difficult to frame. Vague, open-ended queries frequently fail to elicit information about possible bias. Jurors may not understand what information is prejudicial or even may not be aware that they have been exposed to prejudicial publicity. Specific questions, on the other hand, may give the potential juror precisely the information the attorney wants to be certain the juror does not have.

In some cases, the judge may conduct no individualized *voir dire* at all before excluding members of the venire because they had been exposed to press accounts about the case. Judge Sporkin stated that, in one trial which was the subject of considerable publicity, "I just merely asked the panel how many of you have heard about this, and maybe a third said they had. I excluded them. . . ."

At heart, the answer to the problem of ensuring impartiality is not provided by existing judicial remedies. Rather, the answer lies in the public's and the court's understanding that mass communications make the world today fundamentally different from the past, when only men and women who neither had seen nor heard of a controversy were thought to be suitable jurors.

The Supreme Court has identified a number of essential roles that juries play in the American judicial system. For instance, one important function is to protect citizens against "arbitrary law enforcement," "the corrupt or overzealous prosecutor," and "the compliant, biased, or eccentric judge." The Court has written, juries "interpos[e] between the accused and his accuser . . . the commonsense judgment of a group of laymen." Juries also play an important role in preserving social order.

None of these roles involve discerning the truth and, in fact, objective truth may not be a goal of the judicial system. Alexis de Tocqueville wrote in *Democracy in America:* "If it were a question of deciding how far the jury, especially the jury in civil cases, facilitates the good administration of justice, I admit that its usefulness can be contested." Far removed from any role they play in making decisions or doing justice, de Tocqueville concluded: "Juries are wonderfully effective in shaping a nation's judgment and increasing its natural lights. That, in my view, is its greatest advantage. It should be regarded as a free school which is always open and in which each juror learns his rights . . . and is given practical lessons in the law."

The various remedies used by courts to identify bias, and the all-too-frequent association of "impartial" with "unaware," create an assumption that ideal jurors are ignorant ones and that the jury is a blank slate on which the court may write freely. This assumption is inaccurate and unrealistic.

Other countries which rely on juries, such as Canada and Great Britain, have rejected the practice of questioning them about their background and attitudes except in unusual circumstances. These nations recognize the obvious fact that every juror brings to the jury box opinions, biases, and prejudices. It is because they are supposed to represent the interests and the breadth of their communities' moral sense that juries are used, rather than a judge or individual jurors, and why they have more than one or two members.

One British barrister declared: "Certainly in this country the whole basis of the system is that you are presuming you are entrusting cases to jurors. And so you must; if you're going to ask people to do a job, then I think you must trust them."

If the jury is to perform the many functions assigned to it—safeguard liberty, protect against the government, represent the community, preserve social order, *and* determine guilt or innocence—it must be composed of informed citizens who are representative of the community. Jurors need to reflect its collective interests and experiences. The logic that supports the Supreme Court's refusal to permit the exclusion of blacks and women from serving applies to the exclusion of well-informed, curious, even opinionated people as well.

The U.S. Attorney for the District of Columbia, Jay B. Stephens, stated at the Annenberg forum: "From the perspective of the government it is to our advantage generally, I think, to have intelligent jurors who listen to the evidence, who evaluate the evidence, and who do not go off on extraneous kinds of issues. That purpose is served, I think, by informed jurors, by jurors who are an integral part of the community, who participate in the community, who are very much into what is going on in the world and in the community and stay informed."

The Sixth Amendment guarantees a defendant's right to trial by impartial jury, not impartial *jurors.* Perhaps the nation's founders recognized that impartial people —in the sense of men and women without bias, opinion, or prejudice—do not exist. Rather than base the protection of fundamental judicial rights on an unrealistic and unobtainable concept, the Sixth Amendment depends instead on the interaction of 12 members of the community. Each of those citizens brings his or her own experiences and knowledge into the jury box. Their verdict is not merely the sum of 12 independent votes; rather, it is the product of deliberation, of the interaction between their individual experiences and knowledge.

The term "jury selection" is a misnomer. Lawyers and judges do not select juries. Instead, in the words of defense attorney and former American Bar Association Litigation Section president Ronald Olson, they *de*select those potential jurors "who have particular biases against you that you think would be unfair." Extensive *voir dire* and challenges—permitting attorneys to deselect their way to a panel less representative of the community—may prove a far greater threat to the fundamental fairness of the verdict than exposure to any media coverage. If the membership of the panel is skewed by the selection process, then the fundamental guarantee of fairness—the diversity and breadth of experiences and views—is likely to be compromised.

Regular exposure to media may increase the likelihood of an impartial jury. In fact, the skills of discernment that most citizens exercise and refine daily in evaluating the barrage of news, advertising, and rhetoric may help jurors to be both capable and impartial.

Moreover, competent jurors are not led so easily by the media. The recent inability of the jury to reach a verdict on 12 counts in the cocaine and perjury trial of Marion Barry should give pause to those who believe that a jury easily is swayed by the press. In that case, following a barrage of stories about the Mayor's arrest and legal maneuvers, the jury watched a videotape of Barry smoking crack cocaine and heard his defense counsel acknowledge that the Mayor had used drugs, while Barry testified before a grand jury that he never had used drugs. Still, they acquitted him on one count and refused to convict him on 12 of the 13 others. A similarly dramatic result was reached in the drug trial of John DeLorean, where a jury acquitted the former car manufacturer despite a videotape showing him purchasing cocaine and toasting the success of his illegal venture.

## Looking ahead

To think that jurors wholly unacquainted with the facts of a notorious case can be impaneled today is to dream. Anyone meeting that standard of ignorance should be suspect. The search for such a jury is a chimera. It is also unnecessary. Knowledgeable jurors today—like 800 years ago—can form an impartial jury. In fact, the very diversity of views and experiences that they possess is the best guarantee of impartiality.

Faced with escalating media coverage of people and events that subsequently become embroiled in trials, and practical as well as constitutional hurdles to stymieing that interest, courts are betting the constitutional rights of criminal defendants—not to mention their liberty and, in some cases, their lives—on ineffective judicial remedies for identifying and remedying bias. As a result, some courts mistake "unaware" for "impartial," and so search at great length for jurors who know nothing about the case. The quest for "unaware" jurors also excludes qualified citizens, thereby denying the defendant's right to a representative, competent jury and media-literate citizens the opportunity to study in de Tocqueville's "free school . . . in which each juror learns his rights . . . and is given practical lessons in the law. . . ."

Courts neither need ignore the impact of media coverage on the selection of an impartial jury nor become hopelessly enmeshed in examining the amount and type of it through extended and far-reaching *voir dire.* The language of the Sixth Amendment, dictates of the Supreme Court, and realities of modern society require that courts impanel juries which are impartial, but not without knowledge and opinions.

Mark Twain's words of outrage that informed citizens were being excluded from juries, penned more than a century ago, continue to argue forcefully against the judicial practice of keeping them off juries: "In this age, when a gentleman of high social standing, intelligence, and probity swears that testimony given under solemn oath will outweigh, with him, street talk and newspaper reports based upon mere hearsay, he is worth a hundred jurymen who will swear to their own ignorance and stupidity, and justice would be far safer in his hands than in theirs. Why could not the jury law be so altered as to give men of brains and honesty an *equal chance* with fools and miscreants?"

# Jurors Hear Evidence and Turn It Into Stories

*Studies show they arrange details to reflect their beliefs.*

## Daniel Goleman

Despite the furor over the verdict in the Rodney G. King beating case, scientists who study juries say the system is by and large sound. Many also believe that it is susceptible to manipulation and bias, and could be improved in various specific ways suggested by their research findings.

If there is any lesson to be learned from the research findings, it is that juries are susceptible to influence at virtually every point, from the moment members are selected to final deliberation.

Much of the newest research on the mind of the juror focuses on the stories that jurors tell themselves to understand the mounds of disconnected evidence, often presented in a confusing order. The research suggests that jurors' unspoken assumptions about human nature play a powerful role in their verdicts.

"People don't listen to all the evidence and then weigh it at the end," said Dr. Nancy Pennington, a psychologist at the University of Colorado. "They process it as they go along, composing a continuing story throughout the trial that makes sense of what they're hearing."

That task is made difficult by the way evidence is presented in most trials, in an order dictated for legal reasons rather than logical ones. Thus, in a murder trial, the first witness is often a coroner, who establishes that a death occurred.

"Jurors have little or nothing to tie such facts to, unless an attorney suggested an interpretation in the opening statement," in the form of a story line to follow, Dr. Pennington said.

---

*Studies show jurors are often more merciful than judges.*

---

In an article in the November 1991 issue of Cardozo Law Review, Dr. Pennington, with Dr. Reid Hastie, also a psychologist at the University of Colorado, reported a series of experiments that show just how important jurors' stories are in determining the verdict they come to. In the studies, people called for jury duty but not involved in a trial were recruited for a simulation in which they were to act as jurors for a murder trial realistically re-enacted on film.

In the case, the defendant, Frank Johnson, had quarreled in a bar with the victim, Alan Caldwell, who threatened him with a razor. Later that evening they went outside, got into a fight, and Johnson knifed Caldwell, who died. Disputed points included whether or not Caldwell was a bully who had started the first quarrel when his girlfriend had asked Johnson for a ride to the racetrack, whether Johnson had stabbed Caldwell or merely held his knife out to protect himself, and whether Johnson had gone home to get a knife.

In detailed interviews of the jurors, Dr. Pennington found that in explaining how they had reached their verdicts, 45 percent of the references they made were to events that had not been included in the courtroom testimony. These included inferences about the men's motives and psychological states, and assumptions the jurors themselves brought to the story from their own experience.

The stories that jurors told themselves pieced together the evidence in ways that could lead to opposite verdicts. One common story among the jurors, which led to a verdict of first-degree murder, was that the threat with the razor by Caldwell had so enraged Johnson that he went home to get his knife—a point that was in dispute—with the intention of picking a fight, during which he stabbed him to death.

By contrast, just as many jurors told themselves a story that led them to a verdict of not guilty: Caldwell started the fight with Johnson and threatened him with a razor, and Caldwell ran into the knife that Johnson was using to protect himself.

### Role of Jurors' Backgrounds

The study found that jurors' backgrounds could lead to crucial differences in the assumptions they brought to their explanatory stories. Middle-class jurors were more likely to find the defendant guilty than were working-class jurors. The difference mainly hinged on how they interpreted the fact that Johnson had a knife with him during the struggle.

Middle-class jurors constructed stories that saw Johnson's having a knife as strong evidence that he planned a murderous assault on Caldwell in their second confrontation. But working-class jurors said it was likely that a man like Johnson would be in the habit of carrying a knife with him for protection, and so they saw nothing incriminating about his having the knife.

"Winning the battle of stories in the opening statements may help determine what evidence is attended to, how it is interpreted, and what is recalled both during and after the trial," Dr. Richard Lempert, a psychologist at the University of Michigan Law School, wrote in commenting on Dr. Pennington's article.

---

*One juror might invent a story of self-defense; another calls it homicide.*

---

Verdicts that do not correspond to one's own "story" of a case are shocking. In the King case, "we didn't hear the defense story of what was going on, but only saw the strongest piece of the prosecution's evidence, the videotape," said Dr. Stephen Penrod, a psychologist at the University of Minnesota Law School. "If we had heard the defense theory, we may not have been so astonished by the verdict."

In the contest among jurors to recruit fellow members to one or another version of what happened, strong voices play a disproportionate role. Most juries include some people who virtually never speak up, and a small number who dominate the discussion, typically jurors of higher social status, according to studies reviewed in "Judging the Jury" (Plenum Press,

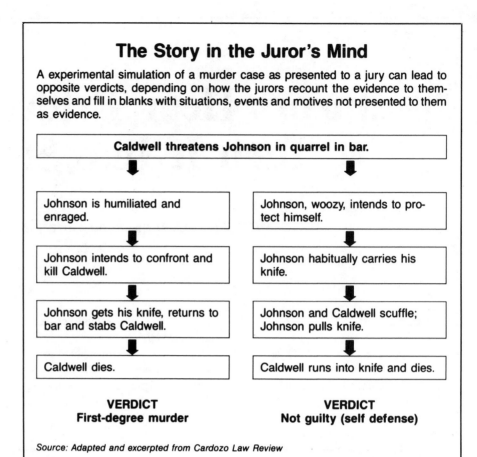

## The Story in the Juror's Mind

A experimental simulation of a murder case as presented to a jury can lead to opposite verdicts, depending on how the jurors recount the evidence to themselves and fill in blanks with situations, events and motives not presented to them as evidence.

**Caldwell threatens Johnson in quarrel in bar.**

| | |
|---|---|
| Johnson is humiliated and enraged. | Johnson, woozy, intends to protect himself. |
| Johnson intends to confront and kill Caldwell. | Johnson habitually carries his knife. |
| Johnson gets his knife, returns to bar and stabs Caldwell. | Johnson and Caldwell scuffle; Johnson pulls knife. |
| Caldwell dies. | Caldwell runs into knife and dies. |
| **VERDICT** First-degree murder | **VERDICT** Not guilty (self defense) |

*Source: Adapted and excerpted from Cardozo Law Review*

---

1986) by two psychologists, Dr. Valerie Hans of the University of Delaware and Dr. Neil Vidmar of Duke University.

The research also reveals that "juries are more often merciful to criminal defendants" than judges in the same cases would be, said Dr. Hans.

**Blaming the Victim**

In recent research, Dr. Hans interviewed 269 jurors in civil cases and found that many tended to focus on the ability of victims to have avoided being injured. "You see the same kind of blaming the victim in rape cases, too, especially among female jurors," Dr. Hans said. "Blaming the victim is reassuring to jurors because if victims are responsible for the harm that befell them, then you don't have to worry about becoming a victim yourself because you know what to do to avoid it."

That tendency may have been at work among the King jurors, Dr. Hans said, "when the jurors said, King was

in control and that if he stopped moving the police would have stopped beating him."

"Of course, the more they saw King as responsible for what happened, the less to blame the officers were in their minds," Dr. Hans said.

Perhaps the most intensive research has focused on the selection of a jury. Since lawyers can reject a certain number of prospective jurors during jury selection without having to give a specific reason, the contest to win the mind of the jury begins with the battle to determine who is and is not on the jury.

The scientific selection of juries began in the early 1970's when social scientists volunteered their services for the defense in a series of political trials, including proceedings arising from the 1971 Attica prison uprising in upstate New York. One method used was to poll the community where the trial was to be held to search for clues to attitudes that might work against the defendant, which the defense lawyers could then use to eliminate jurors.

For example, several studies have shown that people who favor the death penalty are generally pro-prosecution in criminal cases, and so more likely to convict a defendant. Defense lawyers can ask prospective jurors their views on the death penalty, and eliminate those who favor it.

On the basis of such a community survey for a trial in Miami, Dr. Elizabeth Loftus, a psychologist at the University of Washington, found that as a group, whites trust the honesty and fairness of the police far more than blacks. "If you knew nothing else, you'd use that demographic variable in picking a jury in the King case," she said. "But in Ventura County, there's a jury pool with almost no blacks. It was a gift to the defense, in retrospect."

Over the last two decades, such methods have been refined to the point that 300 more consulting groups now advise lawyers on jury selection.

"To advise lawyers on how to present their case, we present both sides of a case to a mock jury recruited to represent the jury pool," said Dr. Lois Heaney, a sociologist at the National Jury Project in Oakland, Calif. The arguments are made to groups ranging from 24 to 100 jurors, who, after hearing the arguments, break into jury-size groups to deliberate.

"More than the verdict, it's the process," Dr. Heaney said. "Where did they bog down; what was most important to them; what issues did they focus on." With that information, the consultants can then advise lawyers on such tactics as their opening statement, and the points where visual aids would help the jury better understand the argument.

Depending on the complexity and how many rounds of mock juries a lawyer requires, the service can cost from $5,000 to more than $100,000.

Among the suggestions for improving jury performance is making juries smaller than the traditional 12. But research data suggest at least one reason for keeping their present size: the more members of a jury, the better its collective memory. In a study of more than 700 jurors, Dr. Pennington and colleagues found that the average rate at which individual jurors remembered evidence from a trial was 60 percent; for judge's instructions the average was 44 percent. But for the jury as a whole, the memory rates were far better: 93 percent for facts and 82 percent for instructions.

Several recommendations for improving the quality of jury decisions have been made by researchers. One is that judges give instructions to the jury at the start of the case rather than only at the end. This would allow jurors to focus on the most relevant evidence and keep them from giving undue weight to facts that matter little from a legal standpoint.

With the cooperation of judges, jurors were allowed to change the usual rules by asking questions of witnesses or taking notes during trials, in a series of experiments conducted by Dr. Penrod of the University of Minnesota and Dr. Larry Heuer, a psychologist at Columbia University. With both changes, the jurors reported a higher level of satisfaction with their verdicts than did jurors who could neither ask questions nor take notes.

# GRAND ILLUSION

**Summary: The grand jury is a secret but critical first step in a serious criminal proceeding. Yet some wonder if it is worth preserving. The account of one juror in the District of Columbia, where a grand jury indictment is mandatory in every felony case, opens the door on the judicial system.**

## Charlotte Allen

It was a late November afternoon, and the group of 23 men and women, minus an absentee or two, had been sitting in a smallish room at the District of Columbia Superior Court since 9 a.m. They were supposed to be discussing a criminal case. Instead, some of them were arguing. One woman was crying. Another had stormed from the room. There were calls to go find someone from the outside — a prosecutor, a marshal — to restore order. It was a day of frayed nerves, of official business mixed with the personal. And there would be more like it before the group — strangers just a month before — would finally wrap up its business.

Everyone knows something about trial by jury, the body of 12 citizens whose secret deliberations decide the fate of defendants in a trial. Hardly anyone knows much about the grand jury, the body of 23 citizens that in all federal courts and in the courts of every state but one render equally secret deliberations that determine whether there is enough evidence in a felony case to charge a defendant in the first place.

The grand jury is a critical preliminary stage in a criminal proceeding. Operating without any direct guidance from judges, it has been called a mere rubber stamp for the prosecutor. There have been calls for its abolition. There have been calls for major reforms. Nonetheless, grand juries keep meeting, day in and day out, holding in their hands the power to decide who shall be forced to go to the time, trouble and expense of standing trial on criminal charges.

In the District of Columbia, where a grand jury indictment is mandatory in every felony case, 868 men and women put in 25 days of grand jury service at the Superior Court in 1990, the last year for which there are figures and likely a typical year (their term is theoretically 18 months but most of that is inactive time). One grand jury is not enough to handle the more than 9,000 indictments that go through the court every year (the rest of the cases are dismissed or plea-bargained), so at any given time four separate grand juries are sitting.

Jurors usually put in three full days a week of virtually uncompensated time for eight weeks or five days a week for five weeks. In return, they get an unparalleled view of the criminal justice system. They meet a parade of prosecutors and assistants, police officers and witnesses. For many, there is satisfaction in playing some role in the fight against crime.

One such grand jury, which included this writer, handed down indictments in more than 200 felony cases, starting in October and wrapping up in mid-January. Many cases were fascinating; the jury learned a great deal about crimes and how and why they are committed. But its role was often redundant and superfluous. In most cases, a judge at a preliminary hearing had already decided there was enough evidence for prosecutors to proceed.

In many of the drug cases—and there were scores of them in drug-plagued Washington—the prosecutors asked for indictments on felony charges carrying mandatory prison terms, when their real aim was to persuade the suspect to plead guilty to a misdemeanor. In other words, the grand jury was helping the prosecutors create plea bargaining chips, for out of the approximately 14,000 felony cases filed every year in the District of Columbia Superior Court, fewer than 800 go as far as a jury trial.

In the few cases where the jury's duties were not redundant—"grand jury originals," where there was no arrest or preliminary hearing until the jurors voted to indict—its function was to help the prosecutors investigate, and build, their cases.

"A good prosecutor gets his case all tried before the grand jury," says veteran Washington criminal defense lawyer Robert Bennett, a former federal prosecutor who recently acted as Senate special counsel in the savings and loan investigations. In fact, Justice Department guidelines forbid prosecutors from going forward on cases unless they think they have enough legally admissible evidence to obtain a conviction.

The investigative process was fascinating, especially in cases when several alibi witnesses told different stories. And it was educational for the prosecutors, too. But was it appropriate? Grand juries are supposed to be representatives of the community who act as buffers between the government and the accused. But this grand jury, just as the civil libertarians always say, usually did exactly what the prosecutors wanted.

Are the civil libertarians right? Are grand juries fair? More pressing, are they obsolete? Two-thirds of the states have made them optional, or reserved them for capital cases or investigations of public scandals. Pennsylvania's grand juries can only investigate. States with limited or optional grand juries use preliminary hearings to establish probable cause. On the other hand, the voters of California, where prosecutors had to contend with expensive procedural protections for defendants at preliminary hearings, approved an anticrime initiative in 1990 that brought back grand juries, at least in principle. (The state Supreme Court had effectively abolished their use.)

Because all its courts are federal courts, the District of Columbia is bound by the Constitution to use grand juries in every felony case, from joyriding to murder. The Fifth Amendment requires that, except in certain kinds of military cases, "no person shall be held to answer for a capital, or otherwise infamous crime, unless on a presentment or indictment of a grand jury." The clause covers all the federal courts, though it doesn't apply to the states.

The constitutional issue hasn't quelled complaints from some lawyers in the District, echoing critics elsewhere, that grand juries are cumbersome, expensive and sometimes force criminal defendants to spend more time in jail waiting for their trials. "We're spending $1 million a year on grand juries" in Washington, complains San Harahan, executive director of the Washington-based Council for Court Excellence. The figure does not seem to be out of line for the rest of the country. In 1990, Sol Wachtler chief judge of New York's highest court,

wrote an article for the *New York Times* complaining that grand juries in that state, which also requires an indictment in every felony case, ate up $2 million in public funds, not counting work time lost by police officers coming to the jury room to testify.

The grand jury is a creation of medieval England, and some of the ambiguity about its proper role—sword of the prosecutor or shield of the innocent?—stems from its com-

> In many of the drug cases — and there were scores of them — the prosecutors asked for indictments on felony charges carrying mandatory prison terms, when their real aim was to persuade the suspect to plead guilty to a misdemeanor.

plicated history. The original mandate of grand juries was not to protect against zealous prosecutors but to ferret out criminals for the Norman kinds on the basis of the grand jurors' knowledge of their communities. By the end of the 14th century, today's two-jury system of processing felony cases was already in place: a 23-person grand jury to issue the accusing document and a 12-person petit jury to hear evidence at trial.

By the late 17th century, grand juries had taken on a more independent function and often refused to allow prosecutions of the politically unpopular. The grand juries of the American Colonies were particularly uncooperative with the British crown, so it was not surprising that the right to have a grand jury review serious charges became part of the Bill of Rights.

Until relatively recently, judges personally picked the grand jury — typically one for each county — from a so-called blue-ribbon list of outstanding citizens. That was partly because grand juries served for a year,

18 months or sometimes two years. It was supposed to be an honor to be called for the grand jury, and only solid citizens of middle years could afford to contribute so much of their time. Blue-ribbon grand juries are still a feature of localities where the jurors' function is strictly investigatory. Starting in the 1960s, however, democracy came to the grand jury. Court rulings and federal law began requiring the random selection of jurors, including grand jurors, from voter registration and driver's license lists, in order to ensure that a true cross section of the community weighed the evidence.

n 1990, 3,211 adult residents of the District of Columbia were sent grand jury summonses. The vast majority either did not receive the notice, had a legal excuse for not serving — a past felony conviction, illness or a critical job — or simply did not show up. (This is supposed to be a crime, but no-shows are never arrested.) In large U.S. cities, the no-response and disqualification rate for jury summonses is staggering: up to 75 percent in some localities, according to a 1990 study by the National Center for State Courts.

Washington is losing population. According to the Census Bureau, there has been a net loss of 9,000 residents since the 1990 census, leaving only 598,000 people in a city that housed 802,000 in 1950. This trend has meant a gradual reduction in the number of Washingtonians available to sit on juries. Unfortunately, felony filings have not dropped proportionately with the population — they reached an all-time high in 1988 of nearly 15,000 (more than twice the 1983 number). As a result, residents who vote or drive can expect to get called for jury duty, grand or petit, every other year. It is no wonder that, in an effort to boost juror morale and encourage those who are called to serve, the Council for Court Excellence has established a "Jury Service Appreciation Week," observed each fall.

The District of Columbia is 70 percent black, so it was not surprising that when grand jury No. 3 was finally sorted out in late October, there were relatively few whites: two men of retirement age and two women, one of them this writer. The other woman, Rose (grand jurors' names have been changed to protect their privacy), was a gregarious woman who befriended everyone.

She had pimento-colored hair and one front tooth. A variety of ailments had put her on Social Security disability and made it, as she forthrightly explained, unprofitable for her to work. She would have lost her Medicaid.

That first day, Rose made it clear that the personal lives and feelings of the jurors would intermingle with day-to-day business. "I hope they'll let us out early today," she confided as the jurors walked from the main courthouse to the grand jury room in an adjacent building that also houses the offices of the U.S. attorney, whose assistants prosecute felonies in both the federal District Court for Washington and the D.C. Superior Court. "I have a legal matter at 2 p.m."

"What kind of legal matter?"

"The parole board. They picked up my husband yesterday. It was so unfair. He was just standing on the sidewalk minding his own business. But he had an open can of beer. I told him not to do that, but he won't listen to me. Now they've got him back at Lorton [Washington's main prison, in Northern Virginia], and they might keep him in there for 10 years if I don't do something. I'm so worried."

"What did they pick him up for?"

"Escape."

It turned out that Ben, as she called him, was actually her fiance. The two had set up housekeeping at Rose's condominium in anticipation of their upcoming marriage. Ben had a checkered penal past, mainly for theft crimes, and Rose would be on one of the free telephones in the grand jury lounge every day, conferring with his lawyer. Together they managed to broker down Ben's total sentence from the anticipated 10 years to a mere 75 days. He would be released in late December, just after the grand jury started a three-week holiday break. "I'm going to bring him in here to meet you," Rose promised the rest of the jurors.

The first task of grand jury No. 3 was to learn how to do its job. A team of grand jury coordinators handed out ID badges and led the group to a small room — with a double bank of chairs, a witness box and a desk for the court reporter — where jurors would spend the next few weeks. The rules were simple: no smoking, no eating, no sleeping, no leaving except on official breaks. A photocopied sheet explaining the steps in a felony prosecution was handed out, as was another that translated in-house abbreviations for crimes: PWID for "possession with intent to distribute,"

and so forth. There had to be a quorum of 16 in the room to hear a case and a vote of 12 to indict.

A coordinator picked a sergeant at arms from several volunteers; she had the duty of fetching witnesses from the waiting room and delivering the votes to the marshal. A foreman (officially foreperson) had earlier been selected to keep order and sign the indictments, and a deputy foreman to swear in witnesses and help the foreman tally votes. A volunteer

> Most jurors on grand jury No. 3 were working and trying to raise families in neighborhoods where theft and violence seemed to be near-daily occurrences. Many commuted on long bus rides from corners of the city that figured strongly in the case files.

secretary kept the case log in a huge book. The foreman, deputy foreman and secretary sat at a long table at the front of the room with the prosecutor.

Most grand jurors complain of boredom waiting for cases, but the high crime rate in Washington kept a parade of prosecutors marching in and out, vying with each other for the grand jury's time. The result was a long day's work, occasionally until 6:30 in the evening. Breaks? The prosecutors often forgot about them. Jurors learned how to slip out between cases to the rest rooms or, for the half who smoked, to the "cancer canyon" of chairs in the hallway just outside the room.

That first afternoon was spent watching a two-hour videotape in which an assistant U.S. attorney went through all the paperwork that leads up to an indictment. She was a literal talking head, and the video camera had just two angles: a close-up and a middle-distance shot. Everyone in the room broke the no-sleeping rule on the very first day. The next day's training session was more lively, fea-

turing the drug man and the stolen car man, both from the Police Department. Jurors learned how to make crack cocaine on the kitchen stove and how to start a car without the keys. Then grand jury No. 3 was in business, and the prosecutors started coming in with their case files and their witnesses.

Grand juries work in secret in order to protect the reputations of innocent people who may never be indicted and the skins of witnesses called to testify. The hearings are closed to the public, and the prosecutor, court reporter and all witnesses must leave the room when the jurors discuss the evidence and vote. Jurors take an oath never to reveal witnesses' names or anything else about the cases, which can be described in only the most general terms.

Suffice it to say that the cases fell into two categories: crimes of appalling violence involving guns, knives, heavy boots applied to the skull or all three, and run-of-the mill car thefts and drug sales. In fact, 70 percent of the arrests in the District of Columbia are drug arrests. The prosecutors bring the drug or stolen car cases straight to the grand jury for a quickie indictment procedure called a "same-day presentment," in which only the undercover officer who had bought the cocaine rocks or the uniformed officer who had tracked down the car testifies.

"We're losing the war on drugs," Vince Caputy, the deputy assistant U.S. attorney in charge of the grand jury, cheerfully announced. "But, what the hell, we're trying."

There were almost no crimes between those two extremes: no burglary cases, except when someone got caught in the act, only two forged checks and no simple thefts.

"Are we going to have any interesting cases like Oliver North?" a juror asked on the first day. The answer was no (North's case went to U.S. District Court because he was accused of violating federal laws) — except that many of the cases were highly interesting in themselves, snapshots of the sociology of the underclass. For example, it is illegal for almost anyone to carry a gun in the District of Columbia. That meant that for every crime in which a gun was used, there was also a charge of "carrying a pistol without a license" or CPWL (no one except a police officer can get a license, not even a retired officer).

This complete ban on gun carrying and sales — the District has one of the strictest gun-control laws in the nation — has had no apparent effect on the use of firearms. Washington has the nation's highest per capita homicide rate, its 489 slayings last year topping 1990's 483.

Almost all the violent crimes reviewed by grand jury No. 3 — slayings, maimings, robberies and rapes — involved guns, sometimes war-strength arsenals, .357s and .45s and TAC 9 semiautomatics with clips containing dozens of bullets. Drug dealers were armed. Kids riding around in stolen cars were armed. Scores of CPWL charges were handed down, as well as scores of charges of UF (unregistered firearm) and UA (unregistered ammunition) and PFDCV (possession of a firearm during a crime of violence). Those few who could not get their hands on a gun made lethal use of knives, scissors, garden tools, Timberland boots and two-by-fours.

Gun control was a frequent topic of cynical conversation among the jurors, many of whom lived in the very neighborhoods where the crimes being reviewed had been committed. The general view was that gun control was a pantywaist idea cooked up by "yuppies" with little appreciation of the day-to-day dangers of living in an urban neighborhood.

"How come you can buy a gun in Maryland and Virginia, and you can't buy one in the District of Columbia?" one fellow asked. "How can you protect yourself?"

All in all, the jurors were extraordinarily socially conservative. Many were regular churchgoers who talked about their faith unabashedly. Jackie, the sergeant at arms, read the Bible during breaks between cases. She and others often engaged in debates over the interpretation of passages and the faults and virtues of various translations. There was little patience with psychological and class explanations for crime. Jurors were aghast when teenagers came in to testify about shootings and beatings dressed in designer warmup suits. They joked about a case involving a clearly homosexual man stabbed by someone he had apparently picked up (they indicted the assailant anyway).

In fact, except for Rose with her Ben ("He's a big baby"), these grand jurors felt no empathy whatsoever with criminals. A majority appeared to favor the death penalty (abolished years ago in the District of Columbia). One man thought that convicted

murderers ought to be made to serve as organ donors. One day a girl testified, hands over her face in shame, how she had been repeatedly raped by her father. "That man shouldn't be in jail," declared Sam, the deputy foreman, after she left the room. "He should be *under* the jail."

Pay for grand jury service was $30 a day plus $2 for carfare. This meant that anyone who could not persuade his employer to compensate him for the time off work paid a severe financial penalty for serving. This in turn meant that almost everyone on the grand jury was either retired, unemployed or employed by the District or federal governments, they being among the few employers with a policy of encouraging jury service.

With the recession, there were even rumors of "professional grand jurors" — people on unemployment who are called for the petit jury but switch to the grand so as to serve longer (petit jurors in Washington serve for either one day or one trial, which usually lasts less than a week).

No professionals appeared to be on grand jury No. 3. Most jurors were working and trying to raise families in neighborhoods where theft and violence seemed to be near-daily occurrences. Many of them commuted on long bus rides from corners of the city that were far from the world of lobbying and politicking associated with the nation's capital.

Jurors tended to regard white Washingtonians as hopeless naifs who became targets for trouble, like the pair of aging hippies in one case who cruised onto one of the tougher streets of Southeast Washington looking to buy cocaine; one was shot dead in the car. Sam and the foreman, Mary, rolled their eyes and shook their heads after the testimony. They did the same after hearing the case of a woman whose gentrified row house was burglarized.

"White people," said Mary. "They don't pull their blinds. They want that *House Beautiful* look, that *Architectural Digest* look. You go anywhere, Georgetown, Capitol Hill, and you see no blinds. They don't have that fear.

"Yuppies." She smiled a smile of infinite patience.

Once a week there was a process, regarded as farcical, called "Gaith-erization." It was named after Tyrone Gaither, who in the late 1960s was indicted and convicted along with an accomplice for shoplifting five sport coats from a Washington department store. The grand jury had voted to

indict the two for grand larceny, and the foreman signed the indictment document later when it was typed up.

Reviewing the case in 1969, the U.S. Circuit Court of Appeals for the District of Columbia ruled that the procedure the grand jury had followed was incorrect. In order to avoid the possibility that the written indictment might differ from the one the grand jury actually voted on, the court said, the grand jury should take a second vote on the exact wording of the indictment. Though there was no evidence that the grand jury had actually made a mistake on Gaither, and there was plenty of evidence that he and his accomplice had stolen the coats, the appellate court decided to reward the pair's lawyers for pointing out the error, and it overturned the convictions.

"I'd like to kill Mr. Gaither," one of the assistant U.S. attorneys told grand jury No. 3.

The ruling, apparently unique to the District of Columbia, threatened to make every grand jury proceeding twice as long, with the prosecutor having to read aloud every typed-up indictment and then wait for a second vote and after that a foreman's signature. Eventually the judges and prosecutors worked out a compromise: As long as the reading, second vote and signing took place at approximately the same time, the Gaither ruling would be deemed complied with. So each Wednesday an assistant U.S. attorney came in with a stack of indictments representing the week's work and speed-read them. Mary signed them. Then the prosecutor left the room and the grand jury voted again. Often more jurors voted to approve the written indictment than had voted to indict the defendant in the first place.

In grand jury proceedings in the federal system and in most states, the rights of the targets — the potential defendants — are severely limited. Although the targets cannot be forced to testify or even appear, unless the grand jury specifically directs them to show for a lineup or supply blood samples or other physical evidence, all other witnesses subpoenaed to appear must testify or be held in contempt of court (though they can invoke their Fifth Amendment right not to answer particular questions that call for self-incriminating answers).

No one, target or witness, has a right to have a lawyer present during the proceedings, although a lawyer can sit outside the door for consultation. No witnesses other than the one actually testifying are allowed in the room; even the target must stay outside. The prosecutor can make unlimited use of hearsay evidence—declarations by third parties that in most cases cannot be used at trial. The prosecutor does not have to furnish a transcript of the entire hearing to the defendant after indictment, only of the testimony of witnesses to be called at trial. The one important right a grand jury target does have, established by the Supreme Court in 1963, is the right to have the prosecutor present to the grand jury all known evidence that favors the target.

"Under federal law, the indictment is not considered a guilt-finding step," explains Joseph Russoniello, a former U.S. attorney for Northern California and now a criminal defense lawyer in San Francisco. "It's merely an investigative step."

What that means is that prosecutors' control over a grand jury is fairly complete. The assistant U.S. attorneys who brought cases before grand jury No. 3 were generally bright, personable and well-prepared. They worked to ingratiate themselves with jurors, as though they were honing themselves for the tougher sell to the trial jury, where the standard of proof is more difficult to meet: not just probable cause, but proof beyond a reasonable doubt.

"How about those Redskins?" was a Monday morning greeting, a way to create a common bond of support for the Super Bowl-bound Washington team. Most of the witnesses were police officers testifying about their on-the-scene reports. But more imaginative prosecutors in the more complex cases loaded on other witnesses, documents and photographs to make the cases come alive.

And so it was that in every case, grand jury No. 3 voted to indict every defendant, mostly on exactly the charges the prosecutors asked for. The closest call for prosecutors was in a multiple-defendant drug-dealing case, where some defendants were not indicted on some charges. Most of the jurors were not interested in even discussing potential weaknesses in the prosecutors' cases. "He shouldn't have been there," said Sam about one defendant who seemed to have done nothing to further the crime. "Get real!" said one juror when another questioned whether the Ziploc storage bags in which crack dealers package their wares

really qualified as illegal drug paraphernalia.

This attitude is apparently typical of grand jurors. "There was almost no discussion of the cases," recalls Curtis Berger, a Columbia University law professor; he sat for three weeks on a state-court grand jury in New York last August. Although the jurors on his panel were mostly white Manhattan professionals, they behaved exactly like the District of Columbia jurors, voting for indictment in 44 of

> In every case, grand jury No. 3 voted to indict every defendant, mostly on exactly the charges the prosecutors asked for. Most of the jurors were not interested in even discussing potential weaknesses in the prosecutors' cases. This attitude is apparently typical.

the 45 cases they heard.

"Most members had the mind-set that if there were any problems with a case, they would get straightened out down the road," says Berger. "I guess I was naive enough to believe that a grand jury was a deliberative body. Of course in general the [assistant district attorneys] who prosecuted the cases did a good job."

"When I was in the U.S. attorney's office, there was one case the grand jury rejected," says Michael Lightfoot, a former Justice Department civil rights lawyer who now practices criminal defense law in Los Angeles. "The guy who handled it was the laughingstock of the office."

The sympathy of jurors means that prosecutors can get away with forgetting, as they occasionally did in the more tedious drug and weapons cases, to present any evidence at all on some element of a crime. The most frequent example of this came in CPWL cases, carrying a pistol without a license. Even though everyone knows it is next to impossible to get a license in Washington, the assistant U.S. attorneys would sometimes ne-

glect to ask the police to run a license check. Then they would leave it to jurors to decide whether to indict on the count. Grand jury No. 3 always went ahead, and because the defendants and their lawyers do not see the full transcripts, it is unlikely they would ever find out that the prosecution's case was technically defective.

One day, an assistant U.S. attorney let it slip that not one of the charges of possession with intent to distribute that had been voted on — and there were dozens of them representing hundreds of cocaine rocks and heroin packets — would likely stick until trial. In fact, given the District's overcrowded prisons, the judges would throttle the prosecutors if they tried to make them all stick, because possession with intent to distribute carries a mandatory four-year sentence unless the defendant is underage or an addict. The defendant is supposed to plead guilty to simple possession, a misdemeanor, and the PWID charge is there in order to persuade him to do so.

A few years ago, a D.C. Superior Court judge issued a ruling ending a practice among prosecutors of issuing grand jury subpoenas from their offices, in the name of the grand jury, without there actually being an open case.

"I have mixed feelings about the grand jury system," says Washington lawyer Bennett. "A prosecutor pretty much gets the grand jury to do what he or she wants. One of its functions is as an insulation of citizens against the government. But an honest person would tell you that function is not being served very well. What protects you is the good faith and personal integrity of the prosecutor."

In fact the very issue of independent action by grand jurors became an irritant that exacerbated already festering personal rancor between factions of jurors.

Grand jurors were encouraged to add their own questions to the prosecutor's inquiries of witnesses. Several targets made the mistake of deciding that the alibi "I was with my girlfriend that night" might not be convincing enough. They elaborated it to something like "I was with my girlfriend and my aunt and my sister and my mother and her cousin." All five would be subpoenaed to testify as possible exculpatory witnesses, and all five would tell dramatically conflicting stories.

Two women on the grand jury became skilled amateur sleuths, nailing alibi witnesses in long rounds of cross-examination. This irritated Mary, a stickler for respectability who worried that the prosecutors would stop sending cases to grand jury No. 3, perceiving it as too slow. Mary had raised six children, and she did not brook insubordination or dissent from anyone. Jackie the sergeant at arms was a friend of the two sleuths, as was a young woman named Dawn; all four sat in a row.

Soon enough, there were fearful quarrels between Mary and the Gang of Four over tiny procedural points: whether and when a matter would be discussed and the order in which votes would be taken. Dawn and one of the sleuths would storm out of the room. Jackie would cry. Mary would stand shaken but firm. Vince Caputy or a marshal would be called in to mediate. By Christmas, many jurors were not speaking to each other. Only Rose remained upbeat, for Ben's release was just days away.

"I'm going to keep him out of trouble," she told anyone who would listen.

Twenty years ago, grand juries became highly controversial. A 1975 book by Leroy D. Clark, *The Grand Jury: The Use and Abuse of Political Power*, detailed how the Justice Department's internal security division prosecutors manipulated grand juries to track down Weather Underground members and other radical leftists; granting immunity from prosecution to their friends and forcing them to testify was a favorite Justice tool, Clark charged. Groups began to lobby for the abolition of the grand jury. The year before, the American Bar Association had set up a committee that eventually issued a model act containing 30 different proposals for grand jury reform, such as allowing lawyers in the grand jury room, using the same evidence rules as apply at trial (restricting the current unlimited use of hearsay evidence) and automatically supplying a full transcript to the defendant instead of the more common custom of supplying only the testimony of witnesses who will also testify at trial.

The federal court system declined to implement any of these proposals, although it made changes designed to inform witnesses of their rights. About half the states picked up some of the ABA's reforms; 16 now allow

lawyers at the proceeding, if in a limited capacity, according to a study for the Justice Department by Abt Associates, a criminal justice research organization, and 20 states now require preparation of a full transcript.

Sentiment for abolishing the grand jury reached a peak when the California Supreme Court ruled in 1978 that the state constitution required a preliminary hearing even for defendants who had gone through a grand jury indictment. Preliminary hearings are perfunctory affairs designed to establish probable cause in most states and the federal system, but not in California, where they are full-fledged minitrials and defense lawyers play an aggressive role, sounding out the prosecution's case. The state high court, then under the leadership of ultraliberal Chief Justice Rose Bird, decided that all felony suspects in the state should enjoy these advantages. The ruling pretty much killed off grand jury indictments in California state proceedings. One other state, Wisconsin, followed California's lead via statute.

Complaints about the time and expense of preliminary hearings in California culminated when the McMartin preschool child abuse case included a record 18-month preliminary hearing that led to no convictions. The 1990 anticrime initiative approved by voters dropped the universal preliminary hearing requirement and for the first time allowed unrestricted hearsay evidence at the hearings, a provision upheld recently by a more conservative California Supreme Court. And grand juries are slowly coming back, says Trish Peckham, a law student at Loyola Marymount University in Los Angeles who has studied them.

Civil libertarians seem to have forgotten about their calls for reform. On Jan. 22, the U.S. Supreme Court heard argument in the case of a Tulsa, Okla., businessman who was tried on bank fraud charges. The question is whether the government's failure to put evidence before a grand jury tending to exonerate him is grounds for overturning his conviction. The American Civil Liberties Union decided not to get involved in *United States vs. Williams*.

"The issue used to be whether the rubber-stamp grand jury was an incursion on rights," says Vivian Berger, a former Manhattan prosecutor

who is now vice dean of Columbia's law school as well as the ACLU's general counsel (and the wife of Columbia's Curtis Berger). "The big issue now isn't incursion of rights so much as relevance," she says. "It's more like, what does it all matter? In New York, it's the [prosecutors] who want to get rid of the grand jury."

What does it all matter? That might be a good question for the federal system. In fact, the District of Columbia has its own preliminary hearing procedure, designed to ensure that people arrested for felonies do not languish in jail waiting for overworked grand juries to make a decision on their indictments. Everyone arrested in Washington and denied bail is entitled to a preliminary hearing — a perfunctory proceeding with usually a single police officer testifying — within 10 days of arrest (20 days for those on bail), unless a grand jury indicts first.

Prosecutors in Washington obviously like grand jury proceedings, for they have set up the quick same-day presentment route for drug and other simple cases to beat the clock. Yet what about the cases that are too complicated for a same-day presentment but too simple for an elaborate gathering of evidence? In those, grand juries plow the same ground as preliminary hearings, adding to the expense of prosecution. This might be an argument for amending the Constitution, but that in itself is not an easy task.

"In criminal law, there's a constant war between relevance and fairness," says Michael Uhlmann, a former Justice official. As to the grand jury, "We have to ask: Is it relevant enough to overcome its presumption of unfairness?"

Grand jury No. 3 was too busy for such speculations. After a holiday break, there were two last days of Gaitherizing and wrapping up a handful of unresolved cases. Then the presiding judge, Fred B. Ugast, addressed the jury. "You've done a real service for your community," he declared. Certificates of appreciation were distributed. There were hugs and handshakes. Jackie cried.

Rose disappointed everyone by not showing up either day. She had called in sick with pneumonia, the marshal said. Then came the knowing looks, the shaking heads and laughter. Grand jury No. 3 said almost in unison: "That's Ben!"

# The Court's 2 Visions of Free Speech

## Linda Greenhouse

*Special to* The New York Times

WASHINGTON, June 23—Two competing visions of the First Amendment, of the role of speech in a democratic society, were on display Monday as the Justices of the Supreme Court wrestled with the question of whether the Constitution permits government to declare that some speech is so hateful that it may be punished as a crime.

In four separate opinions filling 61 pages, these two visions clashed, in emotional and even vitriolic terms. When the smoke cleared, one was the winner, although by the narrowest of margins. The result was a Supreme Court decision of landmark dimension, a declaration in favor of more speech rather than less, even if the speech sometimes carries a painfully high price.

Government may not opt for "silencing speech on the basis of its content," Justice Antonin Scalia said for a five-member majority. The remaining four Justices, while agreeing that the St. Paul "bias-motivated crime ordinance" was unconstitutional, would have struck it down on the far less sweeping ground that this particular law was written in too broad and sloppy a manner; they accepted its goal as worthy while finding its means flawed.

But to the majority, the goal itself was illegitimate. "The point of the First Amendment is that majority preferences must be expressed in some fashion other than silencing speech on the basis of its content," Justice Scalia said.

### An End, or a Means?

The fault line that split the Court reflects a debate with deep roots in political theory and the history of the First Amendment. Essentially, the debate is between those who see free speech as an end in itself and those who see it as a means to an end.

In an article in The New York Review of Books this month, the constitutional scholar Ronald Dworkin wrote that there have been two principal historic justifications for free speech, sometimes overlapping and sometimes in tension with each other. One theory sees free speech as an essential part of a free and just society that treats all its members as "responsible moral agents," according to Professor Dworkin.

"Government insults its citizens, and denies their moral responsibility, when it decrees that they cannot be trusted to hear opinions that might persuade them to dangerous or offensive convictions," he wrote.

The other theory, which Professor Dworkin calls "instrumental," justifies free speech on the ground that it serves a greater good and creates a better country, helping to produce a better informed electorate or a more accountable government, for example.

Without ever being so theoretical, the Court's majority opinion on Monday in R.A.V. v. St Paul was an endorsement of the first theory, of free speech as valuable for its own sake. From that starting point, the majority's conclusion flowed: if free speech itself is the good, rather than the particular ends to which speech is put, then it follows that government may not legitimately pick and choose among the words that autonomous adults can be permitted to say.

---

*In a hate-crime case, Justices split on the First Amendment.*

---

But despite its expansiveness, the majority opinion does not indicate that the Court is about to embrace every free-speech argument it hears in cases concerning libel, the press or other First Amendment matters. Just last year, for example, the Court ruled in Rust v. Sullivan that the Federal Government was free to suppress speech about abortion at family planning clinics as a condition of the receipt of Federal funds.

Chief Justice William H. Rehnquist and Justices Anthony M. Kennedy, David H. Souter and Clarence Thomas joined Justice Scalia's opinion for the Court. The Chief Justice was perhaps the most surprising supporter of an opinion with strong libertarian overtones.

Three years ago, he and Justice Scalia parted company on another important First Amendment issue, the question of whether the Government could make it a crime to burn an American flag as a political protest. Justice Scalia joined Justice William J. Brennan's majority opinion, which declared that "the Government may not prohibit expression of any idea simply because society finds the idea itself offensive or disagreeable." Chief Justice Rehnquist filed an emotional dissenting opinion that included the patriotic poem "Barbara Frietchie":

> "Shoot, if you must, this old gray head,
> But spare your country's flag," she said.

### Speech as Instrument

In their separate opinions on Monday, the other Justices expressed the "instrumental" view of free speech, that speech has value insofar as it serves a constructive, civilizing or decent purpose, and little or no value if it hurts or destroys.

Justice Byron R. White, in an opinion that Justices Harry A. Blackmun, Sandra Day O'Connor and John Paul Stevens also signed, said it was entirely justifiable for St. Paul to have placed hateful speech on the subject of race, religion or sex in a category separate from all other speech.

"This selective regulation reflects the city's judgment that harms based on race, color, creed, religion or gender are more pressing public concerns than the harms caused by other fighting words," Justice White said. "In light of our nation's long and painful experience with discrimination, this determination is plainly reasonable."

Justice Stevens, in his separate opinion, expressed a similar idea. "Conduct that creates special risks or causes special harms may be prohibited by special rules," he said.

In a long footnote referring to the Los Angeles riot, Justice Stevens said, "One need look no further than the recent social unrest in the nation's cities to see that race-based threats may cause more harm to society and to individuals than other threats." While that is "regrettable," he said, "until the nation matures beyond that condition, laws such as St. Paul's ordinance will remain reasonable and justifiable."

Justice Stevens' choice of image, the urban race riot, emphasized the fundamental difference in perspective between the two sides of the Court. To Justice Stevens and his allies, the greatest danger presented by hate speech was the hurtful, destructive nature of the speech or expression itself, in this case a cross burned on the lawn of a black family who had recently moved into a white neighborhood.

But to the majority, the greater danger lay in the threat that a Government-imposed orthodoxy would be put in the service of stamping out the hateful speech.

While Justice Scalia acknowledged in passing that hate speech directed at race or religion was hurtful, he did not concede that there was any difference in kind between a racial epithet and an insult directed at union membership or political affiliation, two examples he gave. The "only interest distinctively served" by the St. Paul ordinance, he said, "is that of displaying the city council's special hostility towards the particular biases thus singled out."

It was this bland insistence on the moral equivalency of all speech that appeared particularly to trouble, even enrage, the Justices on the other side. They wanted some recognition from the majority of the terrible power of words in the mouths of bigots. That they got no such acknowledgement underscores a paradox at the heart of an opinion that will probably stand as one of the Supreme Court's most far-reaching interpretations of the First Amendment.

In expanding the freedom of speech, this decision, in its tone of arid absolutism, may have made freedom more painful to bear.

# Juvenile Justice

A century ago, children found guilty of committing crimes were punished as if they were adults. Since there were few specialized juvenile detention institutions, children were thrown into jails and prisons with murderers, thieves, drunks, tramps, and prostitutes, with no protection and no programs for rehabilitation.

The establishment of a special criminal justice system for the handling of juvenile offenders was hailed in the 1920s by humanitarians, reformers, and social scientists, and accepted, somewhat reluctantly, by the legal profession and the police. Only recently has the cry of dissent been heard.

Judge Ben Lindsay and others who pioneered the juvenile court movement believed that juveniles sinned out of ignorance, because of the growing pains of adolescence, or because they were corrupted by adults. They believed that a juvenile court should concern itself with finding out why a juvenile was in trouble and what society could do to help him or her. They saw the juvenile judge as parental, concerned, and sympathetic, rather than prosecutive and punitive.

The proponents of this system were, of course, thinking of the delinquents of their time—the runaway, the truant, the petty thief, the beggar, the sexual experimenter, and the insubordinate. Now, however, the juvenile in court is more likely to be on trial for murder, gang rape, arson, or mugging. The 1990s also differ from the 1920s in other ways. Juvenile courts are everywhere, as are juvenile police, juvenile probation officers, and juvenile prisons. Literally hundreds of thousands of American juveniles enter this system annually.

It is clear at this time that the winds of change are blowing across the nation's juvenile justice system. Traditional reforms are being replaced by a new and more conservative agenda. This new reform movement emphasizes the welfare of victims, a punitive approach toward serious juvenile offenders, and protection of children from physical and sexual exploitation. Policies that favor diversion and deinstitutionalization are less popular. After many years of attempting to remove status offenders from the juvenile justice system, there are increasing calls for returning truants, runaways, and other troubled youth to juvenile court jurisdiction. In spite of these developments, however, there are many juvenile justice reformers who remain dedicated to advancing due process rights for children and reducing reliance on incarceration.

Clearly, there is conflict and tension between the old and new juvenile justice reform agendas. The articles in this section evaluate problems with the current juvenile justice system and present some possible solutions.

The first essay, "Handling of Juvenile Cases," draws distinctions between juvenile cases and adult cases, explains the circumstances under which juveniles may be tried in criminal courts, and reveals that juveniles receive dispositions rather than sentences.

Transformation in the philosophy and underlying goals of the juvenile justice system has been well documented over the past decade, according to "Punishment, Accountability, and the New Juvenile Justice." Because of the change in the mission of juvenile justice, critical issues need to be addressed.

Are existing delinquency causation theories adequate to the task of explaining female delinquency and official reactions to girls' deviance? The answer is clearly no, according to the author of the next essay, "Girls' Crime and Woman's Place." She maintains that the academic study of delinquent behavior usually focuses on male delinquency alone.

The ultimate authority for the resolution of problems of dysfunctional families is the juvenile court. "The Juvenile Court and the Role of the Juvenile Court Judge" surveys the origin, purposes, and duties of this court and the unique role of the judge.

Nine young people from three cities tell what growing up in urban America is really like in the essay titled "Teenagers Talk About Life."

Ronald Henkoff, author of "Kids Are Killing, Dying, Bleeding," maintain that we should focus on prevention, not just punishment, to curb the epidemic of violence among juveniles in America.

The unit closes with "Children in Gangs." To understand the youth gang problem requires insight into the social context within which gangs emerge. Preventing youths from getting involved with gangs in the first place is the viable long-term solution.

### Looking Ahead: Challenge Questions

When the juvenile court was first conceived, what convictions did its pioneers hold about juvenile offenders?

Some argue that the failure of the juvenile court to fulfill its rehabilitative and preventive promise stems from a grossly oversimplistic view of the phenomenon of juvenile criminality. Do you agree? Why or why not?

Do you believe the departure of the juvenile justice system from its original purpose is warranted?

Why do some young people become members of gangs?

# Handling of Juvenile Cases

## Cases involving juveniles are handled much differently than adult cases

**The juvenile court and a separate process for handling juveniles resulted from reform movements of the late 19th century**

Until that time juveniles who committed crimes were processed through the criminal courts. In 1899 Illinois established the first juvenile court based on the concepts that a juvenile was a salvageable human being who needed treatment rather than punishment and that the juvenile court was to protect the child from the stigma of criminal proceedings. Delinquency and other situations such as neglect and adoption were deemed to warrant the court's intervention on the child's behalf. The juvenile court also handled "status offenses" (such as truancy, running away, and incorrigibility), which are not applicable to adults.

While the juvenile courts and the handling of juveniles remain separated from criminal processing, the concepts on which they are based have changed. Today, juvenile courts usually consider an element of personal responsibility when making decisions about juvenile offenders.

Juvenile courts may retain jurisdiction until a juvenile becomes legally an adult (at age 21 or less in most States). This limit sets a cap on the length of time juveniles may be institutionalized that is often much less than that for adults who commit similar offenses. Some jurisdictions transfer the cases of juveniles accused of serious offenses or with long criminal histories to criminal court so that the length of the sanction cannot be abridged.

**Juvenile courts are very different from criminal courts**

The language used in juvenile courts is less harsh. For example, juvenile courts—
• accept "petitions" of "delinquency" rather than criminal complaints
• conduct "hearings," not trials
• "adjudicate" juveniles to be "delinquent" rather than find them guilty of a crime
• order one of a number of available "dispositions" rather than sentences.

Despite the wide discretion and informality associated with juvenile court proceedings, juveniles are protected by most of the due process safeguards associated with adult criminal trials.

**Most referrals to juvenile court are for property crimes, but 17% are for status offenses**

Reasons for referrals to juvenile courts

| | | |
|---|---|---:|
| 11% | **Crimes against persons** | |
| | Criminal homicide | 1% |
| | Forcible rape | 2 |
| | Robbery | 17 |
| | Aggravated assault | 20 |
| | Simple assault | 59 |
| | | 100% |
| 46% | **Crimes against property** | |
| | Burglary | 25% |
| | Larceny | 47 |
| | Motor vehicle theft | 5 |
| | Arson | 1 |
| | Vandalism and trespassing | 19 |
| | Stolen property offenses | 3 |
| | | 100% |
| 5% | **Drug offenses** | 100% |
| 21% | **Offenses against public order** | |
| | Weapons offenses | 6% |
| | Sex offenses | 6 |
| | Drunkenness and disorderly conduct | 23 |
| | Contempt, probation, and parole violations | 21 |
| | Other | 44 |
| | | 100% |
| 17% | **Status offenses** | |
| | Running away | 28% |
| | Truancy and curfew violations | 21 |
| | Ungovernability | 28 |
| | Liquor violations | 23 |
| | | 100% |
| 100% | Total all offenses | |

Note: Percents may not add to 100 because of rounding.
Source: *Delinquency in the United States 1983*, National Center for Juvenile Justice, July 1986.

**Arrest is not the only means of referring juveniles to the courts**

While adults may begin criminal justice processing only through arrest, summons, or citation, juveniles may be referred to court by law enforcement agencies, parents, schools, victims, probation officers, or other sources.

Law enforcement agencies refer three-quarters of the juvenile cases, and they are most likely to be the referral source in cases involving curfew violations, drug offenses, and property crimes. Other referral sources are most likely in cases involving status offenses (truancy, ungovernability, and running away).

From *Report to the Nation on Crime and Justice*, Bureau of Justice Statistics, U.S. Department of Justice, March 1988, pp. 78-79, 95.

**"Intake" is the first step in the processing of juveniles**

At intake, decisions are made about whether to begin formal proceedings. Intake is most frequently performed by the juvenile court or an executive branch intake unit, but increasingly prosecutors are becoming involved. In addition to beginning formal court proceedings, officials at intake may refer

- **Concurrent jurisdiction**—the prosecutor has the discretion of filing charges for certain offenses in either juvenile or criminal courts
- **Excluded offenses**—the legislature excludes from juvenile court jurisdiction certain offenses usually either very minor, such as traffic or fishing violations, or very serious, such as murder or rape
- **Judicial waiver**—the juvenile court

**As of 1987, 36 States excluded certain offenses from juvenile court jurisdictions**

Eighteen States excluded only traffic, watercraft, fish, or game violations. Another 13 States excluded serious offenses; the other 5 excluded serious offenses and some minor offenses. The serious offenses most often excluded are capital crimes such as murder, but

# Under certain circumstances, juveniles may be tried in criminal courts

the juvenile for psychiatric evaluation, informal probation, or counseling, or, if appropriate, they may close the case altogether.

**For a case involving a juvenile to proceed to a court adjudication, the intake unit must file a petition with the court**

Intake units handle most cases informally without a petition. The National Center for Juvenile Justice estimates that more than half of all juvenile cases disposed of at intake are handled informally without a petition and are dismissed and/or referred to a social service agency.

**Initial juvenile detention decisions are usually made by the intake staff**

Prior to holding an adjudicatory hearing, juveniles may be released in the custody of their parents, put in protective custody (usually in foster homes or runaway shelters), or admitted to detention facilities. In most States juveniles are not eligible for bail, unlike adults.

**Relatively few juveniles are detained prior to court appearance**

One juvenile case in five involved secure detention prior to adjudication in 1983. Status offenders were least likely to be detained. The proportion of status offenders detained has declined from 40% in 1975 to 11% in 1983.

**All States allow juveniles to be tried as adults in criminal courts**

Juveniles are referred to criminal courts in one of three ways—

waives its jurisdiction and transfers the case to criminal court (the procedure is also known as "binding over" or "certifying" juvenile cases to criminal courts).

**Age at which criminal courts gain jurisdiction of young offenders ranges from 16 to 19**

| Age of offender when under criminal court jurisdiction | States |
|---|---|
| 16 years | Connecticut, New York, North Carolina |
| 17 | Georgia, Illinois, Louisiana, Massachusetts, Missouri, South Carolina, Texas |
| 18 | Alabama, Alaska, Arizona, Arkansas, California, Colorado, Delaware, District of Columbia, Florida, Hawaii, Idaho, Indiana, Iowa, Kansas, Kentucky, Maine, Maryland, Michigan, Minnesota, Mississippi, Montana, Nebraska, Nevada, New Hampshire, New Jersey, New Mexico, North Dakota, Ohio, Oklahoma, Oregon, Pennsylvania, Rhode Island, South Dakota, Tennessee, Utah, Vermont, Virginia, Washington, West Virginia, Wisconsin, Federal districts |
| 19 | Wyoming |

Source: "Upper age of juvenile court jurisdiction statutes analysis," Linda A. Szymanski, National Center for Juvenile Justice, March 1987.

**12 States authorize prosecutors to file cases in the juvenile or criminal courts at their discretion**

This procedure, known as concurrent jurisdiction, may be limited to certain offenses or to juveniles of a certain age. Four States provide concurrent jurisdiction over juveniles charged with traffic violations. Georgia, Nebraska, and Wyoming have concurrent criminal jurisdiction statutes.

several States exclude juveniles previously convicted in criminal courts.

**48 States, the District of Columbia, and the Federal Government have judicial waiver provisions**

| Youngest age at which juvenile may be transferred to criminal court by judicial waiver | States |
|---|---|
| No specific age | Alaska, Arizona, Arkansas, Delaware, Florida, Indiana, Kentucky, Maine, Maryland, New Hampshire, New Jersey, Oklahoma, South Dakota, West Virginia, Wyoming, Federal districts |
| 10 years | Vermont |
| 12 | Montana |
| 13 | Georgia, Illinois, Mississippi |
| 14 | Alabama, Colorado, Connecticut, Idaho, Iowa, Massachusetts, Minnesota, Missouri, North Carolina, North Dakota, Pennsylvania, South Carolina, Tennessee, Utah |
| 15 | District of Columbia, Louisiana, Michigan, New Mexico, Ohio, Oregon, Texas, Virginia |
| 16 | California, Hawaii, Kansas, Nevada, Rhode Island, Washington, Wisconsin |

Note: Many judicial waiver statutes also specify offenses that are waivable. This chart lists the States by the youngest age for which judicial waiver may be sought without regard to offense.

Source: "Waiver/transfer/certification of juveniles to criminal court: Age restrictions: Crime restrictions," Linda A. Szymanski, National Center for Juvenile Justice, February 1987.

**A small proportion of juvenile cases are referred to criminal court**

Recent studies found that most juveniles

## 5. JUVENILE JUSTICE

referred to criminal court were age 17 and were charged with property offenses. However, juveniles charged with violent offenses or with serious prior offense histories were more likely to be adjudicated in criminal court. Waiver of juveniles to criminal court is less likely where court jurisdiction extends for several years beyond the juvenile's 18th birthday.

offending behavior has been corrected, whichever is sooner.

Of the 45 States and the District of Columbia that authorize indeterminate periods of confinement—
• 32 grant releasing authority to the State juvenile corrections agency
• 6 delegate it to juvenile paroling agencies

fixed range of time for commitment, or mandate a minimum length of stay in a type of placement, such as a secure institution.

**Dispositions for serious juvenile offenders tend to look like those for adults**

Aggregate statistics on juvenile court

---

# Juveniles receive dispositions rather than sentences

---

**Juveniles tried as adults have a very high conviction rate, but most receive sentences of probation or fines**

More than 90% of the judicial waiver or concurrent jurisdiction cases in Hamparian's study resulted in guilty verdicts, and more than half the convictions led to fines or probation. Sentences to probation often occur because the criminal courts view juveniles as first offenders regardless of their prior juvenile record. However, serious violent juvenile offenders are more likely to be institutionalized. In a study of 12 jurisdictions with Habitual Serious or Violent Juvenile Offender Programs, 63% of those convicted were sentenced to prison and 14% to jail. The average prison sentence was 6.8 years.

**Correctional activities for juveniles tried as adults in most States occur within the criminal justice system**

In 1978, in more than half the States, youths convicted as adults and given an incarcerative sentence could only be placed in adult corrections facilities. In 18 jurisdictions, youths convicted as adults could be placed in either adult or juvenile corrections facilities, but sometimes this discretion was limited by special circumstances. Only 6 jurisdictions restricted placements of juveniles convicted as adults to State juvenile corrections institutions. Generally, youths sentenced in this manner will be transferred to adult facilities to serve the remainder of their sentence on reaching majority.

**Juvenile court dispositions tend to be indeterminate**

The dispositions of juveniles adjudicated to be delinquent extend until the juvenile legally becomes an adult (21 years of age in most States) or until the

• 5 place such authority with the committing judges
• 3 have dual or overlapping jurisdiction.

**Most juvenile cases are disposed of informally**

In 1982 about 54% of all cases referred to juvenile courts by the police and other agencies were handled informally without the filing of a petition. About 20% of all cases involved some detention prior to disposition.

Of about 600,000 cases in which petitions were filed, 64% resulted in formal adjudication. Of these, 61% resulted in some form of probation, and 29% resulted in an out-of-home placement.

**The juvenile justice system is also undergoing changes in the degree of discretion permitted in confinement decisions**

Determinate dispositions are now used in six States, but they do not apply to all offenses or offenders. In most cases they apply only to specified felony cases or to the juveniles with prior adjudications for serious delinquencies.

California imposes determinate periods of confinement for delinquents committed to State agencies based on the standards and guidelines of its paroling agency. Four States have similar procedures, administered by the State agencies responsible for operating their juvenile corrections facilities.

As of 1981 eight States had serious-delinquent statutes requiring that juveniles who are either serious, violent, repeat, or habitual offenders be adjudicated and committed in a manner that differs from the adjudication of other delinquents. Such laws require minimum lengths of commitment, prescribe a

dispositions do not provide an accurate picture of what happens to the more serious offenders because many of the cases coming before juvenile courts involve minor criminal or status offenses. These minor cases are more likely to be handled informally by the juvenile court.

An analysis of California cases involving older juveniles and young adults charged by the police with robbery or burglary revealed more similarities in their disposition patterns than the aggregate juvenile court statistics would suggest. For both types of offenses, juvenile petitions were filed and settled formally in court about as often as were complaints filed and convictions obtained in the cases against adults. The juveniles charged with the more serious offenses and those with the more extensive prior records were the most likely to have their cases reach adjudication. At the upper limits of offense and prior record severity, juveniles were committed to secure institutions about as frequently as were young adults with comparable records.

**Most juveniles committed to juvenile facilities are delinquents**

| | Percent of juveniles |
|---|---|
| Total | 100% |
| Delinquents | 74 |
| Nondelinquents | |
| Status offenders | 12 |
| Nonoffenders (dependency, neglect, abuse, etc.) | 14 |

Source: BJS Children in Custody, 1985, unpublished data.

**The outcomes of juvenile and adult proceedings are similar, but some options are not available in juvenile court**

For example, juvenile courts cannot

160

order the death penalty, life terms, or terms that could exceed the maximum jurisdiction of the court itself. In Arizona the State Supreme Court held that, despite statutory jurisdiction of the juvenile courts to age 21, delinquents could not be held in State juvenile corrections facilities beyond age 18.[3]

Yet, juvenile courts may go further than criminal courts in regulating the lifestyles of juvenile offenders placed in the community under probation supervision. For example, the court may order them to—
• live in certain locations
• attend school
• participate in programs intended to

improve their behavior.

The National Center for Juvenile Justice estimates that almost 70% of the juveniles whose cases are not waived or dismissed are put on probation; about 10% are committed to an institution.

# Punishment, Accountability, and the New Juvenile Justice

## by Martin L. Forst, D. Crim. and Martha-Elin Blomquist, Ph.D.

*The juvenile justice system has undergone radical change in the past three decades. The procedural revolution that began at the end of the 1960s with the Gault decision has more recently evolved into a substantive revolution. The changes in juvenile justice have been many and in some instances drastic, particularly in the apparent demise of the rehabilitative ideal. New theories or models have emerged, incorporating terminology such as punishment, justice, and accountability into the vocabulary of juvenile justice practitioners and the lexicon of state juvenile codes.*

*The transformation in the philosophy and underlying goals of the system has been well-documented over the past decade or so.[1] It is now time to ask critical questions about the significance and meaning of this transformation and to bring attention to unresolved issues. This article suggests the issues that need to be addressed in order to make both practical and philosophical sense out of the changes in the mission of "juvenile justice."*

### The Background

Based on a variety of criticisms,[2] a movement arose within the last decade to make substantive changes in the philosophy of juvenile court and juvenile corrections law, including dispositional decision-making policy. This movement has rejected the rehabilitative ideal as traditionally conceived and has renewed interest in public protection, punishment, justice and accountability. As Gardner summarizes: "...[a] revolution in substantive theory is presently taking place as one jurisdiction after another expresses disenchantment with the rehabilitative ideal and embraces explicitly punitive sanctions as appropriate for youthful offenders."[3]

Notwithstanding their incongruities and unknown consequences, proposals to orient the philosophy and administration of the juvenile justice system around punishment and public protection have been supported by a diverse set of scholars, lawmakers, and practitioners. For example, the prestigious Joint Commission on Juvenile Justice Standards of the Institute of Judicial Administration and the American Bar Association (IJA/ABA) proposed in 1980 that the principles of criminal law and procedure replace the rehabilitative model of juvenile justice.[4] The Joint Commission advocated that juvenile justice sanctions be offense-based rather than based on the needs of the offender and that determinate sentencing should replace the traditional indeterminate sentencing system.

Moreover, these ideas have been supported by a variety of children's rights advocates who believe that a youth has a right to be punished for the offense committed rather than a need to be treated for what others perceive to be wrong with him or her. Other commentators have been concerned with the inequities and injustices resulting from the traditional offender-based system. Offense-based dispositions, by contrast, presumably prevent unjust and disproportionate periods of incarceration often found under a rehabilitation-oriented system. As Fox notes, "punishment clearly implies limits, whereas treatment does not."[5] Under this theory, a youth would not be incarcerated longer than is justified by the nature of the delinquent conduct, and certainly no longer than an adult convicted of the same offense.

Much of the philosophical and structural transformation, despite its lofty theory, is a direct result of public pressure to crack down on juveniles -- to get tough with kids. Drs. Norman and Gillespie conclude, "The mood of the nation continues to move toward punishment and incapacitation of offenders."[6] Many statutory revisions are clearly designed to mollify the public's sense of fear and anger over juvenile crime.[7] Cracking down on juveniles has been accomplished in a variety of ways. Revising transfer laws to allow more juveniles to be tried as adults in criminal courts is but one example.[8] Moreover, numerous statutory changes have made sanctions meted out *within* the juvenile justice system more punitive. For example, the new Texas determinate sentencing law for juveniles, passed in 1987, provides that juveniles who have been adjudicated delinquent for one of six serious, violent offenses may receive a determinate sentence of as long as 30 years' confinement.[9]

Law and order groups have continued to propose more restrictive policies for controlling and sanctioning juvenile crime. The goal of these proposals is to make the juvenile justice system more like the criminal justice system. These proposals have resulted in "criminalizing" the juvenile justice system.

## Moving To New Models

To institute these substantive reforms, many state legislatures have modified -- sometimes extensively -- the purpose clauses of their juvenile court or juvenile corrections statutes.[10] In some states, policy-makers simply added new phrases to the traditional language of *parens patriae* and "the best interests of the child"; in other states they replaced these time-honored goals all together. The new phraseology more closely approximates the underlying purposes of the criminal justice system -- e.g., public protection, accountability, justice, punishment, deterrence, and incapacitation. Although these theoretical concepts are familiar to the criminal process, they remain confused and ill-defined in the juvenile justice system, particularly to the extent that they are merely grafted onto existing child welfare-based philosophies of traditional juvenile court law.

Examples of the new philosophies in juvenile justice abound. In passing the Juvenile Justice Act of 1977, Washington became the first state drastically to revamp its juvenile justice philosophy and enact a determinate sentencing statute for juvenile offenders. Mary Kay Becker, principal sponsor of the bill, said of the new statute:

"[T]he broad purpose of [the bill] should

be fairly clear. In terms of the philosophical polarities that have characterized the juvenile court debate for more than a century, the new law moves away from the *parens patriae* doctrine of benevolent coercion, and closer to a more classical emphasis on justice. The law requires the court to deal more consistently with youngsters who commit offenses. The responsibility of providing services to youngsters whose behavior, while troublesome, is noncriminal, is assigned to the Department of Social and Health Services and the agencies with whom it may contract. The juvenile court is to view itself primarily as an instrument of justice rather than as a provider of services."[11]

This dramatic philosophical change is also demonstrated in the specific objectives of the legislation: (1) "Make the juvenile offender accountable for his or her criminal behavior," and (2) "Provide punishment commensurate with the age, crime, and criminal history of the juvenile offender."[12] This requirement of commensurate punishment creates the foundation for Washington's determinate sentencing system for juveniles.

Maine's statutes also permit the juvenile court to punish a child. Specifically, juvenile court law authorizes judges to remove a juvenile from parental custody for the minor's welfare or safety, or when "the protection of the public would otherwise be endangered, or where necessary *to punish* a child adjudicated...as having committed a...crime (emphasis added).[13]

The California legislature has made a number of significant changes in the codes pertaining to the philosophy and operation of the juvenile court as well. Statutory revisions enacted in the past ten years have made accountability, victims' rights, and public safety high priorities in the juvenile justice system. The current statement of purpose of the juvenile court law reads, in relevant part:

"The purpose of the [Arnold-Kennick Juvenile Court Law] is to provide for the protection and safety of the public and each minor under the jurisdiction of the juvenile court. . . . Minors under the jurisdiction of the juvenile court as a consequence of delinquent conduct, shall in conformity with the interests of public safety and protection, receive care, treatment and guidance which is consistent with their best interest, which holds them accountable for their behavior, and which is appropriate for their circumstances. *Such guidance may include punishment. . . . "* (emphasis added)[14]

But unlike Maine's statute, California law places a restriction on the punishment to be imposed: "Punishment for the purposes of this chapter does not include retribution."[15]

Minnesota's juvenile law incorporates slightly different terminology, requiring the juvenile court and system "promote public safety and reduce juvenile delinquency by maintaining the integrity of the substantive law by prohibiting certain behavior and by developing individual responsibility for lawful behavior."[16] The use of the phrase "promote the public safety" in the Minnesota statute suggests a social defense or public protection rationale, rather than a "justice" model. But the combined usage of "public safety" and "individual responsibility" is confusing. While these terms have some commonsensical appeal, their meaning or relationship to one another is unclear. Is public safety promoted by enhancing individual responsibility? If protecting the public conflicts with the promotion of individual responsibility, how would Minnesota law resolve the conflict?

Experts have used different terms to describe this shift in juvenile justice philosophy and structure. Scholars speak of new "models" of the juvenile justice system. Among others, these include the "criminal" model,[17] "punitive" model,[18] "penal" model,[19] "justice" model,[20] "accountability" model,[21] and "determinate sentencing" model.[22] Often these new terms or concepts are used interchangeably; insufficient thought has been given to the differences, sometimes subtle, among these models. In addition, the logical corollaries of the models have not been adequately explored. A number of issues need further clarification and analysis.

## Addressing Unresolved Issues

### Exploring The Nature of Punishment

Punishment is what the founders of the juvenile justice system presumably wanted to avoid. The idea was to extricate juveniles from the punitive adult system and to treat their underlying problems. As Melton explains, "At its deepest roots, [the] paternalistic vision of the juvenile court was based on the moral premise that youth do not deserve punishment for their violations of the law."[23]

But times have changed -- and so have statutes. The juvenile justice statutes in Washington, Maine, and California, as noted above, specifically mention the goal of punishment. And in Judge McGee's opinion, "There should be some form of punishment involved in every delinquency disposition, clearly identified to the perpetrator as being his just deserts."[24]

But what is punishment, particularly within the context of the juvenile justice system? There appear to be two substantially different conceptions. Punishment is viewed as retributive by some and utilitarian by others.

Gardner clearly summarizes the retributivist position. In his view, ". . . punishment entails the purposeful infliction of suffering upon an offender for his offense. . . ."[25] Moreover, ". . . the primary thrust of punishment, rather than seeking to benefit the offender, is to exact from the recipient his debt to society, a payment of which nullifies his guilt."[26] This is a common theme. The retributivist position is thus "backward looking." That is, the key factor in disposition is the offense that took place in the past; the sanctioning system is based on the *offense.* The treatment needs of the offender are of little or no importance to the retributivist.[27]

By contrast, some commentators, particularly practitioners within the system, conceive of punishment in utilitarian, even humanitarian terms. They view punishment as an instrument of change for misbehaving youths. Some contend, for example, that punishment can be useful in helping foster a sense of responsibility in juveniles.[28] For this reason, according to Judge McGee, the juvenile court should punish juvenile offenders. "By doing so, the juvenile court is not repudiating its mission, it is helping to fulfill it."[29] Thus, punishment is miraculously transformed into rehabilitation.

California's statute is unique and raises profound issues. As noted above, the juvenile court in California is authorized to punish a juvenile offender; but the statute also provides that the punishment cannot be *retributive.* What does this mean? What is the difference between "retributive" punishment and "regular" or non-retributive punishment? Are the goals of these two types of punishment the same or different?

Presumably if the juvenile court is allowed to dispense punishment, the child must be protected from disproportionate punishment. As Fox asserts, "punishment implies limits."[30] If the idea is to punish the child and punishment implies limits, then the limits should be based on the seriousness of the offense. How is this reflected in California law? Does non–retributive punishment also imply limits? Or can non–retributive punishment be disproportionate to the seriousness of the offense? Is non–retributive punishment meant to right a wrong that has taken place in the past or is it intended to change a juvenile's personality or attitude?

To the extent that there is a move to punishment in juvenile justice, the logical corollaries must be more fully explored and articulated. Changing to a punishment–based system, particularly with a retributivist basis, has profound implications for sentencing structure, dispositional alternatives, and the internal logic of the entire juvenile justice system.

### What Is "Justice" In Juvenile Justice?

The meaning of "justice" in juvenile justice has long been confused and the subject of debate. It might be argued that the concept does not belong in the juvenile system to the extent that the system's focus is on the best interests of the child and his or her rehabilitation. Thus under the rehabilitative model, with its indeterminate sentencing scheme, there is no necessary relationship between the offense committed and the disposition –– that is, between the harm done and, for example, the length of stay in an institution.

Conversely, it could be argued that justice is what has long been missing from the juvenile justice system. But this begs the question: what is, or should be, "justice" within the context of the juvenile justice system? Moreover, what is the relationship between justice and punishment?

Justice and punishment seem somehow to be related. To be just, punishment must be proportionate to the seriousness of the offense committed. Seriousness is generally determined by the harmfulness of the act and the degree of culpability of the offender.[31] This notion is summarized in the simple phrase: "let the punishment fit the crime." This, in turn, implies a gradation of offenses by seriousness. It also implies some corresponding ranking of severity of punishment. Based on this internal logic, Washington state has adopted a determinate sentencing scheme for juvenile offenders.

California has at least partially adopted a just deserts schema. Prompted by the State Supreme Court's ruling in *People v. Olivas* to extend equal protection of the law to the term of confinement served by youthful offenders committed to the California Youth Authority,[32] the legislature modified the indeterminate sentencing law applicable to juveniles. As part of a major reform package adopted in 1976 which affected several aspects of the juvenile justice system, legislators enacted the provision that:

> ". . . in any case in which the minor is removed from the physical custody of his . . . guardian as a result of an order of wardship, the order shall specify that the minor may not be held in physical confinement for a period in excess of the maximum term of confinement which would be imposed upon an adult convicted of the offense . . . which brought the minor under the jurisdiction of the juvenile court."[33]

With a justice or just deserts philosophy, it follows that limits must be placed on dispositional alternatives, and specifically on the degree of punishment meted out to juvenile offenders. These limits can be, and often are, in direct conflict with the traditional goals and structure of the juvenile justice system.

### Accountability

Some authorities use the term "accountability" to describe the new models of juvenile justice. Maloney, Romig, and Armstrong, for example, claim that accountability is one of the core values in the recent juvenile court and probation movement. According to them, "Accountability is firmly grounded in the justice theme that the system must respond to illegal behavior in such a way that the offender is made aware of and responsible for the loss, damage, or injury perpetrated upon the victim."[34]

But even this simple assertion raises questions. What is the relationship between accountability and justice or punishment? What is the relationship of accountability to individual responsibility? Does holding a youth accountable mean that the youth will be made to understand and appreciate the wrongfulness of his or her acts? Or does it mean the youth will be held personally responsible for the harm done and punished in direct proportion (no more and no less) to the offense?

Maloney, Romig, and Armstrong seem to use the term in the former way. That is, accountability appears to mean making the juvenile aware of and accept responsibility for his or her wrongful acts. Through the juvenile justice experience, accountability is something to be instilled into the misbehaving youth. For example, Maloney, Romig, and Armstrong suggest that restitution is one of the more promising approaches available to the court "for imposing a tangible and enforceable form of accountability on juvenile offenders."[35] Moreover, "Accountability has taken the form of imparting some sense of individual responsibility and social awareness to the youthful offender."[36] But is accountability something that one *instills* in a juvenile? Or is it something that one inflicts, like punishment, proportionate to the offense?

It is easy to envision the conflicts that could arise with differing notions of accountability -- that is, instilling a sense of responsibility or inflicting punishment for wrongdoing. Take, for example, a 16-year-old armed robber with one prior adjudication for the same offense. Suppose that "justice" (i.e., proportionate punishment as defined by the legislature or a sentencing commission) dictates that a youth spend two years in confinement at a training school. Suppose further that at the end of the two year period the youth does not appreciate or acknowledge the wrongfulness of his or her acts? Should the youth be released at the end of the two year period? If accountability is related to instilling values and fostering responsibility, the answer is no. If accountability is related to just and proportionate punishment, the answer is yes.

## Individual Responsibility

Punishment and accountability are related, in some manner, to responsibility. Generally, the infliction of punishment on a person for his or her acts presumes that a person is responsible for those acts. The law does not allow the punishment of the mentally ill or idiots, because they to not possess the requisite mental intent *(mens rea)* to be morally culpable. For the state to punish, the person receiving the punishment must be viewed as a responsible actor. One of the emerging issues in juvenile justice is whether juveniles -- or which juveniles under what circumstances -- are responsible moral actors.

The traditional view is that juveniles are not fully responsible, especially for criminal activity. Even the IJA/ABA Standards provide, "Juveniles may be viewed as incomplete adults, lacking in full moral and experiential development."[37] This leads some authorities, like Zimring, to conclude that juvenile offenders must be protected from the

full burden of adult responsibility while being "pushed along by degrees toward moral and legal accountability, that we consider appropriate to adulthood."[38]

But the current trend is to hold juveniles responsible (and accountable) for their actions. Melton observes, "As the rehabilitative underpinnings of the juvenile court have withered away, courts have increasingly been faced with the problem of determining individual juveniles' responsibility, especially in those jurisdictions in which punitive purposes have been expressly recognized in juvenile codes."[39] Gardner, moreover, concludes, "Because punishment is justifiable only if its recipient is a 'person' capable of moral agency, the movement toward a punitive model seriously questions the existing view that juveniles lack capacity for rational decision-making."[40]

Some states have officially adopted the view that juveniles are, at least in some instances, responsible moral actors. For example, in California, the administrative policies instituted by correctional officials in the California Youth Authority (CYA) system have begun to focus on the goals of accountability and public protection. In the comprehensive statement of mission and directions used by the Department of the Youth Authority in 1983, the Director stated that, "the most effective way to protect the public is to ensure that offenders are held accountable for their antisocial behavior."[41] According to this policy document, accountability "refers to the ward accepting *full responsibility* for his or her own behavior, including the commitment offense and behavior while in the institution and on parole" (emphasis added).[42]

As noted, this view of the individual responsibility of juveniles conflicts with traditional conceptions of juvenile responsibility and compelling legal precedent. In *Eddings v. Oklahoma,* the United States Supreme Court mentioned that children have a "special place" in the law, and this is evidenced by the fact that every state in the country has a separate juvenile court system.[43] The Court also expressed in *Eddings* that juveniles possess a lower level of maturity than adults: "Our [American] history is replete with laws and judicial recognitions that minors, especially in their earlier years, generally are less mature and responsible than adults."[44] The Court also stated, ". . . Even the normal 16-year-old customarily lacks the maturity of an adult."[45]

The issue of maturity -- and responsibility -

- of juveniles surfaced again in *Thompson v. Oklahoma.* The Supreme Court stated:

> "There is also broad agreement on the proposition that adolescents as a class are less mature and responsible than adults. We stressed this difference in explaining the importance of treating the defendant's youth as a mitigating factor in capital cases. . . . [Moreover] . . . [i]nexperience, less education, and less intelligence make a teenager less able to evaluate the consequences of his or her conduct while at the same time he or she is much more apt to be motivated by mere emotion or peer pressure than is an adult. The reasons why juveniles are not trusted with the privileges and responsibilities of an adult also explain why their irresponsible conduct is not as morally responsible as that of an adult."[46]

This logic led the Court to conclude that ". . . less culpability should attach to a crime committed by a juvenile than to a comparable crime by an adult."[47]

A conflict -- or Catch 22 -- is becoming apparent. On the one hand, juvenile law traditionally holds that juveniles should not be punished because they are *not* responsible actors. On the other hand, some authorities now hold that juveniles should be punished in order to *make* them more responsible. But issues remain unresolved: are juveniles fully responsible for their criminal actions? Under what conditions, if any, are they as responsible as adults? And how is punishment related to levels of responsibility?

### The Infancy Defense

To the extent that the juvenile court has historically not been concerned with culpability, responsibility and punishment, the infancy defense was deemed to be irrelevant. Some states have continued to maintain this traditional view. As recently as a 1981, for example, the Rhode Island Supreme Court held,

> "Once one accepts the principle that a finding of delinquency or waywardness in a juvenile proceeding is not the equivalent of a finding that the juvenile has committed a crime, there is no necessity of a finding that the juvenile has such maturity that he or she knew what he or she was doing was wrong."[48]

In the trend toward punishment, an opposing position is set forth: "Juvenile proceedings are 'criminal' in nature when punishment is the sanction imposed."[49] If juvenile court proceedings are now deemed criminal in nature, should not the infancy defense be relevant? Some jurisdictions are coming to that conclusion. For example, in *State v. Q.D.,* the Washington Supreme Court held, "The principles of construction of criminal statutes, made necessary by our recognition of the criminal nature of juvenile court proceedings, also compel us to conclude that [the infancy defense] applies to proceedings in juvenile courts."[50]

Thus, to the extent that juvenile codes now authorize punishment for juveniles, it follows that juveniles should be allowed to use the traditional criminal defenses. As Melton contends, "If juveniles are to be subjected to *any* punishment, then they should be provided the protections embedded within criminal procedure, modified as necessary to ensure that such proceedings meet the special demands of fundamental fairness as applied to youth."[51]

### Mixed Goals and Continuing Confusion

Some states, as well as some scholars, have tried to blend the new goals of the juvenile justice system with the traditional goals. This mixed bag is evident in the statutory provisions of a few states. For example, the purpose of Florida's revised juvenile code is:

> *"to protect society* more effectively by *substituting for retributive punishment,* whenever possible, methods of offender *rehabilitation and rehabilitative restitution,* recognizing that the application of *sanctions* which are consistent with the *seriousness of the offense* is appropriate *in all cases"* (emphasis added).[52]

The language of the Florida law is particularly confusing. On the one hand, the law appears to retain the traditional goal of rehabilitation, which implies variable lengths of confinement based on the ability of each youth to meet his or her treatment goals. On the other hand, the law implies a just deserts orientation, stressing that sanctions be proportionate to the seriousness of the criminal conduct in all cases. These two principles appear to be diametrically opposed. Which one is it going to be?

In a similar vein, Maloney, Romig, and Armstrong advocate a "balanced approach" to juvenile probation -- and presumably to the rest of the juvenile court and correctional process. They claim that there are four "core values" that shape the juvenile court and probation movement: community protection, accountability, competency development, and individualized assessment and treatment.[53]

But these values can -- and often do -- conflict. Accountability, to the extent that it is associated with justice and punishment, may dictate that a youth stay in an institution for a specified period of time, based on the seriousness of the offense. However, community protection may demand that the youth remain incarcerated for a longer period; conversely, a youth's progress in treatment and rehabilitation may suggest a shorter period of confinement. Which core value is to be followed? How are conflicts to be resolved? Who is to resolve these conflicting principles? It may be difficult, but it may be necessary to acknowledge that some principles do not fit well with other principles. It simply will not work to say that the juvenile court should punish a juvenile offender in direct proportion to his or her offense (just deserts) and at the same time individualize the youth's sentence depending on his or her treatment needs.

The new "balanced" approach is probably not much different than in the "good old days" when statutes provided little, if any, guidance to juvenile court judges or officials (parole board or correctional personnel) who were responsible for deciding when juveniles were to be released from institutional placement. In reality, the balanced approach used to mean a lack of standards or guidelines for decision-making. In practice, some judges and correctional officials would emphasize public protection, others rehabilitation, and still others accountability for misdeeds. The same situation appears true today. The modern balanced approach perpetuates a muddled jurisprudence for responding to different types of juvenile offenders under different fact situations. It does not clearly delineate how much weight is to be given to each of the core values under different circumstances. Without such guidance, judges and correctional officials are likely to rely on their own values, and the "balance" may become skewed by personal bias or community pressures.

## Conclusion

The juvenile justice system is wrestling with a changing philosophy. Disenchantment with the old system has demanded revision. But because of the lack of clarity of the emerging concepts, there is no consensus about the nature and purpose of the new vision of juvenile justice. Enormous confusion remains over the meaning of the new models and how they should be operationalized.

In responding to demands from the public to "crack down on crime" and give public protection a higher priority in crime control policies, lawmakers have used various terms to describe the juvenile justice system's new mission. Some of the new terms conflict with the traditional juvenile justice language that continues to govern the legal framework of many state juvenile justice systems.

Ambiguity over the new terms or models gives juvenile court judges, as well as correctional officials and staff, confused messages as to the purpose or purposes of the system and the relative priority of the system's various goals. "Accountability," for example, is currently an ill-defined concept that means substantially different things to different people. The accountability model is broad enough to encompass all of the ideas of justice, just deserts, punishment, non-retributive punishment, public safety, preventive detention, responsibility, and culpability. Accountability has also given rebirth to the tarnished concepts of treatment and rehabilitation to the extent that it has been associated with the moral improvement of the youthful offender.

Perhaps all of the philosophical debate is simply a guise or smokescreen, used to gloss over an underlying political and social agenda: crack down on kids and put them away for longer periods of time to satisfy the public's thirst for vengeance and demand for public protection. The new models in juvenile justice may not have grown out of an evolving jurisprudence of juvenile justice, but rather out of a political expediency to give juveniles longer and harsher sentences. Whatever the motivations for moving to new models, policy-makers must begin to clarify the goals and mission of the juvenile justice system, and must specify exactly how the system should respond to different types of offenders and offenses.

### Biographical Sketches

Martin L. Forst is Senior Research Associate at the URSA Institute in San Francisco. He received a doctorate in Criminology from the University of California at Berkeley, and is the author or co-author of several books and articles.

Martha–Elin Blomquist is Assistant Professor of Criminal Justice Administration at California State University, Bakersfield. She received her Ph.D in Jurisprudence and Social Policy from Boalt Hall School of Law, University of California at Berkeley. She is the co–author of *Missing Children: Rhetoric and Reality*.

*Authors' Addresses:*
Martin L. Forst, D. Crim
Senior Research Associate
URSA Institute
185 Berry Street, Suite 6600
San Francisco, California 94107
and

Martha–Elin Blomquist, Ph.D.
Assistant Professor
Criminal Justice Administration
California State University
Bakersfield, California 93302

# Notes

[1]For example, see: P. Tamilia, "The Recriminalization of the Juvenile Justice System –– The Demise of the Socialized Court," 31(2) *Juvenile and Family Court Journal,* 15–22 (1980); B. Feld, "Criminalizing Juvenile Justice: Rules of Procedure for the Juvenile Court," 69 *Minnesota Law Review* 141–276 (1984); J. Glen, "Juvenile Court Reform: Procedural Process and Substantive Stasis," 1970 *Wisconsin Law Review* 431–449; B. Feld, "The Juvenile Court Meets the Principle of Offense: Punishment, Treatment and the Difference It Makes," 68 *Boston University Law Review* 821–915 (1988); M. Forst and M. Blomquist, "Cracking Down on Juveniles: The Changing Ideology of Youth Corrections," 5 *Notre Dame Journal of Law, Ethics and Public Policy* 323–375 (1991).

[2]For example, see: F. A. Allen, "The Juvenile Court and the Limits of Juvenile Justice," 11 *Wayne Law Review* 676–687 (1965); M. Wolfgang, "Abolish the Juvenile Court System," 2(10) *California Lawyer* 12–13 (1982); E. van den Haag, *Punishing Criminals.* New York: Basic Books, Inc. (1975); W. Arnold, "Race and Ethnicity Relative to Other Factors in Juvenile Court Dispositions," 77 *American Journal of Sociology* 211–222 (1971); B. Boland and J.Q. Wilson, "Age, Crime and Punishment," 51 *The Public Interest* 22–34 (1978).

[3]M. Gardner, "Punitive Juvenile Justice: Some Observations on a Recent Trend," 10 *International Journal of Law and Psychiatry* 129–151 (1987), at p. 131–132.

[4]Institute of Judicial Administration/American Bar Association (IJA/ABA) Joint Commission on Juvenile Justice Standards, Standards Relating to Disposition (1980). Also see: F. McCarthy, "Delinquency Dispositions Under the Juvenile Justice Standards: The Consequences of a Change of Rationale," 52 *New York University Law Review*

1093–1119 (1977). McCarthy states, ". . . the standards advocate as the principal aim of the juvenile justice system the effective punishment of juveniles whose conduct endangers public safety" at p. 1094.

[5]S. Fox, "The Reform of the Juvenile Court: The Child's Right to Punishment," 25 *Juvenile Justice* 2–9 (1974), at p. 2.

[6]M. Norman and L. Gillespie, "Changing Horses: Utah's Shift in Adjudicating Serious Juvenile Offenders," 12 *Journal of Contemporary Law* 85–98 (1986), at p. 85.

[7]For example, see: R. Dawson, "The Third Justice System: The New Juvenile–Criminal System of Determinate Sentencing for the Youthful Violent Offender in Texas," 19 *St. Mary's Law Journal* 943–1016 (1988); Note, "The Serious Young Offender Under Vermont's Juvenile Law: Beyond the Reach of *Parens Patriae,"* 8 *Vermont Law Review* 173–202 (1983); R. McNally, "Juvenile Court: An Endangered Species," 47 *Federal Probation* 32–37 (1983).

[8]For example, see: B. Feld, "The Juvenile Court Meets the Principle of the Offense: Legislative Changes in Juvenile Waiver Statutes," 78 *Journal of Criminal Law and Criminology* 471–533 (1987); C. Rudman, E. Hartstone, J. Fagan, and M. Moore, "Violent Youth in Adult Court: Process and Punishment," 32 *Crime and Delinquency* 75–96 (1986).

[9]Dawson (1988), *supra,* note 7.

[10]Feld (1988), *supra,* note 1.

[11]M. K. Becker, "Washington State's New Juvenile Code: An Introduction," 14 *Gonzaga Law Review* 289–312 (1979), at p. 308.

[12]Washington Revised Codes, Section 13.40.010(2)(c)–(d).

[13]Maine Revised Statutes Annotated, Title 15, Section 3002.1(c).

[14]California Welfare and Institutions Code, Section 202.

[15]*Id.*

[16]Minnesota Statutes, Section 260.011(2).

[17]For example, see: McCarthy (1977), *supra,* note 4.

[18]For example, see: M. Gardner (1987), *supra,* note 3.

[19]For example, see: S. Wizner and M. Keller, "The Penal Model of Juvenile Justice: Is Juvenile Court Delinquency Jurisdiction Obsolete?" 52 *New York University Law Review* 1120–1135 (1977).

[20]For example, see: C. Springer, *Justice for Juveniles,* U.S. Department of Justice, Office of Juvenile Justice and Delinquency Prevention, Washington, D.C., April 1986.

[21]For example, see: M. Gardner, "The Right of Juvenile Offenders to be Punished: Some Implications of Treating Kids as Persons," 68 *Nebraska Law Review* 182–215 (1989).

[22]For example, see: B. Benda and D. Waite, "A Proposed Determinate Sentencing Model in Virginia: An Empirical Evaluation," 39(1) *Juvenile and Family Court Journal* 55–71 (1988).

[23]G. Melton, "Taking *Gault* Seriously: Toward a New Juvenile Court," 68 *Nebraska Law Review* 146–181 (1989), at p. 151.

[24]C. McGee, "Measured Steps Toward Clarity and Balance in the Juvenile Justice System," 40(3) *Juvenile and Family Court Journal* 1–23 (1989), at p. 16.

[25]Gardner (1989), *supra,* note 21 at p. 185.

[26]*Id.* at p. 184.

[27]For example, see: A. von Hirsch, *Doing Justice.* New York: Hill and Wang, 1976.

[28]R. Barnum, "The Development of Responsibility: Implications for Juvenile Justice," in Francis X. Hartman (ed.), *From Children to Citizens,* 1987, p. 74. Also see: McGee (1989), *supra,* note 24, at p. 16. He states, "Sometimes punishment alone is enough. ... A young petit thief might *learn* lesson enough by a sentence including a few days of incarceration and an additional restitution order."

[29]McGee (1989), *supra,* note 24, at p. 16.

[30]Fox, *supra,* note 5.

[31]von Hirsch (1976), *supra,* note 27.

[32]*People v. Olivas,* 17 Cal.3d 236, 551 P.2d 375 (1976).

[33]California Welfare and Institutions Code, Section 726(c).

[34]D. Maloney, D. Romig, and T. Armstrong, "Juvenile Probation: The Balanced Approach," 39(3) *Juvenile and Family Court Journal* 5–8 (1988), at p. 6.

[35]*Id.*

[36]*Id.*

[37]IJA/ABA Standards (1980), *supra,* note 4, at p. 19 note 5, (quoting Cohen, Position Paper, Juvenile Justice Standards Project, No. 18, 1974).

[38]F. Zimring, *The Changing Legal World of Adolescence.* New York: The Free Press, (1982), at p. 95–96.

[39]Melton (1989), *supra,* note 23 at p. 178.

[40]Gardner (1989), *supra,* note 21, at p. 195.

[41]Department of the Youth Authority. Mission Statement, Premises, Expanded Directional Statements, Sacramento, CA (1983), at p. 5.

[42]*Id.*

[43]*Eddings v. Oklahoma,* 455 U.S. 104 (1982), quoting from *May v. Anderson,* 345 U.S. 528, 536 (1952).

[44]455 U.S. 104, 115–116 (1982).

[45]*Id.* at p. 116.

[46]*Thompson v. Oklahoma,* 487 U.S. 815, 835 (1988).

[47]*Id.*

[48]*In re Michael,* 423 A.2d 1180, 1183 (1981).

[49]Gardner (1987), *supra,* note 3, at p. 147.

[50]*State v. Q.D.,* 685 P.2d 557, 560 (1984).

[51]Melton (1989), *supra,* note 23 at p. 180.

[52]Florida Statutes Annotated, Section 39.001(2)(a).

[53]Maloney et al. (1988), *supra,* note 34.

# Girls' Crime and Woman's Place: Toward a Feminist Model of Female Delinquency

*This article argues that existing delinquency theories are fundamentally inadequate to the task of explaining female delinquency and official reactions to girls' deviance. To establish this, the article first reviews the degree of the androcentric bias in the major theories of delinquent behavior. Then the need for a feminist model of female delinquency is explored by reviewing the available evidence on girls' offending. This review shows that the extensive focus on disadvantaged males in public settings has meant that girls' victimization and the relationship between that experience and girls' crime has been systematically ignored. Also missed has been the central role played by the juvenile justice system in the sexualization of female delinquency and the criminalization of girls' survival strategies. Finally, it will be suggested that the official actions of the juvenile justice system should be understood as major forces in women's oppression as they have historically served to reinforce the obedience of all young women to the demands of patriarchal authority no matter how abusive and arbitrary.*

## Meda Chesney-Lind

*Meda Chesney-Lind: Associate Professor of Women's Studies and an Associate Researcher with the Center for Youth Research at the University of Hawaii, Manoa.*

I ran away so many times. I tried anything man, and they wouldn't believe me. . . . As far as they are concerned they think I'm the problem. You know, runaway, bad label. (Statement of a 16-year-old girl who, after having been physically and sexually assaulted, started running away from home and was arrested as a "runaway" in Hawaii.)

You know, one of these days I'm going to have to kill myself before you guys are gonna listen to me. I can't stay at home. (Statement of a 16-year-old Tucson runaway with a long history of physical abuse [Davidson, 1982, p. 26].)

Who is the typical female delinquent? What causes her to get into trouble? What happens to her if she is caught? These are questions that few members of the general public could answer quickly. By contrast, almost every citizen can talk about "delinquency," by which they generally mean male delinquency, and can even generate some fairly specific complaints about, for ex-

ample, the failure of the juvenile justice system to deal with such problems as "the alarming increase in the rate of serious juvenile crime" and the fact that the juvenile courts are too lenient on juveniles found guilty of these offenses (Opinion Research Corporation, 1982).

This situation should come as no surprise since even the academic study of delinquent behavior has, for all intents and purposes, been the study of male delinquency. "The delinquent is a rogue male" declared Albert Cohen (1955, p. 140) in his influential book on gang delinquency. More than a decade later, Travis Hirschi, in his equally important book entitled *The Causes of Delinquency,* relegated women to a footnote that suggested, somewhat apologetically, that "in the analysis that follows, the 'non-Negro' becomes 'white,' and the girls disappear."

This pattern of neglect is not all that unusual. All areas of social inquiry have been notoriously gender blind. What is

perhaps less well understood is that theories developed to describe the misbehavior of working- or lower-class male youth fail to capture the full nature of delinquency in America; and, more to the point, are woefully inadequate when it comes to explaining female misbehavior and official reactions to girls' deviance.

To be specific, delinquent behavior involves a range of activities far broader than those committed by the stereotypical street gang. Moreover, many more young people than the small visible group of "troublemakers" that exist on every intermediate and high school campus commit some sort of juvenile offense and many of these youth have brushes with the law. One study revealed, for example, that 33% of all the boys and 14% of the girls born in 1958 had at least one contact with the police before reaching their eighteenth birthday (Tracy, Wolfgang, and Figlio, 1985, p. 5). Indeed, some forms of serious delinquent behavior, such as drug and alcohol abuse, are far more frequent than the stereotypical delinquent behavior of gang fighting and vandalism and appear to cut across class and gender lines.

Studies that solicit from youth themselves the volume of their delinquent behavior consistently confirm that large numbers of adolescents engage in at least some form of misbehavior that could result in their arrest. As a consequence, it is largely trivial misconduct, rather than the commission of serious crime, that shapes the actual nature of juvenile delinquency. One national study of youth aged 15-21, for example, noted that only 5% reported involvement in a serious assault, and only 6% reported having participated in a gang fight. In contrast, 81% admitted to having used alcohol, 44% admitted to having used marijuana, 37% admitted to having been publicly drunk, 42% admitted to having skipped classes (truancy), 44% admitted having had sexual intercourse, and 15% admitted to having stolen from the family (McGarrell and Flanagan, 1985, p. 363). Clearly, not all of these activities are as serious as the others. It is important to remember that young people can be arrested for all of these behaviors.

Indeed, one of the most important points to understand about the nature of delinquency, and particularly female delinquency, is that youth can be taken into custody for both criminal acts and a wide variety of what are often called "status offenses." These offenses, in contrast to criminal violations, permit the arrest of youth for a wide range of behaviors that are violations of parental authority: "running away from home," "being a person in need of supervision," "minor in need of supervision," being "incorrigible," "beyond control," truant, in need of "care and protection," and so on. Juvenile delinquents, then, are youths arrested for either criminal or noncriminal status offenses; and, as this discussion will establish, the role played by uniquely juvenile offenses is by no means insignificant, particularly when considering the character of female delinquency.

Examining the types of offenses for which youth are actually arrested, it is clear that again most are arrested for the less serious criminal acts and status offenses. Of the one and a half million youth arrested in 1983, for example, only 4.5% of these arrests were for such serious violent offenses as murder, rape, robbery, or aggravated assault (McGarrell and Flanagan, 1985, p. 479). In contrast, 21% were arrested for a single offense (larceny, theft) much of

which, particularly for girls, is shoplifting (Sheldon and Horvath, 1986).

Table 1 presents the five most frequent offenses for which male and female youth are arrested and from this it can be seen that while trivial offenses dominate both male and female delinquency, trivial offenses, particularly status offenses, are more significant in the case of girls' arrests; for example the five offenses listed in Table 1 account for nearly three-quarters of female offenses and only slightly more than half of male offenses.

More to the point, it is clear that, though routinely neglected in most delinquency research, status offenses play a significant role in girls' official delinquency. Status offenses accounted for about 25.2% of all girls' arrests in 1986 (as compared to 26.9% in 1977) and only about 8.3% of boys' arrests (compared to 8.8% in 1977). These figures are somewhat surprising since dramatic declines in arrests of youth for these offenses might have been expected as a result of the passage of the Juvenile Justice and Delinquency Prevention Act in 1974, which, among other things, encouraged jurisdictions to divert and deinstitutionalize youth charged with noncriminal offenses. While the figures in Table 1 do show a decline in these arrests, virtually all of this decline occurred in the 1970s. Between 1982 and 1986 girls' curfew arrests increased by 5.1% and runaway arrests increased by a striking 24.5%. And the upward trend continues; arrests of girls for running away increased by 3% between 1985 and 1986 and arrests of girls for curfew violations increased by 12.4% (Federal Bureau of Investigation, 1987, p. 171).

Looking at girls who find their way into juvenile court populations, it is apparent that status offenses continue to play an important role in the character of girls' official delinquency. In total, 34% of the girls, but only 12% of the boys, were referred to court in 1983 for these offenses (Snyder and Finnegan, 1987, pp. 6–20). Stating these figures differently, they mean that while males constituted about 81% of all delinquency referrals, females constituted 46% of all status offenders in courts (Snyder and Finnegan, 1987, p. 20). Similar figures were reported for 1977 by Black and Smith (1981). Fifteen years earlier, about half of the girls and about 20% of the boys were referred to court for these offenses (Children's Bureau, 1965). These data do seem to signal a drop in female status offense referrals, though not as dramatic a decline as might have been expected.

For many years statistics showing

large numbers of girls arrested and referred for status offenses were taken to be representative of the different types of male and female delinquency. However, self-report studies of male and female delinquency do not reflect the dramatic differences in misbehavior found in official statistics. Specifically, it appears that girls charged with these noncriminal status offenses have been and continue to be significantly overrepresented in court populations.

Teilmann and Landry (1981) compared girls' contribution to arrests for runaway and incorrigibility with girls' self-reports of these two activities, and found a 10.4% overrepresentation of females among those arrested for runaway and a 30.9% overrepresentation in arrests for incorrigibility. From these data they concluded that girls are "arrested for status offenses at a higher rate than boys, when contrasted to their self-reported delinquency rates" (Teilmann and Landry, 1981, pp. 74–75). These findings were confirmed in another recent self-report study. Figueira-McDonough (1985, p. 277) analyzed the delinquent conduct of 2,000 youths and found "no evidence of greater involvement of females in status offenses." Similarly, Canter (1982) found in the National Youth Survey that there was no evidence of greater female involvement, compared to males, in any category of delinquent behavior. Indeed, in this sample, males were significantly more likely than females to report status offenses.

Utilizing Canter's national data on the extensiveness of girls self-reported delinquency and comparing these figures to official arrests of girls (see Table 2) reveals that girls are underrepresented in every arrest category with the exception of status offenses and larceny theft. These figures strongly suggest that official practices tend to exaggerate the role played by status offenses in girls' delinquency.

Delinquency theory, because it has virtually ignored female delinquency, failed to pursue anomalies such as these found in the few early studies examining gender differences in delinquent behavior. Indeed, most delinquency theories have ignored status offenses. As a consequence, there is considerable question as to whether existing theories that were admittedly developed to explain male delinquency can adequately explain female delinquency. Clearly, these theories were much influenced by the notion that class and protest masculinity were at the core of delinquency. Will the "add women and stir approach" be sufficient? Are these really theories of delin-

TABLE 1: Rank Order of Adolescent Male and Female Arrests for Specific Offenses, 1977 and 1986

| Male | | | | Female | | | |
|---|---|---|---|---|---|---|---|
| 1977 | % of Total Arrests | 1986 | % of Total Arrests | 1977 | % of Total Arrests | 1986 | % of Total Arrests |
| (1) Larceny-Theft | 18.4 | (1) Larceny-Theft | 20.4 | (1) Larceny-Theft | 27.0 | (1) Larceny-Theft | 25.7 |
| (2) Other Offenses | 14.5 | (2) Other Offenses | 16.5 | (2) Runaway | 22.9 | (2) Runaway | 20.5 |
| (3) Burglary | 13.0 | (3) Burglary | 9.1 | (3) Other Offenses | 14.2 | (3) Other Offenses | 14.8 |
| (4) Drug Abuse Violations | 6.5 | (4) Vandalism | 7.0 | (4) Liquor Laws | 5.5 | (4) Liquor Laws | 8.4 |
| (5) Vandalism | 6.4 | (5) Vandalism | 6.3 | (5) Curfew & Loitering Violations | 4.0 | (5) Curfew & Loitering Violations | 4.7 |

| | 1977 | 1986 | % N Change | | 1977 | 1986 | % N Change |
|---|---|---|---|---|---|---|---|
| Arrests for Serious Violent Offenses[a] | 4.2% | 4.7% | 2.3 | Arrests for Serious Violent Offenses | 1.8% | 2.0% | +1.7 |
| Arrests of All Violent Offenses[b] | 7.6% | 9.6% | +10.3 | Arrests of All Violent Offenses | 5.1% | 7.1% | +26.0 |
| Arrests for Status Offenses[c] | 8.8% | 8.3% | −17.8 | Arrests for Status Offenses | 26.9% | 25.2% | −14.7 |

SOURCE: Compiled from Federal Bureau of Investigation (1987, p. 169).
a. Arrests for murder and nonnegligent manslaughter, robbery, forcible rape, and aggravated assault.
b. Also includes arrests for other assaults.
c. Arrests for curfew and loitering law violation and runaway.

quent behavior as some (Simons, Miller, and Aigner, 1980) have argued?

This article will suggest that they are not. The extensive focus on male delinquency and the inattention the role played by patriarchal arrangements in the generation of adolescent delinquency and conformity has rendered the major delinquency theories fundamentally inadequate to the task of explaining female behavior. There is, in short, an urgent need to rethink current models in light of girls' situation in patriarchal society.

To understand why such work must occur, it is first necessary to explore briefly the dimensions of the androcentric bias found in the dominant and influential delinquency theories. Then the need for a feminist model of female delinquency will be explored by reviewing the available evidence on girls' offending. This discussion will also establish that the proposed overhaul of delinquency theory is not, as some might think, solely an academic exercise. Specifically, it is incorrect to assume that because girls are charged with less serious offenses, they actually have few problems and are treated gently when they are drawn into the juvenile justice system. Indeed, the extensive focus on disadvantaged males in public settings has meant that girls' victimization and the relationship between that experience and girls' crime has been systematically ignored. Also missed has been the central role played by the juvenile justice system in the sexualization of girls' delinquency and the criminalization of girls' survival strategies. Finally, it will be suggested that the

official actions of the juvenile justice system should be understood as major forces in girls' oppression as they have historically served to reinforce the obedience of all young women to demands of patriarchal authority no matter how abusive and arbitrary.

## THE ROMANCE OF THE GANG OR THE *WEST SIDE STORY* SYNDROME

From the start, the field of delinquency research focused on visible lower-class male delinquency, often justifying the neglect of girls in the most cavalier of terms. Take, for example, the extremely important and influential work of Clifford R. Shaw and Henry D. McKay who beginning in 1929, utilized an ecological approach to the study of juvenile delinquency. Their impressive work, particularly *Juvenile Delinquency in Urban Areas* (1942) and intensive biographical case studies such as Shaw's *Brothers in Crime* (1938) and *The Jackroller* (1930), set the stage for much of the subcultural research on gang delinquency. In their ecological work, however, Shaw and McKay analyzed only the official arrest data on male delinquents in Chicago and repeatedly referred to these rates as "delinquency rates" (though they occasionally made parenthetical reference to data on female delinquency) (see Shaw and McKay, 1942, p. 356). Similarly, their biographical work traced only male experiences with the law; in *Brothers in Crime*, for example, the delinquent and criminal careers of five brothers were followed for fifteen years. In none of these works was any justification given for the equation of male delinquency with delinquency.

Early fieldwork on delinquent gangs in Chicago set the stage for another style of delinquency research. Yet here too researchers were interested only in talking to and following the boys. Thrasher studied over a thousand juvenile gangs in Chicago during roughly the same period as Shaw and McKay's more quantitative work was being done. He spent approximately one page out of 600 on the five of six female gangs he encountered in his field observation of juvenile gangs. Thrasher (1927, p. 228) did mention, in passing, two factors he felt accounted for the lower number of girl gangs: "First, the social patterns for the behavior of girls, powerfully backed by the great weight of tradition and custom, are contrary to the gang and its activities; and secondly, girls, even in urban disorganized areas, are much more closely supervised and guarded than boys and usually well incorporated into the family groups or some other social structure."

Another major theoretical approach to delinquency focuses on the subculture of lower-class communities as a generating milieu for delinquent behavior. Here again, noted delinquency researchers concentrated either exclusively or nearly exclusively on male lower-class culture. For example, Cohen's work on the subculture of delinquent gangs, which was written nearly twenty years after Thrasher's, deliberately considers only boys' delinquency. His justification for the exclusion of the girls is quite illuminating:

My skin has nothing of the quality of down or silk, there is nothing limpid or flute-like about my voice, I am a total

TABLE 2: Comparison of Sex Differences in Self-Reported and Official Delinquency for Selected Offenses

| | Self-Report[a] M/F Ratios (1976) | Official Statistics[b] M/F Arrest Ratio | |
| --- | --- | --- | --- |
| | | 1976 | 1986 |
| Theft | 3.5:1 (Felony Theft) 3.4:1 (Minor Theft) | 2.5:1 | 2.7:1 |
| Drug Violation | 1:1 (Hard Drug Use) | 5.1:1 | 6.0:1 (Drug Abuse Violations) |
| Vandalism | 5.1:1 | 12.3:1 | 10.0:1 |
| Disorderly Conduct | 2.8:1 | 4.5:1 | 4.4:1 |
| Serious Assault | 3.5:1 (Felony Assault) | 5.6:1 | 5.5:1 (Aggravated Assault) |
| Minor Assault | 3.4:1 | 3.8:1 | 3.4:1 |
| Status Offenses | 1.6:1 | 1.3:1 | 1.1:1 (Runaway, Curfew) |

a. Extracted from Rachelle Canter (1982, p. 383).
b. Compiled from Federal Bureau of Investigation (1986, p. 173).

loss with needle and thread, my posture and carriage are wholly lacking in grace. These imperfections cause me no distress—if anything, they are gratifying—because I conceive myself to be a man and want people to recognize me as a full-fledged, unequivocal representative of my sex. My wife, on the other hand, is not greatly embarrassed by her inability to tinker with or talk about the internal organs of a car, by her modest attainments in arithmetic or by her inability to lift heavy objects. Indeed, I am reliably informed that many women—I do not suggest that my wife is among them—often affect ignorance, frailty and emotional instability because to do otherwise would be out of keeping with a reputation for indubitable femininity. In short, people do not simply want to excel; they want to excel as a man or as a woman [Cohen, 1955, p. 138.]

From this Cohen (1955, p. 140) concludes that the delinquent response "however it may be condemned by others on moral grounds has least one virtue; it incontestably confirms, in the eyes of all concerned, his essential masculinity." Much the same line of argument appears in Miller's influential paper on the "focal concerns" of lower-class life with its emphasis on importance of trouble, toughness, excitement, and so on. These, the author concludes, predispose poor youth (particularly male youth) to criminal misconduct. However, Cohen's comments are notable in their candor and probably capture both the allure that male delinquency has had for at least some male theorists as well as the fact that sexism has rendered the female delinquent as irrelevant to their work.

Emphasis on blocked opportunities (sometimes the "strain" theories) emerged out of the work of Robert K. Merton (1938) who stressed the need to consider how some social structures exert a definite pressure upon certain persons in the society to engage in nonconformist rather than conformist conduct. His work influenced research largely through the efforts of Cloward and Ohlin who discussed access to "legitimate" and "illegitimate" opportunities for male youth. No mention of female delinquency can be found in their *Delinquency and Opportunity* except that women are blamed for male delinquency. Here, the familiar notion is that boys, "engulfed by a feminine world and uncertain of their own identification . . . tend to 'protest' against femininity" (Cloward and Ohlin, 1960, p. 49). Early efforts by Ruth Morris to test this hypothesis utilizing different definitions of success based on the gender of respondents met with mixed success. Attempting to assess boys' perceptions about access to economic power status while for girls the variable concerned itself with the ability or inability of girls to maintain effective relationships, Morris was unable to find a clear relationship between "female" goals and delinquency (Morris, 1964).

The work of Edwin Sutherland emphasized the fact that criminal behavior was learned in intimate personal groups. His work, particularly the notion of differential association, which also influenced Cloward and Ohlin's work, was similarly male oriented as much of his work was affected by case studies he conducted of male criminals. Indeed, in describing his notion of how differential association works, he utilized male examples (e.g., "In an area where the delinquency rate is high a boy who is sociable, gregarious, active, and athletic is very likely to come in contact with the other boys, in the neighborhood, learn delinquent behavior from them, and become a gangster" [Sutherland, 1978, p. 131]). Finally, the work of Travis Hirschi on the social bonds that control delinquency ("social control theory") was, as was stated earlier, derived out of research on male delinquents (though he, at least, studied delinquent behavior as reported by youth themselves rather than studying only those who were arrested).

Such a persistent focus on social class and such an absence of interest in gender in delinquency is ironic for two reasons. As even the work of Hirschi demonstrated, and as later studies would validate, a clear relationship between social class position and delinquency is problematic, while it is clear that gender has a dramatic and consistent effect on delinquency causation (Hagan, Gillis, and Simpson, 1985). The second irony, and one that consistently eludes even contemporary delinquency theorists, is the fact that while the academics had little interest in female delinquents, the same could not be said for the juvenile justice system. Indeed, work on the early history of the separate system for youth, reveals that concerns about girls' immoral conduct were really at the center of what some have called the "childsaving movement" (Platt, 1969) that set up the juvenile justice system.

## "THE BEST PLACE TO CONQUER GIRLS"

The movement to establish separate institutions for youthful offenders was part of the larger Progressive movement, which among other things was keenly concerned about prostitution and other "social evils" (white slavery and the like) (Schlossman and Wallach, 1978; Rafter, 1985, p. 54). Childsaving was also a celebration of women's domesticity, though ironically women were influential in the movement (Platt, 1969; Rafter, 1985). In a sense, privileged women found, in the moral purity crusades and the establishment of family courts, a safe outlet for their energies. As the legitimate guardians of the moral sphere, women were seen as uniquely suited to patrol the normative boundaries of the social order. Embracing rather than challenging these stereotypes, women carved out for themselves a role in the policing of women and girls (Feinman, 1980; Freedman, 1981; Messerschmidt, 1987). Ultimately, many of the early childsavers' activities revolved around the monitoring of young girls', particularly immigrant girls', behavior to prevent their straying from the path.

This state of affairs was the direct consequence of a disturbing coalition between some feminists and the more conservative social purity movement. Concerned about female victimization and distrustful of male (and to some degree female) sexuality, notable women leaders, including Susan B. Anthony, found common cause with the social purists around such issues as opposing the regulation of prostitution and raising the age of consent (see Messerschmidt, 1987). The consequences of such a partnership are an important lesson for contemporary feminist movements that are, to some extent, faced with the same possible coalitions.

Girls were the clear losers in this reform effort. Studies of early family court activity reveal that virtually all the girls who appeared in these courts were charged for immorality or waywardness (Chesney-Lind, 1971; Schlossman and Wallach, 1978; Shelden, 1981). More to the point, the sanctions for such misbehavior were extremely severe. For example, in Chicago (where the first family court was founded), one-half of the girl delinquents, but only one-fifth of the boy delinquents, were sent to reformatories between 1899–1909. In Milwaukee, twice as many girls as boys were committed to training schools (Schlossman and Wallach, 1978, p. 72); and in Memphis females were twice as likely as males to be committed to training schools (Shelden, 1981, p. 70).

In Honolulu, during the period 1929–1930, over half of the girls referred to court were charged with "immorality," which meant evidence of sexual intercourse. In addition, another 30% were charged with "waywardness." Evidence of immorality was vigorously pursued by both arresting officers and social workers through lengthy questioning of the girl and, if possible, males with whom she was suspected of having sex. Other evidence of "exposure" was provided by gynecological examinations that were routinely ordered in virtually all girls' cases. Doctors, who understood the purpose of such examinations, would routinely note the condition of the hymen: "admits intercourse hymen rupture," "no laceration," "hymen ruptured" are typical of the notations on the forms. Girls during this period were also twice as likely as males to be detained where they spent five times as long on the average as their male counterparts. They were also nearly three times more likely to be sentenced to the training school (Chesney-Lind, 1971). Indeed, girls were half of those commit-

ted to training schools in Honolulu well into the 1950s (Chesney-Lind, 1973).

Not surprisingly, large numbers of girls' reformatories and training schools were established during this period as well as places of "rescue and reform." For example, Schlossman and Wallach note that 23 facilities for girls were opened during the 1910–1920 decade (in contrast to the 1850–1910 period where the average was 5 reformatories per decade [Schlossman and Wallach, 1985, p. 70]), and these institutions did much to set the tone of official response to female delinquency. Obsessed with precocious female sexuality, the institutions set about to isolate the females from all contact with males while housing them in bucolic settings. The intention was to hold the girls until marriageable age and to occupy them in domestic pursuits during their sometimes lengthy incarceration.

The links between these attitudes and those of juvenile courts some decades later are, of course, arguable; but an examination of the record of the court does not inspire confidence. A few examples of the persistence of what might be called a double standard of juvenile justice will suffice here.

A study conducted in the early 1970s in a Connecticut training school revealed large numbers of girls incarcerated "for their own protection." Explaining this pattern, one judge explained, "Why most of the girls I commit are for status offenses, I figure if a girl is about to get pregnant, we'll keep her until she's sixteen and then ADC (Aid to Dependent Children) will pick her up" (Rogers, 1972). For more evidence of official concern with adolescent sexual misconduct, consider Linda Hancock's (1981) content analysis of police referrals in Australia. She noted that 40% of the referrals of girls to court made specific mention of sexual and moral conduct compared to only 5% of the referrals of boys. These sorts of results suggest that all youthful female misbehavior has traditionally been subject to surveillance for evidence of sexual misconduct.

Gelsthorpe's (1986) field research on an English police station also revealed how everyday police decision making resulted in disregard of complaints about male problem behavior in contrast to active concern about the "problem behavior" of girls. Notable, here, was the concern about the girls' sexual behavior. In one case, she describes police persistence in pursuing a "moral danger" order for a 14-year-old picked up in a truancy run. Over the objections of both the girl's parents and the Social Services Department and in the face of a written confirmation from a surgeon

that the girl was still premenstrual, the officers pursued the application because, in one officer's words, "I know her sort . . . free and easy. I'm still suspicious that she might be pregnant. Anyway, if the doctor can't provide evidence we'll do her for being beyond the care and control of her parents, no one can dispute that. Running away is proof" (Gelsthorpe, 1986, p. 136). This sexualization of female deviance is highly significant and explains why criminal activities by girls (particularly in past years) were overlooked so long as they did not appear to signal defiance of parental control (see Smith, 1978).

In their historic obsession about precocious female sexuality, juvenile justice workers rarely reflected on the broader nature of female misbehavior or on the sources of this misbehavior. It was enough for them that girls' parents reported them out of control. Indeed, court personnel tended to "sexualize" virtually all female defiance that lent itself to that construction and ignore other misbehavior (Chesney-Lind, 1973, 1977; Smith, 1978). For their part, academic students of delinquency were so entranced with the notion of the delinquent as a romantic rogue male challenging a rigid and unequal class structure, that they spent little time on middle-class delinquency, trivial offenders, or status offenders. Yet it is clear that the vast bulk of delinquent behavior is of this type.

Some have argued that such an imbalance in theoretical work is appropriate as minor misconduct, while troublesome, is not a threat to the safety and well-being of the community. This argument might be persuasive if two additional points could be established. One, that some small number of youth "specialize" in serious criminal behavior while the rest commit only minor acts, and, two, that the juvenile court rapidly releases those youth that come into its purview for these minor offenses, thus reserving resources for the most serious youthful offenders.

The evidence is mixed on both of these points. Determined efforts to locate the "serious juvenile offender" have failed to locate a group of offenders who specialize only in serious violent offenses. For example, in a recent analysis of a national self-report data set, Elliott and his associates noted "there is little evidence for specialization in serious violent offending; to the contrary, serious violent offending appears to be embedded in a more general involvement in a wide range of serious and non-serious offenses" (Elliott, Huizinga, and Morse, 1987). Indeed, they went so far as to speculate that arrest histories that tend to highlight particular types of offenders reflect variations in police policy, practices, and processes of uncovering crime as well as underlying offending patterns.

More to the point, police and court personnel are, it turns out, far more interested in youth they charge with trivial or status offenses than anyone imagined. Efforts to deinstitutionalize "status offenders," for example, ran afoul of juvenile justice personnel who had little interest in releasing youth guilty of noncriminal offenses (Chesney-Lind, 1988). As has been established, much of this is a product of the system's history that encouraged court officers to involve themselves in the noncriminal behavior of youth in order to "save" them from a variety of social ills.

Indeed, parallels can be found between the earlier Progressive period and current national efforts to challenge the deinstitutionalization components of the Juvenile Justice and Delinquency Prevention Act of 1974. These come complete with their celebration of family values and concerns about youthful independence. One of the arguments against the act has been that it allegedly gave children the "freedom to run away" (Office of Juvenile Justice and Delinquency Prevention, 1985) and that it has hampered "reunions" of "missing" children with their parents (Office of Juvenile Justice, 1986). Suspicions about teen sexuality are reflected in excessive concern about the control of teen prostitution and child pornography.

Opponents have also attempted to justify continued intervention into the lives of status offenders by suggesting that without such intervention, the youth would "escalate" to criminal behavior. Yet there is little evidence that status offenders escalate to criminal offenses, and the evidence is particularly weak when considering female delinquents (particularly white female delinquents) (Datesman and Aickin, 1984). Finally, if escalation is occurring, it is likely the product of the justice system's insistence on enforcing status offense laws, thereby forcing youth in crisis to live lives of escaped criminals.

The most influential delinquency theories, however, have largely ducked the issue of status and trivial offenses and, as a consequence, neglected the role played by the agencies of official control (police, probation officers, juvenile court judges, detention home workers, and training school personnel) in the shaping of the "delinquency problem." When confronting the less than distinct picture that emerges from the actual distribution of delinquent behavior, however, the conclusion that agents of social control have considerable discretion in labeling or choosing not to label particular behavior as "delinquent" is inescapable. This symbiotic relationship between delinquent behavior and the official response to that behavior is particularly critical when the question of female delinquency is considered.

## TOWARD A FEMINIST THEORY OF DELINQUENCY

To sketch out completely a feminist theory of delinquency is a task beyond the scope of this article. It may be sufficient, at this point, simply to identify a few of the most obvious problems with attempts to adapt male-oriented theory to explain female conformity and deviance. Most significant of these is the fact that all existing theories were developed with no concern about gender stratification.

Note that this is not simply an observation about the power of gender roles (though this power is undeniable). It is increasingly clear that gender stratification in patriarchal society is as powerful a system as is class. A feminist approach to delinquency means construction of explanations of female behavior that are sensitive to its patriarchal context. Feminist analysis of delinquency would also examine ways in which agencies of social control—the police, the courts, and the prisons—act in ways to reinforce woman's place in male society (Harris, 1977; Chesney-Lind, 1986). Efforts to construct a feminist model of delinquency must first and foremost be sensitive to the situations of girls. Failure to consider the existing empirical evidence on girls' lives and behavior can quickly lead to stereotypical thinking and theoretical dead ends.

An example of this sort of flawed theory building was the early fascination with the notion that the women's movement was causing an increase in women's crime; a notion that is now more or less discredited (Steffensmeier, 1980; Gora, 1982). A more recent example of the same sort of thinking can be found in recent work on the "power-control" model of delinquency (Hagan, Simpson, and Gillis, 1987). Here, the authors speculate that girls commit less delinquency in part because their behavior is more closely controlled by the patriarchal family. The authors' promising beginning quickly gets bogged down in a very limited definition of patriarchal control (focusing on parental supervision and variations in power within the family). Ultimately, the authors' narrow formulation of patriarchal control results in their arguing that mother's work force participation (particularly in high status occupations) leads to increases in daughters' delinquency since these girls find themselves in more "egalitarian families."

This is essentially a not-too-subtle variation on the earlier "liberation" hypothesis. Now, mother's liberation causes daughter's crime. Aside from the methodological problems with the study (e.g., the authors argue that female-headed households are equivalent to upper-status "egalitarian" families where both parents work, and they measure delinquency using a six-item scale that contains no status offense items), there is a more fundamental problem with the hypothesis. There is no evidence to suggest that as women's labor force participation accelerated and the number of female-headed households soared, aggregate female delinquency measured both by self-report and official statistics either declined or remained stable (Ageton, 1983; Chilton and Datesman, 1987; Federal Bureau of Investigation, 1987).

By contrast, a feminist model of delinquency would focus more extensively on the few pieces of information about girls' actual lives and the role played by girls' problems, including those caused by racism and poverty, in their delinquency behavior. Fortunately, a considerable literature is now developing on girls' lives and much of it bears directly on girls' crime.

## CRIMINALIZING GIRLS' SURVIVAL

It has long been understood that a major reason for girls' presence in juvenile courts was the fact that their parents insisted on their arrest. In the early years, conflicts with parents were by far the most significant referral source; in Honolulu 44% of the girls who appeared in court in 1929 through 1930 were referred by parents.

Recent national data, while slightly less explicit, also show that girls are more likely to be referred to court by "sources other than law enforcement agencies" (which would include parents). In 1983, nearly a quarter (23%) of all girls but only 16% of boys charged with delinquent offenses were referred to court by non-law enforcement agencies. The pattern among youth referred for status offenses (for which girls are overrepresented) was even more pronounced. Well over half (56%) of the girls charged with these offenses and 45% of the boys were referred by sources other than law enforcement (Snyder and Finnegan, 1987, p. 21; see also Pope and Feyerherm, 1982).

The fact that parents are often committed to two standards of adolescent behavior is one explanation for such a disparity—and one that should not be discounted as a major source of tension even in modern families. Despite expectations to the contrary, gender-specific socialization patterns have not changed very much and this is especially true for parents' relationships with their daughters (Katz, 1979). It appears that even parents who oppose sexism in general feel"uncomfortable tampering with existing traditions" and "do not want to risk their children becoming misfits" (Katz, 1979, p. 24). Clearly, parental attempts to adhere to and enforce these traditional notions will continue to be a source of conflict between girls and their elders. Another important explanation for girls' problems with their parents, which has received attention only in more recent years, is the problem of physical and sexual abuse. Looking specifically at the problem of childhood sexual abuse, it is increasingly clear that this form of abuse is a particular problem for girls.

Girls are, for example, much more likely to be the victims of child sexual abuse than are boys. Finkelhor and Baron estimate from a review of community studies that roughly 70% of the victims of sexual abuse are female (Finkelhor and Baron, 1986, p. 45). Girls' sexual abuse also tends to start earlier than boys (Finkelhor and Baron, 1986, p. 48); they are more likely than boys to be assaulted by a family member (often a stepfather)(DeJong, Hervada, and Emmett, 1983; Russell, 1986), and as a consequence, their abuse tends to last longer than male sexual abuse (De-Jong,Hervada, and Emmett, 1983). All of these factors are associated with more severe trauma—causing dramatic short- and long-term effects in victims (Adams-Tucker, 1982). The effects noted by researchers in this area move from the more well known "fear, anxiety, depression, anger and hostility, and inappropriate sexual behavior" (Browne and Finkelhor, 1986, p. 69) to behaviors of greater familiarity to criminologists, including running away from home, difficulties in school, truancy, and early marriage (Browne and Finkelhor, 1986).

Herman's study of incest survivors in therapy found that they were more likely to have run away from home than a matched sample of women whose fathers were "seductive" (33% compared to 5%). Another study of women patients found that 50% of the victims of child sexual abuse, but only 20% of the nonvictim group, had left home before the age of 19 (Meiselman, 1978).

Not surprisingly, then, studies of girls on the streets or in court populations are showing high rates of both physical and sexual abuse. Silbert and Pines

(1981, p. 409) found, for example, that 60% of the street prostitutes they interviewed had been sexually abused as juveniles. Girls at an Arkansas diagnostic unit and school who had been adjudicated for either status or delinquent offenses reported similarly high levels of sexual abuse as well as high levels of physical abuse; 53% indicated they had been sexually abused, 25% recalled scars, 38% recalled bleeding from abuse, and 51% recalled bruises (Mouzakitas, 1981).

A sample survey of girls in the juvenile justice system in Wisconsin (Phelps et al., 1982) revealed that 79% had been subjected to physical abuse that resulted in some form of injury, and 32% had been sexually abused by parents or other persons who were closely connected to their families. Moreover, 50% had been sexually assaulted ("raped" or forced to participate in sexual acts)(Phelps et al., 1982, p. 66). Even higher figures were reported by McCormack and her associates (McCormack, Janus, and Burgess, 1986) in their study of youth in a runaway shelter in Toronto. They found that 73% of the females and 38% of the males had been sexually abused. Finally, a study of youth charged with running away, truancy, or listed as missing persons in Arizona found that 55% were incest victims (Reich and Gutierres, 1979).

Many young women, then, are running away from profound sexual victimization at home, and once on the streets they are forced further into crime in order to survive. Interviews with girls who have run away from home show, very clearly, that they do not have a lot of attachment to their delinquent activities. In fact, they are angry about being labeled as delinquent, yet all engaged in illegal acts (Koroki and Chesney-Lind, 1985). The Wisconsin study found that 54% of the girls who ran away found it necessary to steal money, food, and clothing in order to survive. A few exchanged sexual contact for money, food, and/or shelter (Phelps et al., 1982, p. 67). In their study of runaway youth, McCormack, Janus, and Burgess (1986, pp. 392–393) found that sexually abused female runaways were significantly more likely than their nonabused counterparts to engage in delinquent or criminal activities such as substance abuse, petty theft, and prostitution. No such pattern was found among male runaways.

Research (Chesney-Lind and Rodriguez, 1983) on the backgrounds of adult women in prison underscores the important links between women's childhood victimizations and their later criminal careers. The interviews revealed that virtually all of this sample were the victims of physical and/or sexual abuse as youngsters; over 60% had been sexually abused and about half had been raped as young women. This situation prompted these women to run away from home (three-quarters had been arrested for status offenses) where once on the streets they began engaging in prostitution and other forms of petty property crime. They also begin what becomes a lifetime problem with drugs. As adults, the women continue in these activities since they possess truncated educational backgrounds and virtually no marketable occupational skills (see also Miller, 1986).

Confirmation of the consequences of childhood sexual and physical abuse on adult female criminal behavior has also recently come from a large quantitative study of 908 individuals with substantiated and validated histories of these victimizations. Widom (1988) found that abused or neglected females were twice as likely as a matched group of controls to have an adult record (16% compared to 7.5). The difference was also found among men, but it was not as dramatic (42% compared to 33%). Men with abuse backgrounds were also more likely to contribute to the "cycle of violence" with more arrests for violent offenses as adult offenders than the control group. In contrast, when women with abuse backgrounds did become involved with the criminal justice system, their arrests tended to involve property and order offenses (such as disorderly conduct, curfew, and loitering violations) (Widon, 1988, p. 17).

Given this information, a brief example of how a feminist perspective on the causes of female delinquency might look seems appropriate. First, like young men, girls are frequently the recipients of violence and sexual abuse. But unlike boys, girls' victimization and their response to that victimization is specifically shaped by their status as young women. Perhaps because of the gender and sexual scripts found in patriarchal families, girls are much more likely than boys to be victim of family-related sexual abuse. Men, particularly men with traditional attitudes toward women, are likely to define their daughters or stepdaughters as their sexual property (Finkelhor, 1982). In a society that idealizes inequality in male/female relationships and venerates youth in women, girls are easily defined as sexually attractive by older men (Bell, 1984). In addition, girls' vulnerability to both physical and sexual abuse is heightened by norms that require that they stay at home where their victimizers have access to them.

Moreover, their victimizers (usually males) have the ability to invoke official agencies of social control in their efforts to keep young women at home and vulnerable. That is to say, abusers have traditionally been able to utilize the uncritical commitment of the juvenile justice system toward parental authority to force girls to obey them. Girls' complaints about abuse were, until recently, routinely ignored. For this reason, statutes that were originally placed in law to "protect" young people have, in the case of girls' delinquency, criminalized their survival strategies. As they run away from abusive homes, parents have been able to employ agencies to enforce their return. If they persisted in their refusal to stay in that home, however intolerable, they were incarcerated.

Young women, a large number of whom are on the run from homes characterized by sexual abuse and parental neglect, are forced by the very statutes designed to protect them into the lives of escaped convicts. Unable to enroll in school or take a job to support themselves because they fear detection, young female runaways are forced into the streets. Here they engage in panhandling, petty theft, and occasional prostitution in order to survive. Young women in conflict with their parents (often for very legitimate reasons) may actually be forced by present laws into petty criminal activity, prostitution, and drug use.

In addition, the fact that young girls (but not necessarily young boys) are defined as sexually desirable and, in fact, more desirable than their older sisters due to the double standard of aging means that their lives on the streets (and their survival strategies) take on unique shape—one again shaped by patriarchal values. It is no accident that girls on the run from abusive homes, or on the streets because of profound poverty, get involved in criminal activities that exploit their sexual object status. American society has defined as desirable youthful, physically perfect women. This means that girls on the streets, who have little else of value to trade, are encouraged to utilize this "resource" (Campagna and Poffenberger, 1988). It also means that the criminal subculture views them from this perspective (Miller, 1986).

## FEMALE DELINQUENCY, PATRIARCHAL AUTHORITY, AND FAMILY COURTS

The early insights into male delinquency were largely gleaned by intensive field observation of delinquent boys. Very little of this sort of work has been done in the case of girls' delinquency, though it is vital to an understanding of girls' definitions of their own situations, choices, and behavior (for exceptions to this see Campbell, 1984; Peacock, 1981; Miller, 1986; Rosenberg and Zimmerman, 1977). Time must be spent listening to girls. Fuller research on the settings, such as families and schools, that girls find themselves in and the impact of variations in those settings should also be undertaken (see Figueira-McDonough, 1986). A more complete understanding of how poverty and racism shape girls' lives is also vital (see Messerschmidt, 1986; Campbell, 1984). Finally, current qualitative research on the reaction of official agencies to girls' delinquency must be conducted. This latter task, admittedly more difficult, is particularly critical to the development of delinquency theory that is as sensitive to gender as it is to race and class.

It is clear that throughout most of the court's history, virtually all female delinquency has been placed within the larger context of girls' sexual behavior. One explanation for this pattern is that familial control over girls' sexual capital has historically been central to the maintenance of patriarchy (Lerner, 1986). The fact that young women have relatively more of this capital has been one reason for the excessive concern that both families and official agencies of social control have expressed about youthful female defiance (otherwise much of the behavior of criminal justice personnel makes virtually no sense). Only if one considers the role of women's control over their sexuality at the point in their lives that their value to patriarchal society is so pronounced, does the historic pattern of jailing of huge numbers of girls guilty of minor misconduct make sense.

This framework also explains the enormous resistance that the movement to curb the juvenile justice system's authority over status offenders encountered. Supporters of the change were not really prepared for the political significance of giving youth the freedom to run. Horror stories told by the opponents of deinstitutionalization about victimized youth, youthful prostitution, and youthful involvement in pornography (Office of Juvenile Justice and Delinquency Prevention, 1985) all neglect the unpleasant reality that most of these behaviors were often in direct response to earlier victimization, frequently by parents, that officials had, for years, routinely ignored. What may be at stake in efforts to roll back deinstitutionaliza-tion efforts is not so much "protection" of youth as it is curbing the right of young women to defy patriarchy.

In sum, research in both the dynamics of girls' delinquency and official reactions to that behavior is essential to the development of theories of delinquency that are sensitive to its patriarchal as well as class and racial context.

## REFERENCES

Adams-Tucker, Christine. 1982. "Proximate Effects of Sexual Abuse in Childhood." *American Journal of Psychiatry* 193: 1252–1256.

Ageton, Suzanne S. 1983. "The Dynamics of Female Delinquency, 1976–1980.," *Criminology* 21:555–584.

Bell, Inge Powell. 1984. "The Double Standard: Age." in *Women: A Feminist Perspective,* edited by Jo Freeman. Palo Alto, CA: Mayfield.

Black, T. Edwin and Charles P. Smith, 1981. *A Preliminary National Assessment of the Number and Characteristics of Juveniles Processed in the Juvenile Justice System.* Washington, DC: Government Printing Office.

Browne, Angela and David Finkelhor, 1986. "Impact of Child Sexual Abuse: A Review of Research," *Psychological Bulletin* 99:66–77.

Campagna, Daniel S. and Donald I. Poffenberger, 1988. *The Sexual Trafficking in Children,* Dover, DE; Auburn House.

Campbell, Ann. 1984. *The Girls in the Gang.* Oxford: Basil Blackwell.

Canter, Rachelle J. 1982. "Sex Differences in Self-Report Delinquency," *Criminology* 20:373–393.

Chesney-Lind, Meda. 1971, *Female Juvenile Delinquency in Hawaii,* Master's thesis, University of Hawaii.

_____1973. "Judicial Enforcement of the Female Sex Role," *Issues in Criminology* 3:51–71.

_____1978. "Young Women in the Arms of the Law," In *Women, Crime and the Criminal Justice System,* edited by Lee H. Bowker, Boston: Lexington.

_____1986. "Women and Crime: The Female Offender," *Signs* 12:78–96.

_____1988. "Girls and Deinstitutionalization: Is Juvenile Justice Still Sexist?" *Journal of Criminal Justice Abstracts* 20:144–165.

_____and Noelie Rodriguez 1983. "Women Under Lock and Key," *Prison Journal* 63:47–65.

Children's Bureau, Department of Health, Education and Welfare, 1965. *1964 Statistics on Public Institutions for Delinquent Children.* Washington, DC; Government Printing Office.

Chilton, Roland and Susan K. Datesman, 1987, "Gender, Race and Crime: An Analysis of Urban Arrest Trends, 1960–1980," *Gender and Society* 1:152–171.

Cloward, Richard A. and Lloyd E. Ohlin, 1960. *Delinquency and Opportunity,* New York: Free Press.

Cohen, Albert K., 1955. *Delinquent Boys: The Culture of the Gang,* New York: Free Press.

Datesman, Susan and Mikel Aickin, 1984, "Offense Specialization and Escalation Among Status Offenders," *Journal of Criminal Law and Criminology,* 75:1246–1275.

Davidson, Sue, ed. 1982. *Justice for Young Women.* Tucson, AZ; New Directions for Young Women.

DeJong, Allan R., Arturo R. Hervada, and Gary A. Emmett, 1983. "Epidemiologic Variations in Childhood Sexual Abuse," *Child Abuse and Neglect* 7:155–162.

Elliott, Delbert, David Huizinga, and Barbara Morse, 1987, "A Career Analysis of Serious Violent Offenders," In *Violent Juvenile Crime: What Can We Do About It?* edited by Ira Schwartz, Minneapolis, MN: Hubert Humphrey Institute.

Federal Bureau of Investigation, 1987. *Crime in the United States 1986,* Washington, DC; Government Printing Office.

Feinman, Clarice, 1980. *Women in the Criminal Justice System,* New York; Praeger.

Figueira-McDonough, Josefina, 1985. "Are Girls Different? Gender Discrepancies Between Delinquent Behavior and Control," *Child Welfare* 64:273–289.

_____1986, "School Context, Gender, and Delinquency," *Journal of Youth and Adolescence* 15:79–98.

Finkelhor, David, 1982. "Sexual Abuse: A Sociological Perspective," *Child Abuse and Neglect* 6:95–102.

_____and Larry Baron. 1986. "Risk Factors for Child Sexual Abuse," *Journal of Interpersonal Violence* 1:43–71.

Freedman, Estelle, 1981. *Their Sisters' Keepers,* Ann Arbor; University of Michigan Press.

Geltshorpe, Loraine, 1986. "Towards a Sceptical Look at Sexism," *International Journal of the Sociology of Law* 14:125–152.

Gora, JoAnn, 1982. *The New Female Criminal: Empirical Reality or Social Myth,* New York: Praeger.

Hagan, John, A. R. Gillis, and John Simpson, 1985. "The Class Structure of Gender and Delinquency: Toward a Power-Control Theory of Common Delinquent Behavior," *American Journal of Sociology* 90:1151–1178.

Hagan, John, John Simpson, and A. R. Gillis, 1987. "Class in the Household: A Power-Control Theory of Gender and Delinquency," *American Journal of Sociology* 92:788–816.

Hancock, Linda. 1981. "The Myth that Females are Treated More Leniently than Males in the Juvenile Justice System." *Australian and New Zealand Journal of Criminology* 16:4–14.

Harris, Anthony, 1977. "Sex and Theories of Deviance," *American Sociological Review* 42:3–16.

Herman, Jullia L. 1981. *Father-Daughter Incest.* Cambridge, MA; Harvard University Press.

Katz, Phyllis A. 1979. "The Development of Female Identity," In *Becoming Female: Perspectives on Development,* edited by Claire B. Kopp, New York; Plenum.

Koroki, Jan and Meda Chesney-Lind. 1985, *Everything Just Going Down the Drain.* Hawaii; Youth Development and Research Center.

Lerner, Gerda. 1986. *The Creation of Patriarchy.* New York: Oxford.

McCormack, Arlene, Mark-David Janus, and Ann Wolbert Burgess, 1986. "Runaway Youths and Sexual Victimization: Gender Differences In an Adolescent Runaway Population," *Child Abuse and Neglect* 10:387–395.

McGarrell, Edmund F. and Timothy J. Flanagan, eds. 1985. *Sourcebook of Criminal Justice Statistics—1984.* Washington, DC; Government Printing Office.

Meiselman, Karen. 1978. *Incest.* San Francisco: Jossey-Bass.

Merton, Robert K. 1938. "Social Structure and Anomie." *American Sociological Review* 3(October):672–782.

Messerschmidt, James, 1986. *Capitalism, Patriarchy, and Crime: Toward a Socialist Feminist Criminology,* Totowa, NJ: Rowman & Littlefield.

_____1987. "Feminism, Criminology, and the Rise of the Female Sex Delinquent, 1880–1930," *Contemporary Crises* 11:243–263.

Miller, Eleanor, 1986. *Street Woman,* Philadelphia: Temple University Press.

Miller, Walter B. 1958. "Lower Class Culture as the Generating Milieu of Gang Delinquency," *Journal of Social Issues* 14:5–19.

Morris, Ruth, 1964, "Female Delinquency and Relational Problems," *Social Forces* 43:82–89.

Mouzakitas, C. M. 1981, "An Inquiry into the Problem of Child Abuse and Juvenile Delinquency," In *Exploring the Relationship Between Child Abuse and Delinquency,* edited by R. J. Hunner and Y. E. Walkers, Montclair, NJ: Allanheld, Osmun.

National Female Advocacy Project, 1981. *Young Women and the Justice System: Basic Facts and Issues.* Tucson, AZ; New Directions for Young Women.

Office of Juvenile Justice and Delinquency Prevention, 1985. *Runaway Children and the Juvenile Justice and Delinquency Prevention Act: What is the Impact?* Washington, DC; Government Printing Office.

Opinion Research Corporation, 1982, "Public Attitudes Toward Youth Crime: National Public Opinion Poll." Mimeographed. Minnesota; Hubert Humphrey Institute of Public Affairs, University of Minnesota.

Peacock, Carol, 1981. *Hand Me Down Dreams.* New York: Shocken.

Phelps, R. J. et al. 1982. *Wisconsin Female Juvenile Offender Study Project Summary Report,* Wisconsin: Youth Policy and Law Center, Wisconsin Council of Juvenile Justice.

Platt, Anthony M. 1969. *The Childsavers,* Chicago: University of Chicago Press.

Pope, Carl and William H. Feyerherm. 1982. "Gender Bias in Juvenile Court Dispositions," *Social Service Review* 6:1–17.

Rafter, Nicole Hahn, 1985. *Partial Justice.* Boston: Northeastern University Press.

Reich, J. W. And S. E. Gutierres, 1979, "Escape/Aggression Incidence in Sexually Abused Juvenile Delinquents," *Criminal Justice and Behavior* 6:239–243.

Rogers, Kristine, 1972. "For Her Own Protection. . . . Conditions of Incarceration for Female Juvenile Offenders in the State of Connecticut," *Law and Society Review* (Winter):223–246.

Rosenberg, Debby and Carol Zimmerman, 1977. *Are My Dreams Too Much To Ask For?* Tucson, A. Z: New Directions for Young Women.

Russell, Diana E. 1986. *The Secret Trauma: Incest in the Lives of Girls and Women,* New York: Basic Books.

Schlossman, Steven and Stephanie Wallach, 1978. "The Crime of Precocious Sexuality: Female Juvenile Delinquency in the Progressive Era," *Harvard Educational Review* 48:65–94.

Shaw, Clifford R. 1930. *The Jack-Roller,* Chicago: University of Chicago Press.

_____1938. *Brothers in Crime,* Chicago: University of Chicago Press.

_____and Henry D. McKay, 1942. *Juvenile Delinquency in Urban Areas,* Chicago: University of Chicago Press.

Shelden, Randall, 1981. "Sex Discrimination in the Juvenile Justice System: Memphis, Tennessee, 1900–1917." In *Comparing Female and Male Offenders,* edited by Marguerite Q. Warren. Beverly Hills, CA: Sage.

_____and John Horvath, 1986. "Processing Offenders in a Juvenile Court: A Comparison of Males and Females." Paper presented at the annual meeting of the Western Society of Criminology, Newport Beach, CA, February 27–March 2.

Silbert, Mimi and Ayala M. Pines, 1981. "Sexual Child Abuse as an Antecedent to Prostitution," *Child Abuse and Neglect* 5:407–411.

Simons, Ronald L., Martin G. Miller, and Stephen M. Aigner, 1980. "Contemporary Theories of Deviance and Female Delinquency: An Empirical Test," *Journal of Research in Crime and Delinquency* 17:42–57.

Smith, Lesley Shacklady, 1978. "Sexist Assumptions and Female Delinquency," In *Women, Sexuality and Social Control,* edited by Carol Smart and Barry Smart, London: Routledge & Kegan Paul.

Snyder, Howard N. and Terrence A. Finnegan, 1987. *Delinquency in the United States.* Washington, DC: Department of Justice.

Steffensmeier, Darrell J. 1980 "Sex Differences in Patterns of Adult Crime, 1965–1977," *Social Forces* 58:1080–1109.

Sutherland, Edwin, 1978. "Differential Association." in *Children of Ishmael: Critical Perspectives on Juvenile Justice,* edited by Barry Krisberg and James Austin. Palo Alto, CA: Mayfield.

Teilmann, Katherine S. and Pierre H. Landry, Jr. 1981. "Gender Bias in Juvenile Justice." *Journal of Research in Crime and Delinquency* 18:47–80.

Thrasher, Frederic M. 1927. *The Gang.* Chicago: University of Chicago Press.

Tracy, Paul E., Marvin E. Wolfgang, and Robert M. Figlio. 1985. *Delinquency in Two Birth Cohorts: Executive Summary.* Washington, DC: Department of Justice.

Widom, Cathy Spatz. 1988. "Child Abuse, Neglect, and Violent Criminal Behavior." Unpublished manuscript.

# The Juvenile Court and the Role of the Juvenile Court Judge

## Judge Leonard P. Edwards

### Introduction

One of the principal tasks of a democratic society is to nurture its children to a successful, productive adult life. In the United States we rely primarily upon the family to provide to children most of what they need.

It is cardinal with us that the custody, care and nurture of the child reside first in the parents, whose primary function and freedom include preparation for obligations the state can neither supply nor hinder.[1]

Other institutions participate in the socialization process, notably schools, churches, and recreational groups, but the fundamental authority for child rearing resides with a child's family.

When the family fails or is unable to rear its child within acceptable norms, society has an interest in intervening to achieve its own goals. Dysfunctional families which are unable to raise their children within societal norms threaten the viability of the social order.[2]

Our legislatures and courts have recognized the importance of responding to family dysfunction. Numerous laws detail society's response to a family which cannot control a child's delinquent behavior,

a family which cannot adequately provide for a child, a family which cannot protect a child from abuse, or a family which cannot or refuses to educate its child.

The ultimate authority for the resolution of these problems is the juvenile court. The person given the responsibility for carrying out the mandates of the legislature is the juvenile court judge. There are many other persons and institutions the child and family may encounter prior to reaching the court, but if all else fails, the legislatures in the United States have entrusted the authority to address the problems facing dysfunctional families and children to the juvenile court.

Our government's selection of the juvenile court as the institution to fulfill these functions raises a number of important questions:

Is the juvenile court a wise choice? Are there better alternatives than turning to the court system for the resolution of these problems? Are the tasks facing the juvenile court judge consistent with the traditional judicial role? Is the judiciary prepared to meet the challenges set by the legislature? What changes are necessary in the judiciary in order to meet these challenges?

By Judge Leonard P. Edwards, "The Juvenile Court and the Role of the Juvenile Court Judge," Volume 43, No. 2. *Juvenile and Family Court Journal,* National Council of Family Court Judges (1992), pp. 1-2, 25-32. Reprinted by permission.

*This paper . . . discusses the role of the juvenile court judge. . . .*

*[A] conclusion of this paper is that . . . the role of juvenile court judge must be recognized and supported by the judiciary and by the community. . . . Finally, it must be recognized by all that the juvenile court and the agencies serving it cannot alone solve the problems facing children and families in our society today. While the juvenile court must play a key leadership role, the entire community must join in the efforts to support children and preserve families.*

[Editor's Note: This article is part four of a six-part essay. Parts one, two, three, five, and six review the origin of the juvenile court, the status of and alternatives to the juvenile court, expectations fulfillment for the juvenile court judge, and, finally, the conclusion. These parts may be referenced in Volume 43, No. 2, 1992 edition of *Juvenile Family Court Journal.*]

# IV.  The Role of the Juvenile Court Judge

The most important person in the juvenile court is the juvenile court judge.[172] The descriptions of the different systems reveal the unique role of the juvenile court judge, a role that includes many non-traditional functions.  The role of the juvenile court judge combines judicial, administrative, collaborative and advocacy components.

The most traditional role of the juvenile court judge is to decide the legal issues in each of the described categories of cases.  The judge must determine issues such as whether certain facts are true, whether a child should be removed from a parent, what types of services should be offered to the family and whether the child should be returned to the family and the community or placed permanently in another setting.

Clearly these are critical decisions, not only for the family before the court, but also for society.  Given the importance of the family in the United States, such determinations have profound implications for the manner in which families will survive. Juvenile court judges are the gatekeepers for systems which incarcerate society's youth and place society's children in foster care.  Their decisions provide a measure of our society's confidence in the viability of the family.

Moreover, the attitude of the juvenile court judge will significantly influence the manner in which others view children before the court.  An exchange in the Manhattan Family Court reflects one way in which the court can have an impact upon the care of children.  The father's attorney commented on the conditions in the home for seventeen adopted children (urine smell, limited food, poor lighting, no bed sheets).

It may not be the best of care out in Nassau County, but the children are surviving. They're doing okay.

The judge responded: I don't want the children to survive.  I want them to thrive.[173]

Juvenile court judges' decisions also set standards within the community and in the systems connected to the court. The juvenile court judge who removes a child for selling drugs, who refuses to hear a truancy petition because it is not important enough or who returns a child to her family in spite of drug abuse by one of the family members is setting standards which may have a significant impact on how police, probation, social services and other service providers respond to similar cases in the future. Unless an appellate court overturns these decisions, the standards set in the juvenile court will remain as the community's standards for these types of cases.

As an integral part of the decision-making process, the judge must make certain that the parties appearing before the court receive the legal and constitutional rights to which they are entitled. These rights include notice of the legal proceedings, the right to have counsel, and counsel at state expense in many situations,[174] the right to a hearing, to confront and cross examine witnesses, the right to remain silent and the right to a timely hearing on the truth of the allegations. In many cases the court must make certain that families have been provided with services before formal legal action was initiated. With regard to many of these rights, it is the duty of the judge to determine in court whether the party understands the right and wishes to exercise or waive it.

The role of the juvenile court judge includes ensuring that the systems which detect, investigate, resolve and bring cases to court are working efficiently and fairly and that adequate resources exist to respond to the caseloads. For example, the juvenile court judge must ensure that there are enough judicial officers to complete the work of the court.[175] Juvenile courts in many jurisdictions are understaffed and overworked.[176] Within the judiciary it is often difficult to persuade those judicial officers with administrative responsibility that the juvenile court must have sufficient judicial resources to manage the caseloads.[177] Sometimes this lack of judicial resources exists throughout the judiciary,[178] but more frequently the juvenile court receives fewer positions because it is perceived as less important.[179] The problem has been exacerbated with the marked increase in dependency cases over the past five years.[180] In the wake of the higher child abuse and neglect reports, dependency caseloads have risen several-fold. Many juvenile court judges have been struggling with local governments to secure adequate judicial resources to manage the new demands upon the juvenile courts.

Judicial officers cannot function without adequate staff and space. Juvenile courts often find themselves with inadequate staff to meet the legal mandates set by the legislature.[181] The juvenile court judge must work with other branches of government to make certain each is available for the court.

Judges do not work in a vacuum. They learn of the situation facing children and their families from the legal proceedings, the reports from social service agencies, probation departments and from the parties and their attorneys. The quality of a judge's decision about children and their families is directly related to the quality of information the judge receives. Our legal system is built upon a process in which attorneys for the parties are given the duty to present evidence to the court and to test any evidence presented from other sources. From the different perspectives of the parties, the court is able to determine what happened and what should be done.

An important role for the juvenile court judge is to make certain that there are adequate numbers of attorneys of satisfactory quality to complete the work of the court.[182] The juvenile court judge must work with the funding authorities to supply these attorneys and to ensure they are trained. Dependency cases are particularly expensive for the government, as attorneys and guardians ad litem[183] may represent the state or petitioning party, the child and each parent if there is a conflict of interest. Compared to civil cases, in which the government supplies no attorneys, the juvenile court is an expensive operation.

The role of the juvenile court judge as the provider of due process and the role as fiscal manager may be in conflict in one or more of these areas. Providing free attorneys for accused delinquents has never been politically popular, and funders demand to know why every accused delinquent child needs to have an attorney. It is no wonder that some juvenile court judges do not appoint counsel for children in every case[184] or are perceived as favoring waiver of that right.[185]

Similarly, in dependency cases, if the government represents both the petitioner and the child, or if one attorney represents both parents, it would save the cost of an attorney, but it may mean that the remaining attorney has conflicting positions to represent to the court. Juvenile court judges understandably have taken different sides of this debate.[186]

The juvenile court also has the responsibility

of setting the standards by which the juvenile system will be governed. In this way the court provides leadership both to the community and to all participants in the juvenile court system.[187] Cases which do not reach the court but which are resolved by police, probation, social workers or the prosecutor also come under the purview of the juvenile court judge. Only the most serious cases should reach the juvenile court. The majority of cases should be resolved fairly and efficiently by other agencies. It is the role of the juvenile court judge to ensure that this process is implicitly fair to all parties.[188]

> The presiding judge of the juvenile court shall initiate meetings and cooperate with the probation department, welfare department, prosecuting attorney, law enforcement, and other persons and agencies performing an intake function to establish and maintain a fair and efficient intake program designed to promote swift and objective evaluation of the circumstances of any referral and to pursue an appropriate course of action.[189]

The juvenile court judge must know how cases which do not reach the juvenile court are being resolved. What types of alternative dispute resolution techniques are being employed and by whom? What standards do police, probation and prosecution utilize and under what authority? Some may argue that such comprehensive knowledge is unnecessary. Upon reflection, however, it becomes clear that the public holds the juvenile court judge accountable for the failings in a system over which he or she presides.[190]

After the court has made its dispositional orders, it must also monitor the progress of the child, the family and the supervising agency to make certain that each one carries out the terms of its orders.[191] This is no easy task. For the court to monitor services effectively, the judge must become knowledgeable about the services available in the community as well as services which should be available.[192] Review hearings provide one vehicle for the court to assess the situation from month to month. While in all types of juvenile cases reviews are a sound judicial policy, in dependency matters the legislature has mandated judges to review regularly the status of children in placement. This judicial review is the principal mechanism ensuring reunification services are being provided and for preventing unnecessarily long placements and

unnecessary movements of children from home to home, so-called foster care drift.

In some jurisdictions the juvenile court judge is the administrator of the juvenile probation department and court staff who work in the juvenile justice system.[193] This administrative oversight may include responsibility over court personnel including other judges, referees, attorneys, social investigators, clerical workers, support personnel, psychologists, psychiatrists and physicians. The role may also include supervision of the operation of foster homes, detention facilities, the court clinic and aftercare facilities. The juvenile court judge may also have some responsibility for the management of financial services. This administrative role will necessarily take time from the judge's judicial duties. It may also expose the judge to liability for administrative errors such as overcrowding of the juvenile detention facility.[194] On the other hand, the juvenile court judge as administrator is ideally situated to coordinate services between the court and probation departments.[195]

Some critics have argued that this administrative role is inappropriate for the juvenile court judge.[196] Other commentators assert that probation services should be under juvenile court control. They point out that probation is an integral part of the judicial function in the juvenile court and that the juvenile court judge has an interest in maintaining a satisfactory level of service.[197] In some states the juvenile court has no administrative oversight of probation services, while in some states the court has limited control over the selection and administration of probation services.[198] Ironically, as Joseph White points out,

> [w]hichever structure the interested reader may consider . . . certain factors . . . have critical impact. These include the amount of money available for these services, the quality of the personnel with which the system is staffed, and the personal leadership of the judiciary in stimulating community interest and support. Each of these attributes is a *sine qua non* of good services, regardless of the formal administrative structure.[199]

Beyond the confines of the courtroom and the boundaries of the delinquency and dependency systems, the juvenile court judge has an even broader role: providing to the community information about how well the juvenile court is completing the tasks assigned to it.[200]  The juvenile court judge both informs and advocates within the community on behalf of children and their families.[201] No other person has the position, perspective or the prestige to speak on behalf of the children and families whose problems are so serious that they must come before the juvenile court. Because of confidentiality laws which restrict the flow of information about most juvenile court cases, it is critical that the juvenile court judge ensure that information about the juvenile court system is made available to the public. Only in this way will the public receive a balanced view of the work of the juvenile court and not rely solely on the spectacular headlines which appear at regular intervals.[202]

> The court must be open to the public and engaged in a continuous dialogue with the public regarding children, parenting, the responsibility of the institutions surrounding children, the responsibilities of the public, and how the court acquits itself of its own responsibilities.[203]

This public role also includes commenting on and, if necessary, drafting legislation which the judge believes is necessary to complete the work of the juvenile court.  It is remarkable that juvenile court legislation is often written without significant input from the juvenile court judiciary and that in some jurisdictions juvenile court judges are among the last to learn of legislative changes in their court system.  Those states with Juvenile Court Judges Associations have had a much greater impact upon state legislation dealing with juvenile court than those states which have not.[204]

The juvenile court judge has a public role beyond providing information to the community. The judge must also take action to ensure that the necessary community resources are available so that the children and families which come before the court can be well-served.[205] This may be the most untraditional role for the juvenile court judge, but it may be the most important.[206]

What should the judge do when drug counseling is ordered and no drug counseling exists in the community? What should the judge do when a child could be safely returned home if reasonable services were available for the family, but no such services exist? Should the juvenile court judge simply rule on the case before the court and remain indifferent or inactive with regards to the results after the court order has been made?

The clear message from legislators and judges alike is to take action in order to address the deficiencies within the various juvenile court systems.

> Judges should take an active part in the formation of a community-wide, multi-disciplinary "Constituency for Children" to promote and unify private and public sector efforts to focus attention and resources on meeting the needs of deprived children who have no effective voice of their own.[207]

Juvenile court judges have heeded these calls to organize within their own communities.  They convene meetings of private and public sector leaders, multi-disciplinary task forces and community-based organizations and provide the information and the leadership to join in concerted efforts to preserve and strengthen families.

Their effectiveness has been noteworthy.[208] In 1978 David Soukoup, a King County, Washington juvenile court judge, asked volunteers within his community to assist abused and neglected children as they went through the dependency court process. His initiative started the Court Appointed Special Advocate Program (CASA), a nationwide endeavor which now has hundreds of programs and over 28,000 volunteers.[209] Other judges have been noteworthy for their leadership in initiating change within their court systems.[210]

In Jefferson Parish, Gretna, Louisiana, Judge Thomas P. McGee used his position as chief judge of the juvenile court to organize within his community on behalf of the children and families who appear in his court.  Under his leadership the juvenile court was able to develop a system to detect learning disabilities in children who appeared before the juvenile court and ensure that each was properly educated.  He has helped other juvenile court judges and communities organize effective responses for learning disabled children. His successes in his own court and nationally are based upon his belief in judges becoming catalysts for reform.[211]

A Nevada Juvenile Court judge, Judge Charles McGee, was instrumental in creating the Children's Cabinet.  A private, non-profit organization, the Children's Cabinet is intended to "fill the gaps" between existing services to children in Nevada and lead in the identification of new programs and resources for families. In its first five years of existence, through the development of new programs this unique public-private venture has served thousands of families.

Among its many programs the cabinet has developed the Truancy Center, the School Early Intervention Program, the Homeless Youth Project and Northern Nevada's first Family preservation program. While volunteers are a critical component in all of its efforts, the Cabinet has sponsored some programs which are managed and staffed exclusively by volunteers. In 1989 the Cabinet published "Nevada's Children: Our Most Precious Resource?", a collection of statistics and information about Nevada's children. Its efforts have added greatly to the lives of children and families in Northern Nevada.[212]

In 1953 in Oakland County, Michigan, Chief Judge Eugene Arthur Moore convened a small group of citizens and community leaders to develop a community-based prevention program. By 1984 there were 26 locally-based youth assistance programs in Oakland County. In 1989 more than 47,000 county residents voluntarily participated in Youth Assistance Primary Prevention programs. The program has been so successful it received the Kendall I. Lingle Community Resources Award from the National Council of Juvenile and Family Court Judges in 1991.[213]

In 1985 in San Bernardino County, California, Juvenile Court Presiding Judge Patrick Morris convened a county-wide meeting of private and public sector persons interested in working on behalf of children. The result was the creation of the Children's Network, now in its seventh year of coordinating agencies, professionals, businesses and citizens and developing resources on behalf of children.[214] Many other examples exist in juvenile courts throughout the country.[215]

Perhaps the best formal expression of the full role of the juvenile court judge was recently adopted by the California Judicial Council. In Rule 24 the Judicial Council wrote that juvenile court judges are encouraged to:

(1) Provide active leadership within the community in determining the needs and obtaining and developing resources and services for at-risk children and families. At-risk children include delinquent, dependent and status offenders.

(2) Investigate and determine the availability of specific prevention, intervention and treatment services in the community for at-risk children and their families.

(3) Exercise their authority by statute or rule to review, order and enforce the delivery of specific services and treatment for children at risk and their families.

(4) Exercise a leadership role in the development and maintenance of permanent programs of interagency cooperation and coordination among the court and the various public agencies that serve at-risk children and their families.

(5) Take an active part in the formation of a community-wide network to promote and unify private and public sector efforts to focus attention and resources for at-risk children and their families.

(6) Maintain close liaison with school authorities and encourage coordination of policies and programs.

(7) Educate the community and its institutions through every available means including the media concerning the role of the juvenile court in meeting the complex needs of at-risk children and their families.

(8) Evaluate the criteria established by child protection agencies for initial removal and reunification decisions and communicate the court's expectations of what constitutes "reasonable efforts" to prevent removal or hasten return of the child.

(9) Encourage the development of community services and resources to assist homeless, truant, runaway and incorrigible children.

(10) Be familiar with all detention facilities, placements and institutions used by the court.

(11) Act in all instances consistently with the public safety and welfare.[216]

Other commentators support this description.[217]

All of these activities may be necessary if the juvenile court judge is going to make it possible for the juvenile court to be an effective institution. Given the nontraditional aspect of many of these tasks, there are numerous challenges facing the judiciary both to educate and socialize juvenile court judges with regard to their distinctive role.

# FOOTNOTES

1. " . . . the state's assertion of authority [over the general welfare of children] . . . is no mere corporate concern of official authority. It is the interest of youth itself, and of the whole community, that children be both safeguarded from abuses and given opportunities for growth into free and independent . . . citizens." *Prince v. Massachusetts,* 321 U.S. 158 (1941), citing *Pierce v. Society of Sisters,* 268 U.S. 510.

2. "The costs of such failed socialization is not immediately apparent except in the case of those physically abused and neglected. Further, payment for the failure is deferred and at the same time remote from many people in society, especially those with power. Nonetheless, few would disagree that the price is enormous." "Conclusion" by Francis Hartman, *From Children to Citizen II, The Role of the Juvenile Court,* ed. Francis Hartmann, N.Y.: Springer-Verlag (1987)385. See also "The High Cost of Failure," Chapter One in "Beyond Rhetoric: A New American Agenda for Children and Families," *Final Report of the National Commission on Children,* Washington, D.C. (1991)3–13.

172. "But within the juvenile court itself the judge, regardless of ability, holds the highest status. The judge is the ultimate decision-maker. The coterie of probation, social service, legal and clerical attendants rivet their eyes and ears on his nonverbal language and his utterances." Rubin, H. Ted., *Juvenile Justice: Policy, Practice and Law, op cit.* footnote 45, at p. 351. "From this it should be clear that the judges, and particularly the chief judge, occupy the crucial formal decision-making positions with regard both to individual cases and their disposition, and to procedural, administrative, and program policy." *Judging Delinquents* by Robert Emerson, Aldine Publishing Company, Chicago (1969) 13.

173. Dugger, C. W., "Care Ordered for Children in Abuse Cases," *The New York Times,* 29 May 1991, section B, p. 1.

174. Children in delinquency cases are entitled to counsel at state expense. *In re Gault, op cit* footnote 3. Parents in those proceedings are entitled to have counsel, but normally not at state expense. In addition there is usually a prosecutor who brings the petition before the juvenile court. Most states have the same rules for status offense cases. In dependency matters, the parents usually have the right to counsel at state expense. The child will have a guardian ad litem, who may be an attorney, a volunteer, or both. In addition there will usually be an attorney who brings the legal action on behalf of the state.

175. "Judicial Authority and Responsibility: 18 Recommendations on Issues in Delinquency and Abuse/Neglect Dispositions," National Council of Juvenile and Family Court Judges, Reno (1989) at p. 7: "Juvenile and family courts must have an adequate number of qualified judicial officers and other court personnel available to assure the optimum handling of each individual case."

176. The present system permits overloading of non-jury calendars. Because the family (juvenile) courts are non-jury courts, there is almost no limit to the number of non-jury matters than might be assigned to those courts." Senate Task Force on Family Relations Court, Final Report, Sacramento (1990), pp. 8–10. Also see *In re Ashley K., op. cit.* footnote 145.

177. *Ibid.* at p. 4.

178. Lucas, Malcolm M., "Is Inadequate Funding Threatening Our System of Justice?" *Judicature* 74.6 (April–May 1991) 292.

179. Senate Task Force on Family Relations Court, Final Report, *op. cit.* footnote 176, at p. 4, and see Section V. A. *infra* on the "structure of the Court System."

180. Gomby and Shiono, *The Future of Children, op. cit.* footnote 103.

181. Senate Task Force on Family Relations Court, Final Report, *op. cit.* footnote 176, at p. 2 and *In re Ashley K, op. cit.* footnote 145, in which the Appellate Court noted: "All other considerations aside, and there are many, humaneness and plain common sense make it imperative that there be proper judicial case management in child custody cases in Cook County, and that there be a sufficient number of judges to cope with the number of cases in the system" at p. 17.

182. The court should "establish a training program for attorneys representing parents and children and require attorneys who are appointed by the court to attend this program." *Making Reasonable Efforts, op. cit.* footnote 161, at p. 62. And see McCullough, *op. cit.* footnote 152, at p. 59.

183. Since the passage of the Child Abuse Prevention and Treatment Act of 1974 (P.L. 93-247) as a condition of states receiving federal funds, the juvenile court must appoint a guardian ad litem to represent a child in child abuse or neglect cases that result in a judicial proceeding. 42, U.S.C., Paragraph 5103(b)(2)(G)(1976). For a summary of the ways in which each state has responded to the federal mandate see National Study of Guardian ad Litem Representation, Administration for Children, Youth and Families, Office of Human Development Services, U.S. Department of Health and Human Services, CSR, Inc., Washington, D.C. (1990).

184. See Feld, Barry, "The Right to Counsel In Juvenile Court: An Empirical Study of When Lawyers Appear and the Differences They Make," 79 *J. Crim.L. & Criminology, op. cit.* footnote 114, pp. 1185–1346, and Schwartz, *op. cit.* footnote 66 at pp. 40–51.

185. See Schwartz, *op. cit.* footnote 66, at pp. 152–158; Feld, Barry C., "The Juvenile Court Meets the Principal of the Office: Legislative Changes in Juvenile Waiver Statutes," *Journal of Criminal Law and Criminology* 78.3, *op. cit.* footnote 39, at pp. 471–533.

Rubin agrees with Schwartz in asserting that a child in a delinquency proceeding should have an unwaivable right to an attorney. Rubin, *op. cit.* footnote 45, at p. 403.

The author prefers rigorous questioning of the child to the unwaivable right to counsel suggested by Schwartz and Rubin. In Santa Clara County the juvenile court judges have an elaborate *voir dire* which stresses the importance of the legal proceedings and the need for counsel. Only if the child can give intelligent responses to the court's inquiry will a waiver be accepted. Often it is the parent advising the child that an attorney is unnecessary and in that situation the court must be prepared to engage the parents in the waiver discussion. More than 95% of the children in delinquency proceedings are represented by attorneys in this county.

Of course, if the jurisdiction has no resources to employ counsel, the judge may be less willing to engage in this type of *voir dire.* The judge will first have to devise a strategy on how to secure sufficient attorneys for the juvenile court. See the suggestions in footnote 127 and Resources discussion in Part V, *supra.*

186. Different jurisdictions handle this representation in different ways. In some an attorney is appointed to represent the dependent child in every case (Santa Clara County and San Mateo County in California are examples). In other jurisdictions an attorney is appointed to represent the child on a case-by-case basis. This seems to be the minimal requirement of independent representation as stated by the appellate court in the case of *In re Patricia E.* (1985) 175 Cal.App.3d 1. Also see *Making Reasonable Efforts, op. cit.,* footnote 161, at pp. 31–32.

187. "Toward Juvenile Justice" by mark Harrison Moore, in *From Children to Citizens, op. cit.* footnote 7, at p. 177.

188. "Court-Approved Alternative Dispute Resolution: A Better Way to Resolve Minor Delinquency, Status Offense and Abuse/Neglect Cases, *op. cit.* footnote 76, at pp. 4–7 and 25–28. In some states the juvenile court has the obligation to respond to

the needs of children and order both legal intervention and services. Thus, when a local social services department was unwilling to file dependency proceedings to protect a child living in a harmful environment, the judge ordered the agency to file a petition. See *People in the Interest of R. E.* 729 P.2d 1032 (Colo.App.1986) and *In the Interest of J. H.*, 770 P.2d 1355 (Colo.App.1989). In California, a juvenile court judge dismissed a dependency petition after evidence showed a child had been abused in the family home, but stated he was unsure as to the person responsible for the abuse. The Court of Appeals reversed the trial court and ruled that the juvenile court must take jurisdiction of a child under those circumstances. *In re Christina T.*, 184 Cal.App.3d 650, 229 Cal.Rptr.247 (1986). See "The Court: A Child's Last Hope for Protection" by Sue Pachota, *The Rocky Mountain Child Advocate* 1.2 (June/July 1991) at pp. 4–5.

189. Rule 1404(a) Juvenile Court Rules, West's California Juvenile Laws and Court Rules (1991).

190. See *Deprived Children: A Judicial Response, op. cit.* footnote 144, at p. 10. "The public reasonably expects the judiciary is, or ought to be, ultimately accountable for what happens to abused or neglected children who are reported to or handled by government agencies."

191. Jones, Judge William G., "The Special Responsibilities of Juvenile Court Judges," *The Rocky Mountain Child Advocate* 1.2 (June/July 1991) 3.

192. "Monitoring services" is itself a catch-all describing a number of important responsibilities. These have been summarized as requiring the juvenile judge to:

(1) Know what child welfare and family preservation services are available in the community and the problems that can be addressed by these services;

(2) Know which agencies and individuals are responsible for developing policies and providing services to children in the community;

(3) Understand child development and, in particular, the importance of attachment and bonding and the effects of separation on young children;

(4) Encourage the child welfare agency to prevent unnecessary removal by using services to protect children instead of resorting to removal of the child from the home;

(5) Encourage the development of cooperative agreements between law enforcement bodies and the child welfare agency so that law enforcement officers do not remove children from their homes without prior consultation and coordination with the agency;

(6) Be aware of the child welfare agency's performance in providing preventative and reunification services, as well as its rules and regulations on providing these services, and monitor the agency's compliance with the reasonable efforts requirement;

(7) Ensure that the child welfare agency is aware that the failure to make reasonable efforts will result in a failure to receive federal reimbursement;

(8) Establish a training program for all attorneys representing parents and children and require attorneys who are appointed by the court to attend this program;

(9) Be aware of local experts who can testify on the reasonableness and appropriateness of services provided to keep a child in the home and what harm, if any, a child will experience if removed from the home or continued in an out-of-home placement; and

(10) Monitor the court's own record on compliance with the reasonable efforts requirement by monitoring court of appeals' affirmances or reversals of decisions on reasonable efforts.

*Making Reasonable Efforts: Steps for Keeping Families Together*, The Edna McConnell Clark Foundation, *op. cit.* footnote 161, pp. 41–59.

193. In 22 states and the District of Columbia probation services are administered either by the local juvenile court or by the state administrative office of the courts. In 14 states probation administration is divided between judicial and executive branches. In other states probation is administered either exclusively from the state, from county government or a split between county and state executive branch departments. See "Organization and Administration of Juvenile Services: Probation, Aftercare, and State Delinquent Institutions," Patricia McFall Torbet, Pittsburgh, National Center for Juvenile Justice (1990) at p. iv.

194. See *Doe v. County of Lake, Indian* (1975) 399 F.Supp.553 and *Santiago v. City of Philadelphia* (1977) 435 F.Supp.136, 146.

195. See Rubin, *op. cit.* footnote 45, at pp. 358–359.

196. "The Constitutionality of Juvenile Court Administration of Court Services" by David Gilman in *Major Issues in Juvenile Justice Information and Training*, Columbus, OH, Academy for Contemporary Problems, (1981) 465–474. "Courts as Social Service Agencies: An Idea Carried to Its Illogical Extension" by Jack D. Foster, pp. 475–490. National Advisory Commission on Criminal Justice Standards and Goals, *Corrections* (Washington, D.C.: Government Printing Office, 1973), Standards 8.2, 10.1, 16.4; Institute of Judicial Administration–American Bar Association, *Court Organization and Administration*, Standard 1.2; National Advisory Committee on Criminal Justice Standards and Goals, *Juvenile Justice and Delinquency Prevention*, Standard 19.2; National Advisory Committee for Juvenile Justice and Delinquency Prevention, *Standards for the Administration of Juvenile Justice*, Standards 3.14, 4.1.

197. "The Juvenile court's Administrative Responsibilities," by Holland M. Gary, pp. 337–342, and Rubin, *op. cit.* footnote 45, at pp. 358–359.

198. Torbet, *op. cit.* footnote 193, at pp. 2–13.

199. White, Joseph L., "Major Issues in Juvenile Justice Information and Training: Services to Children in Juvenile Courts: The Judicial-Executive Controversy," Columbus, Ohio, Academy for Contemporary Problems (1981), cited in Torbet, *op. cit.* footnote 193, at p. i.

200. "To protect the institution, to maintain a proper accountability relationship to the community and to the law, and to strengthen the overall capacity of the community to rear children, the judges of the juvenile court must be prepared to exercise leadership by explaining what the court stands for, why it is making the decisions it is making, and what these decisions imply for the conduct of others. This is how legal values acquire social force and standing." Moore, *op. cit.* footnote 7, at p. 181.

201. "The juvenile court judge of the future will be something special. His skill as a jurist will be secondary to his ability to motivate the community behind juvenile causes." "The Juvenile Justice System: Vision for the Future" by Seymour Gelber, *Juvenile and Family Court Journal* (1990), op.cit. footnote 105, pp. 15–18, at p. 18.

202. "As Mother Killed Her Son, Protectors Observed Privacy" by Celia W. Dugger, *The New York Times* 10 Feb. 1992, at p. A1 and A16; "Child Deaths Reveal Failings of System by Celia W. Dugger, *The New York Times* 23 Jan. 1992.

203. Harmann, *op. cit.* footnote 2 at p. 390.

204. Perhaps the most outstanding example of a juvenile court judges association in the United States is the Juvenile Court Judges' Commission in the Commonwealth of Pennsylvania. Established by the Pennsylvania Legislature in 1959, its members are nominated by the Chief Justice of the Pennsylvania Supreme Court and appointed by the Governor for three-year terms. The Commission is responsible for:

(1) Advising juvenile courts concerning the proper care and maintenance of delinquent children;

(2) Establishing standards governing the administrative practices and judicial procedures used in juvenile courts;

(3) Establishing personnel practices and employment standards used in probation offices;

(4) Collecting, compiling and publishing juvenile court statistics; and

(5) Administering a Grant-In-Aid program to improve country juvenile probation services.

The commission also serves as the liaison between the juvenile courts and the Legislature to ensure passage of legislation that is in the best interest of all children coming within the jurisdiction of the court. It provides a monthly newsletter, an annual report and numerous other publications and offers training for judges and probation staff throughout the state.

All significant legislation relating to children who come before the juvenile court in Pennsylvania is either drafted, suggested or supported by the Commission. For example refer to the testimony of Hon. R. Stanton Wettinck, Jr., and James E. Anderson before the Joint State Government Commission, Task Force of Services to Children, September 11, 1990. The legislative program was recognized by the National Council of Juvenile and Family Court Judges in 1987 as being the nation's most outstanding program.

For further information contact the Juvenile Court Judges' Commission, P.O. Box 3222, Harrisburg, PA 17105-3222.

205. "Juvenile and family court judges should play a leadership role in working with key people from all three branches of government, law enforcement, public health, medical, drug treatment service providers, social service workers, and the private sector to develop a comprehensive continuum of family-focused, multi-disciplinary drug treatment and family strengthening services." *Protocol for Making Reasonable Efforts in Drug-Related Dependency Cases, op. cit.* footnote 86 at p. 4.

206. "He can't go out on the street corner and compete with the Salvation Army. But he can appoint a strong citizens' committee, composed of community leaders interested in youth, as an Advisory Council. He can regularly attend its meetings and invite its members individually to attend court hearings, to visit existing facilities—both state and local—to examine some case histories (both successful and unsuccessful); and he can suggest to them important community goals. Perhaps some static will crackle, perhaps a little unpleasant gas will escape to assault the community's olfactory nerve—and all to the good. What is there to fear? Many of us juvenile court judges have 'resources' that couldn't be worse." "The Juvenile Court Examines Itself" by Judge William S. Fort, *NPPA Journal* 5, 404–413, at p. 411.

207. *Deprived Children, op. cit.* footnote 144, at p. 12. "Juvenile and family court judges should play a leadership role in working with key people from all three branches of government, law enforcement, public health, medical, drug treatment providers, social service workers, and the private sector to develop a comprehensive continuum of family-focused, multi-disciplinary drug treatment and family strengthening services. *Protocol for Making Reasonable Efforts in Drug-Related Dependency Cases, op. cit.* footnote 86, at p. 4.

208. Yet many juvenile judges rise to the challenge and do remarkable jobs. Procedural safeguards and due process rights for juveniles are scrupulously observed in their courts. These judges always are seeking better means of detention and reserve the use of correctional institutions as a last resort. They are very committed, work long hours, and sometimes pass up promotions to more highly paid judgeships with greater prestige. The result is that these judges usually change the quality of juvenile justice in their communities." Clemens Bartollas, *Juvenile Delinquency,* MacMillan, New York (1985) 456.

209. See *Advocating for the Child in Protection Proceedings* by Donald N. Duquette, Lexington Books, Lexington, MA (1990) 1–11. For more information on the National CASA Association, write to: National CASA Association, 2722 Eastlake Avenue East, Suite 220, Seattle, Washington 99102.

210. For example see "Family Court Reform in Six Pennsylvania Counties: Profiles of Judges as Reform Activists," Mastrofski, Jennifer, *Family and Conciliation Courts Review* 29.2 (Apr. 1991) 129–149. "Judge Ernestine Gray throws the book at young offenders—and then expects them to read it" by Sylvia Whitman, *Student Lawyer* (Apr. 1987) 12–13. For different examples of juvenile court judges, their backgrounds and accomplishments see *Behind the Black Robes: Juvenile Court Judges and the Court,* by Rubin, H. Ted, Beverly Hills, Sage Library of Social Research (1985).

211. "Preventing Juvenile Crime: What a Judge Can Do" by Judge Thomas P. McGee, *The Judges' Journal* 24 (1986), at pp. 20–23 and 51–52. Also see *Learning Disabilities and the Juvenile Justice System,* by John B. Sikorsky, M.D. and Judge Thomas P. McGee, National Council of Juvenile and Family Court Judges, Reno (1986).

212. For further information about the Children's Cabinet, contact Judge Charles McGee or Executive Director Sheila Leslie at The Children's Cabinet, 1090 S. Rock Blvd., Reno, Nevada, 89502, (702) 785-4000.

213. For further information contact Chief Judge Eugene Arthur Moore, Probate Court, County of Oakland, 1200 N. Telegraph Road, Pontiac, Michigan 48341-1043.

214. For more information about the Children's Network write: Children's Network, County Government Center, 2nd Floor, 385 North Arrowhead Avenue, San Bernardino, California 92415-0121, (714) 387-8966.

215. For example, Kids in Common, Santa Clara County, California (write c/o Supervisor Dianne McKenna, Board of Supervisors, 70 West Hedding Street, San Jose, California 95110).

216. Standards of Judicial Administration Recommended by the Judicial Council, Rule 24, Juvenile Matters, West (1991). Not all states have identified the role of the juvenile court judge as broadly as California. In some the juvenile court judge may feel constrained by ethical considerations to refrain from some of these activities. Nevertheless, the California Rule is the trend throughout the United States, as the following statements indicate: "I am extremely impressed by the 'Appendix to California Rules of Court Division I: Standards of Judicial Administration' and think they should be given wide dissemination among juvenile and family court judges. . . . If these rules could be adopted everywhere, they would go a long way to resolving the conflicts now experienced, and toward improving the administration of juvenile and family justice." Mark Harrison Moore, Review of "Resolving the Ethical, Moral and Social Mandates of the Juvenile and Family Court," Memo to Hunter Hurst, Pittsburgh, National Center for Juvenile Justice (1990).

217. "Judges must assert community leadership for prevention and treatment of substance abuse among juveniles and their families." *Drugs—The American Family in Crisis,* NCJFCJ, Reno, NV (1989), at p. 25. Judges must provide leadership within the community in determining needs and developing resources and services for deprived children and families. Judges must encourage cooperation and coordination among the courts and various public and private agencies with responsibilities for deprived children. Juvenile and family courts must maintain close liaison and encourage coordination of policies with school authorities. Judges should take an active part in the formation of a community-wide, multi-disciplinary "Constituency for Children" to promote and unify private and public sector efforts to focus attention and resources on meeting the needs of deprived children who have no effective voice of their own. *Recommendations 1, 3, 5, and 7, Deprived Children: A Judicial Response, op. cit.* footnote 144.

# TEENAGERS TALK ABOUT LIFE

Violence, hopes, cops, racism,

drugs, dreams, school, family, neighborhood—

nine kids from three cities

tell what growing up in America

is really like.

*Susan E. Kuhn*

**W**HAT HAPPENS when you ask seventh- and eighth-graders, awash in the formative years, what their life is like? They tell you. Sometimes they tell you about gangs and guns, or a dad that does drugs. Sometimes they tell you about dreams of flying, or of their unsinkable hope. They tell tales that paint the story of growing up in Mondrian starkness, the picket-fence white of the one square next to the Gotham City dark of the other. They are just kids, mostly 13 or 14 years old, and when you talk to two dozen of them in New York City, Albuquerque, and Kansas City, in public, private, and parochial schools, they tell it to you straight.

What they tell you is that a crisis is not always black, white, or brown, that it can't crush your dreams, that it can make you cry. They said that racism is everywhere, guns and drugs too widespread. That the cops are lazy.

That a good neighborhood is one with lots of playmates. Good teachers write raps. Modern-day heroes are rare.

They told what it is like to be an adolescent and in-between. Adolescence, child psychologists say, is that time in life when personal values are set, decision-making is learned, and social skills are refined. It's the training ground for adulthood, when acceptance is everything, experimentation rampant. For some of America's 28 million teens, the worst part is acne or braces. For others, in trouble or on the edge, the struggles are more than adults could bear.

"There's no question adults underestimate kids' intelligence, their ability to view the world," says Chris Baca, chief executive officer of Youth Development Inc., an Albuquerque organization that last year served over 18,000 high-risk kids. Settle in, and hear how nine young adolescents describe their world.

---

**Anthony Fisher**
AGE 14
ALBUQUERQUE PUBLIC SCHOOL

**Diego Baca**
AGE 13
ALBUQUERQUE PUBLIC SCHOOL

*"My mom's my hero. She's really tops. I worry about her every day."* –DIEGO

*Diego:* There's too much violence. A month ago there were two shootings at a Taco Bell.

*Anthony:* We just got a curfew here. [Albuquerque began to enforce an 11:00 curfew for children under 15 in June.] It's mostly around the Heights, where the gangs are.

*Diego:* There's gangs all over. There's gangs in the desert. There's all kinds of gangs.

*Anthony:* In the Heights there's black gangs. Up at the Movie 8, that's where all the gangs hang out. I was meeting some people over there, and the cop came over to me and started telling me off.

*Diego:* Some of the cops jump to conclusions.

*Anthony:* And he said to me, "Do you want to go to the D-home?"

*Diego:* The juvenile detention center.

*Anthony:* It's like a little kid's prison.

*Diego:* I've been there because my mom's a counselor. The kids down there—it's pretty sad—there's cells, like a jail. It's scary.

*Anthony:* There's fights in school. The *cholos*, that's the Mexicans. The Mexican gangs usually wear their socks up like this. And they wear their hats over their eyes, and they sag their pants.

*Diego:* People join gangs for protection, to stand out, to have friends. I don't need it. I have friends, that's fine with me. I'm not going to get shot.

*Anthony:* I know this one guy, he's really bad, he's been on TV, he's a Crip. He went to church wearing a Georgetown shirt and these big pants, and he was sagging them. I mean his butt was out. He went to church with a bandanna and everything. He got the nerve.

I think tensions got worse since what happened to Rodney King. I don't know why it can't be, why it has to be sections. Everybody's a human being. Why can't we just all stick together?

*Diego:* People always used to tell me, when I was a little kid, that everybody's brothers and sisters. It was hard for me to follow when I was little, but as I grew up, I understood. Not literally meaning you're a brother, but that you're equal, and you shouldn't treat anybody any different. That's how it should be.

*Anthony:* Who started gangs in the first place? Who needs them? Kids who don't get no attention at school join gangs to get attention. They start making up gangs. That's the worst thing about school, the gangs. Things could be a lot better. When you take those basic skills tests . . .

*Diego:* You could do a lot better if you didn't have to worry about getting shot when you're taking those tests. You could worry about your test, not about somebody walking in the hall and stabbing you.

See, sometimes the bad shadows the good too much. People used to think my school was a bad school, and then it started getting better. It's a lot better now. People ask me where I go, and I tell them and they say, "Oh, that's a decent school." No, it's not a decent school, it's a good school. I think all schools are good, it just depends on the kids. It's a matter of how much they want to learn.

*Anthony:* The Mexicans, they come up to you and tell you jokes about being black. All those Rodney King jokes and stuff. One guy was doing that to me and I just couldn't take it, so I popped him. This kid deserved it. I just hit him three times. And he was screaming, just screaming, yelling for his friends to help him. And his friends were right there, and they wouldn't help him. 'Cause they're in a gang and, "Oh yeah, we're going to help you, we're on your side," and his friends don't even help him. So that shows you how gangs stick together. They say they are going to help each other, and they never do.

Racism is everywhere. And it's not always blacks and whites.

*Diego:* The Chinese, Asians. In L.A., a lot of the whites, the blacks, the Hispanics, were getting mad because the Asians and stuff were taking what should have been their businesses.

*Anthony:* Yeah, but I mean the blacks—I'm black, and I can say that—the blacks shouldn't even be mad because a lot of the blacks in the ghetto in L.A. didn't go to school or anything and these Chinese people did.

*Diego:* They worked for it.

*Anthony:* So the ones who are saying it are the ones who really don't deserve it.

*Diego:* When I grow up I want to do professional sports, baseball and football. A lot of professional teams are starting to look in New Mexico.

My mom's my hero. She's really tops. I worry about her every day. And nuclear war.

*Anthony:* I want to play basketball. I practice every day. If I don't make it in basketball, I want to be a lawyer. I don't want to get married. I can't do it. I'm a big flirt.

My heroes are my parents, 'cause they teach me how to do things and they stick with me. People say Michael Jordan's their idol, but what did he ever do for you? He never did anything for you. Your parents brought you into this world. They should be your idol. Your parents changed your diapers, brought you food, washed your clothes. All he ever did for you was play basketball for you on TV.

## Anne McDonough
### Age 14
### New York City Public School

*"I was mugged when I was 8. I was going to the store to buy bread."*

I want to write a book. I'd write about my experiences growing up. I'd write about now, going to school and stuff. There's a lot of stuff going on there, even if it doesn't seem like a lot.

I think hunger is a big problem. I think it's strange that there's a lot of stuff being thrown away. But I think it's getting a lot better. More people are going to soup kitchens and stuff. I helped out at a soup kitchen on Sundays this year. There was this fantastic pianist. He never took lessons. He just didn't seem like somebody who would be homeless.

There are four homeless people who live outside the supermarket I go to. You get to know them a little bit. I don't give them any money, but I talk to them. My mom goes out and buys them food. But she won't give them money.

We came from this soup kitchen once and they had a lot of food left over. We went to this guy and said, "Do you want this food?" And he said, "No, I want money." She could tell he didn't want it for food, maybe for drugs or something. I think that most of them are drug addicts or too lazy to work, but not all of them.

I was mugged when I was 8. I was going to the store to buy bread. I had a very short haircut, and when I came out of the store this man said to me, "Little boy, you shouldn't be carrying so much money around." And he took it. I was so scared. He saw me getting money back from the cashier and followed me out. He followed me up my stairs and blocked me. I saw him again the next day. I just crossed the street.

## La Tanya Harry
### Age 13
### New York City Private School

*"I like Wall Street. Stocks are just pieces of paper. No discrimination."*

Most of my friends live with both their parents. Sometimes I envy them. But I know that my parents don't mix, like water and oil. When I was younger I used to dream about them getting together, but as I got older I knew it wouldn't really work out. I wonder if I'll end up like my parents did. But I try to think positive.

First, I want to get my career off the ground, then get married. Acting is a career I've always wanted. It was a dream I always had.

Jesse Owens is my hero. I like the fact that he was the fastest man in the world. It was the title that he had. It always stuck. Even though he was poor, he made it as a track star. It's like with me and acting. If I do like he did and really put my mind to it, I can make it as an actress.

When I get an acting job, it really makes me happy. And good grades. If I get something in the 80s, I cry. I want in the 90s. Sometimes I wonder why people drop out. When you see what's out there as a result— see, this is what you could become—I don't see why people do it. It's not cool, it's not hip. What do you do with yourself if you don't have an education!

I would rate my neighborhood a negative five, anything below zero. When you come home, there is no place to walk. Walk down the street, and all these people are there, sunbathing, throwing bottles around, and playing craps in the street. It reminds me of a bottle, you know, like the bottles of fruit flies in science class. There are so many people in there, they begin to climb on each other. I think of the neighborhood like that. You can't get out, and when you try to get out, everyone's pulling you back in. There's just no space to breathe in, you can't feel comfortable.

In my neighborhood there's a store, and people deal drugs. They just talk people into doing drugs. I mean, it's not hip! I don't know why people are doing it! It's scary just to look at. Even if you know you aren't going to do drugs, there's nothing positive to see. A lot of people I know, they see drugs on the street, and even if they are really good at doing something they'll say, "Jesus, will I end up this way?"

People just do it in front of kids. There was two guys and a woman in front of this ice-cream truck, and they were fighting over a needle. They were arguing over drugs in front of this little girl, and they didn't care. They didn't care.

It's annoying when people say we have to live in these kinds of neighborhoods because, you know, the white man put us here. I don't believe that.

And what about the police officers who are supposed to be walking the beats in our area? When I walk home at 9 P.M., you'll see drug city right in front of you. Who needs to see *New Jack City* when you can see that down there? They just ride around in their cars and look at you. Like, "What are you doing in my face? I'm going into the coffee shop to get a doughnut, you take care of this crack yourself." This guy was beating his wife up in the streets, and the cops came by and said, "Oh, have a nice day," and kept on going.

I guess you can't blame it only on the cops. If people wanted to do something, they would try to help their society. They'd rather sit around and talk about the problem then actually get it resolved.

When I was younger, I used to go outside to play. Now when I go outside I have to look around to see, my God, is someone shooting or what? Two days ago I was outside and all these people came running and there was this guy, he was shooting out of a window for fun. He was looking at people and saying, "Got you," bang. I couldn't play outside, because I had to watch to see if I was going to get shot.

I like Wall Street. I like the way it's set up. It's really preppy. It seems like they always have control of what's going on. Wall Street is the only place where it seems to me it's free from racial prejudice. Wall Street deals with stocks, which are just pieces of paper. No discrimination against it. You lose, you lose.

---

## Douglas Perkowski
### AGE 13
### NEW YORK CITY PRIVATE SCHOOL

*"Suicide's stupid. I know a lot of kids who have thought about it."*

I grew up in New Jersey and went to a public school. The public school system where we lived sorta went down. And my parents didn't want that so they bought an apartment here in New York City, and now I go to a private school. But I want to move to the country. I don't like the city.

When I think of school, I think of talking to my friends. I don't think of going to class. I have about two hours of homework every night. I used to think it was pretty hard, but now I sorta got the swing of things. I know a lot of kids, their parents are on them constantly, they check their assignments, but it still doesn't help much. You have to be willing to work.

I think suicide's stupid. I know a lot of kids who have thought about it. They seem real serious, and the next day they're fine. I'm sure a lot of the people that jump off the building, the next day, they'd feel better. Whenever I'm in a bad mood, I try to realize it and not let it take control.

After school one day, I was walking down the street and there were a lot of groups of people, just troublemakers. Bunch of 20-year-olds, and one of them came up to bump me, just to start something. I sort of dodged him, and the next one bumped me and I just kept walking, and then they were all talking behind me and I looked back and they started walking towards me, and then I just ran.

A lot, a lot of things like that have happened to me, kids just trying to make trouble, kids hassling me. But I think a lot of times you can avoid it, and I think that's why the tourists think New York is so bad, because they don't know how to avoid trouble. There have been other times when I've seen guys walking down the street, you know, looking posse, hats backwards. From now on, when I see anyone suspicious, I'm not going to get scared off, I'll just cross the street. The tourists think it's so bad, because they get mugged.

Where life is simple, there is more love. That's why I want to live in the country.

---

## Ralph Oberhuber
### AGE 12
### NEW YORK CITY PUBLIC SCHOOL

*"I want to be an officer. Narcotics. I'd try to arrest all the crackheads."*

I live with my mom and my dad and my two sisters and my brother. I've always lived here, except for three years in Puerto Rico when I was younger. I'm the oldest. I like it. I'm responsible for my sisters and my brother. I tell them what to do and they listen. I take them everywhere I go.

School's all right. I like science and math, I could become an astronaut. I don't have homework. If I get good grades, I'm happy. Kids who drop out of school, they're dumb. They ain't gonna get an education, no jobs, no future. Sometimes people drop out because of their parents. My parents care, they tell me to be good, get good grades—

parent talk. I've seen drugs in school. Kids sell them.

The police are scared. They don't want to go out in the streets and get shot. I want to be an officer so the little kids can play in the park. Narcotics. I want to take bad people off the street. I'd try to arrest all the crackheads.

Love, hate, the world's like a scale. Some people are good, some people are bad. When I think about dying, it gives me the chills. I'm afraid.

I want to die peacefully, not to have someone shoot me. I believe in God. I go to church every Sunday. I think God feels the same way we do about war and stuff. The whole world, just peace, that would be perfect.

---

### Adrianne and Andrea Clayton
#### AGE 13
#### KANSAS CITY PUBLIC SCHOOL

*"If you don't have a goal for yourself, there's no use for living."* –ANDREA

*Andrea:* I think the problem is, people aren't dedicated to the goals they've set. Most people that you see on the streets, when they were in school they wanted to become doctors or nurses or lawyers, but when they get in school then they hang out with other groups and then it seems like their goals just fall.

They gotta learn how to set goals and put them up on a brick wall so nobody can get them down. I mean, if you don't have a goal for yourself, there's really no real use for living and being in this world. You have to have some reason to wake up in the morning and go to school.

*Adrianne:* I try to learn something new every day. I think the problem is a lack of self-confidence. Most of the people—and you can pick them out, too—the teacher will say, "Do this," and they'll say, "I can't." The teacher at my cousin's school will say, "Show me a can," and the girl went to get her a can, and she said,

"Show me a can't." And she couldn't show her a can't because there is no such thing as can't.

I want to be a commercial artist. Mostly I want to go to CMU, that's Central Missouri University. My mother was trying to tell me to figure out exactly what I wanted to do in life. I was thinking about being an architect, but then I started really looking at the things they did and I wasn't interested. So my next guess was an artist. My mother said I'd probably have to take something else. So one guy said to me, "Why don't you try to go one step higher and work for yourself?" So I'm taking business too.

The first thing I'd do with a lot of money is save up for college in case I don't get a scholarship. I'd also give some to my family, just to spread it around, or I'd get a big house and just let everyone move in. I believe in giving lots of money to charities because I don't know what I'd do if I didn't have anywhere to sleep.
*Andrea:* The first thing I'd do is go out in the streets and pick up a family, take them in, give them a house, clothing, help get the kids in school.

My grandmother, we have a food pantry in the church, and this woman came down there with a baby in the stroller and this kid that wasn't walking right and she was asking for food. They've got all this food in there, doughnuts and orange juice, but they said they weren't open. And I had $5 I was going to give her, but she left. That really made me feel bad that day.
*Adrianne:* Our neighborhood's okay. It's boring because the old people don't like you to turn up the music, but the only time there's any action is on Sunday evening. That's when all the kids come outside and we play football.
*Andrea:* Sometimes there's shoot-outs. Don't forget that. You hear guns, say, every two nights.
*Adrianne:* I don't have any heroes. I look up to famous artists. Maybe my picture will be on the wall some day.
*Andrea:* I have a whole bunch. One is my writing teacher, who never wants to hear you say can't, because can't means won't.

My other hero is Langston Hughes. I don't know that much about him, but I love the way he writes. "Mother to Son" is my favorite poem. It begins, "Well, son, I'll tell you: Life for me ain't been no crystal stair. It's had tacks in it, and splinters . . ." She was mostly talking about all that time, back in slavery, she's been fighting and she's kept working. She's been out picking cotton and working to the bone, but she still has to tell him don't sit down on the steps 'cause you can find something hard. She's still going and she's still climbing and life for her ain't been no crystal stair.

---

### Bernadette Hall
#### AGE 13
#### ALBUQUERQUE PAROCHIAL SCHOOL

*"Heroes? I don't have any. You hear about Superman, but he's so fake."*

The neighborhood I'm in is like the Brady Bunch. You look around and there's lots of kids. School's okay. Nobody likes the uniforms, but it's really small and safe and everybody's nice.

Our math teacher's great. When we were doing integers, he would sing this song: "Change the sign of the subtrehend and add, add, add." The subtrehend is the number on the bottom. And he told jokes.

I've never seen any guns or drugs. I've seen water guns.

Heroes? I don't have any. You hear about Superman, but he's so fake.

Sometimes I think you can be anything you want to if you have enough determination. I'm not trying to sound like one of the people that's a feminist. It's just if people will accept you as that.

I've heard about a woman and man having the same job, and the woman is paid less. I don't know what the real reason for that is. But I think if you can prove yourself you can be anything you want to be.

# KIDS ARE KILLING, DYING, BLEEDING

America is in the midst of a raging epidemic of juvenile homicide, suicide, and abuse. To cure it, we need to focus on prevention, not just punishment.

*Ronald Henkoff*

**T**HE CHILDREN *who killed 12-year-old Amanda Simpson seared a hole in the American Dream. Just after midnight on April 28, 1991, while Amanda and her mother were sleeping, a group of youngsters broke into their Dayton home and stole a microwave oven. A short while later, some of the juveniles reentered the house, this time with a can of gasoline. They doused the kitchen floor and set the fuel alight. "Fuck 'em, let 'em burn!" the ringleader, a 15-year-old boy, exclaimed. Smoke and flames raced through the tiny structure. Amanda died five days later. Her mother, Judith, was seriously injured, but survived.*

Amanda Simpson was only one recent victim in a raging epidemic of violence against children. You have heard and read a great deal about guns and gangs and ghettos. But this onslaught of childhood violence knows no boundaries of race, geography, or class. Amanda Simpson, a white parochial school student in a medium-size Midwestern city, was killed by a spontaneously organized throng of white children—a bunch of kids loose on the street, unrestrained by their parents, their peers, or their community.

Six boys and two girls, ages 12 to 16 at the time of the crime, were convicted or pled guilty in connection with Amanda's death. The child they killed was an animal lover, a saxophone player, a computer buff, and a volunteer at a local nursing home. One year she sold more than 1,000 boxes of Girl Scout cookies, enough to win a week at the summer camp to which her mother, a single parent, could not afford to send her.

An ever-increasing number of youngsters are caught up in violence—as victims, as witnesses, as perpetrators. The number of children under the age of 18 arrested each year for murder has jumped 55% in the past decade, to 2,674 in 1990. Juvenile arrests for

Reporter Associate *Wilton Woods*

aggravated assault and forcible rape are rising dramatically. Says Colonel Leonard Supenski of the Baltimore County police department: "There are a whole lot of disaffected, alienated youth out there who use violence, and use it with no remorse."

For too many children, there are no safe havens. They are victimized at home, at school, on the street. An astonishing number of youngsters are beaten, maimed, molested, and murdered by parents, relatives, or baby sitters. The National Committee for the Prevention of Child Abuse (NCPCA), using reports filed by all 50 states, calculates that 2.7 million kids—some 4% of American children—suffered from abuse or neglect last year; that's an increase of 40% just since 1985. An estimated 1,383 children (half of them under the age of 1 year) died from maltreatment in 1991, the worst year on record. If anything, says Deborah Daro, the NCPCA's research director, these figures understate the problem.

Among older children, the numbers are even bleaker. More adolescents die from violence—especially gun violence—than from any illness. According to the National Center for Health Statistics, homicide by firearms is now the second-leading cause of death (after motor vehicle crashes) for 15- to 19-year-old whites. For African Americans in that age bracket, homicide is *the* leading cause of death. Altogether, 2,771 children, ages 10 to 19, died from homicide in 1989, up 48% from 1984. Another 2,245 in that age group died from suicide, now the third-leading cause of death among adolescents.

**T**EENAGE VIOLENCE mostly affects urban African Americans (except for suicide, a predominantly white problem). But it is beginning to spread. Under pressure from

big city police departments, gangs are stashing their guns and dope in the suburbs and recruiting high school students as pushers. Says Captain Richard Kozak, chief of intelligence for the Illinois State Police: "We're seeing gang activities in places where they didn't exist two years ago. The gangs are playing off the fact that law enforcement in the suburbs is not prepared to deal with them."

But is *anybody* really prepared to deal with this escalation of childhood violence? In a word, no. The grim trends tell us—or ought to—that our entire approach to the problem has been misguided. We are constantly acting after the fact, trying to mend bodies after they have been broken.

When children are burned or stabbed or shot, we bury them, or we deliver them to overstretched hospitals, shelters, and foster homes. When youngsters commit violent crimes, we send them into an antiquated juvenile justice system that rarely punishes them sufficiently and almost never rehabilitates them. When teenagers kill themselves, we have groups to console their bereaved parents, but we have very few programs to identify and help potentially suicidal kids before they pull the trigger.

"We believe violence in America to be a public health emergency, largely unresponsive to methods thus far used in its control," declared a recent editorial by two physicians in the *Journal of the American Medical Association*. The authors, former surgeon general C. Everett Koop and journal editor George Lundberg, are right. We must address violence against youth the way we treat other public health threats like smoking, drunken driving, or drug abuse: We must focus our efforts on prevention.

The most pressing task is to get guns away from children. The widespread availability of firearms makes it far too easy for kids to kill and be killed. Guns figure in more than 75% of adolescent homicides and more than half of adolescent suicides. Should we really be surprised that so many children are infatuated with firearms? There are more than 200 million privately owned guns in America, and half of all households have at least one. Movies, TV programs, and popular songs are saturated with gun-toting heroes and villains. A five-year study by the American Psychological Association found that the average child has witnessed 8,000 murders and 100,000 other acts of violence on television by the time he or she has completed *sixth* grade.

An astounding number of children either own a gun or know how to get one. Says Baltimore County's Colonel Supenski, whose suburban jurisdiction surrounds Baltimore but excludes the city itself: "For youth today, I don't care where you live, what class you are, or whether you're white, black, or Hispanic, it's cool to carry a gun. Owing to a lot of things, primarily the entertainment industry, it's a macho thing to do."

The teenage arms race shows no signs of abating. A national survey of high school students in 1990 by the Centers for Disease Control found that 4% had carried a gun at least once in the past month. In a more recent study of 11th-graders in Seattle, 6% of boys said they had actually brought a gun into the school building. And these pieces aren't just for show: One-third of the gun-owning students in Seattle reported that they had fired their weapons at another person.

Given the proliferation of guns, it's not surprising that kids say they need to carry one to protect themselves. But the line between "protection" and "aggression" is often so thin that it disappears. At the Henry Horner Homes, a mostly African American

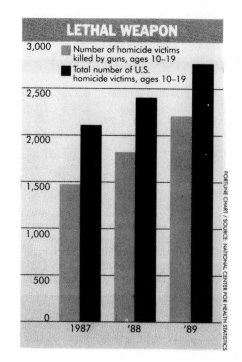

**LETHAL WEAPON**

Number of homicide victims killed by guns, ages 10–19

Total number of U.S. homicide victims, ages 10–19

FORTUNE CHART / SOURCE: NATIONAL CENTER FOR HEALTH STATISTICS

housing project on Chicago's West Side, some teenagers view popping a person as a noble act, a matter of honor and pride. Says David Powell, a counselor at Better Days for Youth, an antigang program: "These kids think if someone is messing with their girlfriend and they shoot him, that's not violence. They see what happens on TV. If the hero has a problem, he shoots. And the hero shows no remorse."

Guns are surprisingly easy to get. In the Seattle study, 34% of the students said they had easy access to a handgun. In Chicago,

where handgun sales have been banned since 1982, an inner-city youngster can take delivery of the weapon of his choice in under two hours. All it requires is a few bucks and a brief chat with the guys hanging out on his front steps. For $20 he can buy a used .22 caliber pistol. For as little as $200 he can own a brand-new, semiautomatic 9-millimeter pistol.

And it takes no skill at all to become a juvenile murderer. The increasingly popular 9-millimeter semiautomatic weighs about 2½ pounds. A teenager can conceal the muzzle in the waistband of his pants and cover up the handle with his sweatshirt or warm-up jacket. The gun's magazine can spew out 15 bullets in less than nine seconds. When one magazine is spent, the shooter can quickly snap on another. This is a point-and-shoot weapon. Aim it at another person and you are likely to inflict great damage, as this writer (who had never used a handgun) discovered when he trained the weapon on a human-shaped firing range target.

*James Love knows all about 9-millimeter pistols. When he was 15, he used one to murder a 22-year-old. He also wounded the young man's teenage brother. Now 20, Love, who was tried and convicted as an adult, is serving a life sentence in the Maryland Penitentiary in Baltimore—eligible for parole in 14 years. As a teenager in an East Baltimore housing project, Love ran a small-time drug ring that netted big money, as much as $10,000 a day. Love says his two victims owed him $15,000. When they didn't pay, he shot them.*

*"When you shoot someone, you don't think about the consequences," says Love, a muscular young African American man dressed in shorts, a T-shirt, and a Nike Air cap. Love now expresses some regret for what he did: "I wish it never would have happened. It ain't worth taking nobody's life for no money."*

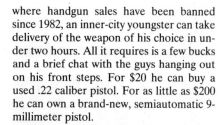

HAT MESSAGE is not getting through to the streets. Teenagers are not only shooting one another, they are also killing, wounding, and terrorizing their younger brothers and sisters. The steady popping of guns can inflict lasting psychological wounds. Children can become withdrawn, mistrustful, fatalistic, defensive, and violent. Says Sharon Brown, a director of programs for children at the Lutheran Social Services center at Cabrini-Green, a housing project on Chicago's North Side: "The kids are all on edge. Brush against them, and they're ready to fight."

Listen to the children of Cabrini-Green describe their world. Says 10-year-old Derrell Ellis: "You can't come outside. You got to duck and dive from the bullets. They be shooting most every day." Eleven-year-old Rachella Thompson used to hurry away from her fifth-floor window when gangs began gunfights in the courtyard of her building. Now, she says, "I don't care. I just sit there and play Nintendo. If they're going to

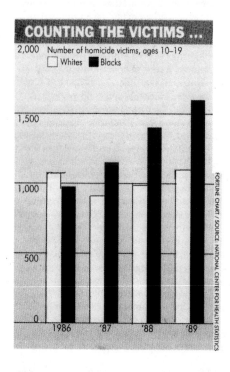

**COUNTING THE VICTIMS ...**

Number of homicide victims, ages 10–19

Whites   Blacks

FORTUNE CHART / SOURCE: NATIONAL CENTER FOR HEALTH STATISTICS

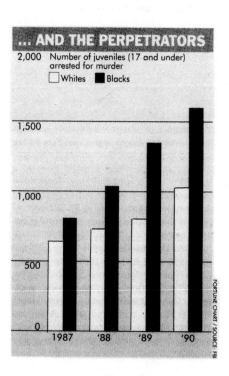

**... AND THE PERPETRATORS**

Number of juveniles (17 and under) arrested for murder

Whites   Blacks

FORTUNE CHART / SOURCE: FBI

shoot, they're going to shoot. Ain't nobody going to stop them."

Children exposed to a single violent event can suffer anxiety and depression for years. Psychologist James Garbarino, co-author of a new book called *Children in Danger*, has studied children in the war zones of Mozambique, Northern Ireland, Kuwait, and Israel's Occupied Territories, as well as the children of the war zones of American cities. Says he: "We haven't begun to address the issue of kids who see violence every day."

These kids don't see violence just in the streets. All too often they witness it in their homes—the result of an altercation between people who know each other. Says Dr. Carl Bell, head of Community Mental Health Council, a psychiatric center on Chicago's South Side: "It's not gang related or drug related or crime related. It's just people getting mad at each other and going off on each other."

This kind of violence sends a powerful message to the children who witness it. Says Bell: "Everyone talks about violence on TV. But they forget that a personal endorsement of violence from someone who is loved, trusted, and respected carries the most weight in the world." African American children are not only more likely to witness violence at home, they are also more likely to be victims of it.

*Dayton resident Delrine Edwards, a 27-year-old African American woman, knows this only too well. Her second-youngest child, Demetri Green, died last December at the age of 3, strangled by her husband, Lorenzo, who said he was high on drugs at the time. Lorenzo, who was not Demetri's father, pleaded guilty to involuntary manslaughter and is serving nine to 25 years in prison. Says Delrine Edwards, who has three other children: "Demetri was a child, so I know he's in heaven. At least I don't have to worry about him like I do the others."*

Children die violently in white suburban homes as well, but there the most critical problem is suicide. Many factors can prompt adolescents to kill themselves—a broken romance, poor grades, concern about their homosexuality, sexual abuse by a parent, an impending divorce, the death of a friend or relative. Reverend Charles Rubey, a Catholic priest who for 13 years has run Loving Outreach to Survivors of Stress (LOSS), a suicide survivors organization in Chicago, thinks parents expect their children to achieve too much too fast. Says he: "There is this intense drive to succeed. Parents say they want the best for their kids, but this can put a tremendous amount of pressure on them."

Rubey also thinks children have been conditioned by fast food, microwave ovens, and 30-minute TV sitcoms to expect instant solutions to complex problems. With ready access to firearms, kids even have a quick way to kill themselves.

*Therese Gump, program director of LOSS, warns parents not to underestimate the potency of their children's feelings. She speaks with tragic authority. Her second-oldest son, Joey, a normally jovial boy, became depressed at 19 during a severe case of mononucleosis. Later he was jilted by a girlfriend and tried to kill himself by swallowing iodine. He survived. Then at 21, shortly after losing a job, Joey climbed into his parked car in a closed garage, turned on the engine, and suffocated. In his note, he said he knew his family loved him but that he couldn't bear to feel love because it caused too much pain.*

THERE ARE NO easy answers to the complex problem of childhood violence. Because a disproportionate number of its victims are poor and African American, the issue overlaps with many other social problems: youth unemployment, welfare, racism, failing schools, sick hospitals, rotten housing, alcoholism, drug abuse, teen pregnancy, and single-parent households.

Our current approach is a de facto policy of containment. While middle-class neighborhoods are still relatively safe, violence festers in the homes, schools, and communities of the 18% of American children who live in poverty. Says Garbarino: "You cannot write off one-fifth of your society for free." The price is more jails, more foster homes, more crime, more deaths, more fear.

Nor is there any guarantee that juvenile violence will stay put. Says Commander Robert Dart, a beefy ex-Marine who heads the Gang Crime Section of the Chicago Police Department: "In some cases we eradicate gangs. In some cases we push them. I was born in Chicago, I live in Chicago, and I work for Chicago. If I have to push the gangs somewhere else, that's what I'll do." That somewhere else may be your home town.

Beyond eliminating poverty or shoving crime from one jurisdiction to another, there are several workable and affordable steps we can take to reduce our children's exposure to violence:

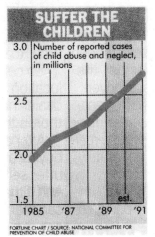

**SUFFER THE CHILDREN**

3.0 | Number of reported cases of child abuse and neglect, in millions

2.5

2.0

1.5 | est.

1985  '87  '89  '91

FORTUNE CHART / SOURCE: NATIONAL COMMITTEE FOR PREVENTION OF CHILD ABUSE

■ **Help parents be parents.** The best place to begin is at the beginning of a child's life. Hawaii's Healthy Start program, funded by the state, intervenes from day one. A case worker interviews new parents in the hospital shortly after their baby is born. The aim is to identify parents at risk of abusing their children: teen mothers, alcoholics, drug users, welfare recipients, or people who have themselves been abused, either by their own parents or their spouses.

Parents who fall into the high-risk category are offered, at no charge, the services of a home visitor. The visitors are paraprofessionals, typically high school graduates who grew up in stable households. A home visitor may counsel a family for as long as five years. Parents are not compelled to enroll in the program, but only a handful refuse the service.

The home visitors, who work for private social service agencies under contract to the state, act as all-purpose advocates for the family. They show parents how to feed and nurture a baby. They ensure that children get regular preventative medical care, including inoculations. In some cases they help parents secure jobs, housing, and, when eligible, welfare and Medicaid.

Healthy Start shows healthy results. Without intervention, some 20% of high-risk parents can be expected to mistreat their children, a figure borne out by research in other states. Among the 1,204 families served by Healthy Start between 1987 and 1989, there were just three cases of abuse and six of neglect—less than 2%. Once the program expands to cover all at-risk families in the state, the total annual cost will be about $16 million. That's substantially less than the $40 million a year Hawaii spends on post-abuse protective custody and foster care.

Healthy Start is also likely to have a salutary effect on crime later in life. Abused children are walking evidence that violence begets violence. A Denver study of first-time juvenile offenders, for example, concluded that 84% had been abused before the age of 6. Says Gail Breakey, the director of the Hawaii Family Stress Center, the leading provider of Healthy Start services: "Child abuse is actually the root cause of so many social problems."

The National Committee for the Prevention of Child Abuse, using a $1 million grant from the Ronald McDonald Children's Charities, is campaigning for the establishment of home visitor programs nationwide. It hopes to have Healthy Start programs in place in 25 states by 1995.

■ **Teach children how to manage anger.** Although anger is a basic human emotion, beginning with a wailing infant's insistent demand for nourishment, many children never learn how to deal with it nonviolently. At the Roth Middle School in Dayton, which is nearly 90% African American, several hundred students take part in a program called Positive Adolescents Choices Training (PACT). Developed by psychologists at nearby Wright State University and incorporated into the middle school's health education classes, PACT aims to defuse violence by teaching African American students how to talk instead of fight.

PACT participants use role playing to reenact the kinds of real-life disputes that can escalate into violence. For example, an adolescent boy confronts a friend who has been spreading false rumors that his sister is pregnant. Instead of cussing his friend out, the boy asks if they can talk, says something positive about their friendship, states what he is angry about and why, tells his friend what action he'd like him to take, asks if he understands, and thanks him for his time. If they can't reach an agreement on the first boy's terms, they try to negotiate a compromise.

Hard as it is to teach kids surrounded by violence to cool their emotions, preliminary studies show that students trained by PACT are less likely to get suspended from school for fighting and more able to handle themselves peaceably in tough situations.

The PACT students who have shown the most progress are those whose parents have enrolled in Impact, a companion program to help them deal with *their* anger. Says Willa Cotten, a parent participant: "I used to get into total screaming matches with my daughter. This program helped me understand all the peer pressure these kids are going through." Cotten now tries to make 13-year-old Wilhemina understand that if she breaks the rules, she won't be shouted at or beaten, but that she will lose privileges.

PACT, like Healthy Start, stresses a most important concept that has eroded in many families: parental responsibility. Says Michelle Hassell, coordinator of the program: "These parents yell at their kids, throw things at them, and threaten them, but they don't discipline them. If you don't discipline your kids, you set them up to fail, because no one is going to love them the way you do."

There are many school-based violence prevention programs, but no one has attempted to evaluate their long-term effectiveness. Cautions Rodney Hammond, PACT's project director: "These programs

are not a panacea. The absence of social skills is not the prime reason for violence. But if our society refuses to deal with the big variables that contribute to violence, like poverty and the easy availability of guns, then we as psychologists need to minimize the casualties as best as we can."

■ **Keep guns away from kids.** We cannot control juvenile violence without controlling guns. Requiring manufacturers to build child-resistant features into firearms could be a small first step. Trigger restraints and other devices would help prevent very young children from accidentally shooting themselves or someone else. But these mis-

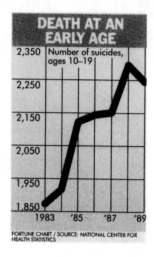

**DEATH AT AN EARLY AGE**

Number of suicides, ages 10–19

2,350
2,250
2,150
2,050
1,950
1,850

1983   '85   '87   '89

FORTUNE CHART / SOURCE: NATIONAL CENTER FOR HEALTH STATISTICS

haps are only part of the problem. Says Stephen Teret, director of the Johns Hopkins University Injury Prevention Center: "What we need to do is gun-proof children rather than child-proof guns."

Three years ago Florida became the first state to make adults partially responsible for the use of guns by children. Any adult who fails to keep a loaded gun safely away from a child under age 16 can be charged with a felony if the child uses the gun to shoot somebody. Laws similar to the Florida act are now on the books in ten states and three cities.

These laws, while helpful, are mere dams erected to stop a tidal wave. Every year about four million new guns are manufactured in the U.S. for civilian use; nearly 1.4 million of those are semiautomatics. Municipalities like Chicago and Washington, D.C., ban the sale of handguns, but the laws are of limited use when firearms can be bought legally just a few steps outside the city limits.

We need action at the federal level, and we need it fast. The public is ahead of politicians on this issue. A Gallup poll last year found that 68% of Americans feel

that laws covering the sale of firearms should be "more strict." A resounding 93% favored imposing a mandatory seven-day waiting period on anyone trying to buy a gun, the so-called Brady Bill now languishing in Congress.

But the Brady Bill, if it passes, would primarily stop convicted felons and mentally ill people from buying firearms. With 200 million guns in circulation, we need to do much more to stanch the flow. Says Dr. Katherine Kaufer Christoffel, professor of pediatrics and community health at Northwestern University's medical school: "The solution is to ban the manufacture, sale, and private possession of handguns." We can start by outlawing assault weapons, like the 9-millimeter semiautomatic pistol, that are wreaking so much havoc on our children.

VIOLENCE against children undermines the very foundation of our nation. Opponents of gun control who cite the Second Amendment to the Constitution should pay more heed to the preamble, especially the phrase about insuring "domestic tranquillity." We the People have created a most untranquil society for our children, where the right to bear arms has been used to sanction a buildup of lethal personal weaponry unprecedented in human history. We cannot "secure the blessings of liberty to ourselves and our posterity" if we continue to allow the slaughter of our offspring.

Beyond controlling guns, we need to reassert the principles of parental and community responsibility. Our children's future is etched in the wan face of Judy Simpson. Amanda Simpson's mother is a frail woman. She is 34 but looks many years older. When she speaks of Amanda, her entire body convulses. Her pain is so palpable that it fills the room. The arsonists who killed her only child left her too ill to work, forcing her to rely on the limited largess of her retired parents and the caring counseling of the victims advocates at the Montgomery County prosecutor's office.

Imbedded in Judy Simpson's anguish is a seething rage, a mission, a purpose: "They took my lovely child from me. I can't do anything to get Amanda back, but I need to get her story out, for the sake of other parents and other children. For too many juveniles, crime seems to be a game. This has to stop."

We owe at least that much to the memory of Amanda Simpson and Demetri Green and Joey Gump and all the rest. We owe it to the frightened kids of Cabrini-Green. They are all our sons. They are all our daughters. They are all our responsibility.

# Children in gangs

**The tragedy of inner-city youth drawn into delinquency and drug trafficking**

# Carl Rogers

**CARL ROGERS,** of the United States, is an expert on child and family issues. He serves as the public policy liaison officer for the American National Council on Child Abuse and Family Violence, a U.S. private sector initiative for the prevention and treatment of child abuse, based in Washington D.C.

THE 1980s witnessed the explosive resurgence of an historic American urban social problem: children and youth in gangs. From New York to Los Angeles, from Chicago to Miami, over forty-five American cities have an identified youth gang problem.

The number of youth gangs in the United States is on the rise and their involvement in the drug trade is resulting in dramatic increases in gang-related violence—including homicide—and arrests for criminal activities in almost every American city. The scope and the nature of the problem vary widely from city to city, but it has been estimated that over 50,000 children and youths are gang members in the city of Los Angeles and that there are over 600 youth gangs in California alone.

Popularized in the 1950s musical *West Side Story,* youth gangs have been a recurring social problem in U.S. cities at least since the second half of the nineteenth century. Their emergence and growth, primarily in poor, urban neighbourhoods, were frequently fuelled by successive waves of immigrants arriving in the United States, and were symptomatic of the problems these groups encountered in trying to adapt to a new and at times radically different culture. Today many youth gangs continue to reflect the difficulties of assimilation of immigrant populations.

Youth gangs are usually defined as groups of young people who frequently engage in illegal activity on a group basis. They are usually territorial in nature, identifying with a particular neighbourhood and protecting their "turf" from encroachment by other gangs. Better organized gangs often control economically motivated crime such as burglary, extortion or drug-trafficking at the neighbourhood level. They may also sell "protection" from criminal activity to legitimate merchants. Youth gangs usually identify themselves by a name ("Crips", and "Bloods" are the names of two Los Angeles-based gangs), and may further distinguish themselves by a particular style or colour of clothing, by use of symbols, or by wearing certain kinds of jewellery.

## A MILLION DOLLARS A WEEK FROM CRACK

The recent dynamic growth of youth gangs and related violence is directly attributed by most sources to the increased sale of cocaine, particularly in the form known as "rock" or "crack". This lucrative illegal activity is helping to transform gangs into drug trafficking criminal organizations. In 1988 Los Angeles police officials acknowledged that they were aware of at least four gangs in their city grossing over $1,000,000 per week through the sale of cocaine. A recent article in the U.S. magazine *Time* ironically noted that the crack cocaine trade may be one of the biggest job programmes for inner city youth in the United States.

One reason why children become involved in drug trafficking is that the laws governing juvenile crime are more lenient than those governing adult crime. Ironically, as the U.S. "war on drugs" has intensified, with both increasing arrests for drug trafficking and more severe penalties for adults convicted of drug-related crime, the value of youth gang members has increased. While an adult convicted of selling drugs in most states is subject to a mandatory prison sentence of anywhere from two years to life imprisonment, a young person under the age of eighteen will seldom be committed to a correctional facility for a first offence, and even if committed is not subject to mandatory sentence lengths. It has become both increasingly profitable and safer for adult criminals to enroll children and youths in the drug trafficking business.

## PEEWEES AND WANNABEES

The average age of youth gang members continues to decline. Most experts place the figure at around thirteen to fifteen years of age, while law enforcement officials in Los Angeles, Chicago and other cities note that children as young as nine or ten years are frequently found in today's gangs. These young recruits, often called "peewees" (slang for little members) or "wannabees" (slang for "want to be" gang members), become casually involved with older gang members who live in their neighbourhood, attend their school, or are members of their own families. Initially, younger children may be asked to perform "favours" for older gang members—to watch for police in the neighbourhood, or to deliver packages which may contain drugs, money or weapons. In exchange, the children often receive expensive gifts or money.

As they demonstrate their trustworthiness and reliability, these children assume more difficult and more dangerous roles. Children as young as ten or eleven years of age are frequently involved in gang-related drug trafficking. Younger children are routinely employed as "spotters" watching and reporting on police activity in their neighbourhood to other gang members, as "weapons carriers" for older gang members, or

in other roles, and earn anywhere from $200 per week to $100 per day. "Runners", usually slightly older children, may earn up to $300 per day keeping street corner dealers supplied with drugs from a hidden cache. Enterprising youths as young as fifteen or sixteen may advance to the level of street corner dealers, routinely earning between $400 and $1,000 per day. In a particularly good market such as New York City, authorities indicate that dealers can make up to $3,000 per day.

Few dealers, however, work full time, and two different studies in Washington, D.C. would suggest that a street corner dealer's average earnings are more likely to be in the range of $4,000 to $7,000 per month. In contrast, most states in the U.S. set a minimum employment age of sixteen years, and most legal entry-level jobs available to young people pay less than $40 per day, or approximately $800 per month.

Once a child is involved with a gang, it may be virtually impossible for him to quit. Gang membership usually leads to truancy and ultimately dropping out of school, closing off escape from a criminal lifestyle through education. The gang member also finds it difficult to give up a more lucrative lifestyle in exchange for unemployment or employment at minimum wage.

The gang member who attempts to quit is also subject to social pressures to continue his or her involvement. At best, attempting to leave the gang may lead to social ostracism; at worst it may lead to direct intimidation.

## IMPOVERISHED INNER-CITY NEIGHBOURHOODS

To truly understand the youth gang problem it is important to understand the social context within which the gangs emerge. First, they are almost universally a product of impoverished urban neighbourhoods, where unemployment routinely exceeds 20 per cent of the workforce and in some cases exceeds 50 per cent. Families consist overwhelmingly of single mothers with children and often rely primarily on public assistance for their livelihood. Nationally, 20 per cent of all children in the United States live in families at or below the established federal poverty level. In many inner-city neighbourhoods this figure approaches 100 per cent. These communities are characterized by generally high crime rates, limited legitimate business activity or employment opportunities, and poorly functioning public education systems.

In contrast to the phenomenon of street children in many Third World countries, or to the problem of runaway or "throwaway" children (children, usually teenagers, expelled from their homes by their parents), most youth gang members live at home with their families. Some parents actively support their child's gang involvement or are totally indifferent, but most parents do care. Even the best intentioned parent, however, can find it difficult, if not impossible, to keep his or her child from becoming involved with a local gang. Every neighbourhood has its history of gang revenge against individual children or their families for resisting the gang. The combined factors of intimidation on the one hand and some financial support on the other eventually result in tacit collusion on the part of these parents. An uneasy truce develops where the parent, while not condoning or supporting the child's gang involvement, nonetheless does little to try to stop this involvement and welcomes the child's periodic financial contributions to the family budget.

So far, the overall public policy approach to this social problem has focused on three broad strategies: suppression of drug use and drug trafficking; suppression of youth gangs; and prevention of youth involvement in gangs. To date, while national statistics suggest an overall decline in the use of illegal drugs, this decline appears to have had little effect on the growth of the gangs or on the frequency of gang-related violence. Similarly, attempts at direct suppression of the gangs through law enforcement activities appear to have had limited effects, despite the mobilization of extensive resources. It is argued

by many, however, that these efforts have slowed the growth and spread of gangs. Alternatively, some have suggested that efforts at gang suppression through arrest and detention of gang members actually lead to increased levels of gang-related violence as other gangs compete for control of territories once controlled by the suppressed gang.

Most experts agree that the only viable long-term solution to the problem is to prevent children and youths from getting involved in gangs in the first place. Most current programmes seek to provide support for high-risk children and their families. They focus on children between the ages of six and fourteen, since it appears to be generally agreed that prevention efforts must begin before young people develop well-established patterns of delinquent behaviour or become seriously involved with gangs. Key elements in many of these programmes include the provision of social and recreational activities, and educational assistance, as well as efforts to prevent the children from dropping out of school and to enhance their self-confidence and self-esteem. The success of prevention efforts ultimately depends on whether these children and young people have a sense of hope in their own future and a belief that through their own efforts they can lead useful, productive lives.

# Punishment and Corrections

In the American system of criminal justice, the term "corrections" has a special meaning. It designates programs and agencies that have legal authority over the custody or supervision of persons who have been convicted of a criminal act by the courts.

The correctional process begins with the sentencing of the convicted offender. The predominant sentencing pattern in the United States encourages maximum judicial discretion and offers a range of alternatives from probation (supervised conditional freedom within the community), through imprisonment, to the death penalty. Selections in this unit focus on the current condition of the penal system in the United States, and the effects that sentencing, probation, imprisonment, and parole have on the rehabilitation of criminals.

"Sentencing and Corrections" illustrates how society, through sentencing, expresses its objectives for the correctional process. The objectives are deterrence, incapacitation, rehabilitation, retribution, and restitution.

The number of state and federal prisoners grew by 48,384 in 1991 and reached another record high at year's end, according to the Bureau of Justice Statistics. As of December 31, 1991, there were 823,414 men and women being held under state or federal jurisdiction. At the end of 1980 there were 329,821 such inmates.

The increased number of drug-law convictions during the last decade has had a dramatic impact on the nation's prisons. Although about one out of every 13 new prisoners had been convicted of a drug offense during 1981, by the end of the decade almost one in three new admissions was for a drug-law violation.

Some 60 percent of inmates released from state and federal lockups return to prison. Recidivism contributes greatly to the overcrowding that plagues prisons throughout the United States. Crowded, tense conditions make survival the principal goal. Rehabilitation is pushed into the background in the effort to manage incipient chaos. Other issues and aspects of the correctional system—women in prison, black imprisonment, boot camps, and the death penalty, are other topics in this unit.

"Women in Jail: Unequal Justice" cites the enormous disparity in the treatment of men and women in prison. Eugene Methvin's article, "Doubling the Prison Population Will Break America's Crime Wave," is a controversial argument for further reliance on imprisonment. "The Crime of Black Imprisonment" cites the high imprisonment rate in America, in general, and for blacks, in particular.

Frank Bentayou asserts that the strategy of battering and demeaning young offenders to "scare them straight" may actually do the opposite. In "The New Chain Gangs," he examines boot camp philosophy.

Finally, the most controversial punishment of all is under discussion in "The Costliest Punishment—A Corrections Administrator Contemplates the Death Penalty" and " 'This Man Has Expired.' "

### Looking Ahead: Challenge Questions

What is your opinion of "boot camps" for young offenders?

If you were to argue the pathology of imprisonment, what points would you make? On the other hand, if you were to justify continued imprisonment of offenders, what would you stress?

If you were a high-level correctional administrator and had the luxury of designing a "humane" prison, what would it be like? What aspects of a traditional prison would you keep? What would you eliminate? What new strategies or programs would you introduce?

What are your feelings about the death penalty? Do you think it is an effective deterrent to murder?

# Unit 6

# Sentencing and Corrections

## Through sentencing, society attempts to express its goals for the correctional process

### The sentencing of criminals often reflects conflicting social goals

These objectives are—
• **Retribution**—giving offenders their "just deserts" and expressing society's disapproval of criminal behavior
• **Incapacitation**—separating offenders from the community to reduce the opportunity for further crime while they are incarcerated
• **Deterrence**—demonstrating the certainty and severity of punishment to discourage future crime by the offender (specific deterrence) and by others (general deterrence)
• **Rehabilitation**—providing psychological or educational assistance or job training to offenders to make them less likely to engage in future criminality
• **Restitution**—having the offender repay the victim or the community in money or services.

### Attitudes about sentencing reflect multiple goals and other factors

Research on judicial attitudes and practices in sentencing revealed that judges vary greatly in their commitment to various goals when imposing sentences. Public opinion also has shown much diversity about the goals of sentencing, and public attitudes have changed over the years. In fashioning criminal penalties, legislators have tended to reflect this lack of public consensus.

Sentencing laws are further complicated by concerns for—
• **Proportionality**—severity of punishment should be commensurate with the seriousness of the crime
• **Equity**—similar crimes and similar criminals should be treated alike
• **Social debt**—the severity of punishment should take into account the offender's prior criminal behavior.

### Judges usually have a great deal of discretion in sentencing offenders

The different sentencing laws give various amounts of discretion to the judge in setting the length of a prison or jail term. In a more fundamental respect, however, the judge often has a high degree of discretion in deciding whether or not to incarcerate the offender at all. Alternatives to imprisonment include—
• probation
• fines
• forfeiture of the proceeds of criminal activity
• restitution to victims
• community service
• split sentences, consisting of a short period of incarceration followed by probation in the community.

Often, before a sentence is imposed a presentence investigation is conducted to provide the judge with information about the offender's characteristics and prior criminal record.

### Disparity and uncertainty arose from a lack of consensus over sentencing goals

By the early 1970s researchers and critics of the justice system had begun to note that trying to achieve the mixed goals of the justice system without new limits on the discretionary options given to judges had—
• reduced the *certainty* of sanctions, presumably eroding the deterrent effect of corrections
• resulted in *disparity* in the severity of punishment, with differences in the sentences imposed for similar cases and offenders
• failed to validate the effectiveness of various rehabilitation programs in changing offender behavior or predicting future criminality.

### Recent sentencing reforms reflect more severe attitudes and seek to reduce disparity and uncertainty

Reforms in recent years have used statutory and administrative changes to—
• clarify the aims of sentencing
• reduce disparity by limiting judicial and parole discretion
• provide a system of penalties that is more consistent and predictable
• provide sanctions consistent with the concept of "just deserts."

The changes have included—
• making prison mandatory for certain crimes and for recidivists
• specifying presumptive sentence lengths
• requiring sentence enhancements for offenders with prior felony convictions
• introducing sentencing guidelines
• limiting parole discretion through the use of parole guidelines
• total elimination of discretionary parole release (determinate sentencing).

### States use a variety of strategies for sentencing

Sentencing is perhaps the most diversified part of the Nation's criminal justice process. Each State has a unique set of sentencing laws, and frequent and substantial changes have been made in recent years. This diversity complicates the classification of sentencing systems. For nearly any criterion that may be considered, there will be some States with hybrid systems that straddle the boundary between categories.

From *Report to the Nation on Crime and Justice,* Bureau of Justice Statistics, U.S. Department of Justice, March 1988, pp. 90-93.

## The basic difference in sentencing systems is the apportioning of discretion between the judge and parole authorities

**Indeterminate sentencing**—the judge specifies minimum and maximum sentence lengths. These set upper and lower bounds on the time to be served. The actual release date (and therefore the time actually served) is determined later by parole authorities within those limits.

**Partially indeterminate sentencing**—a variation of indeterminate sentencing in which the judge specifies only the maximum sentence length. An associated minimum automatically is implied, but is not within the judge's discretion. The implied minimum may be a fixed time (such as 1 year) for all sentences or a fixed proportion of the maximum. In some States the implied minimum is zero; thus the parole board is empowered to release the prisoner at any time.

**Determinate sentencing**—the judge specifies a fixed term of incarceration, which must be served in full (less any "goodtime" earned in prison). There is no discretionary parole release.

## Since 1975 many States have adopted determinate sentencing, but most still use indeterminate sentencing

In 1976 Maine was the first State to adopt determinate sentencing. The sentencing system is entirely or predominantly determinate in these 10 States:

| | |
|---|---|
| California | Maine |
| Connecticut | Minnesota |
| Florida | New Mexico |
| Illinois | North Carolina |
| Indiana | Washington |

The other States and the District of Columbia use indeterminate sentencing in its various forms. One State, Colorado, after changing to determinate sentencing in 1979, went back to indeterminate sentencing in 1985. The Federal justice system has adopted determinate sentencing through a system of sentencing guidelines.

## States employ other sentencing features in conjunction with their basic strategies

**Mandatory sentencing**—Law requires the judge to impose a sentence of incarceration, often of specified length, for certain crimes or certain categories of offenders. There is no option of probation or a suspended sentence.

Mandatory sentencing laws are in force in 46 States (all except Maine, Minnesota, Nebraska, and Rhode Island) and the District of Columbia. In 25 States imprisonment is mandatory for certain repeat felony offenders. In 30 States imprisonment is mandatory if a firearm was involved in the commission of a crime. In 45 States conviction for certain offenses or classes of offenses leads to mandatory imprisonment; most such offenses are serious, violent crimes, and drug trafficking is included in 18 of the States. Many States have recently made drunk driving an offense for which incarceration is mandated (usually for relatively short periods in a local jail rather than a State prison).

**Presumptive sentencing**—The discretion of a judge who imposes a prison sentence is constrained by a specific sentence length set by law for each offense or class of offense. That sentence must be imposed in all unexceptional cases. In response to mitigating or aggravating circumstances, the judge may shorten or lengthen the sentence within specified boundaries, usually with written justification being required.

Presumptive sentencing is used, at least to some degree, in about 12 States.

**Sentencing guidelines**—Explicit policies and procedures are specified for deciding on individual sentences. The decision is usually based on the nature of the offense and the offender's criminal record. For example, the prescribed sentence for a certain offense might be probation if the offender has no previous felony convictions, a short term of incarceration if the offender has one prior conviction, and progressively longer prison terms if the offender's criminal history is more extensive.

Sentencing guidelines came into use in the late 1970s. They are—
• used in 13 States and the Federal criminal justice system
• written into statute in the Federal system and in Florida, Louisiana, Maryland, Minnesota, New Jersey, Ohio, Pennsylvania, and Tennessee
• used systemwide, but not mandated by law, in Utah
• applied selectively in Massachusetts, Michigan, Rhode Island, and Wisconsin
• being considered for adoption in other States and the District of Columbia.

**Sentence enhancements**—In nearly all States, the judge may lengthen the prison term for an offender with prior felony convictions. The lengths of such enhancements and the criteria for imposing them vary among the States.

In some States that group felonies according to their seriousness, the repeat offender may be given a sentence ordinarily imposed for a higher seriousness category. Some States prescribe lengthening the sentences of habitual offenders by specified amounts or imposing a mandatory minimum term that must be served before parole can be considered. In other States the guidelines provide for sentences that reflect the offender's criminal history as well as the seriousness of the offense. Many States prescribe conditions under which parole eligibility is limited or eliminated. For example, a person with three or more prior felony convictions, if convicted of a serious violent offense, might be sentenced to life imprisonment without parole.

Sources: Surveys conducted for the Bureau of Justice Statistics by the U.S. Bureau of the Census in 1985 and by the Pennsylvania Commission on Crime and Delinquency in 1986.

## Sentencing guidelines usually are developed by a separate sentencing commission

Such a commission may be appointed by the legislative, executive, or judicial branch of State government. This is a departure from traditional practice in that sentences are prescribed through

an administrative procedure rather than by explicit legislation.

In some States the guidelines are prescriptive in that they specify whether or not the judge must impose a prison sentence and the presumptive sentence length. In other States the guidelines are advisory in that they provide infor-

mation to the judge but do not mandate sentencing decisions.

To determine whether a prison sentence should be imposed, the guidelines usually consider offense severity and the offender's prior criminal record. A matrix that relates these two factors may be used.

## 6. PUNISHMENT AND CORRECTIONS

### Sentencing matrix

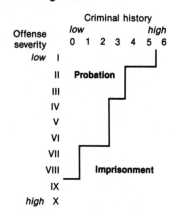

Adapted from *Preliminary report on the development and impact of the Minnesota sentencing guidelines*, Minnesota Sentencing Guidelines Commission, July 1982.

Sentencing guidelines used in the Federal justice system were developed by the United States Sentencing Commission. The guidelines provide for determinate sentencing and the abolition of parole. Ranges of sentence length are specified for various offense classifications and offender characteristics. The judge must provide written justification for any sentence that deviates from the guideline range; sentences that are less severe can be appealed by the prosecution, and sentences that are more severe can be appealed by the defense.

### Changes in sentencing have brought changes in correctional practices

Many sentencing reforms have led to changes in the way correctional systems operate:

The proliferation of determinate and mandatory sentences during the past decade, together with dissatisfaction about the uncertainties of indeterminate sentencing (especially the linking of release decisions to rehabilitative progress or predictions of future behavior), have led to modifications in parole decisionmaking. Many States now use parole guidelines, and many have modified their use of "goodtime" and other incentives for controlling inmate behavior and determining release dates.

New administrative requirements, such as collection of victim restitution funds, operation of community service programs, and levying fees for probation supervision, room and board, and other services, have been added to traditional correctional practices.

Changes in sentencing laws and prac-

tices may be affecting the size of the correctional clientele. Such changes include—
• using determinate and mandatory sentencing
• limiting or abolishing parole discretion

• lowering the age at which youthful offenders become subject to the adult criminal justice system
• enacting in a few jurisdictions laws providing for life imprisonment without the possibility of parole.

## Forfeiture is a relatively new sanction

### What is forfeiture?

Forfeiture is government seizure of property derived from or used in criminal activity. Its use as a sanction aims to strip racketeers and drug traffickers of their economic power because the traditional sanctions of imprisonment and fines have been found inadequate to deter or punish enormously profitable crimes. Seizure of assets aims not only to reduce the profitability of illegal activity but to curtail the financial ability of criminal organizations to continue illegal operations.

### There are two types of forfeiture: civil and criminal

• **Civil forfeiture**—a proceeding against property used in criminal activity. Property subject to civil forfeiture often includes vehicles used to transport contraband, equipment used to manufacture illegal drugs, cash used in illegal transactions, and property purchased with the proceeds of the crime. No finding of criminal guilt is required in such proceedings. The government is required to post notice of the proceedings so that any party who has an interest in the property may contest the forfeiture.

• **Criminal forfeiture**—a part of the criminal action taken against a defendant accused of racketeering or drug trafficking. The forfeiture is a sanction imposed on conviction that requires the defendant to forfeit various property rights and interests related to the violation. In 1970 Congress revived this sanction that had been dormant in American law since the Revolution.

### The use of forfeiture varies greatly among jurisdictions

The Federal Government originally provided for criminal forfeiture in the Racketeer Influenced and Corrupt Organization (RICO) statute and the

Comprehensive Drug Prevention and Control Act, both enacted in 1970. Before that time civil forfeiture had been provided in Federal laws on some narcotics, customs, and revenue infractions. More recently, language on forfeiture has been included in the Comprehensive Crime Control Act of 1984, the Money Laundering Act of 1986, and the Anti-drug Abuse Act of 1986.

Most State forfeiture procedures appear in controlled substances or RICO laws. A few States provide for forfeiture of property connected with the commission of any felony. Most State forfeiture provisions allow for civil rather than criminal forfeiture. A recent survey responded to by 44 States and territories found that under the controlled substances laws most States provide only for civil forfeiture. Eight States (Arizona, Kentucky, Nevada, New Mexico, North Carolina, Utah, Vermont, and West Virginia), however, have criminal forfeiture provisions.[1] Of the 19 States with RICO statutes, all but 8 include the criminal forfeiture sanction.[2]

### What is forfeitable?

Originally most forfeiture provisions aimed to cover the seizure of contraband or modes of transporting or facilitating distribution of such materials. The types of property that may be forfeited have been expanded since the 1970s to include assets, cash, securities, negotiable instruments, real property including houses or other real estate, and proceeds traceable directly or indirectly to violations of certain laws. Common provisions permit seizure of conveyances such as airplanes, boats, or cars; raw materials, products, and equipment used in manufacturing, trafficking, or cultivation of illegal drugs; and drug paraphernalia.

### How long does it take to determine if property can be forfeited?

In most cases some time is provided before the actual forfeiture to allow persons with an interest in seized property to make a claim. Seized property is normally kept for 6 months to 1 year before being declared forfeit and disposed of. Contraband or materials that are illegal *per se*, such as drugs, are disposed of relatively quickly. Cars, airplanes, boats, and other forms of transportation are usually kept for about 6 months before disposal. Real property is often kept for longer periods. Administrative forfeitures usually take less time than ones that require judicial determination.

Because of the depreciation in value of many assets over time and the cost of storing or caring for such assets, forfeiture may result in a cost rather than revenue to the prosecuting jurisdiction.

### What happens to forfeited property?

The disposition of forfeited property is controlled by statute or in some States by their constitutions. In many cases, the seizing agency is permitted to place an asset in official use once it has been declared forfeit by a court. Such assets are usually cars, trucks, boats, or planes used during the crime or proceeds of the crime.

For assets that are sold, the proceeds are usually used first to pay any outstanding liens. The costs of storing, maintaining, and selling the property are reimbursed next. Some States require that, after administrative costs are reimbursed, the costs of law enforcement and prosecution must be paid. More than half the States provide that any outstanding balance go to the State or local treasury, or a part to both.

In eight States law enforcement agencies can keep all property, cash, or sales proceeds. If the State constitution governs distribution, the receiving agency is usually the State or local school system. Some States have specified the recipients to be special programs for drug abuse prevention and rehabilitation.

In 1984 the Federal Government established the Department of Justice Assets Forfeiture Fund to collect proceeds from forfeitures and defray the costs of forfeitures under the Comprehensive Drug Abuse Prevention and Control Act and the Customs Forfeiture Fund for forfeitures under customs laws. These acts also require that the property and proceeds of forfeiture be shared equitably with State and local law enforcement commensurate with their participation in the investigations leading to forfeiture.

# Women in Jail: Unequal Justice

## An unprecedented influx of female inmates leaves prisons overcrowded and overwhelmed

Californians call it The Campus, and with its low-lying, red-brick buildings set against 120 acres of dairy land, the California Institution for Women at Frontera looks deceptively civilized. The illusion ends inside. Constructed in the early 1950s as a repository for 800 or so wayward ladies, Frontera today holds more than 2,500 women at any given moment. The convicts complain that guards spy on them while they're showering or using the toilet. Inspectors have found rodent droppings and roaches in the food. In a lawsuit against the state, inmates charged that shower drains get so backed up, they have to stand on crates to avoid the slime.

A continent away, New York City's Rose M. Singer jail stands as a testimony to penal enlightenment. Because most inmates are young and sometimes high-spirited, the jail can feel a bit like a boarding school for girls. But the starkly lit hallways and pervasive smell of disinfectant are constant reminders of the true purpose of the place. And even though it was completed only two years ago, it is already seriously overcrowded—a dining room has been turned into a dorm. Above all, the inmates hate the lack of privacy. Says Carmen Gonzalez, who is serving nine months for selling crack, "I wish I was in a cell."

**Stiff penalties:** For years, the ranks of convicted criminals have been swelling steadily, bringing the nation's prison system perilously close to an overload. The vast majority—94.4 percent—of those inmates are men. But even in jail, women are breaking down the barriers to equal achievement. The Bureau of Justice Statistics reported last week that the female prison population jumped 21.8 percent from 1988 to 1989—the ninth consecutive year that

the rate of increase at women's institutions far outstripped the men's. The number of women doing time has doubled to 40,000 in the last five years (chart). The main reason is drugs. Stiffer penalties are on the books throughout the country and women, who have turned to crack in a way they never embraced other narcotics, have been caught in the sweep. Judges have also shown a greater willingness to incarcerate women than in the past, when chivalry extended even to lawbreakers. "Courts used to look at it as if they were sentencing a mother," says Gary Maynard, Oklahoma's corrections director. "Now they look at it as if they are sentencing a criminal."

Prisons have been largely unprepared to handle the unique problems of their growing female populations. "We assumed that they could benefit from the same programs as men," says Dan Russell, administrator of Montana's division of corrections. "But women have a lot of psychological and medical needs" that men do not. Often, children are at the heart of the matter. Three quarters of the women are mothers, and many of them single parents. In recent years, a number of prisons have created programs to provide greater contact between kids and inmate moms (box). And public officials have begun to acknowledge—sometimes nudged along by lawsuits—that prisons do not provide women with the same rehabilitation or educational programs as men. Inequities in the correctional system, says Washington, D.C., Superior Court Associate Judge Gladys Kessler, "are a mirror of the sex discrimination that occurs in the nonprison population."

Fed by steamy, seamy '50s movies like "Reform School Girl," Americans have had a long fascination with women behind bars. The reality is a good deal more disturb-

ing—and pathetic. The typical offender, according to a 1988 national study conducted for the American Correctional Association, is a young minority mother. In general, she is slightly better educated and less violent than her male counterpart. Many inmates were victims themselves—of poverty, physical violence or sexual abuse. Though most poor people are obviously law abiding, some analysts say more

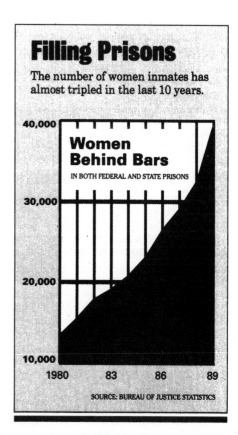

## Filling Prisons

The number of women inmates has almost tripled in the last 10 years.

**Women Behind Bars**

IN BOTH FEDERAL AND STATE PRISONS

SOURCE: BUREAU OF JUSTICE STATISTICS

# 'Dear Mommy, How Are You Doing?'

It is Mother's Day at the Lorton Correctional Complex outside Washington, D.C., and Michael, 10, is waiting impatiently as the women in camouflage pants file into the gym. Finally, Jennifer Nimmons, who is serving 18 months on a drug charge, arrives and Michael rushes into her arms. He has brought his mother a present: a cutout of a dancing bear with a letter on its stomach, which he reads aloud. "Dear Mommy, How are you doing in the hospital? Have a happy mother's day, this is a poem for you. 'Roses are red, Violets are blue, You are the best mother, I ever wrote to'." Then he asks: "Is this a hospital?"

Confused, enraged, hurt—children like Michael are innocent victims of their mothers' crimes. Until recently, prison officials didn't recognize that a child's emotional dependence doesn't stop just because his mother lands behind bars. Now attitudes are changing: institutions around the country have put programs in place to foster that vital relationship.

Some of the most innovative begin at birth. Federal prisons separate mothers and newborns after 24 hours, and few state pens allow inmates to spend time with infants. The Rose M. Singer Center on Rikers Island is a heartening contrast. The mothers' cells surround the glass-walled nursery on three sides, and an intercom system keeps them in constant touch. If kids cry, moms can rush to their aid—the cells are never locked. Because a female federal prisoner is likely to do time far from home, a program called PACT (Parents and Children Together) is designed to improve long-distance parenting. "We counsel inmates to get as involved as possible by calling teachers on a regular basis," says Jaretta Jones, an instructor at the federal penitentiary in Lexington, Ky.

**Psychic costs:** Penal authorities have also become more sensitive about the psychic costs to kids. Some children feel guilty about their parents' predicaments—imagining, for example, if they hadn't opened the door for the cops, Mom would be free. The Huron Valley Women's Facility in Ypsilanti, Mich., provides kids with therapy after visits. "If we are going to lock up these mothers, we have to take some responsibility for those children," says Marilyn Marshall, a vocational counselor at the prison. "They will certainly be our next generation of prisoners unless we pay attention now."

women have taken to crime to support their families as economic conditions have worsened. In Florida last year, more than two thirds of the men were working at the time of their arrest, while 73.8 percent of the women were jobless.

**New Breed:** Women prisoners have always been easier to manage than the men—they're more prone to verbal than physical abuse. But that may be changing. Some penologists worry that the lack of space will not only exacerbate existing problems—for example, fights stemming from lesbian jealousies—but provoke the women into new forms of aggression. "The recidivism, as well as the level of violence, seems to be directly linked to the amount of overcrowding," says Rebecca Jurado, an attorney with the ACLU of southern California.

Drugs, in particular, have stimulated violent outbreaks. More than half the women in the federal system were convicted on drug charges. And the problem doesn't stop at the prison gate. Mary Vermeer, a deputy warden in Perryville, Ariz., says new inmates are delighted to discover that, despite efforts to stem the flow, the drug pipeline makes it almost as easy to get a fix inside as out. At Frontera, crack houses and shooting galleries operate in portable toilets in the yard. Old-timers complain about the new breed of "druggie." "They don't care about nothing," says Delores Lee, 37, who is doing 25 years in Florida on a murder conviction. "They steal; they break things."

AIDS also contributes to the crisis atmosphere in American prisons. So far, there are no national figures measuring the disease among the convict population. An official Massachusetts study based on 400 inmates who volunteered to be tested found that 35 percent of the women were HIV-positive, compared with 13 percent of the men. In California, any woman who tested positive was put into a segregated AIDS unit—whether or not she was actually ill. As a result of a discrimination lawsuit, many HIV inmates at Frontera have been mainstreamed during the day—but must return to their separate quarters to sleep.

Though few would argue that male convicts are socially well adjusted, penal experts tend to agree that female inmates require—and desire—more psychological counseling. Many women feel enormous guilt about their kids. "When men get arrested, they ask for a lawyer," says Brenda Smith, an attorney at the National Women's Law Center in Washington, D.C. "When women get arrested, they ask about their children." The children effectively serve as hostages on the outside, ensuring that the women make few demands. "The No. 1 issue for women is getting their kids back," says Sarah Buel, a battered-women's advocate in Massachusetts. "The unwritten rule is, don't make a fuss and we'll help you get [them] back."

Prison officials have begun to acknowledge the enormous disparity in the treatment of men and women. In a number of recent lawsuits, women plaintiffs have accused the system of gender bias. A major problem is "overincarceration." Because of a lack of facilities, many low-security inmates have landed in medium-security penitentiaries. Many of the women have been subjected to greater restrictions, such as strip searches, than their crimes warrant—and which their male counterparts are largely spared.

Some social critics believe the states should help inmates break the cycle of abuse and poverty that led many of them into crime in the first place. They also argue that the system should recognize that women generally pose less of a threat to public safety than men and deserve more lenient sentences. "Assuming that we want to help offenders, the best place to do this is not in prison," says Nicole Hahn Rafter, author of "Partial Justice," a history of women's prisons. That attitude is unlikely to win much support, particularly now that public opinion favors strict penalties. But it is clear that the overcrowded conditions and lack of rehabilitation programs doubly punish women—and do little to advance the society's interests.

ELOISE SALHOLZ *with* LYNDA WRIGHT *in Los Angeles,* CLARA BINGHAM *in Washington,* TONY CLIFTON *in New York,* GINNY CARROLL *in Houston,* SPENCER REISS *in Miami,* FARAI CHIDEYA *in Boston and bureau reports*

# Doubling the Prison Population Will Break America's Crime Wave

*Editor's note: This thought-provoking article first appeared as an editorial in* The Washington Post *and is reprinted with the author's permission. After its publication, the* Post *ran several letters to the editor taking strong exception to the author's views, including one from ACA Executive Director James A. Gondles, Jr. His letter appears on page 211.*

**Eugene H. Methvin**

*Eugene H. Methvin, a* Reader's Digest *senior editor, has reported on the U.S. criminal justice system for more than 40 years. He served on the 1983-1986 President's Commission on Organized Crime.*

One of America's best-kept secrets is that our huge investment in building prisons—an estimated $30 billion in the last decade to double capacity—has produced a tremendous payoff: Americans are safer and, as the Justice Department reported last week, crime has fallen steadily.

Moreover, some pioneering research and police field testing suggest that if we again double the present federal and state prison population—to somewhere between 1 million and 1.5 million—and leave our city and county jail population at the present 400,000, we will break the back of America's 30-year crime wave.

Liberal opponents will howl, of course. They have convinced many Americans that imprisonment is a failed policy and don't want to hear otherwise. The Edna McConnell Clark Foundation bombards influen-tial media, declaring: "Our prison population has gone up by more than 200 percent in the last 15 years with no resulting decrease in crime." The director of the American Civil Liberties Union's National Prison Project, Alvin Bronstein, writes that "no jurisdiction has ever...had an impact on crime rates by an expanded incarceration policy." *Washington Post* columnist Colman McCarthy insists that prisons don't succeed but "work-release or community-service programs, structured therapy, in-prison job training, restitution, house arrests with electronic monitoring and halfway houses do."

Other pundits and experts will point out that a numerical correlation—between increased incarceration and decreased crime rates—does not prove a causation and that other demographic variables may be at least partly responsible for the trend. They are usually the same people who nonetheless find correlations between crime and joblessness, poverty and illiteracy and who argue that public money is better spent addressing these "root causes."

Despite our high prison population, punishment for crime is near an all-time low, Texas A&M University economist Morgan O. Reynolds observes. He did a 38-year comparison of serious crime and probable punish-ment—that is, the expected days in prison as determined by the median prison sentence for all serious crimes and weighted by probabilities of arrest, prosecution, conviction and imprisonment. He charted the two lines from 1950 to 1988. His chart shows a big horizontal "X."

Probable punishment turned sharply down in 1954, and crime soared. Thus, in 1950 we had 1.8 million serious crimes, and the average offender risked 24 days in prison. By 1964 imprisonment risk dropped in half, to 12.1 days, and crimes had increased to 4.6 million. By 1974, offenders risked a mere 5.5 days in prison and America had 10.3 million crimes. Finally, in 1975, punishment turned slightly up, and the crime increase slowed. In 1988, the prison risk was 8.5 days and the number of crimes was 13.9 million.

**Despite our high prison population, punishment for crime is near an all-time low, according to economist Morgan O. Reynolds.**

"Why is there so much crime?" asks Reynolds. "The main reason is that crime pays for millions of criminals and potential criminals. Only 17 in 100 murders result in a prison sentence. The imprisonment rate for rape is 5.1 percent, for assault 1.5 percent and for auto theft only 0.3 percent. Even though police make 13 million arrests each year, less than 2 percent of them result in a prison sentence."

 From *Corrections Today*, February 1992, pp. 28-40. Copyright © 1992 by the American Correctional Association, Inc.

A related analysis produces similar conclusions. During the 1960s, the total prison population fell from a then-historical peak of about 219,000 in 1961 to about 195,000 in 1968. During the same decade, crimes soared from 3.4 million in 1960 to 8 million in 1970, according to the FBI's Uniform Crime Reports (UCR) based on incidents reported to police.

Only after 1972 did the prison population start upward, surpassing the 1961 peak in 1975, then soaring to 771,243 by last Jan. 1, 1991. And, wonder of wonders, crime declined significantly—whether measured by the FBI's long-standing UCR or by the Justice Department's National Crime Survey of households conducted by its Bureau of Justice Statistics.

The distinction between the two surveys is important. The FBI's UCR, begun in 1929, includes only crimes reported to police: in 1973 the DOJ began its scientific BJS surveys to estimate actual victimization totals, including crimes not reported to police—which the department estimated at 62 percent in 1990 (and more than half of all violent crimes). The two sets of figures frequently produce seeming contradictions and must be interpreted carefully. For example, the latest BJS report shows that the percentage of assaults reported to police increased from 43 to 47 in 1989-90—which alone would produce an increase of almost 10 percent in the FBI's reported assaults even if there were no actual increase.

Moreover, there are differences in crimes. Half or more murders and aggravated assaults are once-in-a-life-time crimes of passion that involve acquaintances; robbery and burglary are almost always crimes of deliberation by predators who repeat and repeat and repeat. I rely more heavily on the latter two categories than on others when measuring the effectiveness of imprisonment rates. There are other variables as well. The crack cocaine epidemic, which began in 1985, clearly has produced an increase in criminality since then—including murderous battles over turf. Rape and theft remain the most underreported

crimes of all, though efforts by police and victims groups to encourage rape reporting are having some success. And much depends on what year is used as a baseline.

Given these caveats, it is not surprising that the FBI could report in October that the number of reported crimes in the nation in the first half of 1991 increased 2 percent over the first half of 1990, continuing an upward trend evident since the mid-1980s—while the BJS could report the same month that actual criminal victimization (reported and unreported) decreased 3.9 percent last year, continuing a "downward trend...that began a decade ago." Contradictory? Not really. They are describing different groups of crimes over different periods of time.

Both surveys, in fact, show a long-term downward trend. Even without adjusting for increased population, increased reporting to police or the crack phenomenon of the late 1980s, the FBI's reported murder rate for the 1981-90 decade declined 8 percent and the burglary rate 26 percent—though the robbery rate increased 5 percent. The broader BJS survey documents an overall 9.2 percent decline in violent crimes since its first survey in 1973; robbery is down 16 percent, burglary 41 percent and rape 33 percent. In sum, the BJS found, the rate of crimes against people was 25 percent lower in 1990 than in 1973 and the rate of household crimes 26 percent lower. The number of personal or household crimes, it added, fell from 41 million in 1981 to 34 million in 1990—a decline of 7 million in a decade.

Michigan, California and Texas in the 1980s have conducted revealing demonstrations of contrasting "deprisonization" and "lock 'em up" policies.

Case 1. Michigan tried it both ways. In the late 1970s, legislators and voters refused to build new prisons, and the state soon was forced to deal with severe overcrowding. The governor granted emergency releases to 20,000 inmates in four years, some

more than two years early. Michigan became the only state to record a prison population decrease in 1981-85, dropping from 15,157 in 1981 to 14,604 in 1984 but then jumping sharply to 17,755 in late 1985 after a *Detroit Free Press* series on early release of prisoners.

The violent-crime rate for Michigan reported by the FBI soared 25 percent, and public outrage mounted. Starting in 1986, a crash prison-building program doubled inmate population in five years. And, wonder of wonders, Michigan's crime rate dropped. Robbery and burglary rates fell more than 25 percent; in Detroit the decline was even more impressive—burglaries down 32 percent, robberies

---

## Half or more murders are once-in-a-lifetime crimes of passion that involve acquaintances.

---

37 percent. (Murders decreased at lesser rates—12 percent in the state and 4 percent in the city, an apparent anomaly probably explained by new and deadly warfare among crack cocaine gangs in Detroit.)

Success in Michigan wasn't cheap. The state voted $888 million to build and expand prisons by 1992, and operating them costs additional millions each year. But there were savings too. In 1988, U.S. Sentencing Commission criminologist Mark A. Cohen calculated the cost of 10 crimes to their victims by combining direct costs such as lost property and wages with estimates of pain, suffering and fear based on known jury awards. Cohen calculated the cost of a rape at $51,050, a robbery at $12,594, an assault at $12,028 and a burglary at $1,372. By this measure, the decrease in just two prominent "fear" crimes—robberies and burglaries—saved Detroiters $113,546,000 in a single year.

Case 2. Since 1982 Californians have approved $3.7 billion in bonds to build prisons. From 1980 to January 1991, inmate population quadrupled from 22,600 to 98,000. By the 1990s, murder, rape and burglary rates fell a whopping 24 to 37 percent from their 1980-82 peaks—which translates as an annual reduction of nearly 1,000 murders, 16,000 robberies and a quarter of a million burglaries.

Case 3. Conversely, Texas learned that skimping on prisons inflates crime disastrously. Prison costs had soared because of a burgeoning inmate population, a doubling of the officer/inmate ratio and a federal judge's order to make costly changes—some indisputably necessary, such as better medical care, but others of dubious value, such as free college courses. The yearly cost per inmate would eventually rise from $2,920 to $14,000 in the '80s, but in an early effort to slow it, the legislature in 1983 adopted a turn-'em-loose-faster approach. Thus, while the imprisoned offender population grew by two-and-a-half times, the average term served dropped from 55 percent of sentence to less than 15 percent and the number of offenders on parole increased by 21 times.

Texas A&M professor Reynolds calculated the consequences. The expected punishment for a serious crime dropped 43 percent (from 13 days to 7.4) from 1980 to 1989, though for the nation as a whole it rose by about 35 percent (from 5.5 days to 8.8) in roughly the same period. Factoring the probability of arrest, conviction and imprisonment, a potential offender in Texas today risks little. Fewer than one out of every 100 serious crimes results in a prison term, and those who land in prison serve an average of only 10 months. For murder an offender risks 24 months, for rape 5.3 months, for robbery 2 months and for burglary 7 days.

Result: The crime rate soared 29 percent in the 1980-89 decade, though nationally it dropped 4 percent, making Texas the second most crime-prone state. In 1980 no Texas city had ranked in the 20 worst American cities in property crimes; in 1988, 13 of the nation's worst 20 cities were in Texas.

If increased incarceration cuts crime, how many inmates should we keep locked away in this "land of the free?" When can we stop? And how much can we afford? We've spent an estimated $430 billion to double our prison population in the past decade, and yet today our prisons crowd in perhaps 140,000 more than they should.

University of Pennsylvania criminologist Marvin Wolfgang compiled arrest records up to the 30th birthday for every male born and raised in Philadelphia in 1945 and 1958 and published a 1990 study comparing the two cohorts. In both, about 35 percent of the young men collected one arrest and most never tangled with the law again. The real hard-core predators were an astonishingly small group of repeaters who were rarely punished; just 7 percent of each age group committed two-thirds of all violent crimes, including three-fourths of the rapes and robberies and virtually all the murders. Moreover, this 7 percent not only had five or more arrests by age 18 but went on committing felonies and, for every arrest made, got away with about a dozen crimes.

Incredibly, only 14 percent of the first five arrests resulted in punishment; in the other 86 percent, no charges were brought. Even the 14 killers among the 1945 cohort averaged an appallingly lenient four years behind bars. Yet when punishment was tried, it worked. The few who were imprisoned committed fewer and less serious crimes afterward.

What can be done? Wolfgang's studies suggest that about 75,000 new young, persistent criminal predators are added to our population every year. They hit their peak rate of offenses at about age 16. Locking up all of them from the time of a third felony conviction until, say, age 30 would almost double our present prison populations to about 1,230,000. But such long-term imprisonments may not prove necessary if punishment is applied early and consistently.

Another measure of the size of our hard-core criminal population comes from a Justice Department program begun in 1983 and based on the Philadelphia findings. The department persuaded 20 cities to have their police, prosecutors, schools and welfare and probation workers pool information and focus on the worst offenders, generally youngsters with three or more arrests by age 18. A serious habitual offender, or SHO, gets priority attention from probation authorities, and if he is arrested anew, investigators and prosecutors throw the book at

---

**Criminologist Marvin Wolfgang's studies suggest that about 75,000 new young, persistent criminal predators are added to our population every year.**

---

him with escalating penalties (coupled with rehabilitation efforts) in an effort to stop the revolving door.

In all 20 cities, SHOs consistently comprised less than 2 percent of all juveniles arrested, or about 18 to 25 youngsters per 100,000 population. Thus, out of 250 million Americans we would have a maximum of maybe 62,500 SHOs between their 14th and 18th birthdays at any one time. Putting them all behind bars until 30 after the third offense—or even permanently, as is the law in many states, though rarely enforced—would be a relatively inexpensive way to cut a huge chunk out of our still atrocious crime rates.

California's only participating city, Oxnard, began a concerted effort to get the city's active SHOs behind bars, and in 1987 violent crimes dropped 38 percent, more than double the drop in any other California city. By 1989 all 30 of Oxnard's identified active SHOs were behind bars—almost exactly the predictable total for a city of 130,000—and its citizens experienced the lowest crime of a decade.

Murders declined 60 percent, robberies 41 percent and burglaries 29 percent.

Based on these social yardsticks, I'd hazard a guess that America's hard-core violent repeaters number upwards of a million. That in turn suggests that if we increase federal and state prison populations to between 1 million and 1.5 million and keep our jails at the present level of about 400,000, we

may see a sharp drop in our horrendous crime rates.

And what about those alternatives to imprisonment Colman McCarthy touts?

The American Institutes for Research in Behavioral Sciences, a nonprofit Washington think tank, studied 350 high-repeat Illinois delinquents and found imprisonment was significantly more effective in reducing subsequent arrests from their previous levels. Judges committed the 159 worst pros-

pects to incarceration and sent another 191 to foster or group homes for community "treatment" programs; the latter recorded subsequent arrest reductions of 56 to 68 percent while those imprisoned registered 71 percent fewer. Moreover, those not imprisoned were free to continue committing untold crimes while in "treatment."

In short, lock 'em up and you slow 'em down. Turn 'em loose and you pay an awful price.

## Executive Director's Reply

# "There Are No Painless Solutions"

**James A. Gondles, Jr.**
**Executive Director**
**American Correctional Association**

Eugene H. Methvin's proposal to "double the present federal and state prison population" is a surprisingly provincial and primitive solution to an ever-evolving and complex social dilemma.

There are no painless solutions to problems like prison crowding. Inmates now are released early to make room for other, more violent offenders. This is usually done under federal court order, because crowding has become so severe that our prisons cannot properly house or feed their existing populations. This being the case, where does Mr. Methvin suggest we put the other half-million people? Where would the money come from? The land? The resources?

And what would we do with this 1.5 million people? Citizens and the state are responsible for inmates' basic welfare. As inmates age, they must be given medication, wheelchairs, walkers, cardiograms, etc. Even the young must be given basic medical care, which increasingly includes AIDS and substance-abuse treatment. The costs of such care can be enormous.

Recall the grim specters of the Attica and the New Mexico prison riots. These were the direct results of piling inmates into insufficient space without concern for treatment and rehabilitation. Crowding can only lead to more harm to society.

From the beginning, history has proven that warehousing inmates treats only the symptom and not the cause. It's estimated that more than 40 percent of all inmates are illiterate; more than half of federal prison inmates are held for drug-related offenses. If we don't at least try to end the source of the trouble, this army of offenders will keep pouring into our prisons.

There are no easy answers. Only a combination of punishment, treatment, education and victim restitution will come close to curing this terrible social ill. It is time for the public to admit ownership of these problems and look for ways to prevent crime, not to continue policies that amount an enormous waste of humanity.

# THE CRIME OF BLACK IMPRISONMENT

## STEVE WHITMAN

*Steve Whitman is a member of the Committee to End the Marion Lock-down. He and the committee may be reached at P.O. Box 578172, Chicago IL 60657-8172.*

HE U.S. "criminal justice" system is the largest in the world. In mid-year 1991 there were over 804,000 people in U.S. prisons, over 405,000 in jails, and more than 4.4 million people—or almost 2 percent of the U.S. population—who were under some form of criminal justice control (including prison, jail, probation, or parole). It is difficult to grasp the enormity of these numbers. For example, the number of people in prison would comprise the 11th largest city in the U.S. The number of people who are incarcerated in jails or prisons is greater than the number of people who live in 13 states. The number of people under the control of the criminal justice system is one and a half times larger than the number of people who live in Chicago or Nicaragua. In 1989, over 14 million people were arrested in the U.S.

### The Sentencing Project's Report

THE SENTENCING PROJECT is an independent organization operating out of Washington D.C. that attempts to propagate ideas about alternatives to incarceration. In January, 1991 the Project issued a report entitled "Americans Behind Bars: A Comparison of International Rates of Incarceration," by Marc Mauer, the assistant director of the organization.

Although incarceration rates are usually calculated by dividing the number of people in prison by the relevant population group, in this report, summarized in the accompanying table, Mauer uses the number of people in prison and jail.

| Country Incarceration Rate per 100,000 | |
|---|---|
| **Country** | **Population: 1989 or 1909** |
| United States | 426 |
| South Africa | 333 |
| Soviet Union | 268 |
| Hungary | 196 |
| Poland | 106 |
| New Zealand | 100 |
| United Kingdom | 97 |
| France | 81 |
| Spain | 76 |
| Italy | 60 |
| Netherlands | 40 |
| United States: Black males | 3,109 |
| South Africa: Black males | 729 |
| United States: white males* | 420 |
| United States: white people* | 210 |
| United States: Black people* | 1,500 |

*\*I have calculated these three rates by using additional data sources. Incarceration rates for other national groupings in the U.S. present still other important issues. Due to limited space I will not discuss rates for other people of color in this article.*

It is important to examine closely the racial dynamics revealed in this table. Imprisonment rates for Black people are about 7.4 times higher than for white people. Indeed, the grotesque distinction of the U.S. having the highest imprisonment rate in the world stems directly from the nature of Black imprisonment in the U.S. While the incarceration rate for white people in the U.S. is twice as high as the rates for other European peoples it is stunning to note that the rate for Black people in the U.S. is four times as high as the rate for Black people in South Africa.

### Returning To The U.S.

WE HAVE EXAMINED the size of the U.S. prison system, international comparisons in incarceration rates, and the racial dynamics of these comparisons. Let us now return to the U.S. and look at the racial dimensions of the criminal justice system. There are many ways of expressing the horrors of Black incarceration:

- as noted above, a Black person in the U.S. is 7.4 times more likely to be imprisoned than a white person;

- one out of every two Black men will be arrested in his lifetime;

- there are more Black men aged 20-29 who are under control of the criminal justice system than there are Black men in college;

- one out of every four Black men are under some form of criminal justice control;

- more than 3 percent of all Black men are in prison (this means only prison, and does not include any of the other criminal justice categories);

 From *Z Magazine*, May 1992, pp. 69-72. Copyright © 1992 by The Institute for Social and Cultural Communications.

- although most (about 94 percent) prisoners are men, the racial differential for women is even greater than it is for men and the increase in the number of women in prison is growing faster (at 4.5 percent) than for men (3.9 percent).

- one out of every four Black men will go to prison at some point in his life. It is important to emphasize that this refers only to prison, not to jail, parole, or probation.

## The Mainstream Media

IMPRISONMENT IS A major social problem in the U.S. While the entire social fabric is disintegrating (schools and hospitals are closing, housing is increasingly unavailable, jobs are disappearing, life expectancy for Black people is decreasing), the only budget items still being funded are tasks of destruction like prisons and war. In this context, even the mainstream media are forced to acknowledge that the bulging prison system is a problem.

This, however, certainly doesn't mean that the media will acknowledge the true nature of the problem. For example, in the past several years, the *New York Times* has printed several very long articles on some issues surrounding the rapidly expanding prison system. All of these uniformly, even studiously, fail to mention Black people. One of the articles contained 36 paragraphs but didn't mention any racial dynamic until the 35th paragraph, and then there was only a brief allusion to "minorities." A short while ago, a major article on imprisonment appeared in the prestigious U.S. journal, *Science*. The central question in the article was what accounts for the soaring imprisonment rate. There was almost no mention of Black imprisonment and its implications. Clearly, it is not to the advantage of the mainstream media to report accurately what is happening in prisons.

## Why Are Imprisonment Rates So High?

IMPRISONMENT RATES IN the U.S. were first compiled on a regular basis in 1925. From then until 1971, or for almost 50 years, the rates stayed more or less constant. Then in 1972 the rates started zooming upward and have not yet stopped. U.S. imprisonment rates have tripled in the past twenty years.

The 1960s saw the birth and rise of groups such as the Black Panther Party (BPP), the Provisional Government of the Republic of New Afrika, and the Black Liberation Army. The government viciously attacked the Black Liberation Movement, murdering many members of the BPP, people like Fred Hampton, Mark Clark and Bunchy Carter, and incarcerating dozens upon dozens of Black revolutionaries. According to one article, in the three years after J. Edgar Hoover's infamous COINTELPRO memorandum, dated August 25, 1967, nearly a thousand members of the BPP were arrested and hundreds of key leaders were sent to jail. Another author notes that the ACLU recorded 48 major police-Panther clashes in Chicago alone in 1969, and that "[T]he killings of Hampton and Clark brought the 1969 death toll of Panthers to 28, according to a *Newsweek* report in 1970." In that same year, police jailed or arrested 749 Panthers.

Perhaps the culminating acts of this period were the murder of George Jackson on August 21, 1971, and the great Attica prison rebellion on September 9-13, 1971. Just a few months later the first control unit section of the United States Penitentiary at Marion was established and imprisonment rates began to soar.

## Do Prisons Deter Crime?

THE QUESTION OF whether or not prisons deter crime is central to this discussion. It may come as a surprise to some that virtually everyone who has studied this question believes that prisons do not deter crime. A few quotes might be illuminating.

- In 1976 the Panel on Research on Deterrent and Incapacitative Effects was established to investigate the appropriate role of prisons in reducing the crime rate. After a meticulous analysis of the existing research and a great deal of original empirical research, the panel reported: "California and Massachusetts, for example, must increase their index prison populations by over 150 percent and 310 percent, respectively, in order to achieve a 10 percent reduction in index crimes through incapacitation.... Thus, policy suggestions, based upon the existing evidence, can only be made with a clear recognition of the inadequacy of the evidence. Accordingly, such suggestions must be very limited and posed with great caution....Policy makers in the criminal justice system are done a great disservice if they are left with the impression that the empirical evidence, which they themselves are frequently unable to evaluate, strongly supports the deterrence hypothesis. Furthermore, such distortions ultimately undermine the credibility of scientific evidence as inputs to public policy choices."

- Again, by a criminologist: "The results reported in the previous section provide no reliable evidence that risk of imprisonment or time served has a measurable impact on the index crime rate."

- In still one more report, "the National Academy of Sciences, in a 1981 summary of previous penal research, concluded that 'caution should be exercised in interpreting the available evidence as establishing a deterrent effect, and especially so for the sanction of imprisonment'."

- And still again, by another criminologist: "Incapacitation appears to have been only slightly more effective in averting crimes in the early 1980s than in the 1970s, despite a near doubling of the U.S. prison populations in less than ten years."

- From Minnesota's Assistant Commissioner of Corrections: "There is no relationship between the incarceration rate and violent crime. We're in the business of tricking people into thinking that spending hundreds of millions [of dollars] for new prisons will make them safe."

- From the Correctional Association of New York: "The state's new policies have been staggeringly expensive, have threatened a crisis of safety and manageability in the prison system, and have failed to reduce the rate of crime or even stop its increase. After almost ten years of getting tough the citizens of New York are more likely to be victims of crime today than in 1971. Moreover, the largest rise in crime came at the end of the decade, during 1980-81, well after the introduction of more severe sentencing practices."

- The American Bar Association's Task Force on Crime has stated: "There is no solid evidence to support the conclusion that sending more convicted offenders to prison for longer periods of time deters others from committing crime."

- Even the Director of Corrections of Alabama understands this situation: "We're on a train that has to be turned around. It doesn't make any sense to pump millions and millions into corrections and have no effect on the crime rate."

- Finally, from the Director of the Department of Corrections of Illinois: "No state has shown that locking up record amounts of people adds benefit to the society."

## What Should We Make of All Of This?

WE HAVE SEEN that prisons incarcerate huge numbers of Black people. We have seen that the initiation of the rapidly spiraling imprisonment rate coincided with the prominence of the Black Liberation movement. We have also seen that prisons do not deter crime. And certainly no one seems to believe any longer that prisons rehabilitate people. Finally, it turns out that prisons are enormously expensive. For example, the entire budget for "justice system expenditures" in 1988 was $60 billion dollars. "Corrections expenditures" accounted for over $19 billion of this. (It has been estimated that all the children of the world could be fully vaccinated for about one billion dollars.) Furthermore, it costs about $20,000 a year to send a person to prison, about what it would cost to send that person to Harvard.

And so it is natural to ask, what is it that a system like this does? What is its purpose. The most reasonable explana-

tion, the one that best fits the facts, is that prison is a control mechanism for people of color, some form of counter-insurgency which has as its purpose the goal of preventing rebellion by people of color within the borders of the U.S.

## Are Activists Interested In Prisons?

WHAT WILL IT take for progressive white people to do something about this gulag system?

Initially, I think that we must stop believing that prisons have anything to do with crime. If the arguments that I have tried to set forward here are not convincing, then any one of the dozens of books are readily available on this topic. If we believe that prisons are not about crime, then they must be about some form of control of Black people.

Except for a few isolated organizations, there is no outside prison movement in this country and there is very little interest in prisons, as far as we can determine. I work with an organization called the Committee to End the Marion Lockdown (CEML). Marion is a federal prison, located in southern Illinois and widely believed to be the most inhumane prison in the country. Among other critics, Marion has been condemned by Amnesty International for violating almost all of the United Nations' Standard Minimum Rules for the Treatment of Prisoners.

This past September, on the 20th anniversary of the great rebellion at Attica prison, we showed the award winning film *Attica* and featured Akil al-Jundi, one of the Attica brothers who was wounded on the yard during the storming of the prison. Few white people attended the program despite the fact that just a few months earlier 300 white people turned out to the very same auditorium to hear someone explain the lies the media tell about Central America. When Noam Chomsky last spoke in the Chicago area, 7,000 people, virtually every one of them white, came to hear him. If these figures in any way represent the interest that white progressive people in this country have in prisons, and I think

they do, then long before there can be any serious large-scale activity against the racist onslaught that is prisons, we must first determine how we can educate ourselves.

## What Could Be Done? What Is Being Done?

THE COMMITTEE TO End the Marion Lockdown has been in existence for almost seven years. During this time we have grown, slowly but steadily, into a Chicago-based organization that has a large mailing list and group of friends across the country. Together, we have been able to bring about some small changes at Marion and, we hope, shape some of the discussion around the process that just recently was described by Human Rights Watch as the "Marionization" of the entire U.S. prison system. We have a large array of resources including several videos, we hold forums, we are invited to speak in other cities—sometimes to discuss our experiences in prison organizing, sometimes to debate wardens, and we demonstrate frequently at Marion and other relevant sites. When J. Michael Qunilan, Director of the Federal Bureau of Prisons, came to Chicago to address the American Society of Criminologists in 1988, we attended his workshop and questioned him about Marion prison. Rather than answer our questions he left the workshop, the conference, and the city all within an hour. When we spoke at a workshop the following day, the room was overflowing with people who had witnessed or heard about our confrontation with Quinlan.

Wherever we go we try to explain how we view prisons in the context of white supremacy and why we think it is important that progressive people fight against prisons and the associated ideology. This year we have set the weekend of May 1 for national demonstrations in many cities. These demonstrations will target some local issue as well as the issue of the growth of control unit prisons like Marion. We hope that some readers of this article will find this area of work important and will become active in it.

# The New Chain Gangs

FRANK BENTAYOU

*Frank Bentayou is a free-lance writer in Shaker Heights, Ohio.*

Shift-change time at Ohio's Southeast Correctional Institution: Guards are laughing as Sergeant J.A. Jeff Scudder, a short bull of a man, struggles to fold up the sleeves of his black uniform. The coarse fabric barely stretches over his upper arms, which are thick as hams.

Scudder's first job today is showing nine new prisoners how to "make a tight rack"—straighten up their beds, he politely explains—and stow their gear. But first he girds himself for battle. After wrestling with the sleeves, he slips a stiff-brim drill-instructor's hat onto his head, bristling with stubble from a close cut.

"You have to teach these guys everything," he says. Calm and neat in his starched uniform, Scudder strolls toward a group of men wearing tattered white jumpsuits and clutching laundry bags. As he approaches, he suddenly explodes and shoots out his hands to grab two prisoners, jerking them toward a wall.

"All right, you pigs, maggots!" Scudder shouts. "Get over here at attention! Now!" A few croak a hasty, "Sir, yes sir!" as they scramble to comply, but Scudder swirls and seizes a youth by the collar.

"What's a matter with you, puke?" Scudder yells in his face, his voice breaking, eyes popping from their sockets. "Haven't you learned how to talk to a guard?"

"Sir, no sir! Yes, sir—" the man stammers.

"You disgusting maggot!" Scudder screams. "Gimme twenty pushups." He hurls him to the floor, then whirls and snatches two laundry bags. In a rage, he dumps them on the floor, too, and kicks the limp garments repeatedly as the prisoners stare at him.

Scudder's dramatic transformation might amaze anybody who hasn't spent time around an institution like this one. It was my second day visiting Camp REAMS, so I understood that the young guard behaved as he is paid to do and that the facility he works for is not like most other prisons.

In fact, REAMS—the acronym stands for Respect, Education, Attitude, Motivation, and Success—is one of at least thirty-four boot camps launched by U.S. prison systems in the past nine years. State corrections officials and lawmakers are so impressed with them that they're planning at least ten more. Aimed at young, usually first-time offenders convicted of nonviolent crimes, they embody military-style discipline, chain-gang labor, and often the kind of brutal treatment Scudder displays. To the chagrin of earnest prison reformers, it is just those features that have made "shock incarceration" the fastest-growing trend in penology, applauded in middle America and embraced by recent Administrations.

According to specialists at the U.S. Justice Department's National Institute of Justice, the new boot camps have sucked up tens of millions in state and Federal corrections dollars for construction and millions more for operations. Yet no one has shown clearly that this approach to punishment actually helps turn young law-breakers away from crime.

In fact, the strategy of battering and demeaning young offenders to "scare them straight" may do the opposite. Some warn that it may instill dangerous resentment in volatile youths and send them a message that such violent behavior as their guards routinely practice has a place in our society. Still, savaging prisoners, working them hard, and subjecting them to strict—and arbitrary—rules seem to appeal to the same public that, in 1988, responded favorably to George Bush's Willie Horton campaign ads.

I think this approach is what people want," says Major Ralph Coyle, the Camp's thirty-three-year-old commander. "They're tired of driving by and seeing a prisoner sitting on a $6,000 John Deere tractor mowing the lawn. I'm tired of it, too. So these guys work hard. And when they mow a lawn, it's with one of those little push-type reel mowers over there. People want to see these guys working."

At boot camps, they work. They clear brush, saw logs, build fences, bust up rocks—all by hand. They also suffer the insults and capricious abuse of tough guards whom they must treat with exaggerated respect.

At REAMS, hard labor starts a few days after inmates arrive; the authoritarian rule starts the moment they step into camp. On Wednesday, intake day, a van stops in a yard surrounded by a tall fence looped with razor wire. The ten passengers, first-time felons recommended for the program, have agreed to work here for three months, followed by time in a halfway house and then probation, in exchange for the shorter sentences.

"They've been briefed on what it's like here," Coyle tells me with a smile. "But they don't really know what to expect."

The guards, like Scudder done up in black drill-instructor uniforms, hats low over their eyes, stand and wait a moment for effect. Then they rush the van. Screaming orders, they throw open the door and begin hurling prisoners out onto the gravel yard.

"Get outta there, you damn maggot!" "Move it, slime!" they shout.

A slender guard with a narrow mustache shoves a prisoner toward the fence, thrusting his chin to within an inch of the youth's cheek. "If I see that smirk on your face again," he growls, saliva flying, "I'm gonna put you through that goddamn fence." He pulls back and yells at the group, "Now we're gonna teach you some damn courtesy."

During the first two days, guards do just that. They shout conflicting orders, march the inmates, shave their heads, belittle them, scream epithets—"fat boy," "crackhead," "geek," and "peter puffer." One drops out, begging to be sent to prison for his full eighteen-month term. Standing in a corner with his hands cuffed behind him, Julius Cheney, a twenty-five-year-old drug dealer, tells me, "I can't take it. I'm just gonna do my time." Then he cries.

"One or two or three will drop out," Coyle says, "usually in the first couple of days. We're not for everybody. But I warn them about what happens to the young guys up the hill," he says, waving vaguely toward Southeast Correctional, the 1,600-inmate medium-security prison on whose ground Camp REAMS is located.

No one has proved prisoners at vast correctional warehouses like SCI are more apt to return to crime than boot-camp alumni, but the bandwagon for shock incarceration keeps rolling. In addition to the thirty-four like REAMS, juvenile systems have opened camps, and there are also camps for women. New York has five boot camps with a population of more than 1,500, and the state plans more. An Ohio guard jokes that "the job market for former Marine DIs [drill instructors] has never been better."

The media have covered shock prisons in a mostly supportive and uncritical manner. Some articles in newspapers and magazines focus on success stories of inmates who, in the course of boot camp, take control of their lives. Others emphasize how caring guards are beneath their rough facades. Jerome G. Miller, a prison reformer, laughs and says, "These places make great TV." In fact, all the positive media coverage, he says, "is one reason politicians love them so much. Of all the human services—if you can call corrections a human service—it's the one most likely to be run by sound bites."

Miller, who heads the Virginia-based National Center for Institutions and Alternatives, a nonprofit organization that develops alternative sentencing options mostly for criminal-defense teams, has been tracking boot camps since their emergence. The former sociology professor, correctional administrator, and author of *Last One Over the Wall*, a book about juvenile corrections, says, "This movement is just the latest corrections fad. I don't think it's necessary. If you treat people in prison decently, you can get good results."

Miller considers good results to be something better than the grim recidivism rate of felons in the United States, where

at least 40 per cent return to criminal behavior, many ending up back behind bars. The national prison population has been growing at a rate of almost 7 per cent a year, according to the Washington-based Sentencing Project, a private research group. Whatever prisons are doing today is not wildly successful.

A visit to any large state institution shows why: Rehabilitation plays virtually no role. Prisoners mostly laze around in their cells or the yard, pump iron, or socialize—if you can call it that. Inmates, particularly young ones, who seek what educational programs are available find themselves shunned, intimidated, and bullied by their more cynical peers.

Prison officials hope shock incarceration will improve things. "We aim everything here at getting these kids to change," Coyle explains. "All of this discipline you've seen and the rough treatment, the hard labor, that's part of it. You have to get their attention to get them to change. Then they can feel positive about having gotten through something challenging."

If the hard work and discipline were all there is to the approach, it might represent just another vengeful response to crime. The rise in both numbers of prisoners—there are 1.1 million felons locked away in the United States, a total that doubled between 1980 and 1990, that tripled between 1970 and 1990—and the toughness of sentences reflect an increasingly harsh public attitude. To Ohio's and some other states' credit, many boot-camp planners also fold in a measure of rehabilitation aimed at these eighteen- to twenty-five-year-olds.

"This is the way we envisioned shock-incarceration camps from the beginning," says Ronald Powell, head of the New Hampshire prison system. "They're aimed at a high-risk population and must combine intensive rehabilitation services with the military boot-camp approach." He believes they need education programs, like the high-school equivalency classes REAMS offers, peer tutoring by inmates who have degrees, drug rehab, and what Powell calls "character-building sessions." Without such features, he predicts, "we'll see some notable failures in the coming years."

In 1983, Powell helped set up the first prison boot camp in Dodge County, Georgia. "Crime, in my mind, is more related to character disorders than to the broader sociological trends some people cite," he says. "We try to get back to individual values. The hope is that we can take a young man with these disorders and produce, well, a man. With a few reservations, I think it works."

Critic Jerry Miller, on the other hand, has many reservations. "Yes, if you include this expensive after-care, maybe there's a possibility the recidivism rate for shock prisons will improve, but who's to

say a traditional prison wouldn't have the same effect if it had all these programs, halfway houses, and probationary terms?"

The point, Miller says, is that "we should concentrate on what we know works—provide rehab programs to inmates, provide alternative sentencing to many of them, get them into community-service projects." All this shouting and shoving only sends young run-amoks the wrong message, he believes: "You get all this sadism from the guards in this situation, and who knows what can happen?"

That's an issue Powell says he considered in New Hampshire. His fear was that guards could too zealously harass a particularly unstable prisoner and cause an incident, even a riot. Someone could get badly hurt or killed. Powell says that in New Hampshire, he has structured his program differently from, say, the camp in Ohio: "We tolerate no physical or verbal abuse of any kind." Coyle, however, thinks of harsh verbal commands and physical prodding as important elements of Camp REAMS.

Some policy-makers and scholars, in their search for answers, are applying standards to corrections that seem to work with other social problems. Much of what they've learned has strengthened the skeptics' position: Shock prisons do some of what the zealots claim—but only when they're set up and operated with tremendous care, a level of care that's hard for a corrections system to approach, let alone sustain.

By being selective about admissions, for instance, a corrections system might save some money, though boot camps can be costly. Oklahoma gave its 1991 boot-camp per-bed cost at $23,500, while beds at its regular prisons cost $17,800. The advantage was that the ninety-day program processes more inmates per bed each year.

"Unfortunately," says Doris MacKenzie, "the planning and training aren't always the best. A system might put offenders who otherwise would get probation or parole in a boot camp, and that would cost quite a lot more." A professor and criminologist at the University of Maryland, she has offered to help the Corrections Institute develop guidelines for operations. So far, no one can tell policymakers what works. The lack of guidelines hasn't stopped corrections systems from buying drill-instructor hats and sharp uniforms, hiring some guards, and diving in.

"As it stands now," MacKenzie explains, "we've got county and city systems setting up boot camps. There are juvenile systems, too. Some of them don't have any idea what they're doing. What we want from a prison is to prompt some attitude change on the part of these young offenders. We frankly don't yet know if this is the way to get it."

Of the prison guards he's seen, Jerry Miller says, "The closest they've ever gotten to a real boot camp is *Gomer Pyle*. And I don't see much sign that the training is getting better."

In response to such concerns, the National Institute of Corrections also urges more research. Last fall, Susan Hunter, chief of the Prisons Division, issued a plea to scholars to submit proposals. The Justice Department will finance some of the efforts, though its apparent largess raises a flag to some. As Miller says, "You've got to remember that Justice under recent Republican Administrations has been a big supporter of boot camps. How likely do you think it is that studies they sponsor will show boot camps don't work?"

In fact, Anna Thompson, a correctional-program specialist at the NIC, says the Institute isn't really testing the underlying value of shock incarceration. It's just developing what she calls "an implementation and training guide for boot camps, sort of a cookbook on how to put them together."

Possibly prison boot camps, as they now operate around the country, may actually help some troubled kids change. But no one knows in what direction or for how long. Considering the kind of model such guards as Jeff Scudder present to the young men whom they pummel and excoriate, we may be unhappy with the outcome.

Back at Camp REAMS, Scudder finishes his hour-long performance playing bad cop, showing new inmates how to make a tight rack and precisely tuck away all personal belongings into a foot locker. Wiping his damp head and neck, he begins to transform himself back into the earnest and friendly young man he was when we first met.

"I feel I'm on a mission," he says. "These guys have lost control, and it's my mission to try to show them how to put some order in their lives."

Scudder has been masterful as a raging DI, and his intention seems laudable. Still, questions hang in the air: What is the shock camp's real effect on prisoners, and what will be its effect on society?

# The Costliest Punishment–A Corrections Administrator Contemplates the Death Penalty

## Paul W. Keve

*The author is professor emeritus, administration of justice, Virginia Commonwealth University, and former director of corrections departments in Delaware and Minnesota.*

It's a provocative question–when most of the Western nations have abolished capital punishment why does the United States go so resolutely against this humane current trend? Also a provocative question–why does this country sentence so many to death and then actually execute so few? The questions and their answers tell us much about the futility and counterproductive nature of this final penalty.

Ostensible support for capital punishment is seen in the fact that in 53 jurisdictions (the 50 states, the District of Columbia, the Federal justice system, and the U.S. Military), there are 38 that authorize the death penalty, and as of the end of 1991 the death rows of 36 of the states were loaded with a total of 2,547 men and women.[1]

The glut of condemned persons reflects an approving attitude which is encouraged by the frequent pronouncements of elected public officials. Every political campaign rings with cries for law and order, including reiterated declarations in favor of capital punishment by most candidates. Indeed, there have been particular campaigns in which the choice between two contestants has seemed to be determined largely by which one has called the loudest for more use of the death penalty.

But despite the proclamations in favor of it, and despite the steady accretions of death row populations, the country is persistently reluctant actually to execute. During the last decade we have been adding an average of about 170 new cases each year to the death rows while the actual executions have been averaging only about 21 annually.[2]

And now in the year just past, 1991, the execution count dropped to only 14![3] Of course the quick response to this from the true believer in capital punishment is to argue that the pace must be stepped up; that the successive appeals must somehow be curtailed and executions expedited. But my argument is that the pace cannot be materially speeded, nor should it be. The only sensible way out of the cumbersome problems with this penalty is in its abolishment.

There are good and practical reasons why the appeals must not be curtailed, but additionally, can it be that even the politicians who demand the penalty actually do not want the executions to go forward any faster? A believable point. A full-scale rate of executions commensurate with the rate of sentencing to death would be the sort of bloodbath that might well cause a revulsion which could reverse or appreciably reduce the present support for the penalty. By loudly demanding the death penalty's availability and use legislators can maintain their image of being "tough on crime," while at the same time feeling assured that the mere token rate of actual executions will prevent what would become unacceptably barbaric results.

Any casual daily reading of the news makes it evident that the average citizen is unaware of the vast difference between the presumed high use of the death penalty and the paucity of executions actually accomplished. And the discrepancy is much greater than that suggested by comparing the execution count with the 170-plus annual additions to the death rows. For if all the original death sentences were sustained the growth rate would be nearly twice what it is, since actual sentences are 300 or more annually.[4] The shrinkage of nearly 50 percent tells much about why the appeals process is so valid and must be unabridged. It means that the appeals are indeed showing up defects in a high proportion of capital convictions.

It is a point on which the public seems to be deceived, and the news media seems quite willing to support the illusion that death sentences always are valid and will be carried out. The media, like the public generally, seems to prefer the illusion to the reality.

This article originally appeared in *Federal Probation*, Vol. 56, No. 1, March 1992, pp. 11-15.

The public ought to be told—repeatedly—that the criminal justice system should not and cannot carry out the rate of executions that is now generally expected. For instance, suppose our rate of executing were to increase, let's say, to 25 per year. It would still take us fully a century to execute all the persons presently waiting on all the death rows! Furthermore, if the present rate of growth were to continue, there would be, during that century, another 17,000 or more new cases added to the backlog on the death rows! One writer calculates that for every person actually executed the U.S. courts are pronouncing 30 death sentences![5] Obviously the vast majority of ordered executions will never be carried out.

### A TOKEN PUNISHMENT

A sober look at the facts should persuade us that our constant effort to implement the capital punishment laws can never bring more than this kind of pretense. In effect, we are resorting to an occasional execution to keep ourselves persuaded that we are being tough on crime. It is a remarkably expensive pretense, and it adds to the anguish of all those involved in any murder and execution. Furthermore, if this corrections administrator's view is valid, the penalty serves no useful purpose and would be even less useful if executions were to keep pace with the sentencing.

The public's unawareness of how unlikely it is that a death sentence will result in actual execution is exceeded only by its unawareness of the exorbitant price we must pay to maintain our token death penalty. The public does know well enough that imprisonment is very expensive, and the mistaken inference, for most people, is that execution consequently must be much cheaper than life imprisonment. In a New York state poll, for instance, a 72 percent support for the death penalty dropped to 56 percent when the persons polled were informed that the death penalty is more costly than life imprisonment.[6]

As a useful example, in my state of Virginia the cost of keeping one person in prison is calculated at a current average of about $17,000 per year.[7] It is much too easy for the public to look at such a figure and think of what it would presumably cost if a young man of 20 or so would come into prison with a life sentence that might keep him inside for perhaps 40 years. The accumulated total would come to a staggering amount. Wouldn't it be much cheaper to sentence him to death and save all that imprisonment cost?

Not so. The dollar argument leads quite the other way.

In the first place, that figure for the annual cost of imprisonment is misleading. The costs in running a prison are mainly fixed costs; as long as the prison is there and operating it has a steady annual cost that is not affected by minor variations in its prisoner population. In other words, as long as we have the prison anyway we do not save money by taking one prisoner out either to turn him loose or to execute him. Nor does it increase the overall cost noticeably to add one more prisoner. So an execution cannot truly be shown to save any imprisonment cost at all, even when compared with a life sentence.

But the cost of executing—now that's another matter.

### CAPITAL PROSECUTIONS: THE TAXPAYER'S BURDEN

A principle that can be counted on absolutely is that the more severe the possible punishment, the more energetic will be the defense and the more costly the prosecution. The death penalty is the ultimate example of this. In 1976 the U.S. Supreme Court approved the principles which, in its opinion, would make the death penalty constitutional. In deciding three capital cases it specified that (1) the sentencing in such cases must be done in trials that are separate from the trials which determine guilt or innocence; (2) the sentencing hearing must examine both mitigating and aggravating factors, including pertinent features of the defendant's life and character as well as the conditions of the crime; and (3) each death sentence must be followed by an automatic right of appeal to the highest state court. Of course, each of these requirements imposes substantial additional costs.

In the first place, defendants in capital cases almost invariably are indigent and so must be served with defense counsel at the expense of the state. In a capital case the number of pretrial motions filed becomes excessive as compared with noncapital cases. "Jury selection is estimated to take, on the average, 5.3 times longer than jury selection for a noncapital case.... [and it takes] approximately 3.5 times longer to try capital cases than to try noncapital murder cases."[8] The trials are longer than in noncapital cases, requiring more time of judges, juries, and all court personnel. And even with all this, the trial is only the first stage of a torturous process.

In preparation for the penalty phase the defense must make extensive investigation of the defendant's life history, with all the costs of special investigators and usually considerable travel expense. The prosecution will also have to go over much of the same ground. And once the sentence is pronounced the required appeal process begins, with a certainty that reversals will occur in a high percentage of cases. According to one count, from 1976 to 1989 more than 1,400 death penalty cases in the U.S. were reversed by appellate courts. About half of death sentences are being overturned on appeals.[9] After a reversal the case must go back to square one and start over again.

Meanwhile the defendant is held in idleness on death row where the operating cost is far greater than in other prison units. Those who are finally executed wait there an average of 6 to 8 years, while those not executed often wait much longer before their sentences are reversed or commuted to life.

Such observations are barely able to suggest the overwhelming complexity that now characterizes legal procedure in capital cases. The extensive literature on the subject details a body of law so specialized and labyrinthine that few defense attorneys can be expected to master it, and few states can be expected to finance the defense of such cases adequately.

Several states have made serious efforts to assess the cost of implementing the death penalty, though the findings have been given remarkably little publicity considering their dramatic quality. In 1982 the New York State Defenders Association made a substantial study of what it would cost to restore the death penalty in that state; it was calculated that "the potential costs of litigating a model New York capital case across just the first three levels of review [would be] $1.9 million per case."[10]

In 1982 New Jersey adopted a death penalty despite an estimate that it would increase the state's criminal justice costs by $16 million annually.[11] In Kansas a move to reestablish the death penalty was defeated partially on the basis of a 1987 study by the Kansas Legislative Research Department that the presence of the death penalty would cost the state an extra $11,420,000 annually.[12] In 1989 a fiscal impact statement produced for the Indiana legislature found that the state would expect to save more than $5 million annually by abolishment of its death penalty.[13]

Florida, the state with the second most populous death row, seems to be paying at the highest level of any, with a calculated cost of each execution figured at $3,178,000.[14] Similar findings have been produced by fiscal studies in Ohio and Oregon. With prices like these it would seem much more practical to spend that money instead on more social services to prevent violent crimes, more police services, and more services to deal constructively with the needs of victims' families.

## HIGH EXPENDITURES WITH NO GAIN

Of course, the issue of cost is the least worthy of any arguments regarding the merits of the death penalty, for we should not flinch at the cost necessary for reduction of such a heinous crime as murder. That raises the controversial question of the deterrent value of the penalty, an issue that cannot be finally resolved to everyone's satisfaction. My own viewpoint comes from experience of more than 50 years in the field of corrections, including responsibility for top administration of correctional systems in two states, one with

the death penalty and one without. Over that half century I have had ample opportunity to know many men and women who had committed murder, some of whom were sentenced to death. Even though their crimes are brutal, it seems impossible to know these offenders well and to conclude that the threat of death would have stopped them. Often chronic misfits with years of failures behind them, they are driven by the towering impulse of the moment and incapable of making any fine distinction between consequences of imprisonment versus death. This observation agrees with the convictions generally of criminologists today who find no deterrent effect in the death penalty.

Some years ago a fellow corrections administrator, with years of experience in the California system, drew the same conclusion and noted the public's refusal to face the facts. "It is the unique deterrent value capital punishment is presumed to have that provides the mainstay of the arguments for retention of the death penalty. That this is true has been refuted year after year before the Legislature by a variety of witnesses—statistical experts, police officials from abolition states, psychiatrists, and criminologists among others"[15]

## THE DEATH PENALTY AS PROVOCATIVE OF MURDER

There is another point about the nonutility of the death penalty—a point also unprovable but made convincing by years of experience. That is, I am convinced that I know of a number of murder victims who would still be alive if the death penalty had not been in effect. Sometimes a person has a wish to commit suicide at the same time that he has an incapacity to do it to himself. For some troubled people, at a subconscious level there is still a residue of the age-old suicide stigma that prevents the person from contriving his own death. But if the state will do it for him then his purpose is accomplished while he is relieved of the stigma. By committing a murder he callously exploits the state's willingness to abet a suicide. Sick and warped as it is, the pattern does exist and can be seen as the psychological condition in more than a few murders. One psychiatrist, observing the same phenomenon, commented that the death penalty "becomes a promise, a contract, a covenant between society and certain (by no means rare) warped mentalities who are moved to kill as part of a self-destructive urge."[16]

The pattern is reflected in the many cases of defendants who refuse to fight their death sentences, sometimes even bringing action to force the state to proceed with the execution. One writer points out that after the death penalty was reinstituted in 1976, five of the first eight men to be executed vigorously opposed any efforts by others to forestall their executions.[17] It becomes a bizarre perversion of the law's intent thus to reward the murderer by implementing the suicide which he wanted but which he could not do for himself.

In a similar category is the individual who suffers inwardly with intense frustration from never having accomplished anything of note in his unrewarding life. For this person the death penalty offers the chance, by committing a murder, to enjoy the spotlight with gripping notoriety for a brief season. Public excitement over his execution guarantees him the reward he seeks, the fame he has otherwise missed.

## RESTRICTING APPEALS: A FALSE CONCEPT

With the prolonged and repetitive stages of appeals that keep capital cases languishing on death rows for years it is altogether natural that persons unfamiliar with the intricacies of the criminal justice system should see as a "solution" a drastic reduction of the prisoner's right to successive appeals. But here again there is vital reason for moving with great caution. The proven fact is that, contrary to popular assumptions about reliability of modern court processes, mistakes are still being made. Evidence for this has been gathered in very recent years by two researchers who have scouted all the U.S. cases since 1900 in which capital convictions were obtained but later set aside.

The project located a total of 350 men and women who were subjects of erroneous capital convictions! A detailed report of the findings was published in 1987, but the researchers still find evidence that such cases continue to occur.[18] And as another research team reports, "Wrongful sentencing of innocent people shows no sign of diminishing with the passage of time. Indeed the capital punishment system seems to be becoming even less reliable over time. In 1987, 1988 and the first seven months of 1989 alone, at least a dozen more men who had received death sentences have been released as innocent."[19]

The conclusion is inescapable that it is still all too easy for fatal mistakes to be made, and as long as this is so we cannot afford to curtail any defendant's right to contest his conviction. If the protracted and costly appeal process is considered too burdensome the only acceptable solution is just to eliminate the death penalty.

Meanwhile, however, if defendants are going to get the quality of defense that our society now considers minimal there must be well funded and well trained defense counsel. But for many states the cost is beyond the resources the state is willing to commit. Adequate defense of a capital case calls for a great amount of time on the part of defense attorneys who have special knowledge and skill in this area of the criminal law that is so complex and so specialized that few are truly qualified. There is so much time involved for the attorney who would undertake it that most of them are reluctant to tolerate the resultant sacrifice of their law practice. An end result may often be to raise a constitutional question; a low limit set by a state on the amount allowed for a defense attorney's fee in a capital case has the likely effect of denying to the defendant the minimum legal defense that today's standards declare to be his right.[20]

## CONSIDER FEELINGS OF THE VICTIMS

But there is still the question—what about the family of the victim? Don't we owe it to them to proceed swiftly to execute the murderer? Proponents of the death penalty seem to infer that if we do not we are grievously failing in the respect due to the victims. The response to that question can be brief. Murder victim families are entitled to all the help, comfort, and consideration that the state can reasonably give. But there is nothing whatever that we can do by executing the murderer which will restore his victim or bring serenity to the family. Experience shows that comfort and healing simply do not come to the victim families by means of the execution. They deserve from us a much more positive kind of help.

A thoughtful look at the alternatives makes clear that in a state with no death penalty the trial and sentencing are much sooner completed, and the ordeal for victims' families is more quickly over. By contrast, where the death penalty is used the families have a greatly prolonged period of anguish. Through successive appeals, successive execution dates, etc., they are repeatedly interviewed by the news media while their anger and distress are repeatedly revived, sometimes never to be resolved. The death penalty, instead of bringing comfort, actually denies the comfort and instead stretches out the agony endlessly.

In the final analysis, my own opposition to the death penalty is not based so much on its excessive cost, or even its failure to deter crime, but is simply found in these three successive points. (1) The act of murder reveals a lack of respect for human life. (2) In consequence then, we need to encourage a higher respect for life. But finally, (3) it defies all logic to suppose that we can encourage a greater respect for human life by the device of taking human life.

## NOTES

1. *Death Row U.S.A.*, NAACP Legal Defense and Educational Fund, Inc., N.Y., Winter 1991
2. Information furnished to author by editorial offices of *Death Row U.S.A.*
3. Ibid.
4. Ibid.
5. Dave Von Drehle, *Miami Herald*, July 11, 1988.
6. James Alan Fox, Michael L. Radelet, and Julie L. Bonesteel, "Death Penalty Opinion in the Post-Furman Years," *New York University Review of Law and Social Change*, 18(2), 1990–1991, p. 515.

# 6. PUNISHMENT AND CORRECTIONS

7. Information supplied to author by accounting services, Virginia Department of Corrections.

8. Margot Garey, "The Cost of Taking a Life: Dollars and Sense of the Death Penalty," *U.C. Davis Law Review, 18*(4), Summer 1985, pp. 1257–1258.

9. Robert E. Spangenberg, in speech (untitled) at Vanderbilt University, February 22, 1989. Also see, Barry Nakell, "The Cost of the Death Penalty," *Criminal Law Bulletin, 14*(1), January/February 1978, p. 69; and Margot Garey, "The Cost of Taking a Life: Dollars and Sense of the Death Penalty," *U.C. Davis Law Review, 18*(4), Summer 1985, pp. 1221–1273.

10. Jonathan E. Gradess, *The Washington Post,* February 28, 1988.

11. Margot Garey, "The Cost of Taking a Life: Dollars and Sense of the Death Penalty," *U.C. Davis Law Review, 18*(4), Summer 1985, p. 1261.

12. Dave Von Drehle, *Miami Herald,* July 13, 1988.

13. Indiana State Legislature, Fiscal Impact Statement for SB0531 (replacing death penalty with life imprisonment), January 23, 1989.

14. Von Drehle, op cit.

15. Richard A. McGee, "Capital Punishment as Seen by a Correctional Administrator," *Federal Probation, 28*(2), June 1964, p. 11.

16. Louis J. West, "Psychiatric Reflections on the Death Penalty," in *Capital Punishment in the United States,* by Hugo Adam Bedau and Chester M. Pierce, AMS Press, 1976.

17. Welsh S. White, *The Death Penalty in the Nineties,* Ann Arbor, University of Michigan Press, 1991, p. 164.

18. Hugo Adam Bedau and Michael L. Radelet, "Miscarriages of Justice in Potentially Capital Cases," *Stanford Law Review, 40*(1).

19. Ronald J. Tabak and J. Mark Lane, "The Execution of Injustice: A Cost and Lack-of-Benefit Analysis of the Death Penalty," *Loyola of L.A. Law Review, 23*(1), November 1989, p. 102.

20. Ronald J. Tabak, "The Death of Fairness: The Arbitrary and Capricious Imposition of the Death Penalty in the 1980s," *New York University Review of Law and Social Change, 14*(4), 1986, p. 76.

# 'THIS MAN HAS EXPIRED'

## WITNESS TO AN EXECUTION

### ROBERT JOHNSON

**ROBERT JOHNSON** *is professor of justice, law, and society at The American University, Washington, D.C. This article is drawn from a Distinguished Faculty Lecture, given under the auspices of the university's senate last spring.*

The death penalty has made a comeback in recent years. In the late sixties and through most of the seventies, such a thing seemed impossible. There was a moratorium on executions in the U.S., backed by the authority of the Supreme Court. The hiatus lasted roughly a decade. Coming on the heels of a gradual but persistent decline in the use of the death penalty in the Western world, it appeared to some that executions would pass from the American scene [cf. *Commonweal*, January 15, 1988]. Nothing could have been further from the truth.

Beginning with the execution of Gary Gilmore in 1977, over 100 people have been put to death, most of them in the last few years. Some 2,200 prisoners are presently confined on death rows across the nation. The majority of these prisoners have lived under sentence of death for years, in some cases a decade or more, and are running out of legal appeals. It is fair to say that the death penalty is alive and well in America, and that executions will be with us for the foreseeable future.

Gilmore's execution marked the resurrection of the modern death penalty and was big news. It was commemorated in a best-selling tome by Norman Mailer, *The Executioner's Song*. The title was deceptive. Like others who have examined the death penalty, Mailer told us a great deal about the condemned but very little about the executioners. Indeed, if we dwell on Mailer's account, the executioner's story is not only unsung; it is distorted.

Gilmore's execution was quite atypical. His was an instance of state-assisted suicide accompanied by an element of romance and played out against a backdrop of media fanfare. Unrepentant and unafraid, Gilmore refused to appeal his conviction. He dared the state of Utah to take his life, and the media repeated the challenge until it became a taunt that may well have goaded officials to action. A failed suicide pact with his lover staged only days before the execution, using drugs she delivered to him in a visit marked by unusual intimacy, added a hint of melodrama to the proceedings. Gilmore's final words, "Let's do it," seemed to invite the lethal hail of bullets from the firing squad. The nonchalant phrase, at once fatalistic and brazenly rebellious, became Gilmore's epitaph. It clinched his outlaw-hero image, and found its way onto tee shirts that confirmed his celebrity status.

Befitting a celebrity, Gilmore was treated with unusual leniency by prison officials during his confinement on death row. He was, for example, allowed to hold a party the night before his execution, during which he was free to eat, drink, and make merry with his guests until the early morning hours. This is not entirely unprecedented. Notorious English convicts of centuries past would throw farewell balls in prison on the eve of their executions. News accounts of such affairs sometimes included a commentary on the richness of the table and the quality of the dancing. For the record, Gilmore served Tang, Kool-Aid, cookies, and coffee, later supplemented by contraband pizza and an unidentified liquor. Periodically, he gobbled drugs obligingly provided by the prison pharmacy. He played a modest arrangement of rock music albums but refrained from dancing.

Gilmore's execution generally, like his parting fete, was decidedly out of step with the tenor of the modern death penalty. Most condemned prisoners fight to save their lives, not to have them taken. They do not see their fate in romantic terms; there are no farewell parties. Nor are they given medication to ease their anxiety or win their compliance. The subjects of typical executions remain anonymous to the public and even to their keepers. They are very much alone at the end.

In contrast to Mailer's account, the focus of the research I have conducted is on the executioners themselves as they carry out typical executions. In my experience executioners—not unlike Mailer himself—can be quite voluble, and sometimes quite moving, in expressing themselves. I shall draw upon their words to describe the death work they carry out in our name.

## DEATH WORK AND DEATH WORKERS

Executioners are not a popular subject of social research, let alone conversation at the dinner table or cocktail party. We simply don't give the subject much thought. When we think of executioners at all, the imagery runs to individual men of disreputable, or at least questionable, character who work stealthily behind the scenes to carry out their grim labors. We picture hooded men hiding in the shadow of the gallows, or anonymous figures lurking out of sight behind electric chairs, gas chambers, firing blinds, or, more recently, hospital gurneys. We wonder who would do such grisly work and how they sleep at night.

This image of the executioner as a sinister and often solitary character is today misleading. To be sure, a few states hire free-lance executioners and traffic in macabre theatrics. Executioners may be picked up under cover of darkness and some may still wear black hoods. But today, executions are generally the work of a highly disciplined and efficient team of correctional officers.

Broadly speaking, the execution process as it is now practiced starts with the prisoner's confinement on death row, an oppressive prison-within-a-prison where the condemned are housed, sometimes for years, awaiting execution. Death work gains momentum when an execution date draws near and the prisoner is moved to the death house, a short walk from the death chamber. Finally, the process culminates in the death watch, a twenty-four-hour period that ends when the prisoner has been executed.

This final period, the death watch, is generally undertaken by correctional officers who work as a team and report directly to the prison warden. The warden or his representative, in turn, must by law preside over the execution. In many states, it is a member of the death watch or execution team, acting under the warden's authority, who in fact plays the formal role of executioner. Though this officer may technically work alone, his teammates view the execution as a shared responsibility. As one officer on the death watch told me in no uncertain terms: "We all take part in it; we all play 100 percent in it, too. That takes the load off this one individual [who pulls the switch]." The formal executioner concurred. "Everyone on the team can do it, and nobody will tell you I did it. I know my team." I found nothing in my research to dispute these claims.

The officers of these death watch teams are our modern executioners. As part of a larger study of the death work process, I studied one such group. This team, comprised of nine seasoned officers of varying ranks, had carried out five electrocutions at the time I began my research. I interviewed each officer on the team after the fifth execution, then served as an official witness at a sixth electrocution. Later, I served as a behind-the-scenes observer during their seventh execution.

The results of this phase of my research form the substance of this essay.

## THE DEATH WATCH TEAM

The death watch or execution team members refer to themselves, with evident pride, as simply "the team." This pride is shared by other correctional officials. The warden at the institution I was observing praised members of the team as solid citizens—in his words, country boys. These country boys, he assured me, could be counted on to do the job and do it well. As a fellow administrator put it, "an execution is something [that] needs to be done and good people, dedicated people who believe in the American system, should do it. And there's a certain amount of feeling, probably one to another, that they're part of that—that when they have to hang tough, they can do it, and they can do it right. And that it's just the right thing to do."

The official view is that an execution is a job that has to be done, and done right. The death penalty is, after all, the law of the land. In this context, the phrase "done right" means that an execution should be a proper, professional, dignified undertaking. In the words of a prison administrator, "We had to be sure that we did it properly, professionally, and [that] we gave as much dignity to the person as we possibly could in the process....If you've gotta do it, it might just as well be done the way it's supposed to be done—without any sensation."

In the language of the prison officials, "proper" refers to procedures that go off smoothly; "professional" means without personal feelings that intrude on the procedures in any way. The desire for executions that take place "without any sensation" no doubt refers to the absence of media sensationalism, particularly if there should be an embarrassing and undignified hitch in the procedures, for example, a prisoner who breaks down or becomes violent and must be forcibly placed in the electric chair as witnesses, some from the media, look on in horror. Still, I can't help but note that this may be a revealing slip of the tongue. For executions are indeed meant to go off without any human feeling, without any sensation. A profound absence of feeling would seem to capture the bureaucratic ideal embodied in the modern execution.

The view of executions held by the execution team members parallels that of correctional administrators but is somewhat more restrained. The officers of the team are closer to the killing and dying, and are less apt to wax abstract or eloquent in describing the process. Listen to one man's observations:

It's a job. I don't take it personally. You know, I don't take it like I'm having a grudge against this person and this person has done something to me. I'm just carrying out a job, doing what I was asked to do....This man has been sentenced to death in the courts. This is the law and he broke this law, and he has to suffer the consequences. And one of the consequences is to put him to death.

I found that few members of the execution team support the death penalty outright or without reservation. Having seen executions close up, many of them have lingering doubts about the justice or wisdom of this sanction. As one officer put it:

I'm not sure the death penalty is the right way. I don't know if there is a right answer. So I look at it like this: if it's gotta be done, at least it can be done in a humane way, if there is such a word for it. . . . The only way it should be done, I feel, is the way we do it. It's done professionally; it's not no horseplaying. Everything is done by documentation. On time. By the book.

Arranging executions that occur "without any sensation" and that go "by the book" is no mean task, but it is a task that is undertaken in earnest by the execution team. The tone of the enterprise is set by the team leader, a man who takes a hard-boiled, no-nonsense approach to correctional work in general and death work in particular. "My style," he says, "is this: if it's a job to do, get it done. Do it and that's it." He seeks out kindred spirits, men who see killing condemned prisoners as a job—a dirty job one does reluctantly, perhaps, but above all a job one carries out dispassionately and in the line of duty.

To make sure that line of duty is a straight and accurate one, the death watch team has been carefully drilled by the team leader in the mechanics of execution. The process has been broken down into simple, discrete tasks and practiced repeatedly. The team leader describes the division of labor in the following exchange:

the execution team is a nine-officer team and each one has certain things to do. When I would train you, maybe you'd buckle a belt, that might be all you'd have to do. . . . And you'd be expected to do one thing and that's all you'd be expected to do. And if everybody does what they were taught, or what they were trained to do, at the end the man would be put in the chair and everything would be complete. It's all come together now.

So it's broken down into very small steps. . . .

*Very small,* yes. Each person has *one* thing to do.

I see. What's the purpose of breaking it down into such small steps?

So people won't get confused. I've learned it's kind of a tense time. When you're executin' a person, killing a person—you call it killin', executin', whatever you want—the man dies anyway. I find the less you got on your mind, why, the better you'll carry it out. So it's just very simple things. And so far, you know, it's all come together, we haven't had any problems.

This division of labor allows each man on the execution team to become a specialist, a technician with a sense of pride in his work. Said one man,

My assignment is the leg piece. Right leg. I roll his pants leg up, place a piece [electrode] on his leg, strap his leg in. . . . I've got all the moves down pat. We train from different posts; I can do any of them. But that's my main post.

The implication is not that the officers are incapable of performing multiple or complex tasks, but simply that it is more efficient to focus each officer's efforts on one easy task.

An essential part of the training is practice. Practice is meant to produce a confident group, capable of fast and accurate performance under pressure. The rewards of practice are reaped in improved performance. Executions take place with increasing efficiency, and eventually occur with precision. "The first one was grisly," a team member confided to me. He explained that there was a certain amount of fumbling, which made the execution seem interminable. There were technical problems as well: The generator was set too high so the body was badly burned. But that is the past, the officer assured me. "The ones now, we know what we're doing. It's just like clockwork."

## THE DEATH WATCH

The death-watch team is deployed during the last twenty-four hours before an execution. In the state under study, the death watch starts at 11 o'clock the night before the execution and ends at 11 o'clock the next night when the execution takes place. At least two officers would be with the prisoner at any given time during that period. Their objective is to keep the prisoner alive and "on schedule." That is, to move him through a series of critical and cumulatively demoralizing junctures that begin with his last meal and end with his last walk. When the time comes, they must deliver the prisoner up for execution as quickly and unobtrusively as possible.

Broadly speaking, the job of the death watch officer, as one man put it, "is to sit and keep the inmate calm for the last twenty-four hours—and get the man ready to go." Keeping a condemned prisoner calm means, in part, serving his immediate needs. It seems paradoxical to think of the death watch officers as providing services to the condemned, but the logistics of the job make service a central obligation of the officers. Here's how one officer made this point:

Well, you can't help but be involved with many of the things that he's involved with. Because if he wants to make a call to his family, well, you'll have to dial the number. And you keep records of whatever calls he makes. If he wants a cigarette, well he's not allowed to keep matches so you light it for him. You've got to pour his coffee, too. So you're aware what he's doing. It's not like you can just ignore him. You've gotta just be with him whether he wants it or not, and cater to his needs.

Officers cater to the condemned because contented inmates are easier to keep under control. To a man, the officers say this is so. But one can never trust even a contented, condemned prisoner.

The death-watch officers see condemned prisoners as men with explosive personalities. "You don't know what, what a man's gonna do," noted one officer. "He's liable to snap, he's liable to pass out. We watch him all the time to prevent him from committing suicide. You've got to be ready—he's liable to do anything." The prisoner is never out of at least one officer's sight. Thus surveillance is constant, and control, for all intents and purposes, is total.

Relations between the officers and their charges during the death watch can be quite intense. Watching and being watched are central to this enterprise, and these are always engaging activities, particularly when the stakes are life and death. These relations are, nevertheless, utterly impersonal; there are no grudges but neither is there compassion or fellow-feeling. Officers are civil but cool; they keep an emotional distance from the men they are about to kill. To do otherwise, they maintain, would make it harder to execute condemned prisoners. The attitude of the officers is that the prisoners arrive as strangers and are easier to kill if they stay that way.

During the last five or six hours, two specific team officers are assigned to guard the prisoner. Unlike their more taciturn and aloof colleagues on earlier shifts, these officers make a conscious effort to talk with the prisoner. In one officer's words, "We keep them right there and keep talking to them—about anything except the chair." The point of these conversations is not merely to pass time; it is to keep tabs on the prisoner's state of mind, and to steer him away from subjects that might depress, anger, or otherwise upset him. Sociability, in other words, quite explicitly serves as a source of social control. Relationships, such as they are, serve purely manipulative ends. This is impersonality at its worst, masquerading as concern for the strangers one hopes to execute with as little trouble as possible.

Generally speaking, as the execution moves closer, the mood becomes more somber and subdued. There is a last meal. Prisoners can order pretty much what they want, but most eat little or nothing at all. At this point, the prisoners may steadfastly maintain that their executions will be stayed. Such bravado is belied by their loss of appetite. "You can see them going down," said one officer. "Food is the last thing they got on their minds."

Next the prisoners must box their meager worldly goods. These are inventoried by the staff, recorded on a one-page checklist form, and marked for disposition to family or friends. Prisoners are visibly saddened, even moved to tears, by this procedure, which at once summarizes their lives and highlights the imminence of death. At this point, said one of the officers, "I really get into him; I watch him real close." The execution schedule, the officer pointed out, is "picking up momentum, and we don't want to lose control of the situation."

This momentum is not lost on the condemned prisoner. Critical milestones have been passed. The prisoner moves in a limbo existence devoid of food or possessions; he has seen the last of such things, unless he receives a stay of execution and rejoins the living. His identity is expropriated as well. The critical juncture in this regard is the shaving of the man's head (including facial hair) and right leg. Hair is shaved to facilitate the electrocution; it reduces physical resistance to electricity and minimizes singeing and burning. But the process has obvious psychological significance as well, adding greatly to the momentum of the execution.

The shaving procedure is quite public and intimidating. The condemned man is taken from his cell and seated in the middle of the tier. His hands and feet are cuffed, and he is dressed only in undershorts. The entire death watch team is assembled around him. They stay at a discrete distance, but it is obvious that they are there to maintain control should he resist in any way or make any untoward move. As a rule, the man is overwhelmed. As one officer told me in blunt terms, "Come eight o'clock, we've got a dead man. Eight o'clock is when we shave the man. We take his identity; it goes with the hair." This taking of identity is indeed a collective process—the team makes a forceful "we," the prisoner their helpless object. The staff is confident that the prisoner's capacity to resist is now compromised. What is left of the man erodes gradually and, according the officers, perceptibly over the remaining three hours before the execution.

After the prisoner has been shaved, he is then made to shower and don a fresh set of clothes for the execution. The clothes are unremarkable in appearance, except that velcro replaces buttons and zippers, to reduce the chance of burning the body. The main significance of the clothes is symbolic: they mark the prisoner as a man who is ready for execution. Now physically "prepped," to quote one team member, the prisoner is placed in an empty tomblike cell, the death cell. All that is left is the wait. During this fateful period, the prisoner is more like an object "without any sensation" than like a flesh-and-blood person on the threshold of death.

For condemned prisoners, like Gilmore, who come to accept and even to relish their impending deaths, a genuine calm seems to prevail. It is as if they can transcend the dehumanizing forces at work around them and go to their deaths in peace. For most condemned prisoners, however, numb resignation rather than peaceful acceptance is the norm. By the account of the death-watch officers, these more typical prisoners are beaten men. Listen to the officers' accounts:

> A lot of 'em die in their minds before they go to that chair. I've never known of one or heard of one putting up a fight. . . . By the time they walk to the chair, they've completely faced it. Such a reality most people can't understand. Cause they don't fight it. They don't seem to have anything to say. It's just something like "Get it over with." They may be numb, sort of in a trance.

> They go through stages. And, at this stage, they're real humble. Humblest bunch of people I ever seen. Most all of 'em is real, real weak. Most of the time you'd only need one or two people to carry out an execution, as weak and as humble as they are.

These men seem barely human and alive to their keepers. They wait meekly to be escorted to their deaths. The people who come for them are the warden and the remainder of the death watch team, flanked by high-ranking correctional officials. The warden reads the court order, known popularly as a death warrant. This is, as one officer said, "the real deal," and nobody misses its significance. The condemned prisoners then go to their deaths compliantly, captives of the inexorable, irresistible momentum of the situation. As one officer put it, "There's no struggle. . . . They just walk right on in there." So too, do the staff "just walk right on in there," following a routine they have come to know well. Both the condemned and the executioners, it would seem, find a relief of sorts in mindless mechanical conformity to the modern execution drill.

## WITNESS TO AN EXECUTION

As the team and administrators prepare to commence the good fight, as they might say, another group, the official witnesses, are also preparing themselves for their role in the execution. Numbering between six and twelve for any given execution, the official witnesses are disinterested citizens in good standing drawn from a cross-section of the state's population. If you will, they are every good or decent person, called upon to represent the community and use their good offices to testify to the propriety of the execution. I served as an official witness at the execution of an inmate.

At eight in the evening, about the time the prisoner is shaved in preparation for the execution, the witnesses are assembled. Eleven in all, we included three newspaper and two television reporters, a state trooper, two police officers, a magistrate, a businessman, and myself. We were picked up in the parking lot behind the main office of the corrections department. There was nothing unusual or even memorable about any of this. Gothic touches were notable by their absence. It wasn't a dark and stormy night; no one emerged from the shadows to lead us to the prison gates.

Mundane considerations prevailed. The van sent for us was missing a few rows of seats so there wasn't enough room for all of us. Obliging prison officials volunteered their cars. Our rather ordinary cavalcade reached the prison but only after getting lost. Once within the prison's walls, we were sequestered for some two hours in a bare and almost shabby administrative conference room. A public information officer was assigned to accompany us and answer our questions. We grilled this official about the prisoner and the execution procedure he would undergo shortly, but little information was to be had. The man confessed ignorance on the most basic points. Disgruntled at this and increasingly anxious, we made small talk and drank coffee.

At 10:40 P.M., roughly two-and-a-half hours after we were assembled and only twenty minutes before the execution was scheduled to occur, the witnesses were taken to the basement of the prison's administrative building, frisked, then led down an alleyway that ran along the exterior of the building. We entered a neighboring cell block and were admitted to a vestibule adjoining the death chamber. Each of us signed a log, and was then led off to the witness area. To our left, around a corner some thirty feet away, the prisoner sat in the condemned cell. He couldn't see us, but I'm quite certain he could hear us. It occurred to me that our arrival was a fateful reminder for the prisoner. The next group would be led by the warden, and it would be coming for him.

We entered the witness area, a room within the death chamber, and took our seats. A picture window covering the front wall of the witness room offered a clear view of the electric chair, which was about twelve feet away from us and well illuminated. The chair, a large, high-back solid oak structure with imposing black straps, dominated the death chamber. Behind it, on the back wall, was an open panel full of coils and lights. Peeling paint hung from the ceiling and walls; water stains from persistent leaks were everywhere in evidence.

Two officers, one a hulking figure weighing some 400 pounds, stood alongside the electric chair. Each had his hands crossed at the lap and wore a forbidding, blank expression on his face. The witnesses gazed at them and the chair, most of us scribbling notes furiously. We did this, I suppose, as much to record the experience as to have a distraction from the growing tension. A correctional officer entered the witness room and announced that a trial run of the machinery would be undertaken. Seconds later, lights flashed on the control panel behind the chair indicating that the chair was in working order. A white curtain, opened for the test, separated the chair and the witness area. After the test, the curtain was drawn. More tests were performed behind the curtain. Afterwards, the curtain was reopened, and would be left open until the execution was over. Then it would be closed to allow the officers to remove the body.

A handful of high-level correctional officials were present in the death chamber, standing just outside the witness area. There were two regional administrators, the director of the Department of Corrections, and the prison warden. The prisoner's chaplain and lawyer were also present. Other than the chaplain's black religious garb, subdued grey pinstripes and bland correctional uniforms prevailed. All parties were quite solemn.

At 10:58 the prisoner entered the death chamber. He was, I knew from my research, a man with a checkered, tragic past. He had been grossly abused as a child, and went on to become grossly abusive of others. I was told he could not describe his life, from childhood on, without talking about confrontations in defense of a precarious sense of self—at home, in school, on the streets, in the prison yard. Belittled by life and choking with rage, he was hungry to be noticed. Paradoxically, he had found his moment in the spotlight, but it was a dim and unflattering light cast before a small and unappreciative audience. "He'd pose for cameras in the chair—for the attention," his counselor had told me earlier in the day. But the truth was that the prisoner wasn't smiling, and there were no cameras.

The prisoner walked quickly and silently toward the chair, an escort of officers in tow. His eyes were turned downward, his expression a bit glazed. Like many before him, the prisoner had threatened to stage a last stand. But that was lifetimes ago, on death row. In the death house, he joined the humble bunch and kept to the executioner's schedule. He appeared to have given up on life before he died in the chair.

En route to the chair, the prisoner stumbled slightly, as if the momentum of the event had overtaken him. Were he not held securely by two officers, one at each elbow, he might have fallen. Were the routine to be broken in this or indeed any other way, the officers believe, the prisoner might faint or panic or become violent, and have to be forcibly placed in the chair. Perhaps as a precaution, when the prisoner reached the chair he did not turn on his own but rather was turned, firmly but without malice, by the officers in his escort. These included the two men at his elbows, and four others who followed behind him. Once the prisoner was seated, again with help, the officers strapped him into the chair.

The execution team worked with machine precision. Like a disciplined swarm, they enveloped him. Arms, legs, stomach, chest, and head were secured in a matter of seconds. Electrodes were attached to the cap holding his head and to the strap holding his exposed right leg. A leather mask was placed over his face. The last officer mopped the prisoner's brow, then touched his hand in a gesture of farewell.

During the brief procession to the electric chair, the prisoner was attended by a chaplain. As the execution team worked feverishly to secure the condemned man's body, the chaplain, who appeared to be upset, leaned over him and placed his forehead in contact with the prisoner's, whispering urgently. The priest might have been praying, but I had the impression he was consoling the man, perhaps assuring him that a forgiving God awaited him in the next life. If he heard the chaplain, I doubt the man comprehended his message. He didn't seem comforted. Rather, he looked stricken and appeared to be in shock. Perhaps the priest's urgent ministrations betrayed his doubts that the prisoner could hold himself together. The chaplain then withdrew at the warden's request, allowing the officers to affix the death mask.

The strapped and masked figure sat before us, utterly alone, waiting to be killed. The cap and mask dominated his face. The cap was nothing more than a sponge encased in a leather shell with a metal piece at the top to accept an electrode. It looked decrepit and resembled a cheap, ill-fitting toupee. The mask, made entirely of leather, appeared soiled and worn. It had two parts. The bottom part covered the chin and mouth, the top the eyes and lower forehead. Only the nose was exposed. The effect of a rigidly restrained body, together with the bizarre cap and the protruding nose, was nothing short of grotesque. A faceless man breathed before us in a tragicomic trance, waiting for a blast of electricity that would extinguish his life. Endless seconds passed. His last act was to swallow, nervously, pathetically, with his Adam's apple bobbing. I was struck by that simple movement then, and can't forget it even now. It told me, as nothing else did, that in the prisoner's restrained body, behind that mask, lurked a fellow human being who, at some level, however primitive, knew or sensed himself to be moments from death.

The condemned man sat perfectly still for what seemed an eternity but was in fact no more than thirty seconds. Finally the electricity hit him. His body stiffened spasmodically, though only briefly. A thin swirl of smoke trailed away from his head and then dissipated quickly. The body remained taut, with the right foot raised slightly at the heel, seemingly frozen

there. A brief pause, then another minute of shock. When it was over, the body was flaccid and inert.

Three minutes passed while the officials let the body cool. (Immediately after the execution, I'm told, the body would be too hot to touch and would blister anyone who did.) All eyes were riveted to the chair; I felt trapped in my witness seat, at once transfixed and yet eager for release. I can't recall any clear thoughts from that moment. One of the death watch officers later volunteered that he shared this experience of staring blankly at the execution scene. Had the prisoner's mind been mercifully blank before the end? I hoped so.

An officer walked up to the body, opened the shirt at chest level, then continued on to get the physician from an adjoining room. The physician listened for a heartbeat. Hearing none, he turned to the warden and said, "This man has expired." The warden, speaking to the director, solemnly intoned: "Mr. Director, the court order has been fulfilled." The curtain was then drawn and the witnesses filed out.

## THE MORNING AFTER

As the team prepared the body for the morgue, the witnesses were led to the front door of the prison. On the way, we passed a number of cell blocks. We could hear the normal sounds of prison life, including the occasional catcall and lewd comment hurled at uninvited guests like ourselves. But no trouble came in the wake of the execution. Small protests were going on outside the walls, we were told, but we could not hear them. Soon the media would be gone; the protestors would disperse and head for their homes. The prisoners, already home, had been indifferent to the proceedings, as they always are unless the condemned prisoner had been a figure of some consequence in the convict community. Then there might be tension and maybe even a modest disturbance on a prison tier or two. But few convict luminaries are executed, and the dead man had not been one of them. Our escort officer offered a sad tribute to the prisoner: "The inmates, they didn't care about this guy."

I couldn't help but think they weren't alone in this. The executioners went home and set about their lives. Having taken life, they would savor a bit of life themselves. They showered, ate, made love, slept, then took a day or two off. For some, the prisoner's image would linger for that night. The men who strapped him in remembered what it was like to touch him; they showered as soon as they got home to wash off the feel and smell of death. One official sat up picturing how the prisoner looked at the end. (I had a few drinks myself that night with that same image for company.) There was some talk about delayed reactions to the stress of carrying out executions. Though such concerns seemed remote that evening, I learned later that problems would surface for some of the officers. But no one on the team, then or later, was haunted by the executed man's memory, nor would anyone grieve for him. "When I go home after one of these things," said one man, "I sleep like a rock." His may or may not be the sleep of the just, but one can only marvel at such a thing, and perhaps envy such a man.

# CRIME CLOCK
## 1991

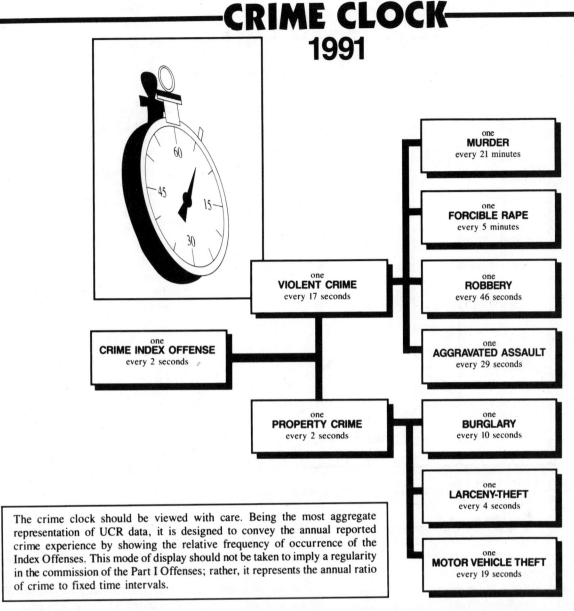

| | |
|---|---|
| one **VIOLENT CRIME** every 17 seconds | one **MURDER** every 21 minutes |
| | one **FORCIBLE RAPE** every 5 minutes |
| one **CRIME INDEX OFFENSE** every 2 seconds | one **ROBBERY** every 46 seconds |
| | one **AGGRAVATED ASSAULT** every 29 seconds |
| one **PROPERTY CRIME** every 2 seconds | one **BURGLARY** every 10 seconds |
| | one **LARCENY-THEFT** every 4 seconds |
| | one **MOTOR VEHICLE THEFT** every 19 seconds |

The crime clock should be viewed with care. Being the most aggregate representation of UCR data, it is designed to convey the annual reported crime experience by showing the relative frequency of occurrence of the Index Offenses. This mode of display should not be taken to imply a regularity in the commission of the Part I Offenses; rather, it represents the annual ratio of crime to fixed time intervals.

# *Crime in the United States 1991*

### Crime Index Total

The Crime Index total rose 3 percent over 1990 to nearly 15 million offenses reported to law enforcement in 1991. Index increases ranged from 2 percent in the Nation's cities to 5 percent in rural counties. Five- and 10-year percent changes showed the 1991 experience was 10 percent above the 1987 level and 15 percent higher than in 1982.

Geographically, the largest volume of Crime Index offenses was reported in the Southern States, which accounted for 37 percent of the total. Following were the Western States with 24 percent, the Midwestern States with 21 percent, and the Northeastern States with 18 percent. All regions except the Northeast showed Crime Index increases from 1990 to 1991.

Crime Index offenses occurred most frequently in August while the lowest totals were recorded in February.

### Rate

Crime rates relate the incidence of crime to population. Nationwide in 1991, there were an estimated 5,898 Crime Index offenses for each 100,000 in population. The Crime Index rate was highest in metropolitan areas and lowest in rural counties. Overall, the 1991 Crime Index rate was 1 percent higher than in 1991, 6 percent higher than in 1987, and 5 percent above the 1982 total.

Regionally, the Crime Index rates ranged from 6,478 in the West to 5,155 in the Northeast. The 2-year percent changes showed a 1-percent rate decline in the Northeast and increases in the remaining regions.

## Table 1.—Index of Crime, United States, 1982–1991

| Population[1] | Crime Index total[2] | Modified Crime Index total[3] | Violent crime[4] | Property crime[4] | Murder and non-negligent man-slaughter | Forcible rape | Robbery | Aggra-vated assault | Burglary | Larceny-theft | Motor vehicle theft | Arson[3] |
|---|---|---|---|---|---|---|---|---|---|---|---|---|
| | | | | | Number of Offenses | | | | | | | |
| **Population by year:** | | | | | | | | | | | | |
| 1982-231,534,000 | 12,974,400 | | 1,322,390 | 11,652,000 | 21,010 | 78,770 | 553,130 | 669,480 | 3,447,100 | 7,142,500 | 1,062,400 | |
| 1983-233,981,000 | 12,108,600 | | 1,258,090 | 10,850,500 | 19,310 | 78,920 | 506,570 | 653,290 | 3,129,900 | 6,712,800 | 1,007,900 | |
| 1984-236,158,000 | 11,881,800 | | 1,273,280 | 10,608,500 | 18,690 | 84,230 | 485,010 | 685,350 | 2,984,400 | 6,591,900 | 1,032,200 | |
| 1985-238,740,000 | 12,431,400 | | 1,328,800 | 11,102,600 | 18,980 | 88,670 | 497,870 | 723,250 | 3,073,300 | 6,926,400 | 1,102,900 | |
| 1986-241,077,000 | 13,211,900 | | 1,489,170 | 11,722,700 | 20,610 | 91,460 | 542,780 | 834,320 | 3,241,400 | 7,257,200 | 1,224,100 | |
| 1987-243,400,000 | 13,508,700 | | 1,484,000 | 12,024,700 | 20,100 | 91,110 | 517,700 | 855,090 | 3,236,200 | 7,499,900 | 1,288,700 | |
| 1988-245,807,000 | 13,923,100 | | 1,566,220 | 12,356,900 | 20,680 | 92,490 | 542,970 | 910,090 | 3,218,100 | 7,705,900 | 1,432,900 | |
| 1989-248,239,000 | 14,251,400 | | 1,646,040 | 12,605,400 | 21,500 | 94,500 | 578,330 | 951,710 | 3,168,200 | 7,872,400 | 1,564,800 | |
| 1990-248,709,873 | 14,475,600 | | 1,820,130 | 12,655,500 | 23,440 | 102,560 | 639,270 | 1,054,860 | 3,073,900 | 7,945,700 | 1,635,900 | |
| 1991-252,177,000 | 14,872,900 | | 1,911,770 | 12,961,100 | 24,700 | 106,590 | 687,730 | 1,092,740 | 3,157,200 | 8,142,200 | 1,661,700 | |
| **Percent change: number of offenses:** | | | | | | | | | | | | |
| 1991/1990 | +2.7 | | +5.0 | +2.4 | +5.4 | +3.9 | +7.6 | +3.6 | +2.7 | +2.5 | +1.6 | |
| 1991/1987 | +10.1 | | +28.8 | +7.8 | +22.9 | +17.0 | +32.8 | +27.8 | -2.4 | +8.6 | +28.9 | |
| 1991/1982 | +14.6 | | +44.6 | +11.2 | +17.6 | +35.3 | +24.3 | +63.2 | -8.4 | +14.0 | +56.4 | |
| | | | | | Rate per 100,000 Inhabitants | | | | | | | |
| **Year:** | | | | | | | | | | | | |
| 1982 | 5,603.6 | | 571.1 | 5,032.5 | 9.1 | 34.0 | 238.9 | 289.2 | 1,488.8 | 3,084.8 | 458.8 | |
| 1983 | 5,175.0 | | 537.7 | 4,637.4 | 8.3 | 33.7 | 216.5 | 279.2 | 1,337.7 | 2,868.9 | 430.8 | |
| 1984 | 5,031.3 | | 539.2 | 4,492.1 | 7.9 | 35.7 | 205.4 | 290.2 | 1,263.7 | 2,791.3 | 437.1 | |
| 1985 | 5,207.1 | | 556.6 | 4,650.5 | 7.9 | 37.1 | 208.5 | 302.9 | 1,287.3 | 2,901.2 | 462.0 | |
| 1986 | 5,480.4 | | 617.7 | 4,862.6 | 8.6 | 37.9 | 225.1 | 346.1 | 1,344.6 | 3,010.3 | 507.8 | |
| 1987 | 5,550.0 | | 609.7 | 4,940.3 | 8.3 | 37.4 | 212.7 | 351.3 | 1,329.6 | 3,081.3 | 529.4 | |
| 1988 | 5,664.2 | | 637.2 | 5,027.1 | 8.4 | 37.6 | 220.9 | 370.2 | 1,309.2 | 3,134.9 | 582.9 | |
| 1989 | 5,741.0 | | 663.1 | 5,077.9 | 8.7 | 38.1 | 233.0 | 383.4 | 1,276.3 | 3,171.3 | 630.4 | |
| 1990 | 5,820.3 | | 731.8 | 5,088.5 | 9.4 | 41.2 | 257.0 | 424.1 | 1,235.9 | 3,194.8 | 657.8 | |
| 1991 | 5,897.8 | | 758.1 | 5,139.7 | 9.8 | 42.3 | 272.7 | 433.3 | 1,252.0 | 3,228.8 | 659.0 | |
| **Percent change: rate per 100,000 inhabitants:** | | | | | | | | | | | | |
| 1991/1990 | +1.3 | | +3.6 | +1.0 | +4.3 | +2.7 | +6.1 | +2.2 | +1.3 | +1.1 | +.2 | |
| 1991/1987 | +6.3 | | +24.3 | +4.1 | +18.6 | +13.1 | +28.2 | +23.3 | -5.8 | +4.8 | +24.5 | |
| 1991/1982 | +5.3 | | +32.7 | +2.1 | +7.6 | +24.4 | +14.1 | +49.8 | -15.9 | +4.7 | +43.6 | |

[1]Populations are Bureau of the Census provisional estimates as of July 1, except 1990, which is the decennial census count.
[2]Because of rounding, the offenses may not add to totals.
[3]Although arson data are included in the trend and clearance tables, sufficient data are not available to estimate totals for this offense.
[4]Violent crimes are offenses of murder, forcible rape, robbery, and aggravated assault. Property crimes are offenses of burglary, larceny-theft, and motor vehicle theft. Data are not included for the property crime of arson.
All rates were calculated on the offenses before rounding.
Data for 1991 were not available for the State of Iowa; therefore, it was necessary that their crime counts be estimated.

## Nature

The Crime Index is composed of violent and property crime categories, and in 1991, 13 percent of the Index offenses reported to law enforcement were violent crimes and 87 percent, property crimes. Larceny-theft was the offense with the highest volume, while murder accounted for the fewest offenses.

Property estimated in value at $16.7 billion was stolen in connection with all Crime Index offenses, with the largest losses due to thefts of motor vehicles; jewelry and precious metals; and televisions, radios, stereos, etc. Law enforcement agencies nationwide recorded a 38-percent recovery rate for dollar losses in connection with stolen property. The highest recovery percentages were for stolen motor vehicles, consumable goods, livestock, clothing and furs, and firearms.

## Law Enforcement Response

Law enforcement agencies nationwide recorded a 21-percent clearance rate for the collective Crime Index offenses in 1991 and made an estimated 3 million arrests for Index crimes. Crimes can be cleared by arrest or by exceptional means when some element beyond law enforcement control precludes the placing of formal charges against the offender. The arrest of one person may clear several crimes, or several persons may be arrested in connection with the clearance of one offense.

The Index clearance rate has remained relatively stable throughout the past 10-year period. Similar to the 1991 experience, it was 21 percent in 1987 and 20 percent in 1982.

Arrests for Index crimes were up 2 percent in 1991 as compared to 1990. Considering longer timeframes, law enforcement agencies in 1991 made 13 and 18 percent more arrests than in the years 1987 and 1982, respectively.

When compared to 1990 figures, 3-percent increases in arrests for murder and robbery were shown in 1991, and the only Crime Index offense indicating a decrease in arrests was motor vehicle theft, 2 percent. Adult arrests for Index crimes were up less than 1 percent, while those of juveniles rose 5 percent. The largest increases in juvenile arrests were shown in arson with 11 percent and robbery at 10 percent.

As in past years, larceny-theft arrests accounted for the highest volume of Crime Index arrests at over 1.2 million.

# CRIME INDEX OFFENSES REPORTED

## MURDER AND NONNEGLIGENT MANSLAUGHTER

### DEFINITION

Murder and nonnegligent manslaughter, as defined in the Uniform Crime Reporting Program, is the willful (nonnegligent) killing of one human being by another.

### TREND

| Year | Number of offenses | Rate per 100,000 inhabitants |
|------|-------------------|------------------------------|
| 1990 | 23,438 | 9.4 |
| 1991 | 24,703 | 9.8 |
| Percent change | +5.4 | +4.3 |

### Volume

Reaching an all-time high during 1991, the total number of murders in the United States for the year was estimated at 24,703. More persons were murdered in August than any other month in 1991, while the fewest were killed during February.

### Murder by Month, 1987-1991

[Percent of annual total]

| Months | 1987 | 1988 | 1989 | 1990 | 1991 |
|--------|------|------|------|------|------|
| January | 7.7 | 8.2 | 8.1 | 7.9 | 8.0 |
| February | 7.9 | 7.2 | 7.1 | 7.0 | 7.0 |
| March | 8.2 | 7.7 | 7.8 | 8.0 | 7.7 |
| April | 7.6 | 7.7 | 7.9 | 7.4 | 7.8 |
| May | 8.6 | 7.8 | 7.8 | 8.1 | 8.1 |
| June | 7.8 | 7.7 | 8.2 | 8.4 | 8.6 |
| July | 8.6 | 8.9 | 9.1 | 9.6 | 9.1 |
| August | 8.9 | 9.5 | 9.0 | 9.3 | 9.4 |
| September | 8.3 | 8.9 | 8.8 | 9.2 | 8.8 |
| October | 8.8 | 8.9 | 8.9 | 8.8 | 8.6 |
| November | 8.3 | 8.2 | 8.5 | 7.6 | 7.8 |
| December | 9.1 | 9.2 | 8.7 | 8.8 | 9.0 |

When viewing the four regions of the Nation, the Southern States, the most populous, accounted for 43 percent of the murders. The Western States reported 21 percent; the Midwestern States, 19 percent; and the Northeastern States, 17 percent. Among the regions, only the Northeast registered a decline from 1990 to 1991, 2 percent.

The murder volume was up 5 percent nationwide in 1991 over 1990. In the Nation's cities overall, murder increased 6 percent, with the greatest increase—21 percent—registered in cities with populations of 50,000 to 99,999. Suburban counties recorded a 2-percent rise in their murder volumes, while rural counties registered a 1-percent decrease.

The[re was] a 23-percent rise nationally in the murder counts from 1987 to 1991. The 10-year trend showed the 1991 total 18 percent above the 1982 level.

### Rate

A murder rate of 10 per 100,000 inhabitants was registered nationwide in 1991. Two-, 5-, and 10-year trends showed the 1991 rate was 4 percent higher than in 1990, 19 percent above the 1987 rate, and 8 percent higher than the 1982 rate.

On a regional basis, the South averaged 12 murders per 100,000 people; the West, 10 per 100,000; and the Northeast and Midwest, 8 per 100,000. Compared to 1990, murder rates in 1991 increased in three of the four geographic regions with the only decline in the Northeast, 2 percent.

The Nation's metropolitan areas reported a 1991 murder rate of 11 victims per 100,000 inhabitants. In the rural counties, the rate was 6 per 100,000, and in cities outside metropolitan areas, the rate was 5 per 100,000.

### Nature

Supplemental data provided by contributing agencies recorded information for 21,505 of the estimated 24,703 murders in 1991. Submitted monthly, the data consist of the age, sex, and race of both victims and offenders; the types of weapons used; the relationships of victims to the offenders; and the circumstances surrounding the murders.

Based on this information, 78 percent of the murder victims in 1991 were males; and 89 percent were persons 18 years of age or older. Forty-eight percent were aged 20 through 34 years. Considering victims for whom race was known, an average of 50 of every 100 were black, 47 were white, and the remainder were persons of other races.

## FORCIBLE RAPE

### DEFINITION

Forcible rape, as defined in the Program, is the carnal knowledge of a female forcibly and against her will. Assaults or attempts to commit rape by force or threat of force are also included; however, statutory rape (without force) and other sex offenses are excluded.

### TREND

| Year | Number of offenses | Rate per 100,000 inhabitants |
|------|-------------------|------------------------------|
| 1990 | 102,555 | 41.2 |
| 1991 | 106,593 | 42.3 |
| Percent change | +3.9 | +2.7 |

### Volume

An estimated 106,593 forcible rapes were reported to law enforcement agencies across the Nation during 1991. The 1991 total was 4 percent higher than the 1990 level.

Geographically, more forcible rapes were reported in the Southern States than in any other region, during 1991. The lowest number of rapes was reported in the Northeast. Even though the South reported the largest volume of rapes, their proportion of the total forcible rapes has remained constant over the past 10 years. The Midwest has shown an increase in its proportion of total rapes, while the Northeast and West have shown declines. All geographic regions recorded increases in the rape volume from 1990 to 1991. Among the population groupings, only cities with populations over 500,000 recorded an increase.

## Forcible Rape by Month, 1987-1991

[Percent of annual total]

| Months | 1987 | 1988 | 1989 | 1990 | 1991 |
|---|---|---|---|---|---|
| January | 7.2 | 7.4 | 7.4 | 7.6 | 7.1 |
| February | 6.8 | 7.3 | 6.3 | 6.7 | 7.0 |
| March | 8.1 | 8.0 | 7.7 | 7.9 | 7.9 |
| April | 8.2 | 8.0 | 8.3 | 8.1 | 8.3 |
| May | 8.9 | 9.0 | 8.6 | 9.1 | 9.2 |
| June | 9.3 | 8.7 | 8.9 | 9.0 | 9.2 |
| July | 9.7 | 9.9 | 10.0 | 9.6 | 9.5 |
| August | 9.8 | 9.8 | 9.5 | 9.4 | 9.7 |
| September | 8.9 | 9.0 | 8.8 | 9.1 | 8.8 |
| October | 8.1 | 8.4 | 8.9 | 8.4 | 8.6 |
| November | 7.7 | 7.6 | 8.3 | 7.7 | 7.8 |
| December | 7.3 | 6.8 | 7.3 | 7.4 | 6.8 |

The greatest numbers of forcible rapes were reported during the summer months.

### Rate

By Uniform Crime Reporting definition, the victims of forcible rape are always female. In 1991, an estimated 83 of every 100,000 females in the country were reported rape victims, an increase of 3 percent over the 1990 rate. Since 1987, the female forcible rape rate has risen 13 percent.

Female forcible rape rates for 1991 showed there were 91 victims per 100,000 females in MSAs, 67 per 100,000 females in cities outside metropolitan areas, and 46 per 100,000 females in rural counties. Although MSAs recorded the highest rape rates, they have shown the smallest change over the past 10 years. During this time, the greatest rate increase was shown in cities outside metropolitan areas, 71 percent. MSAs and rural areas showed lesser increases, 19 percent and 61 percent, respectively.

Regionally, in 1991, the highest female rape rate was in the Western States, which recorded 91 victims per 100,000 females. Following were the Midwestern States with a rate of 89, the Southern States with 88, and the Northeastern States with 57. From 1982-1991, the greatest increase in the female rape rate was shown in the Midwest, followed by the South, and the Northeast. The West remained fairly stable over the past 10 years.

### Nature

Rapes by force constitute the greatest percentage of total forcible rapes, 86 percent of the 1991 experience. The remainder were attempts or assaults to commit forcible rape. The number of rapes by force increased 4 percent in 1991 over the 1990 volume, while attempts to rape decreased 4 percent. Ten years of data show the percentage of rapes by force consistently increasing.

As for all other Crime Index offenses, complaints of forcible rape made to law enforcement agencies are sometimes found to be false or baseless. In such cases, law enforcement agencies "unfound" the offenses and exclude them from crime counts. The "unfounded" rate, or percentage of complaints determined through investigation to be false, is higher for forcible rape than for any other Index crime. In 1991, 8 percent of forcible rape complaints were "unfounded," while the average for all Index crimes was 2 percent.

### Law Enforcement Response

Nationwide, as well as in the cities and suburban counties, over half of the forcible rapes reported to law enforcement were cleared by arrest or exceptional means in 1991. Rural county law enforcement agencies cleared a slightly higher percentage of the offenses brought to their attention than did city and suburban law enforcement agencies.

Clearance rates for the regions were lowest in the Midwestern States and highest in the Southern States.

Of the total clearances for forcible rape in the country as a whole, 13 percent involved only persons under 18 years of age. The percentage of juvenile involvement varied by community type.

The number of arrests for forcible rape rose 1 percent nationwide. Increases were also experienced in the Nation's cities and rural counties from 1990 to 1991, while forcible rape arrests were down 1 percent in the suburban counties.

Of the forcible rape arrestees in 1991, about 3 of every 10 were in the 18- to 24-year age group. Over half of those arrested were white.

## ROBBERY

### DEFINITION

Robbery is the taking or attempting to take anything of value from the care, custody, or control of a person or persons by force or threat of force or violence and/or by putting the victim in fear.

### TREND

| Year | Number of offenses | Rate per 100,000 inhabitants |
|---|---|---|
| 1990 | 639,271 | 257.0 |
| 1991 | 687,732 | 272.7 |
| Percent change | +7.6 | +6.1 |

### Volume

Accounting for 5 percent of all Index crimes and 36 percent of the violent crimes in 1991, robbery was estimated at 687,732 offenses for the year. Robberies occurred most frequently in October and December and least often in April during 1991.

Nationally, the 1991 robbery volume was 8 percent higher than the 1990 level. During the same time period, robberies were up 11 percent in the rural counties, 10

## Robbery by Month, 1987-1991

[Percent of annual total]

| Months | 1987 | 1988 | 1989 | 1990 | 1991 |
|---|---|---|---|---|---|
| January | 8.9 | 8.6 | 8.8 | 8.7 | 8.7 |
| February | 8.1 | 7.9 | 7.4 | 7.3 | 7.5 |
| March | 8.2 | 8.0 | 8.0 | 8.1 | 8.0 |
| April | 7.5 | 7.3 | 7.3 | 7.2 | 7.4 |
| May | 7.5 | 7.6 | 7.6 | 7.7 | 7.8 |
| June | 7.6 | 7.6 | 7.6 | 7.8 | 7.8 |
| July | 8.3 | 8.4 | 8.4 | 8.5 | 8.4 |
| August | 8.7 | 8.7 | 8.6 | 8.8 | 8.8 |
| September | 8.5 | 8.7 | 8.6 | 8.6 | 8.5 |
| October | 8.8 | 9.1 | 9.2 | 8.9 | 9.2 |
| November | 8.5 | 9.0 | 9.0 | 8.7 | 8.7 |
| December | 9.2 | 9.2 | 9.3 | 9.6 | 9.2 |

percent in the suburban counties, and 7 percent in the Nation's cities overall.

Distribution figures for the regions showed that the most populous Southern States registered 32 percent of all reported robberies. Two-year trends show the number of robberies in 1991 was up in three of the four regions as compared to 1990. The increases were 12 percent in the West, 13 percent in the Midwest, and 8 percent in the South. The Northeast showed no change during the same time period.

In 1991, the number of robbery offenses was 33 percent higher than in 1987 and 24 percent above the 1982 total.

### Rate

The national robbery rate in 1991 was 273 per 100,000 people, 6 percent higher than in 1990. In metropolitan areas, the robbery rate was 341; in cities outside metropolitan areas, it was 70; and in the rural areas, it was 17. With 1,189 robberies per 100,000 inhabitants, the highest rate was recorded in cities with a million or more inhabitants.

A comparison of 1990 and 1991 regional rates per 100,000 inhabitants indicated the rate of 287 in the West jumped 9 percent; the rate of 223 in the Midwest was up 12 percent; and the rate of 252 in the South increased 6 percent. The Northeast's rate of 352 was less than 1 percent lower than the previous year.

### Nature

In 1991, a total estimated national loss of $562 million was due to robberies. The value of property stolen during robberies averaged $817 per incident. Average dollar losses ranged from $387 taken during robberies of convenience stores to $3,177 per bank robbery. The impact of this violent crime on its victims cannot be measured in terms of monetary loss alone. While the object of a robbery is to obtain money or property, the crime always involves force or threat of force, and many victims suffer serious personal injury.

As in previous years, robberies on streets or highways accounted for more than half (56 percent) of the offenses in

this category. Robberies of commercial and financial establishments accounted for an additional 22 percent, and those occurring at residences, 10 percent. The remainder

## Robbery, Percent Distribution, 1991

[By region]

| | United States Total | North-eastern States | Mid-western States | Southern States | Western States |
|---|---|---|---|---|---|
| Total[1] | 100.0 | 100.0 | 100.0 | 100.0 | 100.0 |
| Street/highway | 56.2 | 64.8 | 59.1 | 49.9 | 52.1 |
| Commercial house | 11.7 | 9.8 | 10.4 | 12.2 | 14.2 |
| Gas or service station | 2.6 | 2.2 | 3.1 | 2.7 | 2.5 |
| Convenience store | 5.7 | 2.2 | 3.2 | 10.2 | 6.1 |
| Residence | 9.8 | 9.7 | 9.1 | 11.6 | 8.2 |
| Bank | 1.6 | .9 | 1.0 | 1.4 | 3.1 |
| Miscellaneous | 12.3 | 10.4 | 14.0 | 11.9 | 13.8 |

[1]Because of rounding, percentages may not add to totals.

were miscellaneous types. By type, all categories of robbery showed increases from 1990 to 1991. The increases ranged from 2 percent for convenience store robberies to 17 percent for bank robberies.

## AGGRAVATED ASSAULT

### DEFINITION

Aggravated assault is an unlawful attack by one person upon another for the purpose of inflicting severe or aggravated bodily injury. This type of assault is usually accompanied by the use of a weapon or by means likely to produce death or great bodily harm.

### TREND

| Year | Number of offenses | Rate per 100,000 inhabitants |
|---|---|---|
| 1990 | 1,054,863 | 424.1 |
| 1991 | 1,092,739 | 433.3 |
| Percent change | +3.6 | +2.2 |

### Volume

Totaling an estimated 1,092,739 offenses nationally, aggravated assaults in 1991 accounted for 57 percent of the violent crimes. Geographic distribution figures show that 39 percent of the aggravated assault volume was accounted for by the most populous South, 25 percent by the West, 20 percent by the Midwest, and 17 percent by the Northeast. Among the regions, only the Northeast registered a decline in aggravated assaults.

The 1991 monthly figures show that the greatest number of aggravated assaults was recorded during August, while the lowest volume occurred in February.

In 1991, aggravated assaults were up 4 percent nationwide as compared to 1990. For the same time period, cities collectively experienced a 3-percent increase in the aggravated assault volume, with cities from 250,000 to 499,999 recording the greatest rise, 8 percent. Cities with populations from 500,000 to 999,999 experienced the only

## Aggravated Assault by Month, 1987-1991

[Percent of annual total]

| Months | 1987 | 1988 | 1989 | 1990 | 1991 |
|---|---|---|---|---|---|
| January | 7.3 | 7.2 | 7.5 | 7.4 | 6.9 |
| February | 7.0 | 7.0 | 6.6 | 6.7 | 6.6 |
| March | 7.8 | 7.9 | 7.9 | 7.8 | 7.7 |
| April | 8.1 | 8.1 | 8.1 | 8.2 | 8.1 |
| May | 8.9 | 8.9 | 8.9 | 9.0 | 9.1 |
| June | 8.9 | 9.0 | 8.9 | 9.4 | 9.3 |
| July | 9.5 | 9.8 | 9.6 | 10.1 | 9.7 |
| August | 9.5 | 9.8 | 9.2 | 9.3 | 9.9 |
| September | 8.7 | 9.0 | 8.8 | 8.9 | 9.0 |
| October | 8.5 | 8.4 | 9.1 | 8.3 | 8.6 |
| November | 7.9 | 7.5 | 7.9 | 7.4 | 7.6 |
| December | 7.8 | 7.5 | 7.5 | 7.5 | 7.6 |

decline, 2 percent. The suburban counties registered a 2-percent increase and the rural counties, a 5-percent rise for the 2-year period.

Five- and 10-year trends for the country as a whole show aggravated assaults up 28 percent above the 1987 level and 63 percent over the 1982 experience.

### Rate

Up 2 percent above the 1990 rate, there were 433 reported victims of aggravated assault for every 100,000 people nationwide in 1991. The rate was 23 percent higher than in 1987 and 50 percent above the 1982 rate.

Higher than the national average, the rate in metropolitan areas was 487 per 100,000 in 1991. Cities outside metropolitan areas experienced a rate of 372, and rural counties, a rate of 170.

Regionally, the aggravated assault rates ranged from 498 per 100,000 people in the West to 355 per 100,000 in the Midwest. Compared to 1990, 1991 aggravated assault rates were up in three of the four regions, with only the Northeast showing a decline, 1 percent.

### Nature

In 1991, 31 percent of the aggravated assaults were committed with blunt objects or other dangerous weapons. Of the remaining weapon categories, personal weapons such as hands, fists, and feet were used in 27 percent of the

## Aggravated Assault, Type of Weapons Used, 1991

[Percent distribution by region]

| Region | Total all weapons[1] | Fire-arms | Knives or cutting instruments | Other weapons (clubs, blunt objects, etc.) | Personal weapons |
|---|---|---|---|---|---|
| Total | 100.0 | 23.6 | 18.4 | 30.8 | 27.1 |
| Northeastern States | 100.0 | 17.1 | 21.2 | 31.6 | 30.1 |
| Midwestern States | 100.0 | 26.8 | 18.2 | 32.5 | 22.5 |
| Southern States | 100.0 | 27.2 | 20.2 | 30.7 | 21.9 |
| Western States | 100.0 | 21.3 | 14.4 | 29.5 | 34.8 |

[1]Because of rounding, percentages may not add to totals.

offenses; firearms in 24 percent; and knives or cutting instruments in the remainder.

From 1990 to 1991, assaults with firearms and those involving personal weapons increased 7 percent. Those committed with knives or cutting instruments were down 2 percent, and those involving blunt objects or other dangerous weapons decreased less than 1 percent.

## BURGLARY

### DEFINITION

The Uniform Crime Reporting Program defines burglary as the unlawful entry of a structure to commit a felony or theft. The use of force to gain entry is not required to classify an offense as burglary.

### ——— TREND ———

| Year | Number of offenses | Rate per 100,000 inhabitants |
|---|---|---|
| 1990 | 3,073,909 | 1,235.9 |
| 1991 | 3,157,150 | 1,252.0 |
| Percent change | +2.7 | +1.3 |

### Volume

An estimated 3,157,150 burglaries occurred in the United States during 1991. These offenses accounted for 21 percent of the total Crime Index and 24 percent of the property crimes.

Distribution figures for the regions showed that the highest burglary volume occurred in the most populous Southern States, accounting for 41 percent of the total. The Western States followed with 23 percent, the Midwestern States with 20 percent, and the Northeastern States with 16 percent.

In 1991, the greatest numbers of burglaries were recorded during July and August, while the lowest count was reported in February.

## Burglary by Month, 1987-1991

[Percent of annual total]

| Months | 1987 | 1988 | 1989 | 1990 | 1991 |
|---|---|---|---|---|---|
| January | 8.4 | 8.4 | 8.8 | 8.8 | 8.1 |
| February | 7.8 | 7.8 | 7.3 | 7.5 | 7.3 |
| March | 8.3 | 8.1 | 8.2 | 8.1 | 8.1 |
| April | 7.6 | 7.5 | 7.7 | 7.8 | 7.9 |
| May | 8.0 | 8.1 | 8.4 | 8.1 | 8.3 |
| June | 8.0 | 8.0 | 8.3 | 7.9 | 8.2 |
| July | 8.8 | 8.8 | 9.2 | 8.9 | 9.2 |
| August | 9.1 | 9.3 | 9.3 | 9.0 | 9.2 |
| September | 8.4 | 8.6 | 8.6 | 8.3 | 8.6 |
| October | 8.4 | 8.5 | 8.5 | 8.5 | 8.6 |
| November | 8.4 | 8.4 | 8.1 | 8.3 | 8.0 |
| December | 8.8 | 8.5 | 7.8 | 8.7 | 8.6 |

Nationwide, the burglary volume rose 3 percent in 1991 over the 1990 total. By population group, increases were registered in all city groupings except cities with populations of 1 million or more, which showed a 2-percent decline.

Geographically, three of the four regions of the United States reported increases in burglary volumes during 1991 as compared to 1990. The increases were 6 percent in the Midwestern States, 4 percent in the Western States, and 2 percent in the Southern States. The only decrease in the burglary volume occurred in the Northeastern States with a 1-percent decline.

Longer term national trends show burglary down 2 percent from the 1987 volume and 8 percent below the 1982 level.

### Rate

A burglary rate of 1,252 per 100,000 inhabitants was registered nationwide in 1991. The rate rose 1 percent over 1990 but was 16 percent below the 1982 rate. In 1991, for every 100,000 in population, the rate was 1,368 in the metropolitan areas, 1,074 in the cities outside metropolitan areas, and 708 in the rural counties.

Regionally, the burglary rate was 1,498 in the Southern States, 1,324 in the Western States, 1,037 in the Midwestern States, and 1,010 in the Northeastern States. A comparison of 1990 and 1991 rates showed increases of 5 percent in the Midwest and 2 percent in the West. The South's burglary rate showed no change from the previous year, while in the Northeast, a 1-percent decrease was reported.

### Nature

Two of every 3 burglaries in 1991 were residential in nature. Seventy percent of all burglaries involved forcible entry, 23 percent were unlawful entries (without force), and the remainder were forcible entry attempts. Offenses for which time of occurrence was reported were evenly divided between day and night.

Burglary victims suffered losses estimated at $3.9 billion in 1991, and the average dollar loss per burglary was $1,246. The average loss for residential offenses was $1,281, while for nonresidential property, it was $1,180.

Both residential and nonresidential burglary volumes showed increases of 2 percent from 1990 to 1991.

### Law Enforcement Response

Geographically in 1991, a 13-percent clearance rate was recorded for burglaries brought to the attention of law enforcement agencies across the country. In the South, the clearance rate was 15 percent; in the Northeast, 14 percent, in the West, 13 percent; and in the Midwest, 11 percent.

Rural county law enforcement cleared 16 percent of the burglaries in their jurisdictions. Agencies in suburban counties cleared 14 percent, and those in cities, 13 percent.

Adults were involved in 81 percent of all burglary offenses cleared; the remaining 19 percent involved only young people under 18 years of age. Persons under age 18 accounted for 18 percent of the burglary clearances in cities, 20 percent of those in rural counties, and 23 percent of those in suburban counties. The highest degree of

juvenile involvement was recorded in the Nation's smallest cities (under 10,000 in population) where young persons under 18 years of age accounted for 25 percent of the clearances.

## LARCENY-THEFT

### DEFINITION

Larceny-theft is the unlawful taking, carrying, leading, or riding away of property from the possession or constructive possession of another. It includes crimes such as shoplifting, pocket-picking, purse-snatching, thefts from motor vehicles, thefts of motor vehicle parts and accessories, bicycle thefts, etc., in which no use of force, violence, or fraud occurs.

### TREND

| Year | Number of offenses | Rate per 100,000 inhabitants |
|---|---|---|
| 1990 | 7,945,670 | 3,194.8 |
| 1991 | 8,142,228 | 3,228.8 |
| Percent change | +2.5 | +1.1 |

### Volume

Estimated at 8.1 million offenses during 1991, larceny-thefts comprised 55 percent of the Crime Index total and 63 percent of the property crimes. Similar to the experience in previous years, larceny-thefts were recorded most often during the month of August and least frequently in February.

When viewed geographically, the Southern States, the most populous, recorded 38 percent of the larceny-theft total. The Midwest and Western States each registered 23 percent; and the Northeastern States, 16 percent.

### Larceny-Theft by Month, 1987-1991

[Percent of annual total]

| Months | 1987 | 1988 | 1989 | 1990 | 1991 |
|---|---|---|---|---|---|
| January | 7.6 | 7.6 | 8.0 | 8.2 | 7.8 |
| February | 7.5 | 7.5 | 7.2 | 7.4 | 7.5 |
| March | 8.3 | 8.2 | 8.2 | 8.2 | 8.2 |
| April | 8.0 | 7.8 | 8.0 | 7.9 | 8.1 |
| May | 8.2 | 8.3 | 8.6 | 8.3 | 8.4 |
| June | 8.5 | 8.5 | 8.7 | 8.3 | 8.5 |
| July | 9.1 | 9.0 | 9.2 | 8.9 | 9.2 |
| August | 9.2 | 9.5 | 9.5 | 9.1 | 9.3 |
| September | 8.4 | 8.5 | 8.3 | 8.2 | 8.3 |
| October | 8.6 | 8.7 | 8.6 | 8.7 | 8.7 |
| November | 8.1 | 8.2 | 8.0 | 8.1 | 7.9 |
| December | 8.4 | 8.3 | 7.7 | 8.4 | 8.2 |

Compared to 1990, the 1991 volume of larceny-thefts increased 2 percent in the Nation and in all cities collectively. The suburban and rural counties also showed increases, 4 percent and 5 percent, respectively.

Regionally, volume upswings of 3 percent were recorded in both the Midwest and the Southern States. The Western States registered a 2-percent increase, while the Northeastern States showed no change.

The 5- and 10-year national trends indicated larceny was up 9 percent over the 1987 total and 14 percent above the 1982 level.

### Rate

The 1991 larceny-theft rate was 3,229 per 100,000 United States inhabitants. The rate was 1 percent higher than in 1990 and 5 percent above the 1987 and 1982 levels. The 1991 rate was 3,560 per 100,000 inhabitants of metropolitan areas; 3,647 per 100,000 population in cities outside metropolitan areas; and 1,059 per 100,000 people in the rural counties.

Regionally, the rate in the Midwest was 3,082 per 100,000 inhabitants, an increase of 2 percent over the previous year. The South's 1991 rate of 3,518 was up 1 percent, while the rates per 100,000 inhabitants of 2,598 in the Northeast and 3,522 in the West showed no change from 1990 levels.

### Nature

During 1991, the average value of property stolen due to larceny-theft was $478, down slightly from $480 in 1990. When the average value was applied to the estimated number of larceny-thefts, the loss to victims nationally was $3.9 billion for the year. This estimated dollar loss is considered conservative since many offenses in the larceny category, particularly if the value of the stolen goods is small, never come to law enforcement attention. Losses in 24 percent of the thefts reported to law enforcement in 1991 ranged from $50 to $200, while in 36 percent, they were over $200.

Losses of goods and property reported stolen as a result of pocket-picking averaged $366; purse-snatching, $280; and shoplifting, $104. Thefts from buildings resulted in an average loss of $788; from motor vehicles, $544; and from coin-operated machines, $139. The average value loss due to thefts of motor vehicle accessories was $305 and for thefts of bicycles, $233.

Thefts of motor vehicle parts, accessories, and contents made up the largest portion of reported larcenies–37 percent. Also contributing to the high volume of thefts were shoplifting, accounting for 16 percent; thefts from buildings, 14 percent; and bicycle thefts, 6 percent. The remainder was distributed among pocket-picking, purse-snatching, thefts from coin-operated machines, and all other types of larceny-thefts.

## MOTOR VEHICLE THEFT

### DEFINITION

Defined as the theft or attempted theft of a motor vehicle, this offense category includes the stealing of automobiles, trucks, buses, motorcycles, motorscooters, snowmobiles, etc.

### TREND

| Year | Number of offenses | Rate per 100,000 inhabitants |
|---|---|---|
| 1990 ........................ | 1,635,907 | 657.8 |
| 1991 ........................ | 1,661,738 | 659.0 |
| Percent change ......... | +1.6 | +.2 |

### Volume

An estimated total of 1,661,738 thefts of motor vehicles occurred in the United States during 1991. These offenses comprised 13 percent of all property crimes. The regional distribution of motor vehicle thefts showed 32 percent of the volume was in the Southern States, 26 percent in the Western States, 24 percent in the Northeastern States, and 18 percent in the Midwestern States.

The 1991 monthly figures show that the greatest number of motor vehicle thefts was recorded during the month of August, while the lowest count was in February.

### Larceny Analysis by Region, 1991

[Percent distribution]

| | United States Total | North-eastern States | Mid-western States | Southern States | Western States |
|---|---|---|---|---|---|
| Total[1] .................... | 100.0 | 100.0 | 100.0 | 100.0 | 100.0 |
| Pocket-picking ........... | 1.0 | 3.4 | .8 | .4 | .5 |
| Purse-snatching .......... | 1.0 | 1.9 | 1.1 | .8 | .7 |
| Shoplifting ................ | 16.5 | 14.3 | 14.0 | 17.3 | 19.0 |
| From motor vehicles (except accessories) ..... | 22.4 | 22.0 | 18.9 | 20.1 | 29.4 |
| Motor vehicle accessories .............. | 14.1 | 13.5 | 14.4 | 15.9 | 11.7 |
| Bicycles .................. | 5.8 | 6.5 | 5.2 | 4.9 | 7.4 |
| From buildings .......... | 14.2 | 18.0 | 19.2 | 10.8 | 12.3 |
| From coin-operated machines ............... | 1.0 | 2.1 | .6 | .9 | .6 |
| All others ............... | 23.9 | 18.4 | 25.8 | 29.0 | 18.4 |

[1]Because of rounding, percentages may not add to totals.

### Motor Vehicle Theft by Month, 1987-1991

[Percent of annual total]

| Months | 1987 | 1988 | 1989 | 1990 | 1991 |
|---|---|---|---|---|---|
| January ...................... | 7.9 | 8.0 | 8.3 | 8.5 | 8.3 |
| February ..................... | 7.5 | 7.6 | 7.3 | 7.6 | 7.5 |
| March ........................ | 8.4 | 7.9 | 8.1 | 8.4 | 8.2 |
| April ......................... | 7.9 | 7.4 | 7.5 | 7.9 | 7.8 |
| May .......................... | 8.0 | 7.8 | 8.0 | 8.1 | 8.1 |
| June ......................... | 8.1 | 8.0 | 8.2 | 8.1 | 8.2 |
| July ......................... | 8.8 | 8.8 | 8.8 | 8.8 | 8.7 |
| August ....................... | 9.0 | 9.4 | 9.0 | 8.8 | 8.9 |
| September ................... | 8.4 | 8.7 | 8.5 | 8.4 | 8.3 |
| October ...................... | 8.8 | 9.0 | 9.0 | 8.8 | 8.7 |
| November ................... | 8.5 | 8.7 | 8.7 | 8.3 | 8.5 |
| December .................... | 8.7 | 8.7 | 8.5 | 8.4 | 8.8 |

The number of motor vehicle thefts rose 2 percent nationally from 1990 to 1991. During the same period, the Nation's cities overall experienced a 1-percent increase and the suburban counties a 3-percent rise, while rural counties showed a decrease of less than 1 percent.

Geographically, three regions experienced motor vehicle

theft increases, while the Northeastern Region showed a 2-percent decline.

[T]he volume of motor vehicle thefts in 1991 increased 29 percent over the 1987 volume.

## Rate

The 1991 national motor vehicle theft rate—659 per 100,000 people—showed virtually no change from the rate in 1990. The rate was 24 percent higher than in 1987 and 44 percent above the 1982 rate.

For every 100,000 inhabitants living in MSAs, there were 803 motor vehicle thefts reported in 1991. The rate in cities outside metropolitan areas was 233 and in rural counties, 120. As in previous years, the highest rates were in the Nation's most heavily populated municipalities, indicating that this offense is primarily a large-city problem. For every 100,000 inhabitants in cities with populations over 250,000, the 1991 motor vehicle theft rate was 1,681. The Nation's smallest cities, those with fewer than 10,000 inhabitants, recorded a rate of 257 per 100,000.

Among the regions, the motor vehicle theft rates ranged from 791 per 100,000 people in the Western States to 507 in the Midwestern States. The Northeastern States' rate was 795 and the Southern States' rate, 603. All regions except the Northeastern States registered rate increases from 1990 to 1991.

An estimated average of 1 of every 117 registered motor vehicles was stolen nationwide during 1991. Regionally, this rate was greatest in the Northeast where 1 of every 84 motor vehicles registered was stolen. The other three regions reported lesser rates—1 per 101 in the West, 1 per 127 in the South, and 1 per 167 in the Midwest.

## Nature

During 1991, the estimated value of motor vehicles stolen nationwide was nearly $8.3 billion. At the time of theft, the average value per vehicle stolen was $4,983.

Eighty percent of all motor vehicles reported stolen during the year were automobiles, 15 percent were trucks or buses, and the remainder were other types.

### Motor Vehicle Theft, 1991

[Percent distribution by region]

| Region | Total[1] | Autos | Trucks and buses | Other vehicles |
|---|---|---|---|---|
| Total ..................... | 100.0 | 79.7 | 14.7 | 5.6 |
| Northeastern States ....... | 100.0 | 92.7 | 4.4 | 2.9 |
| Midwestern States ........ | 100.0 | 83.0 | 10.5 | 6.5 |
| Southern States .......... | 100.0 | 74.7 | 19.0 | 6.3 |
| Western States ........... | 100.0 | 71.4 | 21.9 | 6.8 |

[1]Because of rounding, percentages may not add to totals.

# Glossary

**Abet**  To encourage another to commit a crime. This encouragement may be by advice, inducement, command, etc. The abettor of a crime is equally guilty with the one who actually commits the crime.

**Accessory after the Fact**  One who harbors, assists, or protects another person, although he knows that person has committed a crime.

**Accessory before the Fact**  One who helps another to commit a crime, even though he is absent when the crime is committed.

**Accomplice**  One who is involved in the commission of a crime with others, whether he actually commits the crime or abets others. The term *principal* means the same thing, except that one may be a principal if he commits a crime without the aid of others.

**Acquit**  To free a person from an accusation of criminal guilt; to find "not guilty."

**Affidavit**  A written declaration or statement sworn to and affirmed by an officer having authority to administer an oath.

**Affirmation**  To swear on one's conscience that what he says is true. An *oath* means that one calls upon God to witness the truth of what he says.

**Alias**  Any name by which one is known other than his true name. *Alias dictus* is the more technically correct term but it is rarely used.

**Alibi**  A claim that one was in a place different from that charged. If the person proves his alibi, he proves that he could not have committed the crime charged.

**Allegation**  The declaration of a party to a lawsuit made in a pleading, that states what he expects to prove.

**Amnesty**  A class or group pardon (e.g., all political prisoners).

**Appeal**  A case carried to a higher court to ask that the decision of the lower court, in which the case originated, be altered or overruled completely.

**Appellate Court**  A court that has jurisdiction to hear cases on appeal; not a trial court.

**Arraignment**  The appearance before the court of a person charged with a crime. He or she is advised of the charges, bail is set, and a plea of "guilty" or "not guilty" is entered.

**Arrest**  To take a person into custody so that he may be held to answer for a crime.

**Autopsy**  A post-mortem examination of a human body to determine the cause of death.

**Bail**  Property (usually money) deposited with a court in exchange for the release of a person in custody to assure later appearance.

**Bail Bond**  An obligation signed by the accused and his sureties, that insures his presence in court.

**Bailiff**  A court attendant whose duties are to keep order in the courtroom and to have custody of the jury.

**Bench Warrant**  An order by the court for the apprehension and arrest of a defendant or other person who has failed to appear when so ordered.

**Bill of Rights**  The first ten amendments to the Constitution of the United States which define such rights as: due process of law, immunity from illegal search and seizure, the ban on cruel and unusual punishment, unreasonably high bail, indictment by a grand jury, and speedy trial.

**Bind Over**  To hold for trial.

**"Blue" Laws**  Laws in some jurisdictions prohibiting sales of merchandise, athletic contests, and the sale of alcoholic beverages on Sundays.

**Booking**  The procedure at a police station of entering the name and identifying particulars relating to an arrested person, the charges filed against him, and the name of the arresting officer.

**Burden of Proof**  The duty of affirmatively proving the guilt of the defendant "beyond a reasonable doubt."

**Calendar**  A list of cases to be heard in a trial court, on a specific day, and containing the title of the case, the lawyers involved, and the index number.

**Capital Crime**  Any crime that may be punishable by death or imprisonment for life.

**Caseload**  The number of cases actively being investigated by a police detective or being supervised by a probation or parole officer.

**Change of Venue**  The removal of a trial from one jurisdiction to another in order to avoid local prejudice.

**Charge**  In criminal law, the accusation made against a person. It also refers to the judge's instruction to the jury on legal points.

**Circumstantial Evidence**  Indirect evidence; evidence from which the principal fact can be proved or disproved by inference. Example: a finger-print found at the crime scene.

**Citizen's Arrest**  A taking into custody of an alleged offender by a person not a law enforcement officer. Such an arrest is lawful if the crime was attempted or committed in his presence.

**Code**  A compilation, compendium, or revision of laws, arranged into chapters, having a table of contents and index, and promulgated by legislative authority. Criminal code; penal code.

**Coercion**  The compelling of a person to do that which he is not obliged to do, or to omit doing what he may legally do, by some illegal threat, force, or intimidation. For example: a forced confession.

**Commit**  To place a person in custody in a prison or other institution by lawful order.

**Common Law**  Law that derives its authority from usage and custom or court decisions.

**Commutation**  To change the punishment meted out to a criminal to one less severe. Executive clemency.

**Complainant**  The victim of a crime who brings the facts to the attention of the authorities.

**Complaint**  A sworn written allegation stating that a specified person committed a crime. Sometimes called an *information*. When issued from a *Grand Jury,* it is called an *indictment.*

**Compulsion**  An irresistible impulse to commit some act, such as stealing, setting a fire, or an illegal sexual act.

**Confession**  An admission by the accused of his guilt; a partial admission (e.g., that he was at the crime scene; that he had a motive) is referred to as "an admission against interest."

**Confinement**  Deprivation of liberty in a jail or prison either as punishment for a crime or as detention while guilt or innocence is being determined.

**Consensual Crime**  A crime without a victim; one in which both parties voluntarily participate (e.g., adultery, sodomy, etc.).

**Conspiracy**  A secret combination of two or more persons who plan for the purpose of committing a crime or any unlawful act or a lawful act by unlawful or criminal means.

**Contempt of Court**  Behavior that impugns the authority of a court or obstructs the execution of court orders.

**Continuance**  A delay in trial granted by the judge on request of either the prosecutor or defense counsel; an adjournment.

**Conviction**  A finding by the jury (or by the trial judge in cases tried without a jury) that the accused is guilty of a crime.

**Corporal**  Corporal punishment is pain inflicted on the body of another. Flogging.

**Corpus Delicti**  The objective proof that a crime has been committed as distinguished from an accidental death, injury or loss.

**Corrections**  Area of criminal justice dealing with convicted offenders in jails, prisons; on probation or parole.

**Corroborating Evidence**  Supplementary evidence that tends to strengthen or confirm other evidence given previously.

**Crime**  An act or omission prohibited and punishable by law. Crimes are divided into *felonies* and *misdemeanors;* and recorded as "crimes against the person" (murder, rape, assault, robbery) and "crimes against property" (burglary, larceny, auto theft). There are also crimes against public morality and against public order.

**Criminal Insanity**  Lack of mental capacity to do or refrain from doing a criminal act; inability to distinguish right from wrong.

**Criminalistics**  Crime laboratory procedures (e.g., ballistics, analysis of stains, etc.).

**Criminology**  The scientific study of crime and criminals.

**Cross-Examination**  The questioning of a witness by the party who did not produce the witness.

**Culpability**  Guilt; *see also mens rea.*

**Defendant**  The person who is being prosecuted.

**Delinquency**  Criminality by a boy or girl who has not as yet reached the age set by the state for trial as an adult (the age varies from jurisdiction to jurisdiction and from crime to crime).

**Demurrer**  In court procedure, a statement that the charge that a crime has been committed has no sufficient basis in law, despite the truth of the facts alleged.

**Deposition**  The testimony of a witness not taken in open court but taken in pursuance of authority to take such testimony elsewhere.

**Detention**  To hold a person in confinement while awaiting trial or sentence, or as a material witness.

**Deterrence**  To prevent criminality by fear of the consequences; one of the rationalizations for punishing offenders.

**Direct Evidence**  Proof of facts by witnesses who actually saw acts or heard words, as distinguished from *Circumstantial Evidence.*

**Direct Examination** The first questioning of a witness by the party who produced him.

**Directed Verdict** An instruction by the judge to the jury to return a specific verdict. A judge may not direct a guilty verdict.

**Discretion** The decision-making powers of officers of the criminal justice system (e.g., to arrest or not, to prosecute or not, to plea-bargain, to grant probation, or to sentence to a penal institution).

**District Attorney** Prosecutor; sometimes County Attorney, (U.S. Attorney in Federal practice).

**Docket** The formal record maintained by the court clerk, listing all cases heard. It contains the defendant's name, index number, date of arrest, and the outcome of the case.

**Double Jeopardy** To be prosecuted twice for the same offense.

**Due Process** Law in its regular course of administration through the courts of justice. Guaranteed by the 5th and 14th Amendments.

**Embracery** An attempt to influence a jury, or a member thereof, in their verdict by any improper means.

**Entrapment** The instigation of a crime by officers or agents of a government who induce a person to commit a crime that he did not originally contemplate in order to institute a criminal prosecution against him.

**Evidence** All the means used to prove or disprove the fact at issue.

**Ex Post Facto** After the fact. An ex post facto law is a criminal law that makes an act unlawful although it was committed prior to the passage of that law.

**Examination** An investigation of a witness by counsel in the form of questions for the purpose of bringing before the court knowledge possessed by the witness.

**Exception** A formal objection to the action of the court during a trial. The indication is that the excepting party will seek to reverse the court's action at some future proceeding. *Objection.*

**Exclusionary Rule** Rule of evidence which makes illegally acquired evidence inadmissible; *see* Mapp vs. Ohio.

**Expert Evidence** Testimony by one qualified to speak authoritatively on technical matters because of his special training or skill.

**Extradition** The surrender by one state to another of an individual accused of a crime.

**False Arrest** Any unlawful physical restraint of another's freedom of movement. Unlawful arrest.

**Felonious** Evil, malicious, or criminal. A felonious act is not necessarily a felony, but is criminal in some degree.

**Felony** Generally, an offense punishable by death or imprisonment in a penitentiary.

**Forensic** Relating to the court. Thus, forensic medicine would refer to medicine in relation to court proceedings and the law in general.

**Grand Jury** A group of 16 to 23 citizens of a county who examine evidence against the person suspected of a crime, and hand down an indictment if there is sufficient evidence to warrant one.

**Habeas Corpus (Writ of)** An order that requires a jailor, warden, police chief, or other public official to produce a person being held in custody before a court in order to show that they have a legal right to hold him in custody.

**Hearsay** Evidence not originating from the witness' personal knowledge.

**Homicide** The killing of a human being; may be murder, negligent or non-negligent manslaughter, or excusable or justifiable homicide.

**Impeach** To discredit. To question the truthfulness of a witness. Also: to charge a president or governor with criminal misconduct.

**Imprisonment** The act of confining a convicted felon in a federal or state prison.

**In Camera** In the judge's private chambers; in secrecy; the general public and press are excluded.

**Indictment** The document prepared by a prosecutor and approved by the grand jury which charges a certain person with a specific crime or crimes for which that person is later to be tried in court. Truebill.

**Inference** A conclusion one draws about something based on proof of certain other facts.

**Injunction** An order by a court prohibiting a defendant from committing an act.

**Intent** A design or determination of the mind to do or not do a certain thing. Intent may be determined from the nature of one's acts. Mens Rea.

**Interpol** International Criminal Police Commission.

**Jail** A short-term confinement institution for the detention of persons awaiting trial and the serving of sentences by those convicted of misdemeanors and offenses.

**Jeopardy** The danger of conviction and punishment that a defendant faces in a criminal trial. *Double Jeopardy.*

**Judicial Notice** The rule that a court will accept certain things as common knowledge without proof.

**Jurisdiction** The power of a court to hear and determine a criminal case.

**Jury** A certain number of persons who are sworn to examine the evidence and determine the truth on the basis of that evidence. Grand jury; trial jury.

**Juvenile Delinquent** A boy or girl who has not reached the age of criminal liability (varies from state to state) and who commits an act which would be a misdemeanor or felony if he were an adult. Delinquents are tried in *Juvenile Court* and confined to separate facilities.

**L.E.A.A.** Law Enforcement Assistance Administration, U.S. Dept. of Justice.

**Leniency** An unusually mild sentence imposed on a convicted offender; clemency granted by the President or a state governor; early release by a parole board.

**Lie Detector** An instrument which measures certain physiological reactions of the human body from which a trained operator may determine whether the subject is telling the truth or lies; polygraph; psychological stress evaluator.

**Mala In Se** Evil in itself. Acts that are made crimes because they are, by their nature, evil and morally wrong.

**Mala Prohibita** Evil because they are prohibited. Acts that are not wrong in themselves but which, to protect the general welfare, are made crimes by statute.

**Malfeasance** The act of a public officer in committing a crime relating to his official duties or powers. Accepting or demanding a bribe.

**Malice** An evil intent to vex, annoy, or injure another; intentional evil.

**Malicious Prosecution** An action instituted in bad faith with the intention of injuring the defendant.

**Mandamus** A writ that issues from a superior court, directed to any person, corporation, or inferior court, requiring it to do some particular thing.

**Mens Rea** A guilty intent.

**Miranda Warning** A police officer when taking a suspect into custody must warn him of his right to remain silent and of his right to an attorney.

**Misdemeanor** Any crime not a *Felony.* Usually, a crime punishable by a fine or imprisonment in the county or other local jail.

**Misprision** Failing to reveal a crime.

**Mistrial** A trial discontinued before reaching a verdict because of some procedural defect or impediment.

**Modus Operandi** Method of operation by criminals.

**Motions** Procedural moves made by either defense attorney or prosecutor and submitted to the court, helping to define and set the ground rules for the proceedings of a particular case. For example: to suppress illegally seized evidence or to seek a change of venue.

**Motive** The reason for committing a crime.

**N.C.C.D.** National Council on Crime and Delinquency.

**No Bill** A phrase used by a *Grand Jury* when they fail to indict.

**Nolle Prosequi** A declaration to a court, by the prosecutor that he does not wish to further prosecute the case.

**Nolo Contendre** A pleading, usually used by a defendant in a criminal case, that literally means "I will not contest."

**Objection** The act of taking exception to some statement or procedure in a trial. Used to call the court's attention to some improper evidence or procedure.

**Opinion Evidence** A witness' belief or opinion about a fact in dispute, as distinguished from personal knowledge of the fact. Expert testimony.

**Ordinance** A statute enacted by the city or municipal government.

**Organized Crime** The crime syndicate; cosa nostra; Mafia; an organized, continuing criminal conspiracy which engages in crime as a business (e.g., loan sharking, illegal gambling, prostitution, extortion, etc.).

**Original Jurisdiction** Trial jurisdiction.

**Over Act** An open or physical act, as opposed to a thought or mere intention.

**Pardon** Executive clemency setting aside a conviction and penalty.

**Parole**  A conditional release from prison, under supervision.

**Penal Code**  The criminal law of a jurisdiction, (sometimes the criminal procedure law is included but in other states it is codified separately).

**Penology**  The study of punishment and corrections.

**Peremptory Challenge**  The act of objecting to a certain number of jurors without assigning a cause for their dismissal. Used during the *voir dire* examination.

**Perjury**  The legal offense of deliberately testifying falsely under oath about a material fact.

**Petit Jury**  The ordinary jury composed of 12 persons who hear criminal cases. Determines guilt or innocence of the accused.

**Plea-Bargaining**  A negotiation between the defense attorney and the prosecutor in which defendant receives a reduced penalty in return for a plea of ''guilty.''

**Police Power**  The authority of the legislation to make laws in the interest of the general public, even at the risk of placing some hardship on individuals.

**Post Mortem**  After death. Commonly applied to examination of a dead body. An autopsy is a post mortem examination to determine the cause of death.

**Preliminary Hearing**  A proceeding in front of a lower court to determine if there is sufficient evidence for submitting a felony case to the grand jury.

**Presumption of Fact**  An inference as to the truth or falsity of any proposition or fact, made in the absence of actual certainty of its truth or falsity or until such certainty can be attained.

**Presumption of Law**  A rule of law that courts and judges must draw a particular inference from a particular fact or evidence, unless the inference can be disproved.

**Prima Facie**  So far as can be judged from the first appearance or at first sight.

**Prison**  Federal or state penal institution for the confinement of convicted felons. Penitentiary.

**Probation**  A penalty placing a convicted person under the supervision of a probation officer for a stated time, instead of being confined.

**Prosecutor**  One who initiates a criminal prosecution against an accused. One who acts as a trial attorney for the government as the representative of the people.

**Provost Marshal**  Military police officer in charge of discipline, crime control and traffic law enforcement at a military post.

**Public Defender**  An appointed or elected public official charged with providing legal representation for indigent persons accused of crimes.

**Reasonable Doubt**  That state of mind of jurors when they do not feel a moral certainty about the truth of the charge and when the evidence does not exclude every other reasonable hypothesis except that the defendant is guilty as charged.

**Rebuttal**  The introduction of contradicting testimony; the showing that statements made by a witness are not true; the point in the trial at which such evidence may be introduced.

**Recidivist**  A repeater in crime; a habitual offender.

**Recognizance**  When a person binds himself to do a certain act or else suffer a penalty, as, for example, with a recognizance bond. Release on recognizance is release without posting bail or bond.

**Relevant**  Applying to the issue in question; related to the issue; useful in determining the truth or falsity of an alleged fact.

**Remand**  To send back. To remand a case for new trial or sentencing.

**Reprieve**  A stay of execution or sentence.

**Search Warrant**  A written order, issued by judicial authority in the name of the state, directing a law enforcement officer to search for personal property and, if found, to bring it before the court.

**Sentence**  The punishment (harsh or lenient) imposed by the trial judge on a convicted offender; major options include: fines, probation, indeterminate sentencing (e.g., three to ten years), indefinite sentencing (e.g., not more than three years), and capital punishment (death).

**Stare Decisis**  To abide by decided cases. The doctrine that once a court has laid down a principle of law as applicable to certain facts, it will apply it to all future cases when the facts are substantially the same.

**State's Evidence**  Testimony given by an accomplice or participant in a crime, tending to convict others.

**Status Offense**  An act which is punishable only because the offender has not as yet reached a statutorily prescribed age (e.g., truancy, running away, drinking alcoholic beverages by a minor, etc.).

**Statute**  A law.

**Stay**  A stopping of a judicial proceeding by a court order.

**Subpoena**  A court order requiring a witness to attend and testify in a court proceeding.

**Subpoena Duces Tecum**  A court order requiring a witness to testify and to bring all books, documents, and papers that might affect the outcome of the proceedings.

**Summons**  An order to appear in court on a particular date, which is issued by a police officer after or instead of arrest. It may also be a notification to a witness or a juror to appear in court.

**Suspect**  One whom the police have determined as very likely to be the guilty perpetrator of an offense. Once the police identify a person as a suspect, they must warn him of his rights (Miranda warning) to remain silent and to have legal advice.

**Testimony**  Evidence given by a competent witness, under oath, as distinguished from evidence from writings and other sources.

**Tort**  A legal wrong committed against a person or property for which compensation may be obtained by a civil action.

**Uniform Crime Reports (U.C.R.)**  Annual statistical tabulation of ''crimes known to the police'' and ''crimes cleared by arrest'' published by the Federal Bureau of Investigation.

**Venue**  The geographical area in which a court with jurisdiction sits. The power of a court to compel the presence of the parties to a litigation. See also *Change of Venue*.

**Verdict**  The decision of a court.

**Victimology**  Sub-discipline of criminology which emphasizes the study of victims; includes *victim compensation*.

**Voir Dire**  The examination or questioning of prospective jurors.

**Waive**  To give up a personal right. For example: to testify before the grand jury.

**Warrant**  A court order directing a police officer to arrest a named person or search a specific premise.

**Witness**  One who has seen, heard, acquired knowledge about some element in a crime. An *expert witness* is one who, though he has no direct knowledge of the crime for which the defendant is being tried, may testify as to the defendant's sanity, the amount of alcohol in the deceased's blood, whether a signature is genuine, that a fingerprint is or is not that of the accused, etc.

# Credits/ Acknowledgments

Cover design by Charles Vitelli

**1. Crime and Justice in America**
Facing overview—The Dushkin Publishing Group photo by Pamela Carley.

**2. Victimology**
Facing overview—EPA Documerica.

**3. Police**
Facing overview—United Nations photo.

**4. The Judicial System**
Facing overview—EPA Documerica.

**5. Juvenile Justice**
Facing overview—United Nations photo.

**6. Punishment and Corrections**
Facing overview—National Archives.

**PHOTOCOPY THIS PAGE!!!***

# ANNUAL EDITIONS ARTICLE REVIEW FORM

■ NAME: _____ DATE: _____

■ TITLE AND NUMBER OF ARTICLE: _____

■ BRIEFLY STATE THE MAIN IDEA OF THIS ARTICLE: _____

_____

_____

_____

_____

■ LIST THREE IMPORTANT FACTS THAT THE AUTHOR USES TO SUPPORT THE MAIN IDEA:

_____

_____

_____

_____

_____

_____

■ WHAT INFORMATION OR IDEAS DISCUSSED IN THIS ARTICLE ARE ALSO DISCUSSED IN YOUR TEXTBOOK OR OTHER READING YOU HAVE DONE? LIST THE TEXTBOOK CHAPTERS AND PAGE NUMBERS:

_____

_____

_____

_____

_____

_____

■ LIST ANY EXAMPLES OF BIAS OR FAULTY REASONING THAT YOU FOUND IN THE ARTICLE:

_____

_____

_____

_____

■ LIST ANY NEW TERMS/CONCEPTS THAT WERE DISCUSSED IN THE ARTICLE AND WRITE A SHORT DEFINITION:

_____

_____

_____

_____

*Your instructor may require you to use this Annual Editions Article Review Form in any number of ways: for articles that are assigned, for extra credit, as a tool to assist in developing assigned papers, or simply for your own reference. Even if it is not required, we encourage you to photocopy and use this page; you'll find that reflecting on the articles will greatly enhance the information from your text.

# We Want Your Advice

## ANNUAL EDITIONS: CRIMINAL JUSTICE 93/94
### Article Rating Form

Here is an opportunity for you to have direct input into the next revision of this volume. We would like you to rate each of the 45 articles listed below, using the following scale:

1. **Excellent: should definitely be retained**
2. **Above average: should probably be retained**
3. **Below average: should probably be deleted**
4. **Poor: should definitely be deleted**

Your ratings will play a vital part in the next revision. So please mail this prepaid form to us just as soon as you complete it.
Thanks for your help!

Annual Editions revisions depend on two major opinion sources: one is our Advisory Board, listed in the front of this volume, which works with us in scanning the thousands of articles published in the public press each year; the other is you—the person actually using the book. Please help us and the users of the next edition by completing the prepaid article rating form on this page and returning it to us. Thank you.

| Rating | Article | Rating | Article |
|---|---|---|---|
| | 1. An Overview of the Criminal Justice System | | 25. The Judicial Process: Prosecutors and Courts |
| | 2. What Is Crime? | | 26. Public Defenders |
| | 3. Are Criminals Made or Born? | | 27. Abuse of Power in the Prosecutor's Office |
| | 4. Race: Our Dilemma Still | | 28. The Search for Justice: Is Impartiality Really Possible? |
| | 5. 20 Years of War on Drugs, and No Victory Yet | | 29. Jurors Hear Evidence and Turn It Into Stories |
| | 6. Organized Crime: Past, Present, and Future | | 30. Grand Illusion |
| | 7. The Siege of L.A. | | 31. The Court's 2 Visions of Free Speech |
| | 8. Understanding Mass Murder: A Starting Point | | 32. Handling of Juvenile Cases |
| | 9. The Fear of Crime | | 33. Punishment, Accountability, and the New Juvenile Justice |
| | 10. Hunted: The Last Year of April LaSalata | | 34. Girls' Crime and Woman's Place: Toward a Feminist Model of Female Delinquency |
| | 11. In the Mind of a Stalker | | 35. The Juvenile Court and the Role of the Juvenile Court Judge |
| | 12. When Is It Rape? | | 36. Teenagers Talk About Life |
| | 13. When Men Hit Women | | 37. Kids Are Killing, Dying, Bleeding |
| | 14. The Unbearable Loss | | 38. Children in Gangs |
| | 15. Abused Women Who Kill Now Seek Way Out of Cells | | 39. Sentencing and Corrections |
| | 16. Incest: A Chilling Report | | 40. Women in Jail: Unequal Justice |
| | 17. Police Response to Crime | | 41. Doubling the Prison Population Will Break America's Crime Wave |
| | 18. Law Enforcement in a Culturally Diverse Society | | 42. The Crime of Black Imprisonment |
| | 19. Blacks and Cops: Up Against a Wall | | 43. The New Chain Gangs |
| | 20. The Most Stressful Job in America: Police Work in the 1990s | | 44. The Costliest Punishment—A Corrections Administrator Contemplates the Death Penalty |
| | 21. Are Women Better Cops? | | 45. 'This Man Has Expired' |
| | 22. Preventing Hate Crime: New Tools, New Expectations for Law Enforcement | | |
| | 23. Cops Get Up-Close and Personal | | |
| | 24. Higher Education and Ethical Policing | | |

*(Continued on next page)*

## ABOUT YOU

Name_____ Date_____

Are you a teacher? ☐   Or student? ☐

Your School Name _____

Department _____

Address _____

City _____ State _____ Zip _____

School Telephone # _____

---

## YOUR COMMENTS ARE IMPORTANT TO US!

Please fill in the following information:

For which course did you use this book? _____

Did you use a text with this Annual Edition?   ☐ yes   ☐ no

The title of the text? _____

What are your general reactions to the Annual Editions concept?

Have you read any particular articles recently that you think should be included in the next edition?

Are there any articles you feel should be replaced in the next edition? Why?

Are there other areas that you feel would utilize an Annual Edition?

May we contact you for editorial input?

May we quote you from above?

---

**ANNUAL EDITIONS: CRIMINAL JUSTICE 93/94**

## BUSINESS REPLY MAIL

First Class          Permit No. 84          Guilford, CT

*Postage will be paid by addressee*

**The Dushkin Publishing Group, Inc.**
**Sluice Dock**
DPG **Guilford, Connecticut 06437**